TREVOR
NOAH
BORN A CRIME

STORIES FROM A SOUTH AFRICAN CHILDHOOD

"When I think of Trevor Noah, the first image I see is from his brilliant memoir, *Born a Crime,* of Trevor's mother throwing him out of a moving vehicle while he's asleep in order to save his life. Through other eyes this could be remembered as traumatic and harrowing. Through Trevor's it is bonding and hilarious, a testament to the love of someone who truly had to think on their feet. That is how Trevor sees the world. A fantastic storyteller, he has always been a defier of rules, which he broke simply by being born in his native country."

—LUPITA NYONG'O, *TIME*

"Noah's not the main character in his own story—his mother is the constant . . . and by the end, Noah lovingly makes clear that the book belongs to her. . . . Noah proves to be a gifted storyteller, able to deftly lace his poignant tales with amusing irony." —*ENTERTAINMENT WEEKLY*

"[An] unforgettable memoir." —*PARADE*

"This isn't your average comic-writes-a-memoir: It's a unique look at a man who is a product of his culture—and a nuanced look at a part of the world whose people have known dark times easily pushed aside." —*REFINERY29*

"[Noah's] electrifying memoir sparkles with funny stories . . . and his candid and compassionate essays deepen our perception of the complexities of race, gender, and class." —*BOOKLIST* (STARRED REVIEW)

Praise for *Born a Crime*

"In the countdown to and aftermath of the election, Mr. [Trevor] Noah has grown more comfortable at moving back and forth between jokes and earnest insights, between humor and serious asides—the way he's done in his stand-up act, and now, in his compelling new memoir. . . . By turns alarming, sad and funny, his book provides a harrowing look, through the prism of Mr. Noah's family, at life in South Africa under apartheid. . . . Mr. Noah offers a series of sharp-edged snapshots. . . . In the end, *Born a Crime* is not just an unnerving account of growing up in South Africa under apartheid, but a love letter to the author's remarkable mother."

—MICHIKO KAKUTANI, *The New York Times*

"You'd be hard-pressed to find a comic's origin story better than the one Trevor Noah serves up in *Born a Crime*. . . . [He] developed his aptitude for witty truth telling [and] . . . every hardscrabble memory of helping his mother scrape together money for food, gas, school fees, and rent, or barely surviving the temper of his stepfather, Abel, reveals the anxious wellsprings of the comedian's ambition and success. If there is harvest in spite of blight, the saying goes, one does not credit the blight—but Noah does manage to wring brilliant comedy from it."

–*O: The Oprah Magazine*

"Noah's not the main character in his own story—his mother is the constant. Foe of the status quo, her presence looms large over every page whether she's mentioned or not, and by the end, Noah lovingly makes clear that this book belongs to her. In other words, this isn't one of those comedian-penned essay collections where the yuks jump out at sitcom speeds. Yet there's still plenty of humor; Noah proves to be a gifted storyteller, able to deftly lace his poignant tales with amusing irony. . . . Longtime fans of *The Daily Show* often wonder why Noah never seems as upset and worked-up as his easily wound predecessor Jon Stewart was. This book seems to hold the answer: He's a master of self-preservation."

—*Entertainment Weekly*

"[H]e thrives with the help of his astonishingly fearless mother. . . . Their fierce bond makes this story soar."

—*People*

"What makes *Born a Crime* such a soul-nourishing pleasure, even with all its darker edges and perilous turns, is reading Noah recount in brisk, warmly conversational prose how he learned to negotiate his way through the bullying and ostracism. . . . What also helped was having a mother like Patricia Nombuyiselo Noah. . . . Consider *Born a Crime* another such gift to her—and an enormous gift to the rest of us."

—*USA Today*

"[Noah] reveals the full brunt of the terror and diabolical absurdity he endured in this substantial collection of staggering personal essays deftly shaped by his stand-up gifts for timing and precision. Incisive, funny, and vivid . . . [his] electrifying memoir sparkles with funny stories. . . . Noah's candid and compassionate essays deepen our perception of the complexities of race, gender, and class. Hopefully, Noah will continue to tell his bracing and redefining story."

—*Booklist* (starred review)

"In eighteen sharp, at times harrowing essays, *The Daily Show* host Trevor Noah reveals his coming-of-age as the son of protective interracial parents in apartheid South Africa."

—*Harper's Bazaar*

"An affecting memoir, *Born a Crime* . . . [is] a love letter to his mother."
—*The Washington Post*

"Remarkable . . . smart . . . extraordinary . . . essential reading on every level."

—*The Seattle Times*

"*The Daily Show* host, born to a black mother and a white father, was a living, breathing 'crime' growing up in apartheid South Africa. His story of surviving—and thriving—is mind-blowing AF."

—*Cosmopolitan*

"[Noah's] compelling new memoir . . . recounts the years before he found fame as a comic and landed one of the top jobs in America. And it reminds us all how to recognize when racism runs riot."

—*Toronto Star*

"You read [*Born a Crime*] for the remarkable perspective of someone born between categories: a biracial kid spit out into an apartheid regime in which marriage between whites and blacks was illegal and his existence a crime. When you go back to watching *The Daily Show*, the jokes sound better."

—NPR

"Noah's childhood stories are told with all the hilarity and intellect that characterizes his comedy, while illuminating a dark and brutal period in South Africa's history that must never be forgotten."

—*Esquire*

"An unforgettable memoir. . . . The book ultimately pays homage to the strength of his mother—who has quite a comedic presence herself—and is a must-read in that it explores Noah's homeland and the way in which being an outsider shaped his life, his stand-up, his work on *The Daily Show* and the lens through which he views race, politics and life itself."

—*Parade*

"This isn't your average comic-writes-a-memoir: It's a unique look at a man who is a product of his culture—and a nuanced look at a part of the world whose people have known dark times easily pushed aside."

—*Refinery29*

"Powerful prose . . . told through stories and vignettes that are sharply observed, deftly conveyed and consistently candid. Growing organically from them is an affecting investigation of identity, ethnicity, language, masculinity, nationality and, most of all, humanity—all issues that the election of Donald Trump in the United States shows are foremost in minds and hearts everywhere. . . . What the reader gleans are the insights that made Noah the thoughtful, observant, empathic man who wrote *Born a Crime*. . . . Here is a level-headed man, forged by remarkable and shocking life incidents, who is quietly determined and who knows where home and the heart lie. Would this unique story have been published had it been about someone not a celebrity of the planet? Possibly not, and to the detriment of potential readers, because this is a warm and very human story of the type that we will need to survive the Trump presidency's imminent freezing of humane values."

—*Mail & Guardian* (South Africa)

"A gritty memoir . . . studded with insight and provocative social criticism . . . with flashes of brilliant storytelling and acute observations on South African culture."

—*Kirkus Reviews*

"Americans will know Trevor Noah much better after reading his terrific new memoir. . . . Noah has a real tale to tell, and he tells it well—the tale of a boyhood in South Africa during and after apartheid. . . . Among the many virtues of *Born a Crime* is a frank and telling portrait of life in South Africa during the 1980s and '90s. . . . *Born a Crime* offers Americans a second introduction to Trevor Noah, and he makes a real impression."

—*Newsday*

"Witty and revealing . . . Noah's story is the story of modern South Africa; though he enjoyed some privileges of the region's slow Westernization, his formative years were shaped by poverty, injustice, and violence. Noah is quick with a disarming joke, and he skillfully integrates the parallel narratives via interstitial asides between chapters. . . . Perhaps the most harrowing tales are those of his abusive stepfather, which form the book's final act (and which Noah cleverly foreshadows throughout earlier chapters), but equally prominent are the laugh-out-loud yarns about going to the prom, and the differences between 'White Church' and 'Black Church.'"

—*Publishers Weekly* (starred review)

BORN A CRIME

BORN A CRIME

STORIES FROM A SOUTH AFRICAN CHILDHOOD

TREVOR NOAH

ANCHOR CANADA

Library and Archives Canada Cataloguing in Publication

Noah, Trevor, 1984-, author
Born a crime / Trevor Noah.

ISBN 978-0-385-68924-3 (paperback)

1. Noah, Trevor, 1984-. 2. Comedians--South Africa--Biography. 3. South African wit and humor. 4. Apartheid--South Africa. I. Title.

PN2988.N62A3 2017   792.702'8092   C2016-902293-5

Born a Crime is a work of nonfiction. Some names and identifying details have been changed.

Book design by Susan Turner
Cover design: Greg Mollica
Cover art: Mark Stutzman, based on a photograph by Kwaku Alston (Trevor Noah); Getty Images (background)

Printed and bound in the USA on acid-free paper

Published in Canada by Anchor Canada,
a division of Random House of Canada Limited,
a Penguin Random House Company

www.penguinrandomhouse.ca

10 9 8 7 6 5 4 3 2 1

For my mother. My first fan.
Thank you for making me a man.

IMMORALITY ACT, 1927

To prohibit illicit carnal intercourse between Europeans and natives and other acts in relation thereto.

B E IT ENACTED by the King's Most Excellent Majesty, the Senate and the House of Assembly of the Union of South Africa, as follows:—

1. Any European male who has illicit carnal intercourse with a native female, and any native male who has illicit carnal intercourse with a European female . . . shall be guilty of an offence and liable on conviction to imprisonment for a period not exceeding five years.

2. Any native female who permits any European male to have illicit carnal intercourse with her and any European female who permits any native male to have illicit carnal intercourse with her shall be guilty of an offence and liable on conviction to imprisonment for a period not exceeding four years. . . .

CONTENTS

I

II

III

PART I

The genius of apartheid was convincing people who were the overwhelming majority to turn on each other. Apart hate, is what it was. You separate people into groups and make them hate one another so you can run them all.

At the time, black South Africans outnumbered white South Africans nearly five to one, yet we were divided into different tribes with different languages: Zulu, Xhosa, Tswana, Sotho, Venda, Ndebele, Tsonga, Pedi, and more. Long before apartheid existed these tribal factions clashed and warred with one another. Then white rule used that animosity to divide and conquer. All nonwhites were systematically classified into various groups and subgroups. Then these groups were given differing levels of rights and privileges in order to keep them at odds.

Perhaps the starkest of these divisions was between South Africa's two dominant groups, the Zulu and the Xhosa. The Zulu man is known as the warrior. He is proud. He puts his head down and fights. When the colonial armies invaded, the Zulu charged into battle with nothing but spears and shields against men with guns. The Zulu were slaughtered by the thousands, but they never stopped fighting. The Xhosa, on the other hand, pride themselves on being the thinkers. My mother is Xhosa. Nelson Mandela was Xhosa. The Xhosa waged a long war against the white man as well, but after experiencing the futility of battle against a better-armed foe, many Xhosa chiefs took a more nimble approach. "These white people are here whether we like it or not," they said. "Let's see what tools they possess that can be useful to us. Instead of being resistant to English, let's learn English. We'll understand what the white man is saying, and we can force him to negotiate with us."

The Zulu went to war with the white man. The Xhosa played chess with the white man. For a long time neither was particularly successful, and each blamed the other for a problem neither had created. Bitterness festered. For decades those feelings were held in check by a common enemy. Then apartheid fell, Mandela walked free, and black South Africa went to war with itself.

———

RUN

Sometimes in big Hollywood movies they'll have these crazy chase scenes where somebody jumps or gets thrown from a moving car. The person hits the ground and rolls for a bit. Then they come to a stop and pop up and dust themselves off, like it was no big deal. Whenever I see that I think, *That's rubbish. Getting thrown out of a moving car hurts way worse than that.*

I was nine years old when my mother threw me out of a moving car. It happened on a Sunday. I know it was on a Sunday because we were coming home from church, and every Sunday in my childhood meant church. We *never* missed church. My mother was—and still is— a deeply religious woman. Very Christian. Like indigenous peoples around the world, black South Africans adopted the religion of our colonizers. By "adopt" I mean it was forced on us. The white man was quite stern with the native. "You need to pray to Jesus," he said. "Jesus will save you." To which the native replied, "Well, we do need to be saved—saved from *you,* but that's beside the point. So let's give this Jesus thing a shot."

My whole family is religious, but where my mother was Team Jesus all the way, my grandmother balanced her Christian faith with the traditional Xhosa beliefs she'd grown up with, communicating with the spirits of our ancestors. For a long time I didn't understand why so many black people had abandoned their indigenous faith for Christianity. But the more we went to church and the longer I sat in those pews the more I learned about how Christianity works: If you're Native American and you pray to the wolves, you're a savage. If you're African and you pray to your ancestors, you're a primitive. But when white people pray to a guy who turns water into wine, well, that's just common sense.

My childhood involved church, or some form of church, at least four nights a week. Tuesday night was the prayer meeting. Wednesday night was Bible study. Thursday night was Youth church. Friday and Saturday we had off. (Time to sin!) Then on Sunday we went to church. Three churches, to be precise. The reason we went to three churches was because my mom said each church gave her something different. The first church offered jubilant praise of the Lord. The second church offered deep analysis of the scripture, which my mom loved. The third church offered passion and catharsis; it was a place where you truly felt the presence of the Holy Spirit inside you. Completely by coincidence, as we moved back and forth between these churches, I noticed that each one had its own distinct racial makeup: Jubilant church was mixed church. Analytical church was white church. And passionate, cathartic church, that was black church.

Mixed church was Rhema Bible Church. Rhema was one of those huge, supermodern, suburban megachurches. The pastor, Ray McCauley, was an ex-bodybuilder with a big smile and the personality of a cheerleader. Pastor Ray had competed in the 1974 Mr. Universe competition. He placed third. The winner that year was Arnold Schwarzenegger.

Every week, Ray would be up onstage working really hard to make Jesus cool. There was arena-style seating and a rock band jamming out with the latest Christian contemporary pop. Everyone sang along, and if you didn't know the words that was okay because they were all right up there on the Jumbotron for you. It was Christian karaoke, basically. I always had a blast at mixed church.

White church was Rosebank Union in Sandton, a very white and wealthy part of Johannesburg. I *loved* white church because I didn't actually have to go to the main service. My mom would go to that, and I would go to the youth side, to Sunday school. In Sunday school we got to read cool stories. Noah and the flood was obviously a favorite; I had a personal stake there. But I also loved the stories about Moses parting the Red Sea, David slaying Goliath, Jesus whipping the money changers in the temple.

I grew up in a home with very little exposure to popular culture. Boyz II Men were not allowed in my mother's house. Songs about some guy grinding on a girl all night long? No, no, no. That was forbidden. I'd hear the other kids at school singing "End of the Road," and I'd have no clue what was going on. I knew *of* these Boyz II Men, but I didn't really know who they were. The only music I knew was from church: soaring, uplifting songs praising Jesus. It was the same with movies. My mom didn't want my mind polluted by movies with sex and violence. So the Bible was my action movie. Samson was my superhero. He was my He-Man. A guy beating a thousand people to death with the jawbone of a donkey? That's pretty badass. Eventually you get to Paul writing letters to the Ephesians and it loses the plot, but the Old Testament and the Gospels? I could quote you anything from those pages, chapter and verse. There were Bible games and quizzes every week at white church, and I kicked everyone's ass.

Then there was black church. There was always some kind of black church service going on somewhere, and we tried them all. In the township, that typically meant an outdoor, tent-revival-style church. We usually went to my grandmother's church, an old-school Methodist congregation, five hundred African grannies in blue-and-white blouses, clutching their Bibles and patiently burning in the hot African sun. Black church was rough, I won't lie. No air-conditioning. No lyrics up on Jumbotrons. And it lasted forever, three or four hours at least, which confused me because white church was only like an hour—in and out, thanks for coming. But at black church I would sit there for what felt like an eternity, trying to figure out why time moved so slowly. *Is it possible for time to actually stop? If so, why does it stop at black church and not at white church?* I eventually decided black people needed more time with Jesus because we suffered more. "I'm here to fill up on my blessings for the week," my mother used to say. The more time we spent at church, she reckoned, the more blessings we accrued, like a Starbucks Rewards Card.

Black church had one saving grace. If I could make it to the third or fourth hour I'd get to watch the pastor cast demons out of people. People possessed by demons would start running up and down the aisles like madmen, screaming in tongues. The ushers would tackle them, like bouncers at a club, and hold them down for the pastor. The pastor would grab their heads and violently shake them back and forth, shouting, "I cast out this spirit in the name of *Jesus*!" Some pastors were more violent than others, but what they all had in common was that they wouldn't stop until the demon was gone and the congregant had gone limp and collapsed on the stage. The person had to fall. Because if he didn't fall that meant the demon was powerful and the pastor needed to come at him even harder. You could be a linebacker in the NFL. Didn't matter. That pastor was taking you *down*. Good Lord, that was fun.

Christian karaoke, badass action stories, and violent faith healers—man, I loved church. The thing I didn't love was the lengths we had to go to in order to get to church. It was an epic slog. We lived in Eden Park, a tiny suburb way outside Johannesburg. It took us an hour to get to white church, another forty-five minutes to get to mixed church, and another forty-five minutes to drive out to Soweto for black church. Then, if that wasn't bad enough, some Sundays we'd double back to white church for a special evening service. By the time we finally got home at night, I'd collapse into bed.

This particular Sunday, the Sunday I was hurled from a moving car, started out like any other Sunday. My mother woke me up, made me porridge for breakfast. I took my bath while she dressed my baby brother Andrew, who was nine months old. Then we went out to the driveway, but once we were finally all strapped in and ready to go, the car wouldn't start. My mom had this ancient, broken-down, bright-tangerine Volkswagen Beetle that she picked up for next to nothing. The reason she got it for next to nothing was because it was always breaking down. To this day I hate secondhand cars. Almost everything that's ever gone wrong in my life I can trace back to a secondhand car. Secondhand cars made me get detention for being late for school. Secondhand cars left us hitchhiking on the side of the freeway. A secondhand car was also the reason my mom got married. If it hadn't been for the Volkswagen that didn't work, we never would have looked for the mechanic who became the husband who became the stepfather who became the man who tortured us for years and put a bullet in the back of my mother's head—I'll take the new car with the warranty every time.

As much as I loved church, the idea of a nine-hour slog, from mixed church to white church to black church then doubling back to white church again, was just too much to contemplate. It was bad enough in a car, but taking public transport would be twice as long and twice as hard. When the Volkswagen refused to start, inside my head I was praying, *Please say we'll just stay home. Please say we'll just stay home.* Then I glanced over to see the determined look on my mother's face, her jaw set, and I knew I had a long day ahead of me.

"Come," she said. "We're going to catch minibuses."

My mother is as stubborn as she is religious. Once her mind's made up, that's it. Indeed, obstacles that would normally lead a person to change their plans, like a car breaking down, only made her more determined to forge ahead.

"It's the Devil," she said about the stalled car. "The Devil doesn't want us to go to church. That's why we've got to catch minibuses."

Whenever I found myself up against my mother's faith-based obstinacy, I would try, as respectfully as possible, to counter with an opposing point of view.

"Or," I said, "the Lord knows that today we *shouldn't* go to church, which is why he made sure the car wouldn't start, so that we stay at home as a family and take a day of rest, because even the Lord rested."

"Ah, that's the Devil talking, Trevor."

"No, because Jesus is in control, and if Jesus is in control and we pray to Jesus, he would let the car start, but he hasn't, therefore—"

"No, Trevor! Sometimes Jesus puts obstacles in your way to see if you overcome them. Like Job. This could be a test."

"Ah! Yes, Mom. But the test could be to see if we're willing to accept what has happened and stay at home and praise Jesus for his wisdom."

"No. That's the Devil talking. Now go change your clothes."

"But, Mom!"

"Trevor! *Sun'qhela!*"

Sun'qhela is a phrase with many shades of meaning. It says "don't undermine me," "don't underestimate me," and "just try me." It's a command and a threat, all at once. It's a common thing for Xhosa parents to say to their kids. Any time I heard it I knew it meant the conversation was over, and if I uttered another word I was in for a hiding—what we call a spanking.

At the time, I attended a private Catholic school called Maryvale College. I was the champion of the Maryvale sports day every single year, and my mother won the moms' trophy every single year. Why? Because she was always chasing me to kick my ass, and I was always running not to get my ass kicked. Nobody ran like me and my mom. She wasn't one of those "Come over here and get your hiding" type moms. She'd deliver it to you free of charge. She was a thrower, too. Whatever was next to her was coming at you. If it was something breakable, I had to catch it and put it down. If it broke, that would be my fault, too, and the ass-kicking would be that much worse. If she threw a vase at me, I'd have to catch it, put it down, and then run. In a split second, I'd have to think, *Is it valuable? Yes. Is it breakable? Yes. Catch it, put it down, now run.*

We had a very Tom and Jerry relationship, me and my mom. She was the strict disciplinarian; I was naughty as shit. She would send me out to buy groceries, and I wouldn't come right home because I'd be using the change from the milk and bread to play arcade games at the supermarket. I loved videogames. I was a master at *Street Fighter*. I could go forever on a single play. I'd drop a coin in, time would fly, and the next thing I knew there'd be a woman behind me with a belt. It was a race. I'd take off out the door and through the dusty streets of Eden Park, clambering over walls, ducking through backyards. It was a normal thing in our neighborhood. Everybody knew: That Trevor child would come through like a bat out of hell, and his mom would be right there behind him. She could go at a full sprint in high heels, but if she really wanted to come after me she had this thing where she'd kick her shoes off while still going at top speed. She'd do this weird move with her ankles and the heels would go flying and she wouldn't even miss a step. That's when I knew, *Okay, she's in turbo mode now.*

When I was little she always caught me, but as I got older I got faster, and when speed failed her she'd use her wits. If I was about to get away she'd yell, *"Stop! Thief!"* She'd do this to her own child. In South Africa, nobody gets involved in other people's business—unless it's mob justice, and then everybody wants in. So she'd yell "Thief!" knowing it would bring the whole neighborhood out against me, and then I'd have strangers trying to grab me and tackle me, and I'd have to duck and dive and dodge them as well, all the while screaming, "I'm not a thief! I'm her son!"

The last thing I wanted to do that Sunday morning was climb into some crowded minibus, but the second I heard my mom say *sun'qhela* I knew my fate was sealed. She gathered up Andrew and we climbed out of the Volkswagen and went out to try to catch a ride.

I was five years old, nearly six, when Nelson Mandela was released from prison. I remember seeing it on TV and everyone being happy. I didn't know why we were happy, just that we were. I was aware of the fact that there was a thing called apartheid and it was ending and that was a big deal, but I didn't understand the intricacies of it.

What I do remember, what I will never forget, is the violence that followed. The triumph of democracy over apartheid is sometimes called the Bloodless Revolution. It is called that because very little white blood was spilled. Black blood ran in the streets.

As the apartheid regime fell, we knew that the black man was now going to rule. The question was, which black man? Spates of violence broke out between the Inkatha Freedom Party and the ANC, the African National Congress, as they jockeyed for power. The political dynamic between these two groups was very complicated, but the simplest way to understand it is as a proxy war between Zulu and Xhosa. The Inkatha was predominantly Zulu, very militant and very nationalistic. The ANC was a broad coalition encompassing many different tribes, but its leaders at the time were primarily Xhosa. Instead of uniting for peace they turned on one another, committing acts of unbelievable savagery. Massive riots broke out. Thousands of people were killed. Necklacing was common. That's where people would hold someone down and put a rubber tire over his torso, pinning his arms. Then they'd douse him with petrol and set him on fire and burn him alive. The ANC did it to Inkatha. Inkatha did it to the ANC. I saw one of those charred bodies on the side of the road one day on my way to school. In the evenings my mom and I would turn on our little black-and-white TV and watch the news. A dozen people killed. Fifty people killed. A hundred people killed.

Eden Park sat not far from the sprawling townships of the East Rand, Thokoza and Katlehong, which were the sites of some of the most horrific Inkatha–ANC clashes. Once a month at least we'd drive home and the neighborhood would be on fire. Hundreds of rioters in the street. My mom would edge the car slowly through the crowds and around blockades made of flaming tires. Nothing burns like a tire—it rages with a fury you can't imagine. As we drove past the burning blockades, it felt like we were inside an oven. I used to say to my mom, "I think Satan burns tires in Hell."

Whenever the riots broke out, all our neighbors would wisely hole up behind closed doors. But not my mom. She'd head straight out, and as we'd inch our way past the blockades, she'd give the rioters this look. *Let me pass. I'm not involved in this shit.* She was unwavering in the face of danger. That always amazed me. It didn't matter that there was a war on our doorstep. She had things to do, places to be. It was the same stubbornness that kept her going to church despite a broken-down car. There could be five hundred rioters with a blockade of burning tires on the main road out of Eden Park, and my mother would say, "Get dressed. I've got to go to work. You've got to go to school."

"But aren't you afraid?" I'd say. "There's only one of you and there's so many of them."

"Honey, I'm not alone," she'd say. "I've got all of Heaven's angels behind me."

"Well, it would be nice if we could *see* them," I'd say. "Because I don't think the rioters know they're there."

She'd tell me not to worry. She always came back to the phrase she lived by: "If God is with me, who can be against me?" She was never scared. Even when she should have been.

That carless Sunday we made our circuit of churches, ending up, as usual, at white church. When we walked out of Rosebank Union it was dark and we were alone. It had been an endless day of minibuses from mixed church to black church to white church, and I was exhausted. It was nine o'clock at least. In those days, with all the violence and riots going on, you did not want to be out that late at night. We were standing at the corner of Jellicoe Avenue and Oxford Road, right in the heart of Johannesburg's wealthy, white suburbia, and there were no minibuses. The streets were empty.

I so badly wanted to turn to my mom and say, "You see? This is why God wanted us to stay home." But one look at the expression on her face, and I knew better than to speak. There were times I could talk smack to my mom—this was not one of them.

We waited and waited for a minibus to come by. Under apartheid the government provided no public transportation for blacks, but white people still needed us to show up to mop their floors and clean their bathrooms. Necessity being the mother of invention, black people created their own transit system, an informal network of bus routes, controlled by private associations operating entirely outside the law. Because the minibus business was completely unregulated, it was basically organized crime. Different groups ran different routes, and they would fight over who controlled what. There was bribery and general shadiness that went on, a great deal of violence, and a lot of protection money paid to avoid violence. The one thing you didn't do was steal a route from a rival group. Drivers who stole routes would get killed. Being unregulated, minibuses were also very unreliable. When they came, they came. When they didn't, they didn't.

Standing outside Rosebank Union, I was literally falling asleep on my feet. Not a minibus in sight. Eventually my mother said, "Let's hitchhike." We walked and walked, and after what felt like an eternity, a car drove up and stopped. The driver offered us a ride, and we climbed in. We hadn't gone ten feet when suddenly a minibus swerved right in front of the car and cut us off.

A Zulu driver got out with an *iwisa*, a large, traditional Zulu weapon—a war club, basically. They're used to smash people's skulls in. Another guy, his crony, got out of the passenger side. They walked up to the driver's side of the car we were in, grabbed the man who'd offered us a ride, pulled him out, and started shoving their clubs in his face. "Why are you stealing our customers? Why are you picking people up?"

It looked like they were going to kill this guy. I knew that happened sometimes. My mom spoke up. "Hey, listen, he was just helping me. Leave him. We'll ride with you. That's what we wanted in the first place." So we got out of the first car and climbed into the minibus.

We were the only passengers in the minibus. In addition to being violent gangsters, South African minibus drivers are notorious for complaining and haranguing passengers as they drive. This driver was a particularly angry one. As we rode along, he started lecturing my mother about being in a car with a man who was not her husband. My mother didn't suffer lectures from strange men. She told him to mind his own business, and when he heard her speaking in Xhosa, that really set him off. The stereotypes of Zulu and Xhosa women were as ingrained as those of the men. Zulu women were well-behaved and dutiful. Xhosa women were promiscuous and unfaithful. And here was my mother, his tribal enemy, a Xhosa woman alone with two small children—one of them a mixed child, no less. Not just a whore but a whore who sleeps with white men. "Oh, you're a *Xhosa*," he said. "That explains it. Climbing into strange men's cars. Disgusting woman."

My mom kept telling him off and he kept calling her names, yelling at her from the front seat, wagging his finger in the rearview mirror and growing more and more menacing until finally he said, "That's the problem with you Xhosa women. You're all sluts—and tonight you're going to learn your lesson."

He sped off. He was driving fast, and he wasn't stopping, only slowing down to check for traffic at the intersections before speeding through. Death was never far away from anybody back then. At that point my mother could be raped. We could be killed. These were all viable options. I didn't fully comprehend the danger we were in at the moment; I was so tired that I just wanted to sleep. Plus my mom stayed very calm. She didn't panic, so I didn't know to panic. She just kept trying to reason with him.

"I'm sorry if we've upset you, *bhuti*. You can just let us out here—"
"No."
"Really, it's fine. We can just walk—"
"No."

He raced along Oxford Road, the lanes empty, no other cars out. I was sitting closest to the minibus's sliding door. My mother sat next to me, holding baby Andrew. She looked out the window at the passing road and then leaned over to me and whispered, "Trevor, when he slows down at the next intersection, I'm going to open the door and we're going to jump."

I didn't hear a word of what she was saying, because by that point I'd completely nodded off. When we came to the next traffic light, the driver eased off the gas a bit to look around and check the road. My mother reached over, pulled the sliding door open, grabbed me, and threw me out as far as she could. Then she took Andrew, curled herself in a ball around him, and leaped out behind me.

It felt like a dream until the pain hit. *Bam!* I smacked hard on the pavement. My mother landed right beside me and we tumbled and tumbled and rolled and rolled. I was wide awake now. I went from half asleep to *What the hell?!* Eventually I came to a stop and pulled myself up, completely disoriented. I looked around and saw my mother, already on her feet. She turned and looked at me and screamed.

"*Run!*"

So I ran, and she ran, and nobody ran like me and my mom.

It's weird to explain, but I just knew what to do. It was animal instinct, learned in a world where violence was always lurking and waiting to erupt. In the townships, when the police came swooping in with their riot gear and armored cars and helicopters, I knew: *Run for cover. Run and hide.* I knew that as a five-year-old. Had I lived a different life, getting thrown out of a speeding minibus might have fazed me. I'd have stood there like an idiot, going, "What's happening, Mom? Why are my legs so sore?" But there was none of that. Mom said "run," and I ran. Like the gazelle runs from the lion, I ran.

The men stopped the minibus and got out and tried to chase us, but they didn't stand a chance. We smoked them. I think they were in shock. I still remember glancing back and seeing them give up with a look of utter bewilderment on their faces. *What just happened? Who'd have thought a woman with two small children could run so fast?* They didn't know they were dealing with the reigning champs of the Maryvale College sports day. We kept going and going until we made it to a twenty-four-hour petrol station and called the police. By then the men were long gone.

I still didn't know why any of this had happened; I'd been running on pure adrenaline. Once we stopped running I realized how much pain I was in. I looked down, and the skin on my arms was scraped and torn. I was cut up and bleeding all over. Mom was, too. My baby brother was fine, though, incredibly. My mom had wrapped herself around him, and he'd come through without a scratch. I turned to her in shock.

"What was *that*?! Why are we running?!"

"What do you mean, 'Why are we running?' Those men were trying to kill us."

"You never told me that! You just threw me out of the car!"

"I did tell you. Why didn't you jump?"

"Jump?! I was asleep!"

"So I should have left you there for them to kill you?"

"At least they would have woken me up before they killed me."

Back and forth we went. I was too confused and too angry about getting thrown out of the car to realize what had happened. My mother had saved my life.

As we caught our breath and waited for the police to come and drive us home, she said, "Well, at least we're safe, thank God."

But I was nine years old and I knew better. I wasn't going to keep quiet this time.

"No, Mom! This was *not* thanks to God! You should have listened to God when he told us to stay at home when the car wouldn't start, because clearly the Devil tricked us into coming out tonight."

"No, Trevor! That's not how the Devil works. This is part of God's plan, and if He wanted us here then He had a reason . . ."

And on and on and there we were, back at it, arguing about God's will. Finally I said, "Look, Mom. I know you love Jesus, but maybe next week you could ask him to meet us at our house. Because this really wasn't a fun night."

She broke out in a huge smile and started laughing. I started laughing, too, and we stood there, this little boy and his mom, our arms and legs covered in blood and dirt, laughing together through the pain in the light of a petrol station on the side of the road in the middle of the night.

Apartheid was perfect racism. It took centuries to develop, starting all the way back in 1652 when the Dutch East India Company landed at the Cape of Good Hope and established a trading colony, Kaapstad, later known as Cape Town, a rest stop for ships traveling between Europe and India. To impose white rule, the Dutch colonists went to war with the natives, ultimately developing a set of laws to subjugate and enslave them. When the British took over the Cape Colony, the descendants of the original Dutch settlers trekked inland and developed their own language, culture, and customs, eventually becoming their own people, the Afrikaners—the white tribe of Africa.

The British abolished slavery in name but kept it in practice. They did so because, in the mid-1800s, in what had been written off as a near-worthless way station on the route to the Far East, a few lucky capitalists stumbled upon the richest gold and diamond reserves in the world, and an endless supply of expendable bodies was needed to go in the ground and get it all out.

As the British Empire fell, the Afrikaner rose up to claim South Africa as his rightful inheritance. To maintain power in the face of the country's rising and restless black majority, the government realized they needed a newer and more robust set of tools. They set up a formal commission to go out and study institutionalized racism all over the world. They went to Australia. They went to the Netherlands. They went to America. They saw what worked, what didn't. Then they came back and published a report, and the government used that knowledge to build the most advanced system of racial oppression known to man.

Apartheid was a police state, a system of surveillance and laws designed to keep black people under total control. A full compendium of those laws would run more than three thousand pages and weigh approximately ten pounds, but the general thrust of it should be easy enough for any American to understand. In America you had the forced removal of the native onto reservations coupled with slavery followed by segregation. Imagine all three of those things happening to the same group of people at the same time. That was apartheid.

———

2

BORN A CRIME

I grew up in South Africa during apartheid, which was awkward because I was raised in a mixed family, with me being the mixed one in the family. My mother, Patricia Nombuyiselo Noah, is black. My father, Robert, is white. Swiss/German, to be precise, which Swiss/Germans invariably are. During apartheid, one of the worst crimes you could commit was having sexual relations with a person of another race. Needless to say, my parents committed that crime.

In any society built on institutionalized racism, race-mixing doesn't merely challenge the system as unjust, it reveals the system as unsustainable and incoherent. Race-mixing proves that races can mix—and in a lot of cases, *want* to mix. Because a mixed person embodies that rebuke to the logic of the system, race-mixing becomes a crime worse than treason.

Humans being humans and sex being sex, that prohibition never stopped anyone. There were mixed kids in South Africa nine months after the first Dutch boats hit the beach in Table Bay. Just like in America, the colonists here had their way with the native women, as colonists so often do. Unlike in America, where anyone with one drop of black blood automatically became black, in South Africa mixed people came to be classified as their own separate group, neither black nor white but what we call "colored." Colored people, black people, white people, and Indian people were forced to register their race with the government. Based on those classifications, millions of people were uprooted and relocated. Indian areas were segregated from colored areas, which were segregated from black areas—all of them segregated from white areas and separated from one another by buffer zones of empty land. Laws were passed prohibiting sex between Europeans and natives, laws that were later amended to prohibit sex between whites and all nonwhites.

The government went to insane lengths to try to enforce these new laws. The penalty for breaking them was five years in prison. There were whole police squads whose only job was to go around peeking through windows—clearly an assignment for only the finest law enforcement officers. And if an interracial couple got caught, God help them. The police would kick down the door, drag the people out, beat them, arrest them. At least that's what they did to the black person. With the white person it was more like, "Look, I'll just say you were drunk, but don't do it again, eh? Cheers." That's how it was with a white man and a black woman. If a black man was caught having sex with a white woman, he'd be lucky if he wasn't charged with rape.

If you ask my mother whether she ever considered the ramifications of having a mixed child under apartheid, she will say no. She wanted to do something, figured out a way to do it, and then she did it. She had a level of fearlessness that you have to possess to take on something like she did. If you stop to consider the ramifications, you'll never do anything. Still, it was a crazy, reckless thing to do. A million things had to go right for us to slip through the cracks the way we did for as long as we did.

· · ·

Under apartheid, if you were a black man you worked on a farm or in a factory or in a mine. If you were a black woman, you worked in a factory or as a maid. Those were pretty much your only options. My mother didn't want to work in a factory. She was a horrible cook and never would have stood for some white lady telling her what to do all day. So, true to her nature, she found an option that was not among the ones presented to her: She took a secretarial course, a typing class. At the time, a black woman learning how to type was like a blind person learning how to drive. It's an admirable effort, but you're unlikely to ever be called upon to execute the task. By law, white-collar jobs and skilled-labor jobs were reserved for whites. Black people didn't work in offices. My mom, however, was a rebel, and, fortunately for her, her rebellion came along at the right moment.

In the early 1980s, the South African government began making minor reforms in an attempt to quell international protest over the atrocities and human rights abuses of apartheid. Among those reforms was the token hiring of black workers in low-level white-collar jobs. Like typists. Through an employment agency she got a job as a secretary at ICI, a multinational pharmaceutical company in Braamfontein, a suburb of Johannesburg.

When my mom started working, she still lived with my grandmother in Soweto, the township where the government had relocated my family decades before. But my mother was unhappy at home, and when she was twenty-two she ran away to live in downtown Johannesburg. There was only one problem: It was illegal for black people to live there.

The ultimate goal of apartheid was to make South Africa a white country, with every black person stripped of his or her citizenship and relocated to live in the homelands, the Bantustans, semi-sovereign black territories that were in reality puppet states of the government in Pretoria. But this so-called white country could not function without black labor to produce its wealth, which meant black people had to be allowed to live near white areas in the townships, government-planned ghettos built to house black workers, like Soweto. The township was where you lived, but your status as a laborer was the only thing that permitted you to stay there. If your papers were revoked for any reason, you could be deported back to the homelands.

To leave the township for work in the city, or for any other reason, you had to carry a pass with your ID number; otherwise you could be arrested. There was also a curfew: After a certain hour, blacks had to be back home in the township or risk arrest. My mother didn't care. She was determined to never go home again. So she stayed in town, hiding and sleeping in public restrooms until she learned the rules of navigating the city from the other black women who had contrived to live there: prostitutes.

Many of the prostitutes in town were Xhosa. They spoke my mother's language and showed her how to survive. They taught her how to dress up in a pair of maid's overalls to move around the city without being questioned. They also introduced her to white men who were willing to rent out flats in town. A lot of these men were foreigners, Germans and Portuguese who didn't care about the law and were happy to sign a lease giving a prostitute a place to live and work in exchange for a steady piece on the side. My mom wasn't interested in any such arrangement, but thanks to her job she did have money to pay rent. She met a German fellow through one of her prostitute friends, and he agreed to let her a flat in his name. She moved in and bought a bunch of maid's overalls to wear. She was caught and arrested many times, for not having her ID on the way home from work, for being in a white area after hours. The penalty for violating the pass laws was thirty days in jail or a fine of fifty rand, nearly half her monthly salary. She would scrape together the money, pay the fine, and go right back about her business.

My mom's secret flat was in a neighborhood called Hillbrow. She lived in number 203. Down the corridor was a tall, brown-haired, brown-eyed Swiss/German expat named Robert. He lived in 206. As a former trading colony, South Africa has always had a large expatriate community. People find their way here. Tons of Germans. Lots of Dutch. Hillbrow at the time was the Greenwich Village of South Africa. It was a thriving scene, cosmopolitan and liberal. There were galleries and underground theaters where artists and performers dared to speak up and criticize the government in front of integrated crowds. There were restaurants and nightclubs, a lot of them foreign-owned, that served a mixed clientele, black people who hated the status quo and white people who simply thought it ridiculous. These people would have secret get-togethers, too, usually in someone's flat or in empty basements that had been converted into clubs. Integration by its nature was a political act, but the get-togethers themselves weren't political at all. People would meet up and hang out, have parties.

My mom threw herself into that scene. She was always out at some club, some party, dancing, meeting people. She was a regular at the Hillbrow Tower, one of the tallest buildings in Africa at that time. It had a nightclub with a rotating dance floor on the top floor. It was an exhilarating time but still dangerous. Sometimes the restaurants and clubs would get shut down, sometimes not. Sometimes the performers and patrons would get arrested, sometimes not. It was a roll of the dice. My mother never knew whom to trust, who might turn her in to the police. Neighbors would report on one another. The girlfriends of the white men in my mom's block of flats had every reason to report a black woman—a prostitute, no doubt—living among them. And you must remember that black people worked for the government as well. As far as her white neighbors knew, my mom could have been a spy posing as a prostitute posing as a maid, sent into Hillbrow to inform on whites who were breaking the law. That's how a police state works—everyone thinks everyone else is the police.

Living alone in the city, not being trusted and not being able to trust, my mother started spending more and more time in the company of someone with whom she felt safe: the tall Swiss man down the corridor in 206. He was forty-six. She was twenty-four. He was quiet and reserved; she was wild and free. She would stop by his flat to chat; they'd go to underground get-togethers, go dancing at the nightclub with the rotating dance floor. Something clicked.

I know that there was a genuine bond and a love between my parents. I saw it. But how romantic their relationship was, to what extent they were just friends, I can't say. These are things a child doesn't ask. All I do know is that one day she made her proposal.

"I want to have a kid," she told him.

"I don't want kids," he said.

"I didn't ask you to have a kid. I asked you to help me to have my kid. I just want the sperm from you."

"I'm Catholic," he said. "We don't do such things."

"You do know," she replied, "that I could sleep with you and go away and you would never know if you had a child or not. But I don't want that. Honor me with your yes so that I can live peacefully. I want a child of my own, and I want it from you. You will be able to see it as much as you like, but you will have no obligations. You don't have to talk to it. You don't have to pay for it. Just make this child for me."

For my mother's part, the fact that this man didn't particularly want a family with her, was prevented by law from having a family with her, was part of the attraction. She wanted a child, not a man stepping in to run her life. For my father's part, I know that for a long time he kept saying no. Eventually he said yes. Why he said yes is a question I will never have the answer to.

Nine months after that yes, on February 20, 1984, my mother checked into Hillbrow Hospital for a scheduled C-section delivery. Estranged from her family, pregnant by a man she could not be seen with in public, she was alone. The doctors took her up to the delivery room, cut open her belly, and reached in and pulled out a half-white, half-black child who violated any number of laws, statutes, and regulations—I was born a crime.

When the doctors pulled me out there was an awkward moment where they said, "Huh. That's a very light-skinned baby." A quick scan of the delivery room revealed no man standing around to take credit.

"Who is the father?" they asked.

"His father is from Swaziland," my mother said, referring to the tiny, landlocked kingdom in the west of South Africa.

They probably knew she was lying, but they accepted it because they needed an explanation. Under apartheid, the government labeled everything on your birth certificate: race, tribe, nationality. Everything had to be categorized. My mother lied and said I was born in Ka-Ngwane, the semi-sovereign homeland for Swazi people living in South Africa. So my birth certificate doesn't say that I'm Xhosa, which technically I am. And it doesn't say that I'm Swiss, which the government wouldn't allow. It just says that I'm from another country.

My father isn't on my birth certificate. Officially, he's never been my father. And my mother, true to her word, was prepared for him not to be involved. She'd rented a new flat for herself in Joubert Park, the neighborhood adjacent to Hillbrow, and that's where she took me when she left the hospital. The next week she went to visit him, with no baby. To her surprise, he asked where I was. "You said that you didn't want to be involved," she said. And he hadn't, but once I existed he realized he couldn't have a son living around the corner and not be a part of my life. So the three of us formed a kind of family, as much as our peculiar situation would allow. I lived with my mom. We'd sneak around and visit my dad when we could.

Where most children are proof of their parents' love, I was the proof of their criminality. The only time I could be with my father was indoors. If we left the house, he'd have to walk across the street from us. My mom and I used to go to Joubert Park all the time. It's the Central Park of Johannesburg—beautiful gardens, a zoo, a giant chessboard with human-sized pieces that people would play. My mother tells me that once, when I was a toddler, my dad tried to go with us. We were in the park, he was walking a good bit away from us, and I ran after him, screaming, "Daddy! Daddy! Daddy!" People started looking. He panicked and ran away. I thought it was a game and kept chasing him.

I couldn't walk with my mother, either; a light-skinned child with a black woman would raise too many questions. When I was a newborn, she could wrap me up and take me anywhere, but very quickly that was no longer an option. I was a giant baby, an enormous child. When I was one you'd have thought I was two. When I was two, you'd have thought I was four. There was no way to hide me.

My mom, same as she'd done with her flat and with her maid's uniforms, found the cracks in the system. It was illegal to be mixed (to have a black parent and a white parent), but it was not illegal to be colored (to have two parents who were both colored). So my mom moved me around the world as a colored child. She found a crèche in a colored area where she could leave me while she was at work. There was a colored woman named Queen who lived in our block of flats. When we wanted to go out to the park, my mom would invite her to go with us. Queen would walk next to me and act like she was my mother, and my mother would walk a few steps behind, like she was the maid working for the colored woman. I've got dozens of pictures of me walking with this woman who looks like me but who isn't my mother. And the black woman standing behind us who looks like she's photobombing the picture, that's my mom. When we didn't have a colored woman to walk with us, my mom would risk walking me on her own. She would hold my hand or carry me, but if the police showed up she would have to drop me and pretend I wasn't hers, like I was a bag of weed.

When I was born, my mother hadn't seen her family in three years, but she wanted me to know them and wanted them to know me, so the prodigal daughter returned. We lived in town, but I would spend weeks at a time with my grandmother in Soweto, often during the holidays. I have so many memories from the place that in my mind it's like we lived there, too.

Soweto was designed to be bombed—that's how forward-thinking the architects of apartheid were. The township was a city unto itself, with a population of nearly one million. There were only two roads in and out. That was so the military could lock us in, quell any rebellion. And if the monkeys ever went crazy and tried to break out of their cage, the air force could fly over and bomb the shit out of everyone. Growing up, I never knew that my grandmother lived in the center of a bull's-eye.

In the city, as difficult as it was to get around, we managed. Enough people were out and about, black, white, and colored, going to and from work, that we could get lost in the crowd. But only black people were permitted in Soweto. It was much harder to hide someone who looked like me, and the government was watching much more closely. In the white areas you rarely saw the police, and if you did it was Officer Friendly in his collared shirt and pressed pants. In Soweto the police were an occupying army. They didn't wear collared shirts. They wore riot gear. They were militarized. They operated in teams known as flying squads, because they would swoop in out of nowhere, riding in armored personnel carriers—hippos, we called them—tanks with enormous tires and slotted holes in the side of the vehicle to fire their guns out of. You didn't mess with a hippo. You saw one, you ran. That was a fact of life. The township was in a constant state of insurrection; someone was always marching or protesting somewhere and had to be suppressed. Playing in my grandmother's house, I'd hear gunshots, screams, tear gas being fired into crowds.

My memories of the hippos and the flying squads come from when I was five or six, when apartheid was finally coming apart. I never saw the police before that, because we could never risk the police seeing me. Whenever we went to Soweto, my grandmother refused to let me outside. If she was watching me it was, "No, no, no. He doesn't leave the house." Behind the wall, in the yard, I could play, but not in the street. And that's where the rest of the boys and girls were playing, in the street. My cousins, the neighborhood kids, they'd open the gate and head out and roam free and come back at dusk. I'd beg my grandmother to go outside.

"Please. *Please,* can I go play with my cousins?"

"No! They're going to take you!"

For the longest time I thought she meant that the other kids were going to steal me, but she was talking about the police. Children could be taken. Children *were* taken. The wrong color kid in the wrong color area, and the government could come in, strip your parents of custody, haul you off to an orphanage. To police the townships, the government relied on its network of *impipis,* the anonymous snitches who'd inform on suspicious activity. There were also the blackjacks, black people who worked for the police. My grandmother's neighbor was a blackjack. She had to make sure he wasn't watching when she smuggled me in and out of the house.

My gran still tells the story of when I was three years old and, fed up with being a prisoner, I dug a hole under the gate in the driveway, wriggled through, and ran off. Everyone panicked. A search party went out and tracked me down. I had no idea how much danger I was putting everyone in. The family could have been deported, my gran could have been arrested, my mom might have gone to prison, and I probably would have been packed off to a home for colored kids.

So I was kept inside. Other than those few instances of walking in the park, the flashes of memory I have from when I was young are almost all indoors, me with my mom in her tiny flat, me by myself at my gran's. I didn't have any friends. I didn't know any kids besides my cousins. I wasn't a lonely kid—I was good at being alone. I'd read books, play with the toy that I had, make up imaginary worlds. I lived inside my head. I still live inside my head. To this day you can leave me alone for hours and I'm perfectly happy entertaining myself. I have to remember to be with people.

Obviously, I was not the only child born to black and white parents during apartheid. Traveling around the world today, I meet other mixed South Africans all the time. Our stories start off identically. We're around the same age. Their parents met at some underground party in Hillbrow or Cape Town. They lived in an illegal flat. The difference is that in virtually every other case they left. The white parent smuggled them out through Lesotho or Botswana, and they grew up in exile, in England or Germany or Switzerland, because being a mixed family under apartheid was just that unbearable.

Once Mandela was elected we could finally live freely. Exiles started to return. I met my first one when I was around seventeen. He told me his story, and I was like, "Wait, *what*? You mean we could have *left*?

That was an *option*?" Imagine being thrown out of an airplane. You hit the ground and break all your bones, you go to the hospital and you heal and you move on and finally put the whole thing behind you—and then one day somebody tells you about parachutes. That's how I felt. I couldn't understand why we'd stayed. I went straight home and asked my mom.

"Why? Why didn't we just leave? Why didn't we go to Switzerland?"

"Because I am not Swiss," she said, as stubborn as ever. "This is my country. Why should I leave?"

South Africa is a mix of the old and the new, the ancient and the modern, and South African Christianity is a perfect example of this. We adopted the religion of our colonizers, but most people held on to the old ancestral ways, too, just in case. In South Africa, faith in the Holy Trinity exists quite comfortably alongside belief in witchcraft, in casting spells and putting curses on one's enemies.

I come from a country where people are more likely to visit *sangomas*—shamans, traditional healers, pejoratively known as witch doctors—than they are to visit doctors of Western medicine. I come from a country where people have been arrested and tried for witchcraft— in a court of law. I'm not talking about the 1700s. I'm talking about five years ago. I remember a man being on trial for striking another person with lightning. That happens a lot in the homelands. There are no tall buildings, few tall trees, nothing between you and the sky, so people get hit by lightning all the time. And when someone gets killed by lightning, everyone knows it's because somebody used Mother Nature to take out a hit. So if you had a beef with the guy who got killed, someone will accuse you of murder and the police will come knocking.

"Mr. Noah, you've been accused of murder. You used witchcraft to kill David Kibuuka by causing him to be struck by lightning."

"What is the evidence?"

"The evidence is that David Kibuuka got struck by lightning and it wasn't even raining."

And you go to trial. The court is presided over by a judge. There is a docket. There is a prosecutor. Your defense attorney has to prove lack of motive, go through the crime-scene forensics, present a staunch defense. And your attorney's argument can't be "Witchcraft isn't real." No, no, no. You'll lose.

3

TREVOR, PRAY

I grew up in a world run by women. My father was loving and devoted, but I could only see him when and where apartheid allowed. My uncle Velile, my mom's younger brother, lived with my grandmother, but he spent most of his time at the local tavern getting into fights.

The only semi-regular male figure in my life was my grandfather, my mother's father, who was a force to be reckoned with. He was divorced from my grandmother and didn't live with us, but he was around. His name was Temperance Noah, which was odd since he was not a man of moderation at all. He was boisterous and loud. His nickname in the neighborhood was "Tat Shisha," which translates loosely to "the smokin' hot grandpa." And that's exactly who he was. He loved the ladies, and the ladies loved him. He'd put on his best suit and stroll through the streets of Soweto on random afternoons, making every-body laugh and charming all the women he'd meet. He had a big, daz-zling smile with bright white teeth—false teeth. At home, he'd take them out and I'd watch him do that thing where he looked like he was eating his own face.

We found out much later in life that he was bipolar, but before that we just thought he was eccentric. One time he borrowed my mother's car to go to the shop for milk and bread. He disappeared and didn't come home until late that night when we were way past the point of needing the milk or the bread. Turned out he'd passed a young woman at the bus stop and, believing no beautiful woman should have to wait for a bus, he offered her a ride to where she lived—three hours away. My mom was furious with him because he'd cost us a whole tank of petrol, which was enough to get us to work and school for two weeks.

When he was up you couldn't stop him, but his mood swings were wild. In his youth he'd been a boxer, and one day he said I'd disrespected him and now he wanted to box me. He was in his eighties. I was twelve. He had his fists up, circling me. "Let's go, Trevah! Come on! Put your fists up! Hit me! I'll show you I'm still a man! Let's go!" I couldn't hit him because I wasn't about to hit my elder. Plus I'd never been in a fight and I wasn't going to have my first one be with an eighty-year-old man. I ran to my mom, and she got him to stop. The day after his pugilistic rage, he sat in his chair and didn't move or say a word all day.

Temperance lived with his second family in the Meadowlands, and we visited them sparingly because my mom was always afraid of being poisoned. Which was a thing that would happen. The first family were the heirs, so there was always the chance they might get poisoned by the second family. It was like *Game of Thrones* with poor people. We'd go into that house and my mom would warn me.

"Trevor, don't eat the food."

"But I'm starving."

"No. They might poison us."

"Okay, then why don't I just pray to Jesus and Jesus will take the poison out of the food?"

"Trevor! *Sun'qhela!*"

So I only saw my grandfather now and then, and when he was gone the house was in the hands of women.

In addition to my mom there was my aunt Sibongile; she and her first husband, Dinky, had two kids, my cousins Mlungisi and Bulelwa. Sibongile was a powerhouse, a strong woman in every sense, big-chested, the mother hen. Dinky, as his name implies, was dinky. He was a small man. He was abusive, but not really. It was more like he tried to be abusive, but he wasn't very good at it. He was trying to live up to this image of what he thought a husband should be, dominant, controlling. I remember being told as a child, "If you don't hit your woman, you don't love her." That was the talk you'd hear from men in bars and in the streets.

Dinky was trying to masquerade as this patriarch that he wasn't. He'd slap my aunt and hit her and she'd take it and take it, and then eventually she'd snap and smack him down and put him back in his place. Dinky would always walk around like, "I control my woman." And you'd want to say, "Dinky, first of all, you don't. Second of all, you don't need to. Because she loves you." I can remember one day my aunt had really had enough. I was in the yard and Dinky came running out of the house screaming bloody murder. Sibongile was right behind him with a pot of boiling water, cursing at him and threatening to douse him with it. In Soweto you were always hearing about men getting doused with pots of boiling water—often a woman's only recourse. And men were lucky if it was water. Some women used hot cooking oil. Water was if the woman wanted to teach her man a lesson. Oil meant she wanted to end it.

My grandmother Frances Noah was the family matriarch. She ran the house, looked after the kids, did the cooking and the cleaning. She's barely five feet tall, hunched over from years in the factory, but rock hard and still to this day very active and very much alive. Where my grandfather was big and boisterous, my grandmother was calm, calculating, with a mind as sharp as anything. If you need to know anything in the family history, going back to the 1930s, she can tell you what day it happened, where it happened, and why it happened. She remembers it all.

My great-grandmother lived with us as well. We called her Koko. She was super old, well into her nineties, stooped and frail, completely blind. Her eyes had gone white, clouded over by cataracts. She couldn't walk without someone holding her up. She'd sit in the kitchen next to the coal stove, bundled up in long skirts and head scarves, blankets over her shoulders. The coal stove was always on. It was for cooking, heating the house, heating water for baths. We put her there because it was the warmest spot in the house. In the morning someone would wake her and bring her to sit in the kitchen. At night someone would come take her to bed. That's all she did, all day, every day. Sit by the stove. She was fantastic and fully with it. She just couldn't see and didn't move.

Koko and my gran would sit and have long conversations, but as a five-year-old I didn't think of Koko as a real person. Since her body didn't move, she was like a brain with a mouth. Our relationship was nothing but command prompts and replies, like talking to a computer.

"Good morning, Koko."

"Good morning, Trevor."

"Koko, did you eat?"

"Yes, Trevor."

"Koko, I'm going out."

"Okay, be careful."

"Bye, Koko."

"Bye, Trevor."

The fact that I grew up in a world run by women was no accident. Apartheid kept me away from my father because he was white, but for almost all the kids I knew on my grandmother's block in Soweto, apartheid had taken away their fathers as well, just for different reasons. Their fathers were off working in a mine somewhere, able to come home only during the holidays. Their fathers had been sent to prison.

Their fathers were in exile, fighting for the cause. Women held the community together. *"Wathint'Abafaẓi Wathint'imbokodo!"* was the chant they would rally to during the freedom struggle. "When you strike a woman, you strike a rock." As a nation, we recognized the power of women, but in the home they were expected to submit and obey.

In Soweto, religion filled the void left by absent men. I used to ask my mom if it was hard for her to raise me alone without a husband. She'd reply, "Just because I live without a man doesn't mean I've never had a husband. God is my husband." For my mom, my aunt, my grandmother, and all the other women on our street, life centered on faith. Prayer meetings would rotate houses up and down the block based on the day. These groups were women and children only. My mom would always ask my uncle Velile to join, and he'd say, "I would join if there were more men, but I can't be the only one here." Then the singing and praying would start, and that was his cue to leave.

For these prayer meetings, we'd jam ourselves into the tiny living area of the host family's house and form a circle. Then we would go around the circle offering prayers. The grannies would talk about what was happening in their lives. "I'm happy to be here. I had a good week at work. I got a raise and I wanted to say thank you and praise Jesus." Sometimes they'd pull out their Bible and say, "This scripture spoke to me and maybe it will help you." Then there would be a bit of song. There was a leather pad called "the beat" that you'd strap to your palm, like a percussion instrument. Someone would clap along on that, keeping time while everyone sang, *"Masango vulekani singene eJerusalema. Masango vulekani singene eJerusalema."*

That's how it would go. Pray, sing, pray. Sing, pray, sing. Sing, sing, sing. Pray, pray, pray. Sometimes it would last for hours, always ending with an "amen," and they could keep that "amen" going on for five minutes at least. *"Ah-men. Ah-ah-ah-men. Ah-ah-ah-ah-men. Ahhhhhhhhah-hhhhhhhhhhahhhhhahhhhhahhhhhmen. Meni-meni-meni. Men-men-men. Ahhhhhhhhhhhhhhhhhhhhhhhhhhhhhhhhhhhhhhhhhhhhhhmmmmmmmennn-nnnnnnnnnnnnnnnnnnnnnnnnnnnnnnnnnnnnnnnnnnnnnnnnnnnnnnnnnnnnnn-*

nnnnnnnnnnnnnnnnnnnnnnnnnnnnnnnnnnnnnnnnnnnnnnnnnnnnnnnnnnnnnnnnnnnnnn-nnnnnnnnnnnnn."Then everyone would say goodbye and go home. Next night, different house, same thing.

Tuesday nights, the prayer meeting came to my grandmother's house, and I was always excited, for two reasons. One, I got to clap along on the beat for the singing. And two, I loved to pray. My grandmother always told me that she loved my prayers. She believed my prayers were more powerful, because I prayed in English. Everyone knows that Jesus, who's white, speaks English. The Bible is in English. Yes, the Bible was not *written* in English, but the Bible came to South Africa in English so to us it's in English. Which made my prayers the best prayers because English prayers get answered first. How do we know this? Look at white people. Clearly they're getting through to the right person. Add to that Matthew 19:14. "Suffer little children to come unto me," Jesus said, "for theirs is the kingdom of heaven." So if a child is praying in English? To White Jesus? That's a powerful combination right there. Whenever I prayed, my grandmother would say, "That prayer is going to get answered. I can *feel* it."

Women in the township always had something to pray for—money problems, a son who'd been arrested, a daughter who was sick, a husband who drank. Whenever the prayer meetings were at our house, because my prayers were so good, my grandmother would want me to pray for everyone. She would turn to me and say, "Trevor, pray." And I'd pray. I loved doing it. My grandmother had convinced me that my prayers got answered. I felt like I was helping people.

There is something magical about Soweto. Yes, it was a prison designed by our oppressors, but it also gave us a sense of self-determination and control. Soweto was ours. It had an aspirational quality that you don't find elsewhere. In America the dream is to make it out of the ghetto. In Soweto, because there was no leaving the ghetto, the dream was to transform the ghetto.

For the million people who lived in Soweto, there were no stores, no bars, no restaurants. There were no paved roads, minimal electricity, inadequate sewerage. But when you put one million people together in one place, they find a way to make a life for themselves. A black-market economy rose up, with every type of business being run out of someone's house: auto mechanics, day care, guys selling refurbished tires.

The most common were the *spaza* shops and the shebeens. The *spaza* shops were informal grocery stores. People would build a kiosk in their garage, buy wholesale bread and eggs, and then resell them piecemeal. Everyone in the township bought things in minute quantities because nobody had any money. You couldn't afford to buy a dozen eggs at a time, but you could buy two eggs because that's all you needed that morning. You could buy a quarter loaf of bread, a cup of sugar. The shebeens were unlawful bars in the back of someone's house. They'd put chairs in their backyard and hang out an awning and run a speakeasy. The shebeens were where men would go to drink after work and during prayer meetings and most any other time of day as well.

People built homes the way they bought eggs: a little at a time. Every family in the township was allocated a piece of land by the government. You'd first build a shanty on your plot, a makeshift structure of plywood and corrugated iron. Over time, you'd save up money and build a brick wall. One wall. Then you'd save up and build another wall. Then, years later, a third wall and eventually a fourth. Now you had a room, one room for everyone in your family to sleep, eat, do everything. Then you'd save up for a roof. Then windows. Then you'd plaster the thing. Then your daughter would start a family. There was nowhere for them to go, so they'd move in with you. You'd add another corrugated-iron structure onto your brick room and slowly, over years, turn that into a proper room for them as well. Now your house had two rooms. Then three. Maybe four. Slowly, over generations, you'd keep trying to get to the point where you had a home.

My grandmother lived in Orlando East. She had a two-room house. Not a two-bedroom house. A two-room house. There was a bedroom, and then there was basically a living room/kitchen/everything-else room. Some might say we lived like poor people. I prefer "open plan." My mom and I would stay there during school holidays. My aunt and cousins would be there whenever she was on the outs with Dinky. We all slept on the floor in one room, my mom and me, my aunt and my cousins, my uncle and my grandmother and my great-grandmother. The adults each had their own foam mattresses, and there was one big one that we'd roll out into the middle, and the kids slept on that.

We had two shanties in the backyard that my grandmother would rent out to migrants and seasonal workers. We had a small peach tree in a tiny patch on one side of the house and on the other side my grandmother had a driveway. I never understood why my grandmother had a driveway. She didn't have a car. She didn't know how to drive. Yet she had a driveway. All of our neighbors had driveways, some with fancy, cast-iron gates. None of them had cars, either. There was no future in which most of these families would ever have cars. There was maybe one car for every thousand people, yet almost everyone had a driveway. It was almost like building the driveway was a way of willing the car to happen. The story of Soweto is the story of the driveways. It's a hopeful place.

Sadly, no matter how fancy you made your house, there was one thing you could never aspire to improve: your toilet. There was no indoor running water, just one communal outdoor tap and one outdoor toilet shared by six or seven houses. Our toilet was in a corrugated-iron outhouse shared among the adjoining houses. Inside, there was a concrete slab with a hole in it and a plastic toilet seat on top; there had been a lid at some point, but it had broken and disappeared long ago. We couldn't afford toilet paper, so on the wall next to the seat was a wire hanger with old newspaper on it for you to wipe. The newspaper was uncomfortable, but at least I stayed informed while I handled my business.

The thing that I couldn't handle about the outhouse was the flies. It was a long drop to the bottom, and they were always down there, eating on the pile, and I had an irrational, all-consuming fear that they were going to fly up and into my bum.

One afternoon, when I was around five years old, my gran left me at home for a few hours to go run errands. I was lying on the floor in the bedroom, reading. I needed to go, but it was pouring down rain. I was dreading going outside to use the toilet, getting drenched running out there, water dripping on me from the leaky ceiling, wet newspaper, the flies attacking me from below. Then I had an idea. Why bother with the outhouse at all? Why not put some newspaper on the floor and do my business like a puppy? That seemed like a fantastic idea. So that's what I did. I took the newspaper, laid it out on the kitchen floor, pulled down my pants, and squatted and got to it.

When you shit, as you first sit down, you're not fully in the experience yet. You are not yet a shitting person. You're transitioning from a person about to shit to a person who is shitting. You don't whip out your smartphone or a newspaper right away. It takes a minute to get the first shit out of the way and get in the zone and get comfortable. Once you reach that moment, that's when it gets really nice.

It's a powerful experience, shitting. There's something magical about it, profound even. I think God made humans shit in the way we do because it brings us back down to earth and gives us humility. I don't care who you are, we all shit the same. Beyoncé shits. The pope shits. The Queen of England shits. When we shit we forget our airs and our graces, we forget how famous or how rich we are. All of that goes away.

You are never more yourself than when you're taking a shit. You have that moment where you realize, *This is me. This is who I am.* You can pee without giving it a second thought, but not so with shitting. Have you ever looked in a baby's eyes when it's shitting? It's having a moment of pure self-awareness. The outhouse ruins that for you. The rain, the flies, you are robbed of your moment, and nobody should be robbed of that. Squatting and shitting on the kitchen floor that day, I was like, *Wow. There are no flies. There's no stress. This is really great. I'm really enjoying this.* I knew I'd made an excellent choice, and I was very proud of myself for making it. I'd reached that moment where I could relax and be with myself. Then I casually looked around the room and I glanced to my left and there, just a few feet away, right next to the coal stove, was Koko.

It was like the scene in *Jurassic Park* when the children turn and the T. rex is right there. Her eyes were wide open, cloudy white and darting around the room. I knew she couldn't see me, but her nose was starting to crinkle—she could sense that something was wrong.

I panicked. I was mid-shit. All you can do when you're mid-shit is finish shitting. My only option was to finish as quietly and as slowly as I could, so that's what I decided to do. Then: the softest *plop* of a little-boy turd on the newspaper. Koko's head snapped toward the sound.

"Who's there? Hallo? *Hallo?!*"

I froze. I held my breath and waited.

"Who's there?! Hallo?!"

I kept quiet, waited, then started again.

"Is somebody there?! Trevor, is that you?! Frances? Hallo? Hallo?"

She started calling out the whole family. "Nombuyiselo? Sibongile? Mlungisi? Bulelwa? Who's there? What's happening?"

It was like a game, like I was trying to hide and a blind woman was trying to find me using sonar. Every time she called out, I froze. There would be complete silence. "Who's there?! Hallo?!" I'd pause, wait for her to settle back in her chair, and then I'd start up again.

Finally, after what felt like forever, I finished. I stood up, took the newspaper—which is not the quietest thing—and I slowwwwwly folded it over. It crinkled. "Who's there?" Again I paused, waited. Then I folded it over some more, walked over to the rubbish bin, placed my sin at the bottom, and gingerly covered it with the rest of the trash. Then I tiptoed back to the other room, curled up on the mattress on the floor, and pretended to be asleep. The shit was done, no outhouse involved, and Koko was none the wiser.

Mission accomplished.

An hour later the rain had stopped. My grandmother came home. The second she walked in, Koko called out to her.

"Frances! Thank God you're here. There's something in the house."

"What was it?"

"I don't know, but I could hear it, and there was a smell."

My gran started sniffing the air. "Dear Lord! Yes, I can smell it, too. Is it a rat? Did something die? It's definitely in the house."

They went back and forth about it, quite concerned, and then, as it was getting dark, my mother came home from work. The second she walked in, my gran called out to her.

"Oh, Nombuyiselo! Nombuyiselo! There's something in the house!"

"What?! What do you mean?"

Koko told her the story, the sounds, the smells.

Then my mom, who has a keen sense of smell, started going around the kitchen, sniffing. "Yes, I can smell it. I can find it . . . I can find it . . ." She went to the rubbish bin. "It's in here." She lifted out the rubbish, pulled out the folded newspaper underneath, and opened it up, and there was my little turd. She showed it to gran.

"Look!"

"What?! How did it get there?!"

Koko, still blind, still stuck in her chair, was dying to know what was happening.

"What's going on?!" she cried. "What's going on?! Did you find it?!"

"It's shit," Mom said. "There's shit in the bottom of the dustbin."

"But how?!" Koko said. "There was no one here!"

"Are you sure there was no one here?"

"Yes. I called out to everyone. Nobody came."

My mother gasped. "We've been bewitched! It's a demon!"

For my mother, this was the logical conclusion. Because that's how witchcraft works. If someone has put a curse on you or your home, there is always the talisman or totem, a tuft of hair or the head of a cat, the physical manifestation of the spiritual thing, proof of the demon's presence.

Once my mom found the turd, all hell broke loose. This was *serious*. They had *evidence*. She came into the bedroom.

"Trevor! Trevor! Wake up!"

"What?!" I said, playing dumb. "What's going on?!"

"Come! There's a demon in the house!"

She took my hand and dragged me out of bed. It was all hands on deck, time for action. The first thing we had to do was go outside and burn the shit. That's what you do with witchcraft; the only way to destroy it is to burn the physical thing. We went out to the yard, and my mom put the newspaper with my little turd on the driveway, lit a match, and set it on fire. Then my mom and my gran stood around the burning shit, praying and singing songs of praise.

The commotion didn't stop there because when there's a demon around, the whole community has to join together to drive it out. If you're not part of the prayer, the demon might leave our house and go to your house and curse you. So we needed everyone. The alarm was raised. The call went out. My tiny old gran was out the gate, going up and down the block, calling to all the other old grannies for an emergency prayer meeting. "Come! We've been bewitched!"

I stood there, my shit burning in the driveway, my poor aged grandmother tottering up and down the street in a panic, and I didn't know what to do. I knew there was no demon, but there was no way I could come clean. The hiding I would have to endure? Good Lord. Honesty was never the best policy when it came to a hiding. I kept quiet.

Moments later the grannies came streaming in with their Bibles, through the gate and up the driveway, a dozen or more at least. Everyone went inside. The house was packed. This was by far the biggest prayer meeting we'd ever had—the biggest thing that had ever happened in the history of our home, period. Everyone sat in the circle, praying and praying, and the prayers were strong. The grannies were chanting and murmuring and swaying back and forth, speaking in tongues. I was doing my best to keep my head low and stay out of it. Then my grandmother reached back and grabbed me, pulled me into the middle of the circle, and looked into my eyes.

"Trevor, pray."

"Yes!" my mother said. "Help us! Pray, Trevor. Pray to God to kill the demon!"

I was terrified. I believed in the power of prayer. I knew that my prayers *worked*. So if I prayed to God to kill the thing that left the shit, and the thing that left the shit was me, then God was going to kill me. I froze. I didn't know what to do. But all the grannies were looking at me, waiting for me to pray, so I prayed, stumbling through as best I could.

> *"Dear Lord, please protect us, um, you know, from whoever did this but, like, we don't know what happened exactly and maybe it was a big misunderstanding and, you know, maybe we shouldn't be quick to judge when we don't know the whole story and, I mean, of course you know best, Heavenly Father, but maybe this time it wasn't actually a demon, because who can say for certain, so maybe cut whoever it was a break . . ."*

It was not my best performance. Eventually I wrapped it up and sat back down. The praying continued. It went on for some time. Pray, sing, pray. Sing, pray, sing. Sing, sing, sing. Pray, pray, pray. Then everyone finally felt that the demon was gone and life could continue, and we had the big "amen" and everyone said good night and went home.

That night I felt terrible. Before bed, I quietly prayed, "God, I am so sorry for all of this. I know this was not cool." Because I knew: God answers your prayers. God is your father. He's the man who's there for you, the man who takes care of you. When you pray, He stops and He takes His time and He listens, and I had subjected Him to two hours of old grannies praying when I knew that with all the pain and suffering in the world He had more important things to deal with than my shit.

When I was growing up we used to get American TV shows rebroadcast on our stations: *Doogie Howser, M.D.; Murder, She Wrote; Rescue 911* with William Shatner. Most of them were dubbed into African languages. *ALF* was in Afrikaans. *Transformers* was in Sotho. But if you wanted to watch them in English, the original American audio would be simulcast on the radio. You could mute your TV and listen to that. Watching those shows, I realized that whenever black people were on-screen speaking in African languages, they felt familiar to me. They sounded like they were supposed to sound. Then I'd listen to them in simulcast on the radio, and they would all have black American accents. My perception of them changed. They didn't feel familiar. They felt like foreigners.

Language brings with it an identity and a culture, or at least the perception of it. A shared language says "We're the same." A language barrier says "We're different." The architects of apartheid understood this. Part of the effort to divide black people was to make sure we were separated not just physically but by language as well. In the Bantu schools, children were only taught in their home language. Zulu kids learned in Zulu. Tswana kids learned in Tswana. Because of this, we'd fall into the trap the government had set for us and fight among ourselves, believing that we were different.

The great thing about language is that you can just as easily use it to do the opposite: convince people that they are the same. Racism teaches us that we are different because of the color of our skin. But because racism is stupid, it's easily tricked. If you're racist and you meet someone who doesn't look like you, the fact that he can't speak like you reinforces your racist preconceptions: He's different, less intelligent. A brilliant scientist can come over the border from Mexico to live in America, but if he speaks in broken English, people say, "Eh, I don't trust this guy."

"But he's a scientist."

"In Mexican science, maybe. I don't trust him."

However, if the person who doesn't look like you speaks like you, your brain short-circuits because your racism program has none of those instructions in the code. "Wait, wait," your mind says, "the racism code says if he doesn't look like me he isn't like me, but the language code says if he speaks like me he . . . is like me? Something is off here. I can't figure this out."

4

CHAMELEON

One afternoon I was playing with my cousins. I was a doctor and they were my patients. I was operating on my cousin Bulelwa's ear with a set of matches when I accidentally perforated her eardrum. All hell broke loose. My grandmother came running in from the kitchen. *"Kwenzeka ntoni?!"* "What's happening?!" There was blood coming out of my cousin's head. We were all crying. My grandmother patched up Bulelwa's ear and made sure to stop the bleeding. But we kept crying. Because clearly we'd done something we were not supposed to do, and we knew we were going to be punished. My grandmother finished up with Bulelwa's ear and whipped out a belt and she beat the shit out of Bulelwa. Then she beat the shit out of Mlungisi, too. She didn't touch me.

Later that night my mother came home from work. She found my cousin with a bandage over her ear and my gran crying at the kitchen table.

"What's going on?" my mom said.

"Oh, Nombuyiselo," she said. "Trevor is so naughty. He's the naughtiest child I've ever come across in my life."

"Then you should hit him."

"I can't hit him."

"Why not?"

"Because I don't know how to hit a white child," she said. "A black child, I understand. A black child, you hit them and they stay black. Trevor, when you hit him he turns blue and green and yellow and red. I've never seen those colors before. I'm scared I'm going to break him. I don't want to kill a white person. I'm so afraid. I'm not going to touch him." And she never did.

My grandmother treated me like I was white. My grandfather did, too, only he was even more extreme. He called me "Mastah." In the car, he insisted on driving me as if he were my chauffeur. "Mastah must always sit in the backseat." I never challenged him on it. What was I going to say? "I believe your perception of race is flawed, Grandfather." No. I was five. I sat in the back.

There were so many perks to being "white" in a black family, I can't even front. I was having a great time. My own family basically did what the American justice system does: I was given more lenient treatment than the black kids. Misbehavior that my cousins would have been punished for, I was given a warning and let off. And I was way naughtier than either of my cousins. It wasn't even close. If something got broken or if someone was stealing granny's cookies, it was me. I was trouble.

My mom was the only force I truly feared. She believed if you spare the rod, you spoil the child. But everyone else said, "No, he's different," and they gave me a pass. Growing up the way I did, I learned how easy it is for white people to get comfortable with a system that awards them all the perks. I knew my cousins were getting beaten for things that I'd done, but I wasn't interested in changing my grandmother's perspective, because that would mean I'd get beaten, too. Why would I do that? So that I'd *feel* better? Being beaten didn't make me feel better. I had a choice. I could champion racial justice in our home, or I could enjoy granny's cookies. I went with the cookies.

At that point I didn't think of the special treatment as having to do with color. I thought of it as having to do with Trevor. It wasn't, "Trevor doesn't get beaten because Trevor is white." It was, "Trevor doesn't get beaten because Trevor is Trevor." Trevor can't go outside. Trevor can't walk without supervision. It's because I'm me; that's why this is happening. I had no other points of reference. There were no other mixed kids around so that I could say, "Oh, this happens to *us*."

Nearly one million people lived in Soweto. Ninety-nine point nine percent of them were black—and then there was me. I was famous in my neighborhood just because of the color of my skin. I was so unique people would give directions using me as a landmark. "The house on Makhalima Street. At the corner you'll see a light-skinned boy. Take a right there."

Whenever the kids in the street saw me they'd yell, *"Indoda yom-lungu!"* "The white man!" Some of them would run away. Others would call out to their parents to come look. Others would run up and try to touch me to see if I was real. It was pandemonium. What I didn't understand at the time was that the other kids genuinely had no clue what a white person was. Black kids in the township didn't leave the township. Few people had televisions. They'd seen the white police roll through, but they'd never dealt with a white person face-to-face, ever.

I'd go to funerals and I'd walk in and the bereaved would look up and see me and they'd stop crying. They'd start whispering. Then they'd wave and say, "Oh!" like they were more shocked by me walking in than by the death of their loved ones. I think people felt like the dead person was more important because a white person had come to the funeral.

After a funeral, the mourners all go to the house of the surviving family to eat. A hundred people might show up, and you've got to feed them. Usually you get a cow and slaughter it and your neighbors come over and help you cook. Neighbors and acquaintances eat outside in the yard and in the street, and the family eats indoors. Every funeral I ever went to, I ate indoors. It didn't matter if we knew the deceased or not. The family would see me and invite me in. *"Awunakuvumela umntana womlungu ame ngaphandle. Yiza naye apha ngaphakathi,"* they'd say. "You can't let the white child stand outside. Bring him in here."

As a kid I understood that people were different colors, but in my head white and black and brown were like types of chocolate. Dad was the white chocolate, mom was the dark chocolate, and I was the milk chocolate. But we were all just chocolate. I didn't know any of it had anything to do with "race." I didn't know what race was. My mother never referred to my dad as white or to me as mixed. So when the other kids in Soweto called me "white," even though I was light brown, I just thought they had their colors mixed up, like they hadn't learned them properly. "Ah, yes, my friend. You've confused aqua with turquoise. I can see how you made that mistake. You're not the first."

I soon learned that the quickest way to bridge the race gap was through language. Soweto was a melting pot: families from different tribes and homelands. Most kids in the township spoke only their home language, but I learned several languages because I grew up in a house where there was no option but to learn them. My mom made sure English was the first language I spoke. If you're black in South Africa, speaking English is the one thing that can give you a leg up. English is the language of money. English comprehension is equated with intelligence. If you're looking for a job, English is the difference between getting the job or staying unemployed. If you're standing in the dock, English is the difference between getting off with a fine or going to prison.

After English, Xhosa was what we spoke around the house. When my mother was angry she'd fall back on her home language. As a naughty child, I was well versed in Xhosa threats. They were the first phrases I picked up, mostly for my own safety—phrases like *"Ndiza kubetha entloko."* "I'll knock you upside the head." Or *"Sidenge ndini somntwana."* "You idiot of a child." It's a very passionate language. Outside of that, my mother picked up different languages here and there. She learned Zulu because it's similar to Xhosa. She spoke German because of my father. She spoke Afrikaans because it is useful to know the language of your oppressor. Sotho she learned in the streets.

Living with my mom, I saw how she used language to cross boundaries, handle situations, navigate the world. We were in a shop once, and the shopkeeper, right in front of us, turned to his security guard and said, in Afrikaans, *"Volg daai swartes, netnou steel hulle iets."* "Follow those blacks in case they steal something."

My mother turned around and said, in beautiful, fluent Afrikaans, *"Hoekom volg jy nie daai swartes sodat jy hulle kan help kry waarna hulle soek nie?"* "Why don't you follow these blacks so you can help them find what they're looking for?"

"Ag, jammer!" he said, apologizing in Afrikaans. Then—and this was the funny thing—he didn't apologize for being racist; he merely apologized for aiming his racism at us. "Oh, I'm so sorry," he said. "I thought you were like the other blacks. You know how they love to steal."

I learned to use language like my mother did. I would simulcast—give you the program in your own tongue. I'd get suspicious looks from people just walking down the street. "Where are you from?" they'd ask. I'd reply in whatever language they'd addressed me in, using the same accent that they used. There would be a brief moment of confusion, and then the suspicious look would disappear. "Oh, okay. I thought you were a stranger. We're good then."

It became a tool that served me my whole life. One day as a young man I was walking down the street, and a group of Zulu guys was walking behind me, closing in on me, and I could hear them talking to one another about how they were going to mug me. *"Asibambe le autie yomlungu. Phuma ngapha mina ngizoqhamuka ngemuva kwakhe."* "Let's get this white guy. You go to his left, and I'll come up behind him." I didn't know what to do. I couldn't run, so I just spun around real quick and said, *"Kodwa bafwethu yingani singavele sibambe umuntu inkunzi? Asenzeni. Mina ngikulindele."* "Yo, guys, why don't we just mug someone together? I'm ready. Let's do it."

They looked shocked for a moment, and then they started laughing.

"Oh, sorry, dude. We thought you were something else. We weren't trying to take anything from you. We were trying to steal from white people. Have a good day, man." They were ready to do me violent harm, until they felt we were part of the same tribe, and then we were cool. That, and so many other smaller incidents in my life, made me realize that language, even more than color, defines who you are to people.

I became a chameleon. My color didn't change, but I could change your perception of my color. If you spoke to me in Zulu, I replied to you in Zulu. If you spoke to me in Tswana, I replied to you in Tswana. Maybe I didn't look like you, but if I spoke like you, I was you.

As apartheid was coming to an end, South Africa's elite private schools started accepting children of all colors. My mother's company offered bursaries, scholarships, for underprivileged families, and she managed to get me into Maryvale College, an expensive private Catholic school. Classes taught by nuns. Mass on Fridays. The whole bit. I started pre-school there when I was three, primary school when I was five.

In my class we had all kinds of kids. Black kids, white kids, Indian kids, colored kids. Most of the white kids were pretty well off. Every child of color pretty much wasn't. But because of scholarships we all sat at the same table. We wore the same maroon blazers, the same gray slacks and skirts. We had the same books. We had the same teachers. There was no racial separation. Every clique was racially mixed.

Kids still got teased and bullied, but it was over usual kid stuff: being fat or being skinny, being tall or being short, being smart or being dumb. I don't remember anybody being teased about their race. I didn't learn to put limits on what I was supposed to like or not like. I had a wide berth to explore myself. I had crushes on white girls. I had crushes on black girls. Nobody asked me what I was. I was Trevor.

It was a wonderful experience to have, but the downside was that it sheltered me from reality. Maryvale was an oasis that kept me from the truth, a comfortable place where I could avoid making a tough decision. But the real world doesn't go away. Racism exists. People are getting hurt, and just because it's not happening to you doesn't mean it's not happening. And at some point, you have to choose. Black or white. Pick a side. You can try to hide from it. You can say, "Oh, I don't pick sides," but at some point life will force you to pick a side.

At the end of grade six I left Maryvale to go to H. A. Jack Primary, a government school. I had to take an aptitude test before I started, and, based on the results of the test, the school counselor told me, "You're going to be in the smart classes, the A classes." I showed up for the first day of school and went to my classroom. Of the thirty or so kids in my class, almost all of them were white. There was one Indian kid, maybe one or two black kids, and me.

Then recess came. We went out on the playground, and black kids were *everywhere*. It was an ocean of black, like someone had opened a tap and all the black had come pouring out. I was like, *Where were they all hiding?* The white kids I'd met that morning, they went in one direction, the black kids went in another direction, and I was left standing in the middle, totally confused. Were we going to meet up later on? I did not understand what was happening.

I was eleven years old, and it was like I was seeing my country for the first time. In the townships you don't see segregation, because everyone is black. In the white world, any time my mother took me to a white church, we were the only black people there, and my mom didn't separate herself from anyone. She didn't care. She'd go right up and sit with the white people. And at Maryvale, the kids were mixed up and hanging out together. Before that day, I had never seen people being together and yet not together, occupying the same space yet choosing not to associate with each other in any way. In an instant I could see, I could feel, how the boundaries were drawn. Groups moved in color patterns across the yard, up the stairs, down the hall. It was insane. I looked over at the white kids I'd met that morning. Ten minutes earlier I'd thought I was at a school where they were a majority. Now I realized how few of them there actually were compared to everyone else.

I stood there awkwardly by myself in this no-man's-land in the middle of the playground. Luckily, I was rescued by the Indian kid from my class, a guy named Theesan Pillay. Theesan was one of the few Indian kids in school, so he'd noticed me, another obvious outsider, right away. He ran over to introduce himself. "Hello, fellow anomaly! You're in my class. Who are you? What's your story?" We started talking and hit it off. He took me under his wing, the Artful Dodger to my bewildered Oliver.

Through our conversation it came up that I spoke several African languages, and Theesan thought a colored kid speaking black languages was the most amazing trick. He brought me over to a group of black kids. "Say something," he told them, "and he'll show you he understands you." One kid said something in Zulu, and I replied to him in Zulu. Everyone cheered. Another kid said something in Xhosa, and I replied to him in Xhosa. Everyone cheered. For the rest of recess Theesan took me around to different black kids on the playground. "Show them your trick. Do your language thing."

The black kids were fascinated. In South Africa back then, it wasn't common to find a white person or a colored person who spoke African languages; during apartheid white people were always taught that those languages were beneath them. So the fact that I did speak African languages immediately endeared me to the black kids.

"How come you speak our languages?" they asked.

"Because I'm black," I said, "like you."

"You're not black."

"Yes, I am."

"No, you're not. Have you not seen yourself?"

They were confused at first. Because of my color, they thought I was a colored person, but speaking the same languages meant that I belonged to their tribe. It just took them a moment to figure it out. It took me a moment, too.

At some point I turned to one of them and said, "Hey, how come I don't see you guys in any of my classes?" It turned out they were in the B classes, which also happened to be the black classes. That same afternoon, I went back to the A classes, and by the end of the day I realized that they weren't for me. Suddenly, I knew who my people were, and I wanted to be with them. I went to see the school counselor.

"I'd like to switch over," I told her. "I'd like to go to the B classes."

She was confused. "Oh, no," she said. "I don't think you want to do that."

"Why not?"

"Because those kids are . . . you know."

"No, I don't know. What do you mean?"

"Look," she said, "you're a smart kid. You don't want to be in that class."

"But aren't the classes the same? English is English. Math is math."

"Yeah, but that class is . . . those kids are gonna hold you back. You want to be in the smart class."

"But surely there must be some smart kids in the B class."

"No, there aren't."

"But all my friends are there."

"You don't want to be friends with those kids."

"Yes, I do."

We went back and forth. Finally she gave me a stern warning.

"You do realize the effect this will have on your future? You do understand what you're giving up? This will impact the opportunities you'll have open to you for the rest of your life."

"I'll take that chance."

I moved to the B classes with the black kids. I decided I'd rather be held back with people I liked than move ahead with people I didn't know.

Being at H. A. Jack made me realize I was black. Before that recess I'd never had to choose, but when I was forced to choose, I chose black. The world saw me as colored, but I didn't spend my life looking at myself. I spent my life looking at other people. I saw myself as the people around me, and the people around me were black. My cousins are black, my mom is black, my gran is black. I grew up black. Because I had a white father, because I'd been in white Sunday school, I got along with the white kids, but I didn't *belong* with the white kids. I wasn't a part of their tribe. But the black kids embraced me. "Come along," they said. "You're rolling with us." With the black kids, I wasn't constantly trying to be. With the black kids, I just was.

Before apartheid, any black South African who received a formal education was likely taught by European missionaries, foreign enthusiasts eager to Christianize and Westernize the natives. In the mission schools, black people learned English, European literature, medicine, the law. It's no coincidence that nearly every major black leader of the anti-apartheid movement, from Nelson Mandela to Steve Biko, was educated by the missionaries—a knowledgeable man is a free man, or at least a man who longs for freedom.

The only way to make apartheid work, therefore, was to cripple the black mind. Under apartheid, the government built what became known as Bantu schools. Bantu schools taught no science, no history, no civics. They taught metrics and agriculture: how to count potatoes, how to pave roads, chop wood, till the soil. "It does not serve the Bantu to learn history and science because he is primitive," the government said. "This will only mislead him, showing him pastures in which he is not allowed to graze." To their credit, they were simply being honest. Why educate a slave? Why teach someone Latin when his only purpose is to dig holes in the ground?

Mission schools were told to conform to the new curriculum or shut down. Most of them shut down, and black children were forced into crowded classrooms in dilapidated schools, often with teachers who were barely literate themselves. Our parents and grandparents were taught with little singsong lessons, the way you'd teach a preschooler shapes and colors. My grandfather used to sing the songs and laugh about how silly they were. *Two times two is four. Three times two is six. La la la la la.* We're talking about fully grown teenagers being taught this way, for generations.

What happened with education in South Africa, with the mission schools and the Bantu schools, offers a neat comparison of the two groups of whites who oppressed us, the British and the Afrikaners. The difference between British racism and Afrikaner racism was that at least the British gave the natives something to aspire to. If they could learn to speak correct English and dress in proper clothes, if they could Anglicize and civilize themselves, one day they *might* be welcome in society. The Afrikaners never gave us that option. British racism said, "If the monkey can walk like a man and talk like a man, then perhaps he is a man." Afrikaner racism said, "Why give a book to a monkey?"

5

THE SECOND GIRL

My mother used to tell me, "I chose to have you because I wanted something to love and something that would love me unconditionally in return." I was a product of her search for belonging. She never felt like she belonged anywhere. She didn't belong to her mother, didn't belong to her father, didn't belong with her siblings. She grew up with nothing and wanted something to call her own.

My grandparents' marriage was an unhappy one. They met and married in Sophiatown, but one year later the army came in and drove them out. The government seized their home and bulldozed the whole area to build a fancy, new white suburb, *Triomf*. Triumph. Along with tens of thousands of other black people, my grandparents were forcibly relocated to Soweto, to a neighborhood called the Meadowlands. They divorced not long after that, and my grandmother moved to Orlando with my mom, my aunt, and my uncle.

My mom was the problem child, a tomboy, stubborn, defiant. My gran had no idea how to raise her. Whatever love they had was lost in the constant fighting that went on between them. But my mom adored her father, the charming, charismatic Temperance. She went gallivanting with him on his manic misadventures. She'd tag along when he'd go drinking in the shebeens. All she wanted in life was to please him and be with him. She was always being swatted away by his girlfriends, who didn't like having a reminder of his first marriage hanging around, but that only made her want to be with him all the more.

When my mother was nine years old, she told my gran that she didn't want to live with her anymore. She wanted to live with her father. "If that's what you want," Gran said, "then go." Temperance came to pick my mom up, and she happily bounded up into his car, ready to go and be with the man she loved. But instead of taking her to live with him in the Meadowlands, without even telling her why, he packed her off and sent her to live with his sister in the Xhosa homeland, Transkei—he didn't want her, either. My mom was the middle child. Her sister was the eldest and firstborn. Her brother was the only son, bearer of the family name. They both stayed in Soweto, were both raised and cared for by their parents. But my mom was unwanted. She was the second girl. The only place she would have less value would be China.

My mother didn't see her family again for twelve years. She lived in a hut with fourteen cousins—fourteen children from fourteen different mothers and fathers. All the husbands and uncles had gone off to the cities to find work, and the children who weren't wanted, or whom no one could afford to feed, had been sent back to the homeland to live on this aunt's farm.

The homelands were, ostensibly, the original homes of South Africa's tribes, sovereign and semi-sovereign "nations" where black people would be "free." Of course, this was a lie. For starters, despite the fact that black people made up over 80 percent of South Africa's population, the territory allocated for the homelands was about 13 percent of the country's land. There was no running water, no electricity. People lived in huts.

Where South Africa's white countryside was lush and irrigated and green, the black lands were overpopulated and overgrazed, the soil depleted and eroding. Other than the menial wages sent home from the cities, families scraped by with little beyond subsistence-level farming. My mother's aunt hadn't taken her in out of charity. She was there to work. "I was one of the cows," my mother would later say, "one of the oxen." She and her cousins were up at half past four, plowing fields and herding animals before the sun baked the soil as hard as cement and made it too hot to be anywhere but in the shade.

For dinner there might be one chicken to feed fourteen children. My mom would have to fight with the bigger kids to get a handful of meat or a sip of the gravy or even a bone from which to suck out some marrow. And that's when there was food for dinner at all. When there wasn't, she'd steal food from the pigs. She'd steal food from the dogs. The farmers would put out scraps for the animals, and she'd jump for it. She was hungry; let the animals fend for themselves. There were times when she literally ate dirt. She would go down to the river, take the clay from the riverbank, and mix it with the water to make a grayish kind of milk. She'd drink that to feel full.

But my mother was blessed that her village was one of the places where a mission school had contrived to stay open in spite of the government's Bantu education policies. There she had a white pastor who taught her English. She didn't have food or shoes or even a pair of underwear, but she had English. She could read and write. When she was old enough she stopped working on the farm and got a job at a factory in a nearby town. She worked on a sewing machine making school uniforms. Her pay at the end of each day was a plate of food. She used to say it was the best food she'd ever eaten, because it was something she had earned on her own. She wasn't a burden to anyone and didn't owe anything to anyone.

When my mom turned twenty-one, her aunt fell ill and that family could no longer keep her in Transkei. My mom wrote to my gran, asking her to send the price of a train ticket, about thirty rand, to bring her home. Back in Soweto, my mom enrolled in the secretarial course that allowed her to grab hold of the bottom rung of the white-collar world. She worked and worked and worked but, living under my grandmother's roof, she wasn't allowed to keep her own wages. As a secretary, my mom was bringing home more money than anyone else, and my grandmother insisted it all go to the family. The family needed a radio, an oven, a refrigerator, and it was now my mom's job to provide it.

So many black families spend all of their time trying to fix the problems of the past. That is the curse of being black and poor, and it is a curse that follows you from generation to generation. My mother calls it "the black tax." Because the generations who came before you have been pillaged, rather than being free to use your skills and education to move forward, you lose everything just trying to bring everyone behind you back up to zero. Working for the family in Soweto, my mom had no more freedom than she'd had in Transkei, so she ran away. She ran all the way down to the train station and jumped on a train and disappeared into the city, determined to sleep in public restrooms and rely on the kindness of prostitutes until she could make her own way in the world.

My mother never sat me down and told me the whole story of her life in Transkei. She'd give me little bursts, random details, stories of having to keep her wits about her to avoid getting raped by strange men in the village. She'd tell me these things and I'd be like, *Lady, clearly you do not know what kind of stories to be telling a ten-year-old*.

My mom told me these things so that I'd never take for granted how we got to where we were, but none of it ever came from a place of self-pity. "Learn from your past and be better because of your past," she would say, "but don't cry about your past. Life is full of pain. Let the pain sharpen you, but don't hold on to it. Don't be bitter." And she never was. The deprivations of her youth, the betrayals of her parents, she never complained about any of it.

Just as she let the past go, she was determined not to repeat it: my childhood would bear no resemblance to hers. She started with my name. The names Xhosa families give their children always have a meaning, and that meaning has a way of becoming self-fulfilling. You have my cousin, Mlungisi. "The Fixer." That's who he is. Whenever I got into trouble he was the one trying to help me fix it. He was always the good kid, doing chores, helping around the house. You have my uncle, the unplanned pregnancy, Velile. "He Who Popped Out of Nowhere." And that's all he's done his whole life, disappear and reappear. He'll go off on a drinking binge and then pop back up out of nowhere a week later.

Then you have my mother, Patricia Nombuyiselo Noah. "She Who Gives Back." That's what she does. She gives and gives and gives. She did it even as a girl in Soweto. Playing in the streets she would find toddlers, three- and four-year-olds, running around unsupervised all day long. Their fathers were gone and their mothers were drunks. My mom, who was only six or seven herself, used to round up the abandoned kids and form a troop and take them around to the shebeens. They'd collect empties from the men who were passed out and take the bottles to where you could turn them in for a deposit. Then my mom would take that money, buy food in the *spaza* shops, and feed the kids. She was a child taking care of children.

When it was time to pick my name, she chose Trevor, a name with no meaning whatsoever in South Africa, no precedent in my family. It's not even a Biblical name. It's just a name. My mother wanted her child beholden to no fate. She wanted me to be free to go anywhere, do anything, be anyone.

She gave me the tools to do it as well. She taught me English as my first language. She read to me constantly. The first book I learned to read was *the* book. The Bible. Church was where we got most of our other books, too. My mom would bring home boxes that white people had donated—picture books, chapter books, any book she could get her hands on. Then she signed up for a subscription program where we got books in the mail. It was a series of how-to books. *How to Be a*

Good Friend. How to Be Honest. She bought a set of encyclopedias, too; it was fifteen years old and way out of date, but I would sit and pore through those.

My books were my prized possessions. I had a bookshelf where I put them, and I was so proud of it. I loved my books and kept them in pristine condition. I read them over and over, but I did not bend the pages or the spines. I treasured every single one. As I grew older I started buying my own books. I loved fantasy, loved to get lost in worlds that didn't exist. I remember there was some book about white boys who solved mysteries or some shit. I had no time for that. Give me Roald Dahl. *James and the Giant Peach, The BFG, Charlie and the Chocolate Factory, The Wonderful Story of Henry Sugar.* That was my fix.

I had to fight to convince my mom to get the Narnia books for me. She didn't like them.

"This lion," she said, "he is a false God—a false idol! You remember what happened when Moses came down from the mountain after he got the tablets . . ."

"Yes, Mom," I explained, "but the lion is a Christ *figure.* Technically, he is Jesus. It's a story to explain Jesus."

She wasn't comfortable with that. "No, no. No false idols, my friend."

Eventually I wore her down. That was a big win.

If my mother had one goal, it was to free my mind. My mother spoke to me like an adult, which was unusual. In South Africa, kids play with kids and adults talk to adults. The adults supervise you, but they don't get down on your level and talk to you. My mom did. All the time. I was like her best friend. She was always telling me stories, giving me lessons, Bible lessons especially. She was big into Psalms. I had to read Psalms every day. She would quiz me on it. "What does the passage mean? What does it mean to *you?* How do you apply it to your life?" That was every day of my life. My mom did what school didn't. She taught me how to think.

• • •

The end of apartheid was a gradual thing. It wasn't like the Berlin Wall where one day it just came down. Apartheid's walls cracked and crumbled over many years. Concessions were made here and there, some laws were repealed, others simply weren't enforced. There came a point, in the months before Mandela's release, when we could live less furtively. It was then that my mother decided we needed to move. She felt we had grown as much as we could hiding in our tiny flat in town.

The country was open now. Where would we go? Soweto came with its burdens. My mother still wanted to get out from the shadow of her family. My mother also couldn't walk with me through Soweto without people saying, "There goes that prostitute with a white man's child." In a black area she would always be seen as that. So, since my mom didn't want to move to a black area and couldn't afford to move to a white area, she decided to move to a colored area.

Eden Park was a colored neighborhood adjacent to several black townships on the East Rand. Half-colored and half-black, she figured, like us. We'd be camouflaged there. It didn't work out that way; we never fit in at all. But that was her thinking when we made the move. Plus it was a chance to buy a home—our own home. Eden Park was one of those "suburbs" that are actually out on the edge of civilization, the kind of place where property developers have said, "Hey, poor people. You can live the good life, too. Here's a house. In the middle of nowhere. But look, you have a yard!" For some reason the streets in Eden Park were named after cars: Jaguar Street. Ferrari Street. Honda Street. I don't know if that was a coincidence or not, but it's funny because colored people in South Africa are known for loving fancy cars. It was like living in a white neighborhood with all the streets named after varietals of fine wine.

I remember moving out there in flashbacks, snippets, driving to a place I'd never seen, seeing people I'd never seen. It was flat, not many trees, the same dusty red-clay dirt and grass as Soweto but with proper houses and paved roads and a sense of suburbia to it. Ours was a tiny house at the bend in the road right off Toyota Street. It was modest and cramped inside, but walking in I thought, *Wow. We are really living*. It was crazy to have my own room. I didn't like it. My whole life I'd slept in a room with my mom or on the floor with my cousins. I was used to having other human beings right next to me, so I slept in my mom's bed most nights.

There was no stepfather in the picture yet, no baby brother crying in the night. It was me and her, alone. There was this sense of the two of us embarking on a grand adventure. She'd say things to me like, "It's you and me against the world." I understood even from an early age that we weren't just mother and son. We were a team.

It was when we moved to Eden Park that we finally got a car, the beat-up, tangerine Volkswagen my mother bought secondhand for next to nothing. One out of five times it wouldn't start. There was no AC. Anytime I made the mistake of turning on the fan the vent would fart bits of leaves and dust all over me. Whenever it broke down we'd catch minibuses, or sometimes we'd hitchhike. She'd make me hide in the bushes because she knew men would stop for a woman but not a woman with a child. She'd stand by the road, the driver would pull over, she'd open the door and then whistle, and I'd come running up to the car. I would watch their faces drop as they realized they weren't picking up an attractive single woman but an attractive single woman with a fat little kid.

When the car did work, we had the windows down, sputtering along and baking in the heat. For my entire life the dial on that car's radio stayed on one station. It was called Radio Pulpit, and as the name suggests it was nothing but preaching and praise. I wasn't allowed to touch that dial. Anytime the radio wasn't getting reception, my mom would pop in a cassette of Jimmy Swaggart sermons. (When we finally found out about the scandal? Oh, man. That was rough.)

But as shitty as our car was, it was a *car*. It was freedom. We weren't black people stuck in the townships, waiting for public transport. We were black people who were out in the world. We were black people who could wake up and say, "Where do we choose to go today?" On the commute to work and school, there was a long stretch of the road into town that was completely deserted. That's where Mom would let me drive. On the highway. I was six. She'd put me on her lap and let me steer and work the indicators while she worked the pedals and the stick shift. After a few months of that, she taught me how to work the stick. She was still working the clutch, but I'd climb onto her lap and take the stick, and she'd call out the gears as we drove. There was this one part of the road that ran deep into a valley and then back up the other side. We'd get up a head of speed, and we'd stick it into neutral and let go of the brake and the clutch, and, *woo-hoo!*, we'd race down the hill and then, *zoom!*, we'd shoot up the other side. We were flying.

If we weren't at school or work or church, we were out exploring. My mom's attitude was "I chose you, kid. I brought you into this world, and I'm going to give you everything I never had." She poured herself into me. She would find places for us to go where we didn't have to spend money. We must have gone to every park in Johannesburg. My mom would sit under a tree and read the Bible, and I'd run and play and play and play. On Sunday afternoons after church, we'd go for drives out in the country. My mom would find places with beautiful views for us to sit and have a picnic. There was none of the fanfare of a picnic basket or plates or anything like that, only baloney and brown bread and margarine sandwiches wrapped up in butcher paper. To this day, baloney and brown bread and margarine will instantly take me back. You can come with all the Michelin stars in the world, just give me baloney and brown bread and margarine and I'm in heaven.

Food, or the access to food, was always the measure of how good or bad things were going in our lives. My mom would always say, "My job is to feed your body, feed your spirit, and feed your mind." That's exactly what she did, and the way she found money for food and books was to spend absolutely nothing on anything else. Her frugality was the stuff of legend. Our car was a tin can on wheels, and we lived in the middle of nowhere. We had threadbare furniture, busted old sofas with holes worn through the fabric. Our TV was a tiny black-and-white with a bunny aerial on top. We changed the channels using a pair of pliers because the buttons didn't work. Most of the time you had to squint to see what was going on.

We always wore secondhand clothes, from Goodwill stores or that were giveaways from white people at church. All the other kids at school got brands, Nike and Adidas. I never got brands. One time I asked my mom for Adidas sneakers. She came home with some knock-off brand, Abidas.

"Mom, these are fake," I said.

"I don't see the difference."

"Look at the logo. There are four stripes instead of three."

"Lucky you," she said. "You got one extra."

We got by with next to nothing, but we always had church and we always had books and we always had food. Mind you, it wasn't necessarily *good* food. Meat was a luxury. When things were going well we'd have chicken. My mom was an expert at cracking open a chicken bone and getting out every last bit of marrow inside. We didn't eat chickens. We obliterated them. Our family was an archaeologist's nightmare. We left no bones behind. When we were done with a chicken there was nothing left but the head. Sometimes the only meat we had was a packaged meat you could buy at the butcher called "sawdust." It was literally the dust of the meat, the bits that fell off the cuts being packaged for the shop, the bits of fat and whatever's left. They'd sweep it up and put it into bags. It was meant for dogs, but my mom bought it for us. There were many months where that was all we ate.

The butcher sold bones, too. We called them "soup bones," but they were actually labeled "dog bones" in the store; people would cook them for their dogs as a treat. Whenever times were really tough we'd fall back on dog bones. My mom would boil them for soup. We'd suck the marrow out of them. Sucking marrow out of bones is a skill poor people learn early. I'll never forget the first time I went to a fancy restaurant as a grown man and someone told me, "You have to try the bone marrow. It's such a delicacy. It's *divine*." They ordered it, the waiter brought it out, and I was like, "Dog bones, motherfucker!" I was not impressed.

As modestly as we lived at home, I never felt poor because our lives were so rich with experience. We were always out doing something, going somewhere. My mom used to take me on drives through fancy white neighborhoods. We'd go look at people's houses, look at their mansions. We'd look at their walls, mostly, because that's all we could see from the road. We'd look at a wall that ran from one end of the block to the other and go, "Wow. That's only *one* house. All of that is for *one* family." Sometimes we'd pull over and go up to the wall, and she'd put me up on her shoulders like I was a little periscope. I would look into the yards and describe everything I was seeing. "It's a big white house! They have two dogs! There's a lemon tree! They have a swimming pool! And a tennis court!"

My mother took me places black people never went. She refused to be bound by ridiculous ideas of what black people couldn't or shouldn't do. She'd take me to the ice rink to go skating. Johannesburg used to have this epic drive-in movie theater, Top Star Drive-In, on top of a massive mine dump outside the city. She'd take me to movies there; we'd get snacks, hang the speaker on our car window. Top Star had a 360-degree view of the city, the suburbs, Soweto. Up there I could see for miles in every direction. I felt like I was on top of the world.

My mom raised me as if there were no limitations on where I could go or what I could do. When I look back I realize she raised me like a white kid—not white culturally, but in the sense of believing that the world was my oyster, that I should speak up for myself, that my ideas and thoughts and decisions mattered.

We tell people to follow their dreams, but you can only dream of what you can imagine, and, depending on where you come from, your imagination can be quite limited. Growing up in Soweto, our dream was to put another room on our house. Maybe have a driveway. Maybe, someday, a cast-iron gate at the end of the driveway. Because that is all we knew. But the highest rung of what's possible is far beyond the world you can see. My mother showed me what was possible. The thing that always amazed me about her life was that no one showed her. No one chose her. She did it on her own. She found her way through sheer force of will.

Perhaps even more amazing is the fact that my mother started her little project, me, at a time when she could not have known that apartheid would end. There was no reason to think it would end; it had seen generations come and go. I was nearly six when Mandela was released, ten before democracy finally came, yet she was preparing me to live a life of freedom long before we knew freedom would exist. A hard life in the township or a trip to the colored orphanage were the far more likely options on the table. But we never lived that way. We only moved forward and we always moved fast, and by the time the law and everyone else came around we were already miles down the road, flying across the freeway in a bright-orange, piece-of-shit Volkswagen with the windows down and Jimmy Swaggart praising Jesus at the top of his lungs.

People thought my mom was crazy. Ice rinks and drive-ins and suburbs, these things were *izinto zabelungu*—the things of white people. So many black people had internalized the logic of apartheid and made it their own. Why teach a black child white things? Neighbors and relatives used to pester my mom. "Why do all this? Why show him the world when he's never going to leave the ghetto?"

"Because," she would say, "even if he never leaves the ghetto, he will know that the ghetto is not the world. If that is all I accomplish, I've done enough."

Apartheid, for all its power, had fatal flaws baked in, starting with the fact that it never made any sense. Racism is not logical. Consider this: Chinese people were classified as black in South Africa. I don't mean they were running around acting black. They were still Chinese. But, unlike Indians, there weren't enough Chinese people to warrant devising a whole separate classification. Apartheid, despite its intricacies and precision, didn't know what to do with them, so the government said, "Eh, we'll just call 'em black. It's simpler that way."

Interestingly, at the same time, Japanese people were labeled as white. The reason for this was that the South African government wanted to establish good relations with the Japanese in order to import their fancy cars and electronics. So Japanese people were given honorary white status while Chinese people stayed black. I always like to imagine being a South African policeman who likely couldn't tell the difference between Chinese and Japanese but whose job was to make sure that people of the wrong color weren't doing the wrong thing. If he saw an Asian person sitting on a whites-only bench, what would he say?

"Hey, get off that bench, you Chinaman!"

"Excuse me. I'm Japanese."

"Oh, I apologize, sir. I didn't mean to be racist. Have a lovely afternoon."

6

LOOPHOLES

My mother used to tell me, "I chose to have you because I wanted something to love and something that would love me unconditionally in return—and then I gave birth to the most selfish piece of shit on earth and all it ever did was cry and eat and shit and say, 'Me, me, me, me me.'"

My mom thought having a child was going to be like having a partner, but every child is born the center of its own universe, incapable of understanding the world beyond its own wants and needs, and I was no different. I was a voracious kid. I consumed boxes of books and wanted more, more, more. I ate like a pig. The way I ate I should have been obese. At a certain point the family thought I had worms. Whenever I went to my cousins' house for the holidays, my mom would drop me off with a bag of tomatoes, onions, and potatoes and a large sack of cornmeal. That was her way of preempting any complaints about my visit. At my gran's house I always got seconds, which none of the other kids got. My grandmother would give me the pot and say, "Finish it." If you didn't want to wash the dishes, you called Trevor. They called me the rubbish bin of the family. I ate and ate and ate.

I was hyperactive, too. I craved constant stimulation and activity. When I walked down the sidewalk as a toddler, if you didn't have my arm in a death grip, I was off, running full-speed toward the traffic. I loved to be chased. I thought it was a game. The old grannies my mom hired to look after me while she was at work? I would leave them in tears. My mom would come home and they'd be crying. "I quit. I can't do this. Your son is a tyrant." It was the same with my schoolteachers, with Sunday school teachers. If you weren't engaging me, you were in trouble. I wasn't a shit to people. I wasn't whiny and spoiled. I had good manners. I was just high-energy and knew what I wanted to do.

My mom used to take me to the park so she could run me to death to burn off the energy. She'd take a Frisbee and throw it, and I'd run and catch it and bring it back. Over and over and over. Sometimes she'd throw a tennis ball. Black people's dogs don't play fetch; you don't throw anything to a black person's dog unless it's food. So it was only when I started spending time in parks with white people and their pets that I realized my mom was training me like a dog.

Anytime my extra energy wasn't burned off, it would find its way into general naughtiness and misbehavior. I prided myself on being the ultimate prankster. Every teacher at school used overhead projectors to put their notes up on the wall during class. One day I went around and took the magnifying glass out of every projector in every classroom. Another time I emptied a fire extinguisher into the school piano, because I knew we were going to have a performance at assembly the next day. The pianist sat down and played the first note and, *foomp!*, all this foam exploded out of the piano.

The two things I loved most were fire and knives. I was endlessly fascinated by them. Knives were just cool. I collected them from pawnshops and garage sales: flick knives, butterfly knives, the Rambo knife, the Crocodile Dundee knife. Fire was the ultimate, though. I loved fire and I especially loved fireworks. We celebrated Guy Fawkes Day in November, and every year my mom would buy us a ton of fireworks, like a mini-arsenal. I realized that I could take the gunpowder out of all the fireworks and create one massive firework of my own. One afternoon I was doing precisely that, goofing around with my cousin and filling an empty plant pot with a huge pile of gunpowder, when I got distracted by some Black Cat firecrackers. The cool thing you could do with a Black Cat was, instead of lighting it to make it explode, you could break it in half and light it and it would turn into a mini-flamethrower. I stopped midway through building my gunpowder pile to play with the Black Cats and somehow dropped a match into the pile. The whole thing exploded, throwing a massive ball of flame up in my face. Mlungisi screamed, and my mom came running into the yard in a panic.

"What happened?!"

I played it cool, even though I could still feel the heat of the fireball on my face. "Oh, nothing. Nothing happened."

"Were you playing with fire?!"

"No."

She shook her head. "You know what? I would beat you, but Jesus has already exposed your lies."

"Huh?"

"Go to the bathroom and look at yourself."

I went to the toilet and looked in the mirror. My eyebrows were gone and the front inch or so of my hair was completely burned off.

From an adult's point of view, I was destructive and out of control, but as a child I didn't think of it that way. I never wanted to destroy. I wanted to create. I wasn't burning my eyebrows. I was creating fire. I wasn't breaking overhead projectors. I was creating chaos, to see how people reacted.

And I couldn't help it. There's a condition kids suffer from, a compulsive disorder that makes them do things they themselves don't understand. You can tell a child, "Whatever you do, don't draw on the wall. You can draw on this paper. You can draw in this book. You can draw on any surface you want. But do not draw or write or color on the wall." The child will look you dead in the eye and say, "Got it." Ten minutes later the child is drawing on the wall. You start screaming. "Why the hell are you drawing on the wall?!" The child looks at you, and he genuinely has no idea why he drew on the wall. As a kid, I remember having that feeling all the time. Every time I got punished, as my mom was whooping my ass, I'd be thinking, *Why did I just do that? I knew not to do that. She told me not to do that.* Then once the hiding was over I'd say to myself, *I'm going to be so good from here on. I'm never ever going to do a bad thing in my life ever ever ever ever ever—and to remember not to do anything bad, let me write something on the wall to remind myself* . . . and then I would pick up a crayon and get straight back into it, and I never understood why.

My relationship with my mom was like the relationship between a cop and a criminal in the movies—the relentless detective and the devious mastermind she's determined to catch. They're bitter rivals, but, damn, they respect the hell out of each other, and somehow they even grow to like each other. Sometimes my mom would catch me, but she was usually one step behind, and she was always giving me the eye. *Someday, kid. Someday I'm going to catch you and put you away for the rest of your life.* Then I would give her a nod in return. *Have a good evening, Officer.* That was my whole childhood.

My mom was forever trying to rein me in. Over the years, her tactics grew more and more sophisticated. Where I had youth and energy on my side, she had cunning, and she figured out different ways to keep me in line. One Sunday we were at the shops and there was a big display of toffee apples. I loved toffee apples, and I kept nagging her the whole way through the shop. "*Please* can I have a toffee apple? *Please* can I have a toffee apple? *Please* can I have a toffee apple? *Please* can I have a toffee apple?"

Finally, once we had our groceries and my mom was heading to the front to pay, I succeeded in wearing her down. "Fine," she said. "Go and get a toffee apple." I ran, got a toffee apple, came back, and put it on the counter at the checkout.

"Add this toffee apple, please," I said.

The cashier looked at me skeptically. "Wait your turn, boy. I'm still helping this lady."

"No," I said. "She's buying it for me."

My mother turned to me. "Who's buying it for you?"

"You're buying it for me."

"No, no. Why doesn't your mother buy it for you?"

"What? My mother? You are my mother."

"I'm your mother? No, I'm not your mother. Where's your mother?"

I was so confused. "*You're* my mother."

The cashier looked at her, looked back at me, looked at her again. She shrugged, like, *I have no idea what that kid's talking about.* Then she looked at me like she'd never seen me before in her life.

"Are you lost, little boy? Where's your mother?"

"Yeah," the cashier said. "Where's your mother?"

I pointed at my mother. "She's my mother."

"What? She can't be your mother, boy. She's black. Can't you see?"

My mom shook her head. "Poor little colored boy lost his mother. What a shame."

I panicked. Was I crazy? Is she not my mother? I started bawling. "*You're* my mother. *You're* my mother. *She's* my mother. *She's* my mother."

She shrugged again. "So sad. I hope he finds his mother."

The cashier nodded. She paid him, took our groceries, and walked out of the shop. I dropped the toffee apple, ran out behind her in tears, and caught up to her at the car. She turned around, laughing hysterically, like she'd really got me good.

"Why are you crying?" she asked.

"Because you said you weren't my mother. Why did you say you weren't my mother?"

"Because you wouldn't shut up about the toffee apple. Now get in the car. Let's go."

By the time I was seven or eight, I was too smart to be tricked, so she changed tactics. Our life turned into a courtroom drama with two lawyers constantly debating over loopholes and technicalities. My mom was smart and had a sharp tongue, but I was quicker in an argument. She'd get flustered because she couldn't keep up. So she started writing me letters. That way she could make her points and there could be no verbal sparring back and forth. If I had chores to do, I'd come home to find an envelope slipped under the door, like from the landlord.

Dear Trevor,

"Children, obey your parents in everything, for this pleases the Lord."
—Colossians 3:20

There are certain things I expect from you as my child and as a young man. You need to clean your room. You need to keep the house clean. You need to look after your school uniform. Please, my child, I ask you. Respect my rules so that I may also respect you. I ask you now, please go and do the dishes and do the weeds in the garden.

Yours sincerely,
Mom

I would do my chores, and if I had anything to say I would write back. Because my mom was a secretary and I spent hours at her office every day after school, I'd learned a great deal about business correspondence. I was extremely proud of my letter-writing abilities.

To Whom It May Concern:
Dear Mom,

I have received your correspondence earlier. I am delighted to say that I am ahead of schedule on the dishes and I will continue to wash them in an hour or so. Please note that the garden is wet and so I cannot do the weeds at this time, but please be assured this task

will be completed by the end of the weekend. Also, I completely
agree with what you are saying with regard to my respect levels and
I will maintain my room to a satisfactory standard.

Yours sincerely,
Trevor

Those were the polite letters. If we were having a real, full-on argument or if I'd gotten in trouble at school, I'd find more accusatory
missives waiting for me when I got home.

Dear Trevor,

"Foolishness is bound up in the heart of a child; the rod of discipline will remove it far from him."
—Proverbs 22:15

Your school marks this term have been very disappointing, and
your behavior in class continues to be disruptive and disrespectful.
It is clear from your actions that you do not respect me. You do
not respect your teachers. Learn to respect the women in your life.
The way you treat me and the way you treat your teachers will
be the way you treat other women in the world. Learn to buck that
trend now and you will be a better man because of it. Because of
your behavior I am grounding you for one week. There will be no
television and no videogames.

Yours sincerely,
Mom

I, of course, would find this punishment completely unfair. I'd take
the letter and confront her.
"Can I speak to you about this?"
"No. If you want to reply, you have to write a letter."
I'd go to my room, get out my pen and paper, sit at my little desk,
and go after her arguments one by one.

To Whom It May Concern:

Dear Mom,

First of all, this has been a particularly tough time in school, and for you to say that my marks are bad is extremely unfair, especially considering the fact that you yourself were not very good in school and I am, after all, a product of yours, and so in part you are to blame because if you were not good in school, why would I be good in school because genetically we are the same. Gran always talks about how naughty you were, so obviously my naughtiness comes from you, so I don't think it is right or just for you to say any of this.

Yours sincerely,

Trevor

I'd bring her the letter and stand there while she read it. Invariably she'd tear it up and throw it in the dustbin. "Rubbish! This is rubbish!" Then she'd start to launch into me and I'd say, "Ah-ah-ah. No. You have to write a letter." Then I'd go to my room and wait for her reply. This sometimes went back and forth for days.

The letter writing was for minor disputes. For major infractions, my mom went with the ass-whooping. Like most black South African parents, when it came to discipline my mom was old school. If I pushed her too far, she'd go for the belt or switch. That's just how it was in those days. Pretty much all of my friends had it the same.

My mom would have given me proper sit-down hidings if I'd given her the opportunity, but she could never catch me. My gran called me "Springbok," after the second-fastest land mammal on earth, the deer that the cheetah hunts. My mom had to become a guerrilla fighter. She got her licks in where she could, her belt or maybe a shoe, administered on the fly.

One thing I respected about my mom was that she never left me in any doubt as to why I was receiving the hiding. It wasn't rage or anger. It was discipline from a place of love. My mom was on her own with a crazy child. I destroyed pianos. I shat on floors. I would screw up, she'd beat the shit out of me and give me time to cry, and then she'd pop back into my room with a big smile and go, "Are you ready for dinner? We need to hurry and eat if we want to watch *Rescue 911*. Are you coming?"

"What? What kind of psychopath are you? You just beat me!"

"Yes. Because you did something wrong. It doesn't mean I don't love you anymore."

"What?"

"Look, did you or did you not do something wrong?"

"I did."

"And then? I hit you. And now that's over. So why sit there and cry? It's time for *Rescue 911*. William Shatner is waiting. Are you coming or not?"

When it came to discipline, Catholic school was no joke. Whenever I got into trouble with the nuns at Maryvale they'd rap me on the knuckles with the edge of a metal ruler. For cursing they'd wash my mouth out with soap. For serious offenses I'd get sent to the principal's office. Only the principal could give you an official hiding. You'd have to bend over and he'd hit your ass with this flat rubber thing, like the sole of a shoe.

Whenever the principal would hit me, it was like he was afraid to do it too hard. One day I was getting a hiding and I thought, *Man, if only my mom hit me like this*, and I started laughing. I couldn't help it. The principal was quite disturbed. "If you're laughing while you're getting beaten," he said, "then something is definitely wrong with you."

That was the first of three times the school made my mom take me to a psychologist to be evaluated. Every psychologist who examined me came back and said, "There's nothing wrong with this kid." I wasn't ADD. I wasn't a sociopath. I was just creative and independent and full of energy. The therapists did give me a series of tests, and they came to the conclusion that I was either going to make an excellent criminal or be very good at catching criminals, because I could always find loopholes in the law. Whenever I thought a rule wasn't logical, I'd find my way around it.

The rules about communion at Friday mass, for example, made absolutely no sense. We'd be in there for an hour of kneeling, standing, sitting, kneeling, standing, sitting, kneeling, standing, sitting, and by the end of it I'd be starving, but I was never allowed to take communion, because I wasn't Catholic. The other kids could eat Jesus's body and drink Jesus's blood, but I couldn't. And Jesus's blood was grape juice. I loved grape juice. Grape juice and crackers—what more could a kid want? And they wouldn't let me have any. I'd argue with the nuns and the priest all the time.

"Only Catholics can eat Jesus's body and drink Jesus's blood, right?"

"Yes."

"But Jesus wasn't Catholic."

"No."

"Jesus was Jewish."

"Well, yes."

"So you're telling me that if Jesus walked into your church right now, Jesus would not be allowed to have the body and blood of Jesus?"

"Well . . . uh . . . um . . ."

They never had a satisfactory reply.

One morning before mass I decided, *I'm going to get me some Jesus blood and Jesus body*. I snuck behind the altar and I drank the entire bottle of grape juice and I ate the entire bag of Eucharist to make up for all the other times that I couldn't.

In my mind, I wasn't breaking the rules, because the rules didn't make any sense. And I got caught only because they broke their own rules. Another kid ratted me out in confession, and the priest turned me in.

"No, no," I protested. "*You've* broken the rules. That's confidential information. The priest isn't supposed to repeat what you say in confession."

They didn't care. The school could break whatever rules it wanted. The principal laid into me.

"What kind of a sick person would eat all of Jesus's body and drink all of Jesus's blood?"

"A hungry person."

I got another hiding and a second trip to the psychologist for that one. The third visit to the shrink, and the last straw, came in grade six. A kid was bullying me. He said he was going to beat me up, and I brought one of my knives to school. I wasn't going to use it; I just wanted to have it. The school didn't care. That was the last straw for them. I wasn't expelled, exactly. The principal sat me down and said, "Trevor, we can expel you. You need to think hard about whether you really want to be at Maryvale next year." I think he thought he was giving me an ultimatum that would get me to shape up. But I felt like he was offering me an out, and I took it. "No," I told him, "I don't want to be here." And that was the end of Catholic school.

Funnily enough, I didn't get into trouble with my mom when it happened. There was no ass-whooping waiting for me at home. She'd lost the bursary when she'd left her job at ICI, and paying for private school was becoming a burden. But more than that, she thought the school was overreacting. The truth is she probably took my side against Maryvale more often than not. She agreed with me 100 percent about the Eucharist thing. "Let me get this straight," she told the principal. "You're punishing a child because he *wants* Jesus's body and Jesus's blood? Why shouldn't he have those things? Of course he should have them." When they made me see a therapist for laughing while the principal hit me, she told the school that was ridiculous, too.

"Ms. Noah, your son was laughing while we were hitting him."

"Well, clearly you don't know how to hit a kid. That's your problem, not mine. Trevor's never laughed when I've hit him, I can tell you."

That was the weird and kind of amazing thing about my mom. If she agreed with me that a rule was stupid, she wouldn't punish me for breaking it. Both she and the psychologists agreed that the school was the one with the problem, not me. Catholic school is not the place to be creative and independent.

Catholic school is similar to apartheid in that it's ruthlessly authoritarian, and its authority rests on a bunch of rules that don't make any sense. My mother grew up with these rules and she questioned them. When they didn't hold up, she simply went around them. The only authority my mother recognized was God's. God is love and the Bible is truth—everything else was up for debate. She taught me to challenge authority and question the system. The only way it backfired on her was that I constantly challenged and questioned her.

When I was seven years old, my mother had been dating her new boyfriend, Abel, for a year maybe, but at that point I was too young to know who they were to each other. It was just "Hey, that's mom's friend who's around a lot." I liked Abel; he was a really nice guy.

As a black person back then, if you wanted to live in the suburbs you'd have to find a white family renting out their servants' quarters or sometimes their garage, which was what Abel had done. He lived in a neighborhood called Orange Grove in a white family's garage, which he'd turned into a cottage-type thing with a hot plate and a bed. Sometimes he'd come and sleep at our house, and sometimes we'd go stay with him. Staying in a garage when we owned our own house wasn't ideal, but Orange Grove was close to my school and my mom's work so it had its benefits.

This white family also had a black maid who lived in the servants' quarters in the backyard, and I'd play with her son whenever we stayed there. At that age my love of fire was in full bloom. One afternoon everyone was at work—my mom and Abel and both of the white parents—and the kid and I were playing together while his mom was inside the house cleaning. One thing I loved doing at the time was using a magnifying glass to burn my name into pieces of wood. You had to aim the lens and get the focus just right and then you got the flame and then you moved it slowly and you could burn shapes and letters and patterns. I was fascinated by it.

That afternoon I was teaching this kid how to do it. We were inside the servants' quarters, which was really more of a toolshed added on to the back of the house, full of wooden ladders, buckets of old paint, turpentine. I had a box of matches with me, too—all my usual fire-making tools. We were sitting on an old mattress that they used to sleep on the floor, basically a sack stuffed with dried straw. The sun was beaming in through the window, and I was showing the kid how to burn his name into a piece of plywood.

At one point we took a break to go get a snack. I set the magnifying glass and the matches on the mattress and we left. When we came back a few minutes later we found the shed had one of those doors that self-locks from the inside. We couldn't get back in without going to get his mother, so we decided to run around and play in the yard. After a while I noticed smoke coming out of the cracks in the window frame. I ran over and looked inside. A small fire was burning in the middle of the straw mattress where we'd left the matches and the magnifying glass. We ran and called the maid. She came, but she didn't know what to do. The door was locked, and before we could figure out how to get into the shed the whole thing caught—the mattress, the ladders, the paint, the turpentine, everything.

The flames moved quickly. Soon the roof was on fire, and from there the blaze spread to the main house, and the whole thing burned and burned and burned. Smoke was billowing into the sky. A neighbor had called the fire brigade, and the sirens were on their way. Me and this kid and the maid, we ran out to the road and watched as the firemen tried to put it out, but by the time they did, it was too late. There was nothing left but a charred brick-and-mortar shell, roof gone, and gutted from the inside.

The white family came home and stood on the street, staring at the ruins of their house. They asked the maid what happened and she asked her son and the kid totally snitched. "Trevor had matches," he said. The family said nothing to me. I don't think they knew what to say.

They were completely dumbfounded. They didn't call the police, didn't threaten to sue. What were they going to do, arrest a seven-year-old for arson? And we were so poor you couldn't actually sue us for anything. Plus they had insurance, so that was the end of it.

They kicked Abel out of the garage, which I thought was hilarious because the garage, which was freestanding, was the only piece of the property left unscathed. I saw no reason for Abel to have to leave, but they made him. We packed up his stuff, put it into our car, and drove home to Eden Park; Abel basically lived with us from then on. He and my mom got into a huge fight. "Your son has burned down my life!" But there was no punishment for me that day. My mom was too much in shock. There's naughty, and then there's burning down a white person's house. She didn't know what to do.

I didn't feel bad about it at all. I still don't. The lawyer in me maintains that I am completely innocent. There were matches and there was a magnifying glass and there was a mattress and then, clearly, a series of unfortunate events. Things catch fire sometimes. That's why there's a fire brigade. But everyone in my family will tell you, "Trevor burned down a house." If people thought I was naughty before, after the fire I was notorious. One of my uncles stopped calling me Trevor. He called me "Terror" instead. "Don't leave that kid alone in your home," he'd say. "He'll burn it to the ground."

My cousin Mlungisi, to this day, cannot comprehend how I survived being as naughty as I was for as long as I did, how I withstood the number of hidings that I got. Why did I keep misbehaving? How did I never learn my lesson? Both of my cousins were supergood kids. Mlungisi got maybe one hiding in his life. After that he said he never wanted to experience anything like it ever again, and from that day he always followed the rules. But I was blessed with another trait I inherited from my mother: her ability to forget the pain in life. I remember the thing that caused the trauma, but I don't hold on to the trauma. I never let the memory of something painful prevent me from trying something new. If you think too much about the ass-kicking your mom gave you, or the ass-kicking that life gave you, you'll stop pushing the boundaries and breaking the rules. It's better to take it, spend some time crying, then wake up the next day and move on. You'll have a few bruises and they'll remind you of what happened and that's okay. But after a while the bruises fade, and they fade for a reason—because now it's time to get up to some shit again.

I grew up in a black family in a black neighborhood in a black country. I've traveled to other black cities in black countries all over the black continent. And in all of that time I've yet to find a place where black people like cats. One of the biggest reasons for that, as we know in South Africa, is that only witches have cats, and all cats are witches.

There was a famous incident during an Orlando Pirates soccer match a few years ago. A cat got into the stadium and ran through the crowd and out onto the pitch in the middle of the game. A security guard, seeing the cat, did what any sensible black person would do. He said to himself, "That cat is a witch." He caught the cat and—live on TV—he kicked it and stomped it and beat it to death with a *sjambok*, a hard leather whip.

It was front-page news all over the country. White people lost their shit. Oh my word, it was insane. The security guard was arrested and put on trial and found guilty of animal abuse. He had to pay some enormous fine to avoid spending several months in jail. What was ironic to me was that white people had spent years seeing video of black people being beaten to death by other white people, but this one video of a black man kicking a cat, that's what sent them over the edge. Black people were just confused. They didn't see any problem with what the man did. They were like, "Obviously that cat was a witch. How else would a cat know how to get out onto a soccer pitch? Somebody sent it to jinx one of the teams. That man had to kill the cat. He was protecting the players."

In South Africa, black people have dogs.

7

FUFI

A month after we moved to Eden Park, my mother brought home two cats. Black cats. Beautiful creatures. Some woman from her work had a litter of kittens she was trying to get rid of, and my mom ended up with two. I was excited because I'd never had a pet before. My mom was excited because she loves animals. She didn't believe in any nonsense about cats. It was just another way in which she was a rebel, refusing to conform to ideas about what black people did and didn't do.

In a black neighborhood, you wouldn't dare own a cat, especially a black cat. That would be like wearing a sign that said, "Hello, I am a witch." That would be suicide. Since we'd moved to a colored neighborhood, my mom thought the cats would be okay. Once they were grown we let them out during the day to roam the neighborhood. Then we came home one evening and found the cats strung up by their tails from our front gate, gutted and skinned and bleeding out, their heads chopped off. On our front wall someone had written in Afrikaans, "*Heks*"—"Witch."

Colored people, apparently, were no more progressive than black people on the issue of cats.

I wasn't exactly devastated about the cats. I don't think we'd had them long enough for me to get attached; I don't even remember their names. And cats are dicks for the most part. As much as I tried they never felt like real pets. They never showed me affection nor did they accept any of mine. Had the cats made more of an effort, I might have felt like I had lost something. But even as a kid, looking at these dead, mutilated animals, I was like, "Well, there you have it. Maybe if they'd been nicer, they could have avoided this."

After the cats were killed, we took a break from pets for a while. Then we got dogs. Dogs are cool. Almost every black family I knew had a dog. No matter how poor you were, you had a dog. White people treat dogs like children or members of the family. Black people's dogs are more for protection, a poor-man's alarm system. You buy a dog and you keep it out in the yard. Black people name dogs by their traits. If it has stripes, you call it Tiger. If it's vicious, you call it Danger. If it has spots, you call it Spotty. Given the finite number of traits a dog can have, pretty much everyone's dogs have the same names; people just recycle them.

We'd never had dogs in Soweto. Then one day some lady at my mom's work offered us two puppies. They weren't planned puppies. This woman's Maltese poodle had been impregnated by the bull terrier from next door, a strange mix. My mom said she'd take them both. She brought them home, and I was the happiest kid on earth.

My mom named them Fufi and Panther. Fufi, I don't know where her name came from. Panther had a pink nose, so she was Pink Panther and eventually just Panther. They were two sisters who loved and hated each other. They would look out for each other, but they would also fight all the time. Like, blood fights. Biting. Clawing. It was a strange, gruesome relationship.

Panther was my mom's dog; Fufi was mine. Fufi was beautiful. Clean lines, happy face. She looked like a perfect bull terrier, only skinnier because of the Maltese mixed in. Panther, who was more half-and-half, came out weird and scruffy-looking. Panther was smart. Fufi was dumb as shit. At least we always thought she was dumb as shit. Whenever we called them, Panther would come right away, but Fufi wouldn't do anything. Panther would run back and get Fufi and then they'd both come. It turned out that Fufi was deaf. Years later Fufi died when a burglar was trying to break into our house. He pushed the gate over and it fell on her back and broke her spine. We took her to the vet and she had to be put down. After examining her, the vet came over and gave us the news.

"It must have been strange for your family living with a dog that was deaf," he said.

"What?"

"You didn't know your dog was deaf?"

"No, we thought it was stupid."

That's when we realized that their whole lives the one dog had been telling the other dog what to do somehow. The smart, hearing one was helping the dumb, deaf one.

Fufi was the love of my life. Beautiful but stupid. I raised her. I potty-trained her. She slept in my bed. A dog is a great thing for a kid to have. It's like a bicycle but with emotions.

Fufi could do all sorts of tricks. She could jump super high. I mean, Fufi could *jump*. I could hold a piece of food out above my own head and she'd leap up and grab it like it was nothing. If YouTube had been around, Fufi would have been a star.

Fufi was a little rascal as well. During the day we kept the dogs in the backyard, which was enclosed by a wall at least five feet high. After a while, every day we'd come home and Fufi would be sitting outside the gate, waiting for us. We were always confused. Was someone opening the gate? What was going on? It never occurred to us that she could actually scale a five-foot wall, but that was exactly what was happening. Every morning, Fufi would wait for us to leave, jump over the wall, and go roaming around the neighborhood.

I caught her one day when I was home for the school holidays. My mom had left for work and I was in the living room. Fufi didn't know I was there; she thought I was gone because the car was gone. I heard Panther barking in the backyard, looked out, and there was Fufi, scaling the wall. She'd jumped, scampered up the last couple of feet, and then she was gone.

I couldn't believe this was happening. I ran out front, grabbed my bicycle, and followed her to see where she was going. She went a long way, many streets over, to another part of the neighborhood. Then she went up to this other house and jumped over their wall and into their backyard. What the hell was she doing? I went up to the gate and rang the doorbell. This colored kid answered.

"May I help you?" he said.

"Yeah. My dog is in your yard."

"What?"

"My dog. She's in your yard."

Fufi walked up and stood between us.

"Fufi, come!" I said. "Let's go!"

This kid looked at Fufi and called her by some other stupid name, Spotty or some bullshit like that.

"Spotty, go back inside the house."

"Whoa, whoa," I said. "Spotty? That's Fufi!"

"No, that's my dog, Spotty."

"No, that's Fufi, my friend."

"No, this is Spotty."

"How could this be Spotty? She doesn't even have spots. You don't know what you're talking about."

"This is Spotty!"

"Fufi!"

"Spotty!"

"Fufi!"

Of course, since Fufi was deaf she didn't respond to "Spotty" or "Fufi." She just stood there. I started cursing the kid out.

"Give me back my dog!"

"I don't know who you are," he said, "but you better get out of here."

Then he went into the house and got his mom and she came out.

"What do you want?" she said.

"That's my dog!"

"This is our dog. Go away."

I started crying. "Why are you stealing my dog?!" I turned to Fufi and begged her. "Fufi, why are you doing this to me?! Why, Fufi?! Why?!" I called to her. I begged her to come. Fufi was deaf to my pleas. And everything else.

I jumped onto my bike and raced home, tears running down my face. I loved Fufi so much. To see her with another boy, acting like she didn't know me, after I raised her, after all the nights we spent together. I was heartbroken.

That evening Fufi didn't come home. Because the other family thought I was coming to steal their dog, they had decided to lock her inside, so she couldn't make it back the way she normally did to wait for us outside the fence. My mom got home from work. I was in tears. I told her Fufi had been kidnapped. We went back to the house. My mom rang the bell and confronted the mom.

"Look, this is our dog."

This lady lied to my mom's face. "This is not your dog. We bought this dog."

"You didn't buy the dog. It's our dog."

They went back and forth. This woman wasn't budging, so we went home to get evidence: pictures of us with the dogs, certificates from the vet. I was crying the whole time, and my mom was losing her patience with me. "Stop crying! We'll get the dog! Calm down!"

We gathered up our documentation and went back to the house. This time we brought Panther with us, as part of the proof. My mom showed this lady the pictures and the information from the vet. She still wouldn't give us Fufi. My mom threatened to call the police. It turned into a whole thing. Finally my mom said, "Okay, I'll give you a hundred rand."

"Fine," the lady said.

My mom gave her some money and she brought Fufi out. The other kid, who thought Fufi was Spotty, had to watch his mother sell the dog he thought was his. Now he started crying. "Spotty! No! Mom, you can't sell Spotty!" I didn't care. I just wanted Fufi back.

Once Fufi saw Panther she came right away. The dogs left with us and we walked. I sobbed the whole way home, still heartbroken. My mom had no time for my whining.

"Why are you crying?!"

"Because Fufi loves another boy."

"So? Why would that hurt you? It didn't cost you anything. Fufi's here. She still loves you. She's still your dog. So get over it."

Fufi was my first heartbreak. No one has ever betrayed me more than Fufi. It was a valuable lesson to me. The hard thing was understanding that Fufi wasn't cheating on me with another boy. She was merely living her life to the fullest. Until I knew that she was going out on her own during the day, her other relationship hadn't affected me at all. Fufi had no malicious intent.

I believed that Fufi was *my* dog, but of course that wasn't true. Fufi was *a* dog. I was *a* boy. We got along well. She happened to live in my house. That experience shaped what I've felt about relationships for the rest of my life: You do not own the thing that you love. I was lucky to learn that lesson at such a young age. I have so many friends who still, as adults, wrestle with feelings of betrayal. They'll come to me angry and crying and talking about how they've been cheated on and lied to, and I feel for them. I understand what they're going through. I sit with them and buy them a drink and I say, "Friend, let me tell you the story of Fufi."

———————

When I was twenty-four years old, one day out of the blue my mother said to me, "You need to find your father."

"Why?" I asked. At that point I hadn't seen him in over ten years and didn't think I'd ever see him again.

"Because he's a piece of you," she said, "and if you don't find him you won't find yourself."

"I don't need him for that," I said. "I know who I am."

"It's not about knowing who you are. It's about him knowing who you are, and you knowing who he is. Too many men grow up without their fathers, so they spend their lives with a false impression of who their father is and what a father should be. You need to find your father. You need to show him what you've become. You need to finish that story."

———————

8

ROBERT

My father is a complete mystery. There are so many questions about his life that I still cannot even begin to answer.

Where'd he grow up? Somewhere in Switzerland.

Where'd he go to university? I don't know if he did.

How'd he end up in South Africa? I haven't a clue.

I've never met my Swiss grandparents. I don't know their names or anything about them. I do know my dad has an older sister, but I've never met her, either. I know that he worked as a chef in Montreal and New York for a while before moving to South Africa in the late 1970s. I know that he worked for an industrial food-service company and that he opened a couple of bars and restaurants here and there. That's about it.

I never called my dad "Dad." I never addressed him "Daddy" or "Father," either. I couldn't. I was instructed not to. If we were out in public or anywhere people might overhear us and I called him "Dad," someone might have asked questions or called the police. So for as long as I can remember I always called him Robert.

While I know nothing of my dad's life before me, thanks to my mom and just from the time I have been able to spend with him, I do have a sense of who he is as a person. He's very Swiss, clean and particular and precise. He's the only person I know who checks into a hotel room and leaves it cleaner than when he arrived. He doesn't like anyone waiting on him. No servants, no housekeepers. He cleans up after himself. He likes his space. He lives in his own world and does his own everything.

I know that he never married. He used to say that most people marry because they want to control another person, and he never wanted to be controlled. I know that he loves traveling, loves entertaining, having people over. But at the same time his privacy is everything to him. Wherever he lives he's never listed in the phone book. I'm sure my parents would have been caught in their time together if he hadn't been as private as he is. My mom was wild and impulsive. My father was reserved and rational. She was fire, he was ice. They were opposites that attracted, and I am a mix of them both.

One thing I do know about my dad is that he hates racism and homogeneity more than anything, and not because of any feelings of self-righteousness or moral superiority. He just never understood how white people could be racist in South Africa. "Africa is full of black people," he would say. "So why would you come all the way to Africa if you hate black people? If you hate black people so much, why did you move into their house?" To him it was insane.

Because racism never made sense to my father, he never subscribed to any of the rules of apartheid. In the early eighties, before I was born, he opened one of the first integrated restaurants in Johannesburg, a steakhouse. He applied for a special license that allowed businesses to serve both black and white patrons. These licenses existed because hotels and restaurants needed them to serve black travelers and diplomats from other countries, who in theory weren't subject to the same restrictions as black South Africans; black South Africans with money in turn exploited that loophole to frequent those hotels and restaurants.

My dad's restaurant was an instant, booming success. Black people came because there were few upscale establishments where they could eat, and they wanted to come and sit in a nice restaurant and see what that was like. White people came because they wanted to see what it was like to sit with black people. The white people would sit and watch the black people eat, and the black people would sit and eat and watch the white people watching them eat. The curiosity of being together overwhelmed the animosity keeping people apart. The place had a great vibe.

The restaurant closed only because a few people in the neighborhood took it upon themselves to complain. They filed petitions, and the government started looking for ways to shut my dad down. At first the inspectors came and tried to get him on cleanliness and health-code violations. Clearly they had never heard of the Swiss. That failed dismally. Then they decided to go after him by imposing additional and arbitrary restrictions.

"Since you've got the license you can keep the restaurant open," they said, "but you'll need to have separate toilets for every racial category. You'll need white toilets, black toilets, colored toilets, and Indian toilets."

"But then it will be a whole restaurant of nothing but toilets."

"Well, if you don't want to do that, your other option is to make it a normal restaurant and only serve whites."

He closed the restaurant.

After apartheid fell, my father moved from Hillbrow to Yeoville, a formerly quiet, residential neighborhood that had transformed into this vibrant melting pot of black and white and every other hue. Immigrants were pouring in from Nigeria and Ghana and all over the continent, bringing different food and exciting music. Rockey Street was the main strip, and its sidewalks were filled with street vendors and restaurants and bars. It was an explosion of culture.

My dad lived two blocks over from Rockey, on Yeo Street, right next to this incredible park where I loved to go because kids of all races and different countries were running around and playing there. My dad's house was simple. Nice, but nothing fancy. I feel like my dad had enough money to be comfortable and travel, but he never spent lavishly on things. He's extremely frugal, the kind of guy who drives the same car for twenty years.

My father and I lived on a schedule. I visited him every Sunday afternoon. Even though apartheid had ended, my mom had made her decision: She didn't want to get married. So we had our house, and he had his. I'd made a deal with my mom that if I went with her to mixed church and white church in the morning, after that I'd get to skip black church and go to my dad's, where we'd watch Formula 1 racing instead of casting out demons.

I celebrated my birthday with my dad every year, and we spent Christmas with him as well. I loved Christmas with my dad because my dad celebrated European Christmas. European Christmas was the best Christmas ever. My dad went all out. He had Christmas lights and a Christmas tree. He had fake snow and snow globes and stockings hung by the fireplace and lots of wrapped presents from Santa Claus. African Christmas was a lot more practical. We'd go to church, come home, have a nice meal with good meat and lots of custard and jelly. But there was no tree. You'd get a present, but it was usually just clothes, a new outfit. You might get a toy, but it wasn't wrapped and it was never from Santa Claus. The whole issue of Santa Claus is a rather contentious one when it comes to African Christmas, a matter of pride. When an African dad buys his kid a present, the last thing he's going to do is give some fat white man credit for it. African Dad will tell you straight up, "No, no, no. *I* bought you that."

Outside of birthdays and special occasions, all we had were our Sunday afternoons. He would cook for me. He'd ask me what I wanted, and I'd always request the exact same meal, a German dish called *Rösti*, which is basically a pancake made out of potatoes and some sort of meat with a gravy. I'd have that and a bottle of Sprite, and for dessert a plastic container of custard with caramel on top.

A good chunk of those afternoons would pass in silence. My dad didn't talk much. He was caring and devoted, attentive to detail, always a card on my birthday, always my favorite food and toys when I came for a visit. But at the same time he was a closed book. We'd talk about the food he was making, talk about the F1 racing we'd watched. Every now and then he'd drop a tidbit of information, about a place he'd visited or his steakhouse. But that was it. Being with my dad was like watching a web series. I'd get a few minutes of information a few minutes at a time, then I'd have to wait a week for the next installment.

When I was thirteen my dad moved to Cape Town, and we lost touch. We'd been losing touch for a while, for a couple of reasons. I was a teenager. I had a whole other world I was dealing with now. Video-games and computers meant more to me than spending time with my parents. Also, my mom had married Abel. He was incensed by the idea of my mom being in contact with her previous love, and she decided it was safer for everyone involved not to test his anger. I went from seeing my dad every Sunday to seeing him every other Sunday, maybe once a month, whenever my mom could sneak me over, same as she'd done back in Hillbrow. We'd gone from living under apartheid to living under another kind of tyranny, that of an abusive, alcoholic man.

At the same time, Yeoville had started to suffer from white flight, neglect, general decline. Most of my dad's German friends had left for Cape Town. If he wasn't seeing me, he had no reason to stay, so he left. His leaving wasn't anything traumatic, because it never registered that we might lose touch and never see each other again. In my mind it was just *Dad's moving to Cape Town for a bit. Whatever.*

Then he was gone. I stayed busy living my life, surviving high school, surviving my early twenties, becoming a comedian. My career took off quickly. I got a radio DJ gig and hosted a kids' adventure reality show on television. I was headlining at clubs all over the country. But even as my life was moving forward, the questions about my dad were always there in the back of my mind, bubbling up to the surface now and then. "I wonder where he is. Does he think about me? Does he know what I'm doing? Is he proud of me?" When a parent is absent, you're left in the lurch of not knowing, and it's so easy to fill that space with negative thoughts. "They don't care." "They're selfish." My one saving grace was that my mom never spoke ill of him. She would always compliment him. "You're good with your money. You get that from your dad." "You have your dad's smile." "You're clean and tidy like your father." I never turned to bitterness, because she made sure I knew his absence was because of circumstance and not a lack of love. She always told me the story of her coming home from the hospital and my dad saying, "Where's my kid? I want that kid in my life." She'd say to me, "Don't ever forget: He chose you." And, ultimately, when I turned twenty-four, it was my mom who made me track him down.

Because my father is so private, finding him was hard work. We didn't have an address. He wasn't in the phone book. I started by reaching out to some of his old connections, German expats in Johannesburg, a woman who used to date one of his friends who knew somebody who knew the last place he stayed. I got nowhere. Finally my mom suggested the Swiss embassy. "They have to know where he is," she said, "because he has to be in touch with them."

I wrote to the Swiss embassy asking them where my father was, but because my father is not on my birth certificate I had no proof that my father is my father. The embassy wrote back and said they couldn't give me any information, because they didn't know who I was. I tried calling them, and I got the runaround there as well. "Look, kid," they said. "We can't help you. We're the *Swiss* embassy. Do you know nothing about the Swiss? Discretion is kind of our thing. That's what we do. Tough luck." I kept pestering them and finally they said, "Okay, we'll take your letter and, if a man such as you're describing exists, we might forward your letter to him. If he doesn't, maybe we won't. Let's see what happens."

A few months later, a letter came back in the post: "Great to hear from you. How are you? Love, Dad." He gave me his address in Cape

Town, in a neighborhood called Camps Bay, and a few months later I went down to visit.

I'll never forget that day. It was probably one of the weirdest days of my life, going to meet a person I knew and yet did not know at all. My memories of him felt just out of reach. I was trying to remember how he spoke, how he laughed, what his manner was. I parked on his street and started looking for his address. Camps Bay is full of older, semiretired white people, and as I walked down the road all these old white men were walking toward me and past me. My father was pushing seventy by that point, and I was so afraid I'd forgotten what he looked like. I was looking in the face of every old white man who passed me, like, *Are* you *my daddy?* Basically it looked like I was cruising old white dudes in a beachfront retirement community. Then finally I got to the address I'd been given and rang the bell, and the second he opened the door I recognized him. *Hey! It's you,* I thought. *Of course it's you. You're the guy. I know you.*

We picked up right where we'd left off, which was him treating me exactly the way he'd treated me as a thirteen-year-old boy. Like the creature of habit he was, my father went straight back into it. "Right! So where were we? Here, I've got all your favorites. Potato *Rösti*. A bottle of Sprite. Custard with caramel." Luckily my tastes hadn't matured much since the age of thirteen, so I tucked right in.

While I was eating he got up and went and picked up this book, an oversized photo album, and brought it back to the table. "I've been following you," he said, and he opened it up. It was a scrapbook of everything I had ever done, every time my name was mentioned in a newspaper, everything from magazine covers to the tiniest club listings, from the beginning of my career all the way through to that week. He was smiling so big as he took me through it, looking at the headlines. "Trevor Noah Appearing This Saturday at the Blues Room." "Trevor Noah Hosting New TV Show."

I felt a flood of emotions rushing through me. It was everything I could do not to start crying. It felt like this ten-year gap in my life closed right up in an instant, like only a day had passed since I'd last seen him.

For years I'd had so many questions. Is he thinking about me? Does he know what I'm doing? Is he proud of me? But he'd been with me the whole time. He'd always been proud of me. Circumstance had pulled us apart, but he was never not my father.

I walked out of his house that day an inch taller. Seeing him had reaffirmed his choosing of me. He chose to have me in his life. He chose to answer my letter. I was wanted. Being chosen is the greatest gift you can give to another human being.

Once we reconnected, I was overcome by this drive to make up for all the years we'd missed. I decided the best way to do it was to interview him. I realized very quickly that that was a mistake. Interviews will give you facts and information, but facts and information weren't really what I was after. What I wanted was a relationship, and an interview is not a relationship. Relationships are built in the silences. You spend time with people, you observe them and interact with them, and you come to know them—and that is what apartheid stole from us: time. You can't make up for that with an interview, but I had to figure that out for myself.

I went down to spend a few days with my father, and I made it my mission: This weekend I will get to know my father. As soon as I arrived I started peppering him with questions. "Where are you from? Where did you go to school? Why did you do this? How did you do that?" He started getting visibly irritated.

"What is this?" he said. "Why are you interrogating me? What's going on here?"

"I want to get to know you."

"Is this how you normally get to know people, by interrogating them?"

"Well . . . not really."

"So how do you get to know people?"

"I dunno. By spending time with them, I guess."

"Okay. So spend time with me. See what you find out."

So we spent the weekend together. We had dinner and talked about politics. We watched F1 racing and talked about sports. We sat quietly in his backyard and listened to old Elvis Presley records. The whole time he said not one word about himself. Then, as I was packing up to leave, he walked over to me and sat down.

"So," he said, "in the time we've spent together, what would you say you've learned about your dad?"

"Nothing. All I know is that you're extremely secretive."

"You see? You're getting to know me already."

PART II

When Dutch colonists landed at the southern tip of Africa over three hundred years ago, they encountered an indigenous people known as the Khoisan. The Khoisan are the Native Americans of South Africa, a lost tribe of bushmen, nomadic hunter-gatherers distinct from the darker, Bantu-speaking peoples who later migrated south to become the Zulu, Xhosa, and Sotho tribes of modern South Africa. While settling in Cape Town and the surrounding frontier, the white colonists had their way with the Khoisan women, and the first mixed people of South Africa were born.

To work the colonists' farms, slaves were soon imported from different corners of the Dutch empire, from West Africa, Madagascar, and the East Indies. The slaves and the Khoisan intermarried, and the white colonists continued to dip in and take their liberties, and over time the Khoisan all but disappeared from South Africa. While most were killed off through disease, famine, and war, the rest of their bloodline was bred out of existence, mixed in with the descendants of whites and slaves to form an entirely new race of people: coloreds. Colored people are a hybrid, a complete mix. Some are light and some are dark. Some have Asian features, some have white features, some have black features. It's not uncommon for a colored man and a colored woman to have a child that looks nothing like either parent.

The curse that colored people carry is having no clearly defined heritage to go back to. If they trace their lineage back far enough, at a certain point it splits into white and native and a tangled web of "other." Since their native mothers are gone, their strongest affinity has always been with their white fathers, the Afrikaners. Most colored people don't speak African languages. They speak Afrikaans. Their religion, their institutions, all of the things that shaped their culture came from Afrikaners.

The history of colored people in South Africa is, in this respect, worse than the history of black people in South Africa. For all that black people have suffered, they know who they are. Colored people don't.

———

9

THE MULBERRY TREE

At the end of our street in Eden Park, right in a bend at the top of the road, stood a giant mulberry tree growing out of someone's front yard. Every year when it bore fruit the neighborhood kids would go and pick berries from it, eating as many as they could and filling up bags to take home. They would all play under the tree together. I had to play under the tree by myself. I didn't have any friends in Eden Park.

I was the anomaly wherever we lived. In Hillbrow, we lived in a white area, and nobody looked like me. In Soweto, we lived in a black area, and nobody looked like me. Eden Park was a colored area. In Eden Park, *everyone* looked like me, but we couldn't have been more different. It was the biggest mindfuck I've ever experienced.

The animosity I felt from the colored people I encountered growing up was one of the hardest things I've ever had to deal with. It taught me that it is easier to be an insider as an outsider than to be an outsider as an insider. If a white guy chooses to immerse himself in hip-hop culture and only hang out with black people, black people will say, "Cool, white guy. Do what you need to do." If a black guy chooses to button up his blackness to live among white people and play lots of golf, white people will say, "Fine. I like Brian. He's safe." But try being a black person who immerses himself in white culture while still living in the black community. Try being a white person who adopts the trappings of black culture while still living in the white community. You will face more hate and ridicule and ostracism than you can even begin to fathom. People are willing to accept you if they see you as an outsider trying to assimilate into their world. But when they see you as a fellow tribe member attempting to disavow the tribe, that is something they will never forgive. That is what happened to me in Eden Park.

When apartheid came, colored people defied easy categorization, so the system used them—quite brilliantly—to sow confusion, hatred, and mistrust. For the purposes of the state, colored people became the almost-whites. They were second-class citizens, denied the rights of white people but given special privileges that black people didn't have, just to keep them holding out for more. Afrikaners used to call them *amperbaas:* "the almost-boss." The almost-master. "You're *almost* there. You're *so close*. You're *this close* to being white. Pity your grandfather couldn't keep his hands off the chocolate, eh? But it's not your fault you're colored, so keep trying. Because if you work hard enough you can erase this taint from your bloodline. Keep on marrying lighter and whiter and don't touch the chocolate and maybe, *maybe,* someday, if you're lucky, you can become white."

Which seems ridiculous, but it would happen. Every year under apartheid, some colored people would get promoted to white. It wasn't a myth; it was real. People could submit applications to the government. Your hair might become straight enough, your skin might become light enough, your accent might become polished enough—and you'd be reclassified as white. All you had to do was denounce your people, denounce your history, and leave your darker-skinned friends and family behind.

The legal definition of a white person under apartheid was "one who in appearance is obviously a white person who is generally not accepted as a coloured person; or is generally accepted as a white person and is not in appearance obviously a white person." It was completely arbitrary, in other words. That's where the government came up with things like the pencil test. If you were applying to be white, the pencil went into your hair. If it fell out, you were white. If it stayed in, you were colored. You were what the government said you were. Sometimes that came down to a lone clerk eyeballing your face and making a snap decision. Depending on how high your cheekbones were or how broad your nose was, he could tick whatever box made sense to him, thereby deciding where you could live, whom you could marry, what jobs and rights and privileges you were allowed.

And colored people didn't just get promoted to white. Sometimes colored people became Indian. Sometimes Indian people became colored. Sometimes blacks were promoted to colored, and sometimes coloreds were demoted to black. And of course whites could be demoted to colored as well. That was key. Those mixed bloodlines were always lurking, waiting to peek out, and fear of losing their status kept white people in line. If two white parents had a child and the government decided that child was too dark, even if both parents produced documentation proving they were white, the child could be classified as colored, and the family had to make a decision. Do they give up their white status to go and live as colored people in a colored area? Or would they split up, the mother taking the colored child to live in the ghetto while the father stayed white to make a living to support them?

Many colored people lived in this limbo, a true purgatory, always yearning for the white fathers who disowned them, and they could be horribly racist to one another as a result. The most common colored slur was *boesman*. "Bushman." "Bushie." Because it called out their blackness, their primitiveness. The worst way to insult a colored person was to infer that they were in some way black. One of the most sinister things about apartheid was that it taught colored people that it was black people who were holding them back. Apartheid said that the only reason colored people couldn't have first-class status was because black people might use coloredness to sneak past the gates to enjoy the benefits of whiteness.

That's what apartheid did: It convinced every group that it was because of the other race that they didn't get into the club. It's basically the bouncer at the door telling you, "We can't let you in because of your friend Darren and his ugly shoes." So you look at Darren and say, "Screw you, Black Darren. You're holding me back." Then when Darren goes up, the bouncer says, "No, it's actually your friend Sizwe and his weird hair." So Darren says, "Screw you, Sizwe," and now everyone hates everyone. But the truth is that none of you were ever getting into that club.

Colored people had it rough. Imagine: You've been brainwashed into believing that your blood is tainted. You've spent all your time assimilating and aspiring to whiteness. Then, just as you think you're closing in on the finish line, some fucking guy named Nelson Mandela comes along and flips the country on its head. Now the finish line is back where the starting line was, and the benchmark is black. Black is in charge. Black is beautiful. Black is powerful. For centuries colored people were told: Blacks are monkeys. Don't swing from the trees like them. Learn to walk upright like the white man. Then all of a sudden it's *Planet of the Apes*, and the monkeys have taken over.

So you can imagine how weird it was for me. I was mixed but not colored—colored by complexion but not by culture. Because of that I was seen as a colored person who didn't want to be colored.

In Eden Park, I encountered two types of colored people. Some colored people hated me because of my blackness. My hair was curly and I was proud of my Afro. I spoke African languages and loved speaking them. People would hear me speaking Xhosa or Zulu and they'd say, *"Wat is jy? 'n Boesman?"* "What are you, a Bushman?" Why are you trying to be black? Why do you speak that click-click language? Look at your light skin. You're almost there and you're throwing it away.

Other colored people hated me because of my whiteness. Even though I identified as being black, I had a white father. I went to an English private school. I'd learned to get along with white people at church. I could speak perfect English, and I barely spoke Afrikaans, the language colored people were supposed to speak. So colored people thought that I thought I was better than them. They would mock my accent, like I was putting on airs. *"Dink jy, jy is grênd?"* "You think you're high class?"—uppity, people would say in America.

Even when I thought I was liked, I wasn't. One year I got a brand-new bike during the summer holidays. My cousin Mlungisi and I were taking turns riding around the block. I was riding up our street when this cute colored girl came out to the road and stopped me. She smiled and waved to me sweetly.

"Hey," she said, "can I ride your bike?"

I was completely shocked. *Oh, wow,* I thought, *I made a friend.*

"Yeah, of course," I said.

I got off and she got on and rode about twenty or thirty feet. Some random older kid came running up to the street, she stopped and got off, and he climbed on and rode away. I was so happy that a girl had spoken to me that it didn't fully sink in that they'd stolen my bicycle. I ran back home, smiling and skipping along. My cousin asked where the bicycle was. I told him.

"Trevor, you've been robbed," he said. "Why didn't you chase them?"

"I thought they were being nice. I thought I'd made a friend."

Mlungisi was older, my protector. He ran off and found the kids, and thirty minutes later he came back with my bike.

Things like that happened a lot. I was bullied all the time. The incident at the mulberry tree was probably the worst of them. Late one afternoon I was playing by myself like I always did, running around the neighborhood. This group of five or six colored boys was up the street picking berries off the mulberry tree and eating them. I went over and started picking some to take home for myself. The boys were a few years older than me, around twelve or thirteen. They didn't talk to me, and I didn't talk to them. They were speaking to one another in Afrikaans, and I could understand what they were saying. Then one of them, this kid who was the ringleader of the group, walked over. *"Mag ek jou moerbeie sien?"* "Can I see your mulberries?" My first thought, again, was, *Oh, cool. I made a friend.* I held up my hand and showed him my mulberries. Then he knocked them out of my hand and smushed them into the ground. The other kids started laughing. I stood there and looked at him a moment. By that point I'd developed thick skin. I was used to being bullied. I shrugged it off and went back to picking berries.

Clearly not getting the reaction he wanted, this kid started cursing me out. *"Fok weg, jou onnosele Boesman!"* "Get the fuck out of here! Go away, you stupid Bushie! Bushman!" I ignored him and went on about my business. Then I felt a *splat!* on the back of my head. He'd hit me with a mulberry. It wasn't painful, just startling. I turned to look at him and, *splat!*, he hit me again, right in my face.

Then, in a split second, before I could even react, all of these kids started pelting me with berries, pelting the shit out of me. Some of the berries weren't ripe, and they stung like rocks. I tried to cover my face with my hands, but there was a barrage coming at me from all sides. They were laughing and pelting me and calling me names. "Bushie! Bushman!" I was terrified. Just the suddenness of it, I didn't know what to do. I started crying, and I ran. I ran for my life, all the way back down the road to our house.

When I ran inside I looked like I'd been beaten to a pulp because I was bawling my eyes out and was covered in red-purple berry juice. My mother looked at me, horrified.

"What happened?"

In between sobs I told her the story. "These kids . . . the mulberry tree . . . they threw berries at me . . ." When I finished, she burst out laughing. "It's not funny!" I said.

"No, no, Trevor," she said. "I'm not laughing because it's funny. I'm laughing out of relief. I thought you'd been beaten up. I thought this was blood. I'm laughing because it's only berry juice."

My mom thought everything was funny. There was no subject too dark or too painful for her to tackle with humor. "Look on the bright side," she said, laughing and pointing to the half of me covered in dark berry juice. "Now you really are half black and half white."

"It's not funny!"

"Trevor, you're okay," she said. "Go and wash up. You're not hurt. You're hurt emotionally. But you're not hurt."

Half an hour later, Abel showed up. At that point Abel was still my mom's boyfriend. He wasn't trying to be my father or even a stepfather, really. He was more like a big brother than anything. He'd joke around with me, have fun. I didn't know him that well, but one thing I did know about him was that he had a temper. Very charming when he wanted to be, incredibly funny, but fuck he could be mean. He'd grown up in the homelands, where you had to fight to survive. Abel was big, too, around six-foot-three, long and lean. He hadn't hit my mom yet. He hadn't hit me yet, either. But I knew he was dangerous. I'd seen it. Someone would cut us off in traffic. Abel would yell out the window. The other guy would honk and yell back. In a flash Abel would be out of our car, over to theirs, grabbing the guy through the driver's-side window, screaming in his face, raising a fist. You'd see the other guy panic. "Whoa, whoa, whoa. I'm sorry, I'm sorry."

When Abel walked in that night, he sat down on the couch and saw that I'd been crying.

"What happened?" he said.

I started to explain. My mother cut me off. "Don't tell him," she said. She knew what would happen. She knew better than me.

"Don't tell me what?" Abel said.

"It's nothing," she said.

"It's not nothing," I said.

She glared at me. "Don't tell him."

Abel was getting frustrated. "What? Don't tell me what?"

He'd been drinking; he never came home from work sober, and the drinking always made his temper worse. It was strange, but in that moment I realized that if I said the right things I could get him to step in and do something. We were almost family, and I knew if I made him feel like his family had been insulted, he'd help me get back at the boys. I knew he had a demon inside him, and I hated that; it terrified me how violent and dangerous he was when he snapped. But in that moment I knew exactly what I had to say to get the monster on my side.

I told him the story, the names they called me, the way they attacked me. My mother kept laughing it off, telling me to get over it, that it was kids being kids, no big deal. She was trying to defuse the situation, but I couldn't see that. I was just mad at her. "You think it's a joke, but it's not funny! It's not *funny*!"

Abel wasn't laughing. As I told him what the bullies had done, I could see the anger building up inside him. With Abel's anger, there was no ranting and raving, no clenched fists. He sat there on the couch listening to me, not saying a word. Then, very calm and deliberate, he stood up.

"Take me to these boys," he said.

Yes, I thought, *this is it. Big brother is going to get my revenge for me.*

We got into his car and drove up the road, stopping a few houses down from the tree. It was dark now except for the light from the streetlamps, but we could see the boys were still there, playing under the tree. I pointed to the ringleader. "That one. He was the main one." Abel slammed his foot on the gas and shot up onto the grass and straight toward the bottom of the tree. He jumped out. I jumped out. As soon as the kids saw me they knew exactly what was happening. They scattered and ran like hell.

Abel was quick. Good Lord, he was fast. The ringleader had made a dash for it and was trying to climb over a wall. Abel grabbed him, pulled him down, and dragged him back. Then he stripped a branch off the tree, a switch, and started whipping him. He whipped the *shit* out of him, and I loved it. I have never enjoyed anything as much as I enjoyed that moment. Revenge truly is sweet. It takes you to a dark place, but, man, it satisfies a thirst.

Then there was the strangest moment where it flipped. I caught a glimpse of the look of terror in the boy's face, and I realized that Abel had gone past getting revenge for me. He wasn't doing this to teach the kid a lesson. He was just beating him. He was a grown man venting his rage on a twelve-year-old boy. In an instant I went from *Yes, I got my revenge* to *No, no, no. Too much. Too much. Oh shit. Oh shit. Oh shit. Dear God, what have I done?*

Once this kid was beat to shit, Abel dragged him over to the car and held him up in front of me. "Say you're sorry." The kid was whimpering, trembling. He looked me in the eye, and I had never seen fear in someone's eyes like I saw in his. He'd been beaten by a stranger in a way I don't think he'd ever been beaten before. He said he was sorry, but it was like his apology wasn't for what he'd done to me. It was like he was sorry for every bad thing he'd ever done in his life, because he didn't know there could be a punishment like this.

Looking in that boy's eyes, I realized how much he and I had in common. He was a kid. I was a kid. He was crying. I was crying. He was a colored boy in South Africa, taught how to hate and how to hate himself. Who had bullied him that he needed to bully me? He'd made me feel fear, and to get my revenge I'd unleashed my own hell on his world. But I knew I'd done a terrible thing.

Once the kid apologized, Abel shoved him away and kicked him. "Go." The kid ran off, and we drove back to the house in silence. At home Abel and my mom got in a huge fight. She was always on him about his temper. "You can't go around hitting other people's children! You're not the law! This anger, this is no way to live!"

A couple of hours later this kid's dad drove over to our house to confront Abel. Abel went out to the gate, and I watched from inside the house. By that point Abel was truly drunk. This kid's dad had no idea what he was walking into. He was some mild-mannered, middle-aged guy. I don't remember much about him, because I was watching Abel the whole time. I never took my eyes off him. I knew that's where the danger was.

Abel didn't have a gun yet; he bought that later. But Abel didn't need a gun to put the fear of God in you. I watched as he got right in this guy's face. I couldn't hear what the other man was saying, but I heard Abel. "Don't fuck with me. I will kill you." The guy turned quickly and got back in his car and drove away. He thought he was coming to defend the honor of his family. He left happy to escape with his life.

When I was growing up, my mom spent a lot of time trying to teach me about women. She was always giving me lessons, little talks, pieces of advice. It was never a full-blown, sit-down lecture about relationships. It was more like tidbits along the way. And I never understood why, because I was a kid. The only women in my life were my mom and my grandmother and my aunt and my cousin. I had no love interest whatsoever, yet my mom insisted. She would go off on a whole range of things.

"Trevor, remember a man is not determined by how much he earns. You can still be the man of the house and earn less than your woman. Being a man is not what you have, it's who you are. Being more of a man doesn't mean your woman has to be less than you."

"Trevor, make sure your woman is the woman in your life. Don't be one of these men who makes his wife compete with his mother. A man with a wife cannot be beholden to his mother."

The smallest thing could prompt her. I'd walk through the house on the way to my room and say, "Hey, Mom" without glancing up. She'd say, "No, Trevor! You look at me. You acknowledge me. Show me that I exist to you, because the way you treat me is the way you will treat your woman. Women like to be noticed. Come and acknowledge me and let me know that you see me. Don't just see me when you need something."

These little lessons were always about grown-up relationships, funnily enough. She was so preoccupied with teaching me how to be a man that she never taught me how to be a boy. How to talk to a girl or pass a girl a note in class—there was none of that. She only told me about adult things. She would even lecture me about sex. As I was a kid, that would get very awkward.

"Trevor, don't forget: You're having sex with a woman in her mind before you're having sex with her in her vagina."

"Trevor, foreplay begins during the day. It doesn't begin in the bedroom."

I'd be like, "What? What is foreplay? What does that even mean?"

———

10

A YOUNG MAN'S LONG, AWKWARD, OCCASIONALLY TRAGIC, AND FREQUENTLY HUMILIATING EDUCATION IN AFFAIRS OF THE HEART, PART 1: VALENTINE'S DAY

It was my first year at H. A. Jack, the primary school I transferred to after leaving Maryvale. Valentine's Day was approaching fast. I was twelve years old, and I'd never done Valentine's Day before. We didn't celebrate it in Catholic school. I understood Valentine's Day, as a concept. The naked baby shoots you with an arrow and you fall in love. I got that part. But this was my first time being introduced to it as an activity. At H. A. Jack, Valentine's Day was used as a fundraiser. Pupils were going around selling flowers and cards, and I had to go ask a friend what was happening.

"What is this?" I said. "What are we doing?"

"Oh, you know," she said, "it's Valentine's Day. You pick a special person and you tell them that you love them, and they love you back."

Wow, I thought, *that seems intense*. But I hadn't been shot by Cupid's arrow, and I didn't know of anyone getting shot on my behalf. I had no clue what was going on. All week, the girls in school kept saying, "Who's your valentine? Who's your valentine?" I didn't know what I was supposed to do. Finally one of the girls, a white girl, said, "You should ask Maylene." The other kids agreed. "Yes, Maylene. You should definitely ask Maylene. You have to ask Maylene. You guys are *perfect* for each other."

Maylene was a girl I used to walk home from school with. We lived in the city now, me, my mom and Abel, who was now my stepfather, and my new baby brother, Andrew. We'd sold our house in Eden Park to invest in Abel's new garage. Then that fell apart, and we ended up moving to a neighborhood called Highlands North, a thirty-minute walk from H. A. Jack. A group of us would leave school together every afternoon, each kid peeling off and going their separate way when we reached their house. Maylene and I lived the farthest, so we'd always be the last two. We'd walk together until we got where we needed to go, and then we'd part ways.

Maylene was cool. She was good at tennis, smart, cute. I liked her. I didn't have a crush on her; I wasn't even thinking about girls that way yet. I just liked hanging out with her. Maylene was also the only colored girl in school. I was the only mixed kid in school. We were the only two people who looked like each other. The white girls were insistent about me asking Maylene to be my valentine. They were like, "Trevor, you *have* to ask her. You're the *only two*. It's your *responsibility*." It was like our species was going to die out if we didn't mate and carry on. Which I've learned in life is something that white people do without even realizing it. "You two look the same, therefore we must arrange for you to have sex."

I honestly hadn't thought of asking Maylene, but when the girls brought it up, that thing happened where someone plants the idea in your head and it changes your perception.

"Maylene's totally got a thing for you."

"*Does* she?"

"Yeah, you guys are great together!"

"*Are* we?"

"Totally."

"Well, okay. If you say so."

I liked Maylene as much as I liked anyone, I suppose. Mostly I think I liked the idea of being liked. I decided I'd ask her to be my valentine, but I had no idea how to do it. I didn't know the first thing about having a girlfriend. I had to be taught the whole love bureaucracy of the school. There was the thing where you don't actually talk straight to the person. You have your group of friends and she has her group of friends, and your group of friends has to go to her group of friends and say, "Okay, Trevor likes Maylene. He wants her to be his valentine. We're in favor. We're ready to sign off with your approval." Her friends say, "Okay. Sounds good. We have to run it by Maylene." They go to Maylene. They consult. They tell her what they think. "Trevor says he likes you. We're in favor. We think you'd be good together. What do you say?" Maylene says, "I like Trevor." They say, "Okay. Let's move forward." They come back to us. "Maylene says she approves and she's waiting for Trevor's Valentine's Day advance."

The girls told me this process was what needed to happen. I said, "Cool. Let's do it." The friends sorted it out, Maylene got on board, and I was all set.

The week before Valentine's, Maylene and I were walking home together, and I was trying to get up the courage to ask her. I was so nervous. I'd never done anything like it. I already knew the answer; her friends had told me she'd say yes. It's like being in Congress. You know you have the votes before you go to the floor, but it's still difficult because anything could happen. I didn't know how to do it, all I knew was I wanted it to be perfect, so I waited until we were standing outside McDonald's. Then I mustered up all of my courage and turned to her.

"Hey, Valentine's Day is coming up, and I was wondering, would you be my valentine?"

"Yes. I'll be your valentine."

And then, under the golden arches, we kissed. It was my first time ever kissing a girl. It was just a peck, our lips touched for only a few seconds, but it set off explosions in my head. *Yes! Oh, yes. This. I don't know what this is, but I like it.* Something had awakened. And it was right outside McDonald's, so it was extra special.

Now I was truly excited. I had a valentine. I had a girlfriend. I spent the whole week thinking about Maylene, wanting to make her Valentine's Day as memorable as I could. I saved up my pocket money and bought her flowers and a teddy bear and a card. I wrote a poem with her name in the card, which was really hard because there aren't many good words that rhyme with Maylene. (Machine? Ravine? Sardine?) Then the big day came. I got my Valentine's card and the flowers and the teddy bear and got them ready and took them to school. I was the happiest boy on earth.

The teachers had set aside a period before recess for everyone to exchange valentines. There was a corridor outside our classrooms where I knew Maylene would be, and I waited for her there. All around me, love was in bloom. Boys and girls exchanging cards and gifts, laughing and giggling and stealing kisses. I waited and waited. Finally Maylene showed up and walked over to me. I was about to say "Happy Valentine's Day!" when she stopped me and said, "Oh, hi, Trevor. Um, listen, I can't be your girlfriend anymore. Lorenzo asked me to be his valentine and I can't have two valentines, so I'm his girlfriend now and not yours."

She said it so matter-of-factly that I had no idea how to process it. This was my first time having a girlfriend, so at first I thought, *Huh, maybe this is just how it goes.*

"Oh, okay," I said. "Well, um . . . happy Valentine's Day."

I held out the card and the flowers and the teddy bear. She took them and said thanks, and she was gone.

I felt like someone had taken a gun and shot holes in every part of me. But at the same time some part of me said, "Well, this makes sense." Lorenzo was everything I wasn't. He was popular. He was *white*. He'd upset the balance of everything by asking out the only colored girl in school. Girls loved him, and he was dumb as rocks. A nice guy, but kind of a bad boy. Girls did his homework for him; he was that guy. He was really good-looking, too. It was like when he was creating his character he traded in all his intelligence points for beauty points. I stood no chance.

As devastated as I was, I understood why Maylene made the choice that she did. I would have picked Lorenzo over me, too. All the other kids were running up and down the corridors and out on the playground, laughing and smiling with their red and pink cards and flowers, and I went back to the classroom and sat by myself and waited for the bell to ring.

P etrol for the car, like food, was an expense we could not avoid, but my mom could get more mileage out of a tank of petrol than any human who has ever been on a road in the history of automobiles. She knew every trick. Driving around Johannesburg in our rusty old Volkswagen, every time she stopped in traffic, she'd turn off the car. Then the traffic would start and she'd turn the car on again. That stop-start technology that they use in hybrid cars now? That was my mom. She was a hybrid car before hybrid cars came out. She was the master of coasting. She knew every downhill between work and school, between school and home. She knew exactly where the gradient shifted to put it into neutral. She could time the traffic lights so we could coast through intersections without using the brakes or losing momentum.

There were times when we would be in traffic and we had so little money for petrol that I would have to push the car. If we were stuck in gridlock, my mom would turn the car off and it was my job to get out and push it forward six inches at a time. People would pitch up and offer to help.

"Are you stuck?"

"Nope. We're fine."

"You sure?"

"Yep."

"Can we help you?"

"Nope."

"Do you need a tow?"

And what do you say? The truth? "Thanks, but we're just so poor my mom makes her kid push the car"?

That was some of the most embarrassing shit in my life, pushing the car to school like the fucking Flintstones. Because the other kids were coming in on that same road to go to school. I'd take my blazer off so that no one could tell what school I went to, and I would bury my head and push the car, hoping no one would recognize me.

———

OUTSIDER

After finishing primary school at H. A. Jack, I started grade eight at Sandringham High School. Even after apartheid, most black people still lived in the townships and the areas formerly designated as homelands, where the only available government schools were the broken remnants of the Bantu system. Wealthy white kids—along with the few black people and colored people and Indians who had money or could get scholarships—were holed up in private schools, which were super-expensive but virtually guaranteed entry into university. Sandringham was what we call a Model C school, which meant it was a mix of government and private, similar to charter schools in America. The place was huge, a thousand kids on sprawling grounds with tennis courts, sports fields, and a swimming pool.

Being a Model C school and not a government school, Sandringham drew kids from all over, making it a near-perfect microcosm of post-apartheid South Africa as a whole—a perfect example of what South Africa has the potential to be. We had rich white kids, a bunch of middle-class white kids, and some working-class white kids. We had black kids who were newly rich, black kids who were middle-class, and black kids from the townships. We had colored kids and Indian kids, and even a handful of Chinese kids, too. The pupils were as integrated as they could be given that apartheid had just ended. At H. A. Jack, race was broken up into blocks. Sandringham was more like a spectrum.

South African schools don't have cafeterias. At Sandringham we'd buy our lunch at what we call the tuck shop, a little canteen, and then have free rein to go wherever we wanted on the school grounds to eat— the quad, the courtyard, the playground, wherever. Kids would break off and cluster into their cliques and groups. People were still grouped by color in most cases, but you could see how they all blended and shaded into one another. The kids who played soccer were mostly black. The kids who played tennis were mostly white. The kids who played cricket were a mix. The Chinese kids would hang out next to the prefab buildings. The matrics, what South Africans call seniors, would hang out on the quad. The popular, pretty girls would hang out over here, and computer geeks would hang out over there. To the extent that the groupings were racial, it was because of the ways race overlapped class and geography out in the real world. Suburban kids hung out with suburban kids. Township kids hung out with township kids.

At break, as the only mixed kid out of a thousand, I faced the same predicament I had on the playground at H. A. Jack: Where was I supposed to go? Even with so many different groups to choose from, I wasn't a natural constituent of any particular one. I obviously wasn't Indian or Chinese. The colored kids would shit on me all the time for being too black. So I wasn't welcome there. As always, I was adept enough with white kids not to get bullied by them, but the white kids were always going shopping, going to the movies, going on trips— things that required money. We didn't have any money, so I was out of the mix there, too. The group I felt the most affinity for was the poor black kids. I hung out with them and got along with them, but most of them took minibuses to school from way out in the townships, from Soweto, from Tembisa, from Alexandra. They rode to school as friends and went home as friends. They had their own groups. Weekends and school holidays, they were hanging out with one another and I couldn't visit. Soweto was a forty-minute drive from my house. We didn't have money for petrol. After school I was on my own. Weekends I was on my own. Ever the outsider, I created my own strange little world. I did it out of necessity. I needed a way to fit in. I also needed money, a way to buy the same snacks and do the things that the other kids were doing. Which is how I became the tuck-shop guy.

Thanks to my long walk to school, I was late every single day. I'd have to stop off in the prefect's office to write my name down for detention. I was the patron saint of detention. Already late, I'd run to join my morning classes—math, English, biology, whatever. The last period before break was assembly. The pupils would come together in the assembly hall, each grade seated row by row, and the teachers and the prefects would get up onstage and go over the business of what was happening in the school—announcements, awards, that sort of thing. The names of the kids with detention were announced at every assembly, and I was always one of them. Always. Every single day. It was a running joke. The prefect would say, "Detentions for today . . ." and I would stand up automatically. It was like the Oscars and I was Meryl Streep. There was one time I stood up and then the prefect named the five people and I wasn't one of them. Everyone burst out laughing. Somebody yelled out, "Where's Trevor?!" The prefect looked at the paper and shook his head. "Nope." The entire hall erupted with cheers and applause. *"Yay!!!!"*

Then, immediately after assembly, there would be a race to the tuck shop because the queue to buy food was so long. Every minute you spent in the queue was working against your break time. The sooner you got your food, the longer you had to eat, play a game of soccer, or hang out. Also, if you got there late, the best food was gone.

Two things were true about me at that age. One, I was still the fastest kid in school. And two, I had no pride. The second we were dismissed from assembly I would run like a bat out of hell to the tuck shop so I could be the first one there. I was *always* first in line. I became notorious for being that guy, so much so that people started coming up to me in line. "Hey, can you buy this for me?" Which would piss off the kids behind me because it was basically cutting the line. So people started approaching me during assembly. They'd say, "Hey, I've got ten rand. If you buy my food for me, I'll give you two." That's when I learned: time is money. I realized people would pay me to buy their food because I was willing to run for it. I started telling everyone at assembly, "Place your orders. Give me a list of what you want, give me a percentage of what you're going to spend, and I'll buy your food for you."

I was an overnight success. Fat guys were my number-one customers. They loved food, but couldn't run. I had all these rich, fat white kids who were like, "This is fantastic! My parents spoil me, I've got money, and now I've got a way I can get food without having to work for it—and I still get my break." I had so many customers I was turning kids away. I had a rule: I would take five orders a day, high bidders only. I'd make so much that I could buy my lunch using other kids' money and keep the lunch money my mom gave me for pocket cash. Then I could afford to catch a bus home instead of walking or save up to buy whatever. Every day I'd take orders, assembly would end, and I'd make my mad dash and buy everybody's hot dogs and Cokes and muffins. If you paid me extra you could even tell me where you'd be and I'd deliver it to you.

I'd found my niche. Since I belonged to no group I learned to move seamlessly between groups. I floated. I was a chameleon, still, a cultural chameleon. I learned how to blend. I could play sports with the jocks. I could talk computers with the nerds. I could jump in the circle and dance with the township kids. I popped around to everyone, working, chatting, telling jokes, making deliveries.

I was like a weed dealer, but of food. The weed guy is always welcome at the party. He's not a part of the circle, but he's invited into the circle temporarily because of what he can offer. That's who I was. Always an outsider. As the outsider, you can retreat into a shell, be anonymous, be invisible. Or you can go the other way. You protect yourself by opening up. You don't ask to be accepted for everything you are, just the one part of yourself that you're willing to share. For me it was humor. I learned that even though I didn't belong to one group, I could be a part of any group that was laughing. I'd drop in, pass out the snacks, tell a few jokes. I'd perform for them. I'd catch a bit of their conversation, learn more about their group, and then leave. I never overstayed my welcome. I wasn't popular, but I wasn't an outcast. I was everywhere with everybody, and at the same time I was all by myself.

I don't regret anything I've ever done in life, any choice that I've made. But I'm consumed with regret for the things I didn't do, the choices I didn't make, the things I didn't say. We spend so much time being afraid of failure, afraid of rejection. But regret is the thing we should fear most. Failure is an answer. Rejection is an answer. Regret is an eternal question you will never have the answer to. "What if . . ." "If only . . ." "I wonder what would have . . ." You will never, never know, and it will haunt you for the rest of your days.

12

A YOUNG MAN'S LONG, AWKWARD, OCCASIONALLY TRAGIC, AND FREQUENTLY HUMILIATING EDUCATION IN AFFAIRS OF THE HEART, PART II: THE CRUSH

In high school, the attention of girls was not an affliction I suffered from. I wasn't the hot guy in class. I wasn't even the cute guy in class. I was ugly. Puberty was not kind to me. My acne was so bad that people used to ask what was wrong with me, like I'd had an allergic reaction to something. It was the kind of acne that qualifies as a medical condition. *Acne vulgaris,* the doctor called it. We're not talking about pimples, kids. We're talking pustules—big, pus-filled blackheads and white-heads. They started on my forehead, spread down the sides of my face, and covered my cheeks and neck and ravaged me everywhere.

Being poor didn't help. Not only could I not afford a decent haircut, leaving me with a huge, unruly Afro, but my mother also used to get angry at the fact that I grew out of my school uniforms too fast, so to save money she started buying my clothes three sizes too big. My blazer was too long and my pants were too baggy and my shoes flopped around. I was a clown. And of course, Murphy's Law, the year my mom started buying my clothes too big was the year that I stopped growing. So now I was never going to grow into my clown clothes and I was stuck being a clown. The only thing I had going for me was the fact that I was tall, but even there I was gangly and awkward-looking. Duck feet. High ass. Nothing worked.

After suffering my Valentine's Day heartbreak at the hands of Maylene and the handsome, charming Lorenzo, I learned a valuable lesson about dating. What I learned was that cool guys get girls, and funny guys get to hang out with the cool guys with their girls. I was not a cool guy; therefore I did not have girls. I understood that formula very quickly and I knew my place. I didn't ask girls out. I didn't have a girlfriend. I didn't even try.

For me to try to get a girl would have upset the natural order of things. Part of my success as the tuck-shop guy was that I was welcome everywhere, and I was welcome everywhere because I was nobody. I was the acne-ridden clown with duck feet in floppy shoes. I wasn't a threat to the guys. I wasn't a threat to the girls. The minute I became somebody, I risked no longer being welcomed as nobody. The pretty girls were already spoken for. The popular guys had staked their claim. They would say, "I like Zuleika," and you knew that meant if you tried anything with Zuleika there'd be a fight. In the interest of survival, the smart move was to stay on the fringe, stay out of trouble.

At Sandringham, the only time girls in class looked at me was when they wanted me to pass a letter to the hot guy in class. But there was one girl I knew named Johanna. Johanna and I had been at the same school intermittently our whole lives. We were in preschool at Maryvale together. Then she left and went to another school. Then we were in primary school at H. A. Jack together. Then she left and went to another school. Then finally we were at Sandringham together. Because of that we became friends.

Johanna was one of the popular girls. Her best friend was Zaheera. Johanna was beautiful. Zaheera was stunning. Zaheera was colored, Cape Malay. She looked like Salma Hayek. Johanna was out and about and kissing boys, so the guys were all into her. Zaheera, as beautiful as she was, was extremely shy, so there weren't as many guys after her.

Johanna and Zaheera were always together. They were one grade below me, but in terms of popularity they were three grades above me. Still I got to hang out with them because I knew Johanna and we had this thing from being in different schools together. Dating girls may have been out of the question for me, but talking to them was not, because I could make them laugh. Human beings like to laugh, and lucky for me pretty girls are human beings. So I could relate to them in that way, but never in the other way. I knew this because whenever they stopped laughing at my jokes and stories they'd say, "So how do you think I can get Daniel to ask me out?" I always had a clear idea of where I stood.

Outwardly, I had carefully cultivated my status as the funny, nonthreatening guy, but secretly I had the hugest crush on Zaheera. She was *so* pretty and *so* funny. We'd hang out and have great conversations. I thought about her constantly, but for the life of me I never considered myself worthy of dating her. I told myself, *I'm going to have a crush on her forever, and that's all that's ever going to happen.*

At a certain point I decided to map out a strategy. I decided I'd be best friends with Zaheera and stay friends with her long enough to ask her to the matric dance, what we call our senior prom. Mind you, we were in grade nine at this point. The matric dance was three years away. But I decided to play the long game. I was like, *Yep, just gonna take my time.* Because that's what happens in the movies, right? I'd seen my American high school movies. You hang around long enough as the friendly good guy and the girl dates a bunch of handsome jerks, and then one day she turns around and goes, "Oh, it's you. It was always you. You're the guy I was supposed to be with all along."

That was my plan. It was foolproof.

I hung out with Zaheera every chance I got. We'd talk about boys, which ones she liked and which ones liked her. I'd give her advice. At one point she got set up with this guy Gary. They started dating. Gary was in the popular group but kind of shy and Zaheera was in the popular group but kind of shy, so his friends and her friends set them up together, like an arranged marriage. But Zaheera didn't like Gary at all. She told me. We talked about everything.

One day, I don't know how, but I plucked up the courage to ask Zaheera for her phone number, which was a big deal back then because it wasn't like cellphone numbers where everybody has everyone's number for texting and everything. This was the landline. To her house. Where her parents might answer. We were talking one afternoon at school and I asked, "Can I get your phone number? Maybe I can call you and we can talk at home sometime." She said yes, and my mind exploded. *What???!!!! A girl is giving me her phone number???!!! This is insane!!! What do I do??!!* I was so nervous. I'll never forget her telling me the digits one by one as I wrote them down, trying to keep my hand from shaking. We said goodbye and went our separate ways to class, and I was like, *Okay, Trevor. Play it cool. Don't call her right away.* I called her that night. At seven. She'd given me her number at two. That was me being cool. *Dude, don't call her at five. That's too obvious. Call her at seven.*

I phoned her house that night. Her mom answered. I said, "May I speak to Zaheera, please?" Her mom called her, and she came to the phone and we talked. For like an hour. After that we started talking more, at school, on the phone. I never told her how I felt. Never made a move. Nothing. I was always too scared.

Zaheera and Gary broke up. Then they got back together. Then they broke up. Then they got back together. They kissed once, but she didn't like it, so they never kissed again. Then they broke up for real. I bided my time through it all. I watched Popular Gary go down in flames, and I was still the good friend. *Yep, the plan is working. Matric dance, here we come. Only two and a half years to go . . .*

Then we had the mid-year school holidays. The day we came back, Zaheera wasn't at school. Then she wasn't at school the next day. Then she wasn't at school the day after that. Eventually I went and tracked down Johanna on the quad.

"Hey, where's Zaheera?" I said. "She hasn't been around for a while. Is she sick?"

"No," she said. "Didn't anyone tell you? She left the school. She doesn't go here anymore."

"What?"

"Yeah, she left."

My first thought was, *Wow, okay. That's news. I should give her a call to catch up.*

"What school did she move to?" I asked.

"She didn't. Her dad got a job in America. During the break they moved there. They've emigrated."

"What?"

"Yeah. She's gone. She was such a good friend, too. I'm really sad. Are you as sad as I am?"

"Uh . . . yeah," I said, still trying to process everything. "I liked Zaheera. She was really cool."

"Yeah, she was super sad, too, because she had such a huge crush on you. She was always waiting for you to ask her out. Okay, I gotta go to class! Bye!"

She ran off and left me standing there, stunned. She'd hit me with so much information at once, first that Zaheera was gone, then that she had left for America, and then that she'd liked me all along. It was like I'd been hit by three successive waves of heartbreak, each one bigger than the last. My mind raced through all the hours we'd spent talking on the quad, on the phone, all the times I could have said, "Hey, Zaheera, I like you. Will you be my girlfriend?" Ten words that might have changed my life if I'd had the courage to say them. But I hadn't, and now she was gone.

In every nice neighborhood there's one white family that Does Not Give a Fuck. You know the family I'm talking about. They don't do their lawn, don't paint the fence, don't fix the roof. Their house is shit. My mom found that house and bought it, which is how she snuck a black family into a place as white as Highlands North.

Most black people integrating into white suburbs were moving to places like Bramley and Lombardy East. But for some reason my mom chose Highlands North. It was a suburban area, lots of shopping. Working people, mostly. Not wealthy but stable and middle-class. Older houses, but still a nice place to live. In Soweto I was the only white kid in the black township. In Eden Park I was the only mixed kid in the colored area. In Highlands North I was the only black kid in the white suburb—and by "only" I mean only. In Highlands North the white never took flight. It was a largely Jewish neighborhood, and Jewish people don't flee. They're done fleeing. They've already fled. They get to a place, build their shul, and hold it down. Since the white people around us weren't leaving, there weren't a lot of families like ours moving in behind us.

I didn't make any friends in Highlands North for the longest time. I had an easier time making friends in Eden Park, to be honest. In the suburbs, everyone lived behind walls. The white neighborhoods of Johannesburg were built on white fear—fear of black crime, fear of black uprisings and reprisals—and as a result virtually every house sits behind a six-foot wall, and on top of that wall is electric wire. Everyone lives in a plush, fancy maximum-security prison. There is no sitting on the front porch, no saying hi to the neighbors, no kids running back and forth between houses. I'd ride my bike around the neighborhood for hours without seeing a single kid. I'd hear them, though. They were all meeting up behind brick walls for play-dates I wasn't invited to. I'd hear people laughing and playing and I'd get off my bike and creep up and peek over the wall and see a bunch of white kids splashing around in someone's swimming pool. I was like a Peeping Tom, but for friendship.

It was only after a year or so that I figured out the key to making black friends in the suburbs: the children of domestics. Many domestic workers in South Africa, when they get pregnant they get fired. Or, if they're lucky, the family they work for lets them stay on and they can have the baby, but then the baby goes to live with relatives in the homelands. Then the black mother raises the white children, seeing her own child only once a year at the holidays. But a handful of families would let their domestics keep their children with them, living in little maids' quarters or flatlets in the back-yard.

For a long time, those kids were my only friends.

———

13

COLORBLIND

At Sandringham I got to know this one kid, Teddy. Funny guy, charming as hell. My mom used to call him Bugs Bunny; he had a cheeky smile with two big teeth that stuck out the front of his mouth. Teddy and I got along like a house on fire, one of those friends where you start hanging out and from that day forward you're never apart. We were both naughty as shit, too. With Teddy, I'd finally met someone who made me feel normal. I was the terror in my family. He was the terror in his family. When you put us together it was mayhem. Walking home from school we'd throw rocks through windows, just to see them shatter, and then we'd run away. We got detention together all the time. The teachers, the pupils, the principal, everyone at school knew: Teddy and Trevor, thick as thieves.

Teddy's mom worked as a domestic for a family in Linksfield, a wealthy suburb near school. Linksfield was a long walk from my house, nearly forty minutes, but still doable. Walking around was pretty much all I did back then, anyway. I couldn't afford to do anything else, and I couldn't afford to get around any other way. If you liked walking, you were my friend. Teddy and I walked all over Johannesburg together. I'd walk to Teddy's house and we'd hang out there. Then we'd walk back to my house and hang out there. We'd walk from my house down to the city center, which was like a three-hour hike, just to hang out, and then we'd walk all the way back.

Friday and Saturday nights we'd walk to the mall and hang out. The Balfour Park Shopping Mall was a few blocks from my house. It's not a big mall, but it has everything—an arcade, a cinema, restaurants, South Africa's version of Target, South Africa's version of the Gap. Then, once we were at the mall, since we never had any money to shop or watch movies or buy food, we'd just wander around inside.

One night we were at the mall and most of the shops were closed, but the cinema was still showing movies so the building was still open. There was this stationery shop that sold greeting cards and magazines, and it didn't have a door, so when it closed at night there was only a metal gate, like a trellis, that was pulled across the entrance and pad-locked. Walking past this shop, Teddy and I realized that if we put our arms through the trellis we could reach this rack of chocolates just inside. And these weren't just any chocolates—they were alcohol-filled chocolates. I loved alcohol. Loved loved loved it. My whole life I'd steal sips of grown-ups' drinks whenever I could.

We reached in, grabbed a few, drank the liquor inside, and then gobbled down the chocolates. We'd hit the jackpot. We started going back again and again to steal more. We'd wait for the shops to start to close, then we'd go and sit against the gate, acting like we were just hanging out. We'd check to make sure the coast was clear, and then one of us would reach in, grab a chocolate, and drink the whiskey. Reach in, grab a chocolate, drink the rum. Reach in, grab a chocolate, drink the brandy. We did this every weekend for at least a month, having the best time. Then we pushed our luck too far.

It was a Saturday night. We were hanging out at the entrance to the stationery shop, leaning up against the gate. I reached in to grab a chocolate, and at that exact moment a mall cop came around the corner and saw me with my arm in up to my shoulder. I brought my hand out with a bunch of chocolates in it. It was almost like a movie. I saw him. He saw me. His eyes went wide. I tried to walk away, acting natural. Then he shouted out, "*Hey! Stop!*"

And the chase was on. We bolted, heading for the doors. I knew if a guard cut us off at the exit we'd be trapped, so we were hauling ass as fast as we could. We cleared the exit. The second we hit the parking lot, mall cops were coming at us from every direction, a dozen of them at least. I was running with my head down. These guards knew me. I was in that mall all the time. The guards knew my mom, too. She did her banking at that mall. If they even caught a glimpse of who I was, I was dead.

We ran straight across the parking lot, ducking and weaving between parked cars, the guards right behind us, yelling. We made it to the petrol station out at the road, ran through there, and hooked left up the main road. They chased and chased and we ran and ran, and it was *awesome*. The risk of getting caught was half the fun of being naughty, and now the chase was on. I was loving it. I was shitting myself, but also loving it. This was my turf. This was my neighborhood. You couldn't catch me in my neighborhood. I knew every alley and every street, every back wall to climb over, every fence with a gap big enough to slip through. I knew every shortcut you could possibly imagine. As a kid, wherever I went, whatever building I was in, I was always plotting my escape. You know, in case shit went down. In reality I was a nerdy kid with almost no friends, but in my mind I was an important and dangerous man who needed to know where every camera was and where all the exit points were.

I knew we couldn't run forever. We needed a plan. As Teddy and I booked past the fire station there was a road off to the left, a dead end that ran into a metal fence. I knew that there was a hole in the fence to squeeze through and on the far side was an empty field behind the mall that took you back to the main road and back to my house. A grown-up couldn't fit through the hole, but a kid could. All my years of imagining the life of a secret agent for myself finally paid off. Now that I needed an escape, I had one.

"Teddy, this way!" I yelled.

"No, it's a dead end!"

"We can get through! Follow me!"

He didn't. I turned and ran into the dead end. Teddy broke the other way. Half the mall cops followed him, half followed me. I got to the fence and knew exactly how to squirm through. Head, then shoulder, one leg, then twist, then the other leg—done. I was through. The guards hit the fence behind me and couldn't follow. I ran across the field to a fence on the far side, popped through there, and then I was right on the road, three blocks from my house. I slipped my hands into my pockets and casually walked home, another harmless pedestrian out for a stroll.

Once I got back to my house I waited for Teddy. He didn't show up. I waited thirty minutes, forty minutes, an hour. No Teddy.

Fuck.

I ran to Teddy's house in Linksfield. No Teddy. Monday morning I went to school. Still no Teddy.

Fuck.

Now I was worried. After school I went home and checked at my house again, nothing. Teddy's house again, nothing. Then I ran back home.

An hour later Teddy's parents showed up. My mom greeted them at the door.

"Teddy's been arrested for shoplifting," they said.

Fuuuck.

I eavesdropped on their whole conversation from the other room. From the start my mom was certain I was involved.

"Well, where was Trevor?" she asked.

"Teddy said he wasn't with Trevor," they said.

My mom was skeptical. "Hmm. Are you *sure* Trevor wasn't involved?"

"No, apparently not. The cops said there was another kid, but he got away."

"So it *was* Trevor."

"No, we asked Teddy, and he said it wasn't Trevor. He said it was some other kid."

"Huh . . . okay." My mom called me in. "Do you know about this thing?"

"What thing?"

"Teddy was caught shoplifting."

"*Whhaaat?*" I played dumb. "Noooo. That's crazy. I can't believe it. *Teddy?* No."

"Where were you?" my mom asked.

"I was at home."

"But you're always with Teddy."

I shrugged. "Not on this occasion, I suppose."

For a moment my mom thought she'd caught me red-handed, but Teddy'd given me a solid alibi. I went back to my room, thinking I was in the clear.

The next day I was in class and my name was called over the PA system. "Trevor Noah, report to the principal's office." All the kids were like, "Ooooohhh." The announcements could be heard in every classroom, so now, collectively, the whole school knew I was in trouble. I got up and walked to the office and waited anxiously on an uncomfortable wooden bench outside the door.

Finally the principal, Mr. Friedman, walked out. "Trevor, come in." Waiting inside his office was the head of mall security, two uniformed police officers, and my and Teddy's homeroom teacher, Mrs. Vorster. A roomful of silent, stone-faced white authority figures stood over me, the guilty young black man. My heart was pounding. I took a seat.

"Trevor, I don't know if you know this," Mr. Friedman said, "but Teddy was arrested the other day."

"What?" I played the whole thing again. "Teddy? Oh, no. What for?"

"For shoplifting. He's been expelled, and he won't be coming back to school. We know there was another boy involved, and these officers are going around to the schools in the area to investigate. We called you here because Mrs. Vorster tells us you're Teddy's best friend, and we want to know: Do you know anything about this?"

I shook my head. "No, I don't know anything."

"Do you know who Teddy was with?"

"No."

"Okay." He stood up and walked over to a television in the corner of the room. "Trevor, the police have video footage of the whole thing. We'd like you to take a look at it."

Fuuuuuuuuuuuuuuuuuck.

My heart was pounding in my chest. *Well, life, it's been fun,* I thought. *I'm going to get expelled. I'm going to go to jail. This is it.*

Mr. Friedman pressed Play on the VCR. The tape started. It was grainy, black-and-white security-camera footage, but you could see what was happening plain as day. They even had it from multiple angles: Me and Teddy reaching through the gate. Me and Teddy racing for the door. They had the whole thing. After a few seconds, Mr. Friedman reached up and paused it with me, from a few meters out, freeze-framed in the middle of the screen. In my mind, this was when he was going to turn to me and say, "Now would you like to confess?" He didn't.

"Trevor," he said, "do you know of any white kids that Teddy hangs out with?"

I nearly shat myself. *"What?!"*

I looked at the screen and I realized: Teddy was dark. I am light; I have olive skin. But the camera can't expose for light and dark at the same time. So when you put me on a black-and-white screen next to a black person, the camera doesn't know what to do. If the camera has to pick, it picks me as white. My color gets blown out. In this video, there was a black person and a white person. But still: It was me. The picture wasn't great, and my facial features were a bit blurry, but if you looked closely: It was me. I was Teddy's best friend. I was Teddy's only friend. I was the *single most likely accomplice*. You had to at least *suspect* that it was me. They didn't. They grilled me for a good ten minutes, but only because they were so sure that I had to know who this white kid was.

"Trevor, you're Teddy's best friend. Tell us the truth. Who is this kid?"

"I don't know."

"You don't recognize him at all?"

"No."

"Teddy never mentioned him to you?"

"Never."

At a certain point Mrs. Vorster just started running through a list of all the white kids she thought it could be.

"Is it David?"

"No."

"Rian?"

"No."

"Frederik?"

"No."

I kept waiting for it to be a trick, for them to turn and say, "It's *you*!" They didn't. At a certain point, I felt so invisible I almost wanted to take credit. I wanted to jump up and point at the TV and say, "Are you people blind?! That's me! Can you not see that that's me?!" But of course I didn't. And they couldn't. These people had been so fucked by their own construct of race that they could not see that the white person they were looking for was sitting right in front of them.

Eventually they sent me back to class. I spent the rest of the day and the next couple of weeks waiting for the other shoe to drop, waiting for my mom to get the call. "We've got him! We figured it out!" But the call never came.

South Africa has eleven official languages. After democracy came, people said, "Okay, how do we create order without having different groups feel like they've been left out of power again?" English is the international language and the language of money and of the media, so we had to keep that. Most people were forced to learn at least some Afrikaans, so it's useful to keep that, too. Plus we didn't want the white minority to feel ostracized in the new South Africa, or else they'd take all their money and leave.

Of the African languages, Zulu has the largest number of native speakers, but we couldn't keep that without also having Xhosa and Tswana and Ndebele. Then there's Swazi, Tsonga, Venda, Sotho, and Pedi. We tried to keep all the major groups happy, so the next thing we knew we'd made eleven languages official languages. And those are just the languages big enough to demand recognition; there are dozens more.

It's the Tower of Babel in South Africa. Every single day. Every day you see people completely lost, trying to have conversations and having no idea what the other person is saying. Zulu and Tswana are fairly common. Tsonga and Pedi are pretty fringe. The more common your tongue, the less likely you are to learn others. The more fringe, the more likely you are to pick up two or three. In the cities most people speak at least some English and usually a bit of Afrikaans, enough to get around. You'll be at a party with a dozen people where bits of conversation are flying by in two or three different languages. You'll miss part of it, someone might translate on the fly to give you the gist, you pick up the rest from the context, and you just figure it out. The crazy thing is that, somehow, it works. Society functions. Except when it doesn't.

14

A YOUNG MAN'S LONG, AWKWARD, OCCASIONALLY TRAGIC, AND FREQUENTLY HUMILIATING EDUCATION IN AFFAIRS OF THE HEART, PART III: THE DANCE

By the end of high school I'd become a mogul. My tuck-shop business had evolved into a mini-empire that included selling pirated CDs I made at home. I'd convinced my mother, as frugal as she was, that I needed a computer for school. I didn't. I wanted it so I could surf the Internet and play *Leisure Suit Larry*. But I was very convincing, and she broke down and got it for me. Thanks to the computer, the Internet, and the fortunate gift of a CD writer from a friend, I was in business.

I had carved out my niche, and was having a great time; life was so good as an outsider that I didn't even think about dating. The only girls in my life were the naked ones on my computer. While I downloaded music and messed around in chat rooms, I'd dabble in porn sites here and there. No video, of course, only pictures. With online porn today you just drop straight into the madness, but with dial-up it took so long for the images to load. It was almost gentlemanly compared to now. You'd spend a good five minutes looking at her face, getting to know her as a person. Then a few minutes later you'd get some boobs. By the time you got to her vagina, you'd spent a lot of quality time together.

In September of grade twelve, the matric dance was coming up. Senior prom. This was the big one. I was again faced with the dilemma of Valentine's Day, confronting another strange ritual I did not understand. All I knew about prom was that, according to my American movies, prom is where *it* happens. You lose your virginity. You go and you ride in the limousine, and then you and the girl do the thing. That was literally my only reference. But I knew the rule: Cool guys get girls, and funny guys get to hang out with the cool guys with their girls. So I'd assumed I wouldn't be going, or if I did go it wouldn't be with a date.

I had two middlemen working for me in my CD business, Bongani and Tom. They sold the CDs that I copied in exchange for a cut. I met Tom at the arcade at the Balfour Park mall. Like Teddy, he lived nearby because his mom was a domestic worker. Tom was in my grade but went to a government school, Northview, a proper ghetto school. Tom handled my CD sales over there.

Tom was a chatterbox, hyperactive and go-go-go. He was a real hustler, too, always trying to cut a deal, work an angle. He could get people to do anything. A great guy, but fucking crazy and a complete liar as well. I went with him once to Hammanskraal, a settlement that was like a homeland, but not really. Hammanskraal, as its Afrikaans name suggests, was the kraal of Hamman, what used to be a white man's farm. The proper homelands, Venda and Gazankulu and Transkei, were places where black people actually lived, and the government drew a border around them and said, "Stay there." Hammanskraal and settlements like it were empty places on the map where deported black people had been relocated. That's what the government did. They would find some patch of arid, dusty, useless land, and dig row after row of holes in the ground—a thousand latrines to serve four thousand families. Then they'd forcibly remove people from illegally occupying some white area and drop them off in the middle of nowhere with some pallets of plywood and corrugated iron. "Here. This is your new home. Build some houses. Good luck." We'd watch it on the news. It was like some heartless, survival-based reality TV show, only nobody won any money.

One afternoon in Hammanskraal, Tom told me we were going to see a talent show. At the time, I had a pair of Timberland boots I'd bought. They were the only decent piece of clothing I owned. Back then, almost no one in South Africa had Timberlands. They were impossible to get, but everyone wanted them because American rappers wore them. I'd scrimped and saved my tuck-shop money and my CD money to buy them. As we were leaving, Tom told me, "Be sure to wear your Timberlands."

The talent show was in this little community hall attached to nothing in the middle of nowhere. When we got there, Tom was going around, shaking hands, chatting with everybody. There was singing, dancing, some poetry. Then the host got up onstage and said, *"Re na le modiragatsi yo o kgethegileng. Ka kopo amogelang . . . Spliff Star!"* "We've got a special performer, a rapper all the way from America. Please welcome . . . Spliff Star!"

Spliff Star was Busta Rhymes's hype man at the time. I sat there, confused. *What? Spliff Star? In Hammanskraal?* Then everyone in the room turned and looked at me. Tom walked over and whispered in my ear.

"Dude, come up onstage."

"What?"

"Come onstage."

"Dude, what are you talking about?"

"Dude, please, you're gonna get me in so much shit. They've already paid me the money."

"*Money?* What money?"

Of course, what Tom had failed to tell me was that he'd told these people he was bringing a famous rapper from America to come and rap in their talent show. He had demanded to be paid up front for doing so, and I, in my Timberlands, was that famous American rapper.

"Screw you," I said. "I'm not going anywhere."

"Please, dude, I'm begging you. Please do me this favor. Please. There's this girl here, and I wanna get with her, and I told her I know all these rappers . . . Please. I'm begging you."

"Dude, I'm not Spliff Star. What am I gonna do?!"

"Just rap Busta Rhymes songs."

"But I don't know any of the lyrics."

"It doesn't matter. These people don't speak English."

"Aw, fuck."

I got up onstage and Tom did some terrible beat-boxing— *"Bff ba-dff, bff bff ba-dff"*—while I stumbled through some Busta Rhymes lyrics that I made up as I went along. The audience erupted with cheers and applause. An American rapper had come to Hammanskraal, and it was the most epic thing they had ever seen.

So that's Tom.

One afternoon Tom came by my house and we started talking about the dance. I told him I didn't have a date, couldn't get a date, and wasn't going to get a date.

"I can get you a girl to go with you to the dance," he said.

"No, you can't."

"Yes, I can. Let's make a deal."

"I don't want one of your deals, Tom."

"No, listen, here's the deal. If you give me a better cut on the CDs I'm selling, plus a bunch of free music for myself, I'll come back with the most beautiful girl you've ever seen in your life, and she'll be your date for the dance."

"Okay, I'll take that deal because it's never going to happen."

"Do we have a deal?"

"We have a deal, but it's not going to happen."

"But do we have a *deal*?"

"It's a deal."

"Okay, I'm going to find you a date. She's going to be the most beautiful girl you've ever seen, and you're going to take her to the matric dance and you're going to be a superstar."

The dance was still two months away. I promptly forgot about Tom and his ridiculous deal. Then he came over to my house one afternoon and popped his head into my room.

"I found the girl."

"Really?"

"Yeah. You have to come and meet her."

I knew Tom was full of shit, but the thing that makes a con man successful is that he never gives you nothing. He delivers just enough to keep you believing. Tom had introduced me to many beautiful women. He was never dating them, but he talked a good game, and was always around them. So when he said he had a girl, I didn't doubt him. The two of us jumped on a bus and headed into the city.

The girl lived in a run-down block of flats downtown. We found her building, and a girl leaned over the balcony and waved us inside. That was the girl's sister Lerato, Tom said. Come to find out, he'd been trying to get with Lerato, and setting me up with the sister was his way in—of course, Tom was working an angle.

It was dark in the lobby. The elevator was busted, so we walked up several flights. This girl Lerato brought us into the flat. In the living room was this giant, but I mean really, really enormous, fat woman. I was like, *Oh, Tom. I see what you've done here. Nicely played.* Tom was a big joker as well.

"Is this my date?" I asked.

"No, no, no," he said. "This is not your date. This is her older sister. Your date is Babiki. Babiki has three older sisters, and Lerato is her younger sister. Babiki's gone to the store to buy groceries. She'll be back in a moment."

We waited, chatted with the older sister. Ten minutes later the door opened and the most beautiful girl I have ever seen in my life walked in. She was . . . good Lord. Beautiful eyes, beautiful golden yellow-brown skin. It was like she glowed. No girl at my high school looked anything like her.

"Hi," she said.

"Hi," I replied.

I was dumbfounded. I had no idea how to talk to a girl that beautiful. She was shy and didn't speak much, either. There was a bit of an awkward pause. Luckily Tom's a guy who just talks and talks. He jumped right in and smoothed everything over. "Trevor, this is Babiki. Babiki, Trevor." He went on and on about how great I was, how much she was looking forward to the dance, when I would pick her up for the dance, all the details. We hung out for a few, and then Tom needed to get going so we headed out the door. Babiki turned and smiled at me and waved as we left.

"Bye."

"Bye."

We walked out of that building and I was the happiest man on earth. I couldn't believe it. I was the guy at school who couldn't get a date. I'd resigned myself to never getting a date, didn't consider myself worthy of having a date. But now I was going to the matric dance with the most beautiful girl in the world.

Over the following weeks we went down to Hillbrow a few more times to hang out with Babiki and her sisters and her friends. Babiki's family was Pedi, one of South Africa's smaller tribes. I liked getting to know people of different backgrounds, so that was fun. Babiki and her friends were what we call *amabhujua*. They're as poor as most other black people, but they try to act like they're not. They dress fashionably and act rich. *Amabhujua* will put a shirt on layaway, one shirt, and spend seven months paying it off. They'll live in shacks wearing Italian leather shoes that cost thousands. An interesting crowd.

Babiki and I never went on a date alone. It was always the two of us in a group. She was shy, and I was a nervous wreck most of the time, but we had fun. Tom kept everyone loose and having a good time. Whenever we'd say goodbye, Babiki would give me a hug, and once she even gave me a little kiss. I was in heaven. I was like, *Yeah, I've got a girlfriend. Cool.*

As the dance approached, I started getting nervous. I didn't have a car. I didn't have any decent clothes. This was my first time taking out a beautiful girl, and I wanted it to be perfect.

We'd moved to Highlands North when my stepfather's garage went out of business, and he moved his workshop to the house. We had a big yard and a garage in the back, and that became his new workshop, essentially. At any given time, we had at least ten or fifteen cars in the driveway, in the yard, and out on the street, clients' cars being worked on and old junkers Abel kept around to tinker with. One afternoon Tom and I were at the house. Tom was telling Abel about my date, and Abel decided to be generous. He said I could take a car for the dance.

There was a red Mazda that we'd had for a while, a complete piece of shit but it worked well enough. I'd borrowed it before, but the car I really wanted was Abel's BMW. It was old and beat-up like the Mazda, but a shit BMW is still a BMW. I begged him to let me take it.

"Please, please, can I use the BMW?"

"Not a fucking chance."

"Please. This is the greatest moment in my life. Please. I'm begging you."

"No."

"Please."

"No. You can take the Mazda."

Tom, always the hustler and the dealmaker, stepped in.

"Bra Abie," he said. "I don't think you understand. If you saw the girl Trevor is taking to the dance, you would see why this is so important. Let's make a deal. If we bring her here and she's the most beautiful girl you've ever seen in your life, you'll let him take the BMW."

Abel thought about it.

"Okay. Deal."

We went to Babiki's flat, told her my parents wanted to meet her, and brought her back to my house. Then we brought her around to the garage in the back where Abel and his guys were working. Tom and I went over and introduced them.

"Abel, this is Babiki. Babiki, this is Abel."

Abel smiled big, was charming as always.

"Nice to meet you," he said.

They chatted for a few minutes. Tom and Babiki left. Abel turned to me.

"Is that the girl?"

"Yes."

"You can take the BMW."

Once I had the car, I desperately needed something to wear. I was taking out this girl who was really into fashion, and, except for my Timberlands, everything I owned was shit. I was limited in my wardrobe choices because I was stuck buying in the shops my mother let me go to, and my mother did not believe in spending money on clothes. She'd take me to some bargain clothing store and tell me what our budget was, and I'd have to find something to wear.

At the time I had no clue about clothes. My idea of fashion was a brand of clothing called Powerhouse. It was the kind of stuff weight lifters wear down in Miami or out at Venice Beach, baggy track pants with baggy sweatshirts. The logo was a cartoon of this giant body-building bulldog wearing wraparound sunglasses and smoking a cigar and flexing his muscles. On the pants he was flexing all the way down your leg. On the shirt he was flexing across your chest. On the underwear, he was flexing on your crotch. I thought Powerhouse was the baddest thing in the world, I can't even front. I had no friends, I loved dogs, and muscles were cool—that's where I was working from. I had Powerhouse everything, the full range, five of the same outfit in five different colors. It was easy. The pants came with the top, so I knew how to make it work.

Bongani, the other middleman from my CD business, found out I had a date, and he made it his mission to give me a makeover. "You need to up your game," he said. "You cannot go to the dance looking the way you look—for her sake, not yours. Let's go shopping."

I went to my mom and begged her to give me money to buy something to wear for the dance. She finally relented and gave me 2,000 rand, for one outfit. It was the most money she'd ever given me for anything in my life. I told Bongani how much I had to spend, and he said we'd make it work. The trick to looking rich, he told me, is to have one expensive item, and for the rest of the things you get basic, good-looking quality stuff. The nice item will draw everyone's eye, and it'll look like you've spent more than you have.

In my mind nothing was cooler than the leather coats everybody wore in *The Matrix*. *The Matrix* came out while I was in high school and it was my favorite movie at the time. I loved Neo. In my heart I knew: *I am Neo*. He's a nerd. He's useless at everything, but secretly he's a badass superhero. All I needed was a bald, mysterious black man to come into my life and show me the way. Now I had Bongani, black, head shaved, telling me, "You can do it. You're the one." And I was like, "*Yes*. I knew it."

I told Bongani I wanted a leather coat like Keanu Reeves wore, the ankle-length black one. Bongani shut that down. "No, that's not practical. It's cool, but you'll never be able to wear it again." He took me shopping and we bought a calf-length black leather jacket, which would look ridiculous today but at the time, thanks to Neo, was very cool. That alone cost 1,200 rand. Then we finished the outfit with a pair of simple black pants, suede square-toed shoes, and a cream-white knitted sweater.

Once we had the outfit, Bongani took a long look at my enormous Afro. I was forever trying to get the perfect 1970s Michael Jackson Afro. What I had was more Buckwheat: unruly and impossible to comb, like stabbing a pitchfork into a bed of crabgrass.

"We need to fix that fucking hair," Bongani said.

"What do you mean?" I said. "This is just my hair."

"No, we *have* to do something."

Bongani lived in Alexandra. He dragged me there, and we went to talk to some girls from his street who were hanging out on the corner.

"What would you do with this guy's hair?" he asked them.

The girls looked me over.

"He has so much," one of them said. "Why doesn't he cornrow it?"

"Shit, yeah," they said. "That's great!"

I said, "What? Cornrows? No!"

"No, no," they said. "Do it."

Bongani dragged me to a hair salon down the street. We went in and sat down. The woman touched my hair, shook her head, and turned to Bongani.

"I can't work with this sheep," she said. "You have to do something about this."

"What do we need to do?"

"You have to relax it. I don't do that here."

"Okay."

Bongani dragged me to a second salon. I sat down in the chair, and the woman took my hair and started painting this creamy white stuff in it. She was wearing rubber gloves to keep this chemical relaxer off her own skin, which should have been my first clue that maybe this wasn't such a great idea. Once my hair was full of the relaxer, she told me, "You have to try to keep it in for as long as possible. It's going to start burning. When it starts burning, tell me and we'll rinse it out. But the longer you can handle it, the straighter your hair will become."

I wanted to do it right, so I sat in the chair and waited and waited for as long as I could.

I waited too long.

She'd told me to tell her when it started burning. She should have told me to tell her when it started tingling, because by the time it was actually burning it had already taken off several layers of my scalp. I was well past tingling when I started to freak out. *"It's burning! It's burning!"* She rushed me over to the sink and started to rinse the relaxer out. What I didn't know is that the chemical doesn't really start to burn until it's being rinsed out. I felt like someone was pouring liquid fire onto my head. When she was done I had patches of acid burns all over my scalp.

I was the only man in the salon; it was all women. It was a window into what women experience to look good on a regular basis. *Why would they ever do this?*, I thought. *This is horrible.* But it worked. My hair was completely straight. The woman combed it back, and I looked like a pimp, a pimp named Slickback.

Bongani then dragged me back to the first salon, and the woman agreed to cornrow my hair. She worked slowly. It took six hours. Finally she said, "Okay, you can look in the mirror." She turned me around in the chair and I looked in the mirror and . . . I had never seen myself like that before. It was like the makeover scenes in my American movies, where they take the dorky guy or girl, fix the hair and change the clothes, and the ugly duckling becomes the swan. I'd been so convinced I'd never get a date that I never tried to look nice for a girl, so I didn't know that I could. The hair was good. My skin wasn't perfect, but it was getting better; the pustules had receded into regular pimples. I looked . . . not bad.

I went home, and my mom squealed when I walked in the door.

"Ooooooh! They turned my baby boy into a pretty little girl! I've got a little girl! You're so pretty!"

"Mom! C'mon. Stop it."

"Is this the way you're telling me that you're gay?"

"What? No. Why would you say that?"

"You know it's okay if you are."

"No, Mom. I'm not gay."

Everyone in my family loved it. They all thought it looked great. My mom did tease the shit out of me, though.

"It's very well done," she said, "but it is way too pretty. You do look like a girl."

The big night finally came. Tom came over to help me get ready. The hair, the clothes, everything came together perfectly. Once I was set, we went to Abel to get the keys to the BMW, and that was the moment the whole night started to go wrong.

It was a Saturday night, end of the week, which meant Abel was drinking with his workers. I walked out to his garage, and as soon as I saw his eyes I knew: He was wasted. *Fuck*. When Abel was drunk he was a completely different person.

"Ah, you look nice!" he said with a big smile, looking me over. "Where are you going?"

"Where am I—Abie, I'm going to the dance."

"Okay. Have fun."

"Um . . . can I get the keys?"

"The keys to what?"

"To the car."

"What car?"

"The BMW. You promised I could drive the BMW to the dance."

"First go buy me some beers," he said.

He gave me his car keys; Tom and I drove to the liquor store. I bought Abel a few cases of beer, drove back, and unloaded it for him.

"Okay," I said, "can I take the BMW now?"

"No."

"What do you mean 'no'?"

"I mean 'no.' I need my car tonight."

"But you promised. You said I could take it."

"Yeah, but I need the car."

I was crushed. I sat there with Tom and begged him for close to half an hour.

"Please."

"No."

"Please."

"Nope."

Finally we realized it wasn't going to happen. We took the shitty Mazda and drove to Babiki's house. I was an hour late picking her up. She was completely pissed off. Tom had to go in and convince her to come out, and eventually she did.

She was even more gorgeous than before, in an amazing red dress, but she was clearly not in a great mood. Inside I was quietly starting to panic, but I smiled and kept trying my gentlemanly best to be a good date, holding the door for her, telling her how beautiful she was. Tom and the sister gave us a send-off and we headed out.

Then I got lost. The dance was being held at some venue in a part of town I wasn't familiar with, and at some point I got completely turned around and had no idea where I was. I drove around for an hour in the dark, going left, going right, doubling back. I was on my cellphone the whole time, desperately calling people, trying to figure out where I was, trying to get directions. Babiki sat next to me in stony silence the whole time, clearly not feeling me or this night *at all*. I was crashing hard. I was late. I didn't know where I was going. I was the worst date she'd ever had in her life.

I finally figured out where I was and we made it to the dance, nearly two hours late. I parked, jumped out, and ran around to get her door. When I opened it, she just sat there.

"Are you ready?" I said. "Let's go in."

"No."

"No? What . . . what do you mean, 'no'?"

"No."

"Okay . . . but why?"

"No."

"But we need to go inside. The dance is inside."

"No."

I stood there for another twenty minutes, trying to convince her to come inside, but she kept saying "no." She wouldn't get out of the car.

Finally, I said, "Okay, I'll be right back."

I ran inside and found Bongani.

"Where have you been?" he said.

"I'm here! But my date's in the car and she won't come in."

"What do you mean she won't come in?"

"I don't know what's going on. Please help me."

We went back out to the parking lot. I took Bongani over to the car, and the second he saw her he lost it. "Jesus in Heaven! This is the most beautiful woman I've ever seen. You said she was beautiful, Trevor, but this is insane." In an instant he completely forgot about helping me with Babiki. He turned and ran back inside and called to the guys. "Guys! You gotta come see this! Trevor got a date! And she's beautiful! Guys! Come out here!"

Twenty guys came running out into the parking lot. They clustered around the car. "Yo, she's so hot!" "Dude, *this* girl came with *Trevor*?" Guys were gawking at her like she was an animal at the zoo. They were asking to take pictures with her. They were calling back to more people inside. "This is insane! Look at Trevor's date! No, no, no, you gotta come and see!"

I was mortified. I'd spent four years of high school carefully avoiding any kind of romantic humiliation whatsoever, and now, on the night of the matric dance, the night of all nights, my humiliation had turned into a circus bigger than the event itself: Trevor the undatable clown thought he was going to have the most beautiful girl at the dance, but he's crashing and burning so let's all go outside and watch.

Babiki sat in the passenger seat, staring straight ahead, refusing to budge. I was outside the car, pacing, stressed out. A friend of mine had a bottle of brandy that he'd smuggled into the dance. "Here," he said, "have some of this." Nothing mattered at that point, so I started drinking. I'd fucked up. The girl didn't like me. The night was done.

Most of the guys eventually wandered back inside. I was sitting on the pavement, taking swigs from the brandy bottle, getting buzzed. At some point Bongani went back over to the car to try one last time to convince Babiki to come in. After a minute his head popped up over the car with this confused look.

"Yo, Trevor," he said, "your date does not speak English."

"What?"

"Your date. She does not speak any English."

"That's not possible."

I got up and walked over to the car. I asked her a question in English and she gave me a blank stare.

Bongani looked at me.

"How did you not know that your date does not speak English?"

"I . . . I don't know."

"Have you never spoken to her?"

"Of course I have—or, wait . . . *have* I?"

I started flashing back through all the times I'd been with Babiki, meeting at her flat, hanging out with her friends, introducing her to Abel. Did I talk to her then? No. Did I talk to her then? No. It was like the scene in *Fight Club* where Ed Norton's character flashes back and realizes he and Brad Pitt have never been in the same room with Helena Bonham Carter at the same time. He realizes he's been punching himself the whole time. *He's* Tyler Durden. In all the excitement of meeting Babiki, the times we were hanging out and getting to know each other, we were never actually speaking to each other. It was always through Tom.

Fucking Tom.

Tom had promised he'd get me a beautiful date for the dance, but he hadn't made any promises about any of her other qualities. Whenever we were together, she was speaking Pedi to Tom, and Tom was speaking English to me. But she didn't speak English, and I didn't speak Pedi. Abel spoke Pedi. He'd learned several South African languages in order to deal with his customers, so he'd spoken with her fluently when they met. But in that moment I realized I'd never actually heard her say anything in English other than: "Yes." "No." "Hi." "Bye." That's it: "Yes." "No." "Hi." "Bye."

Babiki was so shy that she didn't talk much to begin with, and I was so inept with women that I didn't know how to talk to her. I'd never had a girlfriend; I didn't even know what "girlfriend" meant. Someone put a beautiful woman on my arm and said, "She's your girlfriend." I'd been mesmerized by her beauty and just the idea of her—I didn't know I was supposed to talk to her. The naked women on my computer, I'd never had to talk to them, ask them their opinions, ask them about their feelings. And I was afraid I'd open my mouth and ruin the whole thing, so I just nodded and smiled along and let Tom do the talking.

All three of Babiki's older sisters spoke English, and her younger sister Lerato spoke a little. So whenever we hung out with Babiki and her sisters and their friends, a lot of the conversation was in English. The rest of it was going right by me in Pedi or in Sotho, but that's completely normal in South Africa so it never bothered me; I got enough of the gist of the conversation from everyone's English to know what was going on. And the way my mind works with language, even when I'm hearing other languages, they get filtered into English as I'm hearing them. My mind stores them in English. When my grandmother and great-grandmother were hysterically praying to God to destroy the demon that had shit on their kitchen floor, all of that transpired in Xhosa, but it's stored in English. I remember it as English. So whenever I lay in bed at night dreaming about Babiki and the moments we'd spent together, I *felt* like it had transpired in English because that's how I remembered it. And Tom had never said anything about what language she spoke or didn't speak, because why would he care? He just wanted to get his free CDs and get with the sister. Which is how I'd been dating a girl for over a month—the girl I very much believed was my first girlfriend—without ever having had a single conversation with her.

Now the whole night came rushing back and I saw it from her point of view, and it was perfectly obvious to me why she didn't want to get out of the car. She probably hadn't wanted to go to the dance with me in the first place; she probably owed Tom a favor, and Tom can talk anyone into anything. Then I'd left her sitting and waiting for me for an hour and she was pissed off. Then she got into the car and it was the first time we had ever been alone, and she realized I couldn't even hold a conversation with her. I'd driven her around and gotten lost in the dark—a young girl alone in a car in the middle of nowhere with some strange guy, no idea where I was taking her. She was probably terrified. Then we got to the dance and she didn't speak anyone's language. She didn't know anyone. She didn't even know me.

Bongani and I stood outside the car, staring at each other. I didn't know what to do. I tried talking to her in every language I knew. Nothing worked. She only spoke Pedi. I got so desperate that I started trying to talk to her using hand signals.

"Please. You. Me. Inside. Dance. Yes?"

"No."

"Inside. Dance. Please?"

"No."

I asked Bongani if he spoke Pedi. He didn't. I ran inside to the dance and ran around looking for someone who spoke Pedi to help me to convince her to come in. "Do you speak Pedi? Do you speak Pedi? Do you speak Pedi?" Nobody spoke Pedi.

So I never got to go to my matric dance. Other than the three minutes I spent running through it looking for someone who spoke Pedi, I spent the whole night in the parking lot. When the dance ended, I climbed back into the shitty red Mazda and drove Babiki home. We sat in total awkward silence the whole way.

I pulled up in front of her block of flats in Hillbrow, stopped the car, and sat for a moment as I tried to figure out the polite and gentlemanly way to end the evening. Then, out of nowhere, she leaned over and gave me a kiss. Like, a real kiss, a proper kiss. The kind of kiss that made me forget that the whole disaster had just happened. I was so confused. I didn't know what I was supposed to do. She pulled back and I looked deep into her eyes and thought, *I have no idea how girls work*.

I got out of the car, walked around to her side, and opened her door. She gathered up her dress and stepped out and headed toward her flat, and as she turned to go I gave her one last little wave.

"Bye."

"Bye."

PART III

In Germany, no child finishes high school without learning about the Holocaust. Not just the facts of it but the how and the why and the gravity of it—what it means. As a result, Germans grow up appropriately aware and apologetic. British schools treat colonialism the same way, to an extent. Their children are taught the history of the Empire with a kind of disclaimer hanging over the whole thing. "Well, *that* was shameful, now wasn't it?"

In South Africa, the atrocities of apartheid have never been taught that way. We weren't taught judgment or shame. We were taught history the way it's taught in America. In America, the history of racism is taught like this: "There was slavery and then there was Jim Crow and then there was Martin Luther King Jr. and now it's done." It was the same for us. "Apartheid was bad. Nelson Mandela was freed. Let's move on." Facts, but not many, and never the emotional or moral dimension. It was as if the teachers, many of whom were white, had been given a mandate. "Whatever you do, don't make the kids angry."

GO HITLER!

When I was in grade nine, three Chinese kids transferred to Sandringham: Bolo, Bruce Lee, and John. They were the only Chinese kids in the school, out of a thousand pupils. Bolo got his nickname because he looked like Bolo Yeung from the Jean-Claude Van Damme movie *Bloodsport*. Bruce Lee's name really was Bruce Lee, which made our lives. Here was this Chinese guy, quiet, good-looking, in great shape, and his name was Bruce Lee. We were like, *This is magic. Thank you, Jesus, for bringing us Bruce Lee.* John was just John, which was weird because of the other two.

I got to know Bolo because he was one of my tuck-shop clients. Bolo's parents were professional pirates. They pirated videogames and sold them at flea markets. As the son of pirates, Bolo did the same thing—he started selling bootleg PlayStation games around school. Kids would give him their PlayStation, and he'd bring it back a few days later with a chip in it that enabled them to play pirated games, which he would then sell them. Bolo was friends with this white kid and fellow pirate named Andrew, who traded in bootleg CDs. Andrew was two grades above me and a real computer geek; he even had a CD writer at home, back when nobody had CD writers.

One day on my tuck-shop rounds, I overheard Andrew and Bolo complaining about the black kids at school. They'd realized that they could take Andrew's and Bolo's merchandise, say "I'll pay you later," and then not pay, because Andrew and Bolo were too scared of black people to go back to ask for the money. I leaned in to their conversation and said, "Listen, you shouldn't get upset. Black people don't have any money, so trying to get more stuff for less money is just what we do. But let me help. I'll be your middleman. You give me the merchandise and I'll sell it, and then I'll handle getting the money. In return, you give me a cut of the sale." They liked the idea right away, and we became partners.

As the tuck-shop guy, I was perfectly positioned. I had my network set up. All I had to do was tap into it. With the money I made selling CDs and videogames, I was able to save up and add new components and more memory to my own computer. Andrew the computer geek showed me how to do it, where to buy the cheapest parts, how to assemble them, how to repair them. He showed me how his business worked, too, how to download music, where to get rewritable CDs in bulk. The only thing I was missing was my own CD writer, because it was the most expensive component. At the time a CD writer cost as much as the rest of the computer, nearly 2,000 rand.

I worked as a middleman for Bolo and Andrew for a year. Then Bolo left school; the rumor was that his parents got arrested. From that point on I worked for Andrew, and then as he was about to matriculate he decided to quit the game. "Trevor," he told me, "you've been a loyal partner." And, as thanks, he bequeathed unto me his CD writer. At the time, black people barely had access to computers, let's start there. But a CD writer? That was the stuff of lore. It was mythical. The day Andrew gave it to me, he changed my life. Thanks to him, I now controlled production, sales, distribution—I had everything I needed to lock down the bootleg business.

I was a natural capitalist. I loved selling stuff, and I was selling something that everybody wanted and nobody else could provide. I sold my discs for 30 rand, around $3. A regular CD in the store cost 100 to 150 rand. Once people started buying from me, they wouldn't buy real CDs ever again—the deal was too good.

I had an instinct for business, but at the time I knew nothing about music, which was odd for someone running a music-pirating business. The only music I knew, still, was Christian music from church, the only music allowed in my mother's house. The CD writer Andrew gave me was a 1x CD writer, which meant it copied at the speed it played. Every day I'd leave school, go to my room, and sit for five to six hours, copying CDs. I had my own surround-sound system built with old car speakers I'd salvaged from the junkers Abel kept in the yard, and I strung them up around the room. Even though I had to sit there while each CD played, for a long time I didn't really listen to them. I knew it was against the dealer's code: Never get high on your own supply.

Thanks to the Internet, I could get anyone anything. I never judged anyone's taste in music. You wanted the new Nirvana, I got you the new Nirvana. You wanted the new DMX, I got you the new DMX. Local South African music was big, but black American music was what people were desperate for, hip-hop and R&B. Jagged Edge was huge. 112 was huge. I sold a lot of Montell Jordan. So much Montell Jordan.

When I started, I had a dial-up connection and a 24k modem. It would take a day to download an album. But technology kept evolving, and I kept reinvesting in the business. I upgraded to a 56k modem. I got faster CD writers, multiple CD writers. I started downloading more, copying more, selling more. That's when I got two middlemen of my own, my friend Tom, who went to Northview, and my friend Bongani, who lived in Alex.

One day Bongani came to me and said, "You know what would

make a lot of money? Instead of copying whole albums, why don't you put the best tracks of different albums onto one CD, because people only wanna hear the songs they like." That sounded like a great idea, so I started making mix CDs. Those sold well. Then a few weeks later Bongani came back and said, "Can you make the tracks fade into one another so the music moves from track one to track two without a break and the beat carries on? It'll be like a DJ playing a complete set the whole night." That sounded like a great idea, too. I downloaded a program called BPM, "beats per minute." It had a graphical interface that looked like two vinyl records side by side, and I could mix and fade between songs, basically everything a DJ can do live. I started making party CDs, and those started selling like hotcakes, too.

Business was booming. By matric I was balling, making 500 rand a week. To put that in perspective, there are maids in South Africa who still earn less than that today. It's a shit salary if you're trying to support a family, but as a sixteen-year-old living at home with no real expenses, I was living the dream.

For the first time in my life I had money, and it was the most liberating thing in the world. The first thing I learned about having money was that it gives you choices. People don't want to be rich. They want to be able to choose. The richer you are, the more choices you have. That is the freedom of money.

With money, I experienced freedom on a whole new level: I went to McDonald's. People in America don't understand, but when an American chain opens in a third-world country, people go crazy. That's true to this day. A Burger King opened for the first time in South Africa last year, and there was a queue around the block. It was an event. Everyone was going around saying, "I have to eat at Burger King. Have you heard? *It's from America.*" The funny thing was that the queue was actually just white people. White people went bat-shit crazy for Burger King. Black people were like, *whatever.* Black people didn't need Burger King. Our hearts were with KFC and McDonald's. The crazy thing

about McDonald's is that we knew about it long before it came, probably from movies. We never even dreamed we would ever get one in
South Africa; McDonald's seemed to us like one of those American
things that is exclusively American and can't go anywhere else. Even
before we ever tasted McDonald's, we knew we'd love it, and we did.
At one point South Africa was opening more McDonald's than any
other country in the world. With Mandela came freedom—and with
freedom came McDonald's. A McDonald's had opened up just two
blocks from our house not long after we moved to Highlands North,
but my mom would never pay for us to eat there. With my own money
I was like, *Let's do this.* I went all in. They didn't have "supersize" at the
time; "large" was the biggest. So I walked up to the counter, feeling
very impressed with myself, and I put down my money and said, "I'll
have a large number one."

I fell in love with McDonald's. McDonald's, to me, tasted like
America. McDonald's *is* America. You see it advertised and it looks
amazing. You crave it. You buy it. You take your first bite, and it blows
your mind. It's even better than you imagined. Then, halfway through,
you realize it's not all it's cracked up to be. A few bites later you're like,
Hmm, there's a lot wrong with this. Then you're done, you miss it like
crazy, and you go back for more.

Once I'd had a taste of America, I never ate at home. I only ate
McDonald's. McDonald's, McDonald's, McDonald's, McDonald's.
Every night my mother would try to cook me dinner.

"Tonight we're having chicken livers."

"No, I'm gonna have McDonald's."

"Tonight we're having dog bones."

"I think I'm gonna go with McDonald's again."

"Tonight we're having chicken feet."

"Hmmmmm . . . Okay, I'm in. But tomorrow I'm eating McDonald's."

The money kept rolling in and I was balling out of control. This is
how balling I was: I bought a cordless telephone. This was before everyone had a cellphone. The range on this cordless phone was strong

enough that I could put the base outside my window, walk the two blocks to McDonald's, order my large number one, walk back home, go up to my room, and fire up my computer, carrying on a conversation the whole time. I was that dude walking down the street holding a giant phone to my ear with the aerial fully extended, talking to my friend. "Yeah, I'm just goin' down to McDonald's . . ."

Life was good, and none of it would have happened without Andrew. Without him, I would never have mastered the world of music piracy and lived a life of endless McDonald's. What he did, on a small scale, showed me how important it is to empower the dispossessed and the disenfranchised in the wake of oppression. Andrew was white. His family had access to education, resources, computers. For generations, while his people were preparing to go to university, my people were crowded into thatched huts singing, *"Two times two is four. Three times two is six. La la la la la."* My family had been denied the things his family had taken for granted. I had a natural talent for selling to people, but without knowledge and resources, where was that going to get me? People always lecture the poor: "Take responsibility for yourself! Make something of yourself!" But with what raw materials are the poor to make something of themselves?

People love to say, "Give a man a fish, and he'll eat for a day. Teach a man to fish, and he'll eat for a lifetime." What they don't say is, "And it would be nice if you gave him a fishing rod." That's the part of the analogy that's missing. Working with Andrew was the first time in my life I realized you need someone from the privileged world to come to you and say, "Okay, here's what you need, and here's how it works." Talent alone would have gotten me nowhere without Andrew giving me the CD writer. People say, "Oh, that's a handout." No. I still have to work to profit by it. But I don't stand a chance without it.

One afternoon I was in my room making a CD when Bongani came over to pick up his inventory. He saw me mixing songs on my computer.

GO HITLER! | 191

"This is insane," he said. "Are you doing this live?"

"Yeah."

"Trevor, I don't think you understand; you're sitting on a gold mine. We need to do this for a crowd. You need to come to the township and start DJ'ing gigs. No one has ever seen a DJ playing on a computer before."

Bongani lived in Alexandra. Where Soweto is a sprawling, government-planned ghetto, Alexandra is a tiny, dense pocket of a shantytown, left over from the pre-apartheid days. Rows and rows of cinder-block and corrugated-iron shacks, practically stacked on top of one another. Its nickname is Gomorrah because it has the wildest parties and the worst crimes.

Street parties are the best thing about Alexandra. You get a tent, put it up in the middle of the road, take over the street, and you've got a party. There's no formal invitations or guest list. You just tell a few people, word of mouth travels, and a crowd appears. There are no permits, nothing like that. If you own a tent, you have the right to throw a party in your street. Cars creep up to the intersection and the driver will see the party blocking their way and shrug and make a U-turn. Nobody gets upset. The only rule is that if you throw a party in front of somebody's house, they get to come and share your alcohol. The parties don't end until someone gets shot or a bottle gets broken on someone's face. That's how it has to end; otherwise, it wasn't a party.

Back then, most DJs could spin for only a few hours; they were limited by the number of vinyls they could buy. Since parties went all night, you might need five or six DJs to keep the dancing going. But I had a massive hard drive stuffed with MP3s, which is why Bongani was excited when he saw me mixing—he saw a way to corner the market.

"How much music do you have?" he asked.

"Winamp says I can play for a week."

"We'll make a fortune."

Our first gig was a New Year's Eve party the summer we graduated from Sandringham. Bongani and I took my tower, my giant monitor, and all the cables and the keyboard and the mouse. We loaded everything up in a minibus and brought it over to Alex. We took over the street in front of his house, ran the electricity out of his place, set up the computer, set up speakers, and borrowed a tent, and people came. It was explosive. By midnight the whole street was packed from one end to the other. Ours was the biggest New Year's Eve party in Alexandra that year, and to have the biggest party in Alexandra is no joke. All night, from far and wide, people kept coming. The word spread: "There's a light-skinned guy who plays music on a computer. You've never seen anything like it." I DJ'd by myself until dawn. By then me and my friends were so drunk and exhausted that we passed out on the lawn outside Bongani's house. The party was so big it made our reputation in the hood, instantly. Pretty soon we were getting booked all over.

Which was a good thing.

When Bongani and I graduated from high school, we couldn't get jobs. There were no jobs for us to get. The only ways I had to make money were pirating CDs and DJ'ing parties, and now that I'd left Sandringham, the minibus drivers and corner kids in Alexandra were the single biggest market for my CDs. It was also where I was playing the most gigs, so to keep earning I naturally gravitated that way. Most of the white kids I knew were taking a gap year. "I'm going to take a gap year and go to Europe." That's what the white kids were saying. So I said, "I, too, am going to take a gap year. I am going to take a year and go to the township and hang out on the corner." And that's what I did.

There was a low brick wall running down the middle of the road in front of Bongani's house in Alex, and every day Bongani and I and our crew would go sit on the wall. I'd bring my CDs. We'd play music and practice dance moves. We hustled CDs all day and DJ'd parties at night. We started getting booked for gigs in other townships, other hoods.

Thanks to my computer and modem I was getting exclusive tracks few people had access to, but that created a problem for me. Sometimes I'd play the new music at parties and people would stand around going, "What is this? How do you dance to it?" For example, if a DJ plays a song like "Watch Me (Whip/Nae Nae)"—yes, it's a catchy song, but what is a whip? What is a nae nae? For that song to be popular you have to know how to do the whip and the nae nae; new music works at parties only if people know how to dance to it. Bongani decided we needed a dance crew to show people the steps to the songs we were playing. Because we spent our days doing nothing but listening to CDs and coming up with dance moves, our crew from the corner already knew all the songs, so they became our dancers. And hands down the best, most beautiful, most graceful dancer in the crew was Bongani's neighbor, Hitler.

Hitler was a great friend of mine, and good Lord could that guy dance. He was mesmerizing to watch. He had a looseness and a fluidity that defied physics—imagine a jellyfish if it could walk on land. Incredibly handsome, too, tall and lithe and muscular, with beautiful, smooth skin, big teeth, and a great smile, always laughing. And all he did was dance. He'd be up in the morning, blasting house music or hip-hop, practicing moves the whole day.

In the hood, everybody knows who the best dancer in the crew is. He's like your status symbol. When you're poor you don't have cars or nice clothes, but the best dancer gets girls, so that's the guy you want to roll with. Hitler was our guy. There were parties with dance competitions. Kids from every neighborhood would come and bring their best dancers. We'd always bring Hitler, and he almost always won.

When Bongani and I put together a routine for our dance crew, there was no question who was going to be the star attraction. We built the whole set around Hitler. I'd warm the crowd up with a few songs, then the dancers would come out and do a couple of numbers. Once they'd gotten the party started, they'd fan out to form a semicircle around the stage with a gap in the back for Hitler to enter. I'd crank up Redman's "Let's Get Dirty" and start whipping the crowd up even more. *"Are you ready?! I can't hear you! Let me hear you make some noise!"* People would start screaming, and Hitler would jump into the middle of the semicircle and the crowd would lose it. Hitler would do his thing while the guys circled around him, shouting him on. *"Go Hit-ler! Go Hit-ler! Go Hit-ler! Go Hit-ler!"* And because this was hip-hop, the crew would do that thing where you shoot your arm out in front of you with your palm flat, bopping it up and down to the beat. *"Go Hit-ler! Go Hit-ler! Go Hit-ler! Go Hit-ler!"* We'd have the whole crowd in a frenzy, a thousand people in the street chanting along with their hands in the air. *"Go Hit-ler! Go Hit-ler! Go Hit-ler! Go Hit-ler!"*

Hitler, although an unusual name, is not unheard-of in South Africa. Part of it has to do with the way a lot of black people pick names. Black people choose their traditional names with great care; those are the names that have deeply personal meanings. But from colonial times through the days of apartheid, black people in South Africa were required to have an English or European name as well—a name that white people could pronounce, basically. So you had your English name, your traditional name, and your last name: Patricia Nombuy-iselo Noah. Nine times out of ten, your European name was chosen at random, plucked from the Bible or taken from a Hollywood celebrity or a famous politician in the news. I know guys named after Mussolini and Napoleon. And, of course, Hitler.

Westerners are shocked and confused by that, but really it's a case of the West reaping what it has sown. The colonial powers carved up Africa, put the black man to work, and did not properly educate him. White people don't talk to black people. So why would black people know what's going on in the white man's world? Because of that, many black people in South Africa don't really know who Hitler was. My own grandfather thought "a hitler" was a kind of army tank that was helping the Germans win the war. Because that's what he took from what he heard on the news. For many black South Africans, the story of the war was that there was someone called Hitler and he was the reason the Allies were losing the war. This Hitler was so powerful that at some point black people had to go help white people fight against him—and if the white man has to stoop to ask the black man for help fighting someone, that someone must be the toughest guy of all time. So if you want your dog to be tough, you name your dog Hitler. If you want your kid to be tough, you name your kid Hitler. There's a good chance you've got an uncle named Hitler. It's just a thing.

At Sandringham, we were taught more about World War II than the typical black kids in the townships were, but only in a basic way. We weren't taught to think critically about Hitler and anti-Semitism and the Holocaust. We weren't taught, for instance, that the architects of apartheid were big fans of Hitler, that the racist policies they put in place were inspired, in part, by the racist policies of the Third Reich. We weren't taught how to think about how Hitler related to the world we lived in. We weren't being taught to think, period. All we were taught was that in 1939 Hitler invaded Poland and in 1941 he invaded the Soviet Union and in 1943 he did something else. They're just facts. Memorize them, write them down for the test, and forget them.

There is also this to consider: The name Hitler does not offend a black South African because Hitler is not the worst thing a black South African can imagine. Every country thinks their history is the most important, and that's especially true in the West. But if black South Africans could go back in time and kill one person, Cecil Rhodes would come up before Hitler. If people in the Congo could go back in time and kill one person, Belgium's King Leopold would come way before Hitler. If Native Americans could go back in time and kill one person, it would probably be Christopher Columbus or Andrew Jackson.

I often meet people in the West who insist that the Holocaust was the worst atrocity in human history, without question. Yes, it was horrific. But I often wonder, with African atrocities like in the Congo, how horrific were they? The thing Africans don't have that Jewish people do have is documentation. The Nazis kept meticulous records, took pictures, made films. And that's really what it comes down to. Holocaust victims count because Hitler counted them. Six million people killed. We can all look at that number and rightly be horrified. But when you read through the history of atrocities against Africans, there are no numbers, only guesses. It's harder to be horrified by a guess. When Portugal and Belgium were plundering Angola and the Congo, they weren't counting the black people they slaughtered. How many black people died harvesting rubber in the Congo? In the gold and diamond mines of the Transvaal?

So in Europe and America, yes, Hitler is the Greatest Madman in History. In Africa he's just another strongman from the history books. In all my time hanging out with Hitler, I never once asked myself, "*Why* is his name Hitler?" His name was Hitler because his mom named him Hitler.

Once Bongani and I added the dancers to our DJ sets, we blew up. We called our group the Black and White Boys. The dancers were called the Springbok Boys. We started getting booked everywhere. Successful black families were moving to the suburbs, but their kids still wanted to have block parties and stay connected to the culture of the townships, so they'd book us to play their parties. Word of mouth traveled. Pretty soon we were getting booked more and more in the suburbs, meeting white people, playing for white people.

One kid we knew from the township, his mother was involved in creating cultural programs for schools. In America they'd be called "diversity programs." They were springing up all over South Africa because we were supposed to be learning about and embracing one another in this post-apartheid era. This kid's mom asked us if we wanted to play at a cultural day at some school in Linksfield, the wealthy suburb south of Sandringham where my pal Teddy had lived. There was going to be all sorts of different dancing and music, and everyone was going to come together and hang out and be cultural. She offered to pay, so we said sure. She sent us the information with the time and place and the name of the school: the King David School. A Jewish school.

The day of the event, we booked a minibus, loaded it up with our gear, and drove over. Once we arrived we waited in the back of the school's assembly hall and watched the acts that went onstage before us, different groups took their turns performing, flamenco dancers, Greek dancers, traditional Zulu musicians. Then we were up. We were billed as the Hip Hop Pantsula Dancers—the South African B-Boys. We set up our sound system onstage. I looked out, and the whole hall was nothing but Jewish kids in their yarmulkes, ready to party.

I got on the mic. "Are you ready to rock out?!"

"Yeahhhhhh!"

"Make some noise!"

"Yeahhhhhh!"

I started playing. The bass was bumping, my crew was dancing, and everyone was having a great time. The teachers, the chaperones, the parents, hundreds of kids—they were all dancing like crazy. Our set was scheduled for fifteen minutes, and at the ten-minute mark came the moment for me to play "Let's Get Dirty," bring out my star dancer, and shut shit down.

I started the song, the dancers fanned out in their semicircle, and I got on the mic.

"Are you guys ready?!"

"Yeahhhhhh!"

"You guys are not ready! Are you *ready*?!"

"Yeeeaaahhhhhhhh!"

"All right! Give it up and make some noise for *HIIIIIITTTT-LLLLEERRRRRRRRRR*!!!"

Hitler jumped out to the middle of the circle and started killing it. The guys around him were all chanting, *"Go Hit-ler! Go Hit-ler! Go Hit-ler! Go Hit-ler!"* They had their arms out in front of them, bouncing to the rhythm. *"Go Hit-ler! Go Hit-ler! Go Hit-ler! Go Hit-ler!"* And I was right there on the mic leading them along. *"Go Hit-ler! Go Hit-ler! Go Hit-ler! Go Hit-ler!"*

The whole room stopped. No one was dancing. The teachers, the chaperones, the parents, the hundreds of Jewish kids in their yarmulkes—they froze and stared aghast at us up on the stage. I was oblivious. So was Hitler. We kept going. For a good thirty seconds the only sound in the room was the beat of the music and me on the mic yelling, *"Go Hit-ler! Go Hit-ler! Go Hit-ler! Put your hands in the air for Hitler, yo!"*

A teacher ran up behind me and yanked the plug for my system out of the wall. The hall went dead silent, and she turned on me and she was livid. "How *dare* you?! This is disgusting! You horrible, disgusting vile creature! How *dare* you?!"

My mind was racing, trying to figure out what she was talking about. Then it clicked. Hitler had a special dance move called *o spana va*. It means "where you work" and it was very sexual: His hips would gyrate and thrust, like he was fucking the air. That was the move he was doing at the moment the teacher ran out, so clearly the dance was the thing she found so disgusting. But this was a move that African people do all the time. It's a part of our culture. Here we were sharing our culture for a cultural day, and this woman was calling us disgusting. She was offended, and I was offended by her taking offense.

"Lady," I said, "I think you need to calm down."

"I will *not* calm down! How dare you come here and insult us?!"

"This is not insulting anyone. This is who we are!"

"Get out of here! You people are disgusting."

And there it was. *You people*. Now I saw what the deal was: This lady was racist. She couldn't see black men dancing suggestively and not get pissed off. As I started packing up my gear, we kept arguing.

"Listen, lady. We're free now. We're gonna do what we're gonna do. You can't stop us."

"I'll have you know that my people stopped people like you before, and we can stop you again."

She was talking, of course, about stopping the Nazis in World War II, but that's not what I was hearing. Jews in South Africa are just white people. All I was hearing was some white lady shouting about how white people beat us before and they'll beat us again. I said, "You will *never* stop us again, lady"—and here's where I played the trump card— "You'll never stop us, because now we have *Nelson Mandela* on our side! And he *told* us we can do this!"

"*What?!*"

She was so confused. I'd had it. I started cussing her out. "Fuck you, lady. Fuck your program. Fuck your school. Fuck your whole people. Let's go, guys! We're out!"

We didn't walk out of that school. We danced out. We danced down the street pumping our fists in the air. *"Go Hit-ler! Go Hit-ler! Go Hit-ler! Go Hit-ler!"* Because Hitler had shut shit down. Hitler had the most gangster dance moves ever, and those white people didn't know what hit them.

Alexandra was a farm originally named for the wife of the white man who owned it. Like Sophiatown and other black spots populating white areas before apartheid, Alex started out as a squatter settlement where blacks gathered and lived when coming to Johannesburg to find work. What was unique about Alex is that this farmer sold plots of land to some of the black tenants in the time before it was illegal for blacks to own property. So while Sophiatown and other black ghettos were razed and rebuilt as white suburbs, Alex fought and held on and asserted its right to exist. Wealthy white suburbs like Sandton grew around it, but Alex remained. More squatters came and more squatters came, putting up makeshift shacks and shanties. They look like the slums in Mumbai or the favelas in Brazil. The first time I saw the favelas in Rio I said, "Yeah, that's Alexandra, but on a hill."

Soweto was beautiful because, after democracy, you watched Soweto grow. Soweto has become a proper city unto itself. People went from three-room houses to five-room houses to three-bedroom houses with garages. There was room to grow because the piece of land from the government gave you something to build on. Alexandra can't do that. Alex can't get any bigger, because it's pinned in on all sides, and it can't build up, because it's mostly shacks.

When democracy came, people flooded into Alex from the home-lands, building new shacks in the backyards of other shacks with still more shacks attached to the backside of those shacks, growing more dense and more compressed, leaving close to 200,000 people living in a few square kilometers. Even if you go back today, Alex hasn't changed. It can't change. It's physically impossible for it to change. It can only be what it is.

THE CHEESE BOYS

My friend Bongani was a short, bald, super-buff guy. He wasn't always that way. His whole life he'd been skinny, and then a bodybuilding magazine found its way into his hands and changed his life. Bongani was one of those people who brought out the best in everybody. He was that friend who believed in you and saw the potential in you that nobody else did, which was why so many of the township kids gravitated toward him, and why I gravitated toward him as well. Bongani was always popular, but his reputation really took off when he beat up one of the more infamous bullies in the school. That cemented his status as sort of the leader and protector of the township kids.

Bongani lived in Alex, but I never visited him there while we were still in school; he'd always come to my house in Highlands North. I'd been to Alex a few times, for brief visits, but I'd never spent any real time there. I'd never been there at night, let's put it that way. Going to Alex during the day is different from going there at night. The place was nicknamed Gomorrah for a reason.

One day after school, not long before we matriculated, Bongani walked up to me on the quad.

"Hey, let's go to the hood," he said.

"The hood?"

At first I had no idea what he was talking about. I knew the word "hood" from rap songs, and I knew the different townships where black people lived, but I had never used the one to describe the other.

The walls of apartheid were coming down just as American hip-hop was blowing up, and hip-hop made it cool to be from the hood. Before, living in a township was something to be ashamed of; it was the bottom of the bottom. Then we had movies like *Boyz n the Hood* and *Menace II Society,* and they made the hood look cool. The characters in those movies, in the songs, they owned it. Kids in the townships started doing the same, wearing their identity as a badge of honor: You were no longer from the township—you were from the hood. Being from Alex gave you way more street cred than living in Highlands North. So when Bongani said, "Let's go to the hood," I was curious about what he meant. I wanted to find out more.

When Bongani took me to Alex we entered as most people do, from the Sandton side. You ride through one of the richest neighborhoods in Johannesburg, past palatial mansions and huge money. Then you go through the industrial belt of Wynberg that cordons off the rich and white from the poor and black. At the entrance to Alex there's the huge minibus rank and the bus station. It's the same bustling, chaotic third-world marketplace you see in James Bond and Jason Bourne movies. It's Grand Central Station but outdoors. Everything's dynamic. Everything's in motion. Nothing feels like it was there yesterday, and nothing feels like it will be there tomorrow, but every day it looks exactly the same.

Right next to the minibus rank, of course, is a KFC. That's one thing about South Africa: There's always a KFC. KFC found the black people. KFC did not play games. They were in the hood before McDonald's, before Burger King, before anyone. KFC was like, "Yo, we're *here* for you."

Once you go past the minibus rank, you're in Alex proper. I've been in few places where there's an electricity like there is in Alex. It's a hive of constant human activity, all day long, people coming and going, gangsters hustling, guys on the corner doing nothing, kids running around. There's nowhere for all that energy to go, no mechanism for it to dissipate, so it erupts periodically in epic acts of violence and crazy parties. One minute it'll be a placid afternoon, people hanging out, doing their thing, and next thing you know there's a cop car chasing gangsters, flying through the streets, a gun battle going off, helicopters circling overhead. Then, ten minutes later, it's like it never happened—everyone's back to hanging out, back to the hustle, coming and going, running around.

Alex is laid out on a grid, a series of avenues. The streets are paved, but the sidewalks are mostly dirt. The color scheme is cinder block and corrugated iron, gray and dark gray, punctuated by bright splashes of color. Someone's painted a wall lime green, or there's a bright-red sign above a takeaway shop, or maybe somebody's picked up a bright-blue piece of sheet metal just by luck. There's little in the way of basic sanitation. Trash is everywhere, typically a garbage fire going down some side street. There's always something burning in the hood.

As you walk, there's every smell you can imagine. People are cooking, eating takeaways in the streets. Some family has a shack that's jury-rigged onto the back of someone else's shack, and they don't have any running water, so they've bathed in a bucket from the outdoor tap and then dumped the dirty water in the street, where it runs into the river of sewerage that's already there because the water system has backed up again. There's a guy fixing cars who thinks he knows what he's doing, but he doesn't. He's dumping old motor oil into the street, and now the oil is combining with the dirty bathwater to make a river of filth running down the street. There's probably a goat hanging around—there's always a goat. As you're walking, sound washes over you, the steady thrum of human activity, people talking in a dozen different languages, chatting, haggling, arguing. There's music playing constantly. You've got traditional South African music coming from one corner, someone blasting Dolly Parton from the next corner, and somebody driving past pumping the Notorious B.I.G.

The hood was a complete sensory overload for me, but within the chaos there was order, a system, a social hierarchy based on where you lived. First Avenue was not cool at all because it was right next to the commotion of the minibus rank. Second Avenue was nice because it had semi-houses that were built when there was still some sort of formal settlement going on. Third, Fourth, and Fifth Avenues were nicer—for the township. These were the established families, the old money. Then from Sixth Avenue on down it got really shitty, more shacks and shanties. There were some schools, a few soccer fields. There were a couple of hostels, giant projects built by the government for housing migrant workers. You never wanted to go there. That's where the serious gangsters were. You only went there if you needed to buy an AK-47.

After Twentieth Avenue you hit the Jukskei River, and on the far side of that, across the Roosevelt Street Bridge, was East Bank, the newest, nicest part of the hood. East Bank was where the government had gone in, cleared out the squatters and their shacks, and started to build actual homes. It was still low-income housing, but decent two-bedroom houses with tiny yards. The families who lived there had a bit of money and usually sent their kids out of the hood to better schools, like Sandringham. Bongani's parents lived in East Bank, at the corner of Roosevelt and Springbok Crescent, and after walking from the minibus rank through the hood, we wound up there, hanging around outside his house on the low brick wall down the middle of Springbok Crescent, doing nothing, shooting the shit. I didn't know it then, but I was about to spend the next three years of my life hanging out at that very spot.

• • •

I graduated from high school when I was seventeen, and by that point life at home had become toxic because of my stepfather. I didn't want to be there anymore, and my mom agreed that I should move out. She helped me move to a cheap, roach-infested flat in a building down the road. My plan, insofar as I had one, was to go to university to be a computer programmer, but we couldn't afford the tuition. I needed to make money. The only way I knew how to make money was selling pirated CDs, and one of the best places to sell CDs was in the hood, because that's where the minibus rank was. Minibus drivers were always looking for new songs because having good music was something they used to attract customers.

Another nice thing about the hood was that it's super cheap. You can get by on next to nothing. There's a meal you can get in the hood called a *kota*. It's a quarter loaf of bread. You scrape out the bread, then you fill it with fried potatoes, a slice of baloney, and some pickled mango relish called *achar*. That costs a couple of rand. The more money you have, the more upgrades you can buy. If you have a bit more money you can throw in a hot dog. If you have a bit more than that, you can throw in a proper sausage, like a bratwurst, or maybe a fried egg. The biggest one, with all the upgrades, is enough to feed three people.

For us, the ultimate upgrade was to throw on a slice of cheese. Cheese was always the thing because it was so expensive. Forget the gold standard—the hood operated on the cheese standard. Cheese on anything was money. If you got a burger, that was cool, but if you got a cheeseburger, that meant you had more money than a guy who just got a hamburger. Cheese on a sandwich, cheese in your fridge, that meant you were living the good life. In any township in South Africa, if you had a bit of money, people would say, "Oh, you're a cheese boy." In essence: You're not really hood because your family has enough money to buy cheese.

In Alex, because Bongani and his crew lived in East Bank, they were considered cheese boys. Ironically, because they lived on the first street just over the river, they were looked down on as the scruff of East Bank and the kids in the nicer houses higher up in East Bank were the cheesier cheese boys. Bongani and his crew would never admit to being cheese boys. They would insist, "We're not cheese. We're hood." But then the real hood guys would say, "Eh, you're not hood. You're cheese." "We're not cheese," Bongani's guys would say, pointing further up East Bank. "They're cheese." It was all a bunch of ridiculous posturing about who was hood and who was cheese.

Bongani was the leader of his crew, the guy who got everyone together and got things moving. Then there was Mzi, Bongani's henchman. Small guy, just wanted to tag along, be in the mix. Bheki was the drinks man, always finding us booze and always coming up with an excuse to drink. Then there was Kakoatse. We called him G. Mr. Nice Guy. All G was interested in was women. If women were in the mix, he was in the game. Then, finally, there was Hitler, the life of the party. Hitler just wanted to dance.

Cheese boys were in a uniquely fucked situation when apartheid ended. It is one thing to be born in the hood and know that you will never leave the hood. But the cheese boy has been shown the world outside. His family has done okay. They have a house. They've sent him to a decent school; maybe he's even matriculated. He has been given more potential, but he has not been given more opportunity. He has been given an awareness of the world that is out there, but he has not been given the means to reach it.

The unemployment rate, technically speaking, was "lower" in South Africa during apartheid, which makes sense. There was slavery— that's how everyone was employed. When democracy came, everyone had to be paid a minimum wage. The cost of labor went up, and suddenly millions of people were out of work. The unemployment rate for young black men post-apartheid shot up, sometimes as high as 50 percent. What happens to a lot of guys is they finish high school and they can't afford university, and even little retail jobs can be hard to come by when you're from the hood and you look and talk a certain way. So, for many young men in South Africa's townships, freedom looks like this: Every morning they wake up, maybe their parents go to work or maybe not. Then they go outside and chill on the corner the whole day, talking shit. They're free, they've been taught how to fish, but no one will give them a fishing rod.

• • •

One of the first things I learned in the hood is that there is a very fine line between civilian and criminal. We like to believe we live in a world of good guys and bad guys, and in the suburbs it's easy to believe that, because getting to know a career criminal in the suburbs is a difficult thing. But then you go to the hood and you see there are so many shades in between.

In the hood, gangsters were your friends and neighbors. You knew them. You talked to them on the corner, saw them at parties. They were a part of your world. You knew them from before they became gangsters. It wasn't, "Hey, that's a crack dealer." It was, "Oh, little Jimmy's selling crack now." The weird thing about these gangsters was that they were all, at a glance, identical. They drove the same red sports car. They dated the same beautiful eighteen-year-old girls. It was strange. It was like they didn't have personalities; they shared a personality. One could be the other, and the other could be the one. They'd each studied how to be *that* gangster.

In the hood, even if you're not a hardcore criminal, crime is in your life in some way or another. There are degrees of it. It's everyone from the mom buying some food that fell off the back of a truck to feed her family, all the way up to the gangs selling military-grade weapons and hardware. The hood made me realize that crime succeeds because crime does the one thing the government doesn't do: crime cares. Crime is grassroots. Crime looks for the young kids who need support and a lifting hand. Crime offers internship programs and summer jobs and opportunities for advancement. Crime gets involved in the community. Crime doesn't discriminate.

My life of crime started off small, selling pirated CDs on the corner. That in itself was a crime, and today I feel like I owe all these artists money for stealing their music, but by hood standards it didn't even qualify as illegal. At the time it never occurred to any of us that we were doing anything wrong—if copying CDs is wrong, why would they make CD writers?

The garage of Bongani's house opened up onto Springbok Cresent.

Every morning we'd open the doors, run an extension cord out into the street, set up a table, and play music. People would walk by and ask, "What is that? Can I get one, please?" Our corner was also where a lot of minibus drivers ended their routes and turned around to loop back to the minibus rank. They'd swing by, place an order, come back, pick it up. Swing by, place an order, come back, pick it up. We spent our whole day running out to them, going back to the garage to make more mixes, and going back out to sell. There was a converted shipping container around the corner where we'd hang out when we got tired of the wall. It had a pay phone installed inside that we'd use to call people. When things were slow we'd wander back and forth between the container and the wall, talking and hanging out with the other people with nothing to do in the middle of the day. We'd talk to drug dealers, talk to gangsters. Every now and then the cops would come crashing through. A day in the life of the hood. Next day, same thing.

Selling slowly evolved into hustling because Bongani saw all the angles and knew how to exploit them. Like Tom, Bongani was a hustler. But where Tom was only about the short con, Bongani had schemes: If we do this, we get that, then we can flip that for the other thing, which gives us the leverage we need to get something bigger. Some minibus drivers couldn't pay up front, for example. "I don't have the money, because I've just started my shift," they'd say. "But I need new music. Can I owe you guys some form of credit? I'll owe you a ride. I'll pay you at the end of my shift, at the end of the week?" So we started letting drivers buy on credit, charging them a bit of interest.

We started making more money. Never more than a few hundred, maybe a thousand rand at a time, but it was all cash on hand. Bongani was quick to realize the position we were in. Cash is the one thing everyone in the hood needs. Everyone's looking for a short-term loan for something, to pay a bill or pay a fine or just hold things together. People started coming to us and asking for money. Bongani would cut a deal, and then he'd come to me. "Yo, we're going to make a deal with this guy. We're going to loan him a hundred, and he's going to give us back one-twenty at the end of the week." I'd say okay. Then the guy would come back and give us 120 rand. Then we did it again. Then we did it some more. We started to double our money, then triple our money.

Cash gave us leverage in the hood's barter economy as well. It's common knowledge that if you're standing at a corner of a main street in the hood, somebody's going to try to sell you something. "Yo, yo, yo, man. You want some weed?" "You wanna buy a VCR?" "You wanna buy a DVD player?" "Yo, I'm selling a TV." That's just how it works.

Let's say we see two guys haggling on the corner, a crackhead trying to sell a DVD player and some working dude who wants it but doesn't have the money because he hasn't got his wages yet. They're going back and forth, but the crackhead wants the money now. Crackheads don't wait. There's no layaway plan with a crackhead. So Bongani steps in and takes the working guy aside.

"Look, I understand you can't pay for the DVD player now," Bongani says. "But how much are you willing to pay for it?"

"I'll pay one-twenty," he says.

"Okay, cool."

Then Bongani takes the crackhead aside.

"How much do you want for the DVD player?"

"I want one-forty."

"Okay, listen. You're a crackhead. This is a stolen DVD player. I'm going to give you fifty."

The crackhead protests a bit, but then he takes the money because he's a crackhead and it's cash and crack is all about the now. Then Bongani goes back to the working guy.

"All right. We'll do one-twenty. Here's your DVD player. It's yours."

"But I don't have the one-twenty."

"It's cool. You can take it now, only instead of one-twenty you give us one-forty when you get your wages."

"Okay."

So now we've invested 50 rand with the crackhead and that gets us 140 from the working guy. But Bongani would see a way to flip it and grow it again. Let's say this guy who bought the DVD player worked at a shoe store.

"How much do you pay for a pair of Nikes with your staff discount?" Bongani would ask.

"I can get a pair of Nikes for one-fifty."

"Okay, instead of you giving us one-forty, we'll give you ten and you get us a pair of Nikes with your discount."

So now this guy's walking away with a DVD player *and* 10 rand in his pocket. He's feeling like he got a good deal. He brings us the Nikes and then we go to one of the cheesier cheese boys up in East Bank and we say, "Yo, dude, we know you want the new Jordans. They're three hundred in the shops. We'll sell them to you for two hundred." We sell him the shoes, and now we've gone and turned 60 rand into 200.

That's the hood. Someone's always buying, someone's always selling, and the hustle is about trying to be in the middle of that whole thing. None of it was legal. Nobody knew where anything came from. The guy who got us Nikes, did he really have a "staff discount"? You don't know. You don't ask. It's just, "Hey, look what I found" and "Cool, how much do you want?" That's the international code.

At first I didn't know not to ask. I remember one time we bought a car stereo or something like that.

"But who did this belong to?" I said.

"Eh, don't worry about it," one of the guys told me. "White people have insurance."

"Insurance?"

"Yeah, when white people lose stuff they have insurance policies that pay them cash for what they've lost, so it's like they've lost nothing."

"Oh, okay," I said. "Sounds nice."

And that was as far as we ever thought about it: When white people lose stuff they get money, just another nice perk of being white.

It's easy to be judgmental about crime when you live in a world wealthy enough to be removed from it. But the hood taught me that everyone has different notions of right and wrong, different definitions of what constitutes crime, and what level of crime they're willing to participate in. If a crackhead comes through and he's got a crate of Corn Flakes boxes he's stolen out of the back of a supermarket, the poor mom isn't thinking, *I'm aiding and abetting a criminal by buying these Corn Flakes*. No. She's thinking, *My family needs food and this guy has Corn Flakes*, and she buys the Corn Flakes.

My own mother, my super-religious, law-abiding mother who used to shit on me about breaking the rules and learning to behave, I'll never forget one day I came home and in the kitchen was a giant box of frozen burger patties, like two hundred of them, from a takeaway place called Black Steer. A burger at Black Steer cost at least 20 rand.

"What the hell is this?" I said.

"Oh, some guy at work had these and was selling them," she said. "I got a great discount."

"But where did he get it from?"

"I don't know. He said he knew somebody who—"

"Mom, he stole it."

"We don't know that."

"We *do* know that. Where the hell is some guy going to get all of these burger patties from, randomly?"

Of course, we ate the burgers. Then we thanked God for the meal.

When Bongani first said to me, "Let's go to the hood," I thought we were going to sell CDs and DJ parties in the hood. It turned out that we were selling CDs and DJing parties in order to capitalize a payday-lending and pawnshop operation in the hood. Very quickly that became our core business.

Every day in the hood was the same. I'd wake up early. Bongani would meet me at my flat and we'd catch a minibus to Alex with my computer, carrying the giant tower and the giant, heavy monitor the whole way. We'd set it up in Bongani's garage, and start the first batch of CDs. Then we'd walk. We'd go down to the corner of Nineteenth and Roosevelt for breakfast. When you're trying to stretch your money, food is where you have to be careful. You have to plan or you'll eat your profits. So every morning for breakfast we eat *vetkoek*, which is fried dough, basically. Those were cheap, like 50 cents a pop. We could buy a bunch of those and have enough energy to sustain us until later on in the day.

Then we'd sit on the corner and eat. While we ate, we'd be picking up orders from the minibus drivers as they went past. After that we'd go back to Bongani's garage, listen to music, lift weights, make the CDs. Around ten or eleven, the drivers would start coming back from their morning routes. We'd take the CDs and head out to the corner for them to pick up their stuff. Then we'd just be on the corner, hanging out, meeting characters, seeing who came by, seeing where the day was going to take us. A guy needs this. A guy's selling that. You never knew what it was going to be.

There was always a big rush of business at lunch. We'd be all over Alexandra, hitting different shops and corners, making deals with everyone. We'd get free rides from the minibus drivers because we'd hop in with them and use it as an opportunity to talk about what music they needed, but secretly we were riding with the guy for free. "Hey, we want to collect orders. We'll talk to you while you drive. What do you need? What music are you looking for? Do you need the new Maxwell? Okay, we got the new Maxwell. Okay, we'll talk to you later. We'll jump out here." Then we'd hop on another ride going wherever we were going next.

After lunch, business would die down, and that's when we'd get our lunch, usually the cheapest thing we could afford, like a smiley with some maize meal. A smiley is a goat's head. They're boiled and covered with chili pepper. We call them smileys because when you're done eating all the meat off it, the goat looks like it's smiling at you from the plate. The cheeks and the tongue are quite delicious, but the eyes are disgusting. They pop in your mouth. You put the eyeball into your mouth and you bite it, and it's just a ball of pus that pops. It has no crunch. It has no chew. It has no flavor that is appetizing in any way.

After lunch we'd head back to the garage, relax, sleep off the meal, and make more CDs. In the afternoons we'd see a lot of moms. Moms loved us. They were some of our best customers. Since moms run the household, they're the ones looking to buy that box of soap that fell off the back of the truck, and they were more likely to buy it from us than from some crackhead. Dealing with crackheads is unpleasant. We were upstanding, well-spoken East Bank boys. We could even charge a premium because we added that layer of respectability to the transaction. Moms are also often the most in need of short-term loans, to pay for this or that for the family. Again, they'd rather deal with us than with some gangster loan shark. Moms knew we weren't going to break anyone's legs if they couldn't pay. We didn't believe in that. Also we weren't capable of it—let's not forget that part. But that's where Bongani's brilliance came in. He always knew what a person could provide pending their failure to pay.

We made some of the craziest trades. Moms in the hood are protective of their daughters, especially if their daughters are pretty. In Alex there were girls who got locked up. They went to school, came straight home, and went straight into the house. They weren't allowed to leave. Boys weren't allowed to talk to them, weren't even allowed to hang around the house—none of that. Some guy was always going on about some locked-away girl: "She's so beautiful. I'll do anything to get with her." But he couldn't. Nobody could.

Then that mom would need a loan. Once we lent her the money, until she paid us back she couldn't chase us away from her house. We'd go by and hang out, chat, make small talk. The daughter would be right there, but the mom couldn't say, "Don't talk to those boys!" The loan gave us access to establish a relationship with the mom. We'd get invited to stay for dinner. Once the mom knew we were nice, upstanding guys, she'd agree to let us take her daughter to a party as long as we promised to get her home safely. So then we'd go to the guy who'd been so desperate to meet the daughter.

"Hey, let's make a deal. We'll bring the girl to your party and you get to hang out with her. How much can you give us?"

"I don't have money," he'd say, "but I have some cases of beer."

"Okay, so tonight we're going to this party. You give us two cases of beer for the party."

"Cool."

Then we'd go to the party. We'd invite the girl, who was usually thrilled to escape her mother's prison. The guy would bring the beer, he'd get to hang out with the girl, we'd write off the mom's debt to show her our gratitude, and we'd make our money back selling the beer. There was always a way to make it work. And often that was the most fun part: working the angles, solving the puzzle, seeing what goes where, who needs what, whom we can connect with who can then get us the money.

At the peak of our operation we probably had around 10,000 rand in capital. We had loans going out and interest coming in. We had our stockpile of Jordans and DVD players we'd bought to resell. We also had to buy blank CDs, hire minibuses to go to our DJ gigs, feed five guys three times a day. We kept track of everything on the computer. Having lived in my mom's world, I knew how to do spreadsheets. We had a Microsoft Excel document laid out: everybody's name, how much they owed, when they paid, when they didn't pay.

After work was when business started to pick up. Minibus drivers picking up one last order, men coming home from work. The men weren't looking for soap and Corn Flakes. They wanted the gear—DVD players, CD players, PlayStation games. More guys would come through selling stuff, too, because they'd been out hustling and stealing all day. There'd be a guy selling a cellphone, a guy selling some leather jackets, a guy selling shoes. There was this one dude who looked like a black version of Mr. Burns from *The Simpsons*. He'd always come by at the end of his shift with the most random useless crap, like an electric toothbrush without the charger. One time he brought us an electric razor.

"What the hell is this?"

"It's an electric razor?"

"An electric razor? We're black. Do you know what these things do to our skin? Do you see anyone around here who can use an electric razor?"

We never knew where he was getting this stuff from. Because you don't ask. Eventually we pieced it together, though: He worked at the airport. It was all crap he was boosting from people's luggage.

Slowly the rush would start to taper off and we'd wind down. We'd make our last collections, go over our CD stock, balance our accounts. If there was a party to DJ that night we'd start getting ready for that. Otherwise, we'd buy a few beers and sit around and drink, talk about the day, listen to the gunshots in the distance. Gunshots went off every night, and we'd always try to guess what kind of gun it was. "That's a nine-millimeter." Usually there'd be a police chase, cop cars flying through after some guy with a stolen car. Then everyone would go home for dinner with their families. I'd take my computer, get back in a minibus, ride home, sleep, and then come back and do it all again the next day.

A year passed. Then two. I had stopped planning for school, and was no closer to having the money to enroll.

The tricky thing about the hood is that you're always working, working, working, and you feel like something's happening, but really nothing's happening at all. I was out there every day from seven a.m. to seven p.m., and every day it was: How do we turn ten rand into twenty? How do we turn twenty into fifty? How do I turn fifty into a hundred? At the end of the day we'd spend it on food and maybe some beers, and then we'd go home and come back and it was: How do we turn ten into twenty? How do we turn twenty into fifty? It was a whole day's work to flip that money. You had to be walking, be moving, be thinking. You had to get to a guy, find a guy, meet a guy. There were many days we'd end up back at zero, but I always felt like I'd been very productive.

Hustling is to work what surfing the Internet is to reading. If you add up how much you read in a year on the Internet—tweets, Facebook posts, lists—you've read the equivalent of a shit ton of books, but in fact you've read no books in a year. When I look back on it, that's what hustling was. It's maximal effort put into minimal gain. It's a hamster wheel. If I'd put all that energy into studying I'd have earned an MBA.

Instead I was majoring in hustling, something no university would give me a degree for.

When I first went into Alex, I was drawn by the electricity and the excitement of it, but more important, I was accepted there, more so than I'd been in high school or anywhere else. When I first showed up, a couple of people raised an eyebrow. "Who's this colored kid?" But the hood doesn't judge. If you want to be there, you can be there. Because I didn't live in the hood I was technically an outsider in the hood, but for the first time in my life I didn't feel like one.

The hood is also a low-stress, comfortable life. All your mental energy goes into getting by, so you don't have to ask yourself any of the big questions. Who am I? Who am I supposed to be? Am I doing enough? In the hood you can be a forty-year-old man living in your mom's house asking people for money and it's not looked down on. You never feel like a failure in the hood, because someone's always worse off than you, and you don't feel like you need to do more, because the biggest success isn't that much higher than you, either. It allows you to exist in a state of suspended animation.

The hood has a wonderful sense of community to it as well. Everyone knows everyone, from the crackhead all the way through to the policeman. People take care of one another. The way it works in the hood is that if any mom asks you to do something, you have to say yes. "Can I send you?" is the phrase. It's like everyone's your mom, and you're everyone's kid.

"Can I send you?"

"Yeah, whaddya need?"

"I need you to go buy milk and bread."

"Yeah, cool."

Then she gives you some money and you go buy milk and bread. As long as you aren't busy and it doesn't cost you anything, you don't say no.

The biggest thing in the hood is that you have to share. You can't get rich on your own. You have money? Why aren't you helping people? The old lady on the block needs help, everyone pitches in. You're buying beer, you buy beer for everyone. You spread it around. Everyone must know that your success benefits the community in one way or another, or you become a target.

The township polices itself as well. If someone's caught stealing, the township deals with them. If someone's caught breaking into a house, the township deals with them. If you're caught raping a woman, pray to God the police find you before the township does. If a woman is being hit, people don't get involved. There are too many questions with a beating. What's the fight about? Who's responsible? Who started it? But rape is rape. Theft is theft. You've desecrated the community.

The hood was strangely comforting, but comfort can be dangerous. Comfort provides a floor but also a ceiling. In our crew, our friend G was like the rest of us, unemployed, hanging out. Then he got a job at a nice clothing store. Every morning he went to work, and the guys would tease him about going to work. We'd see him headed out all dressed up, and everyone would be laughing at him. "Oh, G, look at you in your fancy clothes!" "Oh, G, going to go see the white man today, huh?" "Oh, G, don't forget to bring some books back from the library!"

One morning, after a month of G working at the place, we were hanging out on the wall, and G came out in his slippers and his socks. He wasn't dressed for work.

"Yo, G, what's going on? What's up with the job?"

"Oh, I don't work there anymore."

"Why?"

"They accused me of stealing something and I got fired."

And I'll never forget thinking to myself that it felt like he did it on purpose. He sabotaged himself so that he'd get accepted back into the group again.

The hood has a gravitational pull. It never leaves you behind, but it also never lets you leave. Because by making the choice to leave, you're insulting the place that raised you and made you and never turned you away. And that place fights you back.

As soon as things start going well for you in the hood, it's time to go. Because the hood will drag you back in. It will find a way. There will be a guy who steals a thing and puts it in your car and the cops find it—something. You can't stay. You think you can. You'll start doing better and you'll bring your hood friends out to a nice club, and the next thing you know somebody starts a fight and one of your friends pulls a gun and somebody's getting shot and you're left standing around going, "What just happened?"

The hood happened.

One night I was DJ'ing a party, not in Alex but right outside Alex in Lombardy East, a nicer, middle-class black neighborhood. The police were called about the noise. They came busting in wearing riot gear and pointing machine guns. That's how our police roll. We don't have small and then big. What Americans call SWAT is just our regular police. They came looking for the source of the music, and the music was coming from me. This one cop came over to where I was with my computer and pulled this massive assault rifle on me.

"You gotta shut this down right now."

"Okay, okay," I said. "I'm shutting it down."

But I was running Windows 95. Windows 95 took *forever* to shut down. I was closing windows, shutting down programs. I had one of those fat Seagate drives that damaged easily, and I didn't want to cut the power and possibly damage the drive. This cop clearly didn't give a fuck about any of that.

"Shut it down! Shut it down!"

"I am! I'm shutting it down! I have to close the programs!"

The crowd was getting angry, and the cop was getting nervous. He turned his gun away from me and shot the computer. Only he clearly didn't know anything about computers because he shot the monitor. The monitor exploded but the music kept playing. Now there was chaos—music blaring and everyone running and panicking because of the gunshot. I yanked the power cord out of the tower to shut the thing down. Then the cops started firing tear gas into the crowd.

The tear gas had nothing to do with me or the music. Tear gas is just what the police use to shut down parties in black neighborhoods, like the club turning on the lights to tell everyone to go home.

I lost the hard drive. Even though the cop shot the monitor the explosion somehow fried the thing. The computer would still boot up, but it couldn't read the drive. My music library was gone. Even if I'd had the money for a new hard drive, it had taken me years to amass the music collection. There was no way to replace it. The DJ'ing business was over. The CD-selling business was done. All of a sudden our crew lost its main revenue stream. All we had left was the hustle, and we hustled even harder, taking the bit of cash we had on hand and trying to double it, buying this to flip it for that. We started eating into our savings, and in less than a month we were running on dust.

Then, one evening after work, our friend from the airport, the black Mr. Burns, came by.

"Hey, look what I found," he said.

"What've you got?"

"A camera."

I'll never forget that camera. It was a digital camera. We bought it from him, and I took it and turned it on. It was full of pictures of a nice white family on vacation, and I felt like shit. The other things we'd bought had never mattered to me. Nikes, electric toothbrushes, electric razors. Who cares? Yeah, some guy might get fired because of the pallet of Corn Flakes that went missing from the supermarket, but that's degrees removed. You don't think about it. But this camera had a face. I went through those pictures, knowing how much my family pictures meant to me, and I thought, *I haven't stolen a camera. I've stolen someone's memories. I've stolen part of someone's life.*

It's such a strange thing, but in two years of hustling I never once thought of it as a crime. I honestly didn't think it was bad. *It's just stuff people found. White people have insurance.* Whatever rationalization was handy. In society, we do horrible things to one another because we don't see the person it affects. We don't see their face. We don't see them as people. Which was the whole reason the hood was built in the first place, to keep the victims of apartheid out of sight and out of mind. Because if white people ever saw black people as human, they would see that slavery is unconscionable. We live in a world where we don't see the ramifications of what we do to others, because we don't live with them. It would be a whole lot harder for an investment banker to rip off people with subprime mortgages if he actually had to live with the people he was ripping off. If we could see one another's pain and empathize with one another, it would never be worth it to us to commit the crimes in the first place.

As much as we needed the money, I never sold the camera. I felt too guilty, like it would be bad karma, which I know sounds stupid and it didn't get the family their camera back, but I just couldn't do it. That camera made me confront the fact that there were people on the other end of this thing I was doing, and what I was doing was wrong.

One night our crew got invited to dance in Soweto against another crew. Hitler was going to compete with their best dancer, Hector, who was one of the best dancers in South Africa at the time. This invitation was a huge deal. We were going over there repping our hood. Alex and Soweto have always had a huge rivalry. Soweto was seen as the snobbish township and Alexandra was seen as the gritty and dirty township. Hector was from Diepkloof, which was the nice, well-off part of Soweto. Diepkloof was where the first million-rand houses were built after democracy. "Hey, we're not a township anymore. We're building nice things now." That was the attitude. That's who we were up against. Hitler practiced a whole week.

We took a minibus over to Diepkloof the night of the dance, me and Bongani, Mzi and Bheki and G, and Hitler. Hector won the competition. Then G was caught kissing one of their girls, and it turned into a fight and everything broke down. On our way back to Alex, around one in the morning, as we were pulling out of Diepkloof to get on the freeway, some cops pulled our minibus over. They made everyone get out and they searched it. We were standing outside, lined up alongside the car, when one of the cops came back.

"We've found a gun," he said. "Whose gun is it?"

We all shrugged.

"We don't know," we said.

"Nope, somebody knows. It's somebody's gun."

"Officer, we really don't know," Bongani said.

He slapped Bongani hard across the face.

"You're bullshitting me!"

Then he went down the line, slapping each of us across the face, berating us about the gun. We couldn't do anything but stand there and take it.

"You guys are trash," the cop said. "Where are you from?"

"Alex."

"Ohhhhh, okay, I see. Dogs from Alex. You come here and you rob people and you rape women and you hijack cars. Bunch of fucking hoodlums."

"No, we're dancers. We don't know—"

"I don't care. You're all going to jail until we figure out whose gun this is."

At a certain point we realized what was going on. This cop was shaking us down for a bribe. "Spot fine" is the euphemism everyone uses. You go through this elaborate dance with the cop where you say the thing without saying the thing.

"Can't we do something?" you ask the officer.

"What do you want me to do?"

"We're really sorry, Officer. What can we do?"

"You tell me."

Then you're supposed to make up a story whereby you indicate to the cop how much money you have on you. Which we couldn't do because we didn't have any money. So he took us to jail. It was a public bus. It could have been anyone's gun, but the guys from Alex were the only ones who got arrested. Everyone else in the car was free to go. The cops took us to the police station and threw us in a cell and pulled us out one by one for questioning. When they pulled me aside I had to give my home address: Highlands North. The cop gave me the most confused look.

"You're not from Alex," he said. "What are you doing with these crooks?" I didn't know what to say. He glared at me hard. "Listen here, rich boy. You think it's fun running around with these guys? This isn't play-play anymore. Just tell me the truth about your friends and the gun, and I'll let you go."

I told him no, and he threw me back in the cell. We spent the night, and the next day I called a friend, who said he could borrow the money from his dad to get us out. Later that day the dad came down and paid the money. The cops kept calling it "bail," but it was a bribe. We were never formally arrested or processed. There was no paperwork.

We got out and everything was fine, but it rattled us. Every day we were out in the streets, hustling, trying to act as if we were in some way down with the gangs, but the truth was we were always more cheese than hood. We had created this idea of ourselves as a defense mechanism to survive in the world we were living in. Bongani and the other East Bank guys, because of where they were from, what they looked like—they just had very little hope. You've got two options in that situation. You take the retail job, flip burgers at McDonald's, if you're one of the lucky few who even gets that much. The other option is to toughen up, put up this facade. You can't leave the hood, so you survive by the rules of the hood.

I chose to live in that world, but I wasn't from that world. If anything, I was an imposter. Day to day I was in it as much as everyone else, but the difference was that in the back of my mind I knew I had other options. I could leave. They couldn't.

Once, when I was ten years old, visiting my dad in Yeoville, I needed batteries for one of my toys. My mom had refused to buy me new batteries because, of course, she thought it was a waste of money, so I snuck out to the shops and shoplifted a pack. A security guard busted me on the way out, pulled me into his office, and called my mom.

"We've caught your son shoplifting batteries," he said. "You need to come and fetch him."

"No," she said. "Take him to jail. If he's going to disobey he needs to learn the consequences."

Then she hung up. The guard looked at me, confused. Eventually he let me go on the assumption that I was some wayward orphan, because what mother would send her ten-year-old child to jail?

THE WORLD DOESN'T LOVE YOU

My mom never gave me an inch. Anytime I got in trouble it was tough love, lectures, punishment, and hidings. Every time. For every infraction. You get that with a lot of black parents. They're trying to discipline you before the system does. "I need to do this to you before the police do it to you." Because that's all black parents are thinking from the day you're old enough to walk out into the street, where the law is waiting.

In Alex, getting arrested was a fact of life. It was so common that out on the corner we had a sign for it, a shorthand, clapping your wrists together like you were being put in handcuffs. Everyone knew what that meant.

"Where's Bongani?"

Wrist clap.

"Oh, shit. When?"

"Friday night."

"Damn."

My mom hated the hood. She didn't like my friends there. If I brought them back to the house, she didn't even want them coming inside. "I don't like those boys," she'd say. She didn't hate them personally; she hated what they represented. "You and those boys get into so much shit," she'd say. "You must be careful who you surround yourself with because where you are can determine who you are."

She said the thing she hated most about the hood was that it didn't pressure me to become better. She wanted me to hang out with my cousin at his university.

"What's the difference if I'm at university or I'm in the hood?" I'd say. "It's not like I'm going to university."

"Yes, but the pressure of the university is going to get you. I know you. You won't sit by and watch these guys become better than you. If you're in an environment that is positive and progressive, you too will become that. I keep telling you to change your life, and you don't. One day you're going to get arrested, and when you do, don't call me. I'll tell the police to lock you up just to teach you a lesson."

Because there were some black parents who'd actually do that, not pay their kid's bail, not hire their kid a lawyer—the ultimate tough love. But it doesn't always work, because you're giving the kid tough love when maybe he just needs love. You're trying to teach him a lesson, and now that lesson is the rest of his life.

One morning I saw an ad in the paper. Some shop was having a clearance sale on mobile phones, and they were selling them at such a ridiculous price I knew Bongani and I could flip them in the hood for a profit. This shop was out in the suburbs, too far to walk and too out-of-the-way to take a minibus. Fortunately my stepfather's workshop and a bunch of old cars were in our backyard.

I'd been stealing Abel's junkers to get around since I was fourteen. I would say I was test driving them to make sure they'd been repaired correctly. Abel didn't think that was funny. I'd been caught many times, caught and subjected to my mother's wrath. But that had never stopped me from doing anything.

Most of these junkers weren't street legal. They didn't have proper registrations or proper number plates. Luckily, Abel also had a stack of old number plates in the back of the garage. I quickly learned I could just put one on an old car and hit the road. I was nineteen, maybe twenty, not thinking about any of the ramifications of this. I stopped by Abel's garage when no one was around, picked up one of the cars, the red Mazda I'd taken to the matric dance, slapped some old plates on it, and set off in search of discounted cell phones.

I got pulled over in Hillbrow. Cops in South Africa don't give you a reason when they pull you over. Cops pull you over because they're cops and they have the power to pull you over; it's as simple as that. I used to watch American movies where cops would pull people over and say, "You didn't signal" or "Your taillight's out." I'd always wonder, *Why do American cops bother lying?* One thing I appreciate about South Africa is that we have not yet refined the system to the point where we feel the need to lie.

"Do you know why I pulled you over?"

"Because you're a policeman and I'm a black person?"

"That's correct. License and registration, please."

When the cop pulled me over, it was one of those situations where I wanted to say, "Hey, I know you guys are racially profiling me!" But I couldn't argue the case because I was, at that moment, actually breaking the law. The cop walked up to my window, asked me the standard cop questions. Where are you going? Is this your car? Whose car is this? I couldn't answer. I completely froze.

Being young, funnily enough, I was more worried about getting in trouble with my parents than with the law. I'd had run-ins with the cops in Alexandra, in Soweto, but it was always more about the circumstance: a party getting shut down, a raid on a minibus. The law was all around me, but it had never come down on me, Trevor, specifically. And when you haven't had much experience with the law, the law appears rational—cops are dicks for the most part, but you also recognize that they're doing a job.

Your parents, on the other hand, are not rational at all. They have served as judge, jury, and executioner for your entire childhood, and it feels like they give you a life sentence for every misdemeanor. In that moment, when I should have been scared of the cop, all I was thinking was *Shit shit shit; I'm in so much trouble when I get home.*

The cop called in the number-plate registration and discovered that it didn't match the car. Now he was really on my case. "This car is not in your name! What's going on with these plates?! Step out of the vehicle!" It was only then that I realized: *Ohhhhh, shit. Now I'm in* real *trouble.* I stepped out of the car, and he put the cuffs on me and told me I was being arrested on suspicion of driving a stolen vehicle. He took me in, and the car was impounded.

The Hillbrow police station looks exactly like every other police station in South Africa. They were all built by the same contractor at the height of apartheid—separate nodes in the central nervous system of a police state. If you were blindfolded and taken from one to the other, you probably wouldn't even know that you'd changed locations. They're sterile, institutional, with fluorescent lights and cheap floor tile, like a hospital. My cop walked me in and sat me down at the front booking desk. I was charged and fingerprinted.

In the meantime, they'd been checking out the car, which wasn't going well for me, either. Whenever I borrowed cars from Abel's workshop, I tried to take the junkers rather than a real client's car; I thought I'd get in less trouble that way. That was a mistake. The Mazda, being one of Abel's junkers, didn't have a clear title of ownership. If it had had an owner, the cops would have called the owner, the owner would have explained that the car had been dropped off for repairs, and the whole thing would have been sorted out. Since the car didn't have an owner, I couldn't prove I hadn't stolen it.

Carjackings were common in South Africa at the time, too. So common you weren't even surprised when they happened. You'd have a friend coming over for a dinner party and you'd get a call.

"Sorry. Got carjacked. Gonna be late."

"Ah, that sucks. Hey, guys! Dave got carjacked."

"Sorry, Dave!"

And the party would continue. And that's if the person survived the carjacking. Often they didn't. People were getting shot for their cars all the time. Not only could I not prove I hadn't stolen the car, I couldn't prove I hadn't murdered someone for it, either. The cops were grilling me. "You kill anyone to get that car, boy? Eh? You a killer?"

I was in deep, deep trouble. I had only one lifeline: my parents. One call would have fixed everything. "This is my stepfather. He's a mechanic. I borrowed his car when I shouldn't have." Done. At worst I'd get a slap on the wrist for driving a car that wasn't registered. But what would I be getting at home?

I sat there in the police station—arrested for suspicion of grand theft auto, a plausible suspect for carjacking or murder—and debated whether I should call my parents or go to jail. With my stepfather I was thinking, *He might actually kill me.* In my mind that was an entirely realistic scenario. With my mother I was thinking, *She's going to make this worse. She's not the character witness I want right now. She won't help me.* Because she'd told me she wouldn't. "If you ever get arrested, don't call me." I needed someone sympathetic to my plight, and I didn't believe she was that person. So I didn't call my parents. I decided I didn't need them. I was a man. I could go it alone. I used my call to phone my cousin and told him not to tell anyone what had happened while I figured out what to do—now I just had to figure out what to do.

I'd been picked up late in the afternoon, so by the time I was processed it was close to lights-out. I was spending the night in jail, like it or not. It was at that point that a cop pulled me aside and told me what I was in for.

The way the system works in South Africa is that you're arrested and held in a cell at the police station until your bail hearing. At the hearing, the judge looks at your case, hears arguments from the opposing sides, and then he either dismisses the charges or sets bail and a trial date. If you can make bail, you pay and go home. But there are all sorts of ways your bail hearing can go wrong: You get some court-appointed lawyer who hasn't read your case and doesn't know what's going on. Your family can't pay your bail. It could even be that the court's backed up. "Sorry, we're too busy. No more hearings today." It doesn't matter the reason. Once you leave jail, you can't go back to jail. If your situation isn't resolved that day, you go to prison to await trial. In prison you're housed with the people awaiting trial, not with the general population, but even the awaiting-trial section is incredibly dangerous because you have people picked up for traffic violations all the way up to proper hardened criminals. You're stuck there together, and you can be there for days, weeks, maybe months. It's the same way in America. If you're poor, if you don't know how the system works, you can slip through the cracks, and the next thing you know you're in this weird purgatory where you're not in prison but you're not not in prison. You haven't been convicted of any crime, but you're still locked up and can't get out.

This cop pulled me aside and said, "Listen, you don't want to go to your bail hearing. They'll give you a state attorney who won't know what's going on. He'll have no time for you. He'll ask the judge for a postponement, and then maybe you'll go free or maybe you won't. Trust me, you don't want to do that. You have the right to stay here for as long as you like. You want to meet with a lawyer and set yourself up before you go anywhere near a court or a judge." He wasn't giving me this advice out of the goodness of his heart. He had a deal with a defense attorney, sending him clients in exchange for a kickback. He handed me the attorney's business card, I called him, and he agreed to take my case. He told me to stay put while he handled everything.

Now I needed money, because lawyers, as nice as they are, don't do anything for free. I called a friend and asked him if he could ask his dad to borrow some money. He said he'd handle it. He talked to his dad, and the lawyer got his retainer the next day.

With the lawyer taken care of, I felt like I had things under control.

I was feeling pretty slick. I'd handled the situation, and, most important, Mom and Abel were none the wiser.

When the time came for lights-out a cop came and took my stuff. My belt, my wallet, my shoelaces.

"Why do you need my shoelaces?"

"So you don't hang yourself."

"Right."

Even when he said that, the gravity of my situation still wasn't sinking in. Walking to the station's holding cell, looking around at the other six guys in there, I was thinking, *This is no big deal. Everything's gonna be cool. I'm gonna get out of this.* I thought that right up until the moment the cell door clanged shut behind me and the guard yelled, "Lights out!" That's when I thought, *Oh, shit. This is real.*

The guards had given me a mat and a scratchy blanket. I rolled them out on the concrete floor and tried to get comfortable. Every bad prison movie I'd ever seen was racing through my head. I was thinking, *I'm gonna get raped. I'm gonna get raped. I'm gonna get raped.* But of course I didn't get raped, because this wasn't prison. It was jail, and there's a big difference, as I would soon come to understand.

I woke up the next morning with that fleeting sensation where you think something has all been a dream. Then I looked around and remembered that it wasn't. Breakfast came, and I settled in to wait.

A day in jail is mostly silence punctuated by passing guards shouting profanities at you, doing roll call. Inside the holding cell nobody says anything. Nobody walks into a jail cell and says, "Hi, guys! I'm Brian!" Because everyone is afraid, and no one wants to appear vulnerable. Nobody wants to be the bitch. Nobody wants to be the guy getting killed. I didn't want anyone to know that I was just a kid in for a traffic charge, so I reached back in my mind for all the stereotypes of what I imagined people act like in prison, and then I tried to act like that.

In South Africa, everyone knows that colored gangsters are the most ruthless, the most savage. It's a stereotype that's fed to you your whole life. The most notorious colored gangs are the Numbers Gangs: the 26s, the 27s, the 28s. They control the prisons. They're known for being brutally violent—maiming, torturing, raping, cutting off people's heads—not for the sake of making money but just to prove how ruthless and savage they are, like Mexican drug cartels. In fact a lot of these gangs base their thing on those Mexican gangs. They have the same look: the Converse All Stars with the Dickies pants and the open shirt buttoned only at the top.

By the time I was a teenager, anytime I was profiled by cops or security guards, it usually wasn't because I was black but because I looked colored. I went to a club once with my cousin and his friend. The bouncer searched Mlungisi, waved him in. He searched our friend, waved him in. Then he searched me and got up in my face.

"Where's your knife?"

"I don't have a knife."

"I know you have a knife somewhere. Where is it?"

He searched and searched and finally gave up and let me in, looking me over like I was trouble.

"No *shit* from you! Okay?"

I figured that if I was in jail people were going to assume I was the kind of colored person who ends up in jail, a violent criminal. So I played it up. I put on this character; I played the stereotype. Anytime the cops asked me questions I started speaking in broken Afrikaans with a thick colored accent. Imagine a white guy in America, just dark enough to pass for Latino, walking around jail doing bad Mexican-gangster dialogue from the movies. *"Shit's about to get loco, ese."* That's basically what I was doing—the South African version of that. This was my brilliant plan to survive incarceration. But it worked. The guys in the cell with me, they were there for drunk driving, for domestic abuse, for petty theft. They had no idea what real colored gangsters were like. Everyone left me alone.

We were all playing a game, only nobody knew we were playing it. When I walked in that first night, everyone was giving me this look: "I'm dangerous. Don't fuck with me." So I went, "Shit, these people are hardened criminals. I shouldn't be here, because I am not a criminal." Then the next day everything turned over quickly. One by one, guys left to go to their hearings, I stayed to wait for my lawyer, and new people started to pitch up. Now I was the veteran, doing my colored-gangster routine, giving the new guys the same look: "I'm dangerous. Don't fuck with me." And they looked at me and went, "Shit, he's a hardened criminal. I shouldn't be here, because I am not like him." And round and round we went.

At a certain point it occurred to me that every single person in that cell might be faking it. We were all decent guys from nice neighborhoods and good families, picked up for unpaid parking tickets and other infractions. We could have been having a great time sharing meals, playing cards, and talking about women and soccer. But that didn't happen, because everyone had adopted this dangerous pose and nobody talked because everyone was afraid of who the other guys were pretending to be. Now those guys were going to get out and go home to their families and say, "Oh, honey, that was rough. Those were some real criminals in there. There was this one colored guy. Man, he was a killer."

Once I had the game sorted out, I was good again. I relaxed. I was back to thinking, *I got this. This is no big deal.* The food was actually decent. For breakfast they brought you these peanut butter sandwiches on thick slices of bread. Lunch was chicken and rice. The tea was too hot, and it was more water than tea, but it was drinkable. There were older, hard-time prisoners close to parole, and their detail was to come and clean the cells and circulate books and magazines for you to read. It was quite relaxing.

There was one point when I remember eating a meal and saying to myself, *This isn't so bad. I hang around with a bunch of dudes. There's no chores. No bills to pay. No one constantly nagging me and telling me what to do. Peanut butter sandwiches? Shit, I eat peanut butter sandwiches all the time. This is pretty sweet. I could do this.* I was so afraid of the ass-whooping waiting for me at home that I genuinely considered going to prison. For a brief moment I thought I had a plan. "I'll go away for a couple of years, come back, and say I was kidnapped, and mom will never know and she'll just be happy to see me."

On the third day, the cops brought in the largest man I'd ever seen. This guy was *huge*. Giant muscles. Dark skin. Hardened face. He looked like he could kill all of us. Me and the other prisoners who'd been acting tough with one another—the second he walked in our tough-guy routines were over. Everyone was terrified. We all stared at him. "Oh, fuck . . ."

For whatever reason this guy was half naked when the cops picked him up. He was wearing clothes the police had scrounged up for him at the station, this torn-up wifebeater that was way too small, pants so short on him they looked like capris. He looked like a black version of the Incredible Hulk.

This guy went and sat alone in the corner. Nobody said a word. Everyone watched and waited, nervously, to see what he would do. Then one of the cops came back and called the Hulk over; they needed information from him. The cop started asking him a bunch of questions, but the guy kept shaking his head and saying he didn't understand. The cop was speaking Zulu. The Hulk was speaking Tsonga. Black person to black person, and neither could understand the other— the Tower of Babel. Few people in South Africa speak Tsonga, but since my stepfather was Tsonga I had picked it up along the way. I overheard the cop and the other guy going back and forth with nothing getting across, so I stepped in and translated for them and sorted everything out.

Nelson Mandela once said, "If you talk to a man in a language he understands, that goes to his head. If you talk to him in his language, that goes to his heart." He was so right. When you make the effort to speak someone else's language, even if it's just basic phrases here and there, you are saying to them, "I understand that you have a culture and identity that exists beyond me. I see you as a human being."

That is exactly what happened with the Hulk. The second I spoke to him, this face that had seemed so threatening and mean lit up with gratitude. *"Ah, na khensa, na khensa, na khensa. Hi wena mani? Mufana wa mukhaladi u xitiela kwini xiTsonga? U huma kwini?"* "Oh, thank you, thank you, thank you. Who are you? How does a colored guy know Tsonga? Where are you from?"

Once we started talking I realized he wasn't the Hulk at all. He was the sweetest man, a gentle giant, the biggest teddy bear in the world. He was simple, not educated. I'd assumed he was in for murder, for squashing a family to death with his bare hands, but it wasn't anything like that. He'd been arrested for shoplifting PlayStation games. He was out of work and needed money to send to his family back home, and when he saw how much these games sold for he thought he could steal a few and sell them to white kids and make a lot of money. As soon as he told me that, I knew he wasn't some hardened criminal. I know the world of pirated things—stolen videogames have no value because it's cheaper and less risky to copy them, like Bolo's parents did.

I tried to help him out a bit. I told him my trick of putting off your bail hearing to get your defense together, so he stayed in the cell, too, biding his time, and we hit it off and hung out for a few days, having a good time, getting to know each other. No one else in the cell knew what to make of us, the ruthless colored gangster and his menacing, Hulk-like friend. He told me his story, a South African story that was all too familiar to me: The man grows up under apartheid, working on a farm, part of what's essentially a slave labor force. It's a living hell but it's at least something. He's paid a pittance but at least he's paid. He's told where to be and what to do every waking minute of his day. Then apartheid ends and he doesn't even have that anymore. He finds his way to Johannesburg, looking for work, trying to feed his children back home. But he's lost. He has no education. He has no skills. He doesn't know what to do, doesn't know where to be. The world has been taught to be scared of him, but the reality is that he is scared of the world because he has none of the tools necessary to cope with it. So what does he do? He takes shit. He becomes a petty thief. He's in and out of jail. He gets lucky and finds some construction work, but then he gets laid off from that, and a few days later he's in a shop and he sees some Play-Station games and he grabs them, but he doesn't even know enough to know that he's stolen something of no value.

I felt terrible for him. The more time I spent in jail, the more I realized that the law isn't rational at all. It's a lottery. What color is your skin? How much money do you have? Who's your lawyer? Who's the judge? Shoplifting PlayStation games was less of an offense than driving with bad number plates. He had committed a crime, but he was no more a criminal than I was. The difference was that he didn't have any friends or family to help him out. He couldn't afford anything but a state attorney. He was going to go stand in the dock, unable to speak or understand English, and everyone in the courtroom was going to assume the worst of him. He was going to go to prison for a while and then be set free with the same nothing he had going in. If I had to guess, he was around thirty-five, forty years old, staring down another thirty-five, forty years of the same.

The day of my hearing came. I said goodbye to my new friend and wished him the best. Then I was handcuffed and put in the back of a police van and driven to the courthouse to meet my fate. In South African courts, to minimize your exposure and your opportunities for escape, the holding cell where you await your hearing is a massive pen below the courtroom; you walk up a set of stairs into the dock rather than being escorted through the corridors. What happens in the holding cell is you're mixed in with the people who've been in prison awaiting trial for weeks and months. It's a weird mix, everything from white-collar criminals to guys picked up on traffic stops to real, hardcore criminals covered with prison tattoos. It's like the cantina scene from *Star Wars*, where the band's playing music and Han Solo's in the corner and all of the bad guys and bounty hunters from all over the universe are hanging out—a wretched hive of scum and villainy, only there's no music and there's no Han Solo.

I was with these people for only a brief window of time, but in that moment I saw the difference between prison and jail. I saw the difference between criminals and people who've committed crimes. I saw the hardness in people's faces. I thought back on how naive I'd been just hours before, thinking jail wasn't so bad and I could handle it. I was now truly afraid of what might happen to me.

When I walked into that holding pen, I was a smooth-skinned, fresh-faced young man. At the time, I had a giant Afro, and the only way to control it was to have it tied back in this ponytail thing that looked really girly. I looked like Maxwell. The guards closed the door behind me, and this creepy old dude yelled out in Zulu from the back, *"Ha, ha, ha! Hhe madoda! Angikaʐe ngibone indoda enhle kangaka! Siʐoba nobusuku obuhle!"* "Yo, yo, yo! Damn, guys. I've never seen a man this beautiful before. It's gonna be a good night tonight!"

Fuuuuuuuuuck.

Right next to me as I walked in was a young man having a complete meltdown, talking to himself, bawling his eyes out. He looked up and locked eyes with me, and I guess he thought I looked like a kindred soul he could talk to. He came straight at me and started crying about how he'd been arrested and thrown in jail and the gangs had stolen his clothes and his shoes and raped him and beat him every day. He wasn't some ruffian. He was well-spoken, educated. He'd been waiting for a year for his case to be heard; he wanted to kill himself. That guy put the fear of God in me.

I looked around the holding cell. There were easily a hundred guys in there, all of them spread out and huddled into their clearly and unmistakably defined racial groups: a whole bunch of black people in one corner, the colored people in a different corner, a couple of Indians off to themselves, and a handful of white guys off to one side. The guys who'd been with me in the police van, the second we walked in, they instinctively, automatically, walked off to join the groups they belonged to. I froze.

I didn't know where to go.

I looked over at the colored corner. I was staring at the most notorious, most violent prison gang in South Africa. I looked like them, but

I wasn't them. I couldn't go over there doing my fake gangster shit and have them discover I was a fraud. No, no, no. That game was over, my friend. The last thing I needed was colored gangsters up against me.

But then what if I went to the black corner? I know that I'm black and I identify as black, but I'm not a black person on the face of it, so would the black guys understand why I was walking over? And what kind of shit would I start by going there? Because going to the black corner as a perceived colored person might piss off the colored gangs even more than going to the colored corner as a fake colored person. Because that's what had happened to me my entire life. Colored people would see me hanging out with blacks, and they'd confront me, want to fight me. I saw myself starting a race war in the holding cell.

"Hey! Why are you hanging out with the blacks?"

"Because I am black."

"No, you're not. You're colored."

"Ah, yes. I know it looks that way, friend, but let me explain. It's a funny story, actually. My father is white and my mother is black and race is a social construct, so . . ."

That wasn't going to work. Not here.

All of this was happening in my head in an instant, on the fly. I was doing crazy calculations, looking at people, scanning the room, assessing the variables. *If I go here, then this. If I go there, then that.* My whole life was flashing before me—the playground at school, the *spaza* shops in Soweto, the streets of Eden Park—every time and every place I ever had to be a chameleon, navigate between groups, explain who I was. It was like the high school cafeteria, only it was the high school cafeteria from hell because if I picked the wrong table I might get beaten or stabbed or raped. I'd never been more scared in my life. But I still had to pick. Because racism exists, and you have to pick a side. You can say that you don't pick sides, but eventually life will force you to pick a side.

That day I picked white. They just didn't look like they could hurt me. It was a handful of average, middle-aged white dudes. I walked over to them. We hung out for a while, chatted a bit. They were mostly in for white-collar crimes, money schemes, fraud and racketeering. They'd be useless if anyone came over looking to start trouble; they'd get their asses kicked as well. But they weren't going to do anything to me. I was safe.

Luckily the time went by fairly quickly. I was in there for only an hour before I was called up to court, where a judge would either let me go or send me to prison to await trial. As I was leaving, one of the white guys reached over to me. "Make sure you don't come back down here," he said. "Cry in front of the judge; do whatever you have to do. If you go up and get sent back down here, your life will never be the same."

Up in the courtroom, I found my lawyer waiting. My cousin Mlungisi was there, too, in the gallery, ready to post my bail if things went my way.

The bailiff read out my case number, and the judge looked up at me. "How are you?" he said.

I broke down. I'd been putting on this tough-guy facade for nearly a week, and I just couldn't do it anymore.

"I-I'm not fine, Your Honor. I'm not fine."

He looked confused. "What?!"

I said, "I'm not fine, sir. I'm really suffering."

"Why are you telling me this?"

"Because you asked how I was."

"Who asked you?"

"You did. You just asked me."

"I didn't say, '*How* are you?' I said, '*Who* are you?' Why would I waste time asking 'How are you?'! This is jail. I know everyone is suffering down there. If I asked everyone 'How are you?' we'd be here all day. I said, '*Who* are you?' State your name for the record."

"Trevor Noah."

"Okay. Now we can carry on."

The whole courtroom started laughing, so then I started laughing, too. But now I was even more petrified because I didn't want the judge to think I wasn't taking him seriously because I was laughing.

It turned out that I needn't have been worried. Everything that happened next took only a few minutes. My lawyer had talked to the prosecutor and everything had been arranged beforehand. He presented my case. I had no priors. I wasn't dangerous. There were no objections from the opposing side. The judge assigned my trial date and set my bail, and I was free to go.

I walked out of court and the light of day hit my face and I said, "Sweet *Jesus*, I am never going back there again." It had been only a week, in a cell that wasn't terribly uncomfortable with food that wasn't half bad, but a week in jail is a long, long time. A week without shoelaces is a long, long time. A week with no clocks, with no sun, can feel like an eternity. The thought of anything worse, the thought of doing real time in a real prison, I couldn't even imagine.

I drove with Mlungisi to his place, took a shower, and slept there. The next day he dropped me back at my mom's house. I strolled up the driveway acting real casual. My plan was to say I'd been crashing with Mlungisi for a few days. I walked into the house like nothing had happened. "Hey, Mom! What's up?" Mom didn't say anything, didn't ask me any questions. I was like, *Okay. Cool. We're good.*

I stayed for most of the day. Later in the afternoon we were sitting at the kitchen table, talking. I was telling all these stories, going on about everything Mlungisi and I had been up to that week, and I caught my mom giving me this look, slowly shaking her head. It was a different look than I had ever seen her give before. It wasn't "One day, I'm going to catch you." It wasn't anger or disapproval. It was disappointment. She was hurt.

"What?" I said. "What is it?"

She said, "Boy, who do you think paid your bail? Hmm? Who do you think paid your lawyer? Do you think I'm an idiot? Did you think no one would tell me?"

The truth came spilling out. Of course she'd known: the car. It had been missing the whole time. I'd been so wrapped up in dealing with jail and covering my tracks I'd forgotten that the proof of my crime was right there in the yard, the red Mazda missing from the driveway. And of course when I called my friend and he'd asked his dad for the money for the lawyer, the dad had pressed him on what the money was for and, being a parent himself, had called my mother immediately. She'd given my friend the money to pay the lawyer. She'd given my cousin the money to pay my bail. I'd spent the whole week in jail thinking I was so slick. But she'd known everything the whole time.

"I know you see me as some crazy old bitch nagging at you," she said, "but you forget the reason I ride you so hard and give you so much shit is because I love you. Everything I have ever done I've done from a place of love. If I don't punish you, the world will punish you even worse. The world doesn't love you. If the police get you, the police don't love you. When I beat you, I'm trying to save you. When they beat you, they're trying to kill you."

My favorite thing to eat as a kid, and still my favorite dessert of all time, was custard and jelly, what Americans would call Jell-O. One Saturday my mom was planning for a big family celebration and she made a huge bowl of custard and jelly and put it in the fridge. It had every flavor: red, green, and yellow. I couldn't resist it. That whole day, every time I walked past the fridge I'd pop my head in with a spoon and sneak a bite. This was a giant bowl, meant to last for a week for the whole family. I finished it in one day by myself.

That night I went to bed and I got absolutely butchered by mosquitoes. Mosquitoes love to feast on me, and when I was a kid it was bad. They would destroy me at night. I would wake up covered with bites and feel ill to my stomach and itchy all over. Which was exactly what happened this particular Sunday morning. Covered with mosquito bites, my stomach bloated with custard and jelly, I could barely get out of bed. I felt like I was going to vomit. Then my mom walked in.

"Get dressed," she said. "We're going to church."

"I don't feel well."

"That's why we're going to church. That's where Jesus is going to heal you."

"Eh, I'm not sure that's how it works."

My mom and I had different ideas about how Jesus worked. She believed that you pray to Jesus and then Jesus pitches up and does the thing that you need. My views on Jesus were more reality-based.

"Why don't I take medicine," I said, "and then pray to Jesus to thank him for giving us the doctors who invented medicine, because medicine is what makes you feel better, not Jesus."

"You don't need medicine if you have Jesus. Jesus will heal you. Pray to Jesus."

"But is medicine not a blessing from Jesus? And if Jesus gives us medicine and we do not take the medicine, are we not denying the grace that he has given us?"

Like all of our debates about Jesus, this conversation went nowhere.

"Trevor," she said, "if you don't go to church you're going to get worse. You're lucky you got sick on Sunday, because now we're going to church and you can pray to Jesus and Jesus is going to heal you."

"That sounds nice, but why don't I just stay home?"

"No. Get dressed. We're going to church."

———

MY MOTHER'S LIFE

Once I had my hair cornrowed for the matric dance, I started getting attention from girls for the first time. I actually went on dates. At times I thought that it was because I looked better. At other times I thought it was because girls liked the fact that I was going through as much pain as they did to look good. Either way, once I found success, I wasn't going to mess with the formula. I kept going back to the salon every week, spending hours at a time getting my hair straightened and cornrowed. My mom would just roll her eyes. "I could never date a man who spends more time on his hair than I do," she'd say.

Monday through Saturday my mom worked in her office and puttered around her garden dressed like a homeless person. Then Sunday morning for church she'd do her hair and put on a nice dress and some high heels and she looked like a million bucks. Once she was all done up, she couldn't resist teasing me, throwing little verbal jabs the way we'd always do with each other.

"Now who's the best-looking person in the family, eh? I hope you enjoyed your week of being the pretty one, 'cause the queen is back, baby. You spent four hours at the salon to look like that. I just took a shower."

She was just having fun with me; no son wants to talk about how hot his mom is. Because, truth be told, she was beautiful. Beautiful on the outside, beautiful on the inside. She had a self-confidence about her that I never possessed. Even when she was working in the garden, dressed in overalls and covered in mud, you could see how attractive she was.

I can only assume that my mother broke more than a few hearts in her day, but from the time I was born, there were only two men in her life, my father and my stepfather. Right around the corner from my father's house in Yeoville, there was a garage called Mighty Mechanics. Our Volkswagen was always breaking down, and my mom would take it there to get it repaired. We met this really cool guy there, Abel, one of the auto mechanics. I'd see him when we went to fetch the car. The car broke down a lot, so we were there a lot. Eventually it felt like we were there even when there was nothing wrong with the vehicle. I was six, maybe seven. I didn't understand everything that was happening. I just knew that suddenly this guy was around. He was tall, lanky and lean but strong. He had these long arms and big hands. He could lift car engines and gearboxes. He was handsome, but he wasn't good-looking. My mom liked that about him; she used to say there's a type of ugly that women find attractive. She called him Abie. He called her Mbuyi, short for Nombuyiselo.

I liked him, too. Abie was charming and hilarious and had an easy, gracious smile. He loved helping people, too, especially anyone in distress. If someone's car broke down on the freeway, he pulled over to see what he could do. If someone yelled "Stop, thief!" he was the guy who gave chase. The old lady next door needed help moving boxes? He's that guy. He liked to be liked by the world, which made his abuse even harder to deal with. Because if you think someone is a monster and the whole world says he's a saint, you begin to think that you're the bad person. *It must be my fault this is happening* is the only conclusion you can draw, because why are you the only one receiving his wrath?

Abel was always cool with me. He wasn't trying to be my dad, and my dad was still in my life, so I wasn't looking for anyone to replace him. *That's mom's cool friend* is how I thought of him. He started coming out to stay with us in Eden Park. Some nights he'd want us to crash with him at his converted garage flat in Orange Grove, which we did. Then I burned down the white people's house, and that was the end of that. From then on we lived together in Eden Park.

One night my mom and I were at a prayer meeting and she took me aside.

"Hey," she said. "I want to tell you something. Abel and I are going to get married."

Instinctively, without even thinking, I said, "I don't think that's a good idea."

I wasn't upset or anything. I just had a sense about the guy, an intuition. I'd felt it even before the mulberry tree. That night hadn't changed my feelings toward Abel; it had only shown me, in flesh and blood, what he was capable of.

"I understand that it's hard," she said. "I understand that you don't want a new dad."

"No," I said. "It's not that. I like Abel. I like him a lot. But you shouldn't marry him." I didn't know the word "sinister" then, but if I had I probably would have used it. "There's just something not right about him. I don't trust him. I don't think he's a good person."

I'd always been fine with my mom dating this guy, but I'd never considered the possibility of him becoming a permanent addition to our family. I enjoyed being with Abel the same way I enjoyed playing with a tiger cub the first time I went to a tiger sanctuary: I liked it, I had fun with it, but I never thought about bringing it home.

If there was any doubt about Abel, the truth was right there in front of us all along, in his name. He was Abel, the good brother, the good son, a name straight out of the Bible. And he lived up to it as well. He was the firstborn, dutiful, took care of his mother, took care of his siblings. He was the pride of his family.

But Abel was his English name. His Tsonga name was Ngisaveni. It means "Be afraid."

Mom and Abel got married. There was no ceremony, no exchange of rings. They went and signed the papers and that was it. A year or so later, my baby brother, Andrew, was born. I only vaguely remember my mom being gone for a few days, and when she got back there was now this thing in the house that cried and shat and got fed, but when you're nine years older than your sibling, their arrival doesn't change much for you. I wasn't changing diapers; I was out playing arcade games at the shop, running around the neighborhood.

The main thing that marked Andrew's birth for me was our first trip to meet Abel's family during the Christmas holidays. They lived in Tzaneen, a town in Gazankulu, what had been the Tsonga homeland under apartheid. Tzaneen has a tropical climate, hot and humid. The white farms nearby grow some of the most amazing fruit—mangoes, lychees, the most beautiful bananas you've ever seen in your life. That's where all the fruit we export to Europe comes from. But on the black land twenty minutes down the road, the soil has been decimated by years of overfarming and overgrazing. Abel's mother and his sisters were all traditional, stay-at-home moms, and Abel and his younger brother, who was a policeman, supported the family. They were all very kind and generous and accepted us as part of the family right away.

Tsonga culture, I learned, is extremely patriarchal. We're talking about a world where women must bow when they greet a man. Men and women have limited social interactions. The men kill the animals, and the women cook the food. Men are not even allowed in the kitchen. As a nine-year-old boy, I thought this was fantastic. I wasn't allowed to do anything. At home my mom was forever making me do chores—wash the dishes, sweep the house—but when she tried to do that in Tzaneen, the women wouldn't allow it.

"Trevor, make your bed," my mom would say.

"No, no, no, no," Abel's mother would protest. "Trevor must go outside and play."

I was made to run off and have fun while my girl step-cousins had to clean the house and help the women cook. I was in heaven.

My mother loathed every moment of being there. For Abel, a first-born son who was bringing home his own firstborn son, this trip was a huge deal. In the homelands, the firstborn son almost becomes the father/husband by default because the dad is off working in the city. The firstborn son is the man of the house. He raises his siblings. His mom treats him with a certain level of respect as the dad's surrogate. Since this was Abel's big homecoming with Andrew, he expected my mother to play her traditional role, too. But she refused.

The women in Tzaneen had a multitude of jobs during the day. They prepared breakfast, prepared tea, prepared lunch, did the washing and the cleaning. The men had been working all year in the city to support the family, so this was their vacation, more or less. They were at leisure, waited on by the women. They might slaughter a goat or something, do whatever manly tasks needed to be done, but then they would go to an area that was only for men and hang out and drink while the women cooked and cleaned. But my mom had been working in the city all year, too, and Patricia Noah didn't stay in anyone's kitchen. She was a free-roaming spirit. She insisted on walking to the village, going where the men hung out, talking to the men as equals.

The whole tradition of women bowing to the men, my mom found that absurd. But she didn't refuse to do it. She overdid it. She made a mockery of it. The other women would bow before men with this polite little curtsy. My mom would go down and cower, groveling in the dirt like she was worshipping a deity, and she'd stay down there for a long time, like a *really* long time, long enough to make everyone very uncomfortable. That was my mom. Don't fight the system. Mock the system. To Abel, it looked like his wife didn't respect him. Every other man had some docile girl from the village, and here he'd come with this modern woman, a Xhosa woman no less, a culture whose women were thought of as particularly loudmouthed and promiscuous. The two of them fought and bickered the whole time, and after that first trip my mother refused to go back.

Up to that point I'd lived my whole life in a world run by women, but after my mom and Abel were married, and especially after Andrew was born, I watched him try to assert himself and impose his ideas of what he thought his family should be. One thing that became clear early on was that those ideas did not include me. I was a reminder that my mom had lived a life before him. I didn't even share his color. His family was him, my mom, and the new baby. My family was my mom and me. I actually appreciated that about him. Sometimes he was my buddy, sometimes not, but he never pretended our relationship was anything other than what it was. We'd joke around and laugh together. We'd watch TV together. He'd slip me pocket money now and again after my mother said I'd had enough. But he never gave me a birthday present or a Christmas present. He never gave me the affection of a father. I was never his son.

Abel's presence in the house brought with it new rules. One of the first things he did was kick Fufi and Panther out of the house.

"No dogs in the house."

"But we've always had the dogs in the house."

"Not anymore. In an African home, dogs sleep outside. People sleep inside."

Putting the dogs in the yard was Abel's way of saying, "We're going to do things around here the way they're supposed to be done." When they were just dating, my mother was still the free spirit, doing what she wanted, going where she wanted. Slowly, those things got reined in. I could feel that he was trying to rein in our independence. He even got upset about church. "You cannot be at church the whole day," he'd say. "My wife is gone all day, and what will people say? 'Why is his wife not around? Where is she? Who goes to church for the whole day?' No, no, no. This brings disrespect to me."

He tried to stop her from spending so much time at church, and one of the most effective tools he used was to stop fixing my mother's car. It would break down, and he'd purposefully let it sit. My mom couldn't afford another car, and she couldn't get the car fixed somewhere else. You're married to a mechanic and you're going to get your car fixed by another mechanic? That's worse than cheating. So Abel became our only transport, and he would refuse to take us places. Ever defiant, my mother would take minibuses to get to church.

Losing the car also meant losing access to my dad. We had to ask Abel for rides into town, and he didn't like what they were for. It was an insult to his manhood.

"We need to go to Yeoville."

"Why are you going to Yeoville?"

"To see Trevor's dad."

"What? No, no. How can I take my wife and her child and drop you off there? You're insulting me. What do I tell my friends? What do I tell my family? My wife is at another man's house? The man who made that child with her? No, no, no."

I saw my father less and less. Not long after, he moved down to Cape Town.

Abel wanted a traditional marriage with a traditional wife. For a long time I wondered why he ever married a woman like my mom in the first place, as she was the opposite of that in every way. If he wanted a woman to bow to him, there were plenty of girls back in Tzaneen being raised solely for that purpose. The way my mother always explained it, the traditional man wants a woman to be subservient, but he never falls in love with subservient women. He's attracted to independent women. "He's like an exotic bird collector," she said. "He only wants a woman who is free because his dream is to put her in a cage."

When we first met Abel, he smoked a lot of weed. He drank, too, but it was mostly weed. Looking back, I almost miss his pothead days because the weed mellowed him out. He'd smoke, chill, watch TV, and fall asleep. I think subconsciously it was something he knew he needed to do to take the edge off his anger. He stopped smoking after he and my mom got married. She made him stop for religious reasons—the body is a temple and so on. But what none of us saw coming was that when he stopped smoking weed he just replaced it with alcohol. He started drinking more and more. He never came home from work sober. An average day was a six-pack of beer after work. Weeknights he'd have a buzz on. Some Fridays and Saturdays he just didn't come home.

When Abel drank, his eyes would go red, bloodshot. That was the clue I learned to read. I always thought of Abel as a cobra: calm, perfectly still, then explosive. There was no ranting and raving, no clenched fists. He'd be very quiet, and then out of nowhere the violence would come. The eyes were my only clue to stay away. His eyes were everything. They were the eyes of the Devil.

Late one night we woke up to a house filled with smoke. Abel hadn't come home by the time we'd gone to bed, and I'd fallen asleep in my mother's room with her and Andrew, who was still a baby. I jerked awake to her shaking me and screaming. *"Trevor! Trevor!"* There was smoke everywhere. We thought the house was burning down.

My mom ran down the hallway to the kitchen, where she discovered the kitchen on fire. Abel had driven home drunk, blind drunk, drunker than we'd ever seen him before. He'd been hungry, tried to heat up some food on the stove, and passed out on the couch while it was cooking. The pot had burned itself out and burned up the kitchen wall behind the stove, and smoke was billowing everywhere. She turned off the stove and opened the doors and the windows to try to air the place out. Then she went over to the couch and woke him up and started berating him for nearly burning the house down. He was too drunk to care.

She came back into the bedroom, picked up the phone, and called my grandmother. She started going on and on about Abel and his drinking. "This man, he's going to kill us one day. He almost burnt the house down . . ."

Abel walked into the bedroom, very calm, very quiet. His eyes were blood red, his eyelids heavy. He put his finger on the cradle and hung up the call. My mom lost it.

"How dare you! Don't you hang up my phone call! What do you think you're doing?!"

"You don't tell people what's happening in this house," he said.

"Oh, please! You're worried about what the world is thinking? Worry about this world! Worry about what your family is thinking!"

Abel towered over my mother. He didn't raise his voice, didn't get angry.

"Mbuyi," he said softly, "you don't respect me."

"Respect?! You almost burned down our house. Respect? Oh, please! Earn your respect! You want me to respect you as a man, then act like a man! Drinking your money in the streets, and where are your child's diapers?! Respect?! Earn your respect—"

"Mbuyi—"

"You're not a man; you're a child—"

"Mbuyi—"

"I can't have a child for a husband—"

"Mbuyi—"

"I've got my own children to raise—"

"Mbuyi, shut up—"

"A man who comes home drunk—"

"Mbuyi, shut up—"

"And burns down the house with his children—"

"Mbuyi, shut up—"

"And you call yourself a father—"

Then out of nowhere, like a clap of thunder when there were no clouds, *crack!*, he smacked her across the face. She ricocheted off the wall and collapsed like a ton of bricks. I'd never seen anything like it. She went down and stayed down for a good thirty seconds. Andrew started screaming. I don't remember going to pick him up, but I clearly remember holding him at some point. My mom pulled herself up and struggled back to her feet and launched right back into him. She'd clearly been knocked for a loop, but she was trying to act more with-it than she was. I could see the disbelief in her face. This had never happened to her before in her life. She got right back in his face and started shouting at him.

"Did you just hit me?"

The whole time, in my head, I kept thinking the same thing Abel was saying. *Shut up, Mom. Shut up. You're going to make it worse.* Because I knew, as the receiver of many beatings, the one thing that doesn't help is talking back. But she wouldn't stay quiet.

"Did you just hit me?"

"Mbuyi, I told you—"

"No man has ever! Don't think you can control me when you can't even control—"

Crack! He hit her again. She stumbled back but this time didn't fall. She scrambled, grabbed me, and grabbed Andrew.

"Let's go. We're leaving."

We ran out of the house and up the road. It was the dead of night, cold outside. I was wearing nothing but a T-shirt and sweatpants. We walked to the Eden Park police station, over a kilometer away. My mom marched us in, and there were two cops on duty at the front desk.

"I'm here to lay a charge," she said.

"What are you here to lay a charge about?"

"I'm here to lay a charge against the man who hit me."

To this day I'll never forget the patronizing, condescending way they spoke to her.

"Calm down, lady. Calm down. Who hit you?"

"My husband."

"Your husband? What did you do? Did you make him angry?"

"Did I . . . what? No. He hit me. I'm here to lay a charge against—"

"No, no. Ma'am. Why do you wanna make a case, eh? You sure you want to do this? Go home and talk to your husband. You do know once you lay charges you can't take them back? He'll have a criminal record. His life will never be the same. Do you really want your husband going to jail?"

My mom kept insisting that they take a statement and open a case, and they actually refused—they refused to write up a charge sheet.

"This is a family thing," they said. "You don't want to involve the police. Maybe you want to think it over and come back in the morning."

Mom started yelling at them, demanding to see the station commander, and right then Abel walked into the station. He'd driven down. He'd sobered up a bit, but he was still drunk, driving into a police station. That didn't matter. He walked over to the cops, and the station turned into a boys' club. Like they were a bunch of old pals.

"Hey, guys," he said. "You know how it is. You know how women can be. I just got a little angry, that's all."

"It's okay, man. We know. It happens. Don't worry."

I had never seen anything like it. I was nine years old, and I still thought of the police as the good guys. You get in trouble, you call the police, and those flashing red-and-blue lights are going to come and save you. But I remember standing there watching my mom, flabbergasted, horrified that these cops wouldn't help her. That's when I realized the police were not who I thought they were. They were men first, and police second.

We left the station. My mother took me and Andrew, and we went out to stay with my grandmother in Soweto for a while. A few weeks later, Abel drove over and apologized. Abel was always sincere and heartfelt with his apologies: He didn't mean it. He knows he was wrong. He'll never do it again. My grandmother convinced my mom that she should give Abel a second chance. Her argument was basically, "All men do it." My grandfather, Temperance, had hit her. Leaving Abel was no guarantee it wouldn't happen again, and at least Abel was willing to apologize. So my mom decided to give him another chance. We drove back to Eden Park together, and for years, nothing—for *years* Abel didn't lay a finger on her. Or me. Everything went back to the way it was.

Abel was an amazing mechanic, probably one of the best around at the time. He'd been to technical college, graduated first in his class. He'd had job offers from BMW and Mercedes. His business thrived on referrals. People would bring their cars from all over the city for him to fix because he could work miracles on them. My mom truly believed in him. She thought she could raise him up, help him make good on his potential, not merely as a mechanic but as the owner of his own workshop.

As headstrong and independent as my mom is, she remains the woman who gives back. She gives and gives and gives; that is her nature. She refused to be subservient to Abel at home, but she did want him to succeed as a man. If she could make their marriage a true marriage of equals, she was willing to pour herself into it completely, the same way she poured herself into her children. At some point, Abel's boss decided to sell Mighty Mechanics and retire. My mom had some money saved, and she helped Abel buy it. They moved the workshop from Yeoville to the industrial area of Wynberg, just west of Alex, and Mighty Mechanics became the new family business.

When you first go into business there are so many things nobody tells you. That's especially true when you're two young black people, a secretary and a mechanic, coming out of a time when blacks had never been allowed to own businesses at all. One of the things nobody tells you is that when you buy a business you buy its debt. After my mom and Abel opened up the books on Mighty Mechanics and came to a full realization of what they'd bought, they saw how much trouble the company was already in.

The garage gradually took over our lives. I'd get out of school and walk the five kilometers from Maryvale to the workshop. I'd sit for hours and try to do my homework with the machines and repairs going on around me. Inevitably Abel would get behind schedule on a car, and since he was our ride, we'd have to wait for him to finish before we could go home. It started out as "We're running late. Go nap in a car, and we'll tell you when we're leaving." I'd crawl in the backseat of some sedan, they'd wake me up at midnight, and we'd drive all the way back out to Eden Park and crash. Then pretty soon it was "We're running late. Go sleep in a car, and we'll wake you for school in the morning." We started sleeping at the garage. At first it was one or two nights a week, then three or four. Then my mom sold the house and put that money into the business as well. She went all in. She gave up everything for him.

From that point on we lived in the garage. It was a warehouse, basically, and not the fancy, romantic sort of warehouse hipsters might one day turn into lofts. No, no. It was a cold, empty space. Gray concrete floors stained with oil and grease, old junk cars and car parts everywhere. Near the front, next to the roller door that opened onto the street, there was a tiny office built out of drywall for doing paperwork and such. In the back was a kitchenette, just a sink, a portable hot plate, and some cabinets. To bathe, there was only an open wash basin, like a janitor's sink, with a showerhead rigged up above.

Abel and my mom slept with Andrew in the office on a thin mattress they'd roll out on the floor. I slept in the cars. I got really good at sleeping in cars. I know all the best cars to sleep in. The worst were the cheap ones, Volkswagens, low-end Japanese sedans. The seats barely reclined, no headrests, cheap fake-leather upholstery. I'd spend half the night trying not to slide off the seat. I'd wake up with sore knees because I couldn't stretch out and extend my legs. German cars were wonderful, especially Mercedes. Big, plush leather seats, like couches. They were cold when you first climbed in, but they were well insulated and warmed up nicely. All I needed was my school blazer to curl up under, and I could get really cozy inside a Mercedes. But the best, hands-down, were American cars. I used to pray for a customer to come in with a big Buick with bench seats. If I saw one of those, I'd be like, *Yes!* It was rare for American cars to come in, but when they did, boy, was I in heaven.

Since Mighty Mechanics was now a family business, and I was family, I also had to work. There was no more time for play. There wasn't even time for homework. I'd walk home, the school uniform would come off, the overalls would go on, and I'd get under the hood of some sedan. I got to a point where I could do a basic service on a car by myself, and often I did. Abel would say, "That Honda. Minor service." And I'd get under the hood. Day in and day out. Points, plugs, condensers, oil filters, air filters. Install new seats, change tires, swap headlights, fix taillights. Go to the parts shop, buy the parts, back to the workshop. Eleven years old, and that was my life. I was falling behind in school. I wasn't getting anything done. My teachers used to come down on me.

"Why aren't you doing your homework?"

"I can't do my homework. I have work, at home."

We worked and worked and worked, but no matter how many hours we put in, the business kept losing money. We lost everything. We couldn't even afford real food. There was one month I'll never forget, the worst month of my life. We were so broke that for weeks we ate nothing but bowls of *marogo*, a kind of wild spinach, cooked with caterpillars. Mopane worms, they're called. Mopane worms are literally the cheapest thing that only the poorest of poor people eat. I grew up poor, but there's poor and then there's "Wait, I'm eating worms." Mopane worms are the sort of thing where even people in Soweto would be like, "Eh . . . no." They're these spiny, brightly colored caterpillars the size of your finger. They're nothing like escargot, where someone took a snail and gave it a fancy name. They're fucking worms. They have black spines that prick the roof of your mouth as you're eating them. When you bite into a mopane worm, it's not uncommon for its yellow-green excrement to squirt into your mouth.

For a while I sort of enjoyed the caterpillars. It was like a food adventure, but then over the course of weeks, eating them every day, day after day, I couldn't take it anymore. I'll never forget the day I bit a mopane worm in half and that yellow-green ooze came out and I thought, "I'm eating caterpillar shit." Instantly I wanted to throw up. I snapped and ran to my mom crying. "I don't want to eat caterpillars anymore!" That night she scraped some money together and bought us chicken. As poor as we'd been in the past, we'd never been without food.

That was the period of my life I hated the most—work all night, sleep in some car, wake up, wash up in a janitor's sink, brush my teeth in a little metal basin, brush my hair in the rearview mirror of a Toyota, then try to get dressed without getting oil and grease all over my school clothes so the kids at school won't know I live in a garage. Oh, I hated it so much. I hated cars. I hated sleeping in cars. I hated working on cars. I hated getting my hands dirty. I hated eating worms. I hated it all.

I didn't hate my mom, or even Abel, funnily enough. Because I saw how hard everyone was working. At first I didn't know about the mistakes being made on the business level that were making it hard, so it just felt like a hard situation. But eventually I started to see why the business was hemorrhaging money. I used to go around and buy auto parts for Abel, and I learned that he was buying his parts on credit. The vendors were charging him a crazy markup. The debt was crippling the company, and instead of paying off the debt he was drinking what little cash he made. Brilliant mechanic, horrible businessman.

At a certain point, in order to try to save the garage, my mother quit her job at ICI and stepped in to help him run the workshop. She brought her office skills to the garage full-time and started keeping the books, making the schedule, balancing the accounts. And it was going well, until Abel started to feel like she was running his business. People started commenting on it as well. Clients were getting their cars on time, vendors were getting paid on time, and they would say, "Hey, Abie, this workshop is going so much better now that your wife has taken over." That didn't help.

We lived in the workshop for close to a year, and then my mom had had enough. She was willing to help him, but not if he was going to drink all the profits. She had always been independent, self-sufficient, but she'd lost that part of herself at the mercy of someone else's failed dream. At a certain point she said, "I can't do this anymore. I'm out of this. I'm done." She went out and got a job as a secretary with a real-estate developer, and somehow, between that and borrowing against whatever equity was left in Abel's workshop, she was able to get us the house in Highlands North. We moved, the workshop was seized by Abel's creditors, and that was the end of that.

Growing up I suffered no shortage of my mother's old school, Old Testament discipline. She spared no rod and spoiled no child. With Andrew, she was different. He got spankings at first, but they tapered off and eventually went away. When I asked her why I got beatings and Andrew didn't, she made a joke about it like she does with everything. "I beat you like that because you could take it," she said. "I can't hit your little brother the same way because he's a skinny little stick. He'll break. But you, God gave you that ass for whipping." Even though she was kidding, I could tell that the reason she didn't beat Andrew was because she'd had a genuine change of heart on the matter. It was a lesson she'd learned, oddly enough, from me.

I grew up in a world of violence, but I myself was never violent at all. Yes, I played pranks and set fires and broke windows, but I never attacked people. I never hit anyone. I was never angry. I just didn't see myself that way. My mother had exposed me to a different world than the one she grew up in. She bought me the books she never got to read. She took me to the schools that she never got to go to. I immersed myself in those worlds and I came back looking at the world a different way. I saw that not all families are violent. I saw the futility of violence, the cycle that just repeats itself, the damage that's inflicted on people that they in turn inflict on others.

I saw, more than anything, that relationships are not sustained by violence but by love. Love is a creative act. When you love someone you create a new world for them. My mother did that for me, and with the progress I made and the things I learned, I came back and created a new world and a new understanding for her. After that, she never raised her hand to her children again. Unfortunately, by the time she stopped, Abel had started.

In all the times I received beatings from my mom, I was never scared of her. I didn't like it, certainly. When she said, "I hit you out of love," I didn't necessarily agree with her thinking. But I understood that it was discipline and it was being done for a purpose. The first time Abel hit me I felt something I had never felt before. I felt terror.

I was in grade six, my last year at Maryvale. We'd moved to Highlands North, and I'd gotten in trouble at school for forging my mom's signature on some document; there was some activity I didn't want to participate in, so I'd signed the release in her name to get out of it. The school called my mom, and she asked me about it when I got home that afternoon. I was certain she was going to punish me, but this turned out to be one of those times when she didn't care. She said I should have just asked her; she would have signed the form anyway. Then Abel, who'd been sitting in the kitchen with us, watching the whole thing, said, "Hey, can I talk to you for a second?" Then he took me into this tiny room, a walk-in pantry off the kitchen, and he closed the door behind us.

He was standing between me and the door, but I didn't think anything of it. It didn't occur to me to be scared. Abel had never tried to discipline me before. He'd never even given me a lecture. It was always "Mbuyi, your son did this," and then my mother would handle it. And this was the middle of the afternoon. He was completely sober, which made what happened next all the more terrifying.

"Why did you forge your mother's signature?" he said.

I started making up some excuse. "Oh, I, uh, forgot to bring the form home—"

"Don't lie to me. Why did you forge your mom's signature?"

I started stammering out more bullshit, oblivious to what was coming, and then out of nowhere it came.

The first blow hit me in the ribs. My mind flashed: *It's a trap!* I'd never been in a fight before, had never learned how to fight, but I had this instinct that told me to get in close. I had seen what those long arms could do. I'd seen him take down my mom, but more important, I'd seen him take down grown men. Abel never hit people with a punch; I never saw him punch another person with a closed fist. But he had this ability to hit a grown man across his face with an open hand and they'd crumple. He was that strong. I looked at his arms and I knew, *Don't be on the other end of those things.* I ducked in close and he kept hitting and hitting, but I was in too tight for him to land any solid blows. Then he caught on and he stopped hitting and started trying to grapple and wrestle me. He did this thing where he grabbed the skin on my arms and pinched it between his thumb and forefinger and twisted hard. Jesus, that hurt.

It was the most terrifying moment of my life. I had never been that scared before, ever. Because there was no purpose to it—that's what made it so terrifying. It wasn't discipline. Nothing about it was coming from a place of love. It didn't feel like something that would end with me learning a lesson about forging my mom's signature. It felt like something that would end when he wanted it to end, when his rage was spent. It felt like there was something inside him that wanted to destroy me.

Abel was much bigger and stronger than me, but being in a confined space was to my advantage because he didn't have the room to maneuver. As he grappled and punched I somehow managed to twist and wriggle my way around him and slip out the door. I was quick, but Abel was quick as well. He chased me. I ran out of the house and jumped over the gate, and I ran and I ran and I ran. The last time I turned around he was rounding the gate, coming out of the yard after me. Until I turned twenty-five years old, I had a recurring nightmare of the look on his face as he came around that corner.

The moment I saw him I put my head down and ran. I ran like the Devil was chasing me. Abel was bigger and faster, but this was my neighborhood. You couldn't catch me in my neighborhood. I knew every alley and every street, every wall to climb over, every fence to slip through. I was ducking through traffic, cutting through yards. I have no idea when he gave up because I never looked back. I ran and ran and ran, as far as my legs would carry me. I was in Bramley, three neighborhoods away, before I stopped. I found a hiding place in some bushes and crawled inside and huddled there for what felt like hours.

You don't have to teach me a lesson twice. From that day until the day I left home, I lived like a mouse in that house. If Abel was in a room, I was out of the room. If he was in one corner, I was in the other corner. If he walked into a room, I would get up and act like I was going to the kitchen, then when I reentered the room, I would make sure I was close to the exit. He could be in the happiest, friendliest mood. Didn't matter. Never again did I let him come between me and a door. Maybe a couple of times after that I was sloppy and he'd land a punch or a kick before I could get away, but I never trusted him again, not for a moment.

It was different for Andrew. Andrew was Abel's son, flesh of his flesh, blood of his blood. Despite being nine years younger than me,

Andrew was really the eldest son in that house, Abel's firstborn, and that accorded him a respect that I and even my mother never enjoyed. And Andrew had nothing but love for that man, despite his shortcomings. Because of that love, I think, out of all of us, Andrew was the only one who wasn't afraid. He was the lion tamer, only he'd been raised by the lion—he couldn't love the beast any less despite knowing what it was capable of. For me, the first glint of anger or madness from Abel and I was gone. Andrew would stay and try to talk Abel down. He'd even get between Abel and Mom. I remember one night when Abel threw a bottle of Jack Daniel's at Andrew's head. It just missed him and exploded on the wall. Which is to say that Andrew stayed long enough to get the bottle thrown at him. I wouldn't have stuck around long enough for Abel to get a bead on me.

When Mighty Mechanics went under, Abel had to get his cars out. Someone was taking over the property; there were liens against his assets. It was a mess. That's when he started running his workshop out of our yard. It's also when my mother divorced him.

In African culture there's legal marriage and traditional marriage. Just because you divorce someone legally doesn't mean they are no longer your spouse. Once Abel's debts and his terrible business decisions started impacting my mother's credit and her ability to support her sons, she wanted out. "I don't have debts," she said. "I don't have bad credit. I'm not doing these things with you." We were still a family and they were still traditionally married, but she divorced him in order to separate their financial affairs. She also took her name back.

Because Abel had started running an unlicensed business in a residential area, one of the neighbors filed a petition to get rid of us. My mom applied for a license to be able to operate a business on the property. The workshop stayed, but Abel kept running it into the ground, drinking his money. At the same time, my mother started moving up at the real-estate company she worked for, taking on more responsibilities and earning a better salary. His workshop became like a side hobby almost. He was supposed to pay for Andrew's school fees and groceries, but he started falling behind even on that, and soon my mom was paying for everything. She paid the electricity. She paid the mortgage. He literally contributed nothing.

That was the turning point. When my mother started making more money and getting her independence back—that's when we saw the dragon emerge. The drinking got worse. He grew more and more violent. It wasn't long after coming for me in the pantry that Abel hit my mom for the second time. I can't recall the details of it, because now it's muddled with all the other times that came after it. I do remember that the police were called. They came out to the house this time, but again it was like a boys' club. "Hey, guys. These women, you know how they are." No report was made. No charges were filed.

Whenever he'd hit her or come after me, my mom would find me crying afterward and take me aside. She'd give me the same talk every time.

"Pray for Abel," she'd say. "Because he doesn't hate us. He hates himself."

To a kid this makes no sense. "Well, if he hates himself," I'd say, "why doesn't he kick himself?"

Abel was one of those drinkers where once he was gone you'd look into his eyes and you didn't even see the same person. I remember one night he came home fuckdrunk, stumbling through the house. He stumbled into my room, muttering to himself, and I woke up to see him whip out his dick and start pissing on the floor. He thought he was in the bathroom. That's how drunk he would get—he wouldn't know which room in the house he was in. There were so many nights he would stumble into my room thinking it was his and kick me out of bed and pass out. I'd yell at him, but it was like talking to a zombie. I'd go sleep on the couch.

He'd get wasted with his crew in the backyard every evening after work, and many nights he'd end up fighting with one of them. Someone would say something Abel didn't like, and he'd beat the shit out of him. The guy wouldn't show up for work Tuesday or Wednesday, but then by Thursday he'd be back because he needed the job. Every few weeks it was the same story, like clockwork.

Abel kicked the dogs, too. Fufi, mostly. Panther was smart enough to stay away, but dumb, lovable Fufi was forever trying to be Abel's friend. She'd cross his path or be in his way when he'd had a few, and he'd give her the boot. After that she'd go and hide somewhere for a while. Fufi getting kicked was always the warning sign that shit was about to go down. The dogs and the workers in the yard often got the first taste of his anger, and that would let the rest of us know to lie low. I'd usually go find Fufi wherever she was hiding and be with her.

The strange thing was that when Fufi got kicked she never yelped or cried. When the vet diagnosed her as deaf, he also found out she had some condition where she didn't have a fully developed sense of touch. She didn't feel pain. Which was why she would always start over with Abel like it was a new day. He'd kick her, she'd hide, then she'd be right back the next morning, wagging her tail. "Hey. I'm here. I'll give you another chance."

And he always got the second chance. The Abel who was likable and charming never went away. He had a drinking problem, but he was a nice guy. We had a family. Growing up in a home of abuse, you struggle with the notion that you can love a person you hate, or hate a person you love. It's a strange feeling. You want to live in a world where someone is good or bad, where you either hate them or love them, but that's not how people are.

There was an undercurrent of terror that ran through the house, but the actual beatings themselves were not that frequent. I think if they had been, the situation would have ended sooner. Ironically, the good times in between were what allowed it to drag out and escalate as far as it did. He hit my mom once, then the next time was three years later, and it was just a little bit worse. Then it was two years later, and it was just a little bit worse. Then it was a year later, and it was just a little bit worse. It was sporadic enough to where you'd think it wouldn't happen again, but it was frequent enough that you never forgot it was possible. There was a rhythm to it. I remember one time, after one terrible incident, nobody spoke to him for over a month. No words, no eye contact, no conversations, nothing. We moved through the house as strangers, at different times. Complete silent treatment. Then one morning you're in the kitchen and there's a nod. "Hey." "Hey." Then a week later it's "Did you see the thing on the news?" "Yeah." Then the next week there's a joke and a laugh. Slowly, slowly, life goes back to how it was. Six months, a year later, you do it all again.

One afternoon I came home from Sandringham and my mom was very upset and worked up.

"This man is unbelievable," she said.

"What happened?"

"He bought a gun."

"What? A *gun*? What do you mean, 'He bought a gun'?"

A gun was such a ridiculous thing in my world. In my mind, only cops and criminals had guns. Abel had gone out and bought a 9mm Parabellum Smith & Wesson. Sleek and black, menacing. It didn't look cool like guns in movies. It looked like it killed things.

"Why did he buy a gun?" I asked.

"I don't know."

She said she'd confronted him about it, and he'd gone off on some nonsense about the world needing to learn to respect him.

"He thinks he's the policeman of the world," she said. "And that's the problem with the world. We have people who cannot police themselves, so they want to police everyone else around them."

Not long after that, I moved out. The atmosphere had become toxic for me. I'd reached the point where I was as big as Abel. Big enough to punch back. A father does not fear retribution from his son, but I was not his son. He knew that. The analogy my mom used was that there were now two male lions in the house. "Every time he looks at you he sees your father," she'd say. "You're a constant reminder of another man. He hates you, and you need to leave. You need to leave before you become like him."

It was also just time for me to go. Regardless of Abel, our plan had always been for me to move out after school. My mother never wanted me to be like my uncle, one of those men, unemployed and still living at home with his mother. She helped me get my flat, and I moved out. The flat was only ten minutes away from the house, so I was always around to drop in to help with errands or have dinner once in a while. But, most important, whatever was going on with Abel, I didn't have to be involved.

At some point my mom moved to a separate bedroom in the house, and from then on they were married in name only, not even cohabitating but coexisting. That state of affairs lasted a year, maybe two. Andrew had turned nine, and in my world I was counting down until he turned eighteen, thinking that would finally free my mom from this abusive man. Then one afternoon my mom called and asked me to come by the house. A few hours later, I popped by.

"Trevor," she said. "I'm pregnant."

"Sorry, what?"

"I'm pregnant."

"*What?!*"

Good Lord, I was furious. I was so angry. She herself seemed resolute, as determined as ever, but with an undertone of sadness I had never seen before, like the news had devastated her at first but she'd since reconciled herself to the reality of it.

"How could you let this happen?"

"Abel and I, we made up. I moved back into the bedroom. It was just one night, and then . . . I became pregnant. I don't know how."

She didn't know. She was forty-four years old. She'd had her tubes tied after Andrew. Even her doctor had said, "This shouldn't be possible. We don't know how this happened."

I was boiling with rage. All we had to do was wait for Andrew to grow up, and it was going to be over, and now it was like she'd re-upped on the contract.

"So you're going to have this child with this man? You're going to stay with this man another eighteen years? Are you crazy?"

"God spoke to me, Trevor. He told me, 'Patricia, I don't do anything by mistake. There is nothing I give you that you cannot handle.' I'm pregnant for a reason. I know what kind of kids I can make. I know what kind of sons I can raise. I can raise this child. I will raise this child."

Nine months later Isaac was born. She called him Isaac because in the Bible Sarah gets pregnant when she's like a hundred years old and she's not supposed to be having children and that's what she names her son.

Isaac's birth pushed me even further away. I visited less and less. Then I popped by one afternoon and the house was in chaos, police cars out front, the aftermath of another fight.

He'd hit her with a bicycle. Abel had been berating one of his workers in the yard, and my mom had tried to get between them. Abel was furious that she'd contradicted him in front of an employee, so he picked up Andrew's bike and he beat her with it. Again she called the police, and the cops who showed up this time actually knew Abel. He'd fixed their cars. They were pals. No charges were filed. Nothing happened.

That time I confronted him. I was big enough now.

"You can't keep doing this," I said. "This is not right."

He was apologetic. He always was. He didn't puff out his chest and get defensive or anything like that.

"I know," he said. "I'm sorry. I don't like doing these things, but you know how your mom is. She can talk a lot and she doesn't listen. I feel like your mom doesn't respect me sometimes. She came and disrespected me in front of my workers. I can't have these other men looking at me like I don't know how to control my wife."

After the bicycle, my mom hired contractors she knew through the real-estate business to build her a separate house in the backyard, like a little servants' quarters, and she moved in there with Isaac.

"This is the most insane thing I've ever seen," I told her.

"This is all I can do," she said. "The police won't help me. The government won't protect me. Only my God can protect me. But what

I can do is use against him the one thing that he cherishes, and that is his pride. By me living outside in a shack, everyone is going to ask him, 'Why does your wife live in a shack outside your house?' He's going to have to answer that question, and no matter what he says, everyone will know that something is wrong with him. He loves to live for the world. Let the world see him for who he is. He's a saint in the streets. He's a devil in this house. Let him be seen for who he is."

When my mom had decided to keep Isaac, I was so close to writing her off. I couldn't stand the pain anymore. But seeing her hit with a bicycle, living like a prisoner in her own backyard, that was the final straw for me. I was a broken person. I was done.

"This thing?" I told her. "This dysfunctional thing? I won't be a part of it. I can't live this life with you. I refuse. You've made your decision. Good luck with your life. I'm going to live mine."

She understood. She didn't feel betrayed or abandoned at all.

"Honey, I know what you're going through," she said. "At one point, I had to disown my family to go off and live my own life, too. I understand why you need to do the same."

So I did. I walked out. I didn't call. I didn't visit. Isaac came and I went, and for the life of me I could not understand why she wouldn't do the same: leave. Just leave. Just fucking leave.

I didn't understand what she was going through. I didn't understand domestic violence. I didn't understand how adult relationships worked; I'd never even had a girlfriend. I didn't understand how she could have sex with a man she hated and feared. I didn't know how easily sex and hatred and fear can intertwine.

I was angry with my mom. I hated him, but I blamed her. I saw Abel as a choice she'd made, a choice she was continuing to make. My whole life, telling me stories about growing up in the homelands, being abandoned by her parents, she had always said, "You cannot blame anyone else for what you do. You cannot blame your past for who you are. You are responsible for you. You make your own choices."

She never let me see us as victims. We *were* victims, me and my mom, Andrew and Isaac. Victims of apartheid. Victims of abuse. But I was never allowed to think that way, and I didn't see her life that way. Cutting my father out of our lives to pacify Abel, that was her choice. Supporting Abel's workshop was her choice. Isaac was her choice. She had the money, not him. She wasn't dependent. So in my mind, she was the one making the decision.

It is so easy, from the outside, to put the blame on the woman and say, "You just need to leave." It's not like my home was the only home where there was domestic abuse. It's what I grew up around. I saw it in the streets of Soweto, on TV, in movies. Where does a woman go in a society where that is the norm? When the police won't help her? When her own family won't help her? Where does a woman go when she leaves one man who hits her and is just as likely to wind up with another man who hits her, maybe even worse than the first? Where does a woman go when she's single with three kids and she lives in a society that makes her a pariah for being a manless woman? Where she's seen as a whore for doing that? Where does she go? What does she do?

But I didn't comprehend any of that at the time. I was a boy with a boy's understanding of things. I distinctly remember the last time we argued about it, too. It was sometime after the bicycle, or when she was moving into her shack in the backyard. I was going off, begging her for the thousandth time.

"Why? Why don't you just leave?"

She shook her head. "Oh, baby. No, no, no. I can't leave."

"Why not?"

"Because if I leave he'll kill us."

She wasn't being dramatic. She didn't raise her voice. She said it totally calm and matter-of-fact, and I never asked her that question again.

Eventually she did leave. What prompted her to leave, what the final breaking point was, I have no idea. I was gone. I was off becoming a comedian, touring the country, playing shows in England, hosting radio shows, hosting television shows. I'd moved in with my cousin

Mlungisi and made my own life separate from hers. I couldn't invest myself anymore, because it would have broken me into too many pieces. But one day she bought another house in Highlands North, met someone new, and moved on with her life. Andrew and Isaac still saw their dad, who, by that point, was just existing in the world, still going through the same cycle of drinking and fighting, still living in a house paid for by his ex-wife.

Years passed. Life carried on.

Then one morning I was in bed around ten a.m. and my phone rang. It was on a Sunday. I know it was on a Sunday because everyone else in the family had gone to church and I, quite happily, had not. The days of endlessly schlepping back and forth to church were no longer my problem, and I was lazily sleeping in. The irony of my life is that whenever church is involved is when shit goes wrong, like getting kidnapped by violent minibus drivers. I'd always teased my mom about that, too. "This church thing of yours, all this Jesus, what good has come of it?"

I looked over at my phone. It was flashing my mom's number, but when I answered, it was Andrew on the other end. He sounded perfectly calm.

"Hey, Trevor, it's Andrew."

"Hey."

"How are you?"

"Good. What's up?"

"Are you busy?"

"I'm sort of sleeping. Why?"

"Mom's been shot."

Okay, so there were two strange things about the call. First, why would he ask me if I was busy? Let's start there. When your mom's been shot, the first line out of your mouth should be "Mom's been shot." Not "How are you?" Not "Are you busy?" That confused me. The second weird thing was when he said, "Mom's been shot," I didn't ask, "Who shot her?" I didn't have to. He said, "Mom's been shot," and my mind automatically filled in the rest: "Abel shot mom."

"Where are you now?" I said.

"We're at Linksfield Hospital."

"Okay, I'm on my way."

I jumped out of bed, ran down the corridor, and banged on Mlungisi's door. "Dude, my mom's been shot! She's in the hospital." He jumped out of bed, too, and we got in the car and raced to the hospital, which luckily was only fifteen minutes away.

At that point, I was upset but not terrified. Andrew had been so calm on the phone, no crying, no panic in his voice, so I was thinking, *She must be okay. It must not be that bad.* I called him back from the car to find out more.

"Andrew, what happened?"

"We were on our way home from church," he said, again totally calm. "And Dad was waiting for us at the house, and he got out of his car and started shooting."

"But where? Where did he shoot her?"

"He shot her in her leg."

"Oh, okay," I said, relieved.

"And then he shot her in the head."

When he said that, my body just let go. I remember the exact traffic light I was at. For a moment there was a complete vacuum of sound, and then I cried tears like I had never cried before. I collapsed in heaving sobs and moans. I cried as if every other thing I'd cried for in my life had been a waste of crying. I cried so hard that if my present crying self could go back in time and see my other crying selves, it would slap them and say, "That shit's not worth crying for." My cry was not a cry of sadness. It was not catharsis. It wasn't me feeling sorry for myself. It was an expression of raw pain that came from an inability of my body to express that pain in any other way, shape, or form. She was my mom. She was my teammate. It had always been me and her together, me and her against the world. When Andrew said, "shot her in the head," I broke in two.

The light changed. I couldn't even see the road, but I drove through the tears, thinking, *Just get there, just get there, just get there.* We pulled up to the hospital, and I jumped out of the car. There was an outdoor sitting area by the entrance to the emergency room. Andrew was standing there waiting for me, alone, his clothes smeared with blood. He still looked perfectly calm, completely stoic. Then the moment he looked up and saw me he broke down and started bawling. It was like he'd been holding it together the whole morning and then everything broke loose at once and he lost it. I ran to him and hugged him and he cried and cried. His cry was different from mine, though. My cry was one of pain and anger. His cry was one of helplessness.

I turned and ran into the emergency room. My mom was there in triage on a gurney. The doctors were stabilizing her. Her whole body was soaked in blood. There was a hole in her face, a gaping wound above her lip, part of her nose gone.

She was as calm and serene as I'd ever seen her. She could still open one eye, and she turned and looked up at me and saw the look of horror on my face.

"It's okay, baby," she whispered, barely able to speak with the blood in her throat.

"It's not okay."

"No, no, I'm okay, I'm okay. Where's Andrew? Where's your brother?"

"He's outside."

"Go to Andrew."

"But Mom—"

"*Shh.* It's okay, baby. I'm fine."

"You're not fine, you're—"

"*Shhhhhh.* I'm fine, I'm fine, I'm fine. Go to your brother. Your brother needs you."

The doctors kept working, and there was nothing I could do to help her. I went back outside to be with Andrew. We sat down together, and he told me the story.

They were coming home from church, a big group, my mom and Andrew and Isaac, her new husband and his children and a whole bunch of his extended family, aunts and uncles, nieces and nephews. They had just pulled into the driveway when Abel pulled up and got out of his car. He had his gun. He looked right at my mother.

"You've stolen my life," he said. "You've taken everything away from me. Now I'm going to kill all of you."

Andrew stepped in front of his father. He stepped right in front of the gun.

"Don't do this, Dad, please. You're drunk. Just put the gun away."

Abel looked down at his son.

"No," he said. "I'm killing everybody, and if you don't walk away I will shoot you first."

Andrew stepped aside.

"His eyes were not lying," he told me. "He had the eyes of the Devil. In that moment I could tell my father was gone."

For all the pain I felt that day, in hindsight, I have to imagine that Andrew's pain was far greater than mine. My mom had been shot by a man I despised. If anything, I felt vindicated; I'd been right about Abel all along. I could direct my anger and hatred toward him with no shame or guilt whatsoever. But Andrew's mother had been shot by Andrew's father, a father he loved. How does he reconcile his love with that situation? How does he carry on loving both sides? Both sides of himself?

Isaac was only four years old. He didn't fully comprehend what was happening, and as Andrew stepped aside, Isaac started crying.

"Daddy, what are you doing? Daddy, what are you doing?"

"Isaac, go to your brother," Abel said.

Isaac ran over to Andrew, and Andrew held him. Then Abel raised his gun and he started shooting. My mother jumped in front of the gun to protect everyone, and that's when she took the first bullet, not in her leg but in her butt cheek. She collapsed, and as she fell to the ground she screamed.

"Run!"

Abel kept shooting and everyone ran. They scattered. My mom was struggling to get back to her feet when Abel walked up and stood over her. He pointed the gun at her head point-blank, execution-style. Then he pulled the trigger. Nothing. The gun misfired. *Click!* He pulled the trigger again, same thing. Then again and again. *Click! Click! Click! Click!* Four times he pulled the trigger, and four times the gun misfired. Bullets were popping out of the ejection port, falling out of the gun, falling down on my mom and clattering to the ground.

Abel stopped to see what was wrong with the gun. My mother jumped up in a panic. She shoved him aside, ran for the car, jumped into the driver's seat.

Andrew ran behind and jumped into the passenger seat next to her. Just as she turned the ignition, Andrew heard one last gunshot, and the windshield went red. Abel had fired from behind the car. The bullet went into the back of her head and exited through the front of her face, and blood sprayed everywhere. Her body slumped over the steering wheel. Andrew, reacting without thinking, pulled my mom to the passenger side, flipped over her, jumped into the driver's seat, slammed the car into gear, and raced to the hospital in Linksfield.

I asked Andrew what happened to Abel. He didn't know. I was filled with rage, but there was nothing I could do. I felt completely impotent, but I still felt I had to do something. So I took out my phone and I called him—I called the man who'd just shot my mom, and he actually picked up.

"Trevor."

"You killed my mom."

"Yes, I did."

"You *killed* my *mom*!"

"Yes. And if I could find you, I would kill you as well."

Then he hung up. It was the most chilling moment. It was terrifying. Whatever nerve I'd worked up to call him I immediately lost. To this day I don't know what I was thinking. I don't know what I expected to happen. I was just enraged.

I kept asking Andrew questions, trying to get more details. Then, as we were talking, a nurse came outside looking for me.

"Are you the family?" she asked.

"Yes."

"Sir, there's a problem. Your mother was speaking a bit at first.

She's stopped now, but from what we've gathered she doesn't have health insurance."

"What? No, no. That can't be true. I know my mom has health insurance."

She didn't. As it turned out, a few months prior, she'd decided, "This health insurance is a scam. I never get sick. I'm going to cancel it." So now she had no health insurance.

"We can't treat your mother here," the nurse said. "If she doesn't have insurance we have to send her to a state hospital."

"*State hospital?!* What—no! You can't. My mom's been shot in the head. You're going to put her back on a gurney? Send her out in an ambulance? She'll die. You need to treat her right now."

"Sir, we can't. We need a form of payment."

"I'm your form of payment. I'll pay."

"Yes, people say that, but without a guarantee—"

I pulled out my credit card.

"Here," I said. "Take this. I'll pay. I'll pay for everything."

"Sir, hospital can be very expensive."

"I don't care."

"Sir, I don't think you understand. Hospital can be *really* expensive."

"Lady, I have money. I'll pay anything. Just help us."

"Sir, you don't understand. We have to do so many tests. One test alone could cost two, three thousand rand."

"Three thousan—what? Lady, this is my mother's life we're talking about. I'll pay."

"Sir, you don't understand. Your mother has been shot. In her brain. She'll be in ICU. One night in ICU could cost you fifteen, twenty thousand rand."

"Lady, are you not listening to me? This is my mother's *life*. This is her *life*. Take the money. Take all of it. I don't care."

"*Sir!* You don't understand. I've seen this happen. Your mother could be in the ICU for weeks. This could cost you five hundred thousand, six hundred thousand. Maybe even millions. You'll be in debt for the rest of *your* life."

I'm not going to lie to you: I paused. I paused *hard*. In that moment, what I heard the nurse saying was, "All of your money will be gone," and then I started to think, *Well . . . what is she, fifty? That's pretty good, right? She's lived a good life.*

I genuinely did not know what to do. I stared at the nurse as the shock of what she'd said sunk in. My mind raced through a dozen different scenarios. *What if I spend that money and then she dies anyway? Do I get a refund?* I actually imagined my mother, as frugal as she was, waking up from a coma and saying, "You spent *how much*? You idiot. You should have saved that money to look after your brothers." And what about my brothers? They would be my responsibility now. I would have to raise the family, which I couldn't do if I was millions in debt, and it was always my mother's solemn vow that raising my brothers was the one thing I would never have to do. Even as my career took off, she'd refused any help I offered. "I don't want you paying for your mother the same way I had to pay for mine," she'd say. "I don't want you raising your brothers the same way Abel had to raise his."

My mother's greatest fear was that I would end up paying the black tax, that I would get trapped by the cycle of poverty and violence that came before me. She had always promised me that I would be the one to break that cycle. I would be the one to move forward and not back. And as I looked at that nurse outside the emergency room, I was petrified that the moment I handed her my credit card, the cycle would just continue and I'd get sucked right back in.

People say all the time that they'd do anything for the people they love. But would you really? Would you do anything? Would you give everything? I don't know that a child knows that kind of selfless love. A mother, yes. A mother will clutch her children and jump from a moving car to keep them from harm. She will do it without thinking. But I don't think the child knows how to do that, not instinctively. It's something the child has to learn.

I pressed my credit card into the nurse's hand.

"Do whatever you have to do. Just please help my mom."

We spent the rest of the day in limbo, waiting, not knowing, pacing around the hospital, family members stopping by. Several hours later, the doctor finally came out of the emergency room to give us an update.

"What's happening?" I asked.

"Your mother is stable," he said. "She's out of surgery."

"Is she going to be okay?"

He thought for a moment about what he was going to say.

"I don't like to use this word," he said, "because I'm a man of science and I don't believe in it. But what happened to your mother today was a miracle. I never say that, because I hate it when people say it, but I don't have any other way to explain this."

The bullet that hit my mother in the butt, he said, was a through-and-through. It went in, came out, and didn't do any real damage. The other bullet went through the back of her head, entering below the skull at the top of her neck. It missed the spinal cord by a hair, missed the medulla oblongata, and traveled through her head just underneath the brain, missing every major vein, artery, and nerve. With the trajectory the bullet was on, it was headed straight for her left eye socket and would have blown out her eye, but at the last second it slowed down, hit her cheekbone instead, shattered her cheekbone, ricocheted off, and came out through her left nostril. On the gurney in the emergency room, the blood had made the wound look much worse than it was. The bullet took off only a tiny flap of skin on the side of her nostril, and it came out clean, with no bullet fragments left inside. She didn't even need surgery. They stopped the bleeding, stitched her up in back, stitched her up in front, and let her heal.

"There was nothing we can do, because there's nothing we need to do," the doctor said.

My mother was out of the hospital in four days. She was back at work in seven.

The doctors kept her sedated the rest of that day and night to rest. They told all of us to go home. "She's stable," they said. "There's nothing you can do here. Go home and sleep." So we did.

I went back first thing the next morning to be with my mother in her room and wait for her to wake up. When I walked in she was still asleep. The back of her head was bandaged. She had stitches in her face and gauze covering her nose and her left eye. She looked frail and weak, tired, one of the few times in my life I'd ever seen her look that way.

I sat close by her bed, holding her hand, waiting and watching her breathe, a flood of thoughts going through my mind. I was still afraid I was going to lose her. I was angry at myself for not being there, angry at the police for all the times they didn't arrest Abel. I told myself I should have killed him years ago, which was ridiculous to think because I'm not capable of killing anyone, but I thought it anyway. I was angry at the world, angry at God. Because all my mom does is pray. If there's a fan club for Jesus, my mom is definitely in the top 100, and this is what she gets?

After an hour or so of waiting, she opened her unbandaged eye. The second she did, I lost it. I started bawling. She asked for some water and I gave her a cup, and she leaned forward a bit to sip through the straw. I kept bawling and bawling and bawling. I couldn't control myself.

"*Shh,*" she said. "Don't cry, baby. *Shhhhh.* Don't cry."

"How can I not cry, Mom? You almost died."

"No, I wasn't going to die. I wasn't going to die. It's okay. I wasn't going to die."

"But I thought you were dead." I kept bawling and bawling. "I thought I'd lost you."

"No, baby. Baby, don't cry. Trevor. Trevor, listen. Listen to me. Listen."

"What?" I said, tears streaming down my face.

"My child, you must look on the bright side."

"*What?* What are you talking about, 'the bright side'? Mom, you were shot in the face. There is no bright side."

"Of course there is. Now you're officially the best-looking person in the family."

She broke out in a huge smile and started laughing. Through my tears, I started laughing, too. I was bawling my eyes out and laughing hysterically at the same time. We sat there and she squeezed my hand and we cracked each other up the way we always did, mother and son, laughing together through the pain in an intensive-care recovery room on a bright and sunny and beautiful day.

When my mother was shot, so much happened so quickly. We were only able to piece the whole story together after the fact, as we collected all the different accounts from everyone who was there. Waiting around at the hospital that day, we had so many unanswered questions, like, What happened to Isaac? Where was Isaac? We only found out after we found him and he told us.

When Andrew sped off with my mom, leaving the four-year-old alone on the front lawn, Abel walked over to his youngest, picked him up, put the boy in his car, and drove away. As they drove, Isaac turned to his dad.

"Dad, why did you kill Mom?" he asked, at that point assuming, as we all did, that my mom was dead.

"Because I'm very unhappy," Abel replied. "Because I'm very sad."

"Yeah, but you shouldn't kill Mom. Where are we going now?"

"I'm going to drop you off at your uncle's house."

"And where are you going?"

"I'm going to kill myself."

"But don't kill yourself, Dad."

"No, I'm going to kill myself."

The uncle Abel was talking about was not a real uncle but a friend. He dropped Isaac off with this friend and then he drove off. He spent that day and went to everyone, relatives and friends, and said his goodbyes. He even told people what he had done. "This is what I've done. I've killed her, and I'm now on the way to kill myself. Goodbye." He spent the whole day on this strange farewell tour, until finally one of his cousins called him out.

"You need to man up," the cousin said. "This is the coward's way. You need to turn yourself in. If you were man enough to do this, you have to be man enough to face the consequences."

Abel broke down and handed his gun over to the cousin, the cousin drove him to the police station, and Abel turned himself in.

He spent a couple of weeks in jail, waiting for a bail hearing. We filed a motion opposing bail because he'd shown that he was a threat. Since Andrew and Isaac were still minors, social workers started getting involved. We felt like the case was open-and-shut, but then one day, after a month or so, we got a call that he'd made bail. The great irony was that he got bail because he told the judge that if he was in jail, he couldn't earn money to support his kids. But he wasn't supporting his kids—my mom was supporting the kids.

So Abel was out. The case slowly ground its way through the legal system, and everything went against us. Because of my mother's miraculous recovery, the charge was only attempted murder. And because no domestic violence charges had ever been filed in all the times my mother had called the police to report him, Abel had no criminal record. He got a good lawyer, who continued to lean on the court about the fact that he had children at home who needed him. The case never went to trial. Abel pled guilty to attempted murder. He was given three years' probation. He didn't serve a single day in prison. He kept joint custody of his sons. He's walking around Johannesburg today, completely free. The last I heard he still lives somewhere around Highlands North, not too far from my mom.

The final piece of the story came from my mom, who could only tell us her side after she woke up. She remembered Abel pulling up and pointing the gun at Andrew. She remembered falling to the ground after getting shot in the ass. Then Abel came and stood over her and pointed his gun at her head. She looked up and looked at him straight down the barrel of the gun. Then she started to pray, and that's when the gun misfired. Then it misfired again. Then it misfired again, and again. She jumped up, shoved him away, and ran for the car. Andrew leapt in beside her and she turned the ignition and then her memory went blank.

To this day, nobody can explain what happened. Even the police didn't understand. Because it wasn't like the gun didn't work. It fired, and then it didn't fire, and then it fired again for the final shot. Anyone who knows anything about firearms will tell you that a 9mm handgun cannot misfire in the way that gun did. But at the crime scene the police had drawn little chalk circles all over the driveway, all with spent shell casings from the shots Abel fired, and then these four bullets, intact, from when he was standing over my mom—nobody knows why.

My mom's total hospital bill came to 50,000 rand. I paid it the day we left. For four days we'd been in the hospital, family members visiting, talking and hanging out, laughing and crying. As we packed up her things to leave, I was going on about how insane the whole week had been.

"You're lucky to be alive," I told her. "I still can't believe you didn't have any health insurance."

"Oh but I do have insurance," she said.

"You do?"

"Yes. Jesus."

"Jesus?"

"Jesus."

"Jesus is your health insurance?"

"If God is with me, who can be against me?"

"Okay, Mom."

"Trevor, I prayed. I told you I prayed. I don't pray for nothing."

"You know," I said, "for once I cannot argue with you. The gun, the bullets—I can't explain any of it. So I'll give you that much." Then I couldn't resist teasing her with one last little jab. "But where was your Jesus to pay your hospital bill, hmm? I know for a fact that He didn't pay that."

She smiled and said, "You're right. He didn't. But He blessed me with the son who did."

———

ACKNOWLEDGMENTS

For nurturing my career these past years and steering me down the road that led to this book, I owe many thanks to Norm Aladjem, Derek Van Pelt, Sanaz Yamin, Rachel Rusch, Matt Blake, Jeff Endlich, and Jill Fritzo.

For making this book deal happen and keeping it on track during a very tight and hectic time, I would like to thank Peter McGuigan and his team at Foundry Literary + Media, including Kirsten Neuhaus, Sara DeNobrega, and Claire Harris. Also, many thanks to Tanner Colby for helping me put my story on the page.

For seeing the potential in this book and making it a reality, I would like to thank everyone at Random House and Spiegel & Grau, including my editor Chris Jackson, publishers Julie Grau and Cindy Spiegel,

Tom Perry, Greg Mollica, Susan Turner, Andrea DeWerd, Leigh Marchant, Barbara Fillon, Dhara Parikh, Rebecca Berlant, Kelly Chian, Nicole Counts, and Gina Centrello.

For bringing this book home to South Africa and making sure it is published with the utmost care, I would like to thank everyone at Pan Macmillan South Africa, including Sean Fraser, Sandile Khumalo, Andrea Nattrass, Rhulani Netshivhera, Sandile Nkosi, Nkateko Traore, Katlego Tapala, Wesley Thompson, and Mia van Heerden.

For reading this manuscript in its early stages and sharing thoughts and ideas to make it the finished product you hold in your hands, I owe my deepest gratitude to Khaya Dlanga, David Kibuuka, Anele Mdoda, Ryan Harduth, Sizwe Dhlomo, and Xolisa Dyeshana.

And, finally, for bringing me into this world and making me the man I am today, I owe the greatest debt, a debt I can never repay, to my mother.

TREVOR NOAH is a comedian from South Africa.

trevornoah.com
Facebook.com/OfficialTrevorNoah
Twitter: @Trevornoah
Instagram: @trevornoah

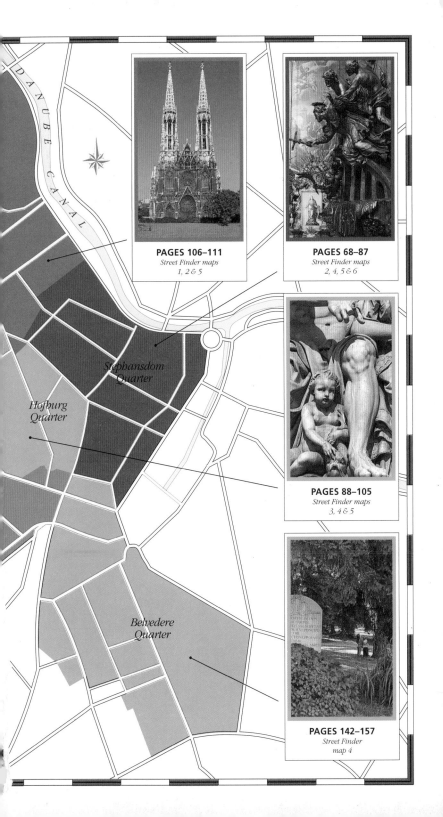

DANUBE CANAL

PAGES 106–111
Street Finder maps
1, 2 & 5

PAGES 68–87
Street Finder maps
2, 4, 5 & 6

Stephansdom
Quarter

Hofburg
Quarter

PAGES 88–105
Street Finder maps
3, 4 & 5

Belvedere
Quarter

PAGES 142–157
Street Finder
map 4

EYEWITNESS TRAVEL

VIENNA

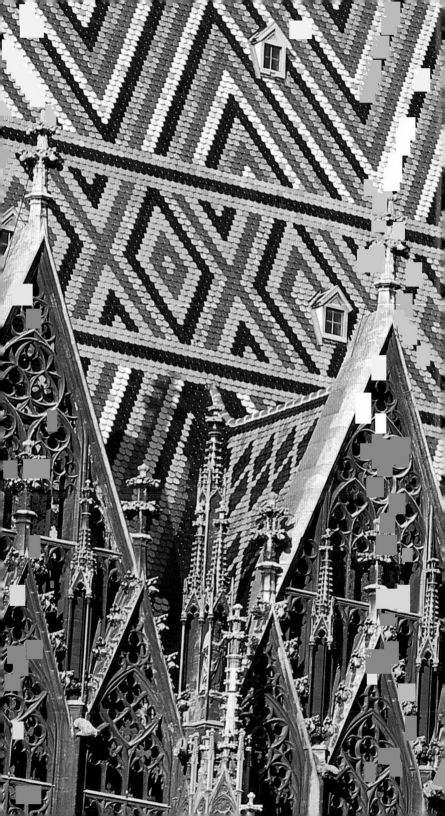

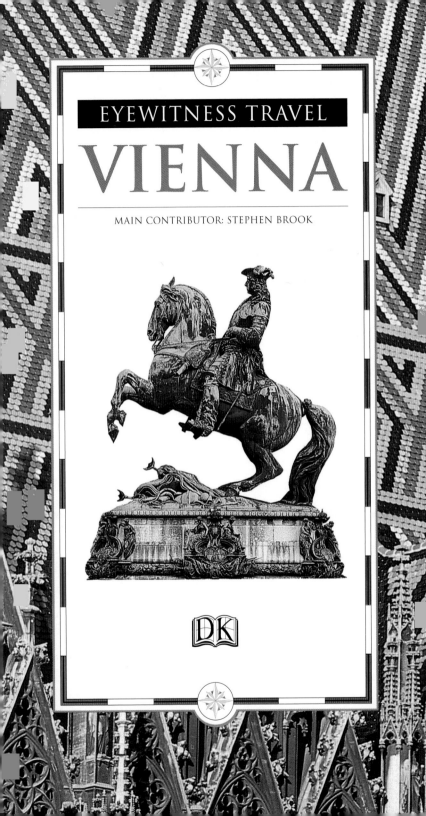

EYEWITNESS TRAVEL

VIENNA

MAIN CONTRIBUTOR: STEPHEN BROOK

DK

LONDON, NEW YORK,
MELBOURNE, MUNICH AND DELHI
www.dk.com

PROJECT EDITOR Carolyn Pyrah
ART EDITOR Sally Ann Hibbard
EDITORS Marcus Hardy, Kim Inglis
USEDITOR Mary Ann Lynch
DESIGNERS Vanessa Hamilton, Andy Wilkinson
DESIGN ASSISTANT Elly King

PRODUCTION Hilary Stephens
PICTURE RESEARCH Ellen Root
DTP DESIGNER Adam Moore

CONTRIBUTORS
Gretel Beer, Rosemary Bircz, Caroline Bugler,
Deirdre Coffey, Fred Mawer

PHOTOGRAPHER
Peter Wilson

ILLUSTRATORS
Richard Draper, Stephen Gyapay, Chris Orr,
Robbie Polley, Ann Winterbotham

Reproduced by Colourscan, Singapore
Printed and bound by L. Rex Printing Company Limited, China

First American Edition, 1994
12 13 14 15 10 9 8 7 6 5 4 3 2 1

Published in the United States by DK Publishing,
375 Hudson Street, New York, New York 10014

**Reprinted with revisions 1996, 1997 (twice), 2000, 2001,
2002, 2003, 2004, 2006, 2008, 2010, 2012**

Copyright © 1994, 2012 Dorling Kindersley Ltd

Published in Great Britain by Dorling Kindersley Limited

ISSN 1542-1554
ISBN 978-0-7566-8428-0

THROUGHOUT THIS BOOK, FLOORS ARE REFERRED TO IN ACCORDANCE WITH
EUROPEAN USAGE, I.E., THE "FIRST FLOOR" IS THE FLOOR ABOVE GROUND LEVEL.

Front cover main image: Upper Belvedere Palace, Vienna

MIX
Paper from
responsible sources
FSC
www.fsc.org   FSC™ C018179

◁ **Close-up of Stephansdom roof**

CONTENTS

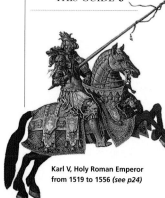

**Karl V, Holy Roman Emperor
from 1519 to 1556 *(see p24)***

INTRODUCING
VIENNA

**Bronze and copper Anker Clock in
Hoher Markt *(see p84)***

Façade of Schönbrunn Palace *(see pp172–75)*

Grinzing restaurant *(see pp186–7)*

Dobostorte *(see p206)*

The Vienna Boys' Choir *(see p39)*

Karlskirche in the Belvedere Quarter *(see pp148–49)*

HOW TO USE THIS GUIDE

This Eyewitness Travel Guide helps you get the most from your stay in Vienna with the minimum of difficulty. The opening section, *Introducing Vienna*, locates the city geographically, sets modern Vienna in its historical context and describes events through the entire year. *Vienna at a Glance* is an overview of the city's main attractions. *Vienna Area by Area* starts on page 66. This is the main sightseeing section,

Plotting the route

which covers all the important sights, with photographs, maps and illustrations. It also includes day trips from Vienna, a river trip and four walks around the city. Carefully researched tips for hotels, restaurants, cafés and bars, markets and shops, entertainment and sports are found in *Travellers' Needs*. The *Survival Guide* has advice from how to make a telephone call to using the transport system and its ticket machines.

FINDING YOUR WAY AROUND THE SIGHTSEEING SECTION

Each of the six sightseeing areas in the city is colour-coded for easy reference. Every chapter opens with an introduction to the part of Vienna it covers, describing its history and character, followed by a Street-by-Street

map illustrating a typical part of the area. Finding your way around each chapter is made simple by the numbering system used throughout. The most important sights are covered in detail in two or more full pages.

Each area has colour-coded thumb tabs.

A locator map shows where you are in relation to other areas in the city centre.

Locator map

A suggested route takes in some of the most interesting and attractive streets in the area.

1 Introduction to the area
For easy reference, the sights in each area are numbered and plotted on an area map. To help the visitor, this map also shows underground stations, train stations and parking areas. The area's key sights are listed by category: Churches and Cathedrals; Museums and Galleries; Streets and Squares; Markets; Historic Buildings and Parks and Gardens.

The area shaded pink is shown in greater detail on the Street-by-Street map on the following pages.

2 Street-by-Street map
This gives a bird's eye view of interesting and important parts of each sightseeing area. The numbering of the sights ties in with the area map and the fuller descriptions on the pages that follow.

The list of star sights recommends the places that no visitor should miss.

VIENNA AREA MAP

The coloured areas shown on this map *(see inside front cover)* are the six main sightseeing areas used in this guide. Each is covered in a full chapter in *Vienna Area by Area (pp66–179)*. They are highlighted on other maps throughout the book. In *Vienna at a Glance (pp40–61)*, for example, they help you locate the top sights. They are also used to help you find the position of the three guided walks *(pp180–87)*.

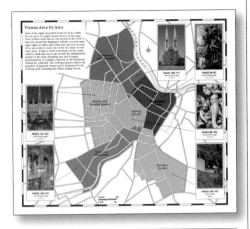

Numbers refer to each sight's position on the area map and its place in the chapter.

Practical information provides all the information you need to visit every sight. Map references pinpoint each sight's location on the *Street Finder* map *(pp262–7)*.

The visitors' checklist provides all the practical information needed to plan your visit.

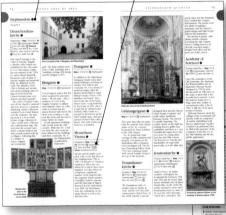

3 Detailed information on each sight

All the important sights in Vienna are described individually. They are listed in order, following the numbering on the area map at the start of the section. Practical information includes a map reference, opening hours, telephone numbers, admission charges and facilities available for each sight. The key to the symbols used is on the back flap.

Stars indicate the features no visitor should miss.

4 Vienna's major sights

Historic buildings are dissected to reveal their interiors; museums and galleries have colour-coded floorplans to help you find important exhibits.

A timeline charts the key events in the history of the building.

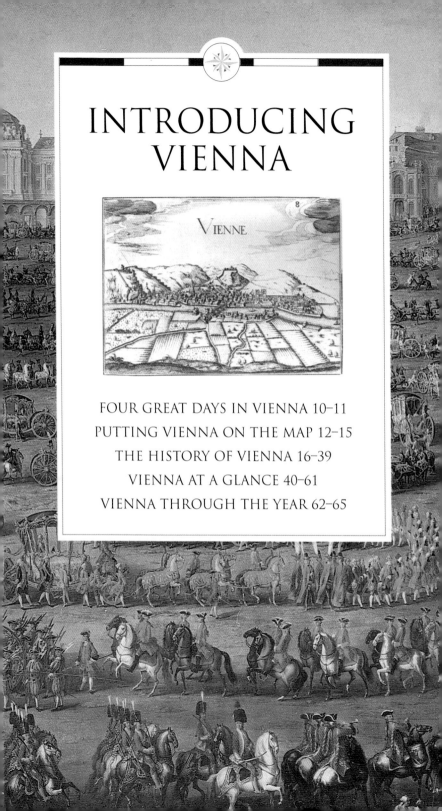

INTRODUCING VIENNA

VIENNE

FOUR GREAT DAYS IN VIENNA

Whether you are a history buff, an art lover, an outdoors' enthusiast or a fan of thrill rides, in Vienna you will be sure to find something that appeals to you. From imperial palaces and art galleries to parks and a funfair, Vienna has

Porcelain Plate

attractions for everyone. Listed here are some ideas for four days of varied activities, with each day tailored to a different interest. Prices include all travel, food and admission costs. Family pricing allows for two adults and two children.

Schönbrunn Palace, whose formal gardens contain a palm house and zoo

VIENNA OF THE HABSBURGS

- **Hofburg: Habsburg Winter Residence**
- **Dine on Emperor's Pancakes**
- **Schönbrunn: Habsburg Summer Home**

TWO ADULTS allow at least €110

Morning
Start the day early with a visit to the huge **Hofburg Complex** *(see pp96–7)*, which includes the former Habsburg winter residence, a church, chapel, the **Spanish Riding School** *(see pp98–9)*, museums and the Austrian National Library. Take a tour of the former **Habsburg State Apartments** *(see pp100–1)*, the **Sisi Museum** (dedicated to Empress Elisabeth of Austria) and the Silberkammer, which houses the Imperial Silver Collection. For lunch, dine in the complex at the **Café Hofburg** *(see p213)*, where traditional specialities such as *Kaiserschmarren* (Emperor's Pancakes) and *Rindsgulasch* (beef goulash) are available.

Afternoon
After lunch, travel to **Schönbrunn Palace and Gardens** *(see pp172–5)*, the former summer residence of the Habsburgs. Take the "Imperial Tour" of the palace, which will guide you through 22 of the palace's state rooms, aided by a free explanatory audio guide. You will be impressed by the palace's grandeur. If you still have time after the tour, wander out into the park and visit the garden's **maze** *(see p172)* and labyrinth for a unique outdoor adventure as well as some picturesque scenery.

One of several statues in the gardens of the Schönbrunn Palace

━━━━━━━━━━━━━━━━

GREEN VIENNA

- **Tour a Butterfly House**
- **Dine in a 1794 café**
- **Take a stroll on a man-made island**
- **Climb a 252-m (827-ft) tower**

TWO ADULTS allow at least €100

Morning
Start the day with a trip to **Burggarten** *(see p102)*, a park in central Vienna that was created by the Habsburgs on land around the Hofburg. Here you can wander among the trees and view statues of Goethe, Mozart and Emperor Franz I. The park is also well-known for its greenhouses, designed by the Jugendstil architect Friedrich Ohmann. Among them is the Butterfly House *(Schmetterlinghaus)*, home to over 150 different species which fly around in a recreated rainforest environment. Next, take a lunch break at the nearby **Café Mozart** *(see p219)*, on Albertinaplatz. In this historic and elegant café, which has been in existence since 1794, you can dine on gourmet vegetarian or traditional Austrian dishes and enjoy some pastries for dessert.

Afternoon
After lunch, pay a visit to **Donau Park** *(see p161)*, which was created in 1964 and is the second largest park in Vienna. Here you can go for a leisurely stroll or jog, or a ride along the cycle paths. For a relaxing moment, sit down by Lake Iris, which is an artificial lake

◁ **The arrival of Isabella of Parma for her marriage to Joseph II, a painting (1760) by Martin Meytens**

Gustav Klimt's Beethoven Frieze on display in the Secession Building

in the centre. A must-see while in the park is the **Donau Turm** *(see p161)*, which is 252 m (827 ft) high and has a revolving restaurant, a café and an observation deck. An elevator will take you to the top of the tower where you can view the whole Vienna metropolitan area. On a clear day, the view stretches to beyond the city.

The elegant exterior of the historic and popular Café Mozart

ART AND ARCHITECTURE

- Tour an art museum designed in Jugendstil
- Dine on classic Greek food
- View an imperial art history museum

TWO ADULTS allow at least €100

Morning
Begin your day with a visit to the **Secession Building** *(see p138)*, which was designed in Jugendstil style and is now used as an exhibition hall for displays of contemporary art. Exhibitions have

included Oswald Oberhuber and Maja Vukoje. The building is also home to Gustav Klimt's famous *Beethoven Frieze*. After viewing the art, try nearby **Kostas** *(see p215)* for a classic Greek lunch of moussaka.

Afternoon
Having eaten, head for the **MuseumsQuartier** *(see pp118–21)* and, for an unforgettable experience, visit the **Kunsthistorisches Museum** (Museum of the History of Art) *(see pp122–3)*. Here you can spend an afternoon viewing magnificent works of art and antiquities, many of which are from imperial Habsburg collections. The Picture Gallery on the first floor is especially impressive and features paintings from the artists Giovanni Bellini, Titian, Pieter Bruegel and Diego Velázquez among others. After a day of browsing, stop off at the **Lux-Gasthaus-Café-Bar** *(see p214)*, just west of the MuseumsQuartier, for a glass of wine or some juice.

A FAMILY DAY

- **Explore the Volksprater Funfair in the Prater**
- **Lunch at the Prater's Schweizerhaus restaurant**
- **Ride a rickshaw along the Hauptallee**

FAMILY OF 4 allow at least €200

Morning
This day starts with a trip to the **Volksprater Funfair** *(see p162)*, the oldest amusement park in the world. Take a spin on the famous Ferris wheel built in 1897. Older kids might then like to ride on the daring Volare roller coaster, while parents with smaller children might enjoy the carousel, or the 4-km (2.5-mile) miniature railway. For lunch, visit the **Schweizerhaus restaurant** *(see p216)* inside the park and sample some hearty fare, such as beef stew and fried chicken.

Afternoon
After lunch, families can rent a rickshaw (or, perhaps, a mountain bike, tandem or children's bike) from the Bicycle Rental Hochschau-bahn stand near the Hochschaubahn roller coaster. Go for a two-hour ride down the **Hauptallee** *(see p163)* in the Prater's green area, which is a boulevard famous for jogging and cycling, or just enjoying a pleasant stroll. Return to one of the funfair's fast-food stands for an ice-cream cone or soft drink.

One of the many attractions at VolksPrater Funfair

Putting Vienna on the Map

Vienna has a population of just over 1.6 million and covers an area of 415 sq km (160 sq miles). The River Danube flows through it and the Danube Canal flows through the city centre. It is the capital of the Republic of Austria, of which it is also a federal state, and is the country's political, economic, cultural and administrative centre. At the heart of Central Europe, it makes a good base from which to explore cities such as Bratislava, Prague, Budapest, Zagreb, Salzburg and Munich, as well as many Austrian towns.

Satellite view of Greater Vienna

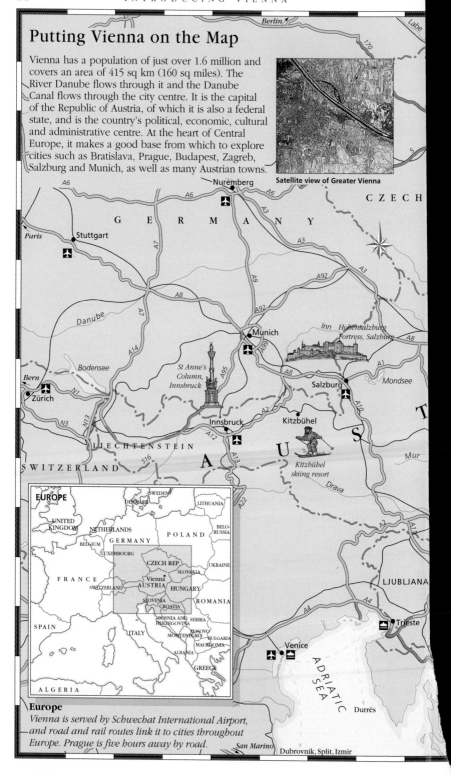

Europe

Vienna is served by Schwechat International Airport, and road and rail routes link it to cities throughout Europe. Prague is five hours away by road.

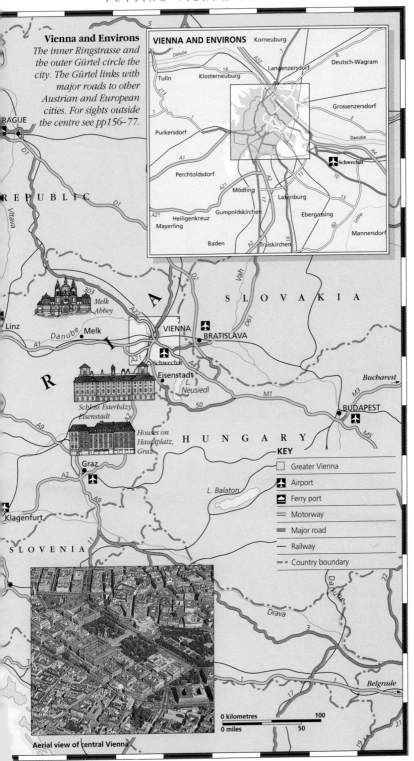

Vienna and Environs
The inner Ringstrasse and the outer Gürtel circle the city. The Gürtel links with major roads to other Austrian and European cities. For sights outside the centre see pp156–77.

VIENNA AND ENVIRONS

Korneuburg

Danube

A22

Langenzersdorf

Deutsch-Wagram

14

8

Tulln

Klosterneuburg

A13

Grossenzersdorf

3

Danube

Purkersdorf

A1

Schwechat

Perchtoldsdorf

A21

A2

A4

15

Mödling

Laxenburg

Ebergassing

Leitha

Heiligenkreuz

Gumpoldskirchen

A21

Mayerling

Mannersdorf

Baden

Traiskirchen

PRAGUE

D1

Vltava

REPUBLIC

D1

303

Melk Abbey

A22

A

S L O V A K I A

D2

Vah

D61

Linz

A1

Danube

Melk

VIENNA

BRATISLAVA

R

A21

Schwechat

Eisenstadt

L. Neusiedl

M1

Bucharest

M3

Schloss Esterházy Eisenstadt

50

BUDAPEST

A9

Houses on Hauptplatz, Graz

H U N G A R Y

M5

Graz

A2

L. Balaton

A9

Klagenfurt

S L O V E N I A

KEY

☐	Greater Vienna
✈	Airport
⛴	Ferry port
═	Motorway
━	Major road
─	Railway
─ ─	Country boundary

Danube

Drava

Belgrade

Aerial view of central Vienna

0 kilometres 100

0 miles 50

Central Vienna

Detail on the door of the Pallavicini Palace (1784) in Josefsplatz

This book divides Vienna into six areas in the centre of town, and has further sections for sights on the outskirts of the city, suggested walks and day trips, as well as practical information. Each of the six main areas has its own chapter, and contains a selection of sights that convey some of that area's history and distinctive character, such as the Stephansdom in the Stephansdom Quarter and the imperial buildings in the Hofburg Quarter. Most of the city's famous sights are in or close to the city centre and are easy to reach on foot or by public transport.

Bars in Sterngasse
Sterngasse, in the Jewish Quarter (see p84), is packed with lively bars like these spilling out into the street (see Restaurants, Cafés and Bars on p218).

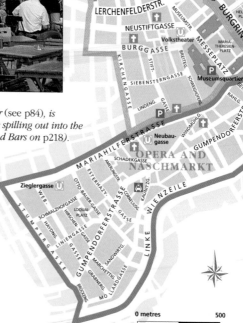

KEY

⬛	Major sight
Ⓤ	U-Bahn station
🔁	Badner Bahn stop
🅿	Parking
ℹ	Tourist information office
🏛	Police station
✝	Church

0 metres   500
0 yards   500

View over the Roof-tops from Am Hof
Am Hof, the largest enclosed square in Vienna, is circled by a number of interesting houses, some with statuary on their roofs and pediments (see p87).

Rathauskeller Façade
The city has plenty of wine cellars – many associated with old vineyards – where wine, beer and simple food is served. This one is located beneath the city hall (see p130).

Pallas Athene Fountain
The figure of Pallas Athene by Karl Kundmann was placed on the fountain in front of the Parliament building in 1902 (see p121).

THE HISTORY OF VIENNA

Vienna was originally a Celtic settlement on the site of the present-day city. Under the Romans it became the garrison of Vindobona, supporting the nearby town of Carnuntum. Its location on the edge of the Hungarian plains, however, made it vulnerable to attack, and Barbarian invasions reduced the town to ruins by the early 5th century. In the 10th century, the German Babenberg dynasty acquired Vienna, and during their reign of almost three centuries the city became a major trading centre. Later, in the 13th century, Vienna came under the control of the Habsburgs. In the 16th century, Turkish invasions threatened Vienna and devastated its outskirts. Only in 1683 were the Turks finally defeated, allowing Vienna to flourish. Immense palaces were built around the court within the city, and in the liberated outskirts, and by the 18th century Vienna was a major imperial and cultural centre. Napoleon's occupation of Vienna in 1809 shook the Habsburgs' confidence, as did the revolution of 1848 – the year Franz Joseph came to the throne. By 1914, Vienna's population had expanded to two million, as people from all over the Habsburg Empire flocked to this vibrant centre. After World War I, the Habsburg Empire collapsed and Vienna's role as the Imperial capital ended. In the following years a strong municipal government – "Red Vienna"– tried to solve the social problems of the city. Austria was annexed by Nazi Germany in the Anschluss of 1938 and then, following Hitler's defeat in 1945, came under Allied control. Vienna regained its independence in 1955, when Austria became a sovereign state.

Maximilian I shield

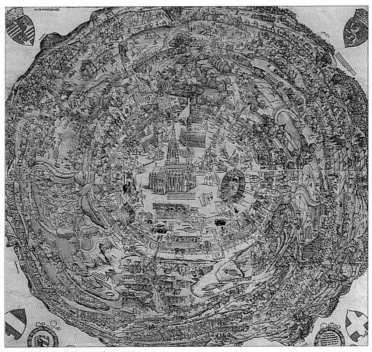

Circular plan of Turkish siege, from 1529

◁ Detail from *The Marriage of Joseph II to Isabella of Parma* (1760) by the Martin van Meytens School

Vienna's Rulers

Vienna emerged from the Dark Ages as a German outpost controlled by Babenberg dukes, who brought great prosperity to the city by the 12th century. There followed a period of social disorder, and intermittent Bohemian rule known as the Interregnum. Vienna fell into Habsburg hands in the 13th century and remained the cornerstone of their domains until the dynasty's downfall in 1918. From 1452 until 1806, Habsburg rulers were almost invariably elected as Holy Roman Emperor, enabling Vienna to develop as an Imperial capital on the grandest scale.

1278–82 Rudolf I of Germany is regent of Austria.

Duke Friedrich II with falconer

1246–50 Interregnum under Margrave Hermann of Baden after death of Duke Friedrich II

900	1000	1100	1200	1300	1400
BABENBERG RULERS				HABSBURG RULERS	
900	1000	1100	1200	1300	1400

976 Leopold of Babenberg

1198–1230 Duke Leopold VI

1177–1194 Duke Leopold V

1358–65 Duke Rudolf IV

1141–77 Duke Heinrich II Jasomirgott

1251–76 Interregnum under Přemysl Ottakar II

1637–57 Emperor
Ferdinand III

1452–93 Friedrich V
(crowned as Holy Roman
Emperor Friedrich III)

1485–90 King Matthias
Corvinus of Hungary
occupies Vienna

1493–1519 Emperor
Maximilian I

1612–19
Emperor Matthias

1657–1705 Emperor Leopold I

Emperor Franz Joseph I

1835–48
Emperor
Ferdinand I
of Austria

1576–1612
Emperor
Rudolf II

1705–11 Emperor
Joseph I

1711–40
Emperor Karl VI

1848–1916 Emperor
Franz Joseph I

1500	1600	1700	1800	1900

1500	1600	1700	1800	1900

1619–37 Emperor
Ferdinand II

1792–1835 Emperor
Franz II (becomes
Franz I of Austria
in 1806)

1918
Habsburgs
exiled

1564–76 Emperor Maximilian II

1916–18 Emperor
Karl I

1556–64 Emperor
Ferdinand I

1790–92 Emperor
Leopold II

1780–90 Emperor
Joseph II

1519–1556
Emperor Karl V

1740–80 Empress Maria Theresa

Early Vienna

The region around Vienna was first inhabited in the late Stone Age, and Vienna itself was founded as a Bronze Age settlement in about 800 BC. Settled by Celts from about 400 BC, the Romans incorporated it into the province of Pannonia in 15 BC, establishing the garrison of Vindo-bona by the 1st century AD. Later overrun by Barbarian tribes, Vindobona diminished in importance until the 8th century, when the Frankish Emperor Charle-magne made it part of his Eastern March and part of the Holy Roman Empire.

Roman urn

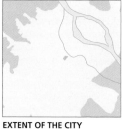

EXTENT OF THE CITY

□ 150 AD   □ Today

Hallstatt Idol
The Iron-Age Hallstatt culture flourished around Vienna from 750 to 400 BC.

Main defensive wall

VINDOBONA
Established around 100 AD, the garrison of Vindobona was allied to the town of Carnuntum.

Vindobona   Carnuntum

Venus of Willendorf
Now in the Natural History Museum (see p126), this late Stone Age figurine was found at Willendorf, close to Vienna, in 1906.

Roman Map
This map of Pannonia shows the position of Roman towns and forts along the Danube.

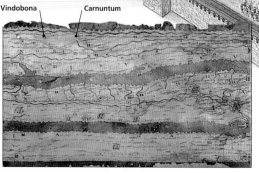

TIMELINE

5000	2000	800	0	100	200
2000 BC Indo-Germanic settlements on northwest wooded slopes	**800 BC** Bronze Age settlements on what is now Hoher Markt	**750 BC** Hallstatt culture **400 BC** Celtic culture	*Marcus Aurelius*	**180** Roman Emperor Marcus Aurelius dies in Vindobona	**280** Roman Emperor Probus authorizes wine-growing in the Danube area
5000 BC Late Stone Age culture			**15 BC** Celtic region of Noricum occupied by Romans	**250** Vindobona, developed as a garrison town, has a population of 20,000	

Preserved shoe from the Hallstatt culture

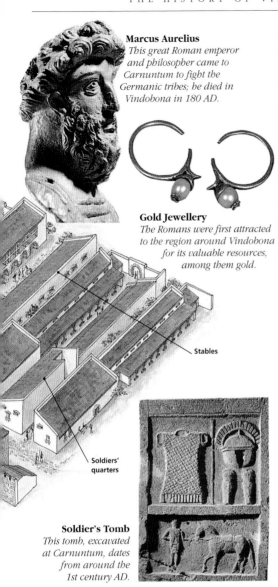

Marcus Aurelius
This great Roman emperor and philosopher came to Carnuntum to fight the Germanic tribes; he died in Vindobona in 180 AD.

Gold Jewellery
The Romans were first attracted to the region around Vindobona for its valuable resources, among them gold.

Stables

Soldiers' quarters

Soldier's Tomb
This tomb, excavated at Carnuntum, dates from around the 1st century AD.

WHERE TO SEE EARLY VIENNA

Many of the Roman walls and ditches have left their mark on the layout of Vienna, but excavations have not been numerous. The most impressive are at Hoher Markt *(see p84)*, at No. 10 Am Hof *(p87)*, and in the Michaelerplatz *(p92)*. The most extensive remains are not in Vienna itself but at Carnuntum, about 25 miles (40 km) east of Vienna, where two amphitheatres and other ruins survive.

The Hoher Markt, *in the very heart of Vienna, is the site of excavations of the Roman garrison of Vindobona.*

This Gorgon's Head, *a large Roman relief of the mythical Medusa, is from Hoher Markt.*

---

see p84

p87

p92

300	400	500	600	700	800

395 First Barbarian invasions approach Vindobona

405 Romans withdraw from Vindobona

500–650 Repeated invasions by Langobards, Goths, Avars and Slav tribes

433 Vindobona destroyed by Huns

Barbarian horseman

883 First mention of Wenia (Vienna) on the borders of the Eastern March founded by Charlemagne

Medieval Vienna

In 955 the Holy Roman Emperor Otto I expelled Hungarian tribes from the Eastern March (see p20). In 976 he made a gift of Vienna to the German Babenbergs, who, despite further incursions by the Hungarians, restored the city's importance as a centre of trade and culture. Following Friedrich II's death in 1246 and the ensuing Interregnum (see p18), the Habsburgs began centuries of rule over Austria. Vienna became a major European city and hub of the Holy Roman Empire.

EXTENT OF THE CITY

▨ 1400　　□ Today

St Ruprecht
St Ruprecht was the patron saint of salt merchants, who brought this precious commodity along the Danube from salt mines in western Austria. Today his statue overlooks the Danube canal.

DEATH OF FRIEDRICH II
Duke Friedrich II was the last of the Babenbergs to rule Vienna. He died in battle against invading Hungarian forces in 1246.

Stephansdom

The Nobility
Often elected as Holy Roman Emperors, the Habsburgs attracted nobility from all over their huge empire.

Duke Friedrich II

Coronation Robe
This magnificent medieval robe (1133), originally from Palermo, formed part of the Habsburg's imperial regalia.

TIMELINE

900	1000	1100
909 Eastern March invaded by Hungarian forces	**955** Otto I of Germany defeats the Hungarians, restoring Christianity and re-establishing the Eastern March ("Ostmark", later renamed Ostarrichi)	**1147** Stephansdom consecrated
	1030 The Hungarians besiege Vienna	**1136** Death of Margave Leopold III
	976 Otto I makes Leopold of Babenberg Margrave of the Eastern March, initiating Babenberg rule	**1137** Vienna becomes a fortified city
		1156 Heinrich II Jasomirgott moves his court to Vienna; builds Am Hof (see p87)

Richard the Lionheart
In 1192, Richard I of England, returning from the crusades in the Holy Land, was captured and held to ransom by Duke Leopold V.

WHERE TO SEE MEDIEVAL VIENNA

Gothic churches include the Stephansdom (*see pp76–9*), Maria am Gestade (*p85*), the Burgkapelle, Minoritenkirche (*p103*), Ruprechtskirche (*p81*) and Augustinerkirche (*p102*). The Michaelerkirche (*p92*) includes some Gothic sculptures and the Schottenkirche medieval art (*p110*). Surviving medieval houses include the Basiliskenhaus in Schönlaterngasse (*p74*).

Tributary of the River Danube

Medieval city wall

Verduner Altar
This masterpiece forms part of the treasury of the huge abbey at Klosterneuburg (see p161). Its 51 panels were completed in 1181 by Nikolaus of Verdun. The abbey itself was consecrated in 1136.

Stained glass *(about 1340) in the Cathedral Museum (p74).*

Hungarian encampment

University
Vienna's University was founded in 1365 by Duke Rudolf IV. This miniature (about 1400) shows the medieval university building and some of the tutors and their students.

Seal of Przemysl Ottakar II

1278–82 Rudolf I becomes ruler of Austria after defeating Ottakar II; 640 years of Habsburg rule follow

1288 Viennese uprising against Habsburgs crushed

1359 Rudolf IV lays foundation stone of the Stephansdom tower

1365 University founded

1477 Friedrich III's son Maximilian I marries Mary of Burgundy, heiress to the Low Countries

1200	1300	1400

1246 Death of Friedrich II followed by Interregnum, during which Przemysl Ottakar II rules Vienna

1273 Count Rudolf of Habsburg crowned Rudolf I of Germany

1278 Vienna granted a city charter

1330 The first Gothic section of Maria am Gestade built

1438 Albrecht V elected Holy Roman Emperor; Vienna made seat of Empire

1452 Friedrich V crowned as Holy Roman Emperor Friedrich III

1485 Vienna occupied by King Matthias Corvinus of Hungary

Renaissance Vienna

Under Maximilian I, Vienna was transformed into a centre for the arts. The Habsburgs were invariably elected Holy Roman Emperor, and by the 16th century their mighty empire had expanded into Spain, Holland, Burgundy, Bohemia and Hungary. But it was under constant threat: from Turkish attacks, the plague, and disputes between Protestants and Catholics that destabilized the city until 1576, when the Jesuits spearheaded the Counter-Reformation.

EXTENT OF THE CITY

▨ *1600*	☐ *Today*

Book Illustration
This Renaissance war wagon (1512) is from Maximilian I's collection of books of engravings and illustrations.

Maximilian I married Mary of Burgundy in 1477 and acquired the Burgundian domains.

Viennese Enamel Casket
This ornate enamel and crystal casket is typical of the skilful craftsmanship practised in Vienna in the 16th century.

Imperial Crown
This beautiful crown was made by Bohemian craftsmen in 1610 for Rudolf II and can now be seen in the Hofburg Treasuries (see pp100–1).

Ferdinand I married Anna of Bohemia and Hungary, and inherited Bohemia in 1526. It was a Habsburg domain until 1918.

TIMELINE

1516 Maximilian's grandson, Karl V, inherits Spain

1519 Karl V inherits Burgundy titles and is elected Holy Roman Emperor; his brother Ferdinand I becomes Austria's archduke

1533 Ferdinand I moves his court to the Hofburg in Vienna

1556 Karl V's son, Philip II, inherits Spain; Ferdinand I takes Bohemia, Austria, Hungary, and imperial title

1571 Protestant Maximilian II allows religious freedom; 80% of city is Protestant

1500	1520	1540	1560	1580

1498 Emperor Maximilian I founds Vienna Boys' Choir

Suleiman the Magnificent

1541 Plague

1572 Spanish Riding School founded

1493 Maximilian I expels Hungarians from Vienna

1529 Graf Niklas Salm vanquishes Turkish army besieging Vienna

1551 Jesuits start Counter-Reformation

1577 Protestant services forbidden by Rudolf II

Triumphal Arch of Maximilian I

The German artist Albrecht Dürer (1471–1528) paid homage to Maximilian I in a famous volume of engravings, which included this design for a triumphal arch.

Philip I married Juana of Castile and Aragon in 1496 and acquired Spain.

THE FAMILY OF MAXIMILIAN I

Painted by Bernhard Strigel (around 1520), this portrait can be read as a document of how, by marrying into prominent European families, the Habsburg family was able to gain control of almost half of Europe.

Mary of Burgundy was married to Maximilian I and was Duchess of the Burgundian domains.

Karl V inherited Spain from his mother, Juana of Castile and Aragon, in 1516.

WHERE TO SEE RENAISSANCE VIENNA

The Schweizertor *(see p97)* in the Hofburg is the most colourful surviving remnant of Renaissance Vienna, though the Salvatorkapelle portal *(p85)* surpasses it in elegance. Also in the Hofburg is the Renaissance Stallburg *(p93)*. Some courtyards, such as those at No. 7 Bäckerstrasse *(p75)* and the Mollard-Clary Palace *(p94)*, preserve a few Renaissance features.

The Schweizertor, *built in the 16th century, forms the entrance to the Schweizerhof of the Hofburg (p97).*

Alte Burg

The medieval core of the Hofburg was constantly being rebuilt. This engraving shows its appearance in the late 15th century, before Ferdinand I had it rebuilt in the 1550s.

Medallion commemorating Maximilian II

	1618 Bohemian rebellion starts Thirty Year's War	**1629** Plague claims 30,000 lives	**1643** Swedish forces threaten Vienna	**1673–9** War with France over the Low Countries
1600	**1620**	**1640**	**1660**	

1598–1618 Protestantism is banned

1620 Ferdinand II defeats Protestant Bohemian aristocracy; Counter-Reformation spreads throughout Habsburg domains

1621 Jews expelled from Inner City

17th-century French infantry

Baroque Vienna

J B Fischer v on Erlach

The Turkish threat to Vienna ended in 1683 when Kara Mustapha's forces were repelled. Under Karl VI the city expanded and the Karlskirche and the Belvedere palaces were constructed. Around the Hofburg, mansions for noble families sprang up, built by architects such as Johann Bernhard Fischer von Erlach *(see p149)* and Johann Lukas von Hildebrandt *(see p152)*. Vienna was transformed into a resplendent Imperial capital.

EXTENT OF THE CITY

▨ *1700*   ☐ *Today*

WINTER PALACE OF PRINCE EUGENE

J B Fischer von Erlach and Johann Lukas von Hildebrandt designed the Winter Palace *(see p80)* for Prince Eugene, hero of the Turkish campaign.

Plague
This lithograph depicts the plague of 1679, which killed around 30,000 Viennese.

Turkish Bed
Ornamented with martial emblems, this bed was designed for Prince Eugene in 1707.

Coffee Houses
The first coffee houses opened in Vienna in the mid-17th century and they have been a prized institution ever since.

Baroque Architecture
Baroque architecture was at its most prolific in Vienna in the early 18th century. Trautson Palace *(see p117)*

TIMELINE

1683 Turkish siege of Vienna by 200,000 soldiers, under Kara Mustapha, from 14 July to 12 September

1700–14 The war of the Spanish Succession

1680		1690		1700

1679 Plague in Vienna

1683–1736 Prince Eugene of Savoy wins more victories over Turks and French, restoring Austria's fortunes

Kara Mustapha

The war of the Spanish Succession: Battle of Blenheim

Turkish Siege

The defeat of the Turks in 1683 was crucial, not only for Vienna, but for Central Europe, which was spared the prospect of Ottoman rule.

Baroque statues

Elaborate window hoods

Baroque porticos

Prince Eugene's entourage

The Prunksaal (1721–6) was built by J B Fischer von Erlach.

Dome ornamentation on the Karlskirche (pp146–7)

Window hood on the Zwölf Apostelkeller (p74)

Prince Eugene

Best remembered for his role in defeating the Turks, Prince Eugene showed great military prowess in the ensuing decades, and died in 1736 laden with honours.

1713 Karl VI proclaims Pragmatic Sanction, allowing succession through the female line

1719 Karlskirche begun

Statue of Maria Theresa holding Pragmatic Sanction

10	1720	1730

1716 Lower Belvedere completed

1713–14 Last plague in Vienna

1722 Vienna becomes an archbishopric

1724–6 Prunksaal and Upper Belvedere completed

Upper Belvedere

Vienna under Maria Theresa

Empress Maria Theresa

The long reign of Maria Theresa was a time of serenity, wealth and sensible administration, despite a background of frequent wars. The vast palace of Schönbrunn was completed by the Empress, who also presided over Vienna's development as the musical capital of Europe. She was succeeded by Joseph II, who introduced many reforms, including religious freedom and public health measures. However, these reforms made him unpopular with his subjects, including the nobility who were angered by the way he handed out titles to bankers and industrialists.

EXTENT OF THE CITY
▨ 1775   ☐ Today

Rococo Table
Wilhelm Martitz designed this Rococo table in 1769 for Maria Theresa, who employed artists committed to the elaborate Rococo style.

Karlskirche   Stephansdom

Young Mozart
Mozart often performed for the Habsburgs, who were highly receptive to his genius.

Burgtheater Programme
This programme was printed for the first performance of Mozart's The Marriage of Figaro in 1786, which took place in the original Burgtheater on Michaelerplatz.

TIMELINE

Christoph von Gluck

1744–9 Schönbrunn Palace is extensively altered by Maria Theresa's court architect, Nikolaus Pacassi

1754 Vienna's first census records a population of 175,000

1740	1750	1760

1740 Maria Theresa comes to the throne; war of the Austrian Succession

Schönbrunn Palace

1762 First performance of Christoph von Gluck's *(see p38) Orpheus and Eurydice* in the Burgtheater

1766 Prater, formerly an imperial game reserve, opened to the public by Joseph II

Damenkarussell

This painting by Martin van Meytens depicts the Damen-karussell (1743), which was held at the Winter Riding School (see pp98–9) to celebrate the defeat of the French army at Prague.

WHERE TO SEE MARIA THERESA'S VIENNA

Schönbrunn Palace (*see pp174–5*) and the Theresianum (*p151*) date from the reign of Maria Theresa. Joseph II later commissioned the Josephinum (*p111*) and the Narrenturm (*p111*), and opened the Augarten (*p164*) and Prater (*pp162–63*) to the public. A Rococo organ is in the Michaelerkirche (*p92*), and some of Maria Theresa's tableware is in the Hofburg Treasuries (*pp100–1*).

VIEW FROM THE BELVEDERE

Under Maria Theresa, the Viennese were able to enjoy a prosperous city. This townscape by Bernardo Bellotto (1759–61) shows them sauntering through the gardens of the Belvedere, with the palaces and churches of the city in the distance.

Belvedere Gardens

Schönbrunn Palace *is filled with Rococo interiors commissioned by Maria Theresa.*

The Pope

In 1782 Pope Pius VI came to Vienna in an attempt to undo the religious reforms of Joseph II.

The Rococo high altar *which is in the Michaelerkirche dates from around 1750.*

1770	1780	1790

1781 Joseph II's Edict of Toleration   *Allgemeine Krankenhaus*

1784 Joseph II founds the Allgemeine Krankenhaus and Narrenturm (*see p111*)

1775 Augarten opened to the public by Joseph II

1782 Pope Pius VI in Vienna

1786 First performance of Mozart's *The Marriage of Figaro* in the Burgtheater

1790–2 Emperor Leopold II

1791 First performance of Mozart's *The Magic Flute*

Biedermeier Vienna

Napoleon's defeat of Austria was a humiliation for Emperor Franz I. The French conqueror briefly occupied Schönbrunn Palace, demolished part of the city walls, and married Franz I's daughter. After the Congress of Vienna, Franz I and his minister, Prince Metternich, imposed autocratic rule in Austria. The middle classes, excluded from political life, retreated into the artistic and domestic pursuits that characterized the Biedermeier age.

Early 19th-century dress

Revolution in 1848 drove Metternich from power but led to a new period of conservative rule under Franz Joseph.

EXTENT OF THE CITY

▨ 1830   ☐ Today

Prince Metternich

The architect of the Congress of Vienna, Metternich gained political supremacy of Austria over four decades. In 1848 revolutionary mobs drove him from Vienna.

THE CONGRESS OF VIENNA

After the defeat of Napoleon in 1814, the victorious European powers gathered in Vienna to restore the established order that had been severely disrupted by the French emperor. The crowned heads and elected rulers of Europe spent a year in the city, where the court and nobility entertained them with a succession of balls and other diversions. The outcome was the restoration of reactionary rule across Europe that, although repressive in many countries, managed to maintain the peace until a series of revolutions swept across Europe in 1848.

The singer Michael Vogl

Franz Schubert playing the piano

TIMELINE

Napoleon Bonaparte

Franz Grillparzer

1800 Vienna's population 232,000

1806 The Holy Roman Empire ends after Franz II abdicates and becomes Emperor Franz I of Austria

1805 First performance of Beethoven's Eroica Symphony and *Fidelio* in Theater an der Wien. Napoleon wins victory at Austerlitz

1809 Napoleon moves into Schönbrunn Palace and marries Franz I's daughter Maria-Louisa

1811 Austria suffers economic collapse and state bankruptcy

1812–14 Napoleon defeated by Russia, Prussia, England and Austria

1815–48 Period of political suppression known as the Vormärz

1814–15 Congress of Vienna held under Presidency of Metternich; Austria loses Belgium but gains parts of Northern Italy

1825 Johann Strauss the Elder forms first waltz orchestra

| 1800 | 1810 | 1820 |

The 1848 Revolution
This painting from 1848 by Anton Ziegler shows the revolution in Vienna, when the middle classes and workers fought together against Metternich.

Biedermeier Chair
This style of furniture characterized the domestic aspirations of Vienna's middle classes in the 1820s.

WHERE TO SEE BIEDERMEIER VIENNA

Napoleon's partial demolition of the city walls led to the creation of the Burggarten *(p102)* and the Volksgarten *(p104)*. Domestic architecture flourished – Biedermeier houses include the Geymüller Schlössl *(p160)* and the Dreimäderlhaus *(p131)* – as did the applied arts *(pp82-3)*.

The Geymüller Schlössl,
dating from 1802, is home to Vienna's Biedermeier museum.

SCHUBERTIADE

Franz Schubert *(see p38)* wrote over 600 songs. These were often performed at musical evenings such as the one shown in this painting, *An Evening at Baron von Spaun's*, by Moritz von Schwind (1804–71).

The Grand Gallop
Waltzes, popularized by Johann Strauss I (the Elder) (see p38), were extremely popular in the 1820s.

1827 Death of Beethoven

1828 Death of Schubert

1830 Vienna's population reaches 318,000

1831–2 Cholera epidemic

1831 The dramatist Franz Grillparzer completes *Des Meeres und der Liebe Wellen*

1830

1837 First railway constructed

1845 Gas lighting introduced

1846 Johann Strauss the Younger becomes music director of the court balls until 1870

1840

1848 Revolution in Vienna; Metternich forced from office, and Emperor Ferdinand I abdicates to be replaced by Franz Joseph

1850 City population reaches 431,000

Ringstrasse Vienna

The Emperor Franz Joseph ushered in a new age of grandeur, despite the dwindling power of the Habsburgs. The city's defences were demolished and a circular boulevard, the Ringstrasse, was built, linking new cultural and political institutions. Vienna attracted gifted men and women from all over the empire, as well as traders from Eastern Europe. However, the resulting ethnic brew often resulted in overcrowding and social tension.

Franz Joseph

EXTENT OF THE CITY

▨ *1885*   ☐ *Today*

Votivkirche (1856–79) *p111*
Heinrich Ferstel

Neues Rathaus (1872–83) *p130*
Friedrich von Schmidt

Parliament (1874–84) *p121*
Theophil Hansen

The Natural History Museum (1871–1890) *pp128–9, Gottfried Semper*

Kunsthistorisches Museum (1871–1890) *pp122–7 Gottfried Semper*

THE SUICIDE OF ARCHDUKE RUDOLF AT MAYERLING

In 1889 the 30-year-old heir to the throne was found dead with his mistress Mary Vetsera. The Archduke's suicide was more than a social scandal. It was a blow to the Habsburg regime, since he was a progressive and intelligent man. His despair may have been aggravated by court protocol that offered no outlet for his ideas.

Theophil Hansen
This Danish-born architect (1813–91) studied in Athens before settling in Vienna. The Greek influence is most evident in his Parliament building on the Ringstrasse.

TIMELINE

Excavation for the Ringstrasse

1867 First performance of *The Blue Danube* by Strauss in Vienna. Hungary granted autonomy, leading to Dual Monarchy with separate governments

| 1850 | 1855 | 1860 | 1865 |

Anton Bruckner

1857–65 Demolition of fortifications and the building of the Ringstrasse

1868 Anton Bruckner *(see p39)* moves from Linz to Vienna

1869 Johannes Brahms settles in Vienna as conductor of the Gesellschaft der Musikfreunde. Opera House opens on Ringstrasse

The Danube
The River Danube often flooded its banks, so its course was altered and regulated in the 1890s by a system of canals and locks.

Vienna Café Society
In the 19th century, Vienna's cafés became the haunts of literary and political cliques.

Museum of Applied Arts (1867–71) *pp82–3, Heinrich Ferstel*

Horse-drawn Trams
Trams appeared on the Ringstrasse in the 1860s. Horseless trams ran along it by the end of the 19th century.

Stadtpark

Opera House (1861–69) *pp140–1 Eduard van der Nüll and August Siccardsburg*

RINGSTRASSE
This great boulevard, built on the orders of Franz Joseph, separates the Stephansdom and Hofburg Quarters from the suburbs. Completed in the 1880s, the Ringstrasse is as grand now as it was then.

The Opening of the Stadtpark
Laid out on either side of the River Wien, the Stadtpark was inaugurated in 1862.

1874 First performance of Strauss's *Die Fledermaus* at the Theater an der Wien. Opening of Central Cemetery

1889 Suicide of Archduke Rudolf at Mayerling

| 1870 | 1875 | 1880 | 1885 |

1873 Stock market crash

1872 Death of Austrian poet and dramatist Franz Grillparzer

1879 Lavish historical parade along the Ringstrasse celebrates Franz Joseph's silver wedding

1890 The suburbs are incorporated into the city

Vienna in the 1900s

Engel Apotheke sign

The turn of the century was a time of intellectual ferment in Vienna. This was the age of Freud, of the writers Karl Kraus and Arthur Schnitzler, and of the Secession and Jugendstil *(see pp54–7)*. At this time artists such as Gustav Klimt and the architects Otto Wagner and Adolf Loos *(see p92)* created revolutionary new styles. This was all set against a decaying Habsburg empire, which Karl I's abdication in 1918 brought to an end. After World War I Austria became a republic.

EXTENT OF THE CITY

▨ *1912*   ☐ *Today*

Wiener Werkstätte
Josef Hoffmann (see p56), designer of this chair, was the principal artist and founder of this Viennese arts workshop (see p83).

KIRCHE AM STEINHOF
This stupendous church was designed by Otto Wagner and decorated by Kolo Moser *(see p57)*.

Loos Haus
The restrained elegance of this former tailoring firm is typical of Loos's style (see p92).

The Secession
This poster by Kolo Moser (see p57) was used to publicize the Secession's exhibitions.

Angels by Othmar Schimkowitz

TIMELINE

1899 First issue of Karl Kraus's periodical *Die Fackel*

1903 Wiener Werkstätte founded

1906 Arnold Schönberg's *Chamber Symphony* and works by Anton von Webern and Alban Berg performed at the Musikverein, provoking a riot

1895 ———————————— **1900** ———————————— **1905**

1897 Secession established when 19 painters and architects break with the Künstlerhaus. Karl Lueger becomes mayor

1902 Gustav Klimt paints the *Beethoven Frieze*. Tramways are electrified

1905 Franz Lehar's operetta *The Merry Widow* first performed. Anti-Semitic riots at the university

1896 Death of the composer Anton Bruckner

Gustav Klimt

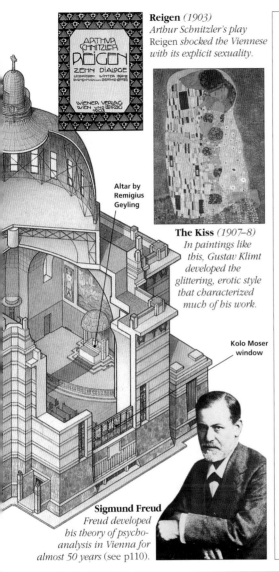

Reigen (*1903*)
Arthur Schnitzler's play
Reigen *shocked the Viennese
with its explicit sexuality.*

**Altar by
Remigius
Geyling**

The Kiss (*1907–8*)
*In paintings like
this, Gustav Klimt
developed the
glittering, erotic style
that characterized
much of his work.*

**Kolo Moser
window**

Sigmund Freud
*Freud developed
his theory of psycho-
analysis in Vienna for
almost 50 years* (see p110).

WHERE TO SEE 1900S VIENNA

Otto Wagner designed the Karlsplatz Pavilions (*see p146*), the Wagner Apartments (*p139*) and the Kirche am Steinhof (*p160*). Adolf Loos designed Loos Haus (*p92*) and the American Bar (*p105*). Suburban architecture includes the Wagner Villas (*p160*). Works by Klimt, Schiele and Kokoschka are displayed at the Upper Belvedere (*pp154–5*), the Museum of Modern Art (*p120*) and the Leopold Museum (*p120*).

The Secession Building *is
where Gustav Klimt's Beethoven Frieze is exhibited* (p55).

The Wagner Apartments *are
decorated with Jugendstil motifs*
(p56) *by Kolo Moser* (p57).

1907 Gustav Mahler resigns as director of Court Opera. Hitler studies art in Vienna

1911 Death of Gustav Mahler

1914 Archduke Ferdinand assassinated in Sarajevo; international crisis follows resulting in World War I

1910

1915

1910 Death of Karl Lueger

1916 Death of Franz Joseph

1908 *The Kiss* by Klimt is first exhibited

1918 Declaration of Austrian Republic after abdication of Emperor Karl I. Austria shrinks from an empire of 50 million to a state of 6.5 million

Modern Vienna

Two decades of struggle between the left and right political parties followed World War I, ending with the union of Austria with Germany – the Anschluss – in 1938. After World War II Vienna was split among the Allies until 1955, when Austria regained its independence.

1929 Ludwig Wittgenstein, a prominent member of the Vienna circle, leaves Vienna for England

1927 Workers, angered by deaths of bystanders during political violence, storm the Palace of Justice

1922 Karl Kraus publishes his immense drama *The Last Days of Mankind*

1944 Allied bombing of Vienna begins

1951 The First Festival of Vienna

1955 On 15 May the Austrian State Treaty brings to an end the Allied occupation. Austria granted independence and declares itself to be permanently neutral

1967 UN Industrial Development Organization (UNIDO) comes to Vienna

1920	1930	1940	1950	1960

1920	1930	1940	1950	1960

1922 Death in Madeira of exiled Karl I, last Habsburg emperor

1920–34 Socialism prevails in so-called "Red Vienna", despite conservative Catholic rule in Austria

1918–20 Severe food shortages and an influenza epidemic afflict the Viennese

1933 Chancellor Dollfuss dissolves Parliament and forms a fascist regime, but refuses to accommodate Hitler

1934 Street fighting in Vienna between socialists and government troops; socialists banned. Murder of Chancellor Dollfuss by the Nazis

1939 Death of novelist Joseph Roth

1945 World War II ends. The second Austrian republic is declared, but Vienna remains divided between the four Allied powers

1955 Reopening of Opera House and Burgtheater

1961 John F Kennedy meets Nikita Khrushchev at East-West summit in Vienna

1938 Chancellor Schuschnigg resigns. Hitler enters Vienna and pronounces Anschluss

1956 Atomic Energy Agency located in Vienna

1959 Ernst Fuchs and Arik Brauer establish the school of fantastic realism

1988 Irmgard Seefried, star of the Vienna Opera House, dies

1986 The controversial Kurt Waldheim elected president; Franz Vranitzky elected Chancellor

1989 Death of Empress Zita, the last Habsburg to have ruled Austria

1979 East-West summit held between Leonid Brezhnev and Jimmy Carter

1983 Pope John Paul visits Vienna

1978 U-Bahn system opened

1970–83 Socialist Bruno Kreisky is Chancellor

1992 Fire in the Hofburg Palace

2010 Red Vienna loses absolute majority – coalition with Green Party

2008 Football European Cup

1970	1980	1990	2000	2010	2020

1970	1980	1990	2000	2010	2020

2006 Mozart year commemorated; 250 years since Mozart's birth

2010 Rise of far-right leader H.C. Strache

2008 Jörg Haider dies in car crash

1995 Austria joins the European Union

2009 Haydn Year

1985 Hundertwasser Haus by Friedensreich Hundertwasser completed

1989 Velvet Revolution in Czechoslovakia heralds Austria's growing economic influence in the new democratic central Europe. Completion of Hans Hollein's Haas Haus in Stephansplatz

1979 UNO city opened

Music in Vienna

From the late 18th to the mid 19th centuries Vienna was the music capital of Europe. At first the Habsburg family and the aristocracy were the city's musical paymasters, but with the rise of the middle classes during the Biedermeier period *(see pp30–31)* music became an important part of bourgeois life. Popular music also flourished as migration from all parts of the Habsburg Empire brought in richly diverse styles of music and dance.

The Waltz became popular following the Congress of Vienna in 1814

a state occasion. The music of Franz Schubert (1797–1828) was little known in his short lifetime. He mostly performed chamber works, piano music and songs at Biedermeier *Schubertiaden* – evenings of music with friends. His music became more popular following his death. After this, "serious" music went through a

CLASSICISM

In the 18th century, Vienna's musical life was dominated by the Imperial Court. Christoph Willibald Gluck (1714–87) was Court *Kapellmeister* (in charge of the court orchestra) to Maria Theresa until 1770, and wrote 10 operas specially for Vienna, including *Orpheus and Eurydice* (1762). His contemporary Wolfgang Amadeus Mozart (1756–91) later built on these foundations. Joseph Haydn (1732–1809) moved to Vienna in the 1790s from Prince Esterházy's palace in Eisenstadt *(see pp176–7)*, and wrote masterpieces such as *The Creation*.

Performance of The Creation (1808) on Haydn's birthday

ROMANTICISM

With the arrival of Ludwig van Beethoven (1770–1827) in Vienna in the mid-1790s, the age of the composer as romantic hero was born. Beethoven was a controversial figure in his time, and many of his most innovative works were only successful outside Vienna. His funeral, however, attended by more than 10,000 people, was

Biedermeier *Schubertiade* evening

fallow period in Vienna, but Johann Strauss I (1804–49) and Joseph Lanner (1801–43) began creating dance music, centred on the waltz.

Performance of The Magic Flute (1791) by Mozart

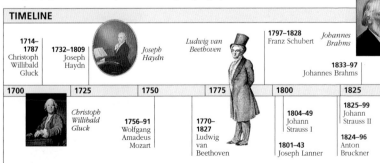

TIMELINE

1700	1725	1750	1775	1800	1825
1714–1787 Christoph Willibald Gluck	**1732–1809** Joseph Haydn	*Joseph Haydn*	*Ludwig van Beethoven*	**1797–1828** Franz Schubert	*Johannes Brahms*
					1833–97 Johannes Brahms
	Christoph Willibald Gluck	**1756–91** Wolfgang Amadeus Mozart	**1770–1827** Ludwig van Beethoven	**1804–49** Johann Strauss I	**1825–99** Johann Strauss II
				1801–43 Joseph Lanner	**1824–96** Anton Bruckner

AGE OF FRANZ JOSEPH

A new era of high musical art began in the 1860s. Johannes Brahms (1833–97) came to Vienna in 1862, and incorporated popular musical styles into works such as his Liebeslieder waltzes and Hungarian Dances. The Romantic composer Anton Bruckner (1824–96) came to the city from Upper Austria in 1868. Johann Strauss II (1825–99) rose to the status of civic hero, composing nearly 400 waltzes, including his famous operetta *Die Fledermaus.* One popular offshoot of the period was *Schrammel* music, named after Joseph Schrammel

Jugendstil poster (1901) for the Waltz depicting Johann Strauss II

(1850–93) and characterized by an ensemble of guitars, violins and accordion. Popular music also influenced Gustav Mahler (1860–1911), director of the Vienna Opera for 10 years.

THE MODERNS

The early years of the 20th century saw the rise of the Second Viennese School: Alban Berg (1885–1935), Arnold Schönberg (1874–1951) and Anton von Webern (1883–1945). These composers were not well received in Vienna, and Schönberg found he had to start his own society to get his works, and those of his colleagues, heard. In 1933 he emigrated to the USA. Since World War II no composers of comparable stature have arisen, though Kurt Schwertsik (born 1935) and H K Gruber (born 1943) now attract international attention. However, the Vienna Philharmonic, established in 1842, is still one of the finest orchestras in the world. The State Opera continues to enjoy a strong reputation, and Vienna has an abundance of fine orchestras, opera and operetta venues, chamber ensembles and choirs.

The Johann Strauss II orchestra at a Court ball

Concert poster (1913) for Arnold Schönberg

1860–1911 Gustav Mahler	1874–1951 Arnold Schönberg
	1875
1883–1945 Anton von Webern	1885–1935 Alban Berg
1850–93 Joseph Schrammel	

VIENNA BOYS' CHOIR

The world-famous Vienna Boys' Choir, the Wiener Sängerknaben, was founded in 1498 by that great patron of the arts, Maximilian I. Today the boys perform masses by Mozart, Schubert or Haydn on Sundays and church holidays at the Burg-kapelle *(see p103).* To obtain a seat you need to book at least eight weeks in advance.

VIENNA AT A GLANCE

Vienna is a compact city and most of its sights are contained within a small area. However, the city boasts an astonishing array of monuments, palaces, parks and museums, which themselves house an impressive array of art and artefacts from all over the world and from all periods of history. Nearly 150 sights are listed in the *Area by Area* section of this book, but to help make the most of your stay, the next 20 pages offer a guide to the very best that Vienna has to offer. As well as churches, palaces, museums and galleries, there are sections on Jugendstil art and coffee houses. Many of the sights listed have a cross-reference to their own full entry. To start with, some of Vienna's top tourist attractions are listed below.

VIENNA'S TOP TOURIST ATTRACTIONS

Opera House
See pp140–41.

Burgtheater
See pp132–33.

Prater
See pp162–63.

Schönbrunn See pp172–75.

Karlskirche
See pp148–49.

Kunsthistorisches Museum
See pp122–27.

Spanish Riding School
See pp98–9.

Stephansdom See pp76–9.

Belvedere
See pp152–57.

Café Central
See p61.

MuseumsQuartier
See p118–20.

◁ The façade of Otto Wagner's Majolikahaus *(see p139)* on the Linke Wienzeile

Vienna's Best: Historic Houses and Palaces

Baroque mansions dominate the streets of the Stephansdom Quarter, while outside the centre of Vienna are the grand summer palaces where the Habsburg emperors and aristocracy lived during warm Middle European summers. The interiors of several of the houses can be visited, while others can only be admired from the outside or from their inner courtyards and staircases. Further details can be found on pages 44–5.

Sigmund Freud's House
This waiting room in the house on Berggasse, where Sigmund Freud lived from 1891 to 1938, has been lovingly restored.

Kinsky Palace
This mansion (1713–16) by Johann Lukas von Hildebrandt (see p152), was built for the Daun family, and is sometimes called the Daun Kinsky Palace. Wirch Philip Daun was commander of the city garrison, and his son Leopold Joseph Daun was Maria Theresa's field marshal.

Schottenring and Alsergrund

Museum and Townhall Quarter

Hofburg
The apartments here are made up of over 20 rooms; among them are ceremonial halls and living quarters which were once occupied by Franz Joseph (see pp32–3) and the Empress Elisabeth.

0 kilometres   0.5

0 miles   0.25

Opera and Naschmarkt

Schönbrunn Palace
This palace, by J B Fischer von Erlach, was built on a scale to rival the palace of Versailles outside Paris. Parts of it were later redesigned by Maria Theresa's architect Nikolaus Pacassi (see p172).

Neidhart Fresco House
Frescoes dating from 1400, depicting the songs of the medieval minnesinger Neidhart van Reuenthal, decorate the dining room of this former house of a wealthy clockmaker.

Mozarthaus Vienna
Mozart lived in this Baroque building for three years between 1784 and 1787, and composed one of his most famous works, The Marriage of Figaro, *here.*

ephansdom Quarter

ofburg uarter

Winter Palace of Prince Eugene
J B Fischer von Erlach and Johann Lukas von Hildebrandt designed this Baroque palace, with its spectacular staircase, for the war hero Prince Eugene (see pp26–7).

Zum Blauen Karpfen
A stucco relief of a blue carp and a frieze of putti *adorn the façade of this 17th-century house on Annagasse.*

Belvedere Quarter

Belvedere
Designed by Johann Lukas von Hildebrandt, Prince Eugene's summer palaces were built on what were originally the southern outskirts of Vienna. The Upper Belvedere now houses the Museum of Austrian Art.

Exploring Vienna's Historic Houses and Palaces

A stroll around Vienna's streets offers the visitor an unparalleled choice of beautifully-preserved historic buildings, from former imperial residences to humbler burgher's dwellings. The majority date from the 17th and 18th centuries, and illustrate the various phases of Baroque architecture. In most cases their original function as residences of the rich and famous has been superseded; a number have now been turned into museums, and their interiors are open to the public.

Façade of the Schönborn-Batthyány Palace

TOWN PALACES

The most extensive town palace is the **Hofburg**, with its museums and imperial apartments. The staircase of the magnificent **Winter Palace of Prince Eugene** is on view to the public, and the 19th-century Neo-Gothic **Ferstel Palace** (1860) houses the Café Central (see p58). The **Obizzi Palace** is home to the Clock Museum (see p86). Town palaces which can be admired from the outside only are the **Kinsky Palace** (1713–16), **Trautson Palace**, **Schönborn-Batthyány Palace**, **Lobkowitz Palace** and **Liechtenstein Palace** (1694–1706), the winter home of the Liechtenstein family.

GARDEN PALACES

Although it seems strange that palaces within the city limits should be termed garden palaces, when they were built they were outside the city boundaries, and offered a cool refuge during the hot summer months for the inhabitants. The most famous example is **Schönbrunn Palace**, where the state apartments can be seen as part of a guided tour. The **Belvedere**, to the south of the city, houses the Museum of Austrian Art, and many of the rooms retain their original splendid decoration. The **Hermes Villa** (1884), a cross between a hunting lodge and a Viennese villa, was commissioned by Franz Joseph for his wife Elisabeth. The interior of the Neo-Classical **Rasumofsky Palace** (1806–7), can sometimes be seen on special occasions. The **Liechtenstein Museum** houses the private art collection of the Liechtenstein family (see p111). The pieces include Renaissance sculpture and Baroque paintings.

Frescoed ceiling of the Liechtenstein Museum

SUBURBAN VILLAS

The Döbling regional museum is housed in the Biedermeier **Villa Wertheimstein** (1834–5), where the interior is furnished in its original flamboyant and overcrowded manner. By contrast, the **Geymüller Schlössl**, containing the Sobek Collection of clocks and watches, is a model of taste and restraint. In Hietzing, the **Villa Primavesi** (1913–15) is a small Jugendstil masterpiece designed by Josef Hoffmann (see p56) for the banker Robert Primavesi.

BURGHERS' HOUSES

On Tuchlauben, the **Neidhart Fresco House** is decorated with secular frescoes from around 1400. Charming Baroque houses of modest dimensions can be seen on **Naglergasse** and **Kurrentgasse** and in inner districts such as **Spittelberg** and **Josefstadt**. A particularly fine example of external decoration can be seen on the Baroque inn **Zum Blauen Karpfen** in Annagasse (see p80). The **Dreimäderlhaus** in Schreyvogelgasse, built in an inter-mediate style between Rococo and Neo-Classicism, is also worth visiting.

Façade and gardens of the Hermes Villa

MEMORIAL HOUSES

Vienna abounds in the former residences of famous composers. They are not all of great architectural merit, and their interest resides mainly in the exhibits they contain. The **Pasqualati Haus** was one of Beethoven's many Viennese residences – it was here that he composed the opera *Fidelio* – and it now houses portraits and other mementoes of the great composer. The **Heiligenstadt Testament House** (at No. 6 Probusgasse, Heiligenstadt), where Beethoven stayed in an attempt to cure his deafness, is now a memorial. The first-floor apartment of the **Haydn Museum** in Haydngasse is pleasantly

Courtyard of the Heiligenstadt Testament House

furnished and filled with letters, manuscripts, personal possessions and the composer's two pianos. Mozart and his family lived from 1784–7 in the **Mozarthaus Vienna**. This is where Mozart

wrote *The Marriage of Figaro*. The **Freud Museum** houses furnishings, documents and photographs, and the waiting room is as it looked when Freud used to see his patients. It is also a study centre.

DECORATIVE DETAILS

Many of the historic houses and palaces of Vienna were built during a period corresponding to the Baroque and late Baroque styles of architecture. Details such as window hoods and pediments over doorways were often extremely ornate.

Caryatid on the doorway of the Liechtenstein Palace

Decorative window hood on the façade of the Trautson Palace

Decorative urns on the Lobkowitz Palace

Decorative pediment with shield on the Schönborn-Batthyány Palace.

Stucco *putti* on the façade of Zum Blauen Karpfen

Vienna's Best: Museums and Galleries

Vienna boasts an astonishing number of museums, and many of the collections are housed in elegant former palaces or handsome buildings specially commissioned for the purpose. Some of the museums are of international importance, while others are of more local or specialist interest. Further details can be found on pages 48–9.

Natural History Museum
This museum has displays of fossils, ethnography, mineralogy and a much-visited dinosaur hall.

Sacred and Secular Treasuries
The Ainkurn sword (around 1450) can be seen in the Imperial Treasuries in the former imperial palace of the Hofburg.

Schottenring and Alsergrund

Museum and Townhall Quarter

Hofburg Quarter

Kunsthistorisches Museum
Hans Holbein's portrait of Jane Seymour (1536) is one of hundreds of Old Master paintings displayed in this fine art museum.

Opera and Naschmarkt

MuseumsQuartier
This vast cultural centre contains the largest Egon Schiele collection in the world, including this Self-portrait with Lowered Head *(1912).*

Albertina
This museum houses temporary exhibitions, mainly based on the Albertina's celebrated collection of prints and drawings (here, Albrecht Dürer's The Hare *dated 1502).*

Wien Museum Karlsplatz
Stained-glass windows from the Stephansdom (around 1390) are among the many items here documenting Vienna's history.

Cathedral Museum
This St Andrew's cross reliquary (about 1440) is one of many medieval religious treasures on display here.

Austrian Museum of Applied Arts
The applied arts of Vienna, such as this early 19th-century beaker and Wiener Werkstätte furniture (see pp54–7), are among the varied artefacts on display in this museum.

Stephansdom Quarter

The Belvedere
The Upper Belvedere displays art from the Middle Ages onwards, including medieval painting and sculpture and Renaissance and Baroque works. Ferdinand Waldmüller's Roses in the Window, *shown here, is displayed on the upper floor, along with Gustav Klimt's* The Kiss. *The Lower Belvedere and Orangery house temporary exhibitions.*

Belvedere Quarter

Heeresgeschichtliches Museum
Paintings of battles and military commanders, such as Sigmund L'Allemand's portrait of Field Marshal Gideon-Ernst Freiherr von Laudon (1878), are part of this museum's collection.

0 kilometres   0.5

0 miles   0.25

DANUBE CANAL

Exploring Vienna's Museums and Galleries

Vienna's museums exhibit an amazing variety of fine, decorative and ethnic art from all periods of history and from different regions of the world. The visitor can see artifacts from all over the ancient world as well as more recent collections, from medieval religious art to 19th- and 20th-century paintings. Silverware is displayed in the city's imperial collections, and Vienna is also unrivalled for its turn-of-the-century exhibits.

Interior of Friedensreich Hundert- wasser's Kunsthaus Wien

ANCIENT AND MEDIEVAL ART

Vienna has marvellous collections of medieval art. The **Neidhart Fresco House** contains medieval secular frescoes, while a number of superb Gothic altarpieces can be seen in the historic Palace Stables at the **Belvedere**. Displayed in the **Cathedral Museum** are outstanding Gothic sculptures as well as masterpieces of applied art; the highlight is a 9th-century Carolingian Gospel. The **Sacred and Secular Treasuries** in the Hofburg are awash with precious medieval objects, including the insignia and crown of the Holy Roman Empire, and a unique collection of medieval objects and Gothic paintings is on display in the treasury of the **Deutschordenskirche**. The splendours of the Verduner Altar at **Klosterneuberg** await

those prepared to make a short journey out of the cen- tre of Vienna. The **Ephesos Museum** of the Hofburg houses ancient Roman and Greek antiquities unearthed at the turn of the century.

OLD MASTERS

The picture gallery in the **Kunsthistorisches Museum** has one of the best collec- tions of Old Masters in the world, reflecting the tastes of the many generations of Habsburg collectors who formed it. There are works by Flemish and Venetian artists, and the best collection of Bruegels on display in any art gallery, as well as Giuseppe Arcimboldo's (1527–93) curious portraits composed of fruit and vegetables. The **Academy of Fine Arts** houses some fine examples of Dutch and Flemish works, its prize exhibit being Hieronymos Bosch's triptych of the *Last Judgement*, which contains

some of the most horrifying images in Christan art. There are also paintings by Johannes Vermeer (1632–75) and Peter Paul Rubens (1577–1640). The ground floor of the Upper Belvedere focuses on Austrian paintings and sculptures from the 17th and 18th centuries. The Bel- vedere itself is a masterpiece of Baroque architecture.

19TH- AND 20TH-CENTURY ART

A permanent display of 19th- and 20th-century Austrian art is housed in the Upper Belvedere. The most famous exhibits are by Gustav Klimt. *Beethoven Frieze* is regarded as one of the masterpieces of Viennese Art Nouveau and can be seen in the **Secession Building.**

The **Museum of Modern Art**, which is located in the MuseumsQuartier *(see p120)*, contains exhibits by 20th- century European artists. They include works by the Viennese avant-garde.

The **Leopold Museum** has an enormous Egon Schiele collection, as well as Expressionist and Austri- an inter-war paintings. The work of Friedensreich Hundertwasser, perhaps Vien- na's best-known modern artist, is on show at the **Kunsthaus Wien**. Prints, drawings and photographs are housed in the **Albertina**.

Parthian monument (around AD 170) in the Ephesos Museum

THE APPLIED ARTS AND INTERIORS

On display in the **Austrian Museum of Applied Arts** is a rich collection of the decorative arts, including Oriental carpets, medieval ecclesiastical garments, Biedermeier and Jugendstil furniture, and the archives of the Wiener Werkstätte. The **Wien Museum Karlsplatz** houses a reconstructed version of the poet Franz Grillparzer's apartment as well as Adolf Loos's *(see p92)* drawing room. In the **Silberkammer** of the Hofburg is a dazzling array of dinner services collected by the Habsburgs. The **Lobmeyr Museum** exhibits glassware designed by Josef Hoffmann.

Glass by Josef Hoffmann in the Lobmeyr Museum

Picture clock in the Clock Museum

SPECIALIST MUSEUMS

Clock enthusiasts can visit the **Clock Museum** and the Sobek Clock and Watch Collection at the **Geymüller Schlössl**. Music is celebrated at the **Sammlung Alter Musikinstrumente**, while the darker side of life can be seen at the **Kriminalmuseum**, and at the **Bestattungsmuseum**, which houses exhibits to do with Viennese funeral rites. The **Heeresgeschichtliches Museum** houses reminders of Austria's military past. The **Hofjagd und Rüstkammer** exhibits historical weaponry. Other specialist museums include the **Österreichisches Filmmuseum** and the **Haus der Musik**.

NATURAL HISTORY AND SCIENCE

Still occupying the building constructed for it in the 19th century is the **Natural History Museum**, which has displays of mineralogy, dinosaur skeletons and zoology. The **Josephinum** houses a range of wax anatomical models, while the **Technical Museum** documents the contribution Austria has made to developments in technology, ranging from home-made items such as an amateur wooden typewriter, to the invention of the car.

ETHNOLOGY AND FOLKLORE

Vienna's Museum of Ethnology in the Hofburg, the **Völkerkundemuseum**, contains objects from all over the world. There are artifacts from Mexico and a collection of musical instruments, masks and textiles from the Far East. The Benin collection from Africa is also on display in the museum *(see p95)*. There is also a section on Eskimo culture. The **Museum für Volks kunde** in Josefstadt houses fascinating exhibits on Austrian folklore and rural life over the centuries.

Benin carving in the Völkerkundemuseum

Vienna's Best: Churches

Vienna's most potent symbol is its cathedral – the
Stephansdom – a masterpiece of Gothic architecture
which stands out in a city where the overwhelming
emphasis is on the Baroque. After the defeat of the
Turks in 1683 *(see pp26–7)*, many churches were
built or remodelled in the Baroque style, although it
is often possible to detect the vestiges of older
buildings beneath later additions. Many church
interiors are lavishly furnished, and several have fine
frescoes. Churches are generally open during the day
except when mass is being held. Stage concerts or
organ recitals are given in the evenings in some
churches. A more detailed overview of Vienna's
churches is on pages 52–3.

Peterskirche
*The tall dome of this late
Baroque church dominates
the view as you approach
from the Graben.*

*Schottenring and
Alsergrund*

*Museum and
Townhall Quarter*

*Hofburg
Quarter*

Michaelerkirche
*This church has one of the most impressive
medieval interiors in Vienna. The Neo-Classical
façade and this cascade of Baroque stucco angels
over the high altar were later additions.*

Maria Treu Kirche
*A statue of Mary
Immaculate graces
the square in front of
this Baroque church
(1716). Its façade
dates from 1860.*

*Opera and
Naschmarkt*

| 0 kilometres | 0.5 |
| 0 miles | 0.25 |

Augustinerkirche
*Antonio Canova's (1753–1822) tomb
for Archduchess Maria Christina is in
the Gothic Augustinerkirche,
which once served as the
Habsburgs' parish church.*

Maria am Gestade
*Dating from the 14th century,
this church was restored in
the 19th century. This 15th-
century Gothic panel, shows
The Annunciation.*

Ruprechtskirche
*Vienna's oldest church has a Romanesque
nave and bell tower, a Gothic aisle and choir,
and stained-glass windows which date back
to the turn of the 14th century.*

Stephansdom
*The richly-carved Wiener
Neustädter Altar from 1447
was a gift from Friedrich III
(see p19).*

*Stephansdom
Quarter*

Jesuitenkirche
*A series of twisted
columns rise up to
support the vault of the
Jesuitenkirche (1623–31),
which also features a
trompe l'oeil dome.*

*Belvedere
Quarter*

Karlskirche
*J B Fischer von
Erlach's eclectic
Baroque masterpiece
(1714–39) boasts a
dome, minarets and
two Chinese-inspired
lateral pavilions.*

Franziskanerkirche
*The dramatic high altar
(1707) by Andrea Pozzo
features a Bohemian
statue of the Virgin
Mary as its centrepiece.*

Exploring Vienna's Churches

Many of Vienna's Churches have undergone modifications over the centuries, and they often present a fascinating mixture of styles, ranging from Romanesque to Baroque. The great era for church building in the city was in the 17th and 18th centuries, when the triumphant Catholic church, in a spate of Counter-Reformation fervour, remodelled several early churches and built new ones. A number of churches were also constructed after the Turks were defeated in 1683 *(see pp26–7)*, and the city as a whole was able to spread out beyond its earlier confines.

MEDIEVAL CHURCHES

At the heart of the city is the **Stephansdom**. Parts date from Romanesque times but most of the cathedral is Gothic; it contains a collection of Gothic sculpture, including a pulpit by Anton Pilgram *(see p78)*. Vienna's oldest church is the **Ruprechtskirche**, which stands in its own square in the Bermuda Triangle *(see p84)*; its plain façade contrasts with the delicate Gothic tracery of **Maria am Gestade**, which has a filigree spire and a lofty, vaulted interior. The early interior of the **Deutschordens-kirche** contains a number of heraldic blazons. A late Romanesque basilica with Gothic modifications lurks behind the façade of the **Michaelerkirche**. The 14th-century

Madonna and Child in the Minoritenkirche

Augustinerkirche contains the hearts of the Habsburg families *(see pp24–5)* down the centuries as well as Antonio Canova's tomb for Maria Christina *(see p102)*. The façade of the **Minoriten-kirche** is built in French Gothic style with an ornate interior; the same is true of the **Burgkapelle**.

17TH-CENTURY CHURCHES

There is little Renaissance architecture in Vienna, but a number of churches built before the Turkish siege survive. The **Franziskaner-kirche**, with its gabled façade and theatrical high altar, and the **Jesuitenkirche** are fine examples of the architecture inspired by the Counter-Reformation *(see p24)*. The **Ursulinenkirche**, built between 1665 and 1675, has a high-galleried interior and **Annakirche** is notable for its beautiful Baroque tower. The **Dominikanerkirche** has a majestic early Baroque façade, built in the 1630s by Antonio Caneval. Although it dates back to Romanesque times, the bulk of the rather squat **Schottenkirche** was built between 1638 and 1648. In the middle of the Baroque square of Am Hof is the impressive façade of the **Kirche am Hof**. It was founded by the Carmelites and is also known as "Church of the Nine Choir Angels".

Carving of St Anne (about 1505) in Annakirche, attributed to Veit Stoss

LATE BAROQUE AND NEO-CLASSICAL CHURCHES

After the Turkish defeat *(see pp26–7)*, a number of Viennese High Baroque churches were built. The most exotic is the **Karlskirche**, and just off the Graben is the great **Peterskirche**. The tiny, ornate **Stanislaus-Kostka Chapel** was once the home of a Polish saint. Two graceful 18th-century churches are to be found on the edge of the inner city: the majestic **Maria Treu Kirche** and the **Ulrichskirche**. Joseph Korn-häusel's **Stadttempel** has a Neo-Classical interior.

TOWERS, DOMES AND SPIRES

Vienna's skyline is punctuated by the domes, spires and towers of its fine churches. Topping **Maria am Gestade** is a delicate openwork lantern, while the **Ruprechtskirche** tower is characteristically squat. The towers of the **Jesuitenkirche** are Baroque and bulbous, and **Karlskirche** has freestanding columns. **Peterskirche** has an oval dome and small towers.

Ruprechts-kirche

Maria am Gestade

Jesuitenkirche

The frescoed interior of the late Baroque Stanislaus-Kostka Chapel

19TH-CENTURY CHURCHES

During the 19th century the prevailing mood of Viennese architecture was one of Romantic historicism. Elements of past styles were adopted and re-created, for churches and for many other municipal buildings, specifically on the Ringstrasse *(see pp32–3)*. The **Griechische Kirche** on Fleischmarkt, took its inspiration from Byzantine architecture, and the inside is replete with iconostases and

frescoes. The **Votivkirche**, built just off the Ringstrasse as an expression of gratitude for Franz Joseph's escape from assassination, is based on French Gothic architecture; its richly-coloured interior contains the marble tomb of Count Niklas Salm, who defended Vienna from the Turks during the siege of 1529 *(see p24)*. On Lerchenfelder Strasse the red-brick **Altlerchenfelder Kirche** is a 19th-century architectural hodge-podge of Gothic and Italian Renaissance styles.

20TH-CENTURY CHURCHES

A masterpiece of early 20th-century church architecture is Otto Wagner's *(see p57)* massive **Kirche am Steinhof**, built to serve a psychiatric hospital. The interior has a slightly clinical air, since it is tiled in white, but the austerity is relieved by Kolo Moser's *(see p57)* stained-glass windows and mosaics.

The haphazard, sculpted blocks of the modern Wotruba Kirche.

The **Dr-Karl-Lueger- Kirche**, located in the Central Cemetery, was built by a protégé of Otto Wagner, Max Hegele, and has the same monumental feel about it. For true devotees of the modern, there is the **Wotruba Kirche** on Georgsgasse in the suburb of Mauer, designed by the sculptor Fritz Wotruba. Not universally liked, this looks as if it is a haphazard assembly of concrete blocks.

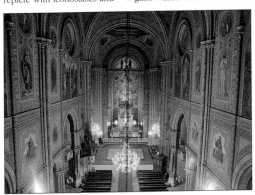

19th-century interior of the Altlerchenfelder Kirche

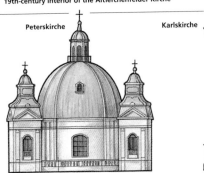

Peterskirche

Karlskirche

Vienna's Best: Jugendstil

A stroll around Vienna's streets will reveal the richness of the city's turn-of-the-century architecture. Some of the buildings are well known and instantly recognizable, and a few of the public ones, such as the Secession building, can be seen inside. However, it can be just as rewarding to discover the lesser-known buildings and monuments of the period and to savour the variety of finely-crafted architectural details. Further details can be found on pages 56–7.

Strudelhof Steps
The setting for a famous novel of the same name by Heimato von Doderer (1896–1966), these magnificent steps were built by Theodore Jäger in 1910.

Schottenri
and
Alsergrun

Kirche am Steinhof
Commissioned for the grounds of a lunatic asylum on the outskirts of the city, this church with its grand copper dome was designed by Otto Wagner in 1905. The stained-glass windows are by Kolo Moser.

Museum and
Townhall
Quarter

Opera and
Naschmarkt

Otto-Wagner-Hofpavillon
Otto Wagner's imperial station pavilion (1899) was built as a showcase for his work.

Wagner Apartments
Otto Wagner's two apartment blocks (1899) overlook the River Wien. No. 40, the Majolikahaus, is covered with ceramic decoration. No. 38 has gold Jugendstil motifs.

Anker Clock

This clock, created by the artist Franz Matsch in 1911, sits on a bridge spanning two buildings on the Hoher Markt. Every hour, on the hour, moving figures parade across the clock face.

Postsparkasse

One of Otto Wagner's masterpieces, this post office savings bank exhibits the finest workmanship outside, and inside. Even the interior ventilator shafts are by Wagner.

Stadtpark Portals

The city's municipal park is adorned with magnificent portals (1903–7), designed by Friedrich Ohmann as part of a project to regulate the flow of the River Wien.

Stephansdom Quarter

Hofburg Quarter

Karlsplatz Pavilions

Two recently-restored pavilions standing in Karlsplatz were built as part of Otto Wagner's scheme for Vienna's turn-of-the-century underground system.

Belvedere Quarter

0 kilometres	1
0 miles	0.5

Secession Building

Nicknamed the Golden Cabbage because of its golden filigree dome, the Secession Building was designed at the turn of the century by Joseph Maria Olbrich for exhibitions of avant-garde art. In the basement is Gustav Klimt's Beethoven Frieze.

Exploring Viennese Jugendstil

The turn of the century saw a flowering of the visual arts in Vienna. A new generation of avant-garde artists formed the Secession in 1896 and, together with architects and designers, forged close ties between the fine and decorative arts, and created new architectural styles.

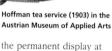

Hoffman tea service (1903) in the Austrian Museum of Applied Arts

PAINTING AND DRAWING

Viennese art at the turn of the century did not conform to one particular style, but there were common elements. These included an obsession with line and rich surface pattern, as well as themes such as the *femme fatale*, love, sex and death. The finest collection of paintings from this period is in the **Belvedere** where pictures by Gustav Klimt (1862–1918) and Egon Schiele (1890–1918) feature prominently. Paintings by both artists and their contemporaries also form part of the permanent display at the **Wien Museum Karlsplatz**. Further examples are at the **Museum of Modern Art** in the MuseumsQuartier. The **Albertina** sometimes shows Schiele drawings. Klimt's *Beethoven Frieze* is in the **Secession Building**, and the decorative schemes he produced for the **Burg-theater** and **Kunsthistorisches Museum** are still in situ.

Decoration (1891) by Gustav Klimt in the Kunsthistorisches Museum

APPLIED ARTS

The Wiener Werkstätte – an arts and crafts studio – was founded by Josef Hoffmann (1870–1956) in 1903, and produced jewellery, fabrics, ceramics, metalwork, cutlery, bookbinding and fashion accessories with the same artistic consideration normally given to painting or sculpture. An outstanding collection is in the **Austrian Museum of Applied Arts**, which also houses a document archive open to researchers. Glass designed by Hoffmann for the Viennese firm of Lobmeyr is displayed in the **Lobmeyr Museum**.

FAVOURITE JUGENDSTIL MOTIFS

Jugendstil motifs were similar to those employed by the French Art Nouveau movement, but were generally made up of a more rigorous, geometric framework. Decorations based on organic plant forms such as sunflowers were very popular, as were female figures, heads and masks. Abstract designs made up of squares and triangles were also used to great effect.

Sunflower motif from the Karlsplatz Pavilions by Otto Wagner

Postcard designed by Joseph Maria Olbrich from *Ver Sacrum*

FURNITURE

The leading Secession designers, such as Hoffmann and Kolo Moser (1868–1918), wanted interior design to return to the simple lines of Biedermeier style *(see pp30–1)* after the excesses of the Ringstrasse era. The **Austrian Museum of Applied Arts** has several interesting displays of their work, as well as that of the Thonet firm, which made the bentwood furniture admired by the Wiener Werkstätte. Furniture was often conceived as just one element of interior design. Unfortunately, many interiors have disappeared or are not open to the public, but the **Wien Museum Karlsplatz**, which also has some pieces of Jugendstil furniture, has a recreation of Adolf Loos's *(see p92)* living room. This is a rare example of a progressive Viennese interior from the turn of the century, created before the architect finally broke with the Secession.

Altar in the Kirche am Steinhof (1905–7)

ARCHITECTURE

Anyone walking around Vienna will notice several buildings with charming Jugendstil details. By the 1890s young architects were beginning to react against buildings of the Ringstrasse era, many of which were pastiches of earlier historical styles. The leading architects at this time were Otto Wagner (1841–1918) and Joseph Maria Olbrich (1867–1908), who collaborated on a number of projects, notably the design and installation of a new city railway and its stations, the most famous examples of which are the **Otto-Wagner-Hofpavillon** at Hietzing and the **Karlsplatz Pavilions**, as well as the **Wagner Apartments** on the Linke Wienzeile. Working independently, Wagner produced the extraordinary **Kirche am Steinhof** as well as the **Postsparkasse**, while Olbrich designed the

Writing desk and chair by Kolo Moser (1903) in the Austrian Museum of Applied Arts

Secession Building as an exhibition space for radical artists and designers. Hoffmann created a number of houses for Secession artists in **Steinfeldgasse**. There are also some Jugendstil houses in **Hietzing**, while the **Anker Clock** by Franz Matsch (1861–1942) is an example of the late flowering of the style. Other examples of street architecture are the **Strudelhof Steps** (1910) by Theodore Jäger and the **Stadtpark Portals** by Friedrich Ohmann (1858–1927) and Joseph Hackhofer (1868–1917).

FINDING JUGENDSTIL VIENNA

Albertina *p102*
Anker Clock *p84*
Austrian Museum of Applied Arts *pp82–3*
Belvedere *p154*
Burgtheater *pp132–33*
Hietzing *pp186–7*
Kaiser Pavilion *p171*
Karlsplatz Pavilions *pp146–7*
Kirche am Steinhof *p160*
Kunsthistorisches Museum *pp122–7*
Lobmeyr Museum *p105*
Museum of Modern Art *p120*
Postsparkasse *p81*
Secession Building *p138*
Steinfeldgasse *p188*
Stadtpark Portals *p182*
Strudelhof Steps, Liechtensteinstrasse. **Map** 1 C3
Wagner Apartments *p139*
Wien Museum Karlsplatz *p146*

Postcard design by Joseph Maria Olbrich from *Ver Sacrum*

Gold leaf detail from the Wagner Apartments

Lettering by Alfred Roller from *Ver Sacrum*

Abstract fabric design by Josef Hoffmann

Vienna's Best: Coffee Houses

Coffee houses have been an essential part of Viennese life for centuries. The coffee house is more than just a place to go to drink coffee. It is a meeting place, somewhere to linger over a snack or a light lunch, and a refuge from city life. Each coffee house attracts its own particular clientele and has its own unique atmosphere. Most of them also serve alcohol. Further details of what coffee houses have to offer can be found on pages 60–61.

Landtmann
This comfortable and formal coffee house used to be frequented by Sigmund Freud. Today it is visited by theatregoers and actors from the nearby Burgtheater, and by journalists and politicians.

Central
Once the meeting place of writers and free thinkers, the most splendid of all the coffee houses in Vienna has now been restored to its former grandeur.

Schottenring and Alsergrund

Museum and Townhall Quarter

Hofburg Quarter

Sperl
Just outside the city centre, the Sperl has a faithful clientele, including many young people who come here for the billiard tables and hot strudels.

Eiles
Its location near various government offices has made the Eiles a favourite haunt of officials and lawyers.

Opera and Naschmarkt

Café Museum
The Café Museum was built in 1899 to designs by Adolf Loos (see p92), but was remodelled in the 1930s. It has now been restored in accordance with Loos's original design.

Hawelka
This famous coffee house has long cultivated its bohemian image. The atmosphere is warm and theatrical, and no visit to Vienna is complete without a late-night cup of coffee or a drink here.

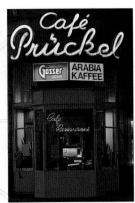

0 kilometres 0.5

0 miles 0.25

Stephansdom Quarter

Prückel
The Prückel has been shabby and run down for as long as anyone can remember, but it has become a mecca for bridge players and locals who crowd into its back room.

Kleines
One of the smallest, quaintest coffee houses in Vienna, the Kleines still attracts a loyal clientele of actors.

Belvedere Quarter

Frauenhuber
The oldest coffee house in Vienna, this is where Mozart once performed. Its location off Kärntner Strasse makes it handy for shoppers and for tourists visiting the nearby Stephansdom.

Exploring Vienna's Coffee Houses

The Viennese coffee house serves many functions and to make the best of the institution it helps to understand the many roles it plays in the lives of local people. In a coffee house you can read the newspapers, share a simple lunch with a friend, or in some play a game of bridge or billiards. Most places serve wines, beers and spirits as well as coffee. The coffee house is a priceless urban resource and, though no longer unique to Vienna, it is here that it has flourished in its most satisfying form. Vienna also has many *Café-Konditoreien (see p203).*

Waiter at the Dommayer café

THE HISTORY OF THE COFFEE HOUSE

Legend maintains that the first coffee house opened its doors after the defeat of the Turks in 1683 *(see p26).* However, historians insist that coffee was known in the city long before this date. Coffee houses took the form we know today in the late 18th century. They reached their heyday in the late 19th century, when they were patronized by cliques of like-minded politicians, artists, writers, composers, doctors or civil servants. In 1890, for instance, the controversial literary

18th-century Viennese girl holding a coffee grinder

group Jung Wien met regularly at the **Griensteidl**, while the essayist Peter Altenberg was reputed to have never been seen outside his favourite café, the **Central**.

Today, as in the past, the **Ministerium**, **Museum**, **Frauenhuber**, **Raimund**, **Eiles**, **Schwarzenberg** and **Zartl** continue to attract their own specific clientele.

COFFEE HOUSE ETIQUETTE

There is a simple but formal etiquette attached to a coffee house. A waiter, almost certainly dressed in a tuxedo, however shabby the coffee house, will take your order, which will often be served with a plain glass of water. Once

you have ordered you are free to occupy your table for as long as you like. A cup of coffee is not cheap, but entitles you to linger for an hour or two and to read the newspapers which are freely available. The grander coffee houses, such as the **Landt-mann** and **Central**, will also have a selection of foreign newspapers and periodicals.

WHAT COFFEE HOUSES HAVE TO OFFER

Coffee houses often function as local clubhouses. At the **Sperl** you can play billiards, at the **Prückel** there are bridge tables, and at

TYPES OF COFFEE

Just as the coffee house is a Viennese institution, so too are the extraordinary varieties of coffee that are available. Just asking for a cup of coffee in Vienna will not always guarantee a result, as the Viennese are exceedingly particular about how they take their coffee; over the centuries they have devised their own specific vocabulary to convey to the waiter precisely how they like their beverage served. The list that follows will cover most variations of the Viennese cup of coffee, although you may well find local ones.

Türkischer: plain, strong black Turkish coffee served in the traditional manner.

Brauner:
coffee with milk (small or large).

Melange:
a blend of coffee and hot milk.

Kurz:
extra strong.

Obers:
with cream.

Mokka:
strong black coffee.

Kapuziner:
black coffee with a dash of milk, usually frothed.

Schwarzer:
black coffee (small or large).

Konsul:
black coffee with a dash of cream.

Kaffeinfreier Kaffee:
decaffeinated coffee.

Espresso: strong black coffee made by machine. Ask for it *gestreckt* for a weak one.

the **Dommayer** you can attend literary readings. The **Central** and **Bräunerhof** both offer live piano music with your coffee. The **Kleines** is, as its name suggests, too tiny to offer entertainment, but still draws a regular crowd. The **Imperial** is part of the hotel of the same name. Coffee houses outside the city centre include the excellent **Westend**.

COFFEE PLAIN AND SIMPLE

Coffee house sign

There are times when you quite simply want a good cup of coffee – when newspapers or a table of your own are luxuries you can dispense with. On such occasions you should keep an eye out for an Espresso bar, where you can lean informally against a counter and order coffee at a half or a third of the price you would normally expect to pay at a coffee house. The *Café-Konditoreien* belonging to the Aida chain, apart from serving delicious cakes and pastries, also function as Espresso bars.

WHAT TO EAT

Most coffee houses offer snack foods throughout the day, simple lunches and occasional specialities, such as pastries, which are served at particular times. The **Hawelka** serves hot jam-filled buns *(Buchteln)* late at night, and the **Sperl** often has fresh strudel late morning. Larger coffee houses, such as **Diglas**, **Landtmann** and Bräunerhof, offer extensive lunch-time menus as well as a range of excellent pastries made on site.

Old Viennese coffee machine in Diglas

Pharisäer: strong black, with whipped cream on top, served with a small liqueur glass of rum.

Schlagobers: strong black coffee served with either plain or whipped cream.

Einspänner: large glass of coffee with whipped cream on top.

Kaisermelange: black coffee with an egg yolk and brandy.

DIRECTORY

Bräunerhof
Stallburggasse 2. **Map** 5 C3.
 Sat & Sun afternoons.

Café Landtmann
See p131.

Central
Palais Ferstel, Herrengasse 14.
Map 2 D5 & 5 B2.

Diglas
Wollzeile 10. **Map** 6 D3.

Dommayer
Dommayergasse 1, Hietzing.
first Sat of month.

Eiles
Josefstädter Strasse 2.
Map 1 B5.

Frauenhuber
Himmelpfortgasse 6.
Map 4 E1 & 6 D4.

Griensteidl
Michaelerplatz 2.
Map 2 D5 & 5 B3.

Hawelka
Dorotheergasse 6.
Map 2 D5 & 5 C3.

Imperial
Hotel Imperial,
Kärntner Ring 16.
Map 4 E2 & 6 D5.

Kleines
Franziskanerplatz 3. **Map** 6 D4.

Ministerium
Georg-Coch-Platz 4.
Map 2 F5 & 6 F3.

Museum
Friedrichstrasse 6.
Map 4 D2.

Prückel
Stubenring 24. **Map** 6 F3.
evenings.

Raimund
Museumstrasse 6.
Map 3 B1.

Schwarzenberg
Kärntner Ring 17.
Map 6 D5.

Sperl
Gumpendorfer Strasse 11.
Map 3 A4.

Westend
Mariahilfer Strasse 128.
Map 3 A3.

Zartl
Rasumofskygasse 7,
Landstrasse.

VIENNA THROUGH THE YEAR

Spring often arrives unexpectedly, with a few days of sunshine and warmth. The climax of spring is the Wiener Festwochen in May. Summers are long and hot, and ideal for swimming and for river trips on the Danube (see pp178–9) during July and August, when some venues officially close. Vienna comes alive again in September when the most important theatres reopen. More often than not,

there is an Indian summer at this time, and it is still warm enough to sit in the Stadtpark. As autumn turns to winter, the streets fill with stalls selling chestnuts and by the feast of St Nicholas on 6 December, snow has often fallen. Christmas is a family occasion, but the New Year is celebrated in style as it heralds the start of the carnival season. The Wiener Tourismusverband (see p239) has details of important events.

SPRING

Vienna is beautiful in spring and is the time for the **Wiener Festwochen** (see May). It is also a season that brings a few days of balmy weather, and when beautiful colours appear in the parks and the Prater woods (see pp162–63). This is the best time of the year to visit the Stadtpark (see p98) with its open-air bandstand and much-photographed resident peacock. The Volksgarten, Burggarten and the great parks of the Belvedere and Schönbrunn also come into their own and there are some splendid views of the city from the Stephansdom tower.

A collection of life-sized dolls on display during the Wiener Festwochen

MARCH

Easter Market (two weeks before Easter), held at the Freyung. Items on sale include arts, crafts and traditional food.
Schönbrunner Schlosskonzerte (until end Oct), at the Orangery, Schönbrunn Palace (see p172). Performances of popular melodies of Johann Strauss.

Runners taking part in the annual Spring Marathon

APRIL

Volksprater Funfair (1 Apr–31 Oct), held in the Prater woods (pp162–63).
Spring Marathon starts from Schönbrunn Palace (see pp172–3), passing the Hofburg, Ringstrasse and Opera House, and ends at the Neues Rathaus (Town Hall).
Frühlingsfestival (2nd week Apr to mid-May). Classical music festival alternating between the Musikverein (p146) and the Konzerthaus (p229).
Spanish Riding School (until Jun). Lipizzaner horses' performances in the Winter Riding School (pp98–9).
Hofburg Orchestra (until Oct). Concerts at Musikverein (p146) and Hofburg (pp96–7).
Kursalon (until end Oct). Open-air concerts (p229). Indoor concerts all year.

MAY

Tag der Arbeit (1 May). Public holiday. Every year, Labour Day is celebrated with parades on Rathausplatz and Ringstrasse.
Maifest (1 May), in the Prater (pp162–63) with music and children's programmes.
Vienna Music Festival (6 May–21 Jun), part of the Wiener Festwochen programme, which begins a few days earlier at the Wiener Konzerthaus (p229) and MuseumsQuartier (p120).
Dancing on the Vindobona (15 May to end Sep). Board the boat at Schwedenplatz for a cruise on the Danube.
Wiener Festwochen (mid-May to mid-Jun). Vienna's greatest festival features operas, plays and performing arts.

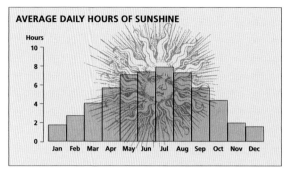

AVERAGE DAILY HOURS OF SUNSHINE

Hours
10
8
6
4
2
0

Jan Feb Mar Apr May Jun Jul Aug Sep Oct Nov Dec

Sunshine Chart
*June, July and August
are the hottest months
in Vienna, with between
six and eight hours of
sunshine each day, but
summer can also be
quite damp and humid.
Although the city cools
down in September,
Indian summers are
quite common.*

SUMMER

Summer can be both the busiest and most relaxing time in Vienna. The great theatres may be officially closed, but the Jazz Festival is on at the Opera House and the Volkstheater in July. The Danube beaches are ideal for sunbathing, swimming and other watersports on sunny days. In the evenings, people relax at the Heuriger wine taverns on the outskirts of the city.

Summer outside the Votivkirche

JUNE

Corpus Christi *(2 Jun)*. Public holiday. Catholic festival held in honour of the Eucharist.
Vinova *(2nd week Jun)*, wine fair in the Prater *(pp162–63)*.

The Concordia Ball
(2nd Fri in Jun) takes place at the Neues Rathaus *(p130)*.
Ball der Universität
(18 Jun). Popular ball held at the University *(p130)*.
Donauinselfest *(last weekend in Jun)*, three-day pop concert on Danube island.

JULY

Outdoor films, operas and concerts *(until Sep)* shown on a giant screen in Rathausplatz. Seating is provided free.
Theater an der Wien
(Jul–Aug). While the State Opera and Volksoper are closed in July and August, opera performances and concerts continue at this theatre *(see p138)*.
Oper Klosterneuburg
(Jul). Performances are in the Kaiserhof courtyard of the palatial religious foundation, Klosterneuburg, a short way north of Vienna *(see p129)*.
Jazzfest *(1st two weeks Jul)*. Well-known artists perform at many venues, including the Opera House *(pp140–41)*, Porgy & Bess Jazz and Music Club *(p229)* and the arcaded courtyard of the Neues Rathaus *(p130)*.

Bathing beside the Danube

International Dance Weeks
(mid-Jul to 3rd week Aug) at the Universitäts Sportzentrum, Schmelz; Volkstheater *(p230)*.
Summer Dance Festival
(Im Puls) *(end Jul to 3rd week Aug)* is held at the Volkstheater *(p230)* and Universitäts Sportzentrum at Schmelz.
Seefestspiele Mörbisch
(Thu–Sun mid-Jul to end Aug). An operetta festival, which takes place in Mörbisch, some 40 km (25 miles) away.

AUGUST

Maria Himmelfahrt
(15 Aug). Public holiday. A Catholic festival, which celebrates the assumption of the Madonna.

Seefestspiele Mörbisch, an annual operetta festival performed against the backdrop of Lake Neusiedl

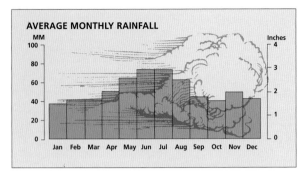

AVERAGE MONTHLY RAINFALL

Rainfall Chart
The summer months are not only the hottest but also the wettest, helping to keep the city cool. During spring and autumn, days can be mild, with some drizzle, until November, which can be very wet. Around 600 mm (23 inches) of rain falls annually.

AUTUMN

In Vienna, autumn means a new start. The theatres, and particularly Vienna's great opera houses, reopen once again. Shops get ready to tempt buyers with their range of autumn fashions. Then, almost overnight, all the shop windows seem to be filled with figures of St Nicholas and his wicked companion Krampus. This cute little furry devil appears everywhere. It is only after 6 December that the shop windows are finally cleared for Christmas displays.

SEPTEMBER

Spanish Riding School performances *(until end Oct)* and training sessions of the Lipizzaner horses *(pp98–9)*.
Vienna Boys' Choir *(mid-Sep to Dec)* perform at Mass at the Burgkapelle *(p103)* on Sunday mornings.
Trotting in the Krieau *(until Jun)*. Trotting races at the Prater *(pp162–63)*.

OCTOBER

National Holiday *(26 Oct)*. Celebrations to mark the passing of the Neutrality

Krampus, the wicked furry devil who accompanies St Nicholas

The Vienna Boys' Choir performing at the Konzerthaus

Act in 1955, which was followed by the withdrawal of the Allied troops stationed in Austria since 1945.
Viennale *(end Oct)*. film festival at Gartenbau, Parkring 12; Metro, Johannesgasse 4; Künstlerhaus, Akademiestrasse 13; and Stadtkino, Schwarzenbergplatz 7–8.
Wien Modern *(until end Nov)*. Modern music festival at the Konzerthaus *(p229)*.

NOVEMBER

Allerheiligen *(1 Nov)*. Public holiday. Catholic festival celebrating All Saints' Day.

Antik-Aktuell *(2nd week Nov)*, art and antiques fair held at the Hofburg.
Schubertiade *(3rd week Nov)* at the Musikverein *(p146)*.
Krippenschau *(until mid-Dec)*, display of historic mangers at Peterskirche *(p87)*.
Christkindlmarkt *(2nd Sat Nov to end Dec)*, Christmas market and children's workshop by the Rathaus *(p130)*.
Christmas markets *(from last Sat Nov)* held at the Freyung, Heiligenkreuzerhof, Schönbrunn, Karlsplatz, Spittelberg and Maria-Theresien-Platz.
International choirs *(last Sat Nov)* at the Town Hall, or Rathaus *(p130)*.

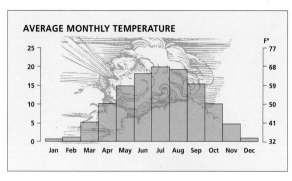

AVERAGE MONTHLY TEMPERATURE

Temperature Chart
The chart shows the average temperatures each month. Top temperatures in July and August can reach 30° C (77° F) although May and September are also quite warm. Winters are icy, and temperatures can be as low as -1.4° C (29.5° F) in January.

WINTER

Roasting chestnuts over hot coals is a regular winter sight on Vienna's streets. As Christmas draws near, stalls offer mulled wine and hot snacks and shops enter into the festive spirit putting up lights and decorations.

The Viennese celebrate Christmas Eve with a traditional meal consisting of *Fisch-beuschelsuppe*, a creamy fish soup, followed by fresh fried carp. The usual dish which is eaten on Christmas Day is goose, although turkey is becoming more popular.

New Year also marks the start of Fasching, Vienna's famous Carnival season.

DECEMBER

Christmas markets *(continue from November)*.

PUBLIC HOLIDAYS

New Year's Day *(1 Jan)*
Epiphany *(6 Jan)*
Easter Sunday
Easter Monday
Tag der Arbeit *(1 May)*
Ascension Day *(6th Thu after Easter)*
Whit Monday *(6th Mon after Easter)*
Corpus Christi *(2 Jun)*
Maria Himmelfahrt *(15 Aug)*
National Holiday *(26 Oct)*
Allerheiligen *(1 Nov)*
Maria Empfängnis *(8 Dec)*
Christmas Day *(25 Dec)*
Stefanitag *(26 Dec)*

Chestnut-roasting in winter

Maria Empfängnis *(8 Dec)*. Public holiday. Catholic festival celebrating the Immaculate Conception.
Midnight Mass *(Christmas Eve)* held in the Stephansdom *(pp76–7)*. No tickets needed but arrive early for seats.
Stefanitag *(26 Dec)*. Public holiday for Boxing Day.
New Year's Eve performance of *Die Fledermaus* *(31 Dec)* at the Opera House *(pp140–41)* and Volksoper *(p229)*. The performance is shown on a large screen in Stephansplatz *(p70)*.
New Year's Eve concerts at the Konzerthaus *(p229)* and Musikverein *(p146)*.
Kaiserball *(31 Dec)* at the Hofburg *(pp96–7)*.
New Year's Eve in the city centre: a street party with snacks and drink. Marquees provide music and cabaret.

JANUARY

New Year's Concert *(31 Dec & 1 Jan)* by the great Vienna Philharmonic at the Musik-verein *(p146)*. Requests for tickets for next year's concert must arrive on 2 Jan *(p228)*.

Beethoven's Ninth Symphony *(31 Dec & 1 Jan)* is performed at the Konzerthaus *(p229)*.
Fasching *(6 Jan to Ash Wed)*, the Vienna Carnival includes the **Heringschmaus** *(Ash Wed)*, a hot and cold buffet.
Holiday on Ice *(mid- to end Jan)*. This is held at the Stadthalle, Vogelweidplatz.
Resonanzen *(2nd to 3rd week Jan)*. Festival of ancient music at the Konzerthaus *(p229)*.
Vienna Ice Dream *(mid-Jan to end Feb)*. Ice-skating in front of City Hall *(p130)*.

FEBRUARY

Opera Ball *(last Thu before Shrove Tue)*, one of the grand-est balls of Fasching *(p141)*.
Wintertanzwoche *(5–13 Feb)*. Part of the Dance Festival *(see below)*. Events are held in the MuseumsQuartier *(p118)*.
Dance Festival *(17 Feb to 27 Mar)*, includes classic and jazz dance at the Universitäts Sportzentrum at Schmelz.
Haydn Tage *(3rd week Feb to 1st week Mar)*. Haydn's music at the Konzerthaus *(see p229)*.

The Christkindlmarkt, in front of the Neues Rathaus

▷ **Johann Strauss II statue in the Stadtpark**

VIENNA AREA BY AREA

STEPHANSDOM QUARTER

The winding streets and spacious squares of this area form the ancient core of Vienna. Following World War II, subterranean excavations uncovered the remains of a Roman garrison from 2,000 years ago, and every succeeding age is represented here, from the Romanesque arches of the Ruprechtskirche to the steel and glass of the spectacular Haas Haus in Stephansplatz. Many of the buildings in the area house government offices, businesses, taverns and stylish shops. Dominating the skyline is the Stephansdom, the focus of the city at its geographical centre.

Plaque on No. 19 Sonnenfelsgasse, once part of the university

SIGHTS AT A GLANCE

Streets and Squares
Am Hof 35
Annagasse 18
Bäckerstrasse 14
Blutgasse 3
Domgasse 4
Fleischmarkt 23
Griechengasse 24
Grünangergasse 6
Hoher Markt 27
Jewish District 26
Judenplatz 31
Kurrentgasse 33
Schönlaterngasse 10
Sonnenfelsgasse 12

Historic Buildings
Academy of Sciences 9
Altes Rathaus 29
Bohemian Court Chancery 28
Haas Haus 15
Heiligenkreuzerhof 13
Postsparkasse 22
Winter Palace of Prince Eugene 17

Churches and Cathedrals
Annakirche 19
Deutschordenskirche 2
Dominikanerkirche 7
Franziskanerkirche 16
Jesuitenkirche 8
Kirche am Hof 34
Maria am Gestade 30
Peterskirche 36
Ruprechtskirche 25
Stephansdom pp76–9 1

Museums and Galleries
Austrian Museum of Applied Arts pp82–3 21
Cathedral Museum 11
Clock Museum 32
Mozarthaus Vienna 5
Haus der Musik 20
Museum Judenplatz 31

GETTING THERE
This area is served by the Stephansplatz (lines U1, U3), Stubentor (line U3) and Schwedenplatz (lines U1, U4) U-Bahn stations. Trams 1 and 2 go along parts of the Ringstrasse. Buses 1A, 2A and 3A stop at the junction of Hoher Markt and Marc-Aurel-Strasse.

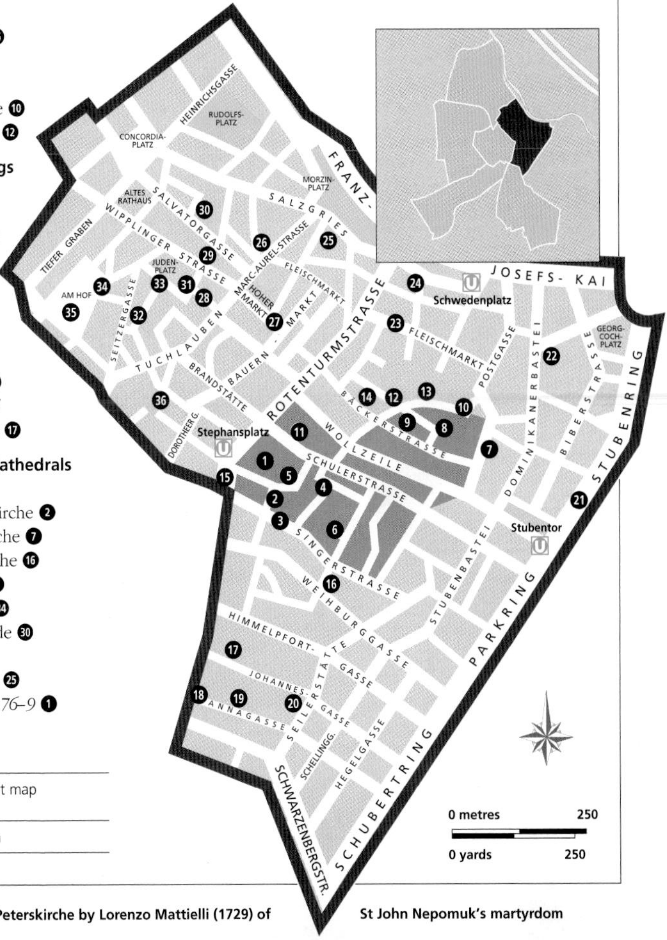

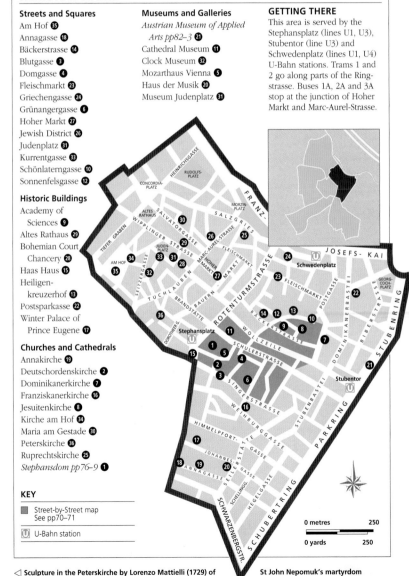

KEY
Street-by-Street map See pp70–71
U-Bahn station

◁ **Sculpture in the Peterskirche by Lorenzo Mattielli (1729) of St John Nepomuk's martyrdom**

Street-by-Street: Old Vienna

This part of the inner city retains its medieval layout, offering a complex of lanes, alleys and spacious courtyards. The influence of the church is particularly evident. You can find remains of monastic orders such as the Dominicans and feudal orders such as the Teutonic Knights, as well as ideological orders, for example the Jesuits. Yet there is nothing ossified about the area: at night the bars and restaurants on Bäckerstrasse and Schönlaterngasse are thronged with people until the early hours of the morning. Dominating everything is the 137-m high (450-ft) spire of the Stephansdom cathedral in the very heart of Vienna.

★ **Cathedral Museum**
Much of this collection was donated by Duke Rudolf IV who is shown here ⓫

★ **Stephansdom**
The cathedral took centuries to build and is rich in medieval and Renaissance monuments ❶

To Rotenturm-strasse

To Kärntner Strasse   STEPHANS-PLATZ

Deutschordenskirche
A remarkable Treasury, with objects collected by German aristocrats, lies alongside this Gothic church ❷

The Haas & Haas Tea House is a charming, informal café and tea house.

Mozarthaus Vienna
Mozart lived here from 1784 to 1787. He had a suite of rooms where he wrote many of his great works ❺

Domgasse
This pretty street includes a bookshop at No. 8, Buchhandlung 777 ❹

Blutgasse
Courtyards like this are typical of the tenement houses on Blutgasse ❸

Schönlaterngasse
The lantern at No. 6 gave this charming street its name ⑩

Dominikaner-kirche
Originally consecrated on this site in 1237, the present Baroque church dates from the 1630s ⑦

LOCATOR MAP
See Street Finder, maps 2 & 6

Jesuitenkirche
This pulpit detail of the apostle Matthew is from the Baroque Jesuitenkirche. One of Vienna's most ornate churches, it was built by the Jesuits in the 1620s ⑧

★ Academy of Sciences
The great hall (Aula) *of the Academy is one of the noblest salons in Vienna* ⑨

Grünanger-gasse
This quiet lane is full of bookshops and art galleries ⑥

KEY

- - - Suggested route

0 metres   50

0 yards   50

STAR SIGHTS

★ Stephansdom

★ Cathedral Museum

★ Academy of Sciences

Stephansdom ●

See pp76–9.

Deutschordens-kirche ●

Singerstrasse 7. **Map** 2 E5 & 6 D3.
Tel 5121065. Ⓤ *Stephansplatz.*
Church ◯ 7am–6pm daily. ⊙
Treasury ◯ 10am–noon Tue, Thu &
Sat, 3–5pm Wed & Fri. ● Sun, Mon
& public hols. ⊘

This church belongs to the
Order of Teutonic Knights,
a chivalric order, which was
established in the 12th century.
It is 14th-century Gothic, but
was restored in the 1720s by
Anton Erhard Martinelli.
Numerous coats of arms of
teutonic knights and memorial
slabs are displayed on the
walls. The altarpiece from
1520 is Flemish and
incorporates panel paintings
and carvings of scenes from
the Passion beneath some very
delicate traceried canopies.

The Order's Treasury is
situated off the church's
courtyard and now serves as
a museum, displaying various
collections acquired by its
Grand Masters over the
centuries. The starting point is
a room, which houses a large
collection of coins, medals and
a 13th-century enthronement
ring. This leads into the second
room containing chalices and
Mass vessels worked with
silver filigree. Following this
is a display of
maces, daggers
and ceremonial

Inner courtyard of No. 9 Blutgasse, the Fähnrichshof

garb. The final exhibits show
some Gothic paintings and a
Carinthian carving of *St George
and the Dragon* (1457).

Blutgasse ●

Map 2 E5 & 6 D3. Ⓤ *Stephansplatz.*

A local legend relates that
this street acquired its
gruesome name – Blood Lane
– after a massacre in 1312
of the Knights Templar (a
military and religious order)
in a skirmish so violent that
the streets flowed with blood.
But there is no evidence to
support this story and the
street's name belies its charm.

Its tall apartment buildings
date mostly from the 18th
century. Walk into No. 3 and
see how the city's restorers
have linked up the buildings
and their courtyards. No. 9,
the Fähnrichshof,
is particularly
impressive.

**Winged altar-
piece in the
Deutschordens-
kirche (1520)**

Domgasse ●

Map 2 E5 & 6 D3. Ⓤ *Stephansplatz.*

In addition to the Figarohaus,
Domgasse boasts some
interesting buildings, including
the Trienter Hof, with its airy
courtyard. No. 6 is a house
of medieval origin called the
Kleiner Bischofshof or small
bishop's house: it has a 1761
Matthias Gerl façade. Next
door is the site of the house
where Franz Georg Kolschitzky
lived and, in 1694, died. It is
said that he claimed some
Turkish coffee beans as a
reward for his bravery in the
1683 Turkish siege, and later
opened Vienna's first coffee
house. The truth of this story,
however, is doubtful.

Mozarthaus Vienna ●

Domgasse 5. **Map** 2 E5 & 6 D3.
Tel 5121791. Ⓤ *Stephansplatz.*
◯ 10am–7pm daily. ⊠ ⊙
www.mozarthausvienna.at

Mozart and his family
occupied a flat on the first
floor of this building from
1784 to 1787. Of Mozart's 11
Viennese residences, this is
the one where he is said to
have been happiest. It is
also where he composed a
significant number of his
masterworks: the exquisite
Haydn quartets, a handful
of piano concerti, and *The
Marriage of Figaro*. Restored
for the anniversary year 2006,
the Mozarthaus now has
exhibitions on two upper floors
as well as the first-floor flat.

Elaborate nave of the Dominikanerkirche

Grünangergasse ❻

Map 4 E1 & 6 D3. Ⓤ *Stephansplatz.*

This quiet lane takes its name from the creperie Zum Grünen Anker at No. 10, a tavern frequented by Franz Schubert in the 19th century.

No. 8's portal has crude carvings of rolls, croissants and pretzels. It is known as the Kipferlhaus after a Viennese crescent-shaped roll. The former Fürstenberg Palace, from 1720, has a Baroque portal with carved hounds racing to the top of the keystone.

Dominikaner- kirche ❼

Postgasse 4. **Map** 2 E5 & 6 E3. **Tel** *5129174.* Ⓤ *Stephansplatz, Schwedenplatz.* ⏰ *7am–7pm Mon–Sat, 7am–9pm Sun.* 📷

The Dominican order of monks came to Vienna in 1226, and by 1237 they had consecrated a church here. In the 1630s Antonio Canevale designed their present church, which boasts a majestic and really rather handsome Baroque façade. The interior is equally imposing. The central chapel on the right has swirling Rococo grilles and candelabra, and there is a very beautiful gilt organ above the west door. Its casing dates from the mid-18th century. The frescoes by Tencala and Rauchmiller are especially noteworthy, as is the high altar.

Jesuitenkirche ❽

Dr-Ignaz-Seipel-Platz 1. **Map** 2 E5 & 6 E3. **Tel** *5125232.* Ⓤ *Stubentor, Stephansplatz, Schwedenplatz.* ⏰ *7am–6:30pm daily.* 📷

Andrea Pozzo, an Italian architect, redesigned the Jesuitenkirche between 1703 and 1705 and its broad, high façade dominates the Dr-Ignaz-Seipel-Platz. In the 1620s the Jesuits decided to move their headquarters here in order to be near the Old University, which they controlled. The

Jesuit order was the dominant force behind the Counter-Reformation. The Jesuits were not afraid of making a statement, and the church's grand design and high façade reflects this dominance.

The interior is gaudy, with plump marble columns screening the side chapels. Pozzo's ceiling frescoes are cleverly executed using a *trompe l'oeil* effect and the pews are richly carved.

Academy of Sciences ❾

Dr-Ignaz-Seipel-Platz 2. **Map** 2 E5 & 6 E3. Ⓤ *Schwedenplatz, Stubentor.* **Tel** *515810.* ⏰ *8am–5pm Mon–Fri.*

Once the centrepiece of the Old University, the Akademie der Wissenschaften has an impressive Baroque façade. Designed in 1753 by Jean Nicolas Jadot de Ville-Issey as the *Aula*, or great hall, it has since been restored. A double staircase leads up to a huge salon that, despite its reconstruction after a fire in 1961, is still one of the great rooms of Vienna.

Elaborate frescoes adorn the ceilings of the Ceremonial Hall and the walls are composed of marble embellished with Rococo plasterwork. Haydn's *Creation* was performed here in 1808 in the presence of the composer: it was the eve of his 76th birthday and his last public appearance.

Fountain by Salomon Kleiner on the Academy of Sciences (about 1755)

The Baroque Bernhardskapelle *(left)*, seen from Schönlaterngasse

Schönlaterngasse ❿

Map 2 E5 & 6 E3. ⓤ *Stephansplatz, Schwedenplatz.* **Alte Schmiede** **Tel** *5128329.* ☐ *10am–3pm Mon–Fri.*

The attractive curving lane derives its name (Pretty Lantern Lane) from the handsome wrought-iron lantern which is clamped to No. 6. This is a copy of the 1610 original which is now in the Wien Museum Karlsplatz *(see p146).* At No. 4, a solid early 17th-century house guards the curve of the street. No. 7, the Basilisken-haus, which is of medieval origin, displays on its façade an artist's impression of a mythical serpent, dating from 1740. A serpent is reputed to have been discovered in 1212 in a well by the house.

The composer Robert Schumann lived at No. 7a from 1838 to 1839. No. 9 is the Alte Schmiede – the large

smithy from which it takes its name has been reassembled in the basement. This complex also contains an art gallery and a hall used for poetry readings and musical workshops.

Cathedral Museum ⓫

Stephansplatz 6. **Map** 2 E5 & 6 D3. **Tel** *515523560.* ⓤ *Stephansplatz.* ☐ *10am–5pm Tue–Sat.* ● *24 & 31 Dec, Maundy Thu & Easter Mon.* 🖼 📷 ♿

Known in German as the Dom und Diözesanmuseum, its exhibits include 18th-century religious paintings by important Austrian artists such as Franz Anton Maulbertsch, and some 16th- and 17th-century rustic carvings. There are also works by the Dutch painter Jan van

Hemessen. Not to be missed is the display of medieval carvings, many of which are of the Madonna and Child.

The Treasury is spectacular as many of the items were the personal gift of Duke Rudolf IV to the Cathedral. His shroud is housed here as well as a famous portrait of him by a Bohemian master dating from the 1360s *(see p70).* Other items include the St Leopold reliquary from 1592, which is encrusted with figures of saints and coats of arms, and some outstanding enamels from the 12th-century.

Sonnenfelsgasse ⓬

Map 2 E5 & 6 E3. ⓤ *Stephansplatz, Schwedenplatz.*

Fine houses line this pleasant street. Though by no means uniform in style, most of the dwellings on the north side of the street are solid merchant and patrician houses dating from the late 16th century. No. 19, which was built in 1628 and renovated in 1721, was once part of the Old University *(see p73).* No. 11 has an impressive courtyard. Many of the balconies overlooking the courtyard have been glassed in to their full height so as to provide extra living space. No. 3 has the most elaborate façade, and contains a *Stadtheuriger* called the Zwölf Apostelkeller *(see p218).* This is an urban equivalent of the *Heurige*, the wine growers' inns found in the villages outside Vienna *(see p219).* The street was named after a soldier called Joseph von Sonnenfels. He became Maria Theresa's legal adviser and under his guidance, she totally reformed the penal code and abolished torture.

Gothic Madonna (1325) in the Cathedral Museum

Heiligen-kreuzerhof ⑬

Schönlaterngasse 5. **Map** 2 E5 & 6 E3.
Tel 5125896. Ⓤ *Schwedenplatz.*
◯ 6am–9pm Mon–Sat. ◯ Sun.
◉ ◻ *Bernhardskapelle*
◯ on request

In the Middle Ages, the rural-monasteries expanded by establishing a presence in the cities. Secularization in the 1780s diminished such holdings, but this one, belonging to the abbey of Heiligenkreuz *(see p176)*, survived.

The buildings around the courtyard housing the city's Applied Arts College present a serene 18th-century face. On the south side of the courtyard is the Bernhardskapelle. Dating from 1662, but altered in the 1730s, the chapel is a Baroque gem. Across from the chapel a patch of wall from Babenberg times *(see pp22–3)* has been exposed to remind you that, as so often in Vienna, the building is much older in origin than it at first appears.

Fresco at No. 12 Bäckerstrasse

Bäckerstrasse ⑭

Map 2 E5 & 6 D3. Ⓤ *Stephansplatz.*

Nowadays people visit this street, which used to house the city's bakers in medieval times, to sample its nightlife rather than its bread. The architecture is also of considerable interest: No. 2 sits beneath a 17th-century tower, and has a pretty courtyard. Opposite, at No. 1, is the site of the Alte Regensburgerhof, the outpost of Bavarian merchants who were given incentives to work in Vienna in the 15th century. No. 8 is the former palace of Count Seilern dating from 1722, and No. 7 is famous for its arcaded Renaissance courtyard and

stables, which is the only surviving example in Vienna. Two other houses of Renaissance origin are located at Nos. 12 and 14.

Haas Haus ⑮

Stephansplatz 12. **Map** 2 E5 & 6 D3.
Tel 5356083. Ⓤ *Stephansplatz.*
◯ 8am–2am daily. ◉ ◻

Commissioning a modern-building directly opposite the Stephansdom was a sensitive task, and the city entrusted its design to one of Austria's leading architects, Hans Hollein. The result is the 1990 Haas Haus, a shining structure of glass and blue-green marble that curves elegantly round right into the Graben. The building has a very pleasing asymmetrical appearance, with decorative elements such as lopsided cubes of marble attached to the façade, a protruding structure high up resembling a diving board and a Japanese bridge inside. The atrium within is surrounded by cafés, shops, a restaurant, Do & Co *(see p214)* and offices.

Franziskaner-kirche ⑯

Franziskanerplatz 4. **Map** 4 E1 & 6 D4.
Tel 5124578. Ⓤ *Stephansplatz.*
◯ 6:30am–noon & 2–5:30pm
Mon–Sat, 7am–5:30pm Sun. ◉ ◻

The Franciscans were fairly late arrivals in Vienna and one of their first tasks was to build a church on the site of a former medieval convent. Dating from 1603, the church totally dominates the Franziskanerplatz.

The façade is in South German Renaissance style, and is topped by an elaborate scrolled gable with obelisks.

Detail from Andrea Pozzo's altar (1707) in the Franziskanerkirche

The Moses Fountain in front of the church was designed by the Neo-Classicist Johann Martin Fischer in 1798.

The interior is in full-blown Baroque style and includes a finely-modelled pulpit dating from 1726, and richly-carved pews. A dramatic high altar by Andrea Pozzo rises to the full height of the church. Only the front part of the structure is three-dimensional – the rest is *trompe l'oeil*. Look out for a 1725 *Crucifixion* by Carlo Carlone among the paintings in the side altars.

You usually have to ask a passing monk for permission to see the church organ. It is worth being persistent, as this is the oldest organ in Vienna (1642), designed by Johann Wöckerl. It has statues of angel musicians and beautifully painted doors on religious themes.

Gleaming façade of Haas Haus (1990)

Stephansdom ❶

Situated in the centre of Vienna, the Stephansdom is the soul of the city itself; it is no mere coincidence that the urns containing the entrails of some of the Habsburgs lie in a vault beneath its main altar. A church has stood on the site for over 800 years, but all that remains of the original 13th-century Romanesque church are the Giants' Doorway and Heathen Towers. The Gothic nave, choir and side chapels are the result of a rebuilding programme in the 14th and 15th centuries, while some of the outbuildings, such as the Lower Vestry, are Baroque additions.

Carving of Rudolf IV

The North Tower, according to legend, was never completed because its master builder, Hans Puchsbaum, broke a pact he had made with the devil, by pronouncing a holy name. The devil then caused him to fall to his death.

★ **Giants' Doorway and Heathen Towers**
The entrance and twin towers apparently stand on the site of an earlier heathen shrine.

Entrance to the catacombs

Pilgram's Pulpit
(see p78)

STAR FEATURES

★ Giants' Doorway and Heathen Towers

★ *Steffl* or Spire

★ Tiled Roof

★ Singer Gate

The symbolic number "O5" of the Austrian Resistance Movement was carved here in 1945.

Main entrance

★ **Singer Gate**
This was once the entrance for male visitors. A sculpted relief above the door depicts scenes from the life of St Paul.

Lower Vestry

★ Steffl or Spire
The 137-m high (450-ft) Gothic spire is a famous landmark. From the Sexton's Lodge (see p79), visitors can climb the stairs as far as a viewing platform.

VISITORS' CHECKLIST

Stephansplatz 3, A-1010.
Map 2 E5 & 6 D3. *Tel*
515523526. ⊤ *Stephansplatz.*
🚌 *1A.* ⬤ *6am–10pm daily.* ✝
High Mass: 10:15am Sun & hols;
Jul & Aug: 9:30am. Guided tours
in English: Apr–Oct: 3:45pm
daily; Pummerin Bell (lift) 8:30am–
5:30pm daily; catacomb tours
daily. 📷 ♿ 🎁 🎁 🎁 🎵
organ concerts May–Nov: Wed.
www.stephanskirche.at

★ Tiled Roof
Almost a quarter of a million glazed tiles cover the roof; they were meticulously restored after the damage caused in the last days of World War II.

JOHANNES CAPISTRANO

On the exterior north-eastern wall of the choir is a pulpit built after the victory over the Turks at Belgrade in 1456. It was from here that the Italian Franciscan, Johannes Capistrano, (1386–1456) is said to have preached against the Turkish invasion in 1451. The 18th-century Baroque statue above it depicts the triumphant saint trampling on a defeated Turkish invader.

South-eastern entrance

TIMELINE

1100	1200	1300	1400	1500	1600	1700	1800	1900	2000

1147 The first Romanesque building on the site consecrated by the Bishop of Passau

1304 Duke Rudolf IV initiates work on High Gothic Albertine Choir

1515 Anton Pilgram carves his pulpit

1711 Pummerin bell cast from remains of guns left by Turks on their retreat from Vienna

1948 Reconstruction and restoration carried out

1230 Second Romanesque building erected on the same ground

1359–1440 Main aisle, southern arches and southern tower built

1515 Double wedding of grandchildren of Maximilian with children of the King of Hungary takes place

1556 North Tower is roofed over

1783 Stephansdom churchyard closed after plague

1916 Emperor Franz Joseph's funeral

1945 Cathedral catches fire during bombing

Inside the Stephansdom

The lofty vaulted interior of the Stephansdom contains an impressive collection of works of art spanning several centuries. Masterpieces of Gothic sculpture include the fabulously intricate pulpit, several of the figures of saints adorning the piers, and the canopies or baldachins over many of the side altars. To the left of the High Altar is the early 15th-century winged Wiener Neustädter Altar bearing the painted images of 72 saints. The altar panels open out to reveal delicate sculpture groups. The most spectacular Renaissance work is the tomb of Friedrich III, while the High Altar adds a flamboyant Baroque note.

The Catacombs
A flight of steps leads down to the catacombs, which extend under the cathedral square.

Christ with Toothache (1420) is the irreverent name of this figure; an old legend has it that Christ afflicts mockers with toothache.

Lift to the Pummerin Bell

Portrait of Pilgram
Master craftsman Anton Pilgram left a portrait of himself, holding a square and compass, below the corbel of the original organ.

Bishop's Gate

The Tirna Chapel houses the grave of the military hero Prince Eugene.

The Statue of Crucified Christ above the altar has, according to legend, a beard of human hair that is still growing.

Main entrance

★ **Pilgram's Pulpit**
Pilgram's intricate Gothic pulpit is decorated with portraits of the Four Fathers of the Church (theologians representing four physiognomic temperaments), while Pilgram himself looks out from a "window" below.

Organ Gallery and Case
In 1960 this modern organ was installed in the loft above the entrance. A more recent organ is in the south choir area.

The Canopy with Pötschen Madonna is a 16th-century canopy that shelters a 1697 icon of the Madonna, to which Prince Eugene's victory over the Turks at Zenta was attributed. It comes from Pecs, a village in Hungary.

★ **Wiener Neustädter Altar**
Friedrich III commissioned the elaborate altarpiece in 1447. Painted panels open out to reveal an earlier carved interior showing scenes from the life of the Virgin Mary and Christ. This panel portrays the Adoration of the Magi *(1420).*

Albertine Choir

Exit from crypt

Emperor Friedrich III's tomb is made from ornate red marble and has a lid bearing a life-like carved portrait of the Emperor. It dates from the 15th century.

The Sexton's Lodge houses the stairs that lead up the steeple.

Chapel of St Catherine

The Madonna of the Servants

The Füchsel Baldachin is a fine Gothic canopy.

The Trinity Altar probably dates from around 1740.

★ **High Altar**
Tobias Pock's altarpiece shows the martyrdom of St Stephen. The sculptures were fashioned by Johann Jakob Pock in 1647.

STAR SIGHTS

★ Pilgram's Pulpit

★ Wiener Neustädter Altar

★ High Altar

THE PUMMERIN BELL

The bell that hangs in the North Tower, known as the *Pummerin* or "Boomer", is a potent symbol for the city reflecting Vienna's turbulent past. The original bell was made from melted-down cannons abandoned when the Turks fled Vienna in 1683. The bell crashed down through the roof in 1945 when fire swept through the Stephansdom, so a new and even larger bell was cast using the remains of the old.

Statuary in the hall of the Winter Palace of Prince Eugene

Winter Palace of Prince Eugene ❶

Himmelpfortgasse 4–8. **Map** 4 E1 & 6 D4. **Tel** 51433. 🚇 Stephansplatz. **Vestibule** 🕐 8am–4pm Mon–Fri. 📷

The Winter Palace was commissioned in 1694 by Prince Eugene of Savoy (see p27), hero of the 1683 Turkish siege. It was begun by Johann Bernhard Fischer von Erlach (see p149) and taken over by Johann Lukas von Hildebrandt (see p152) in 1702. The result is an imposing town mansion, considered one of the most magnificent Baroque edifices in Vienna. Maria Theresa bought it for the state in 1752. Access is limited, but you can view the Baroque staircase (see p43) and glance into the courtyard with its lovely Rococo fountain.

Annagasse ❶

Map 4 E1 & 6 D4. 🚇 Stephansplatz. **Zum Blauen Karpfen** ● to the public.

Now splendidly Baroque, Annagasse dates from medieval times. It is pedestrianized and a pleasant place to browse in the bookshops.

Of note are the luxurious Mailberger Hof and the stucco-decorated Römischer Kaiser hotels (see p195). No. 14's lintel has a Baroque carving of babes making merry, while above this is a relief of the blue carp that gives the house, once a pub, its name: Zum Blauen Karpfen. No. 2 is the 17th-century Esterházy Palace, which is now a casino. It used to be possible to see the Countess Esterházy sweeping her front doorstep!

Annakirche ❶

Annagasse 3b. **Map** 4 E1 & 6 D4. **Tel** 5124797. 🚇 Stephansplatz. 🕐 7am–7pm daily. 📷

There has been a chapel in Annagasse since 1320, but the present Annakirche dates from 1629 to 1634, and it was renovated by the Jesuits during the early 18th century. Devotion to St Anne has deep roots in Vienna and this very intimate church is often full of quiet worshippers.

The finest exterior feature of the church is the moulded copper cupola over the tower. Daniel Gran's ceiling frescoes are now fading and his richly-coloured painting glorifying St Anne on the High Altar is more striking. Gran, together with Franz Anton Maulbertsch, was a leading painter of the Austrian Baroque period. The first chapel on the left houses a copy of a carving of St Anne

from about 1505 – the original is in the cathedral museum (see p74). St Anne is portrayed as a powerfully maternal figure and shown with her daughter, the Virgin Mary, who in turn has the baby Jesus on her knee. The carving is attributed to the sculptor Veit Stoss.

Haus der Musik ❷

Seilerstätte 30. **Map** 4 E1. **Tel** 51648. 🚇 Stephansplatz, Stubenring. 🕐 10am–10pm daily. 📷 📷 on request. 📷 📱 **www.hdm.at**

The House of Music makes the most of the latest audio-visual and interactive technologies to explain and demonstrate all aspects of music. Visitors move through "experience zones" such as the Instrumentarium, with its giant instruments, and the Polyphonium, which is a collection of different sounds.

Moulded copper cupola over the tower of the Annakirche

Detail on the façade of the Griechische Kirche on Griechengasse

Austrian Museum of Applied Arts ㉑

See pp82–3.

Postsparkasse ㉒

Georg-Coch-Platz 2. **Map** 2 F5 & 6 F3. **Tel** 514000. Ⓤ *Schwedenplatz.* ◯ *8am–3pm Mon–Wed & Fri, 8am–5:30pm Thu.* ⊙

This building is the Austrian Post Office Savings Bank and is a wonderful example of Secession architecture *(see pp54–57)*. Designed between 1904 and 1906 by Otto Wagner, it still looks unashamedly modern. The building features the architect's characteristic overhanging eaves, spindly aluminium columns supporting a canopy, heroic sculptures of angels and ornament-like nailheads protruding from the surface of the building.

Wagner was a pioneer in incorporating many functional elements into his decorative schemes. Inside the banking hall the metal columns are clad in aluminium, and tubular heating ducts encircle the hall.

Fleischmarkt ㉓

Map 2 E5 & 6 D2–E3. Ⓤ *Schwedenplatz.* **Griechische Kirche Tel** 5122133. ◯ *9am–4pm Mon–Fri.*

Fleischmarkt, the former meat market, dates from 1220. The small cosy inn called the Griechenbeisl *(see p213)* is its best-known landmark. On its façade is a woodcarving of a bagpiper known as *Der liebe Augustin* (Dear old Augustin). Rumour has it that during the 1679 plague, this bagpiper slumped drunk into the gutter one night and, taken for dead, was put in the plague pit. He woke, attracted attention by playing his pipes and was rescued. Miraculously, he did not catch the plague.

Next to the Griechenbeisl is the Neo-Byzantine Griechische Kirche (Greek church of the Holy Trinity). The versatile architect Theophil Hansen *(see p32)* created its rich, gilt appearance in the 1850s.

A passage links the Griechenbeisl to Griechengasse.

Griechengasse ㉔

Map 2 E5 & 6 E2. Ⓤ *Schwedenplatz.* **Griechische Kirche. Tel** 5122133. ◯ *by appt, 9am–4pm Mon–Fri, 10am–1pm for mass only Sat & Sun.*

This street name refers to the Greek merchants who settled here in the 18th century and it leads up from Rotenturm-strasse. The house on the right dates from 1611 but has since been altered. Opposite is the Griechische Kirche (St George's), not to be confused with the Griechische Kirche in Fleischmarkt. This one was built in 1803 but the gable was added later, in 1898. No. 7 is a 17th-century house. The façade was rebuilt in the late 18th century.

Ruprechtskirche ㉕

Ruprechtsplatz. **Map** 2 E5 & 6 D2. **Tel** 5356003. Ⓤ *Schwedenplatz.* ◯ *9:30–11:30am Mon–Fri & for mass 5pm Sat & 10:30am Sun; Jul–Aug: for mass 6pm Sat only.* ⊙ ♿ *Donation expected.*

Ivy-clad façade of Ruprechtskirche

St Ruprecht *(see p22)* was the patron saint of Vienna's salt merchants and the church that takes his name overlooks the merchants' landing stage on the Danube canal. There is a statue of the saint holding a tub of salt at the foot of the Romanesque tower. Salt was a valuable commodity in the Middle Ages, and evidence suggests that the church dates back to the 11th century, making it the oldest church in Vienna. The interior is less interesting, having been restored at various times, but the chancel has two panes of Romanesque stained glass. The choir is 13th century, the vaulted south aisle 15th century.

Carving of the bagpiper on the façade of the Griechenbeisl, Fleischmarkt

Austrian Museum of Applied Arts ㉑

The MAK (Museum für angewandte Kunst) acts both as a showcase for Austrian decorative arts and as a repository for fine objects from around the world. Originally founded in 1864 as a museum for art and industry, it expanded and diversified over the years to include objects representing new movements and contemporary design. The museum has a fine collection of furniture, including some classical works of the German cabinet-maker David Roentgen, textiles, glass, Islamic and East Asian art and fine Renaissance jewellery. In 1993 the museum was completely renovated and each room was re-designed by a different leading artist. The result is a series of displays that lend the exhibits a unique, unusual flavour.

★ Wiener Werk-stätte Collection
Kolo Moser created this brass vase, inlaid with citrines (false topaz), for the Wiener Werkstätte in 1903.

Stairs to second floor

First floor

First floor mezzanine

★ Dubsky Porcelain Room
A reassembly of a room (around 1724) in the Dubsky Palace at Brno, Czech Republic.

Romanesque, Gothic and Renaissance Room
Blue walls set off the furniture and ceramics in display cases designed by Matthias Esterházy in 1993.

Entrance to MAK Café (see p213)

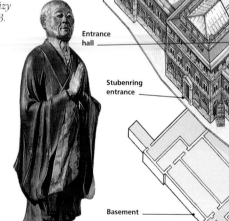

Entrance hall

Stubenring entrance

Basement

MUSEUM GUIDE
The basement houses the individual collections, and the extension is used for special exhibitions. Most of the permanent collection is displayed in the ground-floor galleries, although the Wiener Werkstätte collection plus 20th- and 21st-century architecture is on the first floor. Stairs in the west wing lead to the contemporary design rooms.

KEY

☐	Romanesque, Gothic, Renaissance
☐	Baroque, Rococo
☐	Wiener Werkstätte
☐	Art Nouveau, Art Deco
☐	Islamic Art
☐	Biedermeier
☐	20th-century design
☐	Individual collections
☐	Temporary exhibition space
☐	Non-exhibition space

Monk of the Nichiren Sect
This Japanese wooden sculpture of a praying monk dates from the Muromachi Period (around 1500).

THE WIENER WERKSTATTE

In 1903 Josef Hoffman (pictured) and Kolo Moser founded a co-operative arts and crafts workshop, the Wiener Werkstätte. This promoted all aspects of design from postage stamps and book illustrations to fabric, furniture, jewellery and interiors. The museum houses its archives, which include sketches, fabric patterns and fine pieces.

VISITORS' CHECKLIST

Stubenring 5. **Map** 2 F5 & 6 F3.
Tel 711360. ⓤ *Stubentor.* 🚋 *1A,
74A.* 🚈 *2.* Ⓢ *Landstrasse.* ◯
*10am–midnight Tue, 10am–6pm
Wed–Sun.* ⬤ *1 Jan, 1 May, 1
Nov, 25 Dec (24 & 31 Dec:
10am–3pm).* 📷 ♿ 🚻 📶 www.mak.at

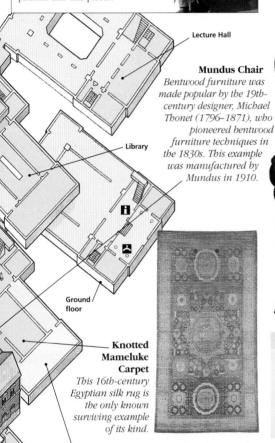

Lecture Hall

Library

Ground floor

Mundus Chair

Bentwood furniture was made popular by the 19th-century designer, Michael Thonet (1796–1871), who pioneered bentwood furniture techniques in the 1830s. This example was manufactured by Mundus in 1910.

Knotted Mameluke Carpet

This 16th-century Egyptian silk rug is the only known surviving example of its kind.

STAR FEATURES

★ Dubsky Porcelain Room

★ Wiener Werkstätte Collection

★ Biedermeier Room

★ Biedermeier Room

This cherrywood sofa (1825–30), designed and manufactured by Danhauser'sche Möbelfabrik, is an outstanding example of Viennese Empire-style Biedermeier design (see pp30–31). The original upholstery has been reproduced.

Jewish District 26

Map 2 F5 & 6 D2. Ⓤ *Schweden-platz.* **Stadttempel Tel** 531040.
🔵 *Mon & Thu for tours at 11:30am and 2pm (take identification).*

Vienna's Jewish District is more famous today for its area of bars and discos called the Bermuda Triangle than for its Jewish community. Judengasse is now a bustling lane lined with clothes shops and bars. There are some solid Biedermeier apartment blocks and on Ruprechts-platz, in the former town hall, a kosher restaurant, the Arche Noah. Behind it is a jutting tower, the Kornhäusel-turm. Named after Josef Kornhäusel, an architect from the Biedermeier period *(see pp30–31)*, it was apparently built as a refuge from his wife.

Close to Arche Noah is Sterngasse. This street has an English-language bookshop called Shakespeare & Co. *(see p225)* and the Neustädter-Hof, a Baroque palace built by Anton Ospel in 1734. A Turkish cannonball, fired in 1683, is embedded in its façade.

Vienna's oldest surviving synagogue, the Stadttempel, designed by Kornhäusel in the 1820s, is on Seitenstetten-gasse. On the same street is the headquarters of Vienna's

The Anker Clock in Hoher Markt

Jewish community. It used to house the Jewish museum, which is now located in Dorotheergasse *(see p93)*.

Hoher Markt 27

Map 2 E5 & 6 D2. Ⓤ *Stephansplatz, Schwedenplatz.* **Roman Museum Tel** 5355606. 🔵 *9am–6pm Tue–Sun & hols.* 📷

Hoher Markt is the oldest square in Vienna. In medieval times fish and cloth markets were held here, and so were

executions. Today it is possible to view the sub-terranean ruins of a former Roman garrison beneath it *(see p21)*. Discovered after World War II, the ancient foundations show groups of houses bisected by straight roads leading to the town gates. It seems probable that they were 2nd- and 3rd-century officers' houses. The excavations are well laid out and exhibits of pottery, reliefs and tiles supplement the ruins.

In the centre of the square is the Vermählungsbrunnen (Nuptial Fountain), or Josefs-brunnen. Emperor Leopold I vowed to commemorate the safe return of his son Joseph from the Siege of Landau and commissioned Johann Bernhard Fischer von Erlach to design this monument, which was built by von Erlach's son Joseph Emanuel between 1729 and 1732. The fountain celebrates the betrothal of Joseph and Mary and bears figures of the high priest and the couple, with gilt urns, statues of angels and fluted columns supporting an elaborate canopy.

Linking two office buildings on the square is the bronze and copper sculptural clock, known as the Anker Clock. Commissioned by the Anker Insurance Company, and designed by Franz Matsch, it was completed in 1914. Every hour a procession of cut-out historical figures, ranging from the Emperor Marcus Aurelius and Duke Rudolf IV to Joseph Haydn, glide from one side of the clock to the other to the sound of organ music. Noon is the best time to see it, as all the figures are on display then.

VIENNA'S JEWS – PAST AND PRESENT

A Jewish community has thrived in Vienna since at least the 12th century, with Judenplatz and, later, the Stadttempel at its core. Unfortunately, the Jews' commercial success caused envy and in 1421, after a charge of ritual murder, almost the entire Jewish population was burnt to death, forcibly baptised or expelled. Thereafter Jewish fortunes fluctuated, with peri-ods of prosperity alternating with expulsions. The 1781 Edict of Tolerance lifted legal constraints that had applied to Jews and by the late 19th century the city's cultural and intellectual life was dominated by Jews. Anti-Semitism spread in the early 20th century and burgeoning Nazism forced many Jews to leave. Of those who remained, 65,000 were murdered. In 1938, 170,000 Jews lived in the city; 50 years later there were 7,000. Now Eastern European Jews are adding to the number.

The interior of the Stadttempel

Bohemian Court Chancery 28

Judenplatz 11. **Map** 2 D5 & 5 C2. **Tel** 53122. Ⓤ *Stephansplatz.* 🔵 *8am–3:30pm Mon–Fri.*

Habsburg rulers were also kings of Bohemia, which was governed from this mag-nificent palace (1709–14). Its architect was the finest of the day: Johann Bernhard Fischer von Erlach *(see p148)*.

Matthias Gerl enlarged the Chancery between 1751 and 1754 to accommodate the Ministry of the Interior. Its glory is the huge Baroque portals, yet the building is as subtle as it is powerful. The elegantly-curved window frames on the first floor are particularly noteworthy.

The building's interior, now a courthouse, and its two courtyards, are less impressive, partly due to reconstruction undertaken after serious bomb damage in World War II.

Altes Rathaus 29

Wipplinger Strasse 8. **Map** 2 D5 & 6 D2. U *Schwedenplatz.* ***Salvatorkapelle Tel*** *5337133.* ◯ *9am–5pm Mon– Thu, or by appointment.* ***Austrian Resistance Archive Tel*** *2289469 319.* ◯ *9am–5pm Mon–Wed, Fri; 9am–7pm Thu.* **www**.doew.at

After the German brothers Otto and Haymo of Neuburg conspired to overthrow the Habsburgs *(see p22)* in 1309,

Ironwork at the Rathaus entrance

their property was confiscated and donated to the city. Over the centuries the site was expanded to form the complex of buildings that until 1883 served as the city hall or *Rathaus.*

The entrance of the Altes Rathaus is festooned with ornamental ironwork. The building is now occupied by offices and shops. The District Museum, which deals with the first municipal district of Vienna (roughly covering the area within the Ring), is also here. Of much greater interest is the Austrian Resistance Archive on

Portal figure by Lorenzo Mattielli in the Bohemian Court Chancery

the first floor, where Austrian Resistance to Nazism is documented. Although many Austrians welcomed Hitler's takeover in 1938, a distin- guished minority fiercely resisted it, and this exhibition pays tribute to them.

In one corner of the Altes Rathaus is the Andromeda Fountain. Located in the main courtyard, it was the last work by sculptor Georg Raphael Donner who designed it in 1741. The relief shows Perseus rescuing Andromeda.

At No. 5 Salvatorplatz is a late 13th-century chapel, the Salvatorkapelle, the only surviving build- ing of the original medieval town house. It has since been enlarged and renovated, but retains its fine Gothic vaults. The walls are lined with old marble tomb slabs, some from the 15th century. Its pretty organ dates from around 1740 and is sometimes used for recitals in the chapel. On the outside wall on Salvatorgasse is an exquisite Renais- sance portal dating from 1520 to 1530 – a rare example of Italianate Renai- ssance style.

Maria am Gestade 30

Salvatorgasse 12. **Map** 2 D5 & 5 C2. ***Tel*** *5339594.* U *Schwedenplatz, Stephansplatz.* ◯ *7:30am–6pm daily & inside at rear by appointment only.* 📷

One of the city's oldest sights is this lofty, Gothic church with its 56-m high (180-ft) steeple and immense choir windows. Mentioned as early as 1158, the present building dates from the late 14th century. It was restored in the 19th century. The church has had a chequered history and during the occupation of Vienna by Napoleon in 1809 his troops used it as an arsenal.

Inside, the nave piers are enlivened with Gothic canopies sheltering statues from various periods: medieval, Baroque and modern. The choir contains two High Gothic panels (1460): they depict the Annunciation, the Crucifixion and the Coronation of the Virgin. Behind the high altar the windows contain medieval stained glass, which is patched with surviving fragments. Tucked away on the north side of the choir is a chapel with a beautiful painted stone altar from 1520. The main parts of the interior are visible from the front entrance, but to walk around inside you need to make an appointment.

Gothic canopies in the Maria am Gestade church

Holocaust memorial in Judenplatz

Judenplatz ③

Map 2 D5 & 5 C2. ⓤ *Stephansplatz, Herrengasse.* **Museum Judenplatz**
Tel 53504310. 🕐 *10am–6pm Sun–Thu, 10am–2pm Fri.* ● *on main Jewish holidays.* 🈲 ♿ *except to synagogue.* 📷 🎫 *free, 2pm & 5pm Thu & Sun. (Take identification).* **www.**jmw.at

Judenplatz was the site of the Jewish ghetto in medieval times. In the centre of the square stands a statue of the German playwright and critic Ephraim Lessing by Siegfried Charoux. The Nazis did not like a tribute to a writer whose works plead for toleration towards Jews, and they destroyed it in 1939. It was later redesigned by the same sculptor and reinstated in the square in 1982.

In 1996 British artist Rachel Whiteread was the controversial winner of a competition to design a monument for the Jewish victims of the Nazi regime, to be unveiled in the square on 9 November 1999, the anniversary of Kristal Nacht. A heated public debate ensued and, following many changes, including the repositioning of the monument by one metre, Judenplatz was reopened on 25 October 2000 as a place of remembrance. It now contains Whiteread's Holocaust-memorial, the Museum Judenplatz at No. 8 and the excavated remains of the medieval synagogue that lie beneath the square. The museum celebrates the vibrant Jewish quarter that was centred on the square until the expulsion of the Jews in 1421, an event gleefully recorded in an inscription, *Zum Grossen Jordan*, on the façade of No. 2. The museum also houses a public data-base of the 65,000 Austrian Jews killed by the Nazis and, in the basement, the excavated synagogue.

Clock Museum ②

Schulhof 2. **Map** 2 D5 & 5 C2.
Tel 5332265. ⓤ *Stephansplatz.* 🕐 *10am–6pm Tue–Sun.* ● *1 Jan, 1 May, 25 Dec.* 📷 **www.**wienmuseum.at

You don't have to be a clock fanatic to enjoy a visit to this wonderful and fascinating museum. Located in the beautiful former Obizzi Palace (1690), the museum contains a fine collection of clocks, some of which were accumulated by an earlier curator, Rudolf Kaftan. Others belonged to the novelist Marie von Ebner-Eschenbach.

Lavish specimen in the Clock Museum

The first floor displays the mechanisms of tower clocks from the 16th century onwards, painted clocks, grandfather clocks and pocket watches. On the other floors are huge astronomical clocks and a wide range of novelty ones.

There are more than 3,000 exhibits. A major highlight is the astronomical clock by David Cajetano, dating from the 18th century. It has over 30 readings and dials that show, among other things, the dates of solar and lunar eclipses. Many other exhibits date from the Biedermeier and *belle époque* periods.

At every full hour the three floors of the museum resound to the incredible sound of numerous clocks striking, chiming and playing. All are carefully maintained to keep the correct time.

The museum gives its visitors a comprehensive account of the history of chronometry through the ages, and of clock technology from the 15th century through to the present day.

Kurrentgasse ③

Map 2 D5 & 5 C2. ⓤ *Stephansplatz.* **Grimm bakery** 🕐 *7am–6:30pm Mon–Fri, 7am–noon Sat.*

This narrow street is shaded by elegant tall Baroque houses, their lower floors filled with cosy bars and pricey Italian restaurants. It's a pleasant place to while away an afternoon. The Grimm bakery at No. 10 is one of the best in Vienna and offers an astonishing variety of breads. No. 12, a house dating from 1730, has an attractive pink cobbled courtyard filled with numerous plants and trees.

One of the many fascinating showrooms in the Clock Museum

Statue on top of No. 10 Am Hof

Kirche am Hof ❹

Schulhof 1. **Map** 2 D5 & 5 C2.
Tel 5338394. Ⓤ *Herrengasse.*
⬜ *7am–noon, 4–6pm daily.* 📷 ♿

This Catholic church, which is picturesquely dedicated to the Nine Choirs of Angels, was founded by Carmelite friars in the late 14th century. The façade, at present being renovated, was redesigned by the Italian architect Carlo Carlone in 1662 to provide space for a large balustraded balcony. The church is now used for services by Vienna's large Croatian community.

It is also worth taking a walk behind the church into Schulhofplatz to look at the tiny restored shops which snuggle happily between the buttresses of the Gothic choir.

Am Hof ❺

Map 2 D5 & 5 C2.
Ⓤ *Stephansplatz, Schottentor.*

This is the largest enclosed square in Vienna. The Romans established a garrison here and, later, the Babenberg ruler Duke Heinrich II Jasomirgott built his castle close to where No. 2 Am Hof stands. In the centre of the square you can see the Marien-säule (Column of Our Lady), a monument that commemorates the end

of the threat of Swedish invasion during the Thirty Years War *(see p25).* Dating from 1667, it was designed by Carlo Carlone and Carlo Canevale.

There are a number of interesting houses around the square. Opposite the church is the palatial Märkleinisches Haus which was designed by Johann Lukas von Hildebrandt *(see p152)* in 1727. Its elegant façade was wrecked by the insertion of a fire station on the ground floor in 1935. The 16th-century red house next door is the headquarters of Johann Kattus, a producer of sparkling wine. No. 10, designed by Anton Ospel, is the Bürgerliche Zeughaus, the citizens' armoury, where the city's fire services are now permanently based. The façade is dominated by the Habsburg coat of arms and military emblems. The allegorical statues above are by Lorenzo Mattielli.

At No. 12 the bay-windowed Urbanihaus dates from the 1730s, and its iron inn sign dates from the same period. Next door is the Collalto Palace – it was here, in 1762, that Mozart made his first public appearance aged just six *(see p38).*

Peterskirche ❻

Petersplatz 6. **Map** 2 D5 & 5 C3.
Tel 5336433. Ⓤ *Stephansplatz.*
⬜ *7am–6pm daily.* 📷

A church has stood here since the 12th century, but the oval structure you see today dates from the early 18th century. It was modelled on St Peter's in Rome and a number of architects collaborated on the design, notably Gabriele Montani. The interior is amazingly lavish, and there's an exuberant, eye-catching pulpit (1716) by the sculptor Matthias Steindl. The richly-clothed skeletons on the right and beneath the altar are the remains of early Christian martyrs originally deposited in the catacombs in Rome. The frescoes inside the huge dome, depicting the Assumption of the Virgin, are by J M Rottmayr.

In 1729 Lorenzo Mattielli designed the sculpture of St John Nepomuk to the right of the choir. This priest earned his sainthood by being thrown into the River Vltava in Prague in 1393 after he refused to reveal the secrets of the confessional to King Wenceslas IV; his martyrdom by drowning later became a favourite subject of artists.

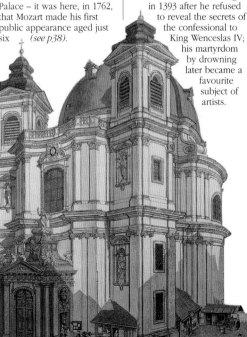

**18th-century engraving
of Peterskirche**

HOFBURG QUARTER

What began as a modest city fortress has grown over the centuries into a vast palace, the Hofburg. The palace was still expanding up until a few years before the Habsburgs fell from power in 1918. The presence of the court had a profound effect on the surrounding area. The former gardens of the palace are now

Portal detail in Josefsplatz

the Volksgarten and Burggarten, and some of the buildings are now splendid museums. Streets such as Herrengasse and Bankgasse are lined with the palaces that the nobility built in their eagerness to be as close as possible to the centre of imperial power. This area is bustling with tourists by day, but at night it is almost deserted.

SIGHTS AT A GLANCE

Streets and Squares
Bankgasse **31**
Dorotheergasse **7**
Graben **8**
Herrengasse **13**
Josefsplatz **6**
Kärntner Strasse **36**
Kohlmarkt **10**
Michaelerplatz **1**
Minoritenplatz **29**
Naglergasse **12**
Neuer Markt **35**
Stock-im-Eisen-Platz **38**

Historic Buildings
American Bar **37**
Bundeskanzleramt **28**
Demel Konditorei **11**
Grosses und Kleines
   Michaelerhaus **3**
Hofburg Complex pp96–7 **15**
Lobkowitz Palace **33**
Loos Haus **2**
Mollard-Clary Palace **14**
Prunksaal **24**
Stallburg **5**
*Spanish Riding School
   pp98–9* **26**

Churches and Cathedrals
Augustinerkirche **23**
Burgkapelle **25**
Kapuzinerkirche
   und Kaisergruft **34**
Michaelerkirche **4**
Minoritenkirche **30**

Museums and Galleries
Albertina **22**
Ephesos Museum **17**
Hofjagd und Rüstkammer **19**
Neue Burg **16**
Sammlung Alter
   Musikinstrumente **18**
*State Apartments and
   Treasuries pp100–101* **27**
Völkerkundemuseum **20**

Parks and Gardens
Burggarten **21**
Volksgarten **32**

Monuments
Pestsäule **9**

```
0 metres          250
0 yards           250
```

GETTING THERE
This area is served by the Herrengasse (line U3) U-Bahn station. Tram 1 runs along the Burgring and Tram 2 leaves the Ring at Parliament. Buses 2A and 3A run along Herrengasse and bus 1A goes from Stubentor to the Graben.

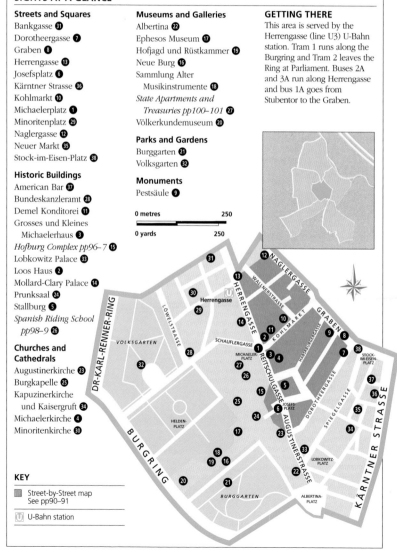

KEY

▢ Street-by-Street map
   See pp90–91

Ⓤ U-Bahn station

◁ **Detail of Danubius fountain by Johann Meixner (1869) outside the Albertina**

Street-by-Street: Imperial Vienna

The streets around the Hofburg are no longer filled with the carriages of the nobility. Most of the palaces have become offices, embassies or apartments. Yet this district remains the most fashionable in Vienna, crammed with elegant shops, art galleries and coffee houses, which offer enjoyable interludes between visits to the many museums and churches in the area.

Mollard-Clary Palace
This mansion, built at the end of the 17th-century, has a façade designed by J L Hildebrandt **14**

Herrengasse
This was a prime site for the palaces of the nobility **13**

Herrengasse U-Bahn

Demel Konditorei
This Café-Konditorei offers delightful decor and exquisite pastries **11**

Grosses und Kleines Michaelerhaus
Joseph Haydn (see p38) once lived in rooms overlooking the handsome courtyard of the Grosses Michaelerhaus **3**

Michaelerplatz
Roman remains have been excavated here **1**

★ Loos Haus
Built in 1912, this unadorned design outraged the conservative sensibilities of the ornament-loving Archduke Franz Ferdinand (see p166) **2**

STAR SIGHTS

★ Loos Haus

★ Michaelerkirche

★ Pestsäule

KEY

— — — Suggested route

0 metres	50
0 yards	50

★ Michaelerkirche
The crypt of this church contains well-preserved corpses from the late 18th century **4**

Josefsplatz
An equestrian statue of Joseph II stands at the centre of this elegant square **6**

Naglergasse
This lane has some of the finest Baroque façades in the city **⑫**

Graben
The Spar-Casse Bank, with its gilt bee on the pediment, is just one of many fine buildings on the pedestrianized Graben **❽**

LOCATOR MAP
See Street Finder, maps 2 & 5

Kohlmarkt
This street has a number of shops by Hans Hollein, one of Austria's finest architects **❿**

★ Pestsäule
Built after the plague of 1679, this is the most imposing of the Baroque plague columns **❾**

Dorotheergasse
Lining this narrow lane are art galleries and auction houses, and the much-loved Café Hawelka (see p58–61) **❼**

Stallburg
Once a royal residence, the Stallburg now houses the Spanish Riding School stables and the Lipizzaner Museum **❺**

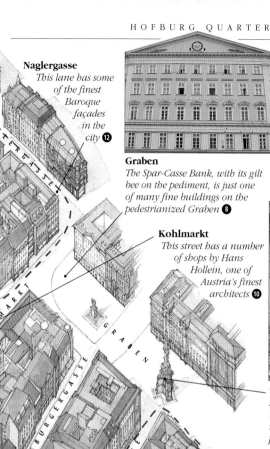

The Palffy Palace
Built in the 16th century, it was a venue for a performance of Mozart's *The Marriage of Figaro.*

The Pallavicini
Palace is a late 18th-century aristocrats' palace, strategically located opposite the Hofburg.

Michaelerplatz ❶

Map 2 D5 & 5 C3. Ⓤ *Herrengasse.*

Michaelerplatz faces the grandiose entrance into the Hofburg, the Michaelertor. Opposite are the Michaelerkirche and Loos Haus. On one side of Michaelerplatz is the Michaelertrakt, commissioned by Franz Joseph in 1888 when the new Burgtheater *(see pp132–33)* on the Ringstrasse opened, and the original theatre dating from 1751, which occupied this site, was demolished. An old design by Joseph Emanuel Fischer von Erlach *(see p149)* was used as the basis for a new design by Ferdinand Kirschner (1821–96). It was finished in 1893, complete with gilt-tasselled cupolas and statuary representing Austria's land and sea power.

Recent excavations have uncovered remains of a Roman encampment, as well as some medieval foundations.

Loos Haus ❷

Michaelerplatz 3. **Map** 2 D5 & 5 C3. **Tel** 53173455. Ⓤ *Herrengasse.* ◯ *8am–3pm Mon–Wed & Fri, 8am–5:30pm Thu.* ♿

Erected opposite the Michaelertor in 1910–12, and designed by Adolf Loos, this building so outraged Franz Ferdinand *(see p166)* that he declared he would

ADOLF LOOS

Unlike his contemporary Otto Wagner *(see p57)*, Adolf Loos (1870–1933) loathed ornament for its own sake. Instead, he used smooth lines and exquisite interior decoration; his buildings' lack of "eyebrows" (the window hoods on many of Vienna's buildings) scandalized Viennese society. Surviving interiors include Knize *(see p93)*, the American Bar *(see p105)* and the Café Museum *(see p137)*.

never use the Michaelertor again. Today it's hard to understand why: the outside is unexceptional but the inside is a lesson in stylish elegance.

Grosses und Kleines Michaelerhaus ❸

Kohlmarkt 11 & Michaelerplatz 6. **Map** 2 D5 & 5 C3. Ⓤ *Herrengasse.* ⬤ *to the public.*

At No. 6 Michaelerplatz a footpath leads to the Baroque Kleines Michaelerhaus (1735). Look out for a vivid painted relief of Christ on the Mount of Olives with a crucifixion in the background (1494) on the side of the Michaelerkirche. The Baroque façade of the Grosses Michaelerhaus is at No. 11 Kohlmarkt. It has a

Michaelerplatz fountain

handsome courtyard and coach house. From here there is a fine view of the older parts of the Michaelerkirche. The buildings around the courtyard were erected in about 1720, and the composer Joseph Haydn *(see p38)* is said to have lived in an unheated attic here in 1749.

Michaelerkirche ❹

Michaelerplatz 1. **Map** 2 D5 & 5 C3. **Tel** 5338000. Ⓤ *Herrengasse/ Stephansplatz.* ◯ *7am–10pm daily.* 📷 📷 ♿ 📷 *Tours of the crypt: 11am & 1:30pm Mon–Sat.*

The Michaelerkirche was once the parish church of the court. Its earliest parts were built in the 13th century, and the choir dates from 1327–40. The Neo-Classical façade is from 1792. Its porch is topped by Baroque statues (1724–25) by Lorenzo Mattielli depicting the Fall of the Angels. Inside are Renaissance and 14th-century frescoes, and a glorious, vividly-carved organ from 1714 by Johann David Sieber. The main choir (1782), replete with tumbling cherubs and sunbursts, is by Karl Georg Merville. The altarpiece of the north choir (1755) is by Franz Anton Maulbertsch.

Off the north choir is the crypt entrance. In the 17th and 18th centuries parishioners were frequently buried beneath their church. Corpses clothed in their burial finery, well-preserved due to the constant temperature, can still be seen in open coffins.

Baroque organ (1714) in the Michaelerkirche

Stallburg ❺

Reitschulgasse 2. **Map** 4 D1 & 5 C3.
Ⓤ *Stephansplatz, Herrengasse.*

The Stallburg was built in the
mid-16th century for Archduke
Maximilian. This former royal
residence was later converted
to stables for the Hofburg.
These are ranged around a
large courtyard with arcades on
three storeys. The Stallburg
houses the Spanish Riding
School stables *(see pp98–9).*

For much of the 18th
century, the Stallburg was
the home of the Imperial art
collection. In 1776, the
collection was transferred to
the Belvedere so that it would
be accessible to the public,
and in 1891 it was moved
to its present home, the
Kunsthistoriches Museum.

Josefsplatz ❻

Augustinerstrasse. **Map** 4 D1 & 5
C4. Ⓤ *Stephansplatz, Herrengasse.*

In the centre of the Josefsplatz is an equestrian statue
(1807) of Joseph II by Franz
Anton Zauner. Despite his
reforms, Joseph II was a true
monarchist, and during the
1848 revolution *(see p31)*
loyalists used the square as
a gathering place.

Facing the Hofburg are
two palaces. No. 5 is
the Pallavicini Palace
(1783–4), a blend of
Baroque and Neo-
Classical styles by
Ferdinand von
Hohenberg.
No. 6 is
the 16th-

century Palffy Palace. On the
right of the Prunksaal *(see
p102)* is the Redoutensaal.
It was built from 1750–60 and
was the venue for masked
balls in imperial times. To
the left is an extension to
the library which was built a
few years later. Both are by
Nikolaus Pacassi, a favourite
architect of Maria Theresa.

Dorotheergasse ❼

Map 4 D1 & 5 C4. Ⓤ *Stephansplatz.*
Jewish Museum Tel *5350431.* ⬜
10am–6pm Sun–Fri. **www**.jmw.at

At No. 11 of this street is the
Eskeles Palace, now home to
the Jewish Museum (Jüdisches
Museum) which, along with
its extension in Judenplatz
(see p86), chronicles the
city's rich Jewish heritage.
At No. 27 is the Dorotheum
(see pp224–5), from the 17th
century. A pawnbrokers and,
more importantly, an auction
house, it has branches all
over Vienna. Halfway along
the street is the Evangelical
church (1783–4), originally
by Gottlieb Nigelli. Towards
the top end, close to Graben,
are two immensely popular
Viennese gathering places,
Café Hawelka at No. 6
(see pp58–61), and the Buffet
Trzesniewski at No. 1 *(see
p218).* There are many
art and antique dealers
in this area.

Baroque plague column (Pestsäule)

Graben ❽

Map 2 D5 & 5 C3. Ⓤ *Stephansplatz.*
Neidhart Fresco House ⬜ *9am–
12:15pm, 1–4:30pm Tue–Sun.*

Facing No. 16 of this
pedestrianized street is the
Joseph Fountain by Johann
Martin Fischer. Further along
is his identical Leopold
Fountain (both 1804). No. 13,
the clothing shop Knize *(see
p223),* is by Adolf Loos. No.
10, the Ankerhaus by Otto
Wagner, is topped by a studio
used by Wagner himself and,
in the 1980s, by Friedensreich
Hundertwasser *(see p164).* No.
21 is Alois Pichl's Spar-Casse
Bank from the 1830s. Just off
the Graben at No. 19 Tuchlauben is the Neidhart Fresco
House, containing medieval
frescoes *(see pp54–7).*

Pestsäule ❾

Graben. **Map** 2 D5 & 5 C3.
Ⓤ *Stephansplatz.*

During the plague of 1679,
Emperor Leopold I vowed
to commemorate Vienna's
eventual deliverance. The
plague over, he commis-
sioned Matthias Rauchmiller,
Lodovico Burnacini and the
young Johann Bernhard
Fischer von Erlach *(see p149)*
to build this Baroque plague
column. Devised by the
Jesuits, its most striking image
shows a saintly figure and an
angel supervising the destruction of a hag representing the
plague, while above the
bewigged Emperor prays.

Statue in Josefsplatz of Joseph II by Franz Anton Zauner (1746–1822)

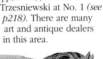

Exterior of Schullin shop *(see p223)*

Kohlmarkt ❿

Map 2 D5 & 5 C3. Ⓤ *Herrengasse.*

Leading directly up to the Imperial Palace, the pedestrianized Kohlmarkt is lined with some of Vienna's most exclusive shops and remarkable shopfronts. No. 9, the Jugendstil Artaria Haus (1901), was the work of Max Fabiani (1865–1962), a protégé of Otto Wagner *(see p57)*. No.16, the book-shop and publishers Manz, boasts a characteristic portal from 1912 by Adolf Loos *(see p92)*. The striking abstract shopfront of jewel-lers Schullin (1982) was designed by the architect Hans Hollein *(see p91)*.

Demel Konditorei ⓫

Kohlmarkt 14. **Map** 2 D5 & 5 C3. *Tel 53517170.* Ⓤ *Stephansplatz.* ◻ *10am–7pm daily.* 📷 ♿

This famous pastry shop at No. 14 Kohlmarkt still bears its imperial patent – K.u.k. Hof-Zuckerbäcker – proudly lettered above the shopfront.

The pastry shop was founded in Michaelerplatz in 1785 and acquired by the pâtissier Christoph Demel in 1857, before moving to its present site on Kohlmarkt in 1888. Its many small rooms are in an ornate late 19th-century style.

Naglergasse ⓬

Map 2 D5 & 5 C2. Ⓤ *Herrengasse.*

During the Middle Ages needle-makers had their shops here, which is how the street acquired its name. This narrow lane also follows the line of a wall that used to stand here in Roman times. Today Naglergasse is lined with a succession of gorgeous Baroque houses. The delight-ful Renaissance bay window of No. 19 is ornamented with carved cherubs. No. 13 dates from the 16th century but has been considerably altered since. No. 21 (1720) is now an inn with a particularly snug and cosy interior.

Herrengasse ⓭

Map 2 D5 & 5 B2. Ⓤ *Herrengasse.*

Flanking the Hofburg, this street was the prime location for the palaces of the Habsburg nobility. In 1843 a visiting writer, J G Kohl, wrote of the street's "silent palaces", and today little has changed.

The base of the provincial government of Lower Austria, the Landhaus, is at No. 13; the façade of the present building dates from the 1830s.

In the courtyard a tablet from 1571 warns visitors not to carry weapons or to fight here. The injunction was famously ignored when the 1848 Revolution *(see p31)* was ignited on this very spot.

The long, low Neo-Classical façade of No. 7 received its present appearance from Ludwig Pichl and Giacomo Quarenghi in 1811. At No. 5 Anton Ospel (1677–1756) gave the Wilczek Palace (built before 1737) an original façade, with angled pilasters lending the central bays an illusion of perspective.

Coat of arms in the courtyard of the Mollard-Clary Palace

Mollard-Clary Palace ⓮

Herrengasse 9. **Map** 2 D5 & 5 B3. *Tel 53410710.* Ⓤ *Herrengasse. Globe Museum* ◻ *10am–6pm Tue–Sun,10am–9pm Thu.*

At No. 9 Herrengasse is the former Mollard-Clary Palace, a mansion constructed by Domenico Martinelli in 1698. The façade was the first commission for Johann Lukas von Hildebrandt *(see p152)*.

From 1923 until 1997 the palace housed the Lower Austrian Provincial Museum, or Landesmuseum. Today the building houses offices and the Globe Museum.

In the courtyard is a 16th-century elaborate wrought-iron well cover and a carved stone coat of arms (1454).

Hofburg Complex ⓯

See pp96–101.

Inside the ornately-decorated Demel Konditorei

Neue Burg ⑯

Heldenplatz. **Map** 4 D1 & 5 B4.
Tel 52524484. Ⓤ *Volkstheater,
Herrengasse.* 🚋 *1, 2, D.*
◯ *10am–6pm Mon, Wed–Sun.*
🖼 📷 www.hofburg.vienna.info

The Neue Burg, a massive
curved building situated on
Heldenplatz, was added to the
Hofburg Complex in 1881–
1913. It embodies the last gasp
of the Habsburg Empire as it
strained under aspirations of
independence from its domains,
when the personal prestige of
Emperor Franz Joseph was all
that seemed able to keep it
intact. It was not the perfect
moment to embark on an
extension to the Hofburg, but
the work was undertaken
nevertheless, and the Neue
Burg was built to designs by
the Ringstrasse architects Karl
von Hasenauer (1833–94) and
Gottfried Semper (1803–79).
Five years after its completion,
the Habsburg empire ended.
   In 1938, Adolf Hitler stood
on the terraced central bay to
proclaim the Anschluss – the
union of Austria and Germany
– to tens of thousands of
Viennese *(see p36).*
   Today the Neue Burg is
home to the reading room of
the National Library, as well
as a number of museums
(see following entries).

Ephesos Museum ⑰

As Neue Burg. **Tel** 525244031.
◯ *10am–6pm Mon, Wed–Sun.*
www.khm.at

For decades Austrian
archaeologists
have been
excavating the
Greek and
Roman site of
Ephesus in Turkey.
Since 1978 their discov-
eries have been on display
in the main block of the Neue
Burg. Also on show are finds
from the Greek island of
Samothrace, excavated in
the 1870s. The main exhibits
include a colossal frieze
commemorating Lucius
Verus's victory over the
Parthians in AD 165, and
many architectural fragments.

Armour at Hofjagd und Rüstkammer

Sammlung Alter Musikinstrumente ⑱

As Neue Burg.

Pianos that belonged to
Beethoven, Schubert and
Haydn, among countless
other items, are housed in the
musical instrument museum.
More important, however, is
the collection of Renaissance
instruments, widely believed
to be the finest in the world.
The claviorgan (1596), the
oldest surviving example of
this instrument, is particularly
fascinating, and features stops
used to create special effects
such as birdsong.

Hofjagd und Rüstkammer ⑲

As Neue Burg.

The Hofburg's weapons
collection is impressive
both for its size and for the
workmanship of its finest
items: ivory and filigree inlay
on weapons, medieval ceremonial saddles and jewelled
Turkish and Syrian maces.
Particularly resplendent are
the 16th-century ceremonial
suits worn by the Habsburgs
for tournaments and military
parades, and the decorative
fighting and hunting weapons.
   The museum was based on
the personal armouries of the
Habsburg emperors and, not
surprisingly, houses one of the
finest collections in Europe.

Völkerkunde-museum ⑳

As Neue Burg. **Tel** 525244031.
◯ *10am–6pm Mon, Wed–Sun.*
www.khm.at

Ranged around an arcaded
Italian Renaissance-style
courtyard, at the west end of
the Neue Burg, is the ethno-
logical museum. To one side
are the Oriental collections:
lacquer screens, clothes,
furniture, weapons, ceramics,
farm tools, masks and musical
instruments. In a neighbouring
room are African figurines
and masks. The artifacts from
Benin are the highlight of the
African collection. Australasia
and Polynesia dominate the
displays upstairs, with fabrics
from Bali, weapons from
Borneo and many musical
instruments from the Far East.
   The large pre-Columbian
collection from Mexico
includes an Aztec feather
headdress, while the permanent collection features a
section on Eskimo culture.

**Renaissance cittern
from the Sammlung
Alter Musikinstrumente**

The Hofburg Complex ⑮

The vast Hofburg Complex contains the former imperial apartments, several museums, a chapel, a church, the Austrian National Library, the Spanish Riding School and the President of Austria's offices. It was the seat of Austrian power for over six centuries, and successive rulers were all anxious to leave their mark. Seven centuries of architectural development can be seen in the 10 or so buildings, ranging from Gothic to late 19th-century historicism.

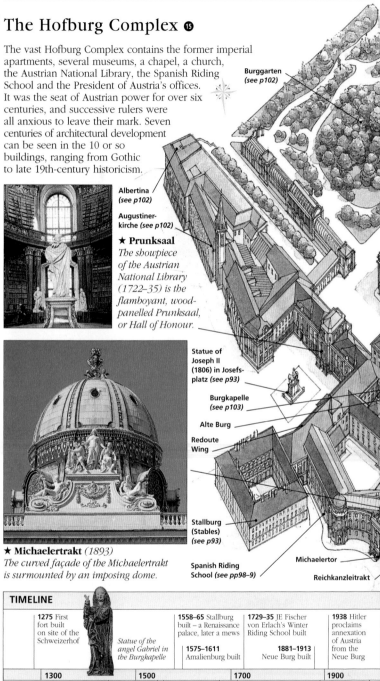

Burggarten
(see p102)

Albertina
(see p102)

Augustiner-kirche *(see p102)*

★ **Prunksaal**
The showpiece of the Austrian National Library (1722–35) is the flamboyant, wood-panelled Prunksaal, or Hall of Honour.

Statue of Joseph II (1806) in Josefs-platz *(see p93)*

Burgkapelle
(see p103)

Alte Burg

Redoute Wing

Stallburg (Stables)
(see p93)

Spanish Riding School *(see pp98–9)*

Michaelertor

Reichkanzleitrakt

★ **Michaelertrakt** *(1893)*
The curved façade of the Michaelertrakt is surmounted by an imposing dome.

TIMELINE

Statue of the angel Gabriel in the Burgkapelle

1275 First fort built on site of the Schweizerhof	**1558–65** Stallburg built – a Renaissance palace, later a mews	**1729–35** JE Fischer von Erlach's Winter Riding School built	**1938** Hitler proclaims annexation of Austria from the Neue Burg
	1575–1611 Amalienburg built	**1881–1913** Neue Burg built	

1300	**1500**	**1700**	**1900**
	1547–52 Ferdinand I reconstructs the Alte Burg	**1552–3** Schweizertor built	**1728** Work begun on J E Fischer von Erlach's Reichskanzleitrakt	**1992** The banqueting hall and ball-room in the Redoute Wing destroyed by fire
1447–9 Alterations carried out on the Burgkapelle under Friedrich III		**1660–80** Leopoldinischertrakt built under Leopold I	**1889–93** Construction of Michaelertrakt and Michaelertor	

Mozart Memorial (1896)
Viktor Tilgner's statue of the composer stands just inside the Ring-strasse entrance.

Neue Burg
(see p95)

Burgtor or outer gate was built to a design by Peter Nobile in 1821–4.

VISITORS' CHECKLIST

Michaelerplatz 1, A-1010.
Map 4 D1 & 5 B4.
Ⓤ *Stephansplatz, Herrengasse.*
2A to Heldenplatz, 3A to Michaelerplatz. D, 1, 2. For opening times of individual museums, see pp92–105.

★ Prince Eugene Statue
Anton Dominik Fernkorn designed this monument of Prince Eugene (1865). The pedestal is by Eduard van der Nüll.

Heldenplatz

★ Schweizertor
This 16th-century Renaissance gateway leads to the Schweizerhof, the oldest part of the Hofburg, originally a stronghold with four towers.

Leopold-inischertrakt

Amalienburg
The oddly-shaped Amalienburg, built in 1575 for emperor Maximilian's son Rudolf, has a Renais-sance façade and an attractive Baroque clock tower.

STAR SIGHTS

★ Prunksaal

★ Prince Eugene Statue

★ Schweizertor

★ Michaelertrakt

Spanish Riding School ㉖

The origins of the Spanish Riding School are obscure, but it is believed to have been founded in 1572 to cultivate the classic skills of *haute école* horsemanship. By breeding and training horses from Spain, the Habsburgs formed the Spanische Reitschule. Today, 80-minute shows take place in the building known as the Winter Riding School. Commissioned by Karl VI, it was built from 1729 to 1735 to a design by Josef Emanuel Fischer von Erlach. There are two entrances to the building – one from door 2, Josefsplatz, the other from the Michaelerkuppel.

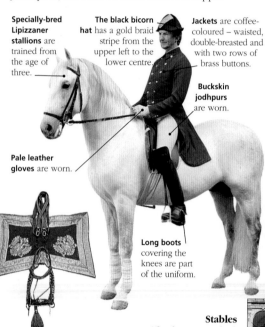

Specially-bred Lipizzaner stallions are trained from the age of three.

The black bicorn hat has a gold braid stripe from the upper left to the lower centre.

Jackets are coffee-coloured – waisted, double-breasted and with two rows of brass buttons.

Buckskin jodhpurs are worn.

Pale leather gloves are worn.

Long boots covering the knees are part of the uniform.

Tack
The elegant saddle with embroidered cloth differs from modern versions and complements the historical dress of the riders; the curb rein is generally used.

Stables
The three storey-high Renaissance former palace of the Stallburg is across the road from the Winter Riding School. It now provides stabling for the horses.

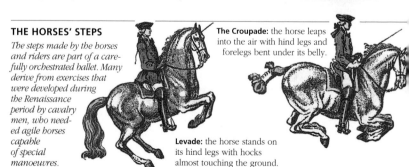

THE HORSES' STEPS

The steps made by the horses and riders are part of a carefully orchestrated ballet. Many derive from exercises that were developed during the Renaissance period by cavalry men, who needed agile horses capable of special manoeuvres.

The Croupade: the horse leaps into the air with hind legs and forelegs bent under its belly.

Levade: the horse stands on its hind legs with hocks almost touching the ground.

Portrait of Karl VI
*An equestrian portrait of
Emperor Karl VI who
commissioned the building,
hangs in the royal box.
Whenever a rider enters the
hall, he must express his
respect to the founder of the
school by raising his bicorn
hat to the portrait.*

**Interior of the Winter
Riding School**
*The gracious interior is lined
with 46 columns and
adorned with elaborate plasterwork, chandeliers and a
coffered ceiling. At the head
of the arena is the court box.
Spectators sit here or watch
from upper galleries.*

THE LIPIZZANER HORSES

The stallions that perform their athletic feats on the sawdust
of the Winter Riding School take their name from the stud at
Lipizza near Trieste in Slovenia *(see below)*, which was
founded by Archduke Karl in 1580. Today the horses are
bred on the Austrian National Stud Farm at Piber near Graz.
The breed was originally produced by crossing Arab, Berber
and Spanish horses. The horses are renowned for their grace
and stamina. You may be able to obtain a ticket without a
reservation to see them at their morning training session.

Capriole: this is a
leap into the air with
a simultaneous kick
of the hind legs.

The Piaffe: the horse
trots on the spot, often
between two pillars.

State Apartments and Treasuries ₂₇

The state apartments in the Reichskanzleitrakt (1723–30) and the Amalienburg (1575) include rooms occupied by Franz Joseph from 1857 to 1916, Empress Elisabeth's apartments from 1854 to 1898 and the rooms where Tsar Alexander I lived during the Congress of Vienna in 1815. The Treasuries hold sacred and secular treasures amassed during centuries of Habsburg rule, They include relics of the Holy Roman Empire, the crown jewels and liturgical objects of the imperial court.

Entrance to Treasuries

★ **10th-Century Crown**
The insignia of the Holy Roman Empire includes this crown set with enamel plaques and cabochons.

Emperor Maximilian I
(around 1500)
This portrait by Bernhard Strigel hangs in the room containing Burgundian treasure. Emperor Maximilian married Mary, Duchess of Burgundy in 1477.

Cradle of the King of Rome
Designed by the French painter Prud'hon, Maria Louisa gave this cradle to her son, the King of Rome (see p175).

Entrance through the Michaelerkuppel to State Apartments and Silberkammer

Crucifix after Giambologna
(around 1590)
This type of crucifix, a Cristo Morto, can be traced back to a similar model by Giambologna which is in Florence.

KEY

- ☐ Franz Joseph's State Apartments
- ☐ Elisabeth's State Apartments
- ☐ Alexander's State Apartments
- ☐ Sacred Treasury
- ☐ Secular Treasury
- ☐ Sisi Museum
- ☐ Non-exhibition space

STAR FEATURES

- ★ 10th-Century Crown
- ★ Imperial Dining Hall
- ★ Empress Elisabeth by Franz Xaver Winterhalter

THE SILBERKAMMER

On display in the ground-floor rooms of the court tableware and silver depot is a dazzling array of items – gold, silver and the finest porcelain – that were once used at the Habsburg state banquets. One of the highlights is a 33-m long (100-ft) gilded bronze centrepiece with accompanying candelabra from around 1800. Visitors can also admire the mid-18th-century Sèvres dinner service that was a diplomatic gift from Louis XV to Maria Theresa.

Goblet from the Laxenburg Service (around 1821)

VISITORS' CHECKLIST

Map 4 D1 & 5 B3. *State Apartments (Kaiserappartements), Sisi Museum & Silberkammer* Michaelerkuppel. Tel 5337570. 9am–5pm daily. Sat & Sun. www.hofburg-wien.at *Secular & Sacred Treasuries (Schatzkammer)* Schweizerhof. Tel 52524031. 10am–6pm Wed–Mon; 24 Dec: to 1pm; 31 Dec: to 3pm. 1 Jan, 1 May, 25 Dec. www.khm.at

Elisabeth's Gymnastic Equipment

The Empress was a fitness enthusiast, and the bars at which she exercised are still in place in her dressing room.

Passage to Neue Burg and Heldenplatz

Sisi Museum

Ticket office

Entrance through the Kaisertor to State Apartments and Silberkammer

Exit from apartments

★ Imperial Dining Hall

The table is laid as it used to be in Emperor Franz Joseph's day (see p32–3), in the room where the Imperial family used to dine.

GUIDE TO TREASURIES

Entering the Secular Treasury, Rooms 1–8 contain items from the Austrian Empire (with Room 5 commemorating Napoleon). Rooms 9–12 exhibit treasures from the Holy Roman Empire, while the Burgundian Inheritance is displayed in Rooms 13–16. Rooms I–V, furthest from the entrance, house the Sacred Treasury.

★ Empress Elisabeth

Winterhalter's portrait of the Empress (1865) with stars in her hair hangs in the Sisi Museum.

Greenhouses in the Burggarten by Friedrich Ohmann (1858–1927)

Burggarten ㉑

Burgring/Opernring. **Map** 4 D1 & 5 B4. ⓤ *Karlsplatz.* 🚊 *1, 2, D.* 🕐 *Apr–Sep: 6am–10pm; Oct–Mar: 6am–8pm daily.*

Before leaving Vienna, Napoleon showed his contempt for the Viennese by razing part of the city walls which had proved so ineffective at preventing his entry. Some of the space left around the Hofburg was later transformed by the Habsburgs into a landscaped garden, planted with a variety of trees. It was opened to the public in 1918.

Overlooking the garden are greenhouses (1901–7) by the Jugendstil architect Friedrich Ohmann, and near the Hofburg entrance is a small equestrian statue (1780) of Emperor Franz I by the sculptor Balthasar Moll. Closer to the Ringstrasse is the Mozart Memorial (1896) by Viktor Tilgner.

Albertina ㉒

Augustinerstrasse 1. **Map** 4 D1 & 5 C4. **Tel** 534830. ⓤ *Karlsplatz, Stephansplatz.* 🕐 *10am–6pm daily (to 9pm Wed).* 📷 ♿ 📷 🔔 🍴 🔔 www.albertina.at

Once hidden away at the Opera end of the Hofburg is the Albertina, now a distinctive landmark. Its raised entrance boasts a controversial freestanding diving-board roof by architect Hans Hollein (*see p91*). The palace once belonged to Maria Theresa's daughter, Maria Christina, and her husband Duke Albert of Sachsen-Teschen, after whom the gallery is named. Today the Albertina houses a collection of one million prints, over 65,000 watercolours and drawings, and some 70,000 photographs. The gems of the collections are by Dürer, with Michelangelo and Rubens also well represented. Picasso heads a fine 20th-century section.

Temporary exhibitions feature paintings on loan along with works from the Albertina. The Batliner Collection, which comprises over 500 works of art and is one of the most significant private collections in Europe, is on permanent loan.

The extension on the Burggarten side houses study facilities and the largest of the three exhibition halls. Comprehensive renovation has restored a number of features of the Albertina to their former glory, including the façades and the central courtyard. Most notably, the Habsburg State Rooms are now open to the public. They represent a remarkable example of Neo-Classical architecture and interior decoration, inspired by the Archduchess Maria Christina herself.

Augustinerkirche ㉓

Augustinerstrasse 3. **Map** 4 D1 & 5 C4. **Tel** 5337099. ⓤ *Stephansplatz.* 🕐 *8am–5pm daily.* 📷

The Augustinerkirche has one of the best-preserved 14th-century Gothic interiors in Vienna; only the modern chandeliers strike a jarring note. The church also houses the Loreto Chapel, dating back to 1724, containing the silver urns that preserve the hearts of the Habsburg family (*see pp24–5*). Here too is one of the most powerful works by the Italian Neo-Classical sculptor Antonio Canova, the tomb of Maria Christina, favourite daughter of Maria Theresa. Like the tomb of Leopold II, which is also here, Maria Christina's tomb is empty; the royal remains lie in the Kaisergruft (*see p104*).

The church is also celebrated for its music, including masses by Schubert or Haydn held here on Sundays.

Prunksaal ㉔

Josefsplatz 1. **Map** 4 D1 & 5 C4. **Tel** 534100. ⓤ *Herrengasse.* 🕐 *10am–6pm Tue–Sun, 10am–9pm Thu.* 📷 📷 www.onb.ac.at

Commissioned as the court library by Karl VI, the main hall, or Prunksaal, of the National Library was designed by Johann Bernhard Fischer von Erlach (*see p149*) in 1719. After his death in 1723, the building was completed by his son. The collection consists of approximately 2.6 million books, and includes the personal library of Prince Eugene (*see pp26–7*), as well as books that were taken from monastic libraries closed during the religious reforms of Joseph II (*see p29*).

The Prunksaal is 77 m (252 ft) long and is the largest Baroque library in Europe. Paired marble columns frame the domed main room, and bookcases line the walls. Spanning the vaults are frescoes by the Baroque painter Daniel Gran (1730), which were restored by Franz

Domed interior of the Prunksaal in the National Library building

Anton Maulbertsch (1769). The many fine statues, including the likeness of Karl VI in the centre of the hall, are the work of Paul Strudel (1648–1708) and his brother Peter (1660–1714).

Burgkapelle ㉕

Hofburg, Schweizerhof. **Map** 4 D1 & 5 B4. **Tel** 5339927. Ⓤ *Herrengasse.* ◯ *11am–3pm Mon–Thu, 11am–1pm Fri for guided tours only.* ◉ *1 Jan, 1 Nov, 8 Dec.* ♿ ✗ **Vienna Boys' Choir** ◯ *Jan–Jun & Sep–Dec: 9:15am Sun (book via website).* 💻 **www**.hofburgkapelle.at

From the Schweizerhof, steps lead up to the Burgkapelle, or Hofburg Chapel, originally constructed in 1296 but modified 150 years later. On Sundays, visitors can hear the Wiener Sängerknaben, the Vienna Boys' Choir *(see p39)*. The chapel interior has Gothic statuary in canopied niches and Gothic carvings, and boasts a bronze crucifix (1720) by Johann Känischbauer.

Spanish Riding School ㉖

See pp98–9.

State Apartments and Treasuries ㉗

See pp100–1.

Bundeskanzleramt ㉘

Ballhausplatz 2. **Map** 1 C5 & 5 B3. **Tel** 531150. Ⓤ *Herrengasse.* ◉ *to the public.*

The Bundeskanzleramt (1717–19), the Austrian Chancery and Foreign Ministry, was designed by Johann Lukas von Hildebrandt *(see p152)*. It was expanded to its present size in 1766 by Nikolaus Pacassi. Major events that shaped Austria's history have taken place here, including meetings of the Congress of Vienna *(see p30)* in 1814–15, the final deliberations in 1914 that led to

No. 4 Minoritenplatz

the outbreak of World War I, and the murder of Chancellor Dollfuss by Nazi terrorists in 1934 *(see p36)*.

Minoritenplatz ㉙

Map 2 D5 & 5 B3. Ⓤ *Herrengasse.*

At No. 1 Minoritenplatz is the Baroque-style State Archives building (the archives are no longer housed here), built on to the back of the Bunderskanzleramt in 1902. There are a number of palaces around the square. No. 3 is the former Dietrichstein Palace of 1755, an early building by Franz Hillebrand. It now contains the offices of the Federal Chancellor and the Foreign Office. No. 4 is the side of the Liechtenstein Palace *(see p104)*. The mid-17th-century Starhemberg Palace is at No. 5. Now housing ministry offices, it was the residence of Count Ernst Rüdiger von Starhemberg, a hero of the 1683 Turkish siege *(see p27)* when he led the Austrian forces within the city.

Minoritenkirche ㉚

Minoritenplatz 2. **Map** 1 C5 & 5 B3. **Tel** 5334162. Ⓤ *Herrengasse.* ◯ *9am–6pm daily.* 📷

This ancient church was established here by the Minor Friars in around 1224, although the present structure dates from 1339. The tower was given its odd pyramidal

shape during the Turkish siege of 1529, when shells sliced the top off the steeple. In the 1780s the Minoritenkirche was restored to its original Gothic style, when Maria Theresa's son, Joseph II *(see p28)*, made a gift of the church to Vienna's Italian community. The church retains a fine west portal (1340) with statues beneath traceried canopies; the carvings above the doorway are modern.

The interior of the church is unexpectedly bright and large and contains a mosaic copy of Leonardo da Vinci's *Last Supper*. Napoleon Bonaparte commissioned Giacomo Raffaelli to execute this work as he proposed to substitute it for the original in Milan and remove the real painting to Paris. Following Napoleon's downfall at Waterloo in 1815, Raffaelli's version was bought by the Habsburgs. In the south aisle is a painted statue of the Madonna and Child (dating from around 1350), while at the same spot in the north aisle is a faded fragment of a 16th-century fresco of St Francis of Assisi.

Gothic statue (about 1400) of Leopold III in the Burgkapelle

Bankgasse ㉛

Map 1 C5 & 5 B3. Ⓤ *Herrengasse.*

Few streets in Vienna are more crammed with the palaces of the nobility.

At Nos. 4–6 is the former Strattmann-Windischgrätz Palace (1692–1734), which was originally designed by Johann Bernhard Fischer von Erlach *(see p149).* The present façade (1783–4) was the work of Franz Hillebrand, who considerably increased the size of the building by incorporating the palace next door. Today, it houses the Hungarian Embassy.

Nos. 5–7 are the back of the Starhemberg Palace. No. 9 is the Liechtenstein Palace, built as a town residence for the Liechtenstein family by Domenico Martinelli (1694–1706). No. 2 is the Schönborn-Batthyány Palace (1695).

Volksgarten ㉜

Dr-Karl-Renner-Ring. **Map** 1 C5 & 5 A3. **Tel** 5339083. Ⓤ *Herrengasse.* ◯ *Apr–Nov: 6am–10pm daily; Dec–Mar: 6:30am–10pm daily.* 📷 ♿

Like the Burggarten landscaped garden *(see p102),* the Volksgarten was created after the destruction of the city

Statuary above the portal to the Lobkowitz Palace

walls by Napoleon, and opened up a space previously occupied by fortifications. Unlike the Burggarten, the Volksgarten was opened to the public soon after its completion in 1820. The formal plantations, especially the splendid rose gardens, are matched in grandeur by the garden's ornaments, notably the Temple of Theseus (1823) by Peter von Nobile. It was built to house Canova's statue of the Greek god, which now graces the staircase of the Kunsthistorisches Museum. Other compositions include Karl von Hasenauer's monument to the poet Franz Grillparzer *(see p33)* and the fountain memorial to the assassinated Empress Elisabeth (1907) by Friedrich Ohmann *(see p57)* and the sculptor Hans Bitterlich.

Lobkowitz Palace ㉝

Lobkowitzplatz 2. **Map** 4 D1 & 5 C4. **Tel** 525244031. Ⓤ *Karlsplatz, Stephansplatz.* ◯ *10am–6pm Tue–Sun.* 📷 ♿ **www.**khm.at

This large palace was built for Count Dietrichstein in 1685–7 by Giovanni Pietro Tencala and altered by Johann Bernhard Fischer von Erlach *(see p149)* in 1710. In 1753 it was acquired by the Lobkowitz family. Balls were held here during the Congress of Vienna *(see p30).*

Since 1991 the palace has been the Austrian Theatre Museum, which houses a model of the first Hofburg theatre and the Eroica-Saal (1724–29) – where many first performances of Beethoven's work took place. The main exhibits chronicle Austrian theatre in the 1940s.

Kapuzinerkirche und Kaisergruft ㉞

Tegetthoffstrasse 2. **Map** 4 D1 & 5 C4. **Tel** 5126852. Ⓤ *Stephansplatz.* **Kaisergruft** ◯ *10am–6pm daily.* **Kapuzinerkirche** ◯ *6am–6pm daily.* 📷 ♿ **www.**kaisergruft.at

Beneath the Kapuziner-kirche are the vaults of the Kaisergruft, the imperial crypt founded in 1619 by the Catholic Emperor Matthias. Here lie the remains of 138 Habsburgs, including Maria Theresa and her husband Franz Stephan in a large tomb by Balthasar Moll (1753). The most poignant tomb is that of Franz Joseph, flanked by his assassinated wife Elisabeth and their son Rudolf, who

Formal rose garden in the Volksgarten

Tomb of Karl VI by Balthasar Moll

committed suicide *(see p32)*. The last reigning Habsburg, Empress Zita, died in 1989 and her remains are also buried in the crypt.

Neuer Markt ❸

Map 4 D1 & 5 C4. Ⓤ *Stephansplatz.*

Known as the Mehlmarkt or flour market until around 1210, the Neuer Markt was also used as a jousting area. Of these origins nothing is left, though a few 18th-century houses remain. In the middle of the Neuer Markt is a replica of the Donner Fountain (1737–9) by Georg Raphael Donner, a symbolic celebration of the role played by rivers in the economic life of the Habsburg Empire. The four figures denote tributaries of the Danube, while the central figure represents Providence. The original figures are in the Lower Belvedere *(see p157)*.

Kärntner Strasse ❸

Map 4 D1 & 5 C5.
Ⓤ *Stephansplatz.* **Malteserkirche**
⬜ 8am–6pm daily. **Lobmeyr**
Museum ⬜ 10am–7pm Mon–Fri,
10am–6pm Sat.

This pedestrianized street was the main highway to Carinthia in medieval times. Now it is the old city's principal shopping street. Day and night, it is packed

with people shopping, buying fresh fruit juice from stands, pausing in cafés, or listening to the street musicians.

No. 37 is the Malteser-kirche. This church was founded by the Knights of Malta who were invited to Vienna early in the 13th century by Leopold VI. The interior retains lofty Gothic windows and vaults.

At No. 1 is the Lobmeyr Museum, which houses glass designed by Josef Hoffmann *(see p56)*, among others, for the Viennese firm of Lobmeyr.

Around the corner at No. 5 Johannesgasse is the superb Questenberg-Kaunitz Palace which dates from the early 18th century. Its design has been attributed to the architect Johann Lukas von Hildebrandt *(see p152)*.

American Bar ❸

Kärntner Strasse 10. **Map** 4 D1 & 6 D3. Ⓤ *Stephansplatz.*

Beneath a garish depiction of the Stars and Stripes is this bar designed by Adolf Loos *(see p92)* in 1908. The interior, restored in 1990, is a gem.

The Donner Fountain in Neuer Markt

The bar is tiny, with every detail worked out by Loos, such as the tables lit from below and the exquisite glass cabinets for storing glasses. One of his hallmarks is the use of mahogany panelling, and this bar is no exception. Mirrors give the impression that the interior is larger than it actually is, and onyx and marble panels reflect a soft light.

Façade of the American Bar

Stock-im-Eisen-Platz ❸

Map 2 D5 & 5 C3. Ⓤ *Stephansplatz.*

This square is at the inter-section of Stephansplatz, Kärntner Strasse and Graben. Opposite Haas Haus *(see p75)* is the Equitable Palace (1891), once headquarters to the Equitable Life Insurance Company. There is also an old tree trunk with nails in it in the square. Passing locksmiths' apprentices would bang in a nail to ensure a safe passage home.

SCHOTTENRING AND ALSERGRUND

This part of the city is dotted with sites of interest, such as the ornate Ferstel Palace and the glass-roofed Ferstel Passage that runs through it. The Schottenring and the Schottentor are named after the Benedictine monks who came here in Babenberg times to found the Schottenkirche Monastery. Later rulers of Austria were responsible for the area's

Relief on the façade of the Schottenkirche

other monuments: Joseph II built a huge public hospital, now the Josephinum, and Franz Joseph founded the Votivkirche as a way of giving thanks after escaping assassination in 1853. To the east, nearer the Danube Canal, quiet residential streets are broken only by the imposing Liechtenstein Museum, one of many summer palaces built beyond the city gates by Vienna's nobility.

SIGHTS AT A GLANCE

Streets and Squares
Freyung ❷
Freyung Passage ❶

Churches and Cathedrals
Schottenkirche ❸
Servitenkirche ❺
Votivkirche ❾

Museums and Galleries
Freud Museum ❹
Josephinum ❼
Liechtenstein Museum ❻
Narrenturm ❽

GETTING THERE
This area is served by the Schottentor (line U2) and Rossauer Lände (line U4) U-Bahn stations. Trams 37, 38, 40, 41 and 42 go along Währinger Strasse. Bus 40A runs the length of Liechtensteinstrasse.

KEY

- ▦ Street-by-Street map See pp108–109
- Ⓤ U-Bahn station

0 metres 250
0 yards 250

◁ **The impressive façade of the 19th-century Votivkirche**

Street-by-Street: Around the Freyung

At the core of this elegant part of the city is the former medieval complex of the Schottenkirche and its courtyards and school. On the other side of the Freyung square are some beautiful Baroque palaces, including Hildebrandt's Kinsky Palace (1713–16), and the Palais Ferstel. The Freyung Passage links the Freyung square with Herrengasse, which is lined with Baroque mansions as well as the city's first skyscraper.

Statue of Turkish soldier, south of the Freyung

Backing onto the Schottenring is the Italianate Börse.

★ **Schottenkirche**
Founded in 1177 and redecorated in the Baroque period, this fine church has a museum and there is a famous school alongside it ❸

★ **Freyung**
This square is overlooked by fine buildings, including the former Schottenkirche priory, originally founded in 1155, then rebuilt in 1744 and, due to its appearance, known by the Viennese as the "chest of drawers house" ❷

Passageway leading from No. 2 Helferstorferstrasse to the Freyung

HELFERSTRFERSTRASSE

SCHOTTENGASSE

★ **Freyung Passage**
The Freyung and Herrengasse are connected by a luxury shopping arcade ❶

FREYUNG

The Café Central
has a papier-mâché statue of the poet Peter Altenberg next to the main entrance. Altenberg spent a great deal of time in various coffee houses around the city *(see pp58–61).*

HERRENGASSE

To Herrengasse U-Bahn

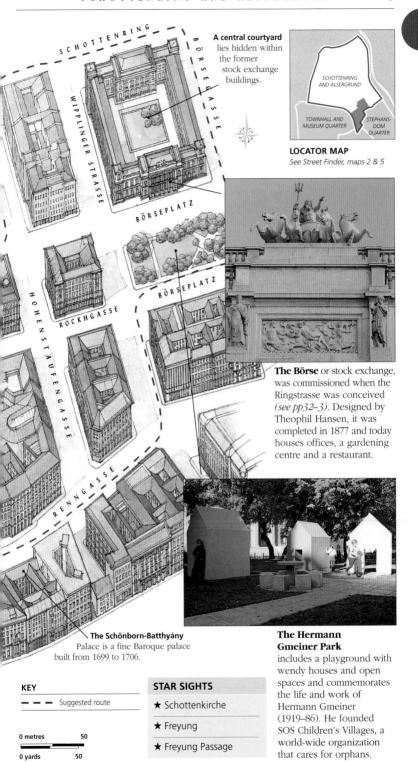

A central courtyard lies hidden within the former stock exchange buildings.

LOCATOR MAP
See Street Finder, maps 2 & 5

SCHOTTENRING AND ALSERGRUND

TOWNHALL AND MUSEUM QUARTER

STEPHANS-DOM QUARTER

The Börse or stock exchange, was commissioned when the Ringstrasse was conceived *(see pp32–3)*. Designed by Theophil Hansen, it was completed in 1877 and today houses offices, a gardening centre and a restaurant.

The Schönborn-Batthyány Palace is a fine Baroque palace built from 1699 to 1706.

The Hermann Gmeiner Park includes a playground with wendy houses and open spaces and commemorates the life and work of Hermann Gmeiner (1919–86). He founded SOS Children's Villages, a world-wide organization that cares for orphans.

KEY

– – – Suggested route

0 metres   50

0 yards   50

STAR SIGHTS

★ Schottenkirche

★ Freyung

★ Freyung Passage

Freyung Passage ❶

Map 2 D5 & 5 B2. 🚇 *Herrengasse.*

Facing the Freyung is the Italian-style *palazzo* known as the Palais Ferstel, dating from 1860 and taking its name from the architect, Heinrich von Ferstel. Wander in and you will find yourself in the glass-roofed Freyung Passage: lined with elegant shops, it converges on a small courtyard of which the centrepiece is a many-tiered statue portraying the lissom water-sprite of the Danube holding a fish. It then emerges on Herrengasse. As an example of civilized urban amenities, the passage is a great success. It also has an entrance into one of Vienna's grandest coffee houses, the Café Central *(see pp59–61)*.

Danube Mermaid's Fountain (1861) in Freyung Passage

Freyung ❷

Map 2 D5 & 5 B2. 🚇 *Herrengasse.* **Kinsky Palace** ⬜ *10am–5pm Mon–Fri.*

The Freyung is a curiously shaped "square". Its name derives from the right of sanctuary granted to the monks of the Schottenkirche that lasted until Maria Theresa abolished it. Fugitives from persecution who entered the area were safe from arrest. No. 4 is the Kinsky Palace (1713–16), by Johann Lukas von Hildebrandt *(see p152)*. Next door is the Porcia Palace of 1546, one of the oldest in Vienna, though much altered. At No. 3 is the Harrach

Façade of the Schottenkirche

Palace; the interior has some fine Rococo doors. Opposite is the Austria Fountain: its four figures symbolize the major rivers of the Habsburgs' lands. Behind is the former Schottenkirche priory, unkindly known as the chest-of-drawers house.

Schottenkirche ❸

Schottenstift, Freyung 6. **Map** 2 D5 & 5 B2. *Tel 53498600.* 🚇 *Schottentor, Herrengasse.* **Museum** ⬜ *11am–5pm Thu–Sat.* 🔴 *Sun & hols.* 🎦 🚫

Despite its name (Scottish church) this 1177 monastic foundation was established by Irish Benedictines. The adjoining buildings have a fine medieval art collection that includes the famous Schotten altarpiece (1475).

The church has been altered repeatedly and has undergone extensive renovation. Today it presents a rather drab Neo-Classical façade, with a rich Baroque interior.

Freud Museum ❹

Berggasse 19. **Map** 1 C3. *Tel 3191596.* 🚇 *Schottentor.* 🚌 *40A.* 🚊 *D.* ⬜ *9am–5pm daily (to 6pm Jul–Sep).* 🎦 📷 **www**.freud-museum.at

No. 19 Berggasse differs little from any other 19th-century apartment in Vienna, yet it is now one of the city's most famous addresses. The father of psychoanalysis, Sigmund Freud, lived, worked and received patients here from 1891 until his departure from Vienna in 1938.

The flat housed Freud's family as well as his practice. The catalogue lists 420 items of memorabilia on display, including letters and books, furnishings, photographs documenting Freud's long life, and various antiquities.

Although quickly abandoned when the Nazis forced Freud to leave the city where he had lived almost all his life, the flat still preserves an intimate domestic atmosphere.

Servitenkirche ❺

Servitengasse 9. **Map** 1 C3. *Tel 317 6195.* 🚇 *Rossauer Lände.* ⬜ *7–9am, 6–7pm Mon–Fri, 7–9am, 5–8pm Sat, 7am–noon, 5–8pm Sun.* 🎦 ♿

Although off the beaten track, this Baroque church (1651–77) is well worth a visit. Inside, a riot of Baroque decoration includes elaborate stucco ornamentation, a fine wrought-iron screen near the entrance, and an exuberant pulpit (1739), partly by Balthasar Moll.

FREUD'S THEORIES

Sigmund Freud (1856–1939) was not only the founder of the techniques of psychoanalysis, but a theorist who wrote many essays and books expounding his contentious ideas. Modern concepts such as subconscious, ego, sublimation and Oedipus complex, evolved from Freudian theories. Freud posited different structural systems within the human psyche that, if seriously out of balance, result in emotional or mental disturbance.

Liechtenstein Museum ❻

Fürstengasse 1. **Map** 1 C2.
Tel 3195767252. 🚇 Friedensbrücke.
🚋 40A. 🚈 D. 🕐 10am–5pm Fri–
Tue. **www.**liechtensteinmuseum.at

Designed by Domenico
Martinelli and completed in
1692, the Liechtenstein Palace
was the summer home of the
Liechtenstein family and now
houses the art collection of
Prince Hans-Adam II von und
zu Liechtenstein. Behind the
imposing Palladian exterior,
notable features include the
Neo-Classical library, and the
Hercules Hall and grand staircase with their magnificent
frescoes. The art collection
centres on the Baroque, with
a special focus on Rubens,
and numerous paintings and
sculptures by German, Dutch
and Italian masters from the
Renaissance through to the
19th century. The palace
stands in an extensive English-
style garden, designed in the
19th century.

Josephinum ❼

Währinger Strasse 25/1. **Map** 1 C4.
Tel 4016026000. 🚇 Schottentor.
🚋 37, 38, 40, 41, 42. 🕐 10am–
6pm daily. ● public hols. 📷 ♿

The ardent reformer Joseph II
(see p28) established this military surgical institute. Designed
by Isidor Canevale in 1785, it
is now a medical museum.
Some rooms contain memorabilia from the 19th century,
when Vienna was a leading
centre for medical research,
but the main attraction is the
unusual collection of wax
anatomical models commis-
sioned by the emperor from
Tuscan artists.

Narrenturm ❽

Spitalgasse 2. **Map** 1 B3. **Tel** 4068672.
🚇 Schottentor. 🚋 5, 33, 43, 44.
🕐 3–6pm Wed, 8–11am Thu,
10am–1pm 1st Sat of month. 📷

What used to be the
Allgemeines Krankenhaus,
founded by Joseph II (see p28)

Detail on the Votivkirche façade

in 1784, has been renovated
and now houses various
faculties of the University
of Vienna. At the far end
of the complex is the Narrenturm Tower, a former lunatic
asylum designed by Isidor
Canevale. The tower now
houses the Museum for
Pathological Anatomy, which
includes a reconstruction of
an apothecary's shop and wax
models. The few ground-floor
rooms open to the public
only show a small part of the
collection, but serious students
can enrol on a guided tour of
the corridors upstairs.

Votivkirche ❾

Rooseveltplatz 8. **Map** 1 C4 & 5 A1.
Tel 4061192. 🚇 Schottentor.
🕐 9am–1pm, 4–6:30pm Tue–Sat,
9am–1pm Sun. 📷 ♿ side entrance.

After a deranged tailor tried
but failed to assassinate
Emperor Franz Joseph on 18
February 1853, a collection
was made to pay for a new
church to be built opposite
the Mölker-Bastei, where the
attempt had been made. The
architect was Heinrich von
Ferstel, who began the church
in 1856 though it was not
dedicated until 1879. The lacy
steeples and spire are very
attractive. Many of the church's
chapels are dedicated to
Austrian regiments and
military heroes. The finest
monument is the Renaissance
sarcophagus tomb of Niklas
Salm in the chapel just west
of the north transept. Salm
commanded Austria's forces
during the 1529 Turkish siege.

Wooden pietà in Gothic style (1470) in the Servitenkirche

MUSEUM AND TOWNHALL QUARTER

The Emperor Franz Joseph commissioned the major institutional buildings of the Habsburg empire, and the city, along the Ringstrasse in the mid-19th century (*see pp32–3*). Today these buildings remain a successful and imposing example of good urban planning. The districts to the west of the Ringstrasse are untouched, including

Der liebe Augustin, Sankt-Ulrichs-Platz

Josefstadt, which still retains an 18th-century atmosphere with its picturesque streets, modest palaces and Baroque churches. The area's cultural institutions are vibrant: the brilliant productions of the Burgtheater and the wide-ranging exhibits of the Natural History Museum and the Kunsthistorisches Museum are all popular today.

SIGHTS AT A GLANCE

Streets and Squares
Mölker-Bastei **17**
Sankt-Ulrichs-Platz **6**
Spittelberg Pedestrian Area **7**

Historic Buildings
Alte Backstube **2**
Burgtheater pp132–33 **19**
Café Landtmann **15**
Dreimäderlhaus **16**
Josefstadt Theater **4**
Neues Rathaus **12**
Parliament **9**
Pasqualati Haus **18**
Trautson Palace **5**
University **14**

Churches and Cathedrals
Dreifaltigkeitskirche **13**
Maria Treu Kirche **3**

Museums and Galleries
Kunsthistorisches Museum pp122–27 **10**
Museum für Volkskunde **1**
MuseumsQuartier **8**
Natural History Museum pp128–9 **11**

GETTING THERE
This area is served by the Rathaus (line U2) and Volkstheater (lines U2, U3) U-Bahn stations. Tram 5 runs from Josefstädter Strasse to Lange Gasse, and 46 goes down Lerchenfelder Strasse. Bus 2A runs from Schwedenplatz to Volkstheater. 13A runs along Piaristengasse, and 48A along Burggasse.

KEY

- Street-by-Street map
  See pp114–115

- **U** U-Bahn station

0 metres   250
0 yards   250

◁ Neues Rathaus façade by night

Street-by-Street: Josefstadt

Tucked behind the grand museums of the Ringstrasse is the 18th-century district known as Josefstadt, named after Emperor Joseph II. Although outside the Inner City, Josefstadt has a vibrant cultural life of its own, with a popular theatre, many good restaurants, and handsome churches and museums. Students from the university and lawyers from the courthouses provide a constantly changing clientele for the district's varied establishments.

★ **Maria Treu Kirche**
Founded by the fathers of the Piarist order, this church was built from 1716 ❸

Josefstadt Theater
Founded in 1788, Vienna's oldest theatre has kept its doors open continuously since it was rebuilt by Josef Kornhäusel (see p84) in 1822 ❹

No. 29 Lange Gasse
Originally built for servants and workers in the 18th century, the cottages lining this courtyard have changed little over the years.

KEY

— — — Suggested route

To Lerchen-
felder Strasse

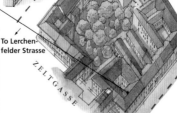

The Plague Column here commemorates an epidemic that occurred in 1713.

STAR SIGHTS

★ Maria Treu Kirche

★ Museum für Volkskunde

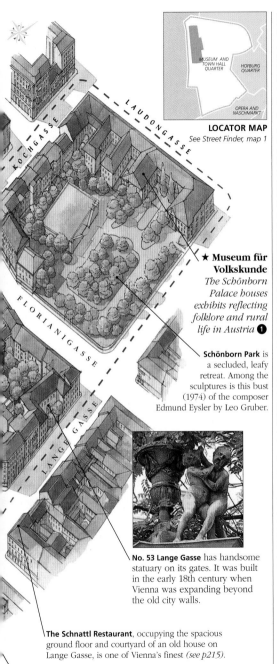

LOCATOR MAP
See Street Finder, map 1

★ Museum für Volkskunde
The Schönborn Palace houses exhibits reflecting folklore and rural life in Austria ❶

Schönborn Park is a secluded, leafy retreat. Among the sculptures is this bust (1974) of the composer Edmund Eysler by Leo Gruber.

No. 53 Lange Gasse has handsome statuary on its gates. It was built in the early 18th century when Vienna was expanding beyond the old city walls.

The Schnattl Restaurant, occupying the spacious ground floor and courtyard of an old house on Lange Gasse, is one of Vienna's finest *(see p215)*.

Alte Backstube
A working bakery from 1701 to 1963, since 1965 it has been a museum and restaurant ❷

| 0 metres | 50 |
| 0 yards | 50 |

Museum für Volkskunde ❶

Laudongasse 15–19. **Map** 1 B4.
Tel 4068905. Ⓤ *Rathaus.* ◯ *10am–5pm Tue–Sun.* ◉ *1 Jan, Easter Mon, 1 May, 1 Nov, 25 Dec.* 🈺 📷 ♿
www.volkskundemuseum.at

The charming Museum of Austrian Folklore is a reminder that Vienna is not only full of imperial grandeur. Here you will find artifacts reflecting the culture of people in Austria and neighbouring countries. Exhibits include objects dating from the 17th to 19th centuries. The museum is housed in the 18th-century Schönborn Palace, designed by Johann Lukas von Hildebrandt as a homely two-storey mansion and altered in 1760 by Isidor Canevale. Today it has a rather imposing façade with statuary running along its top. There is a pleasant park behind the palace.

Alte Backstube ❷

Lange Gasse 34. **Map** 1 B5.
Ⓤ *Rathaus.* **Tel** 4061101.
◯ *11am–midnight Mon–Sat, 5pm–midnight Sun.* ◉ *mid-Jul–mid-Aug and public hols.* 📷 ♿

One of the finest middle-class houses in Vienna was built at No. 34 Lange Gasse in 1697 by the jeweller Hans Bernhard Leopold. The sandstone sculpture that is positioned above the doorway symbolizes the Holy Trinity. Inside is an old bakery, the Alte Backstube, that was in continuous use from 1701 to 1963. The baking ovens were never removed, and today the rooms have been sympathetically restored and incorporated into a traditional restaurant and café. They also contain a museum dedicated to the art of baking where 18th-century equipment is on display.

A few doors away, at No. 29, it's worth glancing into the courtyard to see the rows of single-storey houses facing each other – a rare example of working-class Vienna that is more than 200 years old.

Maria Treu Kirche ❸

Jodok-Fink-Platz. **Map** 1 B5.
Tel 4061453. Ⓤ Rathaus. ☐ for
services and by appointment. 📷

Overlooking Jodok-Fink-
Platz and flanked by monastic
buildings stands the Church
of Maria Treu. It was founded
in 1698 by the fathers of the
Piarist order.

This outstanding church was
originally designed by Johann
Lukas von Hildebrandt in 1716
and altered by Matthias Gerl
in the 1750s. The elegant twin
towers were not completed
until 1854. Inside, there is a
splendid Baroque frescoed
ceiling in vibrant colours from
1752–3 by the great Austrian
painter Franz Anton Maul-
bertsch. A chapel immediately
to the left of the choir contains
an altarpiece of the Crucifixion
dating from about 1774, also
painted by Maulbertsch.

Directly in front of the
church and rising up from the
square is a fine Baroque pillar
topped with a statue of the
Madonna, attended beneath
by statues of saints and angels.
Like many such columns in
Vienna, it was erected to
commemorate an outbreak
of plague, in this case the
epidemic of 1713.

The façade of the glorious Josefstadt Theater

Founded in 1788, it was
rebuilt by Joseph Kornhäusel
(see p84) in 1822, and has
been in operation ever since,
accommodating ballet, opera
and theatre performances.
Beethoven composed and
conducted his overture *The
Consecration of the House*
for the reopening of the
theatre in 1822 after its renovation. The director Max
Reinhardt supervised the
restoration of this attractive
theatre in 1924. Today, it
puts on mostly light plays
and comedies.

Trautson Palace ❺

Museumstrasse 7. **Map** 3 B1.
Ⓤ Volkstheater. ● to the public.

Set back from the street next
to the Volkstheater is this
elegant Baroque palace,
designed in 1710 by Johann
Bernhard Fischer von Erlach
(see p149). Most Viennese
palaces have flat fronts but on
this one the central bays of
the façade jut out with real
panache. Nor is there
anything restrained about the
ornamentation: above the
cornice and pediment is one
of the largest collections of
statuary atop any palace in
the whole of Vienna. This
includes a large statue of
Apollo playing the lyre.
Passing beneath the tall portal
you will see on the left an
immense staircase, with
carvings of bearded giants
bearing its weight, by the
Italian sculptor Giovanni
Giuliani. This leads to the
ceremonial hall.

Originally built for Count
Johann Leopold Donat
Trautson who was in the
service of Joseph I, the palace
was acquired in 1760 by
Maria Theresa *(see pp28–9)*.
She donated it to the Royal
Hungarian Bodyguard that
she had founded. It has
housed the Ministry of Justice
since 1961, so there is no
public access to the interior.

Sankt-Ulrichs-Platz ❻

Between Neustiftgasse and Burggasse.
Map 3 B1. Ⓤ Volkstheater. **Café
Nepomuk Tel** 06766124003. ☐
8am–11pm Mon–Fri, 8am–11pm Sat
& Sun. **Ulrichskirche Tel** 5231246.
☐ on request or for services only.

This tiny sloping square is an
exquisite survival of early
Vienna. The dainty Baroque
house at No. 27 is now the
Café Nepomuk, and adjoining
it is a Renaissance house that
escaped destruction by the
Turks during the sieges of the
city, most probably because
the Turkish commander Kara
Mustafa pitched his own tent
nearby.

The house partly obscures
the façade of the Baroque
Ulrichskirche, built by Josef
Reymund from 1721–4.
Handsome patrician houses
encircle it, of which the
prettiest is No. 2, the
Schulhaus. Elaborately
decorated, it dates from the
mid-18th century. In the
church the composer Gluck
was married and Johann
Strauss the Younger was
christened.

Ceiling frescoes above the altar in
the Maria Treu Kirche

Josefstadt Theater ❹

Josefstädter Strasse 26. **Map** 1 B5.
Tel 427000. Ⓤ Rathaus. ☐ for
performances. **www**.josefstadt.org

This intimate theatre *(see
p230)*, one of the oldest still
standing in Vienna, has
enjoyed a glorious history.

Spittelberg Pedestrian Area ❼

Map 3 B1. 🚇 *Volkstheater.* **Amerlinghaus** ⬜ *2–10pm Mon–Fri.* **Market** ⬜ *Apr–Jun & Sep–Nov: 10am–6pm Sat; Jul & Aug: 2–9pm Sat.* 📷 ♿

A group of streets – the pedestrianized Spittelberggasse, Gutenberggasse and Schrankgasse – has been well restored to present a pretty group of 18th- and 19th-century houses. Traditionally the area was lower class and very lively, home to the actors, artists and strolling players of the day. The houses were mostly tenements, without gardens or courtyards.

The charm of the district was rediscovered in the 1970s and the city authorities set about restoring the buildings. Today, it is a district of restaurants, cafés and boutiques. It hosts a Christmas market, and a regular arts and crafts market from April to November. The Amerlinghaus theatre at No. 8 Stiftgasse is the area's cultural centre and provides a venue for exhibitions and events. The Spittelberg is a great success, and café life keeps the cobbled streets buzzing into the early hours.

Façade detail at No. 20 Spittelberggasse

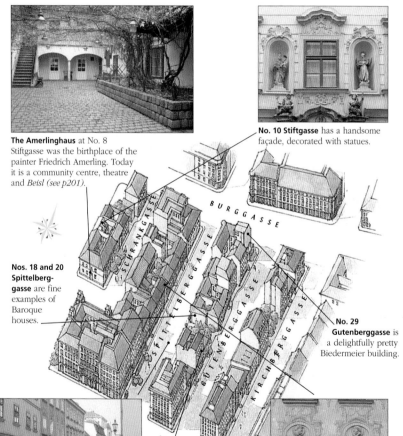

The Amerlinghaus at No. 8 Stiftgasse was the birthplace of the painter Friedrich Amerling. Today it is a community centre, theatre and *Beisl (see p201)*.

No. 10 Stiftgasse has a handsome façade, decorated with statues.

Nos. 18 and 20 Spittelberg-gasse are fine examples of Baroque houses.

No. 29 Gutenberggasse is a delightfully pretty Biedermeier building.

Spittelberggasse acts as the venue for an arts and crafts market that is held on every Saturday from April to November, and daily during Easter and Christmas.

The Witwe Bolte restaurant used to be an inn in the 18th century; legend has it that Emperor Joseph II was thrown out of here in 1778.

No. 9 Spittelberggasse is a beautifully-decorated house, with skilfully-painted *trompe l'oeil* windows, dating from the 18th century.

MuseumsQuartier Wien ❽

Once home to the Imperial stables and carriage houses, the MuseumsQuartier Wien is one of the largest cultural centres in the world. It houses a diverse range of facilities from classical art museums to venues for film, theatre, architecture, dance, new media and a children's creativity centre, as well as a variety of shops, cafés and restaurants. Blending the Baroque architecture of the imperial stables with bold modern buildings, such as the white limestone façade of the Leopold Museum and the dark grey basalt of the Museum of Modern Art Ludwig Foundation Vienna, this impressive and diverse complex aims to provide an almost unprecedented experience.

★ Leopold Museum
Self-portrait with Chinese Lantern *(1912) by Egon Schiele is part of the world's largest collection of Schiele's works, housed in this museum.*

★ ZOOM Kindermuseum
Providing an exciting place to learn, children are encouraged to explore in the ZOOM Lab, play in ZOOM Ocean, be creative in ZOOM Atelier and have fun exploring the ZOOM exhibitions.

math.space

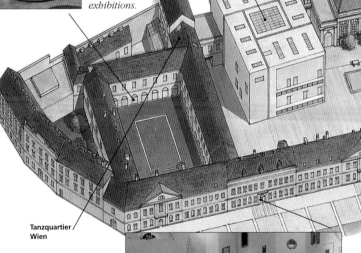

Tanzquartier Wien

STAR SIGHTS

★ ZOOM Kindermuseum

★ Leopold Museum

★ Museum of Modern Art Ludwig Foundation Vienna (MUMOK)

quartier21
As Vienna's centre for contemporary applied art, quartier21 provides a range of frequently changing exhibitions for the public, as well as numerous fashion, design, book and music shops.

Halls E + G

This foyer leads to the former Winter Riding Hall, now Halls E + G showing a variety of concert, theatre and dance performances. The foyer is also the entrance to the Kunsthalle Wien which exhibits international modern art.

Architekturzentrum
Wien

quartier21
(alternate entrance)

Main entrance in the Fischer
von Erlach Wing

Main Courtyard

Often called the largest open-air festival hall in Vienna, from here the diverse architecture of the complex can be appreciated.

★ Museum of Modern Art Ludwig Foundation Vienna

Homme accroupi (1907) by Andre Derain, is part of the collection of European contemporary and modern art in this museum, otherwise known as MUMOK.

Exploring the MuseumsQuartier Wien

Over 20 different cultural institutions are gathered together in the MuseumsQuartier Wien, together with a wide variety of restaurants, cafés and shops. The sight is an ideal starting point for any trip to Vienna, as many other attractions are nearby. It is advisable to begin your visit by going to the Visitor Centre in the Fischer von Erlach Wing, to obtain a programme detailing the events and the exhibitions happening in the complex.

Die Quelle (1923), Leopold Museum

Architekturzentrum Wien
Tel 5223115. ☐ 10am–9pm daily.
🔢 www.azw.at
The permanent exhibition at this venue is concerned with thematic and structural diversity in 20th-century architecture. Committed to providing access to architecture, the venue introduces new architectural work to the public. The four to six temporary exhibitions a year aim to complement this by linking modern architecture with architectural history.

Museum of Modern Art Ludwig Foundation Vienna (MUMOK)
Tel 52500. ☐ 10am–6pm daily (to 9pm Thu). www.mumok.at
This museum contains one of the largest European collections of modern and contemporary art. MUMOK comprises of a variety of genres ranging from American Pop Art, Photo Realism, Fluxus and Nouveau Réalism to Viennese Actionism, Arte Povera, Conceptual and Minimal Art, as well as other contemporary art from Central and Eastern Europe. The galleries are split historically and chronologically over five levels, two underground.

quartier21
Tel 0820 600600. ☐ 10am–8pm daily, except special events.
Over 40 different groups have turned quartier21 into Vienna's centre for contemporary applied art. The attractions for the public, which are on the ground floor, include fashion, design, book and music shops, an exhibition space for art schools, and large event halls.

Leopold Museum
Tel 525700. ☐ 10am–6pm daily (10am–9pm Thu).
www.leopoldmuseum.org
Home to over 5,000 works of art, the Leopold Collection of Austrian art was compiled over five decades by Rudolf Leopold. The exhibition space spans five floors. One of the museum's highlights is the world's largest Egon Schiele collection (on the second floor) along with Expressionist paintings and Austrian inter-war paintings.

Paintings after 1945 and works by Albin Egger-Lienz, including *Die Quelle*, are on the first floor, while an exhibition on Secessionism and Art Nouveau is on the ground level, with major works by Gustav Klimt, Richard Gerstl

and Oskar Kokoschka. The lower two levels include art from other 19th- and early 20th-century Austrian artists.

Tanzquartier Wien
Tel 581359160. www.tqw.at
The Tanzquartier Wien offers facilities and training to dancers and presents dance and other performances to the public.

ZOOM Kindermuseum
Tel 5247908. ☐ 8:30am–5pm Mon–Fri, 10am–5:30pm Sat & Sun, school hols, public hols. Visits must be pre-booked. www.kindermuseum.at
This lively centre offers an unconventional approach to the world of the museum for children from babies to the age of 12. The aim is to encourage learning about exhibition subjects through play and exploration, such as the ZOOM Lab for older children, while younger ones can have a dip in the ZOOM Ocean with their parents.

KUNSTHALLE wien
Tel 5218933. ☐ 10am–7pm daily (to 10pm Thu).
www.kunsthallewien.at
This striking red brick building is a home for innovation and creativity, showing exhibitions of international and contemporary art. The exhibitions emphasize cross-genre and cross-border trends in the arts. Highlights range from experimental architecture, video, photography and film, to new media.

math.space
Tel 5235881/1730. ☐ varies, phone to check. http://math.space.or.at
Linking maths to the arts, this centre for the popularization of maths is aimed at people of all ages, with interactive workshops for children and many programmes for adults.

The Red Horseman (1974) by Roy Lichtenstein in MUMOK

Parliament ❾

Dr-Karl-Renner-Ring 3. **Map** 1 C5 & 5
A3. *Tel* 401102400. Ⓤ *Volkstheater.*
🚋 *1, 2, D.* ⬚ *for* ▨ *except when
parliament is in session: mid-Sep–mid-
Jul: 11am, 2pm, 3pm, 4pm Mon–
Thu; 11am, 1pm, 2pm, 3pm, 4pm Fri;
11am, noon, 1pm, 2pm, 3pm, 4pm
Sat; mid-Jul–mid-Sep: 11am, noon,
1pm, 2pm, 3pm, 4pm Mon–Sat.* ♿
www.parlament.gv.at

Façade of the Parliament building and the Athenebrunnen fountain

The architect Theophil Hansen
(*see p32*) chose a strict Neo-
Classical style when he
designed the Parliament building (and the neighbouring
Palais Epstein). The building
was originally constructed as
part of the Ringstrasse development to act as the *Reichsrat*
building (the Parliament of the
Austrian part of the Habsburg
empire). Construction began
in 1874 and finished in 1884.

The Parliament's entrance is
raised above street level and
approached up a broad ramp.
At the foot of the ramp are the
the bronze Horse Tamers
(1901) by sculptor Josef Lax;
the ramp itself is decorated
with marble figures of Greek
and Roman historians. On the
roof there are chariots and
impressive statues of ancient
scholars and statesmen.

In front of the central
portico is the Athenebrunnen,

a fountain dominated by the
figure of Pallas Athene, the
goddess of Wisdom. It was
designed by Karl Kundmann
and was placed here in 1902.
In this splendid, if chilly, setting
on 11 November 1918 after
the collapse of the Habsburg
empire, the parliamentary
deputies proclaimed the
formation of the republic of

Deutsch-Österreich. It was
renamed the Republic of
Austria in 1919.

During World War II, half
of the Parliament building
was completely destroyed.
Reconstruction was eventually
completed by June 1956, but
the restoration of some of the
damaged artwork, only began
in the 1990s.

THE AUSTRIAN PARLIAMENT

The Austrian parliament is composed of two
houses – the Lower House, or *Nationalrat*, and
the Upper House, or *Bundesrat*. The Lower House
has 183 seats and its members are elected for a
four-year term by proportional representation. It
comprises the governing party and the opposi-
tion. The Upper House is composed of elected
representatives from Austria's nine provinces,
and its function is to approve
legislation passed by the
Lower House. Bills may also
be presented to parliament
by the general public or by
the Chambers of Labour
(representing consumers and
employees) and the Chambers
of the Economy (representing
employers and industry). The
federal President is elected for
a six-year term and is largely
a figurehead. Theoretically, he
or she has the power to veto
bills and dissolve parliament,
though this has never occurred.

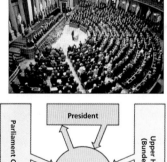

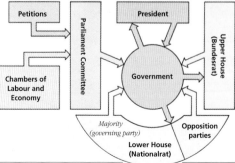

Kunsthistorisches Museum ⑩

More than one and a half million people visit the
Museum of the History of Art every year. Its collections
are based largely on those built up over the centuries by
generations of Habsburg monarchs. Originally the works
of art were housed in the Hofburg and the Belvedere,
but when the Ringstrasse was built *(see pp32–3)*
two magnificent buildings were erected to house
the collections of imperial art and natural
history. The former are on display in this
museum where lavish internal
decoration complements the exhibits.

Second floor

Coin collection

★ **Hunters in the Snow** *(1565)*
*The last painting in Pieter Bruegel the
Elder's series of the seasons shows hunters
returning to the village on a winter's day.*

First floor

★ **The Artist's Studio**
*In this 1665 allegory of art,
Johannes Vermeer shows an
artist in decorative dress
painting a model posing as
Clio, the Muse of History.*

★ **Salt Cellar** *(1540–3)*
*Benvenuto Cellini's sumptuous
gold Saliera shows the sea and
earth united, represented by a
female earth goddess and
the sea god
Neptune.*

KEY

☐	Egyptian and Near Eastern collection
▦	Collection of Greek and Roman Antiquities
☐	Collection of Sculpture and Decorative Arts
☐	Picture gallery
☐	Coin cabinets
☐	Non-exhibition space

Portrait of the Infanta Margarita Teresa *(1659)*
Diego Velázquez captures the fragility of the eight-year-old Spanish princess in all her finery in this official portrait.

Gemma Augustea
The Emperor Augustus dressed as Jupiter sits next to Roma, the personification of Rome, in this Roman cameo carved from onyx.

Ground floor

MUSEUM GUIDE
The ground floor, housing sculpture and the applied arts, is due to reopen in late 2012. Until then, parts of this collection are on display in the picture gallery, on the first floor. Three rooms on the second floor house the impressive coin collection.

Rooms 1–7

King Thutmosis III
Sculpted around 1460 BC, this royal portrait of King Thutmosis III is a remnant of a standing or kneeling figure.

Main entrance from Maria-Theresia-Platz

Rotunda

STAR EXHIBITS

★ Hunters in the Snow by Bruegel

★ The Artist's Studio by Vermeer

★ Salt Cellar by Cellini

THE APOTHEOSIS OF THE RENAISSANCE

Many prominent artists were employed to decorate the museum's interior. As part of an extravagant decorative scheme, the Hungarian painter Michael Munkácsy contributed a fabulous *trompe l'oeil* ceiling painting for the main staircase depicting *The Apotheosis of the Renaissance* (1890). It features Leonardo, Raphael, Veronese, Michelangelo and Titian and their models, presided over by Pope Julius II.

Exploring the Kunsthistorisches' Picture Collection

The collection focuses on Old Masters from the 15th to the 18th centuries, and largely reflects the personal tastes of its Habsburg founders. Venetian and 17th-century Flemish paintings are particularly well represented, and there is an excellent display of works by earlier Netherlandish and German artists. Broadly speaking, the pictures are hung following regional schools or styles of painting, although there is considerable overlap between the various categories.

The Fur (around 1635–40) by Peter Paul Rubens

Three rooms, XIII, XIV and XX, are devoted to Rubens and include large-scale religious works such as the *Ildefonso Altarpiece* (1630–32) and *The Fur*, an intimate portrait of his wife. Rubens' collaborator and pupil, Anthony Van Dyck, is also represented here by some outstanding works in which his sensitivity to human emotion is fully portrayed.

FLEMISH PAINTING

Because of the historic links between the Habsburg monarchy and the Netherlands, there are several works from this part of Europe (present-day Belgium). The works of the early Flemish masters, who pioneered the development of oil painting, are characterized by their luminous colours and close attention to detail. This can be seen in the triptychs by Rogier van der Weyden and Hans Memling, and Jan van Eyck's *Cardinal Niccolo Albergati* (1435). The highlight for many is Room X, in which about half of all Pieter Bruegel the Elder's surviving works are displayed, including his *Tower of Babel* and most of the cycle of *The Seasons*, all from the mid-16th century.

DUTCH PAINTING

Protestant Holland's newly-rich merchants of the 17th century delighted in pictures that reflected their own world rather than the hereafter. The Dutch genre scenes include works of great domestic charm such as Pieter de Hooch's lovely *Woman with Child at her Breast* (1663–5) and Gerard ter Borch's *Woman Peeling Apples* (1661) while Jacob van Ruisdael's *Great Forest* (1655–60) shows the advances made by Dutch painters in their observations of the natural world. All the

Large Self-Portrait (1652) by Rembrandt van Rijn

Rembrandts on show in Room XV are portraits; there is the picture of his mother as the prophetess Hannah (1639) and, in contrast to earlier works, the *Large Self-Portrait* shows the artist wearing a plain smock, with the emphasis on his face. The only painting by Johannes Vermeer is the enigmatic *The Artist's Studio* (Room 24). It is a complicated work with layers of symbolism; whether it is a self portrait or not has never been resolved.

ITALIAN PAINTING

The Italian galleries have a strong collection of 16th-century paintings from Venice and the Veneto. In Room I the broad chronological and stylistic sweep of Titian's work, from his early *Gypsy Madonna*

Susanna and the Elders (1555) by Tintoretto

(1510) to the late *Nymph and Shepherd* (1570–5), can be seen. Other Venetian highlights include Giovanni Bellini's graceful *Young Woman at her Toilette* (1515) and Tintoretto's *Susanna and the Elders*. This is considered to be one of the major works of Venetian Mannerism. Giuseppe Arcimboldo's series of allegorical portrait heads representing the elements and the seasons are usually on show in Room 19, together with other works commissioned by Emperor Rudolf II. Italian Baroque painting includes works by Annibale Carracci and Michelangelo Merisi da Caravaggio, including the huge *Madonna of the Rosary*. Painted between 1606 and 1607, it depicts an intensely realistic Madonna advising St Dominic to distribute rosaries.

FRENCH PAINTING

Although the number of French paintings on show is relatively small, there are some minor masterpieces. The minutely detailed and highly original portrait of *The Court Jester Gonella* (1440–45), is thought to be the work of Jean Fouquet. It depicts a wily old man, seemingly squeezed into the picture, believed to be a famous court jester of the time. A more formal court portrait from 1569 is that of the youthful Charles IX of France by François Clouet. *The Destruction of the Temple in Jerusalem*, a monumental work painted by Nicolas Poussin in 1638, depicts the Emperor Titus watching the Old Testament prophecy of the destruction of the Temple of Solomon come true. It combines agitated movement with thorough archaeological research. Joseph Duplessis' *Christopher Willibald Ritter von Gluck at the Spinet* shows the famous composer gazing at the heavens for inspiration.

Summer (1563) by Giuseppe Arcimboldo

BRITISH AND GERMAN PAINTING

There are few British works. Perhaps the most appealing is the *Landscape of Suffolk* (around 1750) by Thomas Gainsborough. There are also portraits by Gainsborough, Reynolds and Lawrence.

The German collection is rich in 16th-century paintings. There are several Albrecht Dürer works, including his *Madonna with the Pear* (1512). Other works include the *Stag Hunt of Elector Friedrich the Wise* (1529) by Lucas Cranach the Elder and seven portraits by Hans Holbein the Younger.

SPANISH PAINTING

Room 10 houses several fine portraits of the Spanish royal family by the artist Diego Velázquez. He lived from 1599 to 1660 and was the court painter to Philip IV. His works include three portraits of Philip IV's daughter, the Infanta Margarita Teresa (in one aged three, another aged five and in a third aged eight), as well as a portrait of her sickly infant brother, Philip Prosper. Other Spanish works include paintings by Alonso Sánchez Coello and Antonio de Pereda.

Stag Hunt of Elector Friedrich the Wise (1529), by Lucas Cranach the Elder, in the German Collection

Exploring the Kunsthistorisches' Other Collections

Apart from the picture gallery, the Kunsthistorisches-Museum houses several distinct collections of three-dimensional art and objects. Most of the European sculpture and decorative art is from approximately the same period as the paintings (from the 15th to the 18th centuries), but there is also a fine display of medieval objects, while exhibits on show in the Egyptian, Greek and Roman rooms provide an intriguing record of the world's earliest civilizations.

sculptures on display were made to contain deceased souls. Other rooms house mummified animals, Egyptian scripts and artifacts such as pots, clothing and jewellery.

Also shown are a glazed brick relief of a lion from Babylon, and items from Arabia.

ORIENTAL AND EGYPTIAN ANTIQUITIES

Four specially decorated rooms adorned with Egyptian friezes and motifs provide the perfect setting for the bulk of the museum's collection of Egyptian and Near Eastern antiquities. The nucleus of the collection was formed under the earlier Habsburg monarchs. Most of the items were either bought in the 19th century, after Napoleon's Egyptian expedition had increased interest in the area, or added early this century, when Austrian archaeologists excavated at Giza; an outstanding example is the so-called *Reserve Head* (around 26th century BC). The entire 5th-dynasty Tomb Chapel of Ka-Ni-Nisut, from the Pyramid district of Giza, and its well-preserved hieroglyphics (from around 2400BC) are on display in Room II.

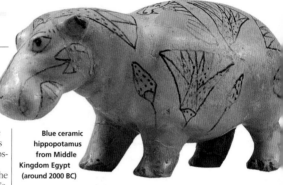

Blue ceramic hippopotamus from Middle Kingdom Egypt (around 2000 BC)

The remarkable collection of objects and sculpture spans a wide chronological period from the Pre-Dynastic era until Roman times. There is a bust of King Thutmosis III *(see p123)* as well as portraits of Egyptian gods and goddesses. In Rooms I and V, where the decorative scheme incorporates Egyptian columns from Aswan, are items associated with the mortuary cult in Ancient Egypt, including sarcophagi, canopic jars (which used to contain the entrails of mummified corpses), scarabs, mummy cases and papyrus books of the dead. In Room VIII there is a small blue ceramic statue of a hippopotamus. These were often found in Middle Kingdom tombs, as hippopotamus hunting was a royal privilege given to citizens who had won the king's favour. Many of the small-scale

Room I from the Egyptian galleries, with papyrus stalk columns from Aswan (around 1410 BC)

GREEK AND ROMAN ANTIQUITIES

Only part of the museum's Greek and Roman collection is housed in the main building; the finds from Ephesus and Samothrace are displayed in the Neue Burg *(see p95)* in the Hofburg.

If you approach the collection from the Egyptian galleries, the first room you come to (Room X) is devoted to early Greek sculpture. Rooms 6–7 house the Austria Romana collection which includes a statue of the *Youth from Magdalensberg*, a 16th-century cast of a lost Roman statue, found buried in an Austrian field. The main gallery (Room XI), decorated in the style of an imperial Roman villa, includes a mosaic of Theseus and the Minotaur, a Roman marble statue of Isis, Greek sculpture and a sarcophagus with fine relief decoration. Rooms XII and XIII house numerous portrait heads.

The collection also boasts figurines and bronzes from Greece and Rome, vases from Tanagra (a town in Ancient Greece) and a large collection of Roman cameos, jewellery, busts of Roman Emperors and Roman glass. Etruscan and Cypriot art are in rooms 1–3. Coptic, Byzantine and Germanic items are shown in the rest of the rooms, where pride of place goes to the Treasure of Nagyszentmiklós, a late 9th-century collection of golden vessels found in Romania in 1799.

Medal of Ulrich II Molitor (1581)

SCULPTURE AND DECORATIVE ARTS

The collection consists of many treasures bought or commissioned by Habsburg connoisseurs, particularly Rudolf II and Archduke Leopold William, for their Kunstkammern, or chambers of art and marvels housed in their Habsburg residences. In addition to sculpture, these princely treasuries contained precious items of high craftsmanship, exotic, highly unusual novelties, and scientific instruments. Among the most intriguing are some intricate automata, including a musical box in the form of a ship, and a moving clock. Some of the royal patrons worked in the studio themselves; on display is some glass blown by the Archduke Ferdinand II and embroidery sewn by Maria Theresa.

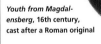

Virgin with Child (about 1495) by Tilman Riemenschneider

As in the Picture Gallery, the main emphasis is on the Renaissance and Baroque, although there is a great display of medieval items. These include fine, late Gothic religious carved statues by artists such as Tilman Riemenschneider, some medieval ivories, drinking horns and communion vessels. The

highlights of the Italian Renaissance rooms are a marble bust of a laughing boy by Desiderio da Settignano, a marble relief of Bacchus and Ariadne and a fine bronze and gilt figurine called Venus Felix after an antique marble statue. Included in the large German Renaissance collection are early playing cards and a table centrepiece, incorporating "vipers' tongues" (in fact, fossilized sharks' teeth), said to ward off poison. Other gems include Benvenuto Cellini's Salt Cellar *(see p122)*, made for the French king François I, and some statuettes by Giambologna. This section is due to reopen in late 2012 but the Italian Renaissance items can be seen in the Italian Renaissance paintings rooms (on the first floor).

Youth from Magdalensberg, 16th century, cast after a Roman original

COINS AND MEDALS

Tucked away on the second floor is one of the most extensive coin and medal collections in the world. For those with a special interest in the area it is exceptional. Once again, the nucleus of the collection came from the former possessions of the Habsburgs, but it has been added to by modern curators and now includes many 20th-century items. Only a fraction of the museum's 500,000 pieces can be seen in the three exhibition rooms.

Room I gives an overview of the development of money. It includes coins from Ancient Greece and Rome, examples of Egyptian, Celtic and Byzantine money, and medieval, Renaissance and European coins, as well as the whole range of Austrian currency.

Also on display is a collection of primitive forms of money such as stone currency from Yap Island in Micronesia.

Rooms II and III house an extensive collection of 19th- and 20th-century medals. The portrait medallions are often miniature works of art in themselves. Particularly noteworthy are the unusual silver and gilt medals belonging to Ulrich Molitor, the Abbot of Heiligenkreuz, and the silver medallion which was engraved by Bertrand Andrieu and minted to commemorate the baptism of Napoleon's son. This shows the emperor as a proud father, lifting aloft his baby, the King of Rome *(see p175)*.

Natural History Museum ⑪

Skull from Upper Paleolithic period

Almost the mirror image of the Kunsthistorisches Museum, the Natural History Museum was designed by the same architects, and opened in 1889. Its carefully devised interior decoration reflects the nature of the collections. These are quite wide ranging and include archaeological, anthro-pological, mineralogical, zoological and geological displays. There are casts of dinosaur skeletons, the world's largest display of skulls illustrating the history of man, one of Europe's most comprehensive collections of gems, prehistoric sculpture, Bronze Age items, and extinct birds and mammals.

★ Hallstatt Archaeo-logical Finds
This reconstructed chariot from the Bycis Kala cave in Moravia dates from the early Iron Age.

Children's centre

Aquariu

Lecture Hall

★ Venus of Willendorf
This ancient fertility figure (see p20) found in Lower Austria is around 24,000 years old.

KEY

☐	Mineralogy
☐	Geology, Paleontology
☐	Archaeology
☐	Anthropology
☐	Zoology
☐	Temporary exhibition space
☐	Non-exhibition space

STAR EXHIBITS

★ Hallstatt Archaeological Finds

★ Venus of Willendorf

★ Cast of *Iguanodon bernissartensis*

Main entrance from Maria-Theresia-Platz

★ Cast of Iguanodon bernissartensis
This is just one of several dinosaur skeletons and casts on show in the paleontology department.

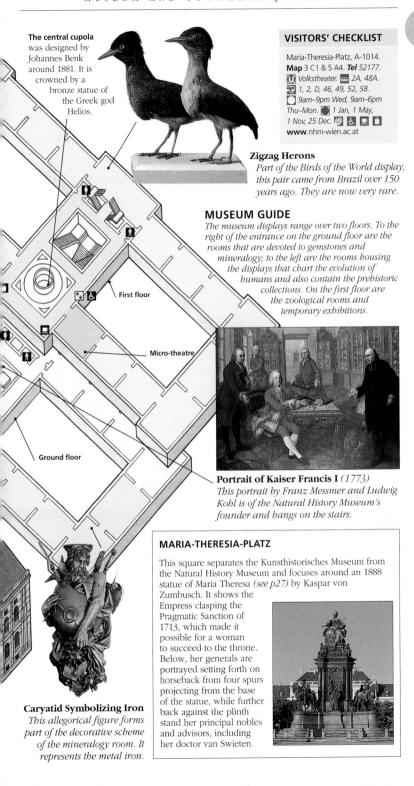

The central cupola was designed by Johannes Benk around 1881. It is crowned by a bronze statue of the Greek god Helios.

Zigzag Herons
*Part of the Birds of the World display,
this pair came from Brazil over 150
years ago. They are now very rare.*

MUSEUM GUIDE

*The museum displays range over two floors. To the
right of the entrance on the ground floor are the
rooms that are devoted to gemstones and
mineralogy; to the left are the rooms housing
the displays that chart the evolution of
humans and also contain the prehistoric
collections. On the first floor are
the zoological rooms and
temporary exhibitions.*

First floor

Micro-theatre

Ground floor

Portrait of Kaiser Francis I *(1773)*
*This portrait by Franz Messmer and Ludwig
Kohl is of the Natural History Museum's
founder and hangs on the stairs.*

MARIA-THERESIA-PLATZ

This square separates the Kunsthistorisches Museum from
the Natural History Museum and focuses around an 1888
statue of Maria Theresa *(see p27)* by Kaspar von
Zumbusch. It shows the
Empress clasping the
Pragmatic Sanction of
1713, which made it
possible for a woman
to succeed to the throne.
Below, her generals are
portrayed setting forth on
horseback from four spurs
projecting from the base
of the statue, while further
back against the plinth
stand her principal nobles
and advisors, including
her doctor van Swieten.

Caryatid Symbolizing Iron
*This allegorical figure forms
part of the decorative scheme
of the mineralogy room. It
represents the metal iron.*

Neues Rathaus ⑫

Friedrich-Schmidt-Platz 1. **Map** 1 B5 & 5 A2. **Tel** 52550. Ⓤ *Rathaus.* 1, 2, D. ◯ for 🎟 1pm Mon, Wed & Fri & through phone bookings for groups. 📷

The new town hall is the seat of the Vienna City and Provincial Assembly. Built from 1872 to 1883 to replace the Altes Rathaus *(see p85)*, it is unashamedly Neo-Gothic in style. The architect, Friedrich von Schmidt, was chosen by the authorities in a competition for the best design.

A huge central tower, 100 m (325 ft) high and topped by the 3-m (11-ft) statue of a knight in armour with a lance, dominates the front façade. Known affectionately as the Rathausmann, it was designed by Franz Gastell and made by the wrought-iron craftsman Alexander Nehr. The most attractive feature is the lofty loggia with its delicate tracery and curved balconies. The building has seven courtyards and concerts are held in the Arkadenhof courtyard. At the top of the first of two grand staircases is the *Festsaal*, a ceremonial hall that stretches the length of the building. Round all four sides are Neo-Gothic arcades and statues of Austrian worthies. In front of the building is the wide Rathausplatz Park.

Dreifaltigkeits-kirche ⑬

Alser Strasse 17. **Map** 1 B4. **Tel** 4057225. Ⓤ *Rathaus.* ◯ 8–11:30am Mon–Sat, 8am–noon Sun. 📷 ♿ *entrance on Schlösselgasse for services.*

Built between 1685 and 1727, the church of the Holy Trinity contains an altarpiece (1708) in the north aisle by the

16th-century crucifix by Veit Stoss, in the Dreifaltigkeitskirche

painter Martino Altomonte, and a graphic crucifix from the workshop of Veit Stoss in the south aisle from the workshop of Veit Stoss. It was to this church that Beethoven's body was brought after he died in 1827. Following the funeral service which was attended by many of his contemporaries, including Schubert and the poet Franz Grillparzer, the cortege bore his coffin to the cemetery at Währing on the city outskirts.

University ⑭

Dr-Karl-Lueger-Ring 1. **Map** 1 C4 & 5 A2. **Tel** 42770. Ⓤ *Schottentor.* ◯ 6:30am–8:30pm Mon–Fri, 8am–1pm Sat. 📷 ♿

Founded in 1365 by Duke Rudolf IV, the University of Vienna now has approximately 50,000 students. The versatile architect Heinrich Ferstel designed its present home in 1883, adopting an Italian Renaissance style.

From the entrance hall, huge staircases lead up to the university's ceremonial halls. In 1895 Gustav Klimt was commissioned to decorate the hall with frescoes, but the degree of nudity portrayed in some panels proved unacceptable to the authorities. Eventually, when no agreement could be reached, Klimt returned his fee to the government and took back the paintings; they were destroyed during World War II.

Front elevation of the Neues Rathaus showing the Rathausmann on his tower some 98 m (320 ft) above the ground

A spacious arcaded courtyard, lined with busts of the university's most distinguished professors, is located in the centre of the building. Among the figures on display include the founder of psychoanalysis, Sigmund Freud (*see p110*), and the philosopher Franz Brentano. Nearby are the smoke-filled and poster-daubed corridors of today's university students.

Café Landtmann **15**

Dr-Karl-Lueger-Ring 4. **Map** 1 C5 & 5 B2. *Tel* 24100. Schottentor, Volkstheater. 1, D. 8am–midnight daily.

If the Café Central (*see p58*) was, and perhaps still is, the coffee house of Vienna's intelligentsia, this café (*see p58*) is undoubtedly the coffee house of the affluent middle classes. With mirrors and elegant panelling, it is an exceedingly comfortable place. Established in 1873 by coffee-maker Franz Landtmann, it is still a popular café. It was Sigmund Freud's (*see p110*) favourite coffee house.

The attractive Dreimäderlhaus (*left*) on Schreyvogelgasse

Dreimäderlhaus **16**

Schreyvogelgasse 10. **Map** 1 C5 & 5 B2. Schottentor.

A delightful remnant of Biedermeier Vienna is found in the houses on one side of the cobbled Schreyvogelgasse. The prettiest is the Dreimäderlhaus (1803). There is a legend that Schubert had three sweethearts (*drei Mäderl*) ensconced here, but it is more likely that the house was named after the 1920s' operetta, *Dreimäderlhaus*, which uses his melodies.

One of the arcades surrounding the University courtyard

Mölker-Bastei **17**

Map 1 C5 & 5 B2. Schottentor.

A few paces away from the bustling Schottentor, a quiet street has been built on to a former bastion of the city walls. It boasts some beautiful late 18th-century houses. Beethoven lived here, and the Emperor Franz Joseph nearly met his death on the bastion in 1853 when a tailor attempted to assassinate him. No. 10 is the

Plaque on the front of the Pasqualati Haus

house where the Belgian Prince Charles de Ligne lived during the Congress of Vienna in 1815 (*see p30*). De Ligne, an elderly aristocrat, wrote a number of cynical commentaries on the various activities of the crowned heads of Europe who came to Vienna at that time. A ladies' man, he caught a fatal chill while waiting for an assignation on the bastion.

Pasqualati Haus **18**

Mölker-Bastei 8. **Map** 1 C5 & 5 B2. *Tel* 5358905. Schottentor. **Museum** 9am–12:15pm & 1–4:30pm Tue–Sun.

The Pasqualati Haus is no different in appearance from any of the other houses along this lane, but it is the most famous of more than 30 places where Ludwig van

Beethoven resided in Vienna. Named after its original owner, Baron Johann von Pasqualati, it was Beethoven's home between 1804 and 1808, and 1810 and 1815. He composed many of his best-loved works here, including the Symphonies 4, 5, 7 and 8, the opera *Fidelio*, the Piano Concerto No. 4, and string quartets.

Today, the rooms on the fourth floor which the composer occupied house a small museum. Various memorabilia, such as a lock of Beethoven's hair, a photograph of his grave at Währing cemetery, a deathbed engraving and early editions of his scores are on display. The museum also contains busts and paintings of Beethoven and his patron Prince Rasumofsky, the Russian ambassador to Vienna.

Liebenberg monument (1890) below the Mölker-Bastei

The Burgtheater ⑲

The Burgtheater is the most prestigious stage in the German-speaking world *(see also p230)*. The original theatre built in Maria Theresa's reign was replaced in 1888 by today's Italian Renaissance-style building by Karl von Hasenauer and Gottfried Semper. It closed for refurbishment in 1897 after the discovery that the auditorium had several seats with no view of the stage. Forty-eight years later a bomb devastated the building, leaving only the side wings containing the Grand Staircases intact. Subsequent restoration was so successful that today its extent is hard to assess.

Two statues of the muses of music and dramatic art adorn the roof.

Busts of playwrights
Lining the walls of the Grand Staircases are busts of playwrights whose works are still performed here, including this one of Johann Nestroy by Hans Knesl.

Ceiling frescoes by the Klimt brothers and Franz Matsch cover the north and south wings.

Entrance for tours

Candelabra lining the staircase

★ **Grand Staircases in North and South Wings**
Two imposing gala staircases lead up from the side entrances to the foyer. Each is a mirror image of the other.

Main entrance on Dr Karl-Lueger-Ring

STAR FEATURES

★ Grand Staircases in North and South Wings

★ Der Thespiskarren by Gustav Klimt

Foyer
The 60-m long (200-ft) curving foyer serves as a waiting area during intervals. Portraits of famous actors and actresses line its walls.

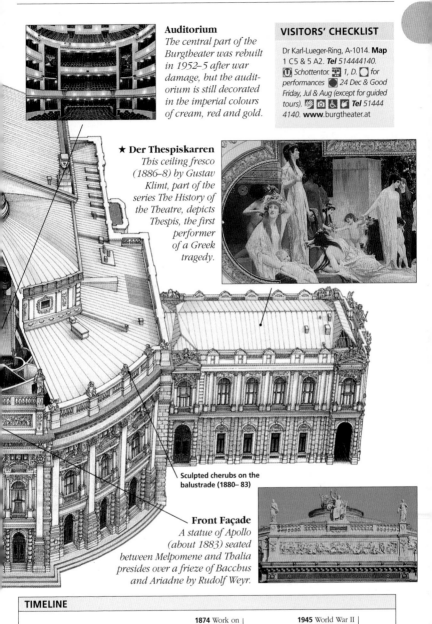

Auditorium
The central part of the Burgtheater was rebuilt in 1952–5 after war damage, but the auditorium is still decorated in the imperial colours of cream, red and gold.

★ Der Thespiskarren
This ceiling fresco (1886–8) by Gustav Klimt, part of the series The History of the Theatre, depicts Thespis, the first performer of a Greek tragedy.

Sculpted cherubs on the balustrade (1880– 83)

Front Façade
A statue of Apollo (about 1883) seated between Melpomene and Thalia presides over a frieze of Bacchus and Ariadne by Rudolf Weyr.

TIMELINE

1741 Maria Theresa founds the Burgtheater in an empty ballroom at the Hofburg

1776 Joseph II reorganizes the theatre and promotes it to the status of a national theatre

The Old Burgtheater in the mid-18th century

1874 Work on the present building begins

1888 The Burgtheater opens on 14 October in the presence of the Emperor Franz Joseph and his family

1897 The auditorium is adapted

1945 World War II fire destroys the auditorium

1955 Theatre reopens with Grillparzer's King Ottokar

| 1750 | | 1850 | 1900 | 1950 |

OPERA AND NASCHMARKT

This is an area of huge contrasts, ranging from the stateliness of the Opera House and the opulence of the Opernring shops to the raucous modernity of

Relief on the façade of the Secession Building

Mariahilfer Strasse. This long street is lined with cinemas and department stores, drawing shoppers not just from Vienna but from much of eastern Europe. The other major thoroughfare in our area is the Linke Wienzeile, which runs parallel to the Rechte Wienzeile. Both roads stretch from

just beyond the Ring-strasse to the city outskirts, following the curving and sometimes subterranean River Wien. Between these roads is the bustling Naschmarkt, which is overlooked by Otto Wagner's Jugendstil apartments on the Linke Wienzeile. Visitors wanting to escape the crowds should visit the celebrated Café Museum, located near the three great cultural institutions of the area – the Academy of Fine Arts, the Opera House and the Secession Building.

SIGHTS AT A GLANCE

Streets and Squares
Mariahilfer Strasse ❽

Historic Buildings
Hotel Sacher ❷
Opera House pp140–1 ❶
Theater an der Wien ❺
Wagner Apartments ❼

Museums and Galleries
Academy of Fine Arts ❸
Haydn Museum ❿
Kaiserliches Hofmobilien-
   depot ❾
Secession Building ❹

Markets
Naschmarkt ❻

GETTING THERE
This area is served by Zieglergasse (line U3), Neubaugasse (line U3) and MuseumsQuartier (line U2) U-Bahn stations. Bus 13A runs from Josefstädter Strasse to Mariahilfer Strasse and to the southern end of the Linke Wienzeile. Bus 57A travels the length of Gumpendorfer Strasse.

KEY

▨	Street-by-Street map See pp136–7
Ⓤ	U-Bahn station

0 metres   250

0 yards   250

◁ **Main staircase and hallway at the Opera House**

Street-by-Street: Opernring

Between the Opera House and the Karl-skirche, two of the great landmarks of Vienna, lies an area that typifies the varied cultural vitality of the city as a whole. Here are an 18th-century theatre, a 19th-century art academy, and the Secession Building. Mixed in with these cultural monuments are emblems of the Viennese devotion to good living: the Hotel Sacher, as sumptuous today as it was a century ago; the Café Museum *(see p58)*, still as popular as it was in the 1900s; and the hurly-burly of the colourful Naschmarkt, where you can buy everything from oysters and exotic fruits to second-hand clothes.

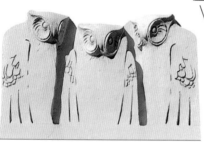

★ Academy of Fine Arts
This Italianate building is home to one of the best collections of old masters in Vienna ❸

The Goethe Statue was designed by Edmund Hellmer in 1890.

The Schiller Statue dominates the park in front of the Academy of Fine Arts.

★ Secession Building
This delightful structure, built in 1898 as a showroom for the Secession artists, houses Gustav Klimt's (see p56) Beethoven Frieze ❹

Theater an der Wien
Today this 18th-century theatre is used as an opera house. It has been the venue for many premieres, among them Beethoven's Fidelio ❺

Naschmarkt
This market sells everything from fresh farm produce to bric-a-brac. It is liveliest on Saturday mornings ❻

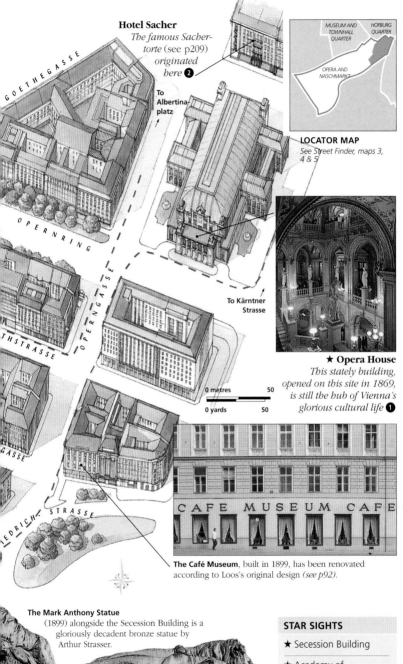

Hotel Sacher
The famous Sacher-torte (see p209) originated here ❷

To Albertina-platz

MUSEUM AND TOWNHALL QUARTER

HOFBURG QUARTER

OPERA AND NASCHMARKT

LOCATOR MAP
See Street Finder, maps 3, 4 & 5

To Kärntner Strasse

0 metres   50

0 yards   50

★ Opera House
This stately building, opened on this site in 1869, is still the hub of Vienna's glorious cultural life ❶

CAFE MUSEUM CAFE

The Café Museum, built in 1899, has been renovated according to Loos's original design *(see p92)*.

The Mark Anthony Statue
(1899) alongside the Secession Building is a gloriously decadent bronze statue by Arthur Strasser.

STAR SIGHTS

★ Secession Building

★ Academy of Fine Arts

★ Opera House

KEY

– – – Suggested route

Opera House ❶

See pp140–141.

Hotel Sacher ❷

Philharmonikerstrasse 4. **Map** 4 D1 & 5 C5. **Tel** 514560. Ⓤ *Karlsplatz.* ◯ *6:30am–midnight daily.* 🅾 ♿ **www**.sacher.com

Founded by the son of Franz Sacher, who, according to some, was the creator of the *Sachertorte* in 1840 *(see p209)*, this hotel *(see p200)* came into its own under Anna Sacher. The cigar-smoking daughter-in-law of the founder ran the hotel from 1892 until her death in 1930. During her time the Sacher became a venue for the extra-marital affairs of the rich and noble. It is still a discreetly sumptuous hotel.

Academy of Fine Arts ❸

Schillerplatz 3. **Map** 4 D2 & 5 B5. **Tel** 588162222. Ⓤ *Karlsplatz.* 🚋 *1, 2, D.* ◯ *10am–6pm Tue–Sun & public hols.* 📷 🅾 ♿ **www**.akademiegalerie.at

Theophil Hansen built the Academy of Fine Arts in Italian Renaissance style from 1872 to 1876. In 1907 Adolf Hitler was barred from entrance on the grounds that he lacked

Façade of the Secession Building

talent. Today the Academy acts as an arts college and has a gallery showing changing exhibitions. These include late Gothic and early Renaissance works, some Rubens' pieces, 17th-century Dutch and Flemish landscapes, as well as a 19th-century Austrian collection.

Secession Building ❹

Friedrichstrasse 12. **Map** 4 D2. **Tel** 5875307. Ⓤ *Karlsplatz.* ◯ *10am–6pm Tue–Sun.* 📷 🅾 ♿ **www**.secession.at

Joseph Maria Olbrich designed the unusual Secession Building in Jugendstil style *(see pp54–7)* as a showcase for the Secession movement's artists *(see p34)*. The almost windowless building, with its filigree globe of entwined laurel leaves on the roof, is a squat cube with four towers. The motto of the founders, emblazoned in gold on the façade, states, *"Der Zeit ihre Kunst, der Kunst ihre Freiheit"*, which translates as: "To every Age its Art, to Art its Freedom". Alongside the building stands the marvellous statue of Mark Anthony in his chariot being

Columned entrance to the Theater an der Wien

drawn by lions (1899), by Arthur Strasser. Gustav Klimt's *Beethoven Frieze* is the Secession's best-known exhibit. Designed in 1902 as a decorative painting, it covers three walls and is 34 m (110 ft) long. It shows interrelated groups of figures and is thought to be a commentary on Beethoven's Ninth Symphony *(see also p35)*.

Theater an der Wien ❺

Linke Wienzeile 6. **Map** 3 C2. **Tel** 58885. Ⓤ *Kettenbrückengasse.* ◯ *for performances.* **www**.theater-wien.at

Emanuel Schikaneder founded this theatre *(see p226)* in 1801; a statue above the entrance shows him playing Papageno in Mozart's *The Magic Flute*. The premiere of Beethoven's *Fidelio* was staged here in 1805. Today it hosts popular opera performances.

Typical stall at the Naschmarkt

Naschmarkt ❻

Map 3 C2–C3. Ⓤ *Kettenbrückengasse.* **Market** ◯ *6am–6:30pm Mon–Fri, 6am–6pm Sat.* **Schubert Museum** ◯ *10am–1pm, 2–6pm Wed & Thu.*

The Naschmarkt is Vienna's liveliest market. It has many well-established shops and some of the best snack bars in Vienna *(see pp217–19)*. As you walk west it gradually becomes less formal, with flower vendors', wine producers' and farmers' stalls spilling out onto the street and offering meats, breads and so on. This area in turn leads into the flea market – a chaos of makeshift stalls.

It's also worth going to No. 6 Kettenbrückengasse, by the U-Bahn, to see the simple flat where Franz Schubert died in 1828. It displays facsimiles, prints and a family piano.

The Majolikahaus, one of the Wagner Apartments

pieces created by artists and designers of the early 20th century. Room after room is filled with outstanding furnishings and royal domestic objects, ranging from a faithful recreation of Empress Elisabeth's Schönbrunn Palace apartments to a simple folding throne that was used while travelling. The exhibits, which range from the mundane to the priceless and often eccentric, provide a fascinating and evocative insight into the everyday lives of the imperial family.

Wagner Apartments ❼

Linke Wienzeile 38 & 40. **Map** 3 C2.
Ⓤ *Kettenbrückengasse.*

Looking onto the Nasch-markt are two remarkable apartment buildings. Designed by Otto Wagner in 1899, they represent the apex of Jugend-stil style (*see pp54–7*). No. 38 has sparkling gilt ornament, mostly by Kolo Moser. The façade of No. 40 has subtle flower patterns in pink, blue and green. Even the sills are moulded and decorated. No. 40, which is called the Majolikahaus after the glazed pottery used for the weather-resistant surface decoration, is the more striking. No. 42 next door, in historicist style (*see pp32–3*), shows what Secession architects were reacting against.

Mariahilfer Strasse ❽

Map 3 A3 & 5 A5. Ⓤ *Zieglergasse, Neubaugasse.* **Stiftkirche**
◻ *7:30am–6pm Mon–Fri, 7am–11pm Sat, 8:30am–9:30pm Sun.* **Mariahilfer Kirche** ◻ *8am–7pm Mon–Sat, 8:30am–7pm Sun.*

This is one of Vienna's busiest shopping streets. On the corner of Stiftgasse is the Stiftkirche. The architect is

unknown, but the church dates from 1739. The façade is an austere pyramidal structure, rising to a bulbous steeple. Of particular interest, there are some lively Rococo reliefs set into the walls.

Across the street at No. 45 is the house where the playwright Ferdinand Raimund was born in 1790. Its cobbled courtyard is lined with shops.

Mariahilfer Kirche is named after a 16th-century cult of the Virgin Mary which was founded at the pilgrimage of Mariahilfer Kirche at Passau. The Viennese church is in the Baroque style and is dominated by two towers with bulbous steeples.

Kaiserliches Hof-mobiliendepot ❾

Andreasgasse 7. **Map** 3 A2.
Tel 52433570. Ⓤ *Zieglergasse.*
◻ *10am–6pm Tue–Sun.*
www.hofmobiliendepot.at

The Imperial furniture collection, founded by Maria Theresa in 1747, gives an intimate portrait of the Habsburg way of life, as well as a detailed historical record of Viennese interior decoration and cabinet-making in the 18th and 19th centuries. Also included in the collection are

Haydn Museum ❿

Haydngasse 19. **Map** 3 A3.
Tel 5961307. Ⓤ *Zieglergasse.*
◻ *10am–1pm, 2–6pm Tue–Sun & hols.* ◼ *1 Jan, 1 May, 25 Dec.*
www.wienmuseum.at

As with many of the museums dedicated to composers, the Haydn Museum does not have a very comprehensive collection of exhibits: only a few copies of documents and scores, a piano and clavichord.

Haydn built this house in what was then a new suburb of Vienna with money he had earned from his successful visits to London between 1791 and 1795. He lived here from 1797 until his death in 1809 and it was here that he com-posed many of his major works, including *The Creation* and *The Seasons*. There is also a room that contains some furniture and mementoes belonging to Johannes Brahms.

Antique wheelchair in the Kaiserliches Hofmobiliendepot.

The Opera House ❶

Vienna's state Opera House, or Staatsoper, was the first of the grand Ringstrasse buildings to be completed (see pp32–3); it opened on 25 May 1869 to the strains of Mozart's *Don Giovanni*. Built in Neo-Renaissance style, it initially failed to impress the Viennese. Yet when it was hit by a bomb in 1945 and largely destroyed, the event was seen as a symbolic blow to the city. With a brand new auditorium and stage incorporating the latest technology, the Opera House reopened on 5 November 1955 with a performance of Beethoven's *Fidelio*.

Gustav Mahler by Rodin

Reliefs of Opera and Ballet (1861–9) *Painted allegorical lunettes by Johann Preleuthner represent ballet, tragic opera and comic opera. The one here depicts comic opera.*

The Auditorium

★ Grand Staircase
A superb marble staircase sweeps up from the main entrance to the first floor. It is embellished with statues by Josef Gasser of the seven liberal arts (such as Music and Dancing) and reliefs of opera and ballet.

★ Schwind Foyer
The foyer is decorated with scenes from operas painted by Moritz von Schwind. Among the busts of famous composers and conductors is Rodin's bronze bust of Mahler (1909).

Main entrance

One of the five bronze statues
by Ernst Julius Hähnel, depicting Heroism, Drama, Fantasy, Humour and Love, standing under the arches of the loggia.

★ Tea Room
Franz Joseph and his entourage used to spend the intervals in this graceful room, which is decorated with silk hangings bearing the Emperor's initials.

STAR FEATURES

★ Grand Staircase

★ Schwind Foyer

★ Tea Room

THE VIENNA OPERA BALL

On the last Thursday of the Vienna Carnival *(see p65)* the stage is extended to cover the seats in the auditorium to create space for the Opera Ball *(see p231)*. This is an expensive society event which opens when the cream of the *jeunesse dorée* – well-to-do girls clad in white and their escorts – take to the floor.

VISITORS' CHECKLIST

Opernring 2, A-1010. **Map** 4 D1 & 5 C5. **Tel** 514442250. Karlsplatz. 1, 2, D. for performances. call 514442606/ 2421 for details. www.wiener-staatsoper.at

The Architects
The architects of the Opera House were August Siccardsburg (right) and Eduard van der Nüll (left).

Fountain
On either side of the Opera House stand two graceful fountains. Designed by Hans Gasser, this one depicts the legendary siren Lorelei supported by figures representing Grief, Love and Vengeance.

The Magic Flute Tapestries
One of the two side salons, the Gustav Mahler Saal, is hung with modern tapestries by Rudolf Eisenmenger illustrating scenes from The Magic Flute.

BELVEDERE QUARTER

The Belvedere Quarter is a grandiose and extravagant district. From the Karlsplatz, with its gardens and statues, there is a lovely view of Johann Bernhard Fischer von Erlach's Baroque Karlskirche. East of this great church, visitors can see more delights, including the two palaces of the Belvedere, now public galleries, and the Schwarzenberg Palace. These huge palaces and beautiful gardens were designed by Johann Lukas

Statue of Leonardo da Vinci in the Künstlerhaus

von Hildebrandt, following the crucial defeat of the Turks in 1683. Only after the Turkish threat had been removed was it possible for Vienna to expand. The turbulent history of the city is excellently documented in the Wien Museum Karlsplatz. Just a few paces away is the Musikverein, home to the Vienna Philharmonic. There is also the Bestattungsmuseum (undertakers' museum), that chronicles the importance the Viennese attach to pomp and death.

SIGHTS AT A GLANCE

Streets and Squares
Rennweg **9**
Schwarzenbergplatz **7**

Historic Buildings
Imperial Hotel **6**
Karlsplatz Pavilions **4**
Musikverein **3**
Schwarzenberg Palace **8**
Theresianum **13**

Museums and Galleries
Bestattungsmuseum **12**
Wien Museum
  Karlsplatz **2**
Künstlerhaus **5**
*Palaces and Gardens
  of the Belvedere
  pp152–57* **10**

Parks and Gardens
Botanical Gardens **11**

Churches
Karlskirche pp148–49 **1**

GETTING THERE
This area is served by the Karlsplatz (lines U1, U2, U4) and Taubstummengasse (line U1) U-Bahn stations. Tram 71 runs along Rennweg and Bus 4A goes from Wittelsbachstrasse to Karlsplatz.

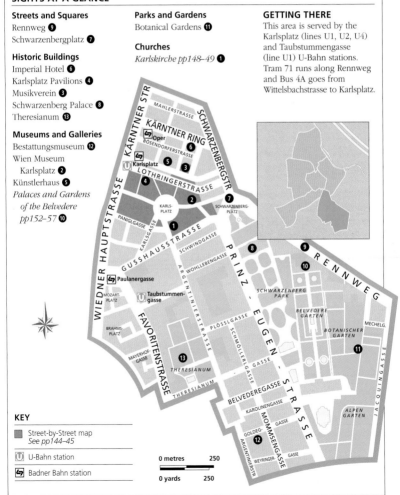

KEY

- ▧ Street-by-Street map
  See pp144–45
- Ⓤ U-Bahn station
- 🚈 Badner Bahn station

0 metres   250
0 yards   250

◁ **Botanical Gardens**

Street-by-Street: Karlsplatz

This part of the city became ripe for development once the threat of Turkish invasion had receded for good in 1683 *(see pp26–7)*. The Ressel Park, at the front of the Karlskirche, gives an unobstructed view of this grandiose church, built on the orders of Karl VI. The park itself is lined with a variety of cultural institutions, notably the Wien Museum Karlsplatz and, across the road, the Musikverein.

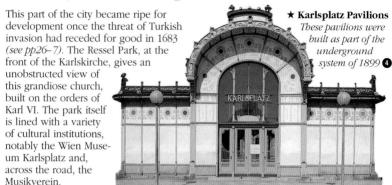

★ Karlsplatz Pavilions
These pavilions were built as part of the underground system of 1899 ❹

Underpass

To Karlsplatz U-Bahn

Ressel Park café

KARLSPLATZ

The Technical University
with its Neo-Classical façade (1816) fronts on to Ressel Park, which contains busts and statues of famous 19th-century Austrian scientists and engineers.

Ressel Statue

STAR SIGHTS

★ Karlsplatz Pavilions

★ Wien Museum Karlsplatz

★ Karlskirche

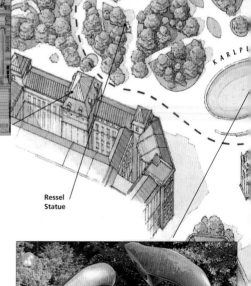

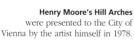

Henry Moore's Hill Arches
were presented to the City of Vienna by the artist himself in 1978.

Musikverein
This Ringstrasse-style (see p146) concert hall, home of the Vienna Philharmonic Orchestra, is renowned for its superb acoustics **3**

LOCATOR MAP
See Street Finder, map 4

OPERA AND NASCH-MARKT

BELVEDERE QUARTER

★ **Wien Museum Karlsplatz**
This museum houses relics of Roman Vienna, stained glass from the Stephansdom and the reconstructed rooms of celebrated Viennese such as Adolf Loos (see p92) **2**

KARLSPLATZ

DUMBASTRASSE

LOTHRINGER STRASSE

MADERSTRASSE

MATTIELLISTRASSE

TECHNIKERSTR

USSHAUSSTRASSE

★ **Karlskirche**
Promised to the people during the 1713 plague, this is Vienna's finest Baroque church **1**

French Embassy

0 metres   50
0 yards   50

THE ART NOUVEAU FRENCH EMBASSY

Built in 1904–12 by the French architect Georges Chédanne, the Embassy is typical of French Art Nouveau, resembling houses along Rue Victor Hugo in Paris. Unaccustomed to this foreign style, some thought the building was oriental, giving rise to a rumour that its plans had been mixed up with those of the French Embassy in Istanbul.

Art Nouveau façade of the French Embassy

KEY

‒ ‒ ‒ Suggested route

Karlskirche ❶

See pp148–9.

Wien Museum Karlsplatz ❷

Karlsplatz. **Map** 4 E2. *Tel 5058747.*
Ⓤ *Karlsplatz.* Ⓞ *10am–6pm
Tue–Sun.* ● *1 Jan, 1 May, 25 Dec.*
📷 ♿ 🎧 www.wienmuseum.at

The Wien Museum Karlsplatz
moved to its current location
in 1959. The ground floor
usually has Roman and
pre-Roman items, as well as
exhibits from the Gothic
period. These include 14th-
and 15th-century gargoyles
and figures, and stained glass
from the Stephansdom, and
carved portraits of early rulers
of Vienna. These displays are
sometimes moved to make
space for visiting exhibitions.

The first-floor 16th- and
17th-century exhibits include
prints depicting Turkish sieges
from 1529 onwards, as well as
a portrait of the Turkish commander Kara Mustafa, captured
banners and weapons, and
prints of the celebrations after
Austria's victory. Here too are
Johann Bernhard Fischer
von Erlach's original plans
for the Schönbrunn Palace
(see pp172–5), and the
original lantern from No. 6
Schönlaterngasse *(see p74).*

The monumental, historicist-style façade of the Musikverein

On the second floor are a
reconstructed 1798 room from
the Caprara-Geymüller Palace
in Wallnerstrasse, panelled
with painted silks, and the
apartment of Austria's most
famous poet, Franz Grillparzer.
There are displays chronicling
the popularity of ballet,
theatre and operetta.

Exhibits from the 20th
century include Richard
Gerstl's portrait of Arnold
Schönberg *(see p39)* and
portraits by Egon Schiele and
Gustav Klimt. There is a room
(1903) from Adolf Loos's
house *(see p92)* in Bösendorferstrasse, silver- and
glassware by Josef Hoffmann,
designs from the Wiener
Werkstätte *(see p56)* and
pictures of Vienna over the
past hundred years.

Musikverein ❸

Bösendorferstrasse 12. **Map** 4 E2.
Tel 5058190. Ⓤ *Karlsplatz.*
Ⓞ *for concerts only.* 📷 ♿
www.musikverein.at

The Musikverein building –
the headquarters of the
Society of the Friends of
Music – was designed from
1867 to 1869 by Theophil
Hansen, in a mixture of styles
employing terracotta statues,
capitals and balustrades. It is
the home of the great Vienna
Philharmonic Orchestra *(see
p229)*, which gives regular
performances here, and forms
the orchestra of the Opera
House. The concert hall seats
almost 2,000. Tickets are sold
on a subscription basis to
Viennese music lovers, but
some are also available on
the day of the performance.
The most famous annual
event here is the New Year's
Day concert *(see p65).*

Karlsplatz Pavilions ❹

Karlsplatz. **Map** 4 D2. *Tel 5058747-
85177.* Ⓤ *Karlsplatz.* Ⓞ *Apr–Oct:
9am–6pm Tue–Sun.* 📷

Otto Wagner *(see pp54–57)*
was responsible for designing
and engineering many
aspects of the early
underground system in the
late 19th century. Some of
these bridges and tunnels are
remarkable in themselves, but
cannot match his stylish pair
of underground railway exit
pavilions (1898–9) alongside

Sunflower motifs on the façade of the Karlsplatz Pavilions

The enormous Hochstrahlbrunnen in Schwarzenbergplatz

Imperial Hotel ❻

Kärntner Ring 16. **Map** 4 E2 & 6 D5.
Tel 50110. 🚇 Karlsplatz. 📷 ♿
www.luxurycollection.com

Along with the Hotel Sacher
(see p138), this is the best
known of the 19th-century
hotels. You can sip tea to the
sound of a pianist playing in
the background or stay in the
same room Richard Wagner
occupied. Adolf Hitler made
the hotel his headquarters
after the Anschluss (see p36).

Schwarzenberg-platz ❼

Map 4 E2. 🚇 Karlsplatz. **Arnold
Schönberg Center Tel** 7121888.

At the centre of this grand
square is the equestrian statue
(1867) of Prince Schwarzenberg, who led the Austrian
and allied armies against Napoleon at the Battle of Leipzig
(1813). The square combines
huge office blocks, the Ringstrasse and the Baroque
splendours of the Schwarzenberg and Belvedere palaces.
Behind the fountain of Hochstrahlbrunnen (1873), at the
intersection of Prinz-Eugen-
Strasse and Gusshausstrasse, is
the monument commemorating
the Red Army's liberation of
the city. It is none too popular
with older Viennese, who still
recall the brutalities endured
in the Russian zone until 1955.

The Arnold Schönberg
Center, at the eastern end of
the square, houses recordings,
scores and memorabilia from
the famous Viennese composer.

the Karlsplatz, which are
among his best-known
buildings. The green copper
colour of the roofs and the
ornamentation complement
the Karlskirche beyond. Gilt
patterns are stamped onto the
white marble cladding and
eaves, with repetitions of
Wagner's beloved sunflower
motif. But the greatest impact
is made by the buildings'
elegantly curving rooflines.
The two pavilions face each
other: one is now a café, the
other is used for exhibitions.

Künstlerhaus ❺

Karlsplatz 5. **Map** 4 D2 & 6 D5.
Tel 5879663. 🚇 Karlsplatz.
⏲ 10am–6pm Fri–Wed; 10am–9pm
Thu. 🚫 ♿ www.k-haus.at

Commissioned by the Vienna
Artists' Society as an exhibition hall for its members, the
Künstlerhaus was built in 1868.
The society favoured grand,
academic styles of painting in
tune with the historicist Ringstrasse architecture. The
Künstlerhaus itself is typical of
this style, which is named
after the Vienna boulevard
where the look is most preva-
lent (see pp32–3). Designed
by August Weber (1836–1903)
in a Renaissance palazzo style,
the Künstlerhaus is now used
for temporary art exhibitions.

Palazzo-style façade of the Künstlerhaus (1868)

Karlskirche ❶

During Vienna's plague epidemic in 1713, Emperor Karl VI vowed that as soon as the city was delivered from its plight he would build a church dedicated to St Charles Borromeo (1538–84), a former Archbishop of Milan and a patron saint of the plague. The following year he announced a competition to design the church, which was won by the architect Johann Bernhard Fischer von Erlach. The result was a richly eclectic Baroque masterpiece: the gigantic dome and portico are borrowed from the architecture of ancient Greece and Rome, while there are Oriental echoes in the gatehouses and minaret-like columns. Building took almost 25 years, and the interior was richly embellished with carvings and altarpieces by the foremost artists of the day, including Daniel Gran and Martino Altomonte.

Angel representing the New Testament

The Pulpit
Two putti surmount the canopy of the richly-gilded pulpit, decorated with rocailles and flower garlands.

Stairway (closed to public)

★ High Altar
The high altar features a stucco relief by Albert Camesina showing St Charles Borromeo being assumed into heaven on a cloud laden with angels and putti.

The two gatehouses leading into the side entrances of the church are reminiscent of Chinese pavilions.

STAR FEATURES

★ High Altar

★ Frescoes in the Cupola

★ The Two Columns

Pediment reliefs by Giovanni Stanetti show the suffering of the Viennese during the 1713 plague.

Angel representing the Old Testament

Main entrance

Cupola
Cross

★ **Frescoes in the Cupola**
*Johann Michael Rottmayr's
fresco, painted between 1725
and 1730, depicts the
Apotheosis of St Charles
Borromeo. It was the
painter's last
commission.*

**JOHANN BERNHARD
FISCHER VON ERLACH**

Many of Vienna's finest buildings, including the Trautson
and Schönbrunn Palaces,
were designed by Fischer
von Erlach (1656–1723).
He died before he finished
the Karlskirche and his son
completed it in 1737.

★ **The Two Columns**
*Inspired by Trajan's Column
in Rome, they are decorated
with spiralling scenes of
St Charles Borromeo's life.
Qualities of Steadfastness
are illustrated on the left,
and Courage on the right.*

Visitors
entrance and
tickets

St Charles Borromeo
*Lorenzo Mattielli's
statue of the patron
saint crowns the
pediment.*

Angel
representing
the New
Testament

Schwarzenberg Palace and Joseph Fischer von Ehrlach's fountain

Schwarzenberg Palace **❽**

Schwarzenbergplatz 9. **Map** 4 E2.

The Palais Schwarzenberg was built by Johann Lukas von Hildebrandt (see p152) in 1697 and then altered by the Fischer von Erlachs (see p149) in the 1720s. The main salon has a domed hall with a magnificent chandelier. Behind the palace are the lawns and shady paths of the park, focused around a pool and fountain designed by Joseph Emanuel Fischer von Erlach. In the past the main reception rooms were used as a venue for concerts and balls, and part of the building now houses a luxury hotel.

One wing is occupied by the Swiss embassy. The present head of the Schwarzenberg family served as an advisor to President Havel after the Velvet Revolution in Czechoslovakia in 1989 and became Czech foreign minister in 2007 and again in 2010.

Rennweg **❾**

Map 4 E2. 🚇 Karlsplatz.
Gardekirche ⬜ 8am–8pm daily.

Rennweg runs from the Schwarzenbergplatz along the edges of the Belvedere palaces. At No. 3, a house built by Otto Wagner (see p57) in 1890 is now the (former) Yugoslav Embassy. Though the façade is in shabby condition, the house remains an interesting example of Wagner's work

just as he was making the transition from Ringstrasse pomp to his later Jugendstil style of architecture.

Next door at No. 5 is where Gustav Mahler (see p39) lived from 1898 to 1909. No. 5a is the Gardekirche (1755–63) by Nikolaus Pacassi (1716–99), Maria Theresa's court architect. It was originally built as the church of the Imperial Hospital and since 1897 has been Vienna's Polish church. A huge dome covers the entire interior, which adds to its spaciousness. One feature of interest is the gilt Rococo embellishment over the side chapels and between the ribs of the dome. Just beyond the Belvedere palace gates at No. 6a stands a Baroque mansion, while the forecourt at No. 8 has formed part of the

Hochschule für Musik since 1988. At No. 10, behind splendid wrought-iron gates, stands the Salesianerinnenkirche of 1717–30. The Baroque façade is flanked by monastic buildings in the same style. The upper storey has scrolled projections that serve as the base for statues. Like the Gardekirche, this church is domed, its design partly attributed to Joseph Emanuel Fischer von Erlach (see p149). Apart from the pulpit, the interior is of little interest.

At No. 27, the present-day Italian Embassy is the palace where Prince Metternich (see p30) lived until he was forced to flee the city in 1848.

Palaces and Gardens of the Belvedere **❿**

See pp152–57.

Botanical Gardens **⓫**

Rennweg 14. **Map** 4 F3. **Tel** 4277 54190. 🚌 71. ⬜ Easter–mid-Oct: 9am–dusk daily; also open in winter (weather permitting). 📷 ♿

The main entrance to the Botanical Gardens is on the corner of Prätoriusgasse and Mechelgasse. Other entrances

Detail of the façade of the Salesianerinnenkirche in Rennweg

are on Jacquingasse, and via a small gate at the rear of the Upper Belvedere which leads to the Alpine Garden and the Botanical Gardens. The latter contains more than 9,000 plant species. The Botanical Gardens were created in 1754 by Maria Theresa and her physician van Swieten for cultivating medicinal herbs. Expanded to their present shape in the 19th century, they remain a centre for the study of plant sciences as part of the University of Vienna's Institute of Botany. Of equal interest to amateurs, the gardens offer a quiet spot to sit and relax after sightseeing.

The Botanical Gardens created by Maria Theresa in 1754

Bestattungs-museum ⓬

Goldeggasse 19. **Map** 4 E4. *Tel* 501954227. Ⓤ *Südtiroler Platz.* 🚊 D, O, 13A, 18. ⬜ Mon–Fri (by appt only). 📷

In Vienna, death and pomp have always been allied with one another, and even today the Viennese like to be buried in style. For the clearest insight into this fascinating feature of Viennese life, it's worth making a visit to this undertakers' museum.

One of the more eerie items, shown immediately after you enter, is the wrought-iron grille (1784) that formed the entrance to the Catholic cemetery at Matzleindorf. Its motif is of a crowned skeleton. You can see the various lanterns and staffs and liveries that were part of the pall-bearers' equipment from the 17th century onwards, as well as the special livery decked around the horses that pulled the hearse. In the 19th century, Viennese specialist couturiers provided widow's mourning attire complete with black handbag and black jewellery. Also in the 19th century a bell was often attached to a rope within the coffin, allowing the recently deceased, should he or she unexpectedly reawaken, to signal the alarm. This device became unnecessary if you requested in your

will to be stabbed in the heart before the coffin lid was nailed down, and the stiletto used for this practice is on display. Other displays show how corpses were dressed up and seated on a chair for one last photograph.

The custodian of the museum will also show you one of Joseph II's *(see p28)* more eccentric innovations from the late 18th century: the economy-model coffin with a trapdoor in the bottom which allowed the shrouded corpse to be dumped into the grave and the coffin to be reused. This story partly illustrates why the tireless reformer was not universally loved by his subjects. His attempts at reform were often perceived as doing more harm than good, or as unnecessary. The emperor was forced to abandon this unpopular idea.

Theresianum ⓭

Favoritenstrasse 15. **Map** 4 E3. Ⓤ *Taubstummengasse.* 🏛 to public.

The original buildings of this former imperial summer palace date from the early 17th century, but were

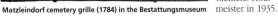
Matzleindorf cemetery grille (1784) in the Bestattungsmuseum

essentially rebuilt after the Turkish siege of 1683 in a Baroque style by the architect and theatre designer Lodovico Burnacini (1636–1707) and others. Known at that time as the Favorita, it became a favourite residence of emperors Leopold I,

Façade of the Theresianum

Joseph I and Karl VI. In 1746 Maria Theresa, who had moved into Schönbrunn *(see pp172–75)*, her summer palace, handed it over to the Jesuits. They established a college here for the education of children from less well-off aristocratic families – the sons of these families were trained to be officials.

Today, the Theresianum is still a school and, since 1964, has also been a college for diplomats and civil servants.

In the Theresianum park on Argentinierstrasse stands Radio House. It has a beautiful entrance hall, which was designed by Clemens Holz-meister in 1935.

Palaces and Gardens of the Belvedere ⓾

Statuary on a gate of Lower Belvedere

The Belvedere was built by Johann Lukas von Hildebrandt as the summer residence of Prince Eugene of Savoy, the brilliant military commander whose strategies helped vanquish the Turks in 1683. Situated on a gently sloping hill, the Belvedere consists of two palaces linked by a formal garden laid out in the French style by Dominique Girard. The garden is sited on three levels, each conveying a complicated programme of Classical allusions: the lower part of the garden represents the domain of the Four Elements, the centre is Parnassus and the upper section is Olympus.

★ **Upper Cascade**
Water flows from the upper basin over five shallow steps into the pool below.

***Putti* on the Steps** *(1852)*
Children and cherubs representing the 12 months adorn the steps to the left and right in the middle area of the gardens.

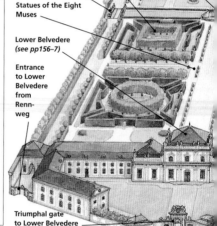

Lower cascade

Bosquet or hedge garden

Statues of the Eight Muses

Lower Belvedere *(see pp156–7)*

Entrance to Lower Belvedere from Renn-weg

Triumphal gate to Lower Belvedere

JOHANN LUKAS VON HILDEBRANDT

Hildebrandt became the court architect in Vienna in 1700 and was one of J B Fischer von Erlach's greatest rivals. In addition to the Belvedere, he designed the Schönborn Palace *(see p110)*, the Kinsky Palace *(see p110)* and the Maria Treu Kirche *(see p116)*.

Coloured etching of the Upper Belvedere and Gardens by Karl Schütz (1784)

TIMELINE

1717–19 Dominique Girard landscapes the gardens	**1765** Lower Belvedere becomes the barracks for the military guard	**1897** Archduke Franz Ferdinand, heir to the throne, moves to the Upper Belvedere		**1953** Museum of Medieval Austrian Art opens to the public
1720 Orangery built	**1781–1891** Belvedere houses the Imperial Picture Gallery, which opens to the public			

1750	1800	1850	1900	1950

1721–3 Upper Belvedere built	**1752** Habsburgs acquire the Belvedere	**1923–9** The Baroque Museum, the 19th-century Gallery and the 20th-century Gallery open to the public	**1955** The Austrian State Treaty signed in the Marble Hall
1714–16 Lower Belvedere built	**1779** Belvedere gardens open to the public		

Detail on Upper Cascade

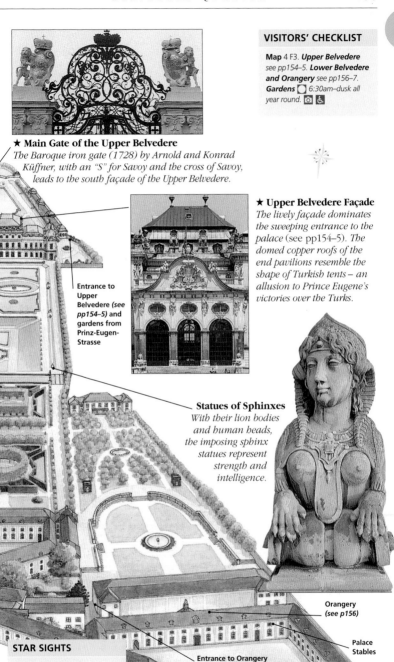

★ **Main Gate of the Upper Belvedere**
The Baroque iron gate (1728) by Arnold and Konrad Küffner, with an "S" for Savoy and the cross of Savoy, leads to the south façade of the Upper Belvedere.

VISITORS' CHECKLIST

Map 4 F3. *Upper Belvedere* see pp154–5. *Lower Belvedere and Orangery* see pp156–7. *Gardens* ○ 6:30am–dusk all year round. ◎ ⚊

Entrance to Upper Belvedere *(see pp154–5)* **and gardens from Prinz-Eugen-Strasse**

★ **Upper Belvedere Façade**
The lively façade dominates the sweeping entrance to the palace (see pp154–5). The domed copper roofs of the end pavilions resemble the shape of Turkish tents – an allusion to Prince Eugene's victories over the Turks.

Statues of Sphinxes
With their lion bodies and human heads, the imposing sphinx statues represent strength and intelligence.

Orangery *(see p156)*

Palace Stables

Entrance to Orangery

STAR SIGHTS

★ Upper Cascade

★ Main Gate of the Upper Belvedere

★ Upper Belvesdere Façade

Upper Belvedere

Standing at the highest point of the garden, the
Upper Belvedere has a more elaborate façade
than the Lower Belvedere: it was intended to be
a symbolic reflection of Prince Eugene's glory. In
addition to the impressive interiors of the Sala
Terrena with its sweeping staircase, the chapel
and the Marble Hall, the building now houses an
Austrian art collection with works ranging from the
Middle Ages to the present day.

★ Chapel
*The centrepiece of this brown, white
and gold interior is an altarpiece,
The Resurrection, by Francesco
Solimena (1723), set among statues
of angels. Prince Eugene could enter
the chapel from his apartments.*

Viewing
balcony for
chapel

**Laughing Self-
Portrait** *(1908)*
*This picture is by Richard
Gerstl, the Viennese artist
who was developing his
own Expressionist style
when he killed himself
in his twenties.*

GALLERY GUIDE
*The ground floor houses
masterpieces of baroque and
medieval art. Art from around
1900 and the late 19th century is
on the ground floor. Early 19th-
century art is on the second floor,
along with a Biedermeier collection.*

KEY

☐	Neo-Classicism-Romanticism
☐	Biedermeier
☐	Early 20th-century art
☐	Historicism-Realism-Impressionism
☐	Masterpieces of baroque and medieval art
☐	Non-exhibition space

Main
entrance
from gardens

★ Sala Terrena
*Four Herculean
figures by Lorenzo
Mattielli support the
ceiling vault of the
Sala Terrena, while
white stuccowork by
Santino Bussi covers
the walls and ceiling.*

★ Gustav Klimt Collection

This marvellous Jugendstil collection by Gustav Klimt is considered by some to be the Belvedere's highlight. In the work here, Judith I *(1901), Klimt depicts the Old Testament heroine as a Viennese* femme fatale.

The Tiger Lion *(1926)*
This savage beast from the 20th-century collection was painted by Oskar Kokoschka, a leading figure in Austrian Expressionism.

Second floor

Marble Hall

The Plain of Auvers *(1890)*
Van Gogh's airy landscape from the 20th-century collection.

First floor

STAR SIGHTS

Stairs to

- ★ Chapel
- ★ Gustav Klimt Collection
- ★ Sala Terrena

Ground floor

Corpus Christi Morning *(1857)*
This bright genre scene is typical of the Austrian Biedermeier painter Ferdinand Georg Waldmüller.

Lower Belvedere and Orangery

The architect Johann Lucas von Hildebrandt (1668–1745) was commissioned by Prince Eugene of Savoy to build the Lower Belvedere in 1714, and it was completed in 1716. It previously housed the Museum of Austrian Baroque Art but now displays temporary exhibitions only. Attractions include the Marble Hall, the state bedroom of Prince Eugene of Savoy, the Hall of Grotesques and the Marble Gallery. The Lower Belvedere also incorporates the Orangery and the palace stables.

Exit to Orangery and stables

Prince Eugene's former bedroom

★ **Golden Cabinet**
A statue of Prince Eugene (1721) by Balthasar Permoser stands in this room, whose walls are covered with huge gilt-framed mirrors.

Hall of Grotesques
The hall is decorated with paintings of grotesques inspired by ancient Roman frescoes of fantastical creatures. They were created by the German painter Jonas Drentwett.

THE ORANGERY

Next door to the Lower Belvedere is the handsome Orangery building, originally used to shelter tender garden plants in winter and now transformed into an exhibition hall retaining its original character. It previously housed the Museum of Austrian Medieval Art but now has regularly-changing temporary exhibitions. Neighbouring the "White Cube", a unique exhibition space, the southern side gallery corridor offers a spectacular view of the Privy Garden and the Upper Belvedere.

The Orangery and gardens in winter

The Palace Stables
Collected here are some 150 items of medieval art, including masterpieces of panel painting and sculpture.

Lower Belvedere Palace *This impressive Baroque palace is set in beautiful landscaped gardens. The façade is adorned with ionic columns and statues.*

VISITORS' CHECKLIST

Rennweg 6a, A-1037. **Map** 4 E3. *Tel* 01796570. 🚋 71, D. ☐ 10am–6pm daily (to 9pm Wed). *Palace Stables* ☐ 10am– noon daily. 📷 🅾 ♿ 🎁 www.belvedere.at

GALLERY GUIDE
All works on display in the Lower Belvedere and Orangery are temporary. Exhibitions include traditional and contemporary painting and sculpture. Pieces are often loaned from galleries and museums worldwide, supplemented by the Belvedere's own collection.

★ **The Marble Hall**
The only two-storey section of the palace, the Marble Hall is clad on all sides with reddish-brown and stucco marble. The magnificent soaring ceiling is dedicated to the sun god Apollo.

The Marble Hall

KEY

☐ Temporary Exhibitions

Main entrance

To gardens

STAR SIGHTS

★ Figures from the Providentia Fountain

★ Golden Cabinet

★ The Marble Hall

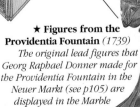

★ **Figures from the Providentia Fountain** *(1739)*
The original lead figures that Georg Raphael Donner made for the Providentia Fountain in the Neuer Markt (see p105) are displayed in the Marble Hall. This central statue represents Providence.

FURTHER AFIELD

or a city of over two million inhabitants, Vienna is suprisingly compact. Nonetheless, some of the most interesting sights are a fair distance from the city centre. At Schönbrunn sprawls the immense palace and gardens so loved by Maria Theresa,

Detail on riding school (1882–6) next to Hermes Villa

and the monastery at Klosterneuburg houses some of Austria's great ecclesiastical art treasures. Many parks and gardens, including the Prater, the Augarten and the Lainzer Tiergarten, all former private Habsburg domaines, are now open to the public.

SIGHTS AT A GLANCE

Historic Buildings
Amalienbad ⑯
Augarten Palace and Park ⑨
Favoriten Water Tower ⑮
Hundertwasser Haus ⑪
Karl Marx Hof ⑦
Otto-Wagner-Hofpavilion
  Hietzing ⑳
Schönbrunn Palace
  and Gardens pp172–5 ⑲
Wagner Villas ①
Werkbundsiedlung ㉑

Churches and Monasteries
Kirche am Steinhof ②
Klosterneuburg ⑥
Wotruba Kirche ㉓

Museums and Galleries
Geymüller Schlössl ③
Heeresgeschichtliches
  Museum pp166–7 ⑬
Kriminalmuseum ⑩
Technical Museum ⑱

Parks and Gardens
Donau Park ⑧
Lainzer Tiergarten ㉒
Prater pp162–3 ⑫

Historic Districts
Grinzing ④
Kahlenberg ⑤

Monuments
Spinnerin am Kreuz ⑰

Cemeteries
Central Cemetery pp168–9 ⑭

10 kilometres = 6 miles

KEY

■	Central Vienna
■	Greater Vienna
⚡	Main line railway station
══	Motorway
····	Motorway tunnel
━━	Major road
══	Minor road

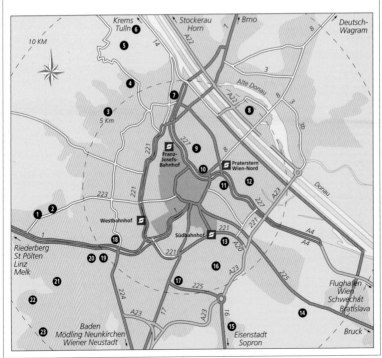

◁ **Part of the façade of the Hundertwasser Haus, built in 1985**

Detail of Ernst Fuchs' Brunnenhaus, next to Wagner Villas

Wagner Villas **❶**

Hüttelbergstrasse 26, Penzing.
Tel 9148575. Ⓤ Hütteldorf. 🚌 148, 152. ◯ 10am–4pm Mon–Fri. 🎒 📷
www.ernstfuchszentrum.com

The Villa Otto Wagner, designed by Wagner from 1886 to 1888 as his own residence, is stylistically midway between his earlier Ringstrasse architecture and the decorative elements of Jugendstil (see pp54–7). The house is built on a grand scale and incorporates classical elements such as Ionic columns, and seems more suited to a north Italian hillside than to Austria. The present owner, the painter Ernst Fuchs (see p36), has imposed his own personality on the villa, adding a fertility statue and garish colours.

The simpler villa next door was built more than 20 years later. Completed in 1913, the house is of steel and concrete rather than brick. It is very lightly decorated in a severe geometrical style with deep blue panels and nailhead ornament. The glass ornament is by Kolo Moser (see p57).

Kirche am Steinhof **❷**

Baumgartner Höhe 1, Penzing.
Tel 9106011007. 🚌 48A. ◯ 4–5pm Sat. 📷 by appointment. 🎒 📷

Completed in 1907, this astonishing church was Otto Wagner's (see pp54–7) last commission. It is set within the grounds of the Psychiatrisches Krankenhaus, a large mental hospital. The exterior is marble clad with nailhead ornament and has spindly screw-shaped pillars, topped by wreaths, supporting the porch. Four stone columns along the façade are adorned with angels by Othmar Schimkowitz (1864–1947). The statues at each corner of the façade are of St Leopold and St Severin to the left and right respectively. They were designed by Richard Luksch and are seated in chairs by Josef Hoffmann (see pp56–7).

The interior is a single space with shallow side chapels. The main decoration consists of gold and white friezes and square roof panels ornamented with gilt nailhead. Illumination is provided by daylight shining through lovely blue glass windows by Kolo Moser (see p57).

Geymüller Schlössl **❸**

Khevenhüllerstrasse 2, Währing.
Tel 711360. 🚌 41A. 🚋 41.
◯ May–Nov: 11am–6pm Sun. 🎒 📷

The Geymüller Schlössl in Pötzleinsdorf, northwest of the city, is a temple to Biedermeier style (see pp30–31). Dating from 1808, the house was built for Johann Heinrich von Geymüller, a rich banker. Now a branch of the Austrian Museum of Applied Arts (see pp82–3), it has a collection of intricate Biedermeier and Empire furniture, such as an apparently simple desk that combines a writing desk with a water-colour cabinet. Gadgets abound: spittoons, still-lifes painted on porcelain, bowls, as well as 200 clocks dating from 1780 to about 1850, the heyday of Viennese clock manufacture.

Jugendstil angels by Othmar Schimkowitz adorning the façade of the Kirche am Steinhof

Grinzing ❹

🚇 *Heiligenstadt.* 🚌 *38A.* 🚋 *38.*

Grinzing is the most famous *Heuriger* village *(see pp186–7)*, but it is also the least authentic, as many of the inns here cater to very large groups of tourists. It is nonetheless very pretty.

It is divided into the Oberer Ort and Unterer Ort (upper and lower towns), the lower town being where you will find more authentic *Heurige* along such lanes as Sandgasse.

Grinzing was repeatedly destroyed by Turkish troops during the many sieges of Vienna *(see p26–7)*, and was again damaged by Napoleon's forces in 1809 *(see p30)*.

Kahlenberg ❺

🚌 *38A.*

Kahlenberg, at 484 m (1,585 ft) *(see pp182–3)*, is the highest point of the Vienna Woods. It has a television mast at the top, as well as a church, an observation terrace and a restaurant. The views over the vineyards below and the city beyond are fabulous, with the Danube bridges to the left and the Vienna Woods to the right. The Kahlenberg played a crucial part in the city's history, in 1683 when the Polish king, Jan Sobieski, led his troops down from this spot to the rescue of Viennese forces who were fighting for the city.

Klosterneuburg ❻

Stift Klosterneuburg. **Tel** *02243-411/212.* 🚇 *Heiligenstadt.* 🚈 *Franz-Josefs-Bahnhof to Klosterneuburg-Kierling.* 🚌 *237, 238, 239.* ⏰ *9am–5pm daily.* 📷 *Daily tours include the Monastery Museum and Imperial Apartments.* 📷 🌐 www.stift-klosterneuburg.at

Above the Danube, 13 km (8 miles) north of Vienna, stands the vast monastery and fortress of Klosterneuburg.

The peach- and salmon-coloured façade of the Karl Marx Hof

Dating originally from the 12th century, it houses the astonishing Verduner Altar, whose 51 panels were completed in 1181 *(see p23)*. In the 18th century it was expanded by Karl VI, who intended to build a complex on the same grand scale as the Escorial palace near Madrid. The work was halted after his death in 1740.

Statue in Grinzing

Karl Marx Hof ❼

Heiligenstädterstrasse 82–92, Döbling. 🚇 *Heiligenstadt.* 🚋 *D.* 🚫 *to the public.*

The Karl Marx Hof, dating from 1927 to 1930, is an immense council block, which contains 1,382 flats. It is the most celebrated of the municipal housing developments built during the period of Red Vienna *(see p36)*, when 63,000 new dwellings went up across the city between 1919 and 1934. The architect of the Karl Marx Hof was Karl Ehn, a pupil of Otto Wagner *(see p54–7)*.

Donau Park ❽

🚇 *Kaisermühlen.* 🚌 *20B.* ⏰ *24 hrs daily.* **Donau Turm Tel** *26335720.* ⏰ *10am–11:30pm daily.* 📷 ♿

Adjoining UNO-city *(see p37)*, the complex of United Nations agencies, is the Donau Park. Laid out in 1964, the park has cycle paths, cafés and other amenities. Rising 252 m (827 ft) above the park is the Donau Turm, with two revolving restaurants and an observation platform. The park and surrounding area have been redeveloped as the Donau City housing project, encompassing the Millennium Tower.

View of the Klosterneuburg monastery with its Baroque dome

Prater ⑫

Originally an Imperial hunting ground, these woods and meadows between the Danube and its canal were opened to the public by Joseph II in 1766. The central avenue, or Hauptallee, was for a long time the preserve of the nobility and their footmen. During the 19th century the western end of the Prater became a massive funfair with booths, sideshows, beer gardens and *Wurst* stands catering for the Viennese workers.

The Miniature Railway
The Liliputbahn travels a 4-km (2 1/2-mile) circuit.

To Praterstern station

Planetarium

Messegelände exhibition centre

Tennisplätze (Tennis Courts)

★ **Ferris Wheel**
The huge wheel circulates very slowly at a speed of about 75 cm (2 1/2 ft) per second, allowing riders spectacular views over the park and funfair.

★ **Volksprater Funfair**
An amusement park has existed here since the last century. Today the enormous funfair is full of high-tech rides ranging from dodgem cars to ghost trains.

The Trotting Stadium
Built in 1913, the Krieau Stadium is the scene of exciting regional and international trotting races from September to June (see p231).

STAR SIGHTS

★ Hauptallee

★ Volksprater Funfair

★ Ferris Wheel

THE HISTORY OF THE FERRIS WHEEL

One of Vienna's most famous landmarks, the giant Ferris Wheel was immortalized in the film of Graham Greene's *The Third Man*. It was built in 1896 by the English engineer Walter Basset, but it has only half the original number of cabins as fire destroyed many of them in 1945.

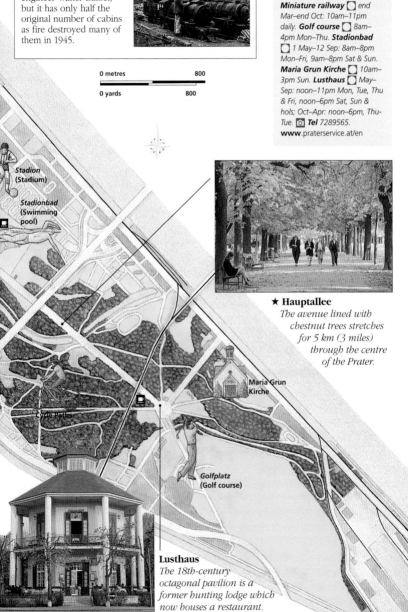

0 metres 800
0 yards 800

Stadion (Stadium)

Stadionbad (Swimming pool)

Cycle paths

★ **Hauptallee**
The avenue lined with chestnut trees stretches for 5 km (3 miles) through the centre of the Prater.

Maria Grun Kirche

Golfplatz (Golf course)

Lusthaus
The 18th-century octagonal pavilion is a former hunting lodge which now houses a restaurant.

Baroque façade of the Augarten Palace set amid 18th-century parkland

Augarten Palace and Park ❾

Obere Augartenstrasse 1. **Map** 2 E2.
Tel 21124201. Ⓤ *Taborstrasse.*
🚌 *5A.* 🚊 *31.* ◯ *6am–dusk daily.*
Porcelain Museum ◯ *10am–5pm
Mon–Sat.* **Augarten Contemporary**
◯ *11am–7pm Thu–Sun.* 📷 ♿

There has been a palace on
this site since the days of
Leopold I, when it was
known as the Alte Favorita,
but it was destroyed by the
Turks in 1683 and then rebuilt
around 1700 to a design
attributed to Johann Bernhard
Fischer von Erlach *(see p149)*.
Since 1948 it has been the
home of the Vienna Boys'
Choir *(see p39)* and consequently it is inaccessible to
the public.
  The park was planted in
the second half of the 17th
century, renewed in 1712, and
opened to the public in 1775
by Joseph II. The handsome

gates by which the public
now enters the gardens were
designed by Isidor Canevale
in 1775. Mozart, Beethoven,
and Johann Strauss I all gave
concerts in the park pavilion.
The Augarten was also used
for royal receptions and
gatherings while the Congress
of Vienna *(see p30)* was
taking place in 1815. The
pavilion used to be the
imperial porcelain factory,
founded in the 18th century,
but has been run since the
1920s by the municipal
authorities. Its showroom has
displays showing the history
of Augarten porcelain. Behind
the pavilion is the studio of
the early 20th-century
sculptor Gustinus Ambrosi,
open to the public as the
Augarten Contemporary.
  The Augarten has the oldest
Baroque garden in Vienna,
with topiary lining long paths
shaded by walls of foliage. In
the distance, you can see two
of the huge and terrifying

flakturms that the Viennese
are unable to rid themselves
of. Built by German forces
in 1942 as defense towers
and anti-aircraft batteries,
these enormous concrete
monoliths could house
thousands of troops. So
thick are their walls that any
explosives powerful enough
to destroy them would have
a similar effect on the
surrounding residential areas.
There are four other such
flakturms still standing in
other parts of the city.

Kriminalmuseum ❿

Grosse Sperlgasse 24. **Map** 6 E1.
Tel 2144678. Ⓤ *Taborstrasse.*
🚌 *5A.* 🚊 *1.* ◯ *10am–5pm
Thu–Sun.* 📷

Since 1991, this house of
medieval origin has been the
home of Vienna's museum of
crime. Once known as the
Seifensiederhaus (the soap

Hundertwasser Haus ⓫

Löwengasse/ Kegelgasse.
Ⓤ *Landstrasse.* 🚌 *4A.* 🚊 *O,1
Hetzgasse.* �𝄐 *to the public.*

The Hundertwasser Haus is a
municipal apartment block
created in 1985 by the artist
Friedensreich Hundertwasser
(see p37), who wished to strike
a blow against what he saw as
soulless modern architecture.
The resulting building, with its
irregular bands of colour and
onion dome cupolas, has been
controversial since its construction. While it is loved by some,
others think it is more like a
stage set than a block of flats.

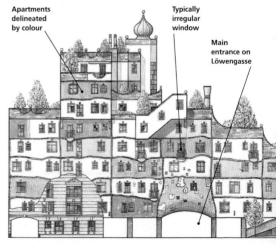

Apartments
delineated
by colour

Typically
irregular
window

Main
entrance on
Löwengasse

boiler's house), this museum's 20 rooms mostly chronicle violent crime, charting the murderous impulses of Vienna's citizenry from the Middle Ages to the 20th century, and the history of the judicial system.

Many of the exhibits come from the archives of the Viennese police force and are distinctly gruesome; there is a wide selection of murder weapons, mummified heads of executed criminals, death masks and case histories

Painting depicting a 1782 robbery

illustrated with photographs and prints. Many of the more unsettling exhibits give a notion of how the Viennese poor of earlier centuries were involved in crime. Political crimes, such as the lynching of a government minister during the revolution of 1848 *(see p30)*, are also covered.

This interesting museum provides a blend of documentary social history and a chamber of horrors which portrays the darker side of Viennese life with gusto.

Prater ⑫

See pp162–3.

Heeresgeschichtliches Museum ⑬

See pp166–7.

Central Cemetery ⑭

See pp168–9.

Favoriten Water Tower ⑮

Windtenstrasse 3, Favoriten.
Tel 5995931071. Ⓤ *Reumannplatz.*
🚌 *15A.* 🚊 *65, 65A, 7A, 15A.* ⬜
for guided tours (phone to arrange).

A complex known the Favoriten pumping station was constructed in 1889 by Franz Borkowitz as part of a municipal scheme for the transportation of drinking water from the Alpine foothills to the rapidly-growing city. By 1910 the construction of other installations around Vienna meant that the operations of the complex had to be scaled down, and of the seven original buildings only the highly decorative yellow-and-red-brick

water tower remains. The fascinating feature of this incongruous-looking tower that soars 67 m (220 ft) into the sky is the original pumping equipment which is still in place. Its utilitarian appearance provides a stark contrast to the ornate turrets, pinnacles and tiles of the building's superstructure. The interior has been restored and guided tours are available to the public. Nearby is the small children's funfair, the Böhmische Prater *(see p234).*

Favoriten Water Tower

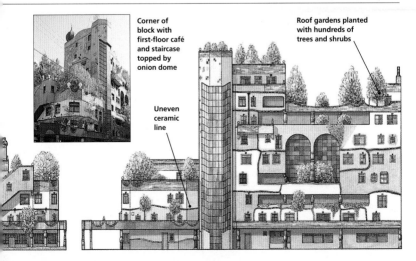

Corner of block with first-floor café and staircase topped by onion dome

Uneven ceramic line

Roof gardens planted with hundreds of trees and shrubs

Heeresgeschichtliches Museum ⑬

This impressive museum of army history is housed in a single block of the military complex known as the Arsenal. It was completed in fortress style in 1856. Theophil Hansen designed the museum itself *(see façade, right)*, which chronicles Austria's military prowess from the 16th century onwards. Exhibits relate to the Turkish siege of 1683, the French Revolution and the Napoleonic wars. Visitors should not miss seeing the car in which Archduke Franz Ferdinand was assassinated, or the modern armaments used in the war that the murder precipitated.

STAR SIGHTS

★ Hall of the Commanders

★ Turkish Standard

★ To the Unknown Soldier by A E Lienz

KEY

☐ Tank park

▨ 16th–19th centuries

☐ 19th and 20th centuries

▨ Non-exhibition space

Ground floor

Sea Power Austria

Republic and Dictatorship 1918–1945

Tank Park
Situated behind the museum are the armoured vehicles used in the Austrian army from 1955 as well as those that belonged to the German army that occupied Austria.

Main entrance from Ghegastrasse

THE ASSASSINATION OF FRANZ FERDINAND
On 28 June 1914 the heir to the throne, Archduke Franz Ferdinand, and his wife Sophie von Hohenberg paid a visit to Sarajevo. Gavrilo Princip, a Serbian nationalist, assassinated the couple, provoking an international crisis that later resulted in World War I. The museum houses the car in which the couple were killed.

MUSEUM GUIDE
The museum is housed on two floors. To view it in chronological order, begin on the first floor on the left, where exhibits relating to the Turkish siege are displayed. Other rooms chronicle the various 18th-century wars and Napoleon's victory over Austria. The 19th and 20th centuries, including heavy artillery used in World War I, are covered on the ground floor. There is also a tank park.

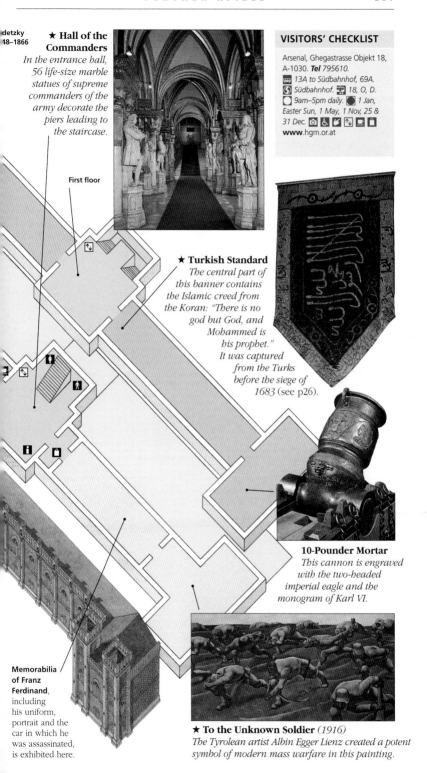

detzky
48–1866

★ **Hall of the Commanders**
In the entrance hall, 56 life-size marble statues of supreme commanders of the army decorate the piers leading to the staircase.

First floor

VISITORS' CHECKLIST

Arsenal, Ghegastrasse Objekt 18, A-1030. **Tel** 795610.
13A to Südbahnhof, 69A.
Südbahnhof. 18, O, D.
9am–5pm daily. 1 Jan, Easter Sun, 1 May, 1 Nov, 25 & 31 Dec.
www.hgm.or.at

★ **Turkish Standard**
The central part of this banner contains the Islamic creed from the Koran: "There is no god but God, and Mohammed is his prophet." It was captured from the Turks before the siege of 1683 (see p26).

10-Pounder Mortar
This cannon is engraved with the two-headed imperial eagle and the monogram of Karl VI.

Memorabilia of Franz Ferdinand, including his uniform, portrait and the car in which he was assassinated, is exhibited here.

★ **To the Unknown Soldier** *(1916)*
The Tyrolean artist Albin Egger Lienz created a potent symbol of modern mass warfare in this painting.

Central Cemetery ⑭

Headstone of Brahms' grave

Austria's largest burial ground, containing two and a half million graves, was opened in 1874 on the city's southern outskirts. The central section includes graves of artists, composers, architects, writers and local politicians. Funerals are usually quite lavish affairs, as the Viennese like to be buried in style, with the pomp appropriate to their station in life. The cemetery contains a vast array of funerary monuments varying from the humble to the bombastic, paying tribute to the city's enduring obsession with death.

★ Dr-Karl-Lueger-Kirche
Max Hegele, a pupil of Otto Wagner, designed this church dedicated to Vienna's mayor in 1907–10.

Arcades around the Dr-Karl-Lueger-Kirche

Presidential Vault
This contains the remains of Dr Karl Renner, the first President of the Austrian Republic after World War II.

Fritz Wotruba's grave *(see p171)*

CEMETERY LAYOUT

The cemetery is divided into specific numbered sections: apart from the central garden of honour where VIPs are buried, there are old and new Jewish cemeteries; a Protestant cemetery; a Russian Orthodox section and various war graves and memorials. It is easier to take the circulating bus that covers the whole area than to walk.

The Monument to the Dead of World War I is a powerful depiction of a mother lamenting by Anton Hanak.

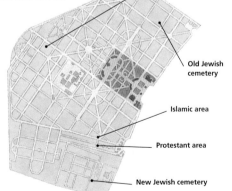

Old Jewish cemetery

Islamic area

Protestant area

New Jewish cemetery

Arnold Schönberg's Cube
The grave of the modernist Viennese composer Arnold Schönberg is marked with this bold cube by Fritz Wotruba.

STAR SIGHTS

★ Musicians' Graves

★ Dr-Karl-Lueger-Kirche

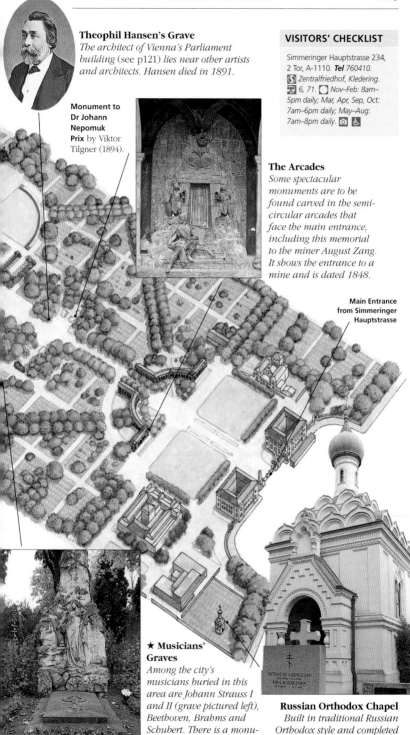

Theophil Hansen's Grave
The architect of Vienna's Parliament building (see p121) lies near other artists and architects. Hansen died in 1891.

Monument to Dr Johann Nepomuk Prix by Viktor Tilgner (1894).

The Arcades
Some spectacular monuments are to be found carved in the semi-circular arcades that face the main entrance, including this memorial to the miner August Zang. It shows the entrance to a mine and is dated 1848.

Main Entrance from Simmeringer Hauptstrasse

★ Musicians' Graves
Among the city's musicians buried in this area are Johann Strauss I and II (grave pictured left), Beethoven, Brahms and Schubert. There is a monument to Mozart, who was buried in St Marx cemetery.

Russian Orthodox Chapel
Built in traditional Russian Orthodox style and completed in 1894, this chapel is used by Vienna's Russian community.

Amalienbad ⑯

Reumannplatz 23, Favoriten.
Tel 6074747. Ⓤ *Reumannplatz.* 🚌
7A, 14A, 66A, 67A, 68A. 🚋 *6, 67.*
Swimming pool 🕐 *9am–6pm Tue,*
9am–9:30pm Wed & Fri, 7am–9:30pm
Thu, 7am–8pm Sat, 7am–6pm Sun.
Sauna 🕐 *1–9:30pm Tue, 9am–*
9:30pm Wed–Fri, 7am–8pm Sat,
7am–6pm Sun. ♿

Public baths may not seem
like an obvious tourist
destination, but the Jugendstil
Amalienbad (1923–6) shows
how the municipal administration in the 1920s not only
provided essential public
facilities, but did so with
stylistic vigour and conviction.
The two designers, Otto
Nadel and Karl Schmalhofer,
were employees of the city's
architectural department.

The magnificent main pool
is covered by a glass roof that
can be opened in minutes and
is surrounded by galleries overlooking the pool. Elsewhere
in the building are saunas
and smaller baths and pools
used for therapeutic purposes.
When first opened, the baths
were one of the largest of
their kind in Europe, designed
to accommodate 1,300 people.
The interior is enlivened by
imaginative mosaic and tile
decoration, which is practical
as well as colourful. The
baths were damaged in World
War II but were impeccably
restored in 1986.

Spinnerin am Kreuz

Spinnerin am Kreuz ⑰

Triesterstrasse 10, Meidling.
Ⓤ *Meidling.* 🚌 *15A, 65A, 7A.* 🚋 *65.*

A medieval column marks the
southernmost boundary
of Vienna's inner suburbs.
Built in 1452 and carved on
all sides, it stands on the spot
where, according to legend, a
woman sat spinning for years
awaiting her husband's return
from the Crusades. Known as
the Spinner at the Cross, it was
designed by Hans Puchsbaum.
Pinnacled canopies shelter
groups of statuary, including a
crucifixion and a grotesque
figure placing the crown of
thorns on the head of Christ.

Technical Museum ⑱

Mariahilfer Strasse 212, Penzing.
Tel 899986000. 🚋 *52, 58.* 🕐 *9am–*
6pm Mon–Fri, 10am–6pm Sat, Sun &
public hols. 🈂 🅾 ♿
www.tmw.ac.at

Franz Joseph founded the
Technisches Museum Wien
in 1908, using the Habsburgs'
personal collections as core
material; it opened its doors
10 years later. It documents all
aspects of technical progress,
from domestic appliances to
large turbines, and includes
exhibitions on heavy industry,
energy, physics and musical
instruments.

A major section of the
museum features interactive
displays on computer technology and oil and gas drilling
and refining, as well as a
reconstruction of a coal mine.

The Railway Museum forms
an integral part of the
Technical Museum. It houses
an extensive collection of
imperial railway carriages
and engines. One of the prize
exhibits is the imperial
carriage that was used by
Franz Joseph's wife, the
Empress Elisabeth.

Schönbrunn Palace and Gardens ⑲

See pp172–5.

Decorative, geometrically-patterned tiling from the 1920s in the Amalienbad

Otto-Wagner-Hofpavillon Hietzing ⑳

Schönbrunner Schlosstrasse 13, Hietzing. **Tel** 8771571. Ⓤ Hietzing. 🚌 51A, 56B, 58B, 156B. 🚊 10, 60, 62. ◯ by appointment only. 📷

Otto Wagner (see p57) designed and built this railway station for the imperial family and royal guests in 1899. This lovely building is in the shape of a white cube with green ironwork and a copper dome. Its waiting room is panelled with wood and glass, and adorned with a peach and russet asymmetrical carpet and a marble and brass fireplace. The cupola is decorated with glass and gilt flower and leaf motifs.

Wagner built the pavilion without a commission from the emperor in an attempt to showcase his work. Unfortunately, Franz Joseph used the station only twice.

The Hofpavillon Hietzing

Werkbund-siedlung ㉑

Jagdschlossgasse, Veitingergasse and Woinovichgasse, Hietzing. 🚌 54B, 55B. 🚊 60.

In the 13th district you can find the 30 or so fascinating "model" houses of the *Werkbundsiedlung* (housing estate) built in the early 1930s for the municipality by some of Europe's leading architects. They are neither beautiful nor lavish, since the idea was to produce a formula for cheap housing, with two bedrooms,

Hermes Villa in the grounds of the Lainzer Tiergarten

that was plain and functional. No. 19 Woinovichgasse is by Adolf Loos (see p92), and Nos. 83–5 Veitingergasse are by Josef Hoffmann (see p56). Each architect had to design a single building, placed side by side with the rest in order to evaluate the different qualities of each. Although intended to be temporary, they have luckily survived.

Lainzer Tiergarten ㉒

Lainzer Tiergarten, Hietzing. **Tiergarten Tel** 400049200. 🚌 60B. ◯ mid-Feb–mid-Nov: 8am–dusk daily. 📷 **Hermes Villa and Garden Tel** 8041324. ◯ for exhibitions 10am–6pm Tue–Sun & public hols. ⚫ 27 Oct–24 Mar. 📷 📷

The Lainzer Tiergarten is a former Habsburg hunting ground which has been converted into an immense nature reserve in the Vienna Woods (see p176). The Tier-garten was opened to the public in 1923 and is still encircled by its 24-km (15-mile) stone wall, protecting its herds of deer and wild boar. From the entrance, a 15-minute walk along paths through woods and meadows brings you to the Hermes Villa, built by Karl von Hasenauer in 1884. It became a retreat for the imperial family, notably the Empress

Elisabeth and her husband Franz Joseph, who had a suite of rooms on the first floor. Inside are murals of scenes from *A Midsummer Night's Dream*, as well as art and historical exhibitions.

Wotruba Kirche ㉓

Georgsgasse/Rysergasse, Mauer. **Tel** 8885003. 🚌 60A. ◯ 2–8pm Sat, 9am–4:30pm Sun & hols or **Tel** 8885003 for appointment to see the church. 📷

Built between 1965 and 1976 in uncompromisingly modern style, this church stands on a hillside very close to the Vienna Woods. It forms a pile of uneven rectangular concrete slabs and glass panels, some of the latter rising to the height of the church. They provide its principal lighting and views for the congregation out on to the woods and hills. The building is raw in style, but powerful and compact. Designed by the sculptor Fritz Wotruba (1907–75), the church looks different from every angle and has a strong sculptural quality. It accommodates a congregation of up to 250.

The exterior of the Wotruba Kirche by Fritz Wotruba, not unlike a modern sculpture

Schönbrunn Palace and Gardens ⑲

The former summer residence of the imperial family takes its name from a beautiful spring that was found on this site. An earlier hunting lodge was destroyed by the Turks, so Leopold I asked Johann Bernhard Fischer von Erlach to design a grand Baroque residence here in 1695. However, it was not until Maria Theresa employed Nikolaus Pacassi that the project was completed in the mid-18th century. The strict symmetry of the architecture is complemented by the gardens with fountains and statues framed by trees and alleyways.

Public swimming pool

Obelisk Cascade

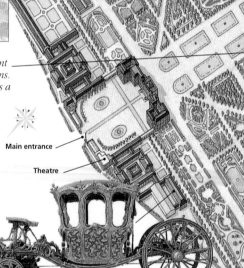

Orangery

Maze
The maze was a favourite element of many European stately gardens. This one at Schönbrunn provides a puzzling detour for visitors.

STAR SIGHTS

★ Gloriette

★ Palm House

★ Coach Museum

Main entrance

Theatre

★ Coach Museum
The former Winter Riding School houses the coaches, sleighs and sedan chairs that were used to transport the imperial family.

TIMELINE

1683 First hunting lodge on site destroyed during the Turkish siege	**1705** Jean Trehet lays out the gardens	**1730** Palace is completed	**1744–9** Nikolaus Pacassi adapts the building for Maria Theresa	**1916** Emperor Franz Joseph dies here, aged 86		**1918** Emperor Karl I abdicates Austrian throne in the Blue Chinese Salon *(p174)*
1650	**1700**	**1750**	**1800**	**1850**	**1900**	**1950**
1696 Leopold I commissions J B Fischer von Erlach to design a new palace		**1775** Gloriette is built	**1805 and 1809** Napoleon uses palace as headquarters		**1882** Palm House is built	**1952** Reconstruction is completed after war damage
Emperor Leopold I		**1752** Maria Theresa's husband, Franz Stephan, founds a menagerie, now the zoo				

★ **Gloriette**
This Neo-Classical arcade, designed by Ferdinand von Hohenberg and built in 1775, is the crowning glory of the hill behind the palace.

Neptune Fountain
This exuberant fountain and basin, at the foot of the hill, was sculpted in 1780 by Franz Anton Zauner.

Schönbrunn Zoo
Founded in 1752 at the order of Franz Stephan, the historic zoo has an octagonal pavilion.

Japanese Gardens

★ **Palm House**
A vast collection of exotic plants flourishes in the magnificent tropical green-house that was erected in 1882.

Hietzing Gate

Façade of Schönbrunn Palace seen from the gardens

Inside Schönbrunn Palace

The Rococo decorative schemes devised by Nikolaus Pacassi dominate the Schönbrunn state rooms, where white panelling, often adorned with gilded ornamental framework, tends to prevail. The rooms vary from extremely sumptuous – such as the Millionen-Zimmer, panelled with fig wood inlaid with Persian miniatures – to the quite plain apartments occupied by Franz Joseph and Empress Elisabeth.

★ **Round Chinese Cabinet**
Maria Theresa used this room for private discussions with her State Chancellor. The walls are adorned with lacquered panels and vases.

★ **Great Gallery**
Once the venue for imperial banquets, the gallery was used for state receptions until 1994.

Hidden staircase which leads to the apartment of the State Chancellor on the floor above and was used for access to secret conferences.

Blue Chinese Salon
The room where Karl I abdicated in 1918 has hand-painted wallpaper with blue insets showing Chinese scenes.

Napoleon Room

Millionen-Zimmer

Memorial Room

First Floor

★ **Vieux-Lacque Room**
During her widowhood, Maria Theresa lived in this room, which is decorated with exquisite oriental lacquered panels.

Main entrance

Large Rosa Room
Landscape scenes of Switzerland and northern Italy by Joseph Rosa give this room its name. The paintings are surrounded by Rococo gilded panels.

Breakfast Room
The imperial family's breakfast room has white wood panelling inlaid with appliqué floral designs worked by Maria Theresa and her daughters.

The Blue Staircase (so called due to its original decorative scheme) leads to the entrance for guided tours of state rooms.

STAR SIGHTS

★ Round Chinese Cabinet

★ Great Gallery

★ Vieux-Lacque Room

ROOM GUIDE

The state rooms open to the public are on the first floor. The suite of rooms to the right of the Blue Staircase were occupied by Franz Joseph and Elisabeth. Two galleries divide these from rooms in the east wing, which include Maria Theresa's bedroom and rooms used by Grand Duke Karl. Two guided tours, the Imperial and the Grand Tour, cover several rooms.

KEY

- ☐ Franz Joseph's apartments
- ▨ Empress Elisabeth's apartments
- ☐ Ceremonial and reception rooms
- ▨ Maria Theresa's rooms
- ☐ Grand Duke Karl's rooms
- ▨ Non-exhibition space

Portrait of Napoleon

Portrait of Maria Louisa

MARIA LOUISA AND THE KING OF ROME

After Napoleon's fall from power, his young son by his Austrian wife Maria Louisa was kept a virtual prisoner in Schönbrunn Palace. In 1832 at the age of 21, after a lonely childhood, he died of consumption in what is known as the Napoleon Room. He was called the Duke of Reichstadt, or the King of Rome, and the Memorial Room contains his portrait as a five-year-old and his effigy. There is also a crested larch under a glass dome; the unhappy boy claimed that he never had a single friend in the palace apart from this bird.

Day Trips from Vienna

Within an hour or two's journey from Vienna there is an astonishing range of countryside from Hungarian-style plains to alpine mountains, majestic rivers and idyllic lakes. Vienna is at the centre of Austria's wine-growing country and is surrounded by historic castles and churches, among which nestle picturesque wine-producing towns and villages. All the sights are accessible by bus or train and trips such as Baden and Mayerling can easily be combined.

Among the trees of Vienna Woods, a popular recreation area

Mayerling and the Vienna Woods **❶**

Vienna Sightseeing organizes trips (see p251). 🚌 *365 from Südtiroler Platz to Mayerling and Heiligenkreuz, or 265 to Heiligenkreuz.* **Mayerling Chapel** *Tel 02258 2275.* ⏲ *summer: 9am–6pm; winter: 9am–5pm Mon–Sat, 10am–5pm Sun & hols.* ⛔ *Maundy Thursday, Good Friday, 24 Dec.* **Heiligenkreuz Abbey** *Tel 02258 8703167.* ⏲ *daily for tours.* 🎫 *10am, 2pm, 3pm & 4pm Mon–Sat, 11am, 2pm, 3pm & 4pm Sun & hols.*

The Vienna Woods extend from within the western bounds of the city and make excellent walking country. A turn around the Lainzer Tiergarten *(see p171)* makes a convenient half- or full-day xouting from Vienna. Further on, where the Vienna Woods stretch out towards the lower slopes of the Alps, there are several interesting sights.

The Mayerling hunting lodge, now the chapel, was the scene in 1889 of the double suicide of Crown Prince Rudolf *(see p32)*, heir to the throne, and his 17-year-old lover Mary Vetsera, daughter of the diplomat Baron Albin Vetsera. Their tragic deaths shook the entire

Austro-Hungarian empire. After his son's death, the Emperor Franz Joseph gave the hunting lodge to a Carmelite convent and it was completely rebuilt.

A few miles north of Mayerling is the medieval Cistercian abbey of Heiligenkreuz. Much of the abbey was rebuilt in the Baroque period, having been destroyed by the Turks in 1529 and 1683. Inside is a 12th-century nave and a 13th-century chapter house. Fine Baroque features include the bell tower and Trinity Column. The abbey houses the tombs of 13 of the Babenbergs who ruled in Austria during the medieval period *(see pp22–3)*.

Baden **❷**

🚌 *552, 360W or 1134 (Mariazell) from Wien Mitte.* 🚆 *or* 🚆 *from Südbahnhof.* 🚋 *Badner Bahn (WLB) from Karlsplatz/Oper. Tel 02252 22600600.*

To the south of Vienna are several spas and wine-growing towns in the hills of the southern Vienna Woods. The most famous is Baden, a spa with curative hot springs dating back to Roman times. As well as bathing in sulphurous water and mud to treat rheumatism, you can enjoy hot pools of 36°C (97°F).

In the early 19th century Baden was popular with the Imperial Court of Vienna. Then many elegant Biedermeier villas, baths, town houses and a square were built, and the gardens of the Kurpark laid out. The park extends from the town centre to the Vienna Woods and has a rose garden and a memorial museum to Beethoven and Mozart. Today you can sample local wines in Baden's restaurants.

Schloss Hof **❸**

🚌 *Shuttle bus operated by Blaguss-Reisen Apr–Oct: Sat, Sun & hols. Book by phone or online. Tel 7982900.* **www**.blaguss.com ⏲ *Apr–Oct: 10am–6pm daily. Tel 02285 200000.* **www**.schlosshof.at

After extensive restoration, Schloss Hof is an appealing destination. In 1725 Prince Eugene made it his principal country seat and laid out the present formal garden. Extended a generation later under Empress Maria Theresa, the palace contains private and state rooms from both periods.

Schloss Esterházy, the 17th-century residence of the Esterházy princes

SIGHTS AT A GLANCE

Day Trips

KEY

🟦	City centre
🟨	Greater Vienna
🛬	Airport
═	Motorway
▬	Major road
═	Minor road

25 kilometres = 15 miles

Eisenstadt ❹

🚌 566 or 766 from Wien Mitte to Eisenstadt Domplatz. 💲 from Süd-bahnhof; change at Bruck an der Leitha. ℹ️ 02682 63384. **Schloss Esterházy Tel** 02682 6385412. ⬜ Jan–Mar & Nov–Dec: 9am–5pm Thu–Sun; Apr–Oct: 9am–5pm daily. 🎫 only. **Haydn Museum Tel** 02682 7193900. ⬜ Mar–Nov: 9am–5pm daily, Nov–Mar: by appt only. **Jewish Museum Tel** 02682 65145. ⬜ May–Oct: 10am–5pm Tue–Sun; Nov–Apr: by appt only (groups only).

To the southeast of Vienna, in Eisenstadt, is Schloss Esterházy, built for Prince Paul Esterházy in 1663–73. It contains the Haydnsaal, a great hall of state in which Joseph Haydn (see pp38–9) conducted the prince's orchestra. He lived nearby on Haydngasse and his house is now a museum. Also nearby is a Jewish Museum.

Rust and Lake Neusiedl ❺

🚌 566 or 766 from Eisenstadt; 666 from Wien Mitte. ℹ️ 02685 502.

Lake Neusiedl, part of which is in Hungary, is surrounded by reeds, the home of dozens of species of wild birds. The reeds are used locally for folk crafts from thatching to basketwork. Around the lake are several wine villages and resorts, of which the prettiest is the town of Rust. It is known for the storks which nest on its roofs and towers.

Mariazell ❻

🚌 552 via Baden or 1150 from Wien Mitte. 💲 from Westbahnhof, change at St Pölten to Mariazell alpine railway. ℹ️ 03882 2366. **Basilica** ⬜ 6am–8pm daily. 🎫 **Tel** 0388 22595 for tours. **Steam tram Tel** 0388 23014. ⬜ Jul–Sep: 10:30am–4:30pm Sat, Sun & hols.

The journey to Mariazell from St Pölten is by the Mariazell alpine railway. The town has long been the main Catholic pilgrim site of Central Europe, and a Gothic and Baroque basilica testifies to its religious significance. Inside the basilica, which was enlarged in the 17th century, there is a wealth of Baroque stucco, painting and decoration. The treasury also forms part of the church.

A cable car up the mountain leaves every 20 minutes from the town centre. An additional attraction is the world's oldest steam tram, built in 1884 and running between Mariazell railway station and a nearby lake.

River Trip from Krems to Melk ❼

See pp178–9.

View of Mariazell, an important Marian shrine since 1377

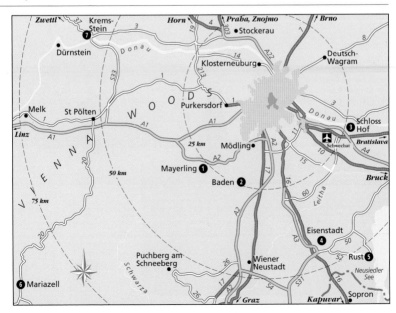

River Trip from Krems to Melk 🕖

Some 80 km (50 miles) west of Vienna is one of the most magnificent stretches of river scenery in Europe. Castles, churches and wine-producing villages rise up on either side of the Danube valley and breathtaking views unfold. Redolent with history (it has been settled for over 30,000 years), this stretch from Krems to Melk is called the Wachau. A river trip is the best way to take in the landmarks, either with one of the tours organized by Cityrama, Vienna Line, Vienna Sightseeing or DDSG Shipping *(see p251)*, or independently *(see box)*.

Wine-producing towns from Rossatz to Wösendorf

On the opposite bank to Dürnstein lies Rossatz ⑤, which has been making wine for centuries and was once a busy port. Findings of Neolithic and Roman remains testify to early settlement. In the 10th century it belonged to a Bavarian convent, but passed to the Babenbergs and became part of their

The perfectly-preserved medieval town of Dürnstein ④

Krems to Dürnstein

The beautiful Renaissance town of Stein has in modern times merged into one with Krems, which has a medieval centre ①. At the end of Steinerstrasse is the house of the Baroque artist Kremser Schmidt. Climb one of the narrow hillside streets and look across the Danube for a fine view of Göttweig Abbey ②, an excellent example of Austrian Baroque, and in the 17th century a centre of the Counter-Reformation. You can also see the small town of Mautern ③, which

developed from a 1st-century Roman fortification, and now boasts the gourmet restaurant Bacher in Südtirolerplatz.

Once on board, after about 8 km (5 miles) you will pass the perfectly-preserved medieval town of Dürnstein ④, with a Baroque church overlooked by the ruins of a castle. From 1192 to 1193, after his return from the Third Crusade, England's King Richard the Lionheart was held prisoner in the castle by Duke Leopold V of Babenberg *(see p23)*. He was released only on payment of a huge ransom. Dürnstein has conserved much of its medieval and Baroque character and has splendid river views and side streets leading to charming river walks. A separate visit is advisable if you want to see the town at leisure.

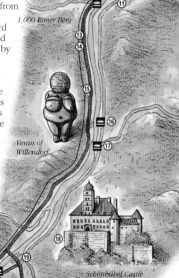

Vineyards at Weissenkirchen ⑥ ⑦ ⑧ ⑨ ⑩

Das Rote Tor ⑫ ⑪

1,000-Eimer Berg ⑬ ⑭

⑮

⑯ ⑰

Venus of Willendorf

⑱

Schönbühel Castle

⑲ ⑳

0 km		5
0 miles		3

KEY

⚓	River boat boarding point
🚉	Railway station
—	Railway line
≈	River
▬	Major road
▭	Minor road

The church at Weissenkirchen which was fortified to hold off the Turks ⑦

Austrian domain. The Renaissance castle and Gothic church were transformed to Baroque around 1700.

At Weissenkirchen ⑥ the church dates mainly from the 15th and 16th centuries. The town is also renowned for its wine, as are Joching ⑦ and Wösendorf ⑧.

Göttweig Abbey

The Benedictine abbey of Melk dominates the river and town ⑳

Spitz to Aggsbachdorf

Spitz ⑫ is another pretty wine town and was also a Protestant stronghold during the Reformation. It lies at the foot of the 1,000-Eimer Berg (1,000-Bucket Mountain), so called because it is claimed that in a good year the vine-clad hills can produce enough wine to fill 1,000 buckets.

Further on is a wall-like rocky precipice jutting out from the bank, the Teufelsmauer or Devil's Wall ⑬. It has given rise to a number of legends. One tells how the devil's grandmother wanted to stop pilgrims and crusaders by creating a dam. At Schwallenbach ⑭ the church was rebuilt after the Bohemians devastated the village in 1463. Although you cannot see it from the boat, you will pass very close to the village of Willendorf ⑮, famous for the prehistoric findings made nearby, including the statue and fertility symbol Venus of Willendorf (*see pp20 and 128*).

Aggstein ⑯ has a ruined castle high above the river. Georg Scheck von Wald, follower of Duke Albrecht I, rebuilt and enlarged the original castle in 1429. Legend has it that he called a rock, placed at the highest point of the castle, his rose garden. He would force his imprisoned enemies to leap to their deaths if the ransom he demanded failed to arrive. Aggsbachdorf ⑰ was settled by the Romans in the 2nd century and owned by the Kuenringer robber-barons during the Middle Ages.

Schönbühel Castle to Melk

The picturesque castle of Schönbühel ⑱ stands on a rocky outcrop overlooking the Danube. Although it has been on record since the 9th century, its present form dates from the early 19th century. Further

The ruined castle above the river at Aggstein ⑯

Churches and ruins

Clearly visible on top of a hill, the fortified Church of St Michael ⑨ was built between 1500 and 1523. An unusual architectural detail is the stone hares on its tower. Local folklore tells how, once, so much snow fell here that hares were able to leap onto the roof.

On the same side of the river is a ruined arch on a hill, Das Rote Tor ⑩, a fragment of a 14th-century gate through which the Swedes walked on their way to Spitz in 1645 during the 30 Years War (*see p25*). The town of Mitterarnsdorf ⑪ has Roman remains.

on, at the mouth of the 70-km long (43-mile) River Pielach ⑲, 30 Bronze Age tombs and the foundations of a Roman tower have been excavated.

The high point of the trip is the Benedictine abbey of Melk ⑳. The pretty town has Renaissance houses, romantic little streets, old towers and remnants of a city wall built in the Middle Ages. The Baroque abbey, where Umberto Eco's novel *The Name of the Rose* begins and ends, is a treasure trove of paintings, sculptures and decorative art. The great library contains 2,000 volumes from the 9th to the 15th centuries alone. The church has a magnificent organ, and skeletons dressed in luxurious materials inside glass coffins. Some of the Abbey's treasures are not on permanent view.

TIPS FOR INDEPENDENT TRAVELLERS

Starting points: Krems, Dürnstein, Melk or any river trip boarding point. River trip tickets are on sale at these points.
Getting there: Take the national network train from Franz-Josefs-Bahnhof to Krems or Dürnstein. For Melk, depart from Westbahnhof.
Stopping-off points: Dürnstein has restaurants and shops.
Melk Abbey Tel 02752 555232.
⏰ Palm Sunday–1st Sun after All Souls: 9am–4:30pm (May–Sep: 9am–5:30pm). 🎧 in English: 10:55am May–Oct.
Cycling: A cycle path runs along the Danube. Hire bikes at Krems, Melk, Spitz and Dürnstein train stations (reduction with train ticket), or from river trip boarding points. Take your passport for identification. www.stiftmelk.at

THREE GUIDED WALKS

Vienna is a comparatively small city, with several main attractions within easy walking distance of each other. All six sightseeing areas in this guide have a suggested short walk marked on a Street-by-Street map. Yet the city's suburbs are also worth exploring on foot. The following guided walks take you through some of the best walking areas in and around the city, all easily accessible by public transport. The first walk takes you through the town itself. Starting in the Stadtpark, it continues past the Karlskirche to the elegant Wagner Apartments and the colourful Naschmarkt on the Linke Wienzeile. Hietzing, on the western edge of the grounds of Schönbrunn

Makart statue *(p182)*

Palace, is our second walk. The former village's quiet streets are lined with an interesting mix of Biedermeier and Jugendstil villas. Towards the end of the walk is Schönbrunn Palace Park, with an area of woodland and the more formally planted Botanical Garden. The third walk takes you to the old wine village of Grinzing, with its many *Heurige*. The route goes through Heiligenstadt, where there are a number of buildings by well-known 20th-century architects. In addition to these walks, there are signposted routes through the Vienna Woods and the Prater, marked *Stadtwanderwege*. For details of these, phone or write to the Wiener Fremdenverkehrsamt *(see p238)*.

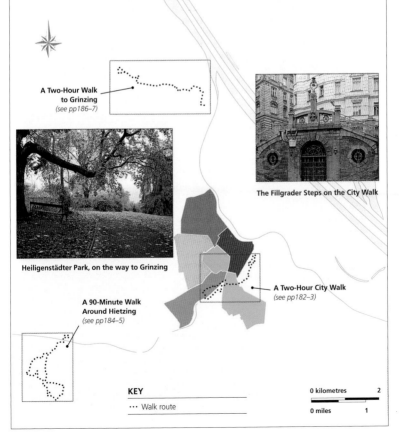

A Two-Hour Walk to Grinzing
(see pp186–7)

The Fillgrader Steps on the City Walk

Heiligenstädter Park, on the way to Grinzing

A Two-Hour City Walk
(see pp182–3)

A 90-Minute Walk Around Hietzing
(see pp184–5)

KEY

··· Walk route

0 kilometres   2

0 miles   1

◁ **Schönbrunn Palace Park** *(see p185)*

A Two-Hour City Walk

This walk skirts the southwestern perimeter of the inner city, following part of the course of the River Wien. It begins with a leisurely stroll through the Stadtpark, which was laid out in English landscape style when the Ringstrasse was built (*see p32*). Continuing past Schwarzenbergplatz and Karlsplatz through the lively Naschmarkt, it ends with a glance at some masterpieces of Jugendstil architecture on the Linke Wienzeile.

The Stadtpark

Begin at the entrance to the Stadtpark opposite Weihburggasse. Almost facing you is an impressive side entrance ① with sculpted portals which was designed between 1857 and 1862.

On the city side, the park contains many monuments to musicians and artists. The first is the gilded statue of Johann Strauss II (*see p39*) playing his violin (1921) ②. Go left past this monument, and left again, into a paved circular seating area with a fountain dedicated to the Sprite of the Danube ③. Turn right out of this area and you come to an iron bridge across the River Wien, from the middle of which you get a view of the embankments ④.

Walk back to the nearby lake ⑤. On its southern side a statue of the Viennese landscape painter Emil Jakob Schindler (1895) ⑥ sits in the bushes. Follow the path until

Jugendstil portal in the Stadtpark, built in 1903–4 as part of the flood defences along the river ⑪

it peters out into a culvert then go left across the bridge. Turn left again until you come to a monument to Franz Schubert (1872) by Karl Kundmann ⑦. Take the path past the lake and turn right at the clock-tower. The painter Hans Makart, who dominated the visual arts in Vienna in the 1870s and 1880s, strikes a rhetorical pose in Viktor Tilgner's 1898 statue ⑧. Walk on past the entrance to the park. On the right is the

bust of Franz Lehár, composer of *The Merry Widow* ⑨. Walk towards the Kursalon ⑩, which opened for concerts, balls and waltzes in the 1860s. Continue past the Kursalon, leaving the park through one of the Jugendstil portals (*see p57*) ⑪.

No. 38 Linke Wienzeile ㉑

Fillgrader Steps

[map of walking route with labelled streets: FILLGRADER GASSE, GUMPENDORFER STRASSE, KÖSTLERGASSE, STIEGENGASSE, LAIMGRUBENGASSE, LEHARGASSE, MILLÖCKERGASSE, WIENZEILE, LINKE WIENZEILE, RECHTE WIENZEILE, HEUMÜHL, KETTENBRÜCKENGASSE, FRANZENGASSE, SCHLEIFMÜHLGASSE, OPERNGASSE, WIEDNER HAUPTSTRASSE, PANIGL..., Karlsplatz Ⓤ, Kettenbrücken-gasse Ⓤ; with numbered stops ⑳ ㉑ ㉒ ㉓ ㉔ ㉕ ㉖]

Statue of Johannes Brahms (1908) by Rudolf Weyr, in the Ressel Park ⑯

JOHANNES BRAHMS

TIPS FOR WALKERS

Starting point: Weihburggasse Tram 2 (on Parkring).
Length: 3 km (1½ miles).
Getting there: Tram 2, which circulates around the Ringstrasse and Franz-Josefs-Kai; or Stubentor U-bahn, then walk.
Stopping-off points: The Kursalon in the Stadtpark serves tea, coffee and cakes on the terrace and has a beer garden to one side. There are also many benches where you can rest. There are cafés in Ressel Park and the Naschmarkt; towards the end of the walk you will find Café Sperl on Gumpendorfer Strasse.

Schwarzenbergplatz

Walk straight ahead, crossing the road into Lothringerstrasse. A monument to Beethoven (1880), showing him surrounded by figures alluding to the Ninth Symphony, stands on the right ⑫. Cross the road to the Konzerthaus (1912–13), home to the Vienna Symphony Orchestra *(see p228)* ⑬.

Cross the busy intersection to get a striking vista of Schwarzenbergplatz to your left, at the end of which is a fountain. It was erected in 1873 to celebrate the city's supply of pure drinking water which comes from the mountains. Behind it is the Memorial to the Red Army which liberated Austria in 1945 ⑭.

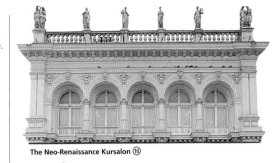

The Neo-Renaissance Kursalon ⑩

(map with labels: Stubentor, Landstrasse (Wien Mitte), PARKRING, WIEN FLUSS, SCHUBERTRING, KÄRNTNER RING, KÄRNTNER RING, PRINZ EUGEN STRASSE, LOTHRINGERSTR., KÖNIG, Stadtpark, AM HEUMARKT, Kursalon, Monument to Beethoven, Brahms Statue, KARLSPLATZ, RENNWEG, GUSSHAUSSTRASSE, ARGENTINIERSTRASSE, SCHWINDGASSE)

```
0 metres        250
0 yards         250
```

KEY

• • • Walk route

☆ Good viewing point

Ⓤ U-Bahn station

Ressel Park

Continue along Lothringerstrasse, pass the Wien Museum Karlsplatz *(see p146)* ⑮, into Ressel Park. On the left is a statue of Brahms with his muse at his feet (1908) by Rudolf Weyr ⑯. Look left past Brahms to the Karlskirche *(see pp148–9)* ⑰. Go on, noting Otto Wagner's pavilions *(see p146)* at road level ⑱. Pass the Neo-Classical Technical High School ⑲ to leave the park. Cross Wiedner Hauptstrasse, go straight ahead then left into Operngasse, crossing the road. Walk through Bärenmühlendurch-gang passage in the building facing you and cross the road into the Naschmarkt ⑳.

Naschmarkt

A lively food market *(see p138)*, originally held in the Karlsplatz, moved here after this part of the river was paved over in the late 19th century. It is a good vantage point from which to admire the elegant 19th-century buildings along the left bank, or Linke Wienzeile. Leave the

Papageno Gate of the Theater an der Wien ㉕

market and cross the road to look at Otto Wagner's Apartments *(see p139)* with golden medallions by Kolo Moser at No. 38 ㉑, and the Majolika-haus at No. 40, so called because of its floral tiles ㉒. As you turn into Köstlergasse alongside No. 38 it is worth pausing to admire the entrance.

Confession box, Karlskirche ⑰

Gumpendorfer Strasse

Turn right at the end of Köstlergasse and walk up Gumpendorfer Strasse. Look left up Fillgradergasse for a glimpse of the Fillgrader Steps ㉓. Continue on to the historic Café Sperl *(see p58)*, once the haunt of the composer Lehár ㉔. Go on and turn right into Millöckergasse to see the famous Papageno Gate of the Theater an der Wien *(see p138)* ㉕. The sculpture above the entrance shows the theatre's first owner, Emanuel Schikaneder, in the character of Papageno from Mozart's *The Magic Flute*. Continue down Millöckergasse to the Linke Wienzeile. Bear left, passing the Secession Building *(see p138)* ㉖, and go on to Karlsplatz U-Bahn.

A 90-Minute Walk Around Hietzing

The former village of Hietzing runs along the western edge of the extensive grounds of Schönbrunn Palace (see p172–5). In Maria Theresa's time it was a fashionable area where the nobility went to spend their summers; later it became a suburb for the wealthy middle classes. The quiet streets contain a marvellous mix of Biedermeier and Jugendstil villas, while the square around the parish church retains an intimate small-town atmosphere.

From the station to Am Platz
Take the Hadikgasse exit from Hietzing U-Bahn ① and cross the tram tracks and road to Kennedybrücke. Turn right down Hadikgasse and after a minute you arrive at Otto-Wagner-Hofpavillon Hietzing (see p171) ②, a former station designed for the use of the imperial family when they were at Schönbrunn. Retrace

The Kaiserstöckl opposite the Park Hotel, now a post office ⑥

your steps to the U-Bahn and cross the road into Hietzinger Hauptstrasse. Notice the attic of No. 6 with cherubs hugging the columns. The building dates from 1901–2, but the lower storey has been altered to accommodate shops ③. On your left through the railings are long avenues of trees at

the side of Schönbrunn ④. Just across the road is the Park Hotel, its ochre façade echoing that of the palace buildings ⑤. Facing it is the Kaiserstöckl (1770) or Emperor's Pavilion ⑥. Today it is a post office, but it used to be the holiday venue of Maria Theresa's foreign ministers. Continue to Am Platz with its plague column dating from 1730 ⑦. Next door to this is the parish church of Maria Geburt ⑧, originally built in the 13th century, and remodelled in the 17th century. The Baroque interior contains altars by the sculptor Matthias Steindl and ceiling frescoes by Georg Greiner. The church was used by Maria Theresa when she was in residence at Schönbrunn, and her box can be seen in the right-hand wall of the choir. In front of the church stands a statue of Franz Joseph's brother

Façade of the Park Hotel ⑤

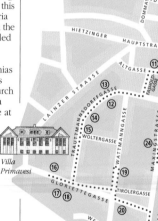

Villa Primavesi

0 metres   250

0 yards   250

KEY

· · · Walk route

Ⓤ U-Bahn station

Elaborate altar by Matthias Steindl in the Maria Geburt Kirche ⑧

TIPS FOR WALKERS

Starting point: *Hietzing U-Bahn.*
Length: *5 km (3 miles).*
Getting there: *the U4 and Tram 58 go to Hietzing.*
Note: *On Sundays you may need to retrace your steps a short distance if the Maxing Gate is locked.*
Stopping-off points: *the BAWAG café in Hietzing's Am Platz is a pleasant place to stop for a coffee.*
Bezirksmuseum Hietzing
🕐 *2–6pm Wed, 2–5pm Sat.*
🔒 *Jul–Aug.* ***Schönbrunn Palace and Park*** *(see pp172–5).*
Villa Primavesi 🔒 *to public.*

Maximilian, the Emperor of Mexico who was executed in 1867 ⑨. Nearby is a Neo-Classical building housing the Bezirksmuseum Hietzing ⑩, and outside the museum is Vienna's last gas lamp.

Trauttmansdorffgasse and Gloriettegasse

Turn left into Maxingstrasse, named after Maximilian, then right into Altgasse. Almost facing Fasholdgasse is an old *Heuriger*, a Biedermeier building with ochre walls ⑪.

Detail from the majolica façade of the Lebkuchenhaus ⑲

across the road, at No. 27, is the house where the composer Alban Berg (*see p39*) once lived ⑬. Nos. 48 and 50 are contrasting examples of Viennese turn-of-the-century architecture ⑭. More examples of Biedermeier style can be seen at Nos. 54 and 56 ⑮.

At the end of the road, turn right into Gloriettegasse. On the right at Nos. 14 and 16 is a villa with sculpted figures in the pediments, built in 1913–15 by Josef Hoffmann for the financier Robert Primavesi ⑯. Note the monumental sculpted figures resting in the pediments.

Cross the road to pass a terrace of Biedermeier houses – Nos. 38 and 40 have lunettes above the windows ⑰. No. 21 is the Villa Schopp, designed by Friedrich Ohmann in 1901–2 ⑱. Turn left down Wattmanngasse to see No. 29, the extraordinary Lebkuchenhaus (Gingerbread House) ⑲, so-called because of its dark brown decoration in majolica. It was built in 1914 to designs by a pupil of Otto Wagner (*see pp54–7*). Turn back into Gloriettegasse. At its southern junction with Wattmanngasse, at No. 9, is the

house that belonged to Katharina Schratt, the actress and confidante of Emperor Franz Joseph during his later years. It is said that the Emperor was in the habit of arriving here for breakfast ⑳.

Maxing Park and Schönbrunn Park

Walk to the end of Gloriettegasse, then turn right up Maxingstrasse and cross the road at Maxing Park. If you would like to add another half hour to the walk, Hietzing cemetery, a little further up the hill, contains the graves of Otto Wagner, Gustav Klimt, Kolo Moser and Franz Grillparzer, among others. Alternatively, enter Maxing Park ㉑ and follow the main path upwards towards the right. At the top, go through the gates marked *Zum Tiergarten Schönbrunn*, passing the forestry research institute on your left. Although you are actually in the grounds of Schönbrunn, this heavily wooded area feels very remote from the formal gardens and you may catch a glimpse of deer. At the crossroads in the path turn left, signposted to the Botanical Garden. You soon arrive at a little wooden hut, which was Crown Prince Rudolf's playhouse ㉒.

The path eventually leads to the formally planted Botanical Garden ㉓, which was laid out in 1848 under Emperor Franz I. Take the path through the garden, keeping to the boundary wall with Hietzing. Exit into Maxingstrasse (this gate may be locked on Sundays) and continue north. At No. 18 is the house where Johann Strauss II wrote *Die Fledermaus* in 1874 ㉔. Carry on north along Maxingstrasse and retrace your steps to Hietzing U-Bahn.

Plaque on No. 50 Trauttmansdorffgasse ⑭

Turn down Fasholdgasse into Trauttmansdorffgasse, a street full of interesting houses. No. 40 is a beautifully-restored, long and low Biedermeier villa ⑫, while

Sculpted figure in a pediment of the Villa Primavesi ⑯

A Two-Hour Walk to Grinzing

This walk through part of Vienna's 19th district begins at the site of one of the most important monuments of 20th-century Vienna, the public housing development of the Karl Marx Hof. It then takes you through a pretty 19th-century park to the old wine village of Grinzing. Although the village suffered destruction at the hands of the Turks in 1529 and 1683 and from Napoleon's army in 1809, and is now feeling the effects of modern tourism, its pretty main street preserves its charm.

Façade of the 16th-century Reinprecht *Heuriger* ⑮

Karl Marx Hof to Heiligenstädter Park

Facing you as you step out of Heiligenstadt station is the long ochre, terracotta and mauve façade of the Karl Marx Hof (*see p161*), a huge housing project designed by the city architect Karl Ehn and built from 1927 to 1930 during the Red Vienna period ①. It sprawls for 1.2 km (³/₄ mile) and has 1,265 flats.

Cross the road and pass through one of the four arches facing you into 12 Februar Platz to see the main façade from the other side. On the keystone of each arch stands a large figure sculpture by Joseph Riedl (1928) ②. Continue through the square, past a statue (1928)

Figure on the Karl Marx Hof ①

by Otto Hofner of a man sowing seeds ③, and you come to Heiligenstädter Strasse. Turn right, cross the road at the second pedestrian crossing and walk through the square opening in the building facing you. Go up the steps and take the path on the left into Heiligenstädter Park. When you come to a fork, take the left path that winds up a hill, going through woods. Turn right at the top into the formal part of the park ④. From here, you get a good view of the vine-clad slopes of the Kahlenberg ⑤.

Steinfeldgasse

Take the second small path on the right, which descends gradually into Steinfeldgasse, where there is a cluster of houses built by the Secessionist

designer Josef Hoffmann. The first one you come to is the Villa Moser-Moll at Nos. 6–8, designed for Carl Moll and Kolo Moser ⑥. Next to it is the Villa Spitzer ⑦, then the more classical Villa Ast, built in 1909–11 ⑧. Where Steinfeldgasse meets Wollergasse is the Villa Henneberg of 1901 ⑨, and at No. 10 Wollergasse ⑩ is the Moll House II of 1906–7. Its black and white details are charming.

Steinfeldgasse to Grinzinger Strasse

At the point where Steinfeldgasse and Wollergasse meet, there is a path leading down through some woods. Follow this and descend the steps to the Church of St Michael, Heiligenstadt ⑪, which has striking

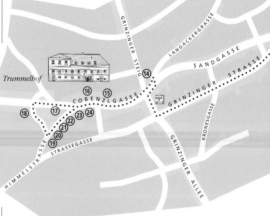
Lawns and trees in the Heiligenstädter Park ④

modern stained-glass windows. Walk past the church, cross Hohe Warte and go up Grinzinger Strasse. You quickly arrive at No. 70, the house where Albert Einstein stayed from 1927 to 1931 ⑫. On the same side of the road is No. 64, the late 18th-century house where Beethoven and the Viennese playwright Franz Grillparzer lodged during the summer of 1808 while Beethoven was composing the Pastoral Symphony ⑬.

Continue up Grinzinger Strasse, passing a number of attractive Biedermeier houses, until you arrive at Grinzinger

Allee. Turn right past a series of wine gardens and immediately right again to get a quick glimpse of the upper part of Sandgasse, where there are a number of more authentic *Heurige* ⑭.

Grinzing

Turning back on yourself and towards the centre of Grinzing, ascend Cobenzlgasse, the upper fork of Grinzing's main street. The Reinprecht *Heuriger* at No. 22 Cobenzlgasse is a 16th-century house, the façade of

Cobenzlgasse, Grinzing's main street

0 metres   500

0 yards   500

Villa Spitzer

No. 64 Grinzinger Strasse

Courtyard at the Passauer Hof, an old wine press house ⑰

KEY

• • • Walk route

☆ Good viewing point

🚋 Tram terminus

Ⓤ U-Bahn station

Ⓢ Schnellbahn station

═ Railway line

TIPS FOR WALKERS

Starting point: Heiligenstadt station.
Length: 3.5 km (2 miles).
Getting there: Heiligenstadt station is served by U-Bahn lines U4 and U6, trains S40 and S45 and buses 10A, 11A, 38A and 39A. Tram D stops on Heiligenstädter Strasse.
Stopping-off points: There are numerous Heurige (usually open from 4pm), coffee shops and restaurants in Grinzing. Avoid the larger Heurige – the smaller ones sell their own wine. Those at the top of Sandgasse are good.

which has a tablet commemorating the composer Robert Stolz ⑮. No. 30 Cobenzlgasse is the Baroque Trummelhof, standing on the site of an 1835 brewery ⑯. Further up on the left, at No. 9, is the Passauer Hof, an old wine press house that contains fragments of a far older, Romanesque building ⑰. On the corner of Cobenzlgasse and Feilergasse is the Altes Presshaus, whose cellar contains an old wine press ⑱.

Turn left into Feilergasse, and you soon come face to face with the impressive white Jugendstil façade of

Nos. 41–3 Himmelstrasse ⑲. Continue down Himmelstrasse to No. 35, another *Heuriger*, Das Alte Haus, which has a charming plaque of the Virgin Mary above its door ⑳. There is a another such painting at No. 31, which shows a holy man carrying various items ㉑. No. 29 ㉒ is another *Heuriger* with a tablet to Sepp Fellner, a *Schrammel* musician *(see p39)* described as "The Schubert of Grinzing". Ironically, at No. 25, a grand building with shields above the doorway, there is a memorial to the real Schubert, described as "The Prince of Song, who loved to tarry in Grinzing" ㉓. Grinzing also has an attractive late Gothic church with a copper cupola and much-restored interior ㉔. Continue down the road to the tram terminus, where the No. 38 tram goes back to town.

Plaque of a holy man on the façade of No. 31 Himmelstrasse ㉑

View down Kohl Markt towards Hofburg ▷

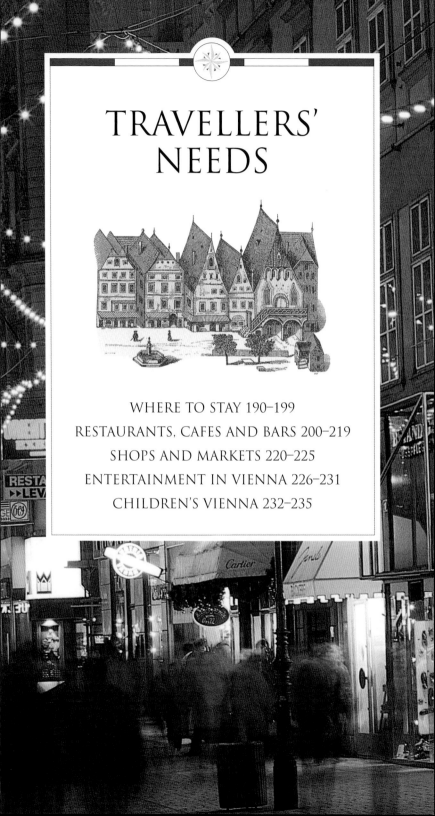

TRAVELLERS' NEEDS

WHERE TO STAY

With more than 500 hotels and pensions, Vienna offers accommodation to suit everyone. From palaces to simple lodgings, it has some of the grandest European city hotels as well as numerous small boarding-houses and self-catering establishments. Hotels are generally larger and better equipped (some also have business facilities), and pensions are always bed and breakfast establishments. Included in this guide is a selection of accommodation to suit all tastes and budgets. Hotels are listed by area and in order of price category. For more details of facilities and for a short description, turn to the listings on pages 194-199. For further types of accommodation available in and on the outskirts of Vienna, see pages 192-193.

Baroque façade of the Mailberger Hof on Annagasse (see p195)

WHERE TO LOOK

One of the thrills of visiting Vienna is that you can stay grandly or cheaply right in the city centre. Almost all of the famous hotels – the Sacher, Bristol, Imperial (see Listings pp194-199) – are on or just off the Ringstrasse, as are most of the large chain hotels. In the city centre lie a number of comfortable hotels and pensions. Most are on fairly quiet side streets. The Townhall and Museum Quarter has some good small hotels and offers affordable lodgings for budget travellers. A few hotels in, or near, wine villages to the north (see p199) are also listed. The **Österreich Werbung** (Austrian Tourist Board) publishes information on over 500 hotels and pensions.

HOTEL PRICES

Accommodation in Vienna can be expensive. Many hotels and pensions in prime locations are highly priced. However, you can expect to pay approximately a fifth to a quarter less for a room in an establishment just outside the Ringstrasse, and less still if you stay further afield.

Most facilities do have rooms at a variety of prices, depending on their size, aspect and, in pensions, whether they have en suite bathrooms. Single rooms are about three-quarters the cost of double rooms. Some places will put an extra bed in the room on request, which can cost less than the price of a single room. Other hotels offer family or triple-bedded rooms.

Vienna's low season is from November-March (excluding Christmas and New Year) and July-August. Few hotels lower prices in summer, although half have winter rates up to

Penthouse suite No. 663 in the Bristol Hotel (see p199)

25% lower. Most of the large chain hotels reduce the room tariff during quiet periods and offer weekend specials.

Out of season, it is worth asking for a discount for payment in cash. Many places offer discounts for longer stays, and it's possible to find packages such as three nights for the price of two.

The **Österreich Werbung** has international offices and provides details of tour operators that offer all-inclusive Vienna packages.

Opulent lobby of the Imperial Hotel (see p199)

HIDDEN EXTRAS

Apart from most five-star hotels, breakfast is included in the tariff. Rates will always include taxes such as VAT (or MWSt). Beware if changing money at your hotel: the official exchange rate could be as much as 10% better.

Parking fees can also mount up. Street parking within the Ringstrasse is restricted to 90 minutes and there are no private garages. Pensions generally leave you to your own devices to find an underground car park, but some hotels have designated spaces. At some hotels a reasonable amount is charged for parking, but at others it can be very expensive. Outlying districts do not have such stringent street parking restrictions, and garage parking is cheaper.

Try to avoid making phone calls from your room. Most hotels charge a flat rate, even though the official rate varies from day-time to night-time and week-days to weekends. The surcharge may be up to three and a half times the standard rate, so it is worth using a public telephone.

Every other Viennese on the street seems to have a four-legged friend, so many of the hotels allow dogs in the rooms. There may be a charge for this.

HOW TO BOOK

Easter, May, June, September, October, Christmas and New Year are considered peak season during which accommodation may be fully booked as early as two months in advance.

Making direct hotel reservations are easy, since many hotel personnel speak English. If you cancel once the booking is made, you may be charged for the room. Check in advance. If arriving after 6pm, let the hotel know or they may re-let your room to someone else.

The **Wiener Tourismusverband** (Vienna Tourist Board) on the corner of Albertinaplatz,

Statue in the reception area of the Hotel Regina *(see p197)*

Sign of a well-known Viennese hotel

Tegethoffstrasse and Meysedergasse *(see p239)*, can reserve hotel rooms in advance. It is also possible to book accommodations by calling the Tourist Board at 24555 or online by visiting www.wien.info. Otherwise, contact the hotel directly. If the hotel accepts credit cards, a phone call to book will suffice; if not, you may have to send booking confirmation to the hotel in writing. Different hotels have different procedures.

FACILITIES

Hotels are rated one to five stars, pensions on a four-star system; a three-star hotel corresponds to a four-star pension. The rating also attempts to cover the quality and ambience of the hotel or

pension. Five-star hotels are upscale and well-run. Many three- and four-star hotels refer to themselves as *Palais*, which equates to a fine town house. At the cheaper end of the scale, small pensions above two stars are often more salubrious than cheap hotels. One- or two-star hotels and pensions tend to cater for travellers on a budget and are generally less pleasant.

Usually, only the top hotels have a full range of public rooms; restaurant, bar, coffee shop and sitting room. In many smaller establishments, the lounge is little more than an extension of the reception. Even if there is no bar, you may find that drinks are served. Almost all hotels and pensions have a breakfast room. While low-priced pensions provide continental breakfast, most hotels offer a hot and cold breakfast buffet.

The Anna Sacher restaurant at the Hotel Sacher *(see p198)*

Because many hotels occupy old buildings, no two bedrooms are the same. Rooms almost always have a phone, though not necessarily a television. Mid-range hotel rooms often have cable TV, mini-bar and a bathroom with a shower or bathtub. Many Viennese buildings back onto quiet courtyards so you can select a peaceful room, or one with a view.

In the 19th century there was a restriction on building heights. To circumvent the regulation, lower floors were (and still are) called *Hochparterre* and *Mezzanin*. Consequently, you may find that the "first floor" is up three stair flights. Additionally, in pensions a communal lift serves the whole building.

The quality of service in the best luxury hotels is as good as anywhere in the world. Wherever you stay, it could be well worth befriending the concierge (by perhaps giving him or her a tip early on in your stay). He or she can be invaluable in directing you to interesting restaurants and bars, and conjuring out of thin air a ticket to the Winter Riding School or a seat at the opera when they have been sold out for months. In general, most of the hotel staff speak English, but the standard of service is variable.

TRAVELLING WITH CHILDREN

Almost all hotels and pensions have cots (some charge) and can arrange a babysitter. Some may charge the same rate for putting a child's bed in the parents' room as they would for an adult's bed. Usually only the larger hotels allow children under various ages to stay free in their parents' room.

DISABLED TRAVELLERS

Information concerning wheelchair access to hotels relies on the individual hotel's assessment of their suitability and it is advisable to check before travelling. The **Wiener Tourismusverband** publishes a detailed leaflet.

HOSTELS

Youth hostels are available in Vienna. The **Wiener Tourismusverband's** youth hostel and camping brochure lists their facilities. Those with better facilities cost around €10–€15 per night including breakfast. Most hostels expect residents to be in by midnight. An International Youth Hostel Federation membership card is required, which can be obtained beforehand or at the hostel. Contact **Österreichischer Jugendherbergsverband** for more information.

SAISONHOTELS

Annually from 1 July to 30 September, two dozen students' hostels become Saisonhotels or seasonal hotels, rated on a scale of one to three stars. At the three-star level expect fairly decent rooms. You may make enquiries at any time of the year at two of the main chains, **Academia Hotels** and **Rosen-Hotel**. Try to reserve well in advance and expect to pay up to €75 for a double room in one of the better places.

CAMPING

Five well-equipped campsites can be found within a radius of 8-15 km (5-9 miles) from the city centre. Most campsites have kitchen facilities; some have a supermarket. For additional camping information, contact the **Wiener Tourismusverband**, **Camping** und **Caravaning Club**

The handsome yellow exterior of the Hotel Josefshof *(see p198)*

Austria, and **Österreichischer Camping Club**. **Wiener Tourismusverband** also produces a camping and youth hostel brochure that provides more details on these sites.

SELF-CATERING

For those who are keen to "go it alone" there are limited opportunities for self-catering in the city. **Pego**, a company that rents homes throughout Austria, has two apartment blocks and a range of flats spread in and around the city; their brochure will give you all the details. You can book by telephone, by fax or in writing. Some apartments have a combined living and sleeping space and most also have a television and telephone. Expect to pay less per night than the price of a pension.

STAYING IN PRIVATE HOMES

It is possible to book a stay in a private home through the **Wiener Tourismusverband**, but the booking has to be made in person. **Mitwohnzentrale**, a private company, offers the same service. Normally you need to stay a few nights and should expect to pay around €36 per person per night.

CHAIN HOTELS

Chain hotels are mostly geared towards business people; rates usually vary according to their level of occupancy, rather than the season. Familiar names include the **Inter-Continental Wien** (*see p199*), **K&K** (*see p195*) and the **Vienna Marriott** (*see p196*) as well as some others listed on pages 194–199.

View of a campsite at No. 40 Hüttelbergstrasse

DIRECTORY

INFORMATION

Österreich Werbung
Margaretenstrasse 1,
A-1040. **Map** 4 D2.
Tel 0810101818.
Fax 5886620.
www.austria.info

Wiener Tourismusverband
Corner of Albertinaplatz,
Tegetthoffstrasse and
Meysedergasse, A-1010.
Map 4 D1 & 6 C4.
Tel 24555. **Fax** 24555-666.
www.wien.info

SAISONHOTELS

Academia Hotels
Pfeilgasse 3a, A-1080.
Map 1 A5. **Tel** 4017655.
Fax 4017620. **www**.
academiahotels.at

Rosen-Hotel
Schelleingasse 36, A-1040.
Map 4 E4. **Tel** 501520.
Fax 50152709.
www.rosenhotels.com

YOUTH HOSTELS

Österreichischer Jugendherbergs-verband
Gonzagagasse 22, A-1010.

Map 2 D4. **Tel** 5335353.
Fax 533535350.
www.oejhv.or.at

CAMPING

Camping und Caravaning Club Austria
Donaustadtstrasse 34,
A-1120. **Tel** 0501232222.
Fax 0501232223.
www.cca-camping.at

Österreichischer Camping Club
Schubertring 1–3, A-1010.
Map 4 E2 & 6 D5.
Tel 7136151.
Fax 711992754.
www.campingclub.at

SELF-CATERING

Pego
Rathausgasse 11, A-6700
Bludenz. *Tel* 05552
65666. **Fax** 05552
656665. **www**.pego.at

PRIVATE HOMES

Mitwohnzentrale
Westbahnstrasse 19,
A-1070. **Map** 3 A2.
Tel 4026061.
Fax 4026061111.

CHAIN HOTELS

Austria Hotels Hotel de France
Schottenring 3, A-1010.
Map 2 D4. **Tel** 313680.
Fax 3195969.
www.hoteldefrance.at

Austria Trend Park-hotel Schönbrunn
Hietzinger Hauptstrasse
10–20, A-1131. **Tel** 87804.
Fax 878043220.
www.austria-trend.at

Clima Cityhotel
Theresianumg 21a,
A-1040. **Map** 4 E4.
Tel 5051696. **Fax** 5043552.
www.climacity-hotel.com

Hilton Vienna
Am Stadtpark, A-1030.
Tel 717000. **Fax** 7130691.
www.hilton.com

Hotel Am Konzerthaus
Am Heumarkt 35–37,
A-1030. **Tel** 716160.
Fax 71616844.
www.accorhotels.com

Hotel Ibis Wien Mariahilf
Mariahilfer Gürtel 22–24,
A-1060. **Tel** 59998. **Fax** 597
9090. **www**.ibishotel.com

Hotel Novotel City
Aspernbrückenstrasse 1,
A-1020. **Tel** 903030.
Fax 90303555.

The Imperial Riding School Vienna, A Renaissance Hotel
Ungargasse 60, A-1030.
Map 4 F1. **Tel** 711750.
Fax 711758143.
www.imperial
renaissance.com

Johann Strauss
Favoritenstrasse 12,
A-1040. **Map** 4 D3.
Tel 5057624.
Fax 5057628. **www**.
hotel-johann-strauss.at

Radisson Blu Palais Hotel
Parkring 16, A-1010. **Map**
4 E1 & 6 E4. **Tel** 515170.
Fax 5122216.
www.radissonblu.com/
palaishotel-vienna

Renaissance Hotel Wien
Ullmannstrasse 71, A-1150.
Tel 89102. **Fax** 89102300.
www.renaissancewien.
com

Choosing a Hotel

The hotels listed here have been selected across a wide price range for their good value, facilities and location. All areas and price categories are covered, and there is additional information to help you choose. Under each area, hotels are listed in alphabetical order within each price category. For map references, *see pp262–5.*

PRICE CATEGORIES
Price categories for a double room with bathroom per night, including tax and service
€ Under €75
€€ €75–110
€€€ €110–145
€€€€ €145–200
€€€€€ over €200

STEPHANSDOM QUARTER

Post
Fleischmarkt 24, 1010 **Tel** *515 83 0* **Fax** *515 83 80 8* **Rooms** *107*   **€€**   **Map** *2 E5, 6 D2*

Located on the site of a former inn patronized by Mozart, Richard Wagner and Friedrich Nietzsche, this traditional hotel has rooms in contemporary style. There are also business rooms with broadband Internet access, and a restaurant/café. Wheelchair accessible. **www.hotel-post-wien.at**

Alma Boutique Hotel
Hafnersteig 7, 1010 **Tel** *533 29 61* **Fax** *533 29 61 81* **Rooms** *26*   **€€€**   **Map** *2 E5, 6 E2*

Located on a quiet, cobbled side street just within the Stephansdom Quarter, this stylish Art Nouveau hotel is fitted with modern amenities. All rooms are luxurious with contemporary decor, and each has a whirlpool bath. Close to the heart of Vienna with all major sights within walking distance. **www.hotel-alma.com**

Am Schubertring
Schubertring 11, 1010 **Tel** *717 02 0* **Fax** *713 99 66* **Rooms** *36*   **€€€**   **Map** *2 F5, 6 D5*

This Ringstrasse-style building contains one of the few Jugendstil hotels in the city. The bedrooms have thick carpets and high-quality reproduction furniture. Some bedrooms are furnished in Jugendstil fashion with dark wood, others in lighter Biedermeier style. Quiet rooms at the back are available. Pets are permitted. **www.schubertring.at**

Austria
Fleischmarkt 20, 1010 **Tel** *515 23* **Fax** *515 23 506* **Rooms** *46*   **€€€**   **Map** *2 E4, 6 D2*

Up a cul-de-sac and close to the Old University is this roomy hotel with high ceilings. A plus point is that it is extremely quiet. Downstairs are a few small sitting rooms and a breakfast room with a fountain. The bedrooms are spacious and have modern furniture and decent, old-fashioned bathrooms. **www.hotelaustria-wien.at**

Domizil
Schulerstrasse 14, 1010 **Tel** *513 31 99 0* **Fax** *512 34 84* **Rooms** *40*   **€€€**   **Map** *2 E5, 6 D3*

Located in central Vienna, near shops, restaurants and a casino, this is a traditional Viennese hotel. Room amenities include a TV, telephone, mini-bar, and in-room safe. A bar is also on site and bicycles are for rent. The staff is friendly and accommodating. Pets are permitted. Wheelchair accessible. **www.hoteldomizil.at**

Hotel Schweizerhof
Bauernmarkt 22, 1010 **Tel** *533 19 31* **Fax** *533 02 14* **Rooms** *55*   **€€€**   **Map** *6 D2*

This family-run hotel, close to St Stephen's Cathedral, aims to spoil its guests with first class service. The friendly staff will organise concert and opera tickets, city tours, restaurant reservations and car rentals, and children under 16 stay free of charge in a room with their parents. **www.schweizerhof.at**

Hotel Tigra
Tiefer Graben 14-20, 1010 **Tel** *533 96 41 0* **Fax** *533 96 45* **Rooms** *79*   **€€€**   **Map** *2 D5, 5 C2*

Located close to Stephansdom, this hotel is located in a historic building which once housed Mozart, as a plaque on the building makes clear. The rooms, however, have been completely modernized. Pets are permitted. Children under the age of 12 can stay for free when accompanied by two adults. **www.hotel-tigra.at**

Kärntnerhof
Grashofgasse 4, 1011 **Tel** *512 19 23* **Fax** *513 22 28 39* **Rooms** *43*   **€€€**   **Map** *2 E5, 6 E3*

A few cafés adjoin this well-run hotel in a cul-de-sac. A gate at the end leads to the lovely Heiligenkreuzerhof where you can park a car. The 19th-century building's best feature behind its imposing façade is a fine Art Deco lift, enclosed within a spiral staircase. Breakfast is served in rustic, beamed surroundings. **www.kartnerhof.com**

Marc Aurel
Marc-Aurel Strasse 8, 1010 **Tel** *533 36 40 0* **Fax** *533 00 78* **Rooms** *31*   **€€€**   **Map** *2 E5, 6 D2*

This smaller hotel offers simple but comfortable rooms as well as an on-site restaurant, café and, in the summer, a garden to dine in. All the rooms can be rented monthly at a discount price. Rooms with a kitchenette are also available. Pets are permitted. Wheelchair accessible. **www.hotel-marcaurel.com**

Key to Symbols *See back cover flap*

Zur Wiener Staatsoper
€€€

Krugerstrasse 11, 1010 **Tel** *513 12 74* **Fax** *513 12 74 15* **Rooms** *22*   **Map** *4 E1, 6 D5*

A tall, thin 19th-century building on a pedestrian street off Kärntner Strasse houses this small hotel. Its façade is great fun, with caryatids over the porch and faces peering out of the plaster-work above. Inside, the breakfast room, bedrooms and bathrooms (all with showers) are squeezed into the space available. **www.zurwienerstaatsoper.at**

Capricorno
€€€€

Schwedenplatz 3-4, 1010 **Tel** *533 31 04 0* **Fax** *533 76 71 0* **Rooms** *46*   **Map** *2 E5, 6 E2*

Located close to shops as well as to the subway, this hotel offers elegantly appointed rooms, most of which feature a balcony. Room amenities include Internet access. Helpful and friendly staff are available round the clock. Wheelchair accessible. **www.schick-hotels.com**

Hotel am Parkring
€€€€

Parkring 12, 1015 **Tel** *51 48 00* **Fax** *51 48 04 0* **Rooms** *58*   **Map** *4 E1, 6 E4*

Located on the "Ring" in the upper floors of a building, this hotel offers a magnificent view of the city below. Most rooms include either a balcony or a terrace where you can enjoy a quiet moment to yourself. The hotel's restaurant features fine brandies and an assortment of Austrian wines *(see p212)*. Pets are permitted. **www.schick-hotels.com**

Mailberger Hof
€€€€

Annagasse 7, 1010 **Tel** *512 06 41* **Fax** *512 06 41 10* **Rooms** *40*   **Map** *4 E1, 6 D4*

This is a lovely hotel that is converted from medieval houses. You can dine in the striking vaulted restaurant or, in the summer, in the garden under parasols. A wide, stone staircase leads to the bedrooms; most overlook the courtyard, are tastefully furnished and have plenty of space. **www.mailbergerhof.at**

Schlosshotel Römischer Kaiser
€€€€

Annagasse 16, 1010 **Tel** *512 77 51 0* **Fax** *512 77 51 13* **Rooms** *24*   **Map** *4 E1, 6 D4*

This terraced house, a classic example of a Viennese miniature Baroque palace, was built for the imperial chancellor in 1684. Stylish public rooms, with chandeliers and rugs on tiles, occupy the ground floor. Upstairs, the bedrooms are cheerful and airy. There are also less expensive attic rooms. Bicycles can be rented. **www.hotel-roemischer-kaiser.at**

Starlight Suiten Hotel Salzgries
€€€€

Salzgries 12, 1010 **Tel** *535 92 22* **Fax** *535 92 22 11* **Rooms** *50*   **Map** *2 E5, 6 D2*

Available here are home-like suites, each with a living room, bedroom, bathroom and work area. All rooms have a mini-bar, microwave oven, telephone and TV. A café and sauna are available on site. Wheelchair accessible. Children up to the age of six can stay for free when accompanied by their parents. **www.starlighthotels.com**

Wandl
€€€€

Petersplatz 9, 1010 **Tel** *534 55 0* **Fax** *534 55 77* **Rooms** *138*   **Map** *2 D5, 5 C3*

This charming, old-fashioned hotel is located close to Peterskirche and has been in the same family for generations. Some of the building's finer stuccoed features are in a few of the bedrooms and in the covered courtyard that serves as a breakfast room. Other rooms are more simple but large, and feature parquet floors. **www.hotel-wandl.com**

Am Stephansplatz
€€€€€

Stephansplatz 9, 1010 **Tel** *534 05 0* **Fax** *534 05 71 0* **Rooms** *56*   **Map** *2 E5, 6 D3*

This hotel features rooms in a sleek, modern style with dark, parquet floors and light-coloured furniture, all designed using ecologically friendly building materials. Taking this a step further, the hotel uses high-quality Grander water throughout for all purposes. Wheelchair accessible. **www.hotelamstephansplatz.at**

Kaiserin Elisabeth
€€€€€

Weihburggasse 3, 1010 **Tel** *515 26 0* **Fax** *515 26 7* **Rooms** *63*   **Map** *4 E1, 6 D4*

This fetching townhouse is located on a side street close to Stephansdom. It dates from the 14th century and in the 1800s played host to many famous musicians such as Wagner and Liszt. The *fin-de-siècle*-style bedrooms are smart, and Persian rugs lie on parquet floors in the public rooms. Pets are permitted. **www.kaiserinelisabeth.at**

K&K Palais
€€€€€

Rudolfsplatz 11, 1010 **Tel** *533 13 53* **Fax** *533 13 53 70* **Rooms** *66*   **Map** *2 E4, 6 D1*

Canary yellow walls abound in this successful, modern establishment that is set within a fine 19th-century building. An impressive, glass-fronted lobby leads to a smart breakfast room and bar, and up a marble staircase to simple bedrooms. The hotel is situated on a quiet, grassy square in a business area. **www.kkhotels.com**

König von Ungarn
€€€€€

Schulerstrasse 10, 1010 **Tel** *515 84 0* **Fax** *515 84 8* **Rooms** *44*   **Map** *2 E5, 6 D3*

In this quality hotel, framed signatures of famous visitors from past centuries cover the walls and Mozart is said to have composed *The Marriage of Figaro* here. The covered central courtyard, with its elegant bar/sitting room, is one of Vienna's loveliest. Most bedrooms are large with appealing rustic furniture. **www.kvu.at**

Palais Coburg
€€€€€

Coburgbastei 4, 1010 **Tel** *518 18 0* **Fax** *518 18 100* **Rooms** *35*   **Map** *6 E4*

This luxurious hotel is situated in a 19th-century building, which gives the Palais Coburg its unique character and historical ambience. Each opulent room is individually decorated with great attention to detail. Hotel facilities include on-site health and beauty rooms, a rooftop spa and indoor pool. **www.palaiscoburg.at**

Radisson Blu Palais Hotel

Parkring 16, 1010 **Tel** *515 17 0* **Fax** *515 17 35 10* **Rooms** *247*

Map *4 E1, 6 E4*

Located across from the Stadtpark and housed in a former Viennese palace, this hotel offers tastefully appointed rooms with amenities that include heated bathroom floors. Also provided are a sauna and a spa that offers beauty treatments. Pets are permitted. Wheelchair accessible. **www.radissonblu.com/palaishotel-vienna**

Vienna Marriott

Parkring 12a, 1010 **Tel** *515 18 0* **Fax** *515 18 67 36* **Rooms** *313*

Map *4 D1, 6 E4*

Numerous shops, cafés, bars and restaurants *(see p212)* fill the open-plan atrium of this modern glass hotel on the Ringstrasse. The hotel lacks a dedicated business centre, but it does have business facilities and a swimming pool. The bedrooms are large; some rooms may be noisier than others. **www.viennamarriott.com**

HOFBURG QUARTER

Pension Nossek

Graben 17, 1010 **Tel** *533 70 41 0* **Fax** *535 36 46* **Rooms** *31*

Map *2 D5, 5 C3*

You will need to book well in advance to obtain a room with a balcony overlooking the Graben in this elegant, but simple family-run pension that is spread over three floors. Most bedrooms have basic bathrooms, but rugs cover the parquet floors, and period furniture and tasteful paintings abound. **www.pension-nossek.at**

Pertschy

Habsburgergasse 5, 1010 **Tel** *534 49 0* **Fax** *534 49 49* **Rooms** *55*

Map *2 D5, 5 C3*

This pension combines simple decor with the features of an 18th-century building. You enter a courtyard through ancient gates and ascend a wide, stone staircase. A walkway connects the bedrooms, which have Rococo-style furnishings. The breakfast room is decorated in dark wood in coffee house style. **www.pertschy.com**

Graben

Dorotheergasse 3, 1010 **Tel** *512 15 31 0* **Fax** *512 15 31 20* **Rooms** *52*

Map *4 D1, 5 C4*

An inn since the 18th century, the Graben has attracted literary figures such as Franz Kafka and Max Brod. Today, it features comfortable rooms with stylish Italian furniture. There is also a business centre, where you can check your emails, and a pizzeria and Italian restaurant. Pets are permitted. **www.kremslehnerhotels.at**

Ambassador

Neuer Markt 5, 1010 **Tel** *961 610* **Fax** *513 299 9* **Rooms** *86*

Map *4 D1, 6 D4*

Vienna's best located five-star hotel has a 19th-century façade looking on to Kärntner Strasse, with an *al fresco* café terrace. Marble pillars, tapestries and chandeliers add to the hotel's regal magnificence. Some of the bedrooms have their own sitting rooms, which are screened behind heavy drapes. Wheelchair accessible. **www.ambassador.at**

Astoria

Kärntner Strasse 32-34, 1015 **Tel** *515 77* **Fax** *515 77 58 2* **Rooms** *128*

Map *5 C4*

This is a cosy turn-of-the-century hotel. The panelled Jugendstil foyer leads to a grand dining room on the first floor. There are some splendid bedrooms, many of which feature their own brass letter boxes. It is worth going to this hotel for the extra space and the interesting period furnishings. **www.austria-trend.at/asw**

Radisson Blu Style Hotel

Herrengasse 12, 1010 **Tel** *22 78 0* **Fax** *22 78 07 7* **Rooms** *78*

Map *2 D5, 5 B2*

Conveniently located, this hotel is in contemporary style and offers uniquely designed rooms with amenities that include a flat-panel LCD TV and a CD/DVD player. The hotel also provides free Wi-Fi facilities as well as a sauna, massage and beauty treatments. Pets are permitted. Wheelchair accessible. **www.radissonblu.de**

SCHOTTERING AND ALSERGRUND

Golderner Bär

Türkenstrasse 27, 1090 **Tel** *317 51 11* **Fax** *31 75 11 122* **Rooms** *27*

Map *1 C4*

This is a simple but comfortable small hotel located close to the "Ring". Here you can enjoy a peaceful night's rest in a room designed and decorated in modern style and with sound-proof windows. Amenities include free Internet access. The staff are friendly and helpful. **www.goldbaerhotel.com**

Hotel Boltzmann

Boltzmanngasse 8, 1090 **Tel** *354 50 0* **Fax** *354 50 81 6* **Rooms** *70*

Map *1 C3*

A charming hotel with all of the amenities of a four-star establishment, the Boltzmann is situated close to the romantic Strudelhof Steps. It is surrounded by gardens and parks and is a short 10-minute walk from the historic centre. The hotel offers cosy rooms full of atmosphere and a private little garden. **www.hotelboltzmann.at**

Key to Price Guide *see p194* **Key to Symbols** *see back cover flap*

Mozart   €€
Nordbergstrasse 4, 1090 **Tel** *317 15 37* **Fax** *317 24 77* **Rooms** *56*   **Map** *1 C2*

Housed in a building that served as quarters for Allied troops after World War II, this hotel uniquely features water that is heated using solar energy. The rooms are tastefully decorated and have contemporary furniture. A private house bar is available. Pets are permitted. Wheelchair accessible. **www.hotelmozart-vienna.at**

Hotel Harmonie   €€€
Harmoniegasse 5-7, 1090 **Tel** *317 66 04* **Fax** *317 66 04 55* **Rooms** *68*   **Map** *1 C3*

Situated in a quiet location, this hotel offers friendly service. Rooms are simple but comfortable, and are designed in a modern style. There is a café and bar, and the staff will assist you in obtaining tickets to concerts. Pets are permitted. Children under the age of 12 can stay for free when accompanied by two adults. **www.bestwestern.at**

Regina   €€€€
Rooseveltplatz 15, 1096 **Tel** *404 46 0* **Fax** *408 83 92* **Rooms** *164*   **Map** *1 C4, 5 A1*

The inside of this hotel has a certain grandeur, with brass chandeliers and classical statues. The building has been a hotel since 1896 and in the restaurant there is a photo of its staff in 1913. Today, the hotel caters mainly to tourist groups. The old-fashioned bedrooms are plain but comfortable. **www.kremslehenerhotels.at**

MUSEUM AND TOWNHALL QUARTER

Arpi   €€
Kochgasse 15, 1080 **Tel** *405 00 33* **Fax** *40 50 03 337* **Rooms** *20*   **Map** *1 B4*

This is a family-owned, centrally located hotel and pension that features rooms in contemporary style. The staff is friendly and will assist you in obtaining tickets to theatres and concerts; they can also help you with arranging sightseeing tours of the city. Breakfast is served in the lounge. **www.hotelarpi.com**

Hotel Academia   €
Pfeilgasse 3a, 1080 **Tel** *401 76 55* **Fax** *401 76 20* **Rooms** *72*   **Map** *1 A5*

During the academic year, this establishment serves as a student residence. However, during the summer break (1 July to 30 September), it opens its doors to the public as a hotel. The rooms are modern and airy, and some include a balcony. Wheelchair accessible. **www.academiahotels.at**

Hotel Korotan   €€
Albertgasse 48, 1080 **Tel** *403 41 93* **Fax** *403 41 93 99* **Rooms** *61*   **Map** *1 A5*

This smaller hotel has an extremely modern and airy style, and friendly staff. All rooms have access to the Internet. Also on the premises are a chapel, library and gallery, making the hotel more of an experience than just a place to sleep. Wheelchair accessible. **www.hotel.korotan.com**

Alpha   €€€
Buchfeldgasse 8, 1080 **Tel** *403 52 91* **Fax** *403 52 91 62* **Rooms** *58*   **Map** *1 B5*

Near the centre of the city, close to the Austrian Parliament building, this is a simple hotel decorated in a modern style. The breakfast room is light and airy. Internet access is available in the public areas. Wheelchair accessible. Wi-Fi is available in all rooms. **www.hotelalpha.at**

Museum   €€€
Museumstrasse 3, 1070 **Tel** *523 44 26* **Fax** *523 44 26 30* **Rooms** *15*   **Map** *3 C1*

Behind a fine façade with wrought-iron balconies, and set above a cinema, is this classic Viennese pension. It is right on the doorstep of the main museums. The spartan, but massive, bedrooms have high ceilings and wooden floors, and the sitting and breakfast rooms have ornate fireplaces and chandeliers. **www.hotelmuseum.at**

Zipser   €€€
Lange Gasse 49, 1080 **Tel** *404 54 0* **Fax** *404 54 13* **Rooms** *53*   **Map** *1 B5*

This pension in the Josefstadt area has smart modern carpets and furniture throughout, and the atmosphere is very friendly. Ask for one of the larger, quieter bedrooms at the rear of the hotel; they have excellent bathrooms and big wooden balconies, which are high up and overlook an attractive leafy courtyard. **www.zipser.at**

Altstadt Vienna   €€€€
Kirchengasse 41, 1070 **Tel** *522 66 66* **Fax** *523 40 01* **Rooms** *42*   **Map** *3 B1*

Situated in an interesting old quarter just west of the main museums, this hotel in a 19th-century patrician house is an extremely popular place to stay. Designer lighting, boldly coloured walls, and striking modern furnishings bring life to the ample rooms. The bedrooms at the rear of the hotel are peaceful. Excellent service. **www.altstadt.at**

Cordial Theaterhotel Wien   €€€€
Josefstädter Strasse 22, 1080 **Tel** *405 36 48 0* **Fax** *405 14 06* **Rooms** *54*   **Map** *1 A5*

Simple but comfortable rooms are to be found at this hotel, close to the Josefstadt Theater. The hotel also has a bar, sauna and solarium. Breakfast can be served in your room for a small, additional fee and the friendly staff will assist you in planning any excursions in and around Vienna. Wheelchair accessible. **www.cordial.at**

Hotel Rathaus
🄿 P 🄱   €€€€

Lange Gasse 13, 1080 **Tel** *400 11 22* **Fax** *400 11 22 88* **Rooms** *40*   **Map** *1 B5*

Located in a historic townhouse in Josefstadt, but with a modern interior, the Rathaus is dedicated to wine and wine culture. Each luxurious double room is named after an Austrian vintner (whose wines are in the mini-bar) and is stocked with wine cosmetics. The service is excellent; expect to be pampered. **www.hotel-rathaus-wien.at**

Mercure Josefshof Wien
🄿 ▤ 🄱   €€€€

Josefsgasse 4-6, 1080 **Tel** *404 19* **Fax** *404 19 15 0* **Rooms** *121*   **Map** *1 B5*

This hotel is on a quiet back street, close to Vienna's English Theatre. There is a marble and glass entry hallway, and the bedrooms are smart with high-quality reproduction furniture and parquet flooring. Pets are permitted. Children under the age of 12 can stay for free when accompanied by an adult. Wheelchair accessible. **www.josefshof.com**

OPERA AND NASCHMARKT

Terminus Hotel
🄽   €

Fillgradergasse 4, 1060 **Tel** *587 73 86 0* **Fax** *587 73 86 16* **Rooms** *45*   **Map** *3 C2*

Located close to the subway, this is a smaller hotel that offers adequate accommodation with the usual range of amenities, such as a TV and telephone. Each room is decorated in a different style. The staff is helpful and pleasant. In the lobby are vending machines selling a variety of items. Pets are permitted. **www.terminus.at**

Hotel Beethoven
🄽 P ▤ 🄱   €€€€

Papagenogasse 6, 1060 **Tel** *587 44 82 0* **Fax** *587 44 42* **Rooms** *36*   **Map** *3 C2*

In this stylishly decorated and conveniently located hotel, which is situated across the street from the Theater an der Wien, you can enjoy professional and friendly service. Internet access is available in the rooms and the staff will assist you in obtaining tickets to the theatre and concerts. Pets are permitted. **www.hotel-beethoven.at**

Le Meridien Vienna
🄽 🄼 ♨ P ▤ 🕐 🄱   €€€€€

Opernring 13-15, 1010 **Tel** *588 90* **Fax** *588 90 90 90* **Rooms** *294*   **Map** *4 D1, 5 B5*

This elegant hotel has rooms that are tastefully decorated in shades of blue, green and pink. In addition to the standard amenities, bathrobes, slippers and umbrellas are provided. There is also a wellness centre with Jacuzzi, sauna and steam room. Pets are permitted. Expect a first-class stay here. **www.lemeridienvienna.com**

Sacher
🄽 🄼 P ▤ 🕐 🄱   €€€€€

Philarmonikerstrasse 4, 1010 **Tel** *514 56 0* **Fax** *514 56 81 0* **Rooms** *152*   **Map** *4 D1, 5 C5*

Since 1876, the Sacher has been a haunt for the wealthy. Now its café is full of tourists and locals who stop by for a slice of their famous chocolate *Sacher Torte (see p215)*. Both the public rooms and more expensive bedrooms are opulent; even the standard rooms have a regal air. The staff provide outstanding service. **www.sacher.com**

BELVEDERE QUARTER

Suzanne
🄽 ▤   €€

Walfischgasse 4, 1010 **Tel** *513 25 07* **Fax** *513 25 00* **Rooms** *26*   **Map** *4 D1, 6 D5*

This popular pension is just a few steps from the Kärntner Strasse and the Opera House. It is above a couple of local shops. However, the bedrooms, with paintings and comfortable armchairs, have old-fashioned charm and are spread over a number of floors. The more expensive rooms have kitchenettes. **www.pension-suzanne.at**

Clima Cityhotel
🄽 P   €€€

Theresianumgasse 21a, 1040 **Tel** *515 16 96* **Fax** *504 35 52* **Rooms** *37*   **Map** *4 E4*

Quiet despite its central location, this hotel offers a great view of the city from the upper floors. Its sleek and airy bedrooms, with good-sized bathrooms, ensure a comfortable and relaxing stay. The friendly staff will assist you in obtaining tickets to events. **www.climacity-hotel.com**

Hotel Erzherzog Rainer
🄽 P 🕐 🄱   €€€

Wiedner Hauptstrasse 27-29, 1040 **Tel** *221 11 1* **Fax** *221 11 35 0* **Rooms** *84*   **Map** *3 C5*

This conveniently located hotel, near the Künstlerhaus, offers traditional Austrian hospitality. The large rooms are decorated tastefully and are quiet as they have sound-proof windows. There is also a comfortable coffee house and bar in which to relax *(see p215)*. Pets are permitted. **www.schick-hotels.com**

Hotel Kaiserhof Wien
🄽 🄼 P ▤ 🄱   €€€€

Frankenberggasse 10, 1040 **Tel** *505 17 01* **Fax** *505 88 75 88* **Rooms** *74*   **Map** *4 D2*

In a central location, this hotel offers tastefully decorated and elegant rooms, all with modern conveniences and some with Wi-Fi Internet access. Pleasant staff are also on hand. For exercise buffs, there is a fitness room, sauna, steam room and sanarium, which features special coloured mood lighting. **www.hotel-kaiserhof.at**

Key to Price Guide *see p194* **Key to Symbols** *see back cover flap*

Bristol 🖼 🍴 P 🗒 🛏 🛎 €€€€€

Kärntner Ring 1, 1015 **Tel** *515 16 0* **Fax** *515 16 55 0* **Rooms** *140*　　　　　　**Map** *4 D2, 6 D5*

The Bristol is a very luxurious hotel. The location is also excellent: on the Ringstrasse and opposite the Opera. Marble, gilt, antiques and paintings are everywhere, creating an atmosphere of dignified opulence. The bedrooms include top-floor penthouses and superb business suites. Wheelchair accessible. **www.luxurycollection.com/bristol**

Imperial 🖼 🍴 P 🗒 🛏 🛎 €€€€€

Kärntner Ring 16, 1015 **Tel** *501 10 0* **Fax** *501 10 41 0* **Rooms** *138*　　　　　　**Map** *4 D2, 6 D5*

The grandest of Vienna's top hotels exudes an air of exclusivity and, if you stay here, you may well be sleeping under the same roof as a head of state or two. In the 1950s, two extra floors were added, containing smaller rooms designed in cherry wood. Small pets are permitted. Wheelchair accessible. **www.luxurycollection.com/imperial**

FURTHER AFIELD

Lindenhof P 🍴 €

Breitenleer Strasse 256, 1220 **Tel** *734 36 37* **Fax** *734 29 80* **Rooms** *24*

Family-owned since 1928, this is a cosy hostelry in a 15th-century building that provides old-world hospitality and simple, but comfortable, rooms. There are also ample dining facilities, including an indoor restaurant and outdoor terrace. Live music and other events take place here occasionally. **www.lindenhof-breitenlee.com**

Gartenhotel Glanzing 🖼 🍴 €€€

Glanzinggasse 23, 1190 **Tel** *470 42 72 0* **Fax** *470 42 72 14* **Rooms** *14*

Built in the 1930s, this interesting ivy-festooned hotel has a rambling garden and stands in leafy suburbs close to the wine villages. It also features big bedrooms and a grand piano in its main room. Pets are permitted. Children under the age of 15 can stay for free when accompanied by an adult. **www.gartenhotel-glanzing.at**

Hotel Capri 🖼 P €€€

Praterstrasse 44-46, 1020 **Tel** *214 84 04* **Fax** *214 27 85* **Rooms** *70*　　　　　　**Map** *6 F4*

This family-run hotel offers spacious, modern rooms that cater for up to four people, ideal for those travelling with families. All rooms have basic amenities with Wi-Fi access. Cots are available on request. Located close to the Prater and only two U-Bahn stops to the bustle of the city. **www.hotelcapri.at**

Hotel Fürstenhof 🖼 €€€

Neubaugürtel 4, 1060 **Tel** *523 32 67* **Fax** *523 32 67 26* **Rooms** *58*

Friendly service and clean and comfortable rooms are provided by this family-run hotel, housed in an early 20th-century building. The rooms are decorated in both traditional and contemporary styles, and some have chandeliers. Cheaper rooms have a shared bathroom, but en-suite rooms are available. **www.hotel-fuerstenhof.com**

Hotel Jäger 🖼 P 🗒 €€€

Hernalser Hauptstrasse 187, 1170 **Tel** *486 66 20 0* **Fax** *486 66 20 8* **Rooms** *17*

Owned and operated by the Jäger family since 1921, this cosy hotel offers first-class and friendly service in a traditional Austrian environment. The accommodation includes apartments with a kitchen. Pets are permitted. Children under the age of 12 can stay for free when accompanied by two adults. **www.hoteljaeger.at**

Hotel Stefanie 🖼 P 🗒 🛏 🛎 €€€

Taborstrasse 12, 1020 **Tel** *211 50* **Fax** *211 50 16 0* **Rooms** *122*　　　　　　**Map** *2 F4, 6 E1*

Dating back to 1703, this is the oldest four-star hotel in Vienna. It is also conveniently located close to Stephansdom. Designed in Classic Viennese or contemporary style, all the bedrooms are comfortable. Wi-Fi Internet access is available in some, as well as in public areas. Pets are permitted. Wheelchair accessible. **www.schick-hotels.com**

Landhaus Fuhrgassl-Huber P 🍴 €€€

Neustift am Walde, Rathstrasse 24, 1190 **Tel** *440 30 33* **Fax** *440 27 14* **Rooms** *38*

This family-run quaint hotel lies in a typical Austrian wine village. There is a *Heuriger (see p201)* next door, and the hotel owner has his own *Heuriger* just up the street. The hotel is prettily decked out in pine, with tiled floors and stencilled furniture. A bus to Vienna is available just outside the hotel. **www.fuhrgassl-huber.at**

Mercure Grand Hotel Biedermeier Wien 🖼 🍴 P 🗒 🛏 🛎 €€€€

Landstrasser Hauptstrasse 28, 1030 **Tel** *716 71 0* **Fax** *716 71 50 3* **Rooms** *203*　　　　　　**Map** *4 F1*

This hotel occupies the whole complex of a superbly restored Biedermeier passage courtyard that lies off one of Vienna's main shopping streets. The large, spacious bedrooms, almost all looking down on the cobbled passage, are particularly quiet. Bicycles are available to rent. Pets are permitted. Wheelchair accessible. **www.mercure.com**

Inter-Continental Wien 🖼 🍴 P 🗒 🛏 🛎 €€€€€

Johannesgasse 28, 1037 **Tel** *711 22 0* **Fax** *713 44 89* **Rooms** *453*　　　　　　**Map** *4 E1, 6 E5*

The Inter-Continental is a modern and cosmopolitan chain hotel, just a 2-minute walk from the Ringstrasse. Classical music is played nightly in the bar area of the elegant, chandeliered foyer, and the upper-floor bedrooms have good views across the Stadtpark. Wheelchair accessible. **www.vienna.intercontinental.com**

RESTAURANTS, CAFÉS AND BARS

The Viennese know how to eat well. The staples of Vienna's cuisine are assimilated from the cooking styles of the Habsburg Empire, and so include *Schnitzels*, originating as North Italian escalopes; dumplings that are a speciality of Bohemia; Hungarian goulash; and even Balkan grills and sausages *(Cevapcici)*. Balkan cuisine is a result of the post-Second World War immigration that has multiplied the ethnic cuisines now available in the city. The range of gastronomy is vast, from

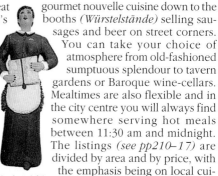
Papier-mâché waitress outside restaurant

gourmet nouvelle cuisine down to the booths *(Würstelstände)* selling sausages and beer on street corners. You can take your choice of atmosphere from old-fashioned sumptuous splendour to tavern gardens or Baroque wine-cellars. Mealtimes are also flexible and in the city centre you will always find somewhere serving hot meals between 11:30 am and midnight. The listings *(see pp210–17)* are divided by area and by price, with the emphasis being on local cuisine, but there is a generous choice of alternatives as well.

TYPES OF EATING PLACE

The humble *Würstelstände* sell hot dogs and *Leberkäse* (only for the adventurous) which is somewhat alarmingly described as "meat remnants worked into an undefined formless mass". On a slightly

Wine cellar sign

higher gastronomic level are the numerous small eateries selling sandwiches, filled rolls, pastries and soft drinks. Mouth-watering open sandwiches are the speciality of **Duran** (several outlets, *see p218*) and the celebrated **Trzesniewski** *(see p218)*, with a coffee or a miniature Pfiff ($^{1}/_{8}$ of a litre) of beer to accompany them.

If something a little more sustaining is required, the numerous *Stehbeisln* (stand-up counters) at some butchers' and food stores offer fresh dishes and sometimes a welcome bowl of hot soup on a winter's day. Some upmarket restaurants advertise a *Gabelfrühstück* (fork breakfast) serving hot delicacies mid-morning. Another extra repast discovered by the Viennese is the *Jause*, typically cold meats and cheese eaten outside regular mealtimes. All these options are preferable to the budget-conscious traveller to the museum restaurants and cafés which, however good, tend to be more expensive.

Local musician performing in a wine cellar

Many self-service restaurants offer a wide selection of cold and hot dishes, including grills made to order, and can be recommended. Among them is **Markt-Restaurant Rosenberger**, which is located in Maysedergasse behind the Opera House. Others can be found in the Ringstrassen shopping mall. Some close early so are better for a quick lunch, while a bustling coffee-house or wine-cellar might be more appealing in the evenings.

WINE CELLARS AND HEURIGEN

Wine cellars represent good value, with cold buffets and a limited range of hot dishes on offer to

Open sandwiches available at Zum Schwarzen Kameel *(see p200)*

accompany local wine from the barrel. The atmosphere is informal, and even more so in the gardens of the *Heurigen* (taverns) in the villages at the periphery of the city at Neustift am Walde, Grinzing, Salmannsdorf, and elsewhere. In theory, *Heurigen* serve only the wine from their own vineyards and of the current vintage. *Heuriger* has two meanings: it refers to the youngest available vintage of the local wine and it also refers to the venues that sell such wines by the glass. According to regulations laid down by Emperor Joseph II, pine twigs placed over or by the door (*ausg'steckt*) remained as long as the vintage lasted, after which they were removed and the tavern closed for the year. You will still see such taverns, but in practice the larger ones are open all year and serve

Garden scene at a *Heuriger* where local wine growers are licensed to sell their own wine

Typical sausage stand *(or Wurst-stand)* in the city centre

an extensive buffet with hot and cold cuts of meat. The wine is mostly white, often a blend of local grapes (the *gemischter Satz*) and is a true *Heuriger* until 11th November of the year after harvest. To sample a genuine local product, look for *Eigenbau* by the entrance.

COFFEE HOUSES AND KONDITOREIEN

Vienna's legendary coffee houses *(see pp58–61)* are culturally specific: politicians favour **Landtmann**, whilst literati swap ideas in **Hawelka** *(see p218)*. Coffee is served in different ways depending on the strength and addition of hot milk or water required.

Prices vary according to location and type: a Ringstraßen café is more expensive than a smoke-filled den with a billiard table at the rear, or somewhere like the **Café Ministerium** *(see p218)* patronised by the proverbially parsimonious bureaucrats from the nearby ministries.

While coffee houses serve a small range of simple hot dishes, the *Konditoreien* concentrate on pastries and cakes, though a few also do a good light lunch. The great *Konditoreien* in the centre can be rather a scrum in the tourist season, but the fare is irresistible (diabetics also catered for). Since there is a complicated nomenclature for the *Konditoreien* themselves, it is best to go to the display counter and point to the item you want. A cheaper alternative is the Aida chain found throughout Vienna, with less comfortable seating but lower prices, even for the *Sachertorte*.

THE VIENNESE BEISL

What the trattoria is to Italy the *Beisl* is to Vienna, a simple restaurant offering local specialities in an agreeably informal atmosphere. The name is thought to be of Jewish origin (in the 18th century,

many inn-keepers were Jewish). Unfortunately many *Beisln* have gone up-market and their prices have lifted accordingly. All of them serve typical Viennese specialities like *Tafelspitz* (boiled beef), *Vanillirostbraten* (pot roast with garlic), *Kalbsbeuschel* (calf's lung and heart) and of course *Schnitzel*, together with enticingly named desserts: *Powidltascherln* (pasta envelopes with plum jam) or *Zwetschkenknödel* (plums in potato dumpling). Viennese cooking is strong in the soup department, one of the more popular soups being *Eierschwammerlsuppe* made with chanterelle mushrooms. Huge portions of *Wiener Schnitzel* are served at **Figlmüller** *(see p210)*.

The most aspiring *Beisln* should have just as good food as a mid-priced restaurant.

A trendy city bar, the Tunnel *(see p219)*, on Florianigasse

The 7th-floor Do & Co restaurant *(see p212)*, with a splendid view of the Stephansdom

MID-PRICED AND ETHNIC RESTAURANTS

The top end of the *Beisln* merge with what Austrians somewhat misleadingly call "*gutbürgerliche Küche*", or "good plain cooking", since at many places so identified, such as **Zum Herkner** in outlying Hernals *(see p217)*, the food is more than good and rather sophisticated. Establishments like **Kern's Beisl** *(see p210)* and **Restaurant Sperl** *(see p215)* offer extremely good value, as do many of the ethnic restaurants throughout the city: **Beim Czaak** *(see p210)* with its roots in Bohemian cuisine, or the Hungarian **Ilona Stüberl** *(see p213)* in the Bräunerstrasse. Some restaurants offer great value

One of the city's many *Café-Konditoreien*

because they only accept cash. The authentic Greek restaurants, such as **Kostas** *(see p215)*, also tend to be inexpensive. The same cannot always be said for the up-market Asian and Japanese restaurants and sushi bars that have enjoyed a boom over the last few years. Some are so popular that they are often booked weeks in advance. Among them are **Tenmaya** *(see p212)*, which offers a traditional Japanese setting, including women dressed in kimonos, and **Kim Kocht** *(see p217)*, which features a tempting gourmet food shop on the premises.

Pizza and pasta establishments are ubiquitous, but many of the genuine Italian restaurants tend to be found at the luxury end of the market. This may be at least partly due to the unique environments in which the food is served; in **Da Capo** *(see p210)*, an authentic wood burning oven is used to cook the pizzas and guests can dine in the restaurant's attractive cellar.

Vegetarian restaurants are slowly on the increase, and one of the longest established is **Wrenkh** *(see p212)*. Other restaurants gaining in popularity are those, such as **Cantino Restaurant**, which offer Spanish cuisine that includes authentic paella and tapas *(see p215)*, and Balkan and Turkish establishments. In **Restaurant Dubróvnik** *(see p216)*, guests can dine on Croatian specialties such as *pljeskavica* and other meals derived from south-east European recipes. Meanwhile, the restaurant **Aux Gazelles** *(see p215)* not only offers authentic French/Moroccan cuisine, but presents a whole North African experience, including Turkish steam baths and a café, bar, bazaar shop and nightclub.

LUXURY RESTAURANTS

Gourmet eating in Vienna generally retains a local flavour. Seriously good cuisines may be found at luxury hotels like the **Hotel Sacher** *(see p198)* or the **Imperial** *(see p216)*. The city's most prestigious restaurant for seafood is the **Restaurant Hummerbar** *(see p216)*, where fresh lobster, scallops and oysters can be had at a price and the menu changes daily. **Steirereck** *(see p217)*, which is located in the leafy surroundings of the Stadtpark, is still considered one of the best gourmet restaurants in the country. Its menus have a strong Austrian theme. In comparison, **Trattoria Martinelli** *(see p214)* serves traditional Tuscan specialties, which can be enjoyed in the Baroque ambience of the Harrach Palace.

Rote Bar, one of two restaurants at the luxurious Hotel Sacher

READING THE MENU

The three main divisions of the menu are *Kalte* or *Warme Vorspeisen* (cold or hot hors d'oeuvres), *Hauptspeisen* (main courses) and *Mehlspeisen* (desserts). There may be separate entries for soups (*Suppen*), fish (*Fisch*), beef (*Rindfleisch*) and pork (*Schweinefleisch*). Many restaurants have a children's menu and usually a selection of vegetarian dishes. Menus may change with the season to make use of the best and freshest produce, and the waiter will often tell you about the day's specialities (*Tagesangebot*) which are not usually mentioned on the standard menu. These are often worth ordering and can be particularly good value for money. You may also see the phrase *Fertige Speisen* for dishes that are not on the fixed-price menu. A specifically Austrian phrase frequently encountered is *Schmankerln*, which implies regional delicacies. Portions tend to be on the generous side, although there is a trend to lighter eating in the more up-market establishments offering nouvelle cuisine.

The house wines are usually served in glasses, which hold exactly a quarter of a litre, though smaller glasses may also be served, and half a litre may come in a carafe. Most restaurants, at least in the city centre, have menus in English but if this is not the case, there is usually a member of staff who can help.

Traditional Austrian musicians at the Heuriger (*see p219*)

Sign for the famous Café-Konditorei Demel

HOW MUCH TO PAY

Vienna's restaurants generally represent good value for money. However over-indulgence in tempting little delicacies (*Leckerbissen*) can make a big dent in the wallet; small items like coffee are also relatively expensive and a cup in one of the congenial old coffee houses or *Konditoreien* costs around €2.50 to €3. Add in an alcoholic drink, such as apricot schnapps, and your costs could easily double. Snack meals and fast-food outlets provide adequate sustenance at around €5, while double that should buy a modest meal in one of the self-service restaurants or less touristy wine cellars. A reasonably priced *Beisl* might cost €20 a head with a glass of wine, but sticking to the fixed-price menu will probably reduce that significantly. There is a large middle swathe of restaurants where you might expect a bill of up to €36, while luxury and gourmet establishments have prices that accelerate well beyond the €40 mark. Prices can be more expensive in the evening or during peak tourist seasons and holidays.

Most restaurants with a regular international clientele take credit cards, but many of the *Beisln* and standard Viennese restaurants only take cash. It is always best to check in advance as to the payment method accepted.

BOOKING AND SERVICE

Always telephone and confirm any special requests especially wheelchair access and facilities for the disabled, if non-smoking seats are available and whether children are catered for. Facilities may be limited and some of the older establish-ments may have narrow corridors or steps. Booking a day ahead or even on the day is usually sufficient. Even a simple *Beisl* can have a faithful local clientele and you may be disappointed if you wander in and expect to find a free table. Assiduous service is the hallmark of many Viennese restaurants. Tips are traditionally 10% and are mandatory everywhere except in the few places where you may find that the service is included.

Kern's Beisl restaurant in the Stephansdom Quarter (*see p210*)

The Flavours of Vienna: Savoury Dishes

Austrian cuisine is a direct legacy of the country's imperial past, when culinary traditions from many parts of Europe influenced Viennese cooks. As a result, it is far more varied and flavoursome than most people realize. There are Italian and Adriatic influences, Polish- and Hungarian- inspired dishes, and even a rich seam of Balkan flavours running through much of the Austrian kitchen repertoire. *Schnitzel*, for example, may have come to Austria via Milan, which was once under Austrian control, while *Gulasch* is the Austrian version of a Hungarian dish that became popular in Vienna in the 19th century.

Chanterelle mushrooms

Cheese stall at a local Austrian farmers' market

MEAT, POULTRY & DAIRY

Beef is narrowly ahead of pork as the nation's favourite meat. Austrian cattle farmers have a long and proud heritage of producing fine beef, which is used in many dishes, such as paprika-rich *Gulasch*. That most famous of Austrian dishes, *Wiener Schnitzel*, is traditionally made with veal. Pork is used primarily to make hams and sausages. The classic Austrian way with pork is to cure it, smoke it and leave it to mature for months in the clean air of the high Alpine pastures. The result is called *Speck*. Lean *Speck* is similar to Italian *prosciutto*, though with a distinctive smoky tang, while fattier cuts are more like *pancetta* or streaky bacon. *Bratwurst*, made with beef, pork and veal, are Austria's preferred sausages, but other types such as *Frankfurters* are also common. Chicken is almost always served breaded *(Backhendl)*, but *Grillhendl* is a whole chicken roasted over an open fire, or on a spit. Duck *(Ente)* is often served with sweet sauces, but sometimes with sour accompaniments such as pickled red cabbage.

Beef frank- furters   Bierwurst   Pork frankfurters

Bratwurst   Lean speck

Speck

Selection of typical Austrian cured pork, sausages and salami

AUSTRIAN DISHES AND SPECIALITIES

While most classic Austrian dishes (especially those originating in Vienna) are found all over the country, there are some regional differences. *Knödel* are more popular in the east, as are carp, game and pork, while beef and lamb appear more often the further west (and higher up the mountains) you travel. Beef is essential for *Tafelspitz*, often called the national dish. *Speck* is used to make *Speck Knödel*, small, dense dumplings, but the one part of the pig that Austrians do love to eat uncured is the knuckle, called *Stelze*, roasted and served chopped with heaps of sauerkraut. *Fischgröstl* is a mix of fish and seafood, fried together with onion, potato and mince (usually leftovers). It is rarely found on menus, but you may be lucky enough to try it in an Austrian home.

Paprika

Tafelspitz *is silverside of beef, boiled with root vegetables and served thickly sliced with gherkins and sauerkraut.*

Spectacular array of vegetables on display in a Viennese market

Roast goose (*Gänsebraten*) is also popular, as are goose livers. The milk of Austrian dairy cows, grazed on sweet Alpine pastures, gives some excellent artisan cheeses, such as fruity Wälder.

FISH

While not great seafood lovers, Austrians have developed a number of their own fish dishes. Trout (*Forelle*) is the most popular fish, usually served grilled with boiled potatoes. Herring (*Hering*) is pickled and eaten as an appetizer. *Heringsschmaus*, a smoked herring and apple salad, is hugely popular at Easter. Carp (*Karpfen*) is a favourite Christmas dish, but is eaten all year, as is plaice (*Scholle* or *Goldbutt*), which is often served with a rich vegetable-based sauce.

VEGETABLES

Vegetables in Austria are of the highest quality and so, while imported produce is available all year round, seasonality is still important to Austrians. That is truest of all

Bunches of pale spears of Austrian *Spargel* (asparagus)

for the nation's favourite, asparagus (*Spargel*). Only local produce is used, and so is found on menus only during the harvesting season, from the end of April to early July. Austrians use asparagus in every way imaginable at this time of year. Wild mushrooms are another seasonal prize, especially chanterelles (*Eierschwammerl*). Potatoes (*Erdäpfel*) feature widely, often in the form of *Knödel*. These are dumplings made of potatoes or stale white bread and are served with venison or pork dishes. White cabbage is often pickled (*Sauerkraut*) and red cabbage is served with venison and most game dishes.

SAVOURY SNACKS

Liptauer: Goat's or sheep's milk cheese is mixed with paprika, caraway seeds, capers, mustard, chives and onions to create this paste, a staple of Austrian wine bars.

Maroni: Roast chestnuts are a winter treat; the aroma of them, toasting over a brazier on a snowy day, is somehow quintessentially Vienna.

Blunzen: Blood sausage is marinated in vinegar and thinly sliced and served with brown bread. A popular "beer snack".

Schmaltzbrot: Brown bread spread thickly with beef or pork dripping, and eaten with onions and pickles.

Wiener Schnitzel *should classically be veal, breaded and fried. In Austria is is never served with sauce.*

Rindsgulasch *is the beef version of Hungarian goulash, a rich stew flavoured with paprika and caraway.*

Forelle Blau, *literally "blue trout", is made by poaching an unscaled fish in stock, which gives it a blueish hue.*

The Flavours of Vienna: Sweet Foods

Few cities in the world can rival Vienna's devotion to all things sweet. The Viennese enjoy cakes mid-morning or afternoon, and set aside time for between-meal snacks. The finest *torten* (gâteaux), pastries and cakes tend to be found in *Konditoreien (see p201)* and are usually consumed with a cup of coffee. Traditional Viennese desserts can be found in all good restaurants, and are typically rich. From the classic Viennese *Apfelstrudel* to *Gugelhupf* from the Tirol, Austrian desserts all carry a regional influence. In Vienna, pastries take pride of place while, to the west, the Italian influence is strong and cakes, ice creams and meringues are preferred.

Poppy seeds

Relaxing over coffee and cake in an elegant Viennese café

CAKES

The Austrian tradition of cake-baking goes back centuries, with competition fierce between towns and cities to produce the finest. Even in small villages, bakeries would try to outdo each other with their sweet creations. Almost every Austrian city now has its trademark cake, with its

citizens quick to boast that theirs is the best. The most famous Austrian cake is a Viennese creation, the *Sacher-torte*, a rich chocolate cake invented by chef Franz Sacher for Chancellor Metternich in 1832. The signature dish of many an Austrian chef, it should be the first cake the visitor tries – with so much choice on offer, it will be difficult to decide on the second. While the Viennese

rave about *Sachertorte*, over in Linz the locals insist their own *Linzertorte* – an almond based cake usually topped with raspberries – is superior. The people of Linz also say that the *Linzertorte* is older, dating back – legend has it – to the 17th century. Around the Hungarian border, they are proud of their *Dobostorte*, named for the Budapest chef who created it in the 19th century. Its layers of sponge

Linzertorte **Stollen** **Sachertorte** **Dobostorte** **Esterházytorte**

Some of the many mouthwatering Austrian cakes available

VIENNESE DESSERTS

Mohr im Hemd, *a hazelnut and chocolate pudding, is served with chocolate sauce and whipped cream.*

From *Topfentascherl* (curd cheese envelopes) to *Kastaniereis* (chestnut purée), Vienna's dessert cuisine uses rich and varied ingredients. Fruits such as plums and apples fill featherlight dumplings, pancakes, fritters and strudels, and although *Mehlspeisen* (puddings) translates literally as "dishes without flour", ground hazelnuts or almonds can be used in its place. Nuts play a key role, especially hazels and pine nuts, the latter often featuring in *Apfelstrudel*. More unusual desserts include sweet "pasta" served with poppyseeds to create *Mohnnudeln*, and *Bohmische Omeletten* (Bohemian omelettes) served with whipped cream and prune sauce. Conversely, *Palatschinken* may also be a savoury snack.

Hazelnuts

Display of traditional pastries and cakes in a *Konditorei*

and chocolate butter cream are topped with a caramel glaze. From Salzburg, the cake of choice is baked meringue, known as *Salzburger Nockerl*, or Salzburg Soufflé. *Esterházytorte* also features meringue, layered with a rich hazelnut cream. Stollen is a marzipan-filled fruit bread originally from Germany and now an integral part of an Austrian Christmas. Regional or not, you'll now find all these classic cakes in Vienna and across the country.

PASTRIES

In the perfect global village, a place on the main street would always be reserved for an Austrian pastry and coffee shop. That the French collective name for sweet pastry is *Viennoiserie* underlines the noble Viennese tradition of sweet baking. Austrian legend has it that the nation's café habit began when the Turks left all their coffee behind as they abandoned Vienna after the failed siege of 1529. The *Kipfel*, a light, crescent-shaped pastry (which later became famous

Entrance to one of the world-famous Mozart chocolate shops

as the croissant) also dates from the time of the Turkish siege, its shape being based on the crescent moon in the Ottoman flag. While such symbolism is often lost today, the importance of the café in Austrian society is not. Modern-day Austrians view cafés as extensions of their home, and spend hours reading, chatting and even watching television in them. Treats on offer in cafés will generally include a classic *Apfelstrudel, Cremeschnitte* (slices of puff pastry filled with custard and glazed with strawberry fondant), and *Punschkrapferl*, a calorie-packed, pink-fondant-topped pastry laced with rum.

MOZARTKUGEL

Fine chocolates, presented in colourfully decorated boxes carrying the portrait of Mozart, are probably the quintessential Austrian souvenir. Known in Austria as *Mozartkugel*, the chocolates originated in Salzburg, where Mozart lived while composing *Cosi fan Tutti*, the opera in which he worships chocolate. In 1890, master confectioner Paul Fürst made the first Mozart chocolates by forming small balls of marzipan which he coated in a praline cream and then dipped in warm chocolate. Viennese confectioners soon adopted the technique and even today producers vie with one another as to whose *Mozartkugel* are the best and most authentic.

Apfelstrudel *rolls paper-thin pastry with apple, sultanas, cinnamon and sometimes pine nuts or poppyseeds.*

Palatschinken *are fat, fluffy crêpes that may be filled with fruit or jam, or served with vanilla or chocolate sauce.*

Topfenknödel *are light curd cheese dumplings rolled in breadcrumbs and served with fruit compôte.*

What to Drink in Vienna

Austria is a source of excellent wine and good rich beers. Vienna itself is a wine-growing region. It is surrounded by vineyards which supply the *Heurige (see p200–1)* in villages on the edge of the city with young local wines. Fine Austrian wines are found in good restaurants *(see* Choosing a Restaurant, *p210)*. Home-produced wine is mainly white but there are some excellent local red wines, especially from the Burgenland and Carnuntum districts. Sweet *Eiswein* is made from grapes left on the vines until the first frosts. Fruit brandies and schnapps, many of them first class, are also produced.

Beyond the villages north and west of Vienna lie vineyards producing *Heurige* wines

Chardonnay from Styria and sparkling wine from Lower Austria

AUSTRIAN WINES

The most popular wine in Austria is Grüner Veltliner *(see below)*. Other wines include superb dry Rieslings, especially from the Wachau, and rich Weissburgunder (Pinot Blanc) from Burgenland. Red wines tend to be soft and lush – robust reds come from the Blaufränkisch grape *(see below)*. Recent good vintages were 1999, 2000, 2002, 2003, 2006, 2007 and 2009.

Riesling from the Wachau can be light, or full bodied like the Smaragd style.

St Laurent is a soft red wine; at its best it is rich and stylish.

Producer's name

Grape variety

Level of ripeness

Style (dry)

Vintage

Producer's address

Alcohol level

Quantity

Grüner Veltliner is a fresh, fruity white wine. It is widely grown in Austria and is usually made in a dry style. It also makes excellent *Eiswein*.

Blaufränkisch is a quality local red – the best comes from Burgenland.

Krügel or ½ litre
tankard

Seidl or standard ⅓
litre measure

Krügel or ½ litre
of pale beer

Pfiff or ⅛ litre
beer glass

AUSTRIAN BEERS

Vienna has been producing good malty beers for more than 150 years. Viennese lagers are bronze in colour and sweet in flavour. They make an excellent accompaniment to the hearty soups and stews found in *Beisln (see p201)*. The local Ottakring brewery's *Gold Fassl* is typical of the style, although lighter Bavarian-type beers such as *Weizengold* are also commonly available. One of Austria's most popular beers is *Gösser*, produced in Styria and found in the pubs and restaurants of Vienna. Speciality beers include the Styrian *Eggenberger Urbock*, one of the strongest beers in the world. It is made by the Schloss Eggenberg brewery founded in the 17th century.

Kaiser beer,
a light beer

Weizengold
wheat beer

Gösser Spezial
is rich

OTHER AUSTRIAN DRINKS

Austria offers a good range of non-alcoholic fruit juices such as *Himbeersaft* (raspberry syrup) or *Johannisbeersaft* (blackcurrant juice). Fruit is also the basis of many types of schnaps (sometimes called *Brand*). This powerful eau de vie is distilled from berries such as juniper and rowan as well as apricots *(Marillen)* and quince *(Quitten)*. It's worth paying the extra to sample the exquisite fruit schnaps produced by the dedicated specialists. *Almdudler* (herbal lemonade) is also a speciality. For a few weeks in autumn, fermenting grape juice, *Sturm*, is available. Milky in colour and quite sweet, it is more alcoholic than its grape flavour suggests.

Apricot
schnaps

Bierhof beer mat
advertising a pub
in the Haarhof.

Null Komma Josef
is a local alcohol-
free beer.

The Wiener Rathauskeller is a popular restaurant
serving a number of beers

Choosing a Restaurant

The restaurants in this guide have been selected because of their good value, good food and attractive interiors. They are listed below by area, and in alphabetical order within each price category. Some of the specialities they serve are mentioned. All have a no-smoking area. For map references, *see pp262-5.*

PRICE CATEGORIES
Price categories for a three-course meal for one, excluding drinks, but including all unavoidable extra charges such as cover, service and tax.
€ Under €20
€€ €20-30
€€€ €30-40
€€€€ €40-50
€€€€€ over €50

STEPHANSDOM QUARTER

Zanoni Luciano   €
Lugeck 7, 1010 **Tel** *512 79 79* **Fax** *512 79 79 76*   **Map** *6 D3*

This popular, casual and inexpensive Italian eatery serves breakfast as well as sandwiches, *crêpes,* ice cream, pastries and cakes. It is a great place to stop if you are in a rush and want a fast meal. The *gelato* is popular with locals who return to try out new flavours. Also available are some food items "to go".

Beim Czaak   €€
Postgasse 15 / Corner Fleischmarkt, 1010 **Tel** *513 72 15* **Fax** *512 74 64*   **Map** *2 E5, 6 E3*

Owned by the same family since 1920, this is a delightfully informal place offering Viennese cuisine and some dishes in the Czech tradition. It has the pleasing atmosphere of the old-style *Beisl,* with few concessions to comfort in the seating. Friendly service, and pets are permitted too. Closed Sun.

Bettelstudent   €€
Johannesgasse 12, 1010 **Tel** *513 20 44* **Fax** *513 20 44 2*   **Map** *4 E1, 6 D4*

Established in 1986, this is an interesting, lively and inexpensive restaurant that features Austrian wines and over 30 different types of beer. Also on offer are local specialities and international cuisine, such as lasagne and spare ribs. The restaurant is well-known for serving meals into the early hours.

Brezl Gwölb   €€
Ledererhof 9, 1010 **Tel/Fax** *533 88 11*   **Map** *2 D4, 5 C2*

Tucked away between Am Hof and Judenplatz this original 16th-century restaurant serves classic Viennese food. The menu includes traditional home-cooked soups, roasts and pastries. Particular highlights include Viennese inn stew, with dumplings and sausages followed by apple strudel and a strong coffee. The beer is highly recommended.

Da Capo   €€
Schulerstrasse 18, 1010 **Tel** *512 44 91* **Fax** *512 44 91 4*   **Map** *2 E5, 6 D3*

An Italian pizzeria and restaurant which feels more up-market than many, Da Capo has a wood-burning oven and offers attractive seating in its cellar. Besides pizza, specialities include antipasti, pasta, meat dishes and seafood. A seasonal menu is also available. Reservations are recommended.

East to West   €€
Seilerstätte 14, 1010 **Tel** *512 91 49* **Fax** *512 91 49*   **Map** *4 E1, 6 D4*

In this popular Asian restaurant, with an attractively understated modern interior, you can enjoy many selections of tongue-tingling Chinese, Japanese and Thai dishes. The food is light and aromatic, and there is a good selection of appropriate wines. Reservations are recommended.

Figlmüller   €€
Wollzeile 5, 1010 **Tel** *512 61 77* **Fax** *320 42 57 20*   **Map** *2 E5, 6 D3*

This is a cosy restaurant and wine tavern that specializes in traditional Austrian fare. It is most famous for its huge *Wiener Schnitzel* and it's a good place to experiment with wines by the glass. Meals for a gluten-free diet are also available. Pets are permitted. Closed end Jul–beg Aug.

Gulaschmuseum   €€
Schulerstrasse 20, 1010 **Tel** *512 10 17* **Fax** *512 10 18*   **Map** *2 E5, 6 D3*

For those who can't get enough of the ever-popular goulash, the Gulaschmuseum is definitely the place to go. It offers many variations of this classic Viennese dish, made with different meats and vegetables. Reservations are recommended.

Kern's Beisl   €€
Keeblattgasse 4, 1010 **Tel** *533 91 88*   **Map** *2 D5, 5 C3*

Popular, cosy and busy, this *Beisl* serves up a variety of authentic Austrian and Viennese dishes, including fried chicken, *Schnitzels* and beef goulash. There is also an extensive and varied Austrian wine and spirits list. For an extra special treat, try the gingerbread for dessert. Closed Sat & Sun.

Key to Symbols *See back cover flap*

Mandarin

Singerstrasse 11, 1010 **Tel** *512 28 04* **Fax** *513 60 84*

This is a popular and busy Asian restaurant that serves up delicious Oriental food in an elegant enviro...
It specializes in Szechuan and Cantonese cuisine and always has some interesting specials on the menu.
Reservations are recommended.

Toko-Ri

€€

Salztorgasse 4, 1010 **Tel** *532 77 77* **Fax** *532 77 77 17*   **Map** *2 E4, 6 D2*

A popular Japanese restaurant – one of a chain of four – Toko-Ri features *sashimi, maki, tempura* and more.
The interior exudes a sleek modern Japanese minimalism and boasts a sushi counter doubling as an aquarium.
It is a good place for devotees of Japanese fish dishes.

Zum Basilisken

€€

Schönlaterngasse 3-5, 1010 **Tel** *513 31 23* **Fax** *513 31 23*   **Map** *6 E5*

A restaurant, bar and café, Zum Basilisken offers traditional Viennese and regional cuisine in a cosy wood-panelled
interior. Specialities include turkey fillets, pork scallops and veal as well as *Tafelspitz*. For something really unique, try
the wild boar dish. For dessert, the pancakes with cranberries are recommended.

Cantinetta Antinori

€€€

Jasomirgottstrasse 3-5, 1010 **Tel** *533 77 22* **Fax** *533 77 22 11*   **Map** *2 D5, 6 D3*

Part of an up-market restaurant chain with locations in Italy, Switzerland and Russia, this restaurant offers classic
Tuscan dishes, including pasta and fish, and wine from its own vineyards. Both the ambience and service have a
discreet Italian stylishness. Reservations are required.

Da Conte

€€€

Kurrentgasse 12, 1010 **Tel** *533 64 64* **Fax** *532 69 97*   **Map** *5 C2*

This is a traditional Italian restaurant that is well-known for its pasta, lamb and veal dishes, as well as its fresh
fish. For dessert, you might also want to try the tiramisu or *crema caramella*. Business lunches are also available.
Reservations are recommended. Closed Sun.

Enoteca Cinque Terre

€€€

Marc-Aurel-Strasse 10, 1010 **Tel** *533 82 65* **Fax** *533 82 65*   **Map** *2 E5, 6 D2*

In this small, but popular, Mediterranean restaurant, watching your meal being cooked is part of the experience. The
emphasis is on Italian cuisine, and specialities include pasta in cream sauces, and mouth-wateringly prepared fish.
Also on offer are excellent Austrian, Italian and Spanish wines. Closed Sat lunch & Sun.

Fadinger

€€€

Wipplingerstrasse 29, 1010 **Tel** *533 43 41* **Fax** *532 44 51*   **Map** *2 D4, 5 C2*

Solid international, vegetarian and regional specialities are served in this elegant restaurant with an airy "Winter
Garden" room. The chef is well-known for making creative use of original sauces and seasonings. Closed Sat & Sun.
Reservations are recommended.

Griechenbeisl

€€€

Fleischmarkt 11, 1010 **Tel** *533 19 77* **Fax** *533 19 77 12*   **Map** *2 E5, 6 D2*

Since 1447, Vienna's oldest inn has been serving generous portions of traditional Viennese fare to its guests. Now
this family-run business has added some international dishes to the menu. Try the pumpkin cream soup, and take a
look at the framed autographs on the walls of the Mark Twain room. Closed 24 Dec.

Ofenloch

€€€

Kurrentgasse 8, 1010 **Tel** *533 88 44* **Fax** *532 98 22*   **Map** *5 C2*

Classic Viennese dishes are served in this historic restaurant with a well-kept *Wirtshaus* interior. The dishes are
prepared using only the very best local products, which are largely organically grown. Weather permitting, diners
can eat outside on one of Vienna's oldest streets. Closed Sun.

Oswald & Kalb

€€€

Bäckerstrasse 14, 1010 **Tel** *512 13 71* **Fax** *512 13 71 10*   **Map** *2 E5, 6 D3*

This small but friendly restaurant behind the Stephansdom has a reputation as a meeting place for artists. While
here, you can enjoy some traditional Austrian and regional fare, including *Wiener Schnitzels*. Both house wine and a
range of beers are available.

Salut

€€€

Wildpretmarkt 3, 1010 **Tel** *533 13 22* **Fax** *533 13 22*   **Map** *2 D5, 6 D3*

There are few French restaurants in Vienna. However, Salut, which offers classic French dishes, does something to
restore the balance. The decor attempts to transplant a little of Paris to the Danube shore. Fish is a speciality,
including *bouillabaisse*. Menu specials are available for lunch. Closed Sun.

Salzamt

€€€

Ruprechtsplatz 1, 1010 **Tel** *533 53 32*   **Map** *2 E5, 6 D2*

Austrian and Viennese cuisine is served in this popular restaurant that opened in the 1980s. Today, it's a favourite
watering hole of sophisticates who linger into the night at the stylish bar. Excellent meat dishes, pastas, fresh fish
and desserts are served here daily. Reservations are recommended.

Weibels Wirtshaus
*Kumpfgasse 2, 1010 **Tel** 512 39 86 **Fax** 512 39 86*

€€€
Map *4 E1, 6 E3*

Austrian cooking at a very high level can be enjoyed in this traditional restaurant with an intimate wood-panelled interior and cosy sitting niches. The menu includes seasonal dishes. When available, try the pumpkinseed soup. Excellent Austrian wines can be ordered by the glass. Reservations are recommended.

Wrenkh
*Bauernmarkt 10, 1010 **Tel** 533 15 26 **Fax** 535 08 40*

€€€
Map *2 E5, 6 D3*

One of the best vegetarian restaurants in Vienna, with a comfortable feel and a modern ambience, the Wrenkh not only serves interesting vegetarian meals but also tasty fresh fruit drinks. Daily specials are available, as are menus in English. Closed Sat lunch & Sun. Reservations are recommended.

Zum Schwarzen Kameel
*Bognergasse 5, 1010 **Tel** 533 81 25 **Fax** 533 81 25 23*

€€€
Map *2 D5, 5 C3*

This popular, family-owned restaurant, bar and café serves both international and regional cuisine, with classics such as *Tafelspitz* (boiled beef) competing with lighter fare, such as delicious ham sandwiches. There are daily fish specials. The Art Deco dining room is a particularly enjoyable place to sit. Closed Sun.

Do & Co
*Stephansplatz 12, 1010 **Tel** 533 39 69 **Fax** 535 39 59*

€€€€
Map *2 E5, 6 D3*

Part of a catering empire as well as a Viennese institution, Do & Co is on the 7th floor of the Haas-Haus building and has a striking view of the Stephansdom. Excellent international and regional dishes are served, and the specialities include kebabs. Reservations are required.

Fabios
*Tuchlauben 6, 1010 **Tel** 532 22 22 **Fax** 532 22 25*

€€€€
Map *2 D5, 5 C3*

This is a very popular international restaurant with a bar and lounge, which offers a variety of food that includes home-made *ravioli*, risotto, venison, rack of lamb and beef fillets. Also on offer is a cookbook featuring some of the restaurant's famous recipes. Closed Sun. Reservations are required.

König von Ungarn Restaurant
*Schulerstrasse 10, 1010 **Tel** 515 84 15 **Fax** 515 848*

€€€€
Map *2 E5, 6 D3*

Located in the historic König von Ungarn Hotel *(see p195)*, in a 16th-century building, this restaurant offers international and regional cuisine either *à la carte* or from a set menu. Try the roasted wild duck or stuffed veal fillet. Alternatively, the platter of roasted mixed meats is recommended.

Parkring Restaurant
*Parkring 12a, 1010 **Tel** 515 18 6653 **Fax** 515 18 6736*

€€€€
Map *4 D1, 6 E4*

Located in the Vienna Marriott Hotel *(see p196)*, this formal restaurant offers fine dining as well as splendid views of the Stadtpark. Viennese cuisine and *à la carte* international dishes are served in an elegant yet relaxed environment. A perfect place to end a busy day. Open Wed–Sun for evening meals and Sun for brunch.

Plachutta
*Wollzeile 38, 1010 **Tel** 512 15 77 **Fax** 512 15 77 20*

€€€€
Map *2 E5, 6E3*

Typical Viennese cuisine is served in elegant, yet comfortable, green and cream-coloured surroundings. The restaurant specializes in meat dishes and is most well-known for its *Tafelspitz*, which is a boiled beef dish. Formal dress is required; men must wear a jacket and tie. Reservations are recommended.

Restaurant Das Schick
*Parkring 12, 1010 **Tel** 514 80 41 7 **Fax** 514 80 40*

€€€€
Map *4 E1, 6 E4*

On the 12th floor of the Hotel Am Parkring, this restaurant serves traditional Austrian cuisine and Viennese specialities while giving diners an exceptional view of the city. Local wines and brandies are also on offer. Four-course menus are available for a set price.

Tenmaya
*Krugerstrasse 3, 1010 **Tel** 512 73 97 **Fax** 512 46 86*

€€€€
Map *6 D5*

Popular with locals and tourists alike, this Japanese restaurant features numerous Asian delicacies, including sushi and *teppanyaki*. The traditional Japanese setting, which includes women dressed in kimonos, also helps to create an enjoyable dining experience. Reservations are recommended.

Walter Bauer
*Sonnenfelsgasse 17, 1010 **Tel** 512 98 71 **Fax** 512 98 71*

€€€€
Map *6 E3*

Popular with Austrian celebrities and other locals, this restaurant serves international and gourmet cuisine as well as traditional and regional specialities. Dishes include yellow-fin tuna, salmon, lobster and rack of venison. For dessert, try the walnut *Schmarrn*. Closed Mon lunch, Sat & Sun. Reservations are recommended.

Le Siècle
*Parkring 16, 1010 **Tel** 515 170 **Fax** 512 22 16*

€€€€
Map *4 E1, 6 E4*

Located in the exceptional Radisson Blu Palais Hotel *(see p196)*, this is an award-winning and elegant international restaurant that also serves a number of regional specialities. For a special evening, order their Candlelight Dinner Menu. Closed Sat, Sun and holidays and for two weeks in summer.

Key to Price Guide *see p210* **Key to Symbols** *see back cover flap*

HOFBURG QUARTER

Ilona Stüberl

♿ 🅥 🍴 📶 €

Bräunerstrasse 2, 1010 **Tel** *533 90 29* **Fax** *533 90 29 6* **Map** *2 D5, 5 C3*

In this small and popular family-owned restaurant that specializes in Hungarian cuisine, large helpings of goulash, stuffed cabbage, paprika chicken and other dishes are served up. Outside, there are tables on a pedestrian-only street. Pets are permitted. Closed Mon Oct–Mar.

Café Hofburg

♿ 🅥 🍴 📶 €€

Hofburg-Innerer Burghof 1, 1010 **Tel** *241 00 420* **Fax** *241 00 419* **Map** *4 D1, 5 B4*

Conveniently located in the Hofburg Palace, this elegant café and restaurant serves traditional Viennese cuisine, including beef goulash, sausages, salads and a variety of pancakes. Try the Emperor's Pancakes filled with apple sauce and plums.

Regina Margherita

♿ 🅥 🍴 📶 €€

Wallnerstrasse 4, Palais Esterhazy, 1010 **Tel** *533 08 12* **Fax** *533 08 12 20* **Map** *2 D5, 5 B3*

This is a popular Italian restaurant and pizzeria that is located just off Kohlmarkt. It claims to serve "perfect pizzas" as they are freshly baked in an authentic Neapolitan pizza oven. The Italian staff provide friendly service. Reservations are recommended.

Reinthaler's Beisl

📑 ♿ 📶 €€

Dorotheergasse 2-4, 1010 **Tel** *513 12 49* **Map** *2 D5, 5 B3*

This typical, down-to-earth Viennese Beisl restaurant is good value, with lunchtime dishes of the day and a wide range of local specialities. There is outside seating in warmer wather, and reservations are recommended, especially at lunchtime.

Yugetsu

♿ 🅥 🍴 €€

Führichgasse 10, 1010 **Tel** *512 27 20* **Fax** *512 27 20 21* **Map** *4 D1, 5 C4*

The number of Japanese patrons inspires confidence in the authenticity and quality of the food served in this Japanese restaurant with an ultra-modern interior. There is a sushi bar on the ground floor and *teppanyaki* on the first floor. Some say this is the best Japanese restaurant in Vienna.

Ephesus

♿ 🅥 🍴 📶 €€€

Bräunerstrasse 8, 1010 **Tel** *533 90 91* **Fax** *533 90 91* **Map** *2 D5, 5 C3*

In the arched interior of Ephesus, with its elegant wall friezes in imitation of the Epheos ruins, Turkish food returns to the traditions of the Ottoman kitchen. As well as Levantine dishes, there are Turko-Greek standbys such as *tsatsiki* and moussaka. The wines are Austrian, Turkish, Greek and Italian. Closed Sun.

Novelli Bacaro con Cucina

🅥 🍴 📶 €€€€

Bräunerstrasse 11, 1010 **Tel** *513 42 00* **Fax** *513 42 00 1* **Map** *5 C3*

This up-market Mediterranean restaurant, located in a palace, specializes in Italian cuisine and has a lovely interior styled with terracotta from Tuscany. The classic Italian dishes on offer include antipasti, home-made pasta, lamb and beef. There is also an excellent wine list. Pets are permitted. Closed Sun.

Palmenhaus

🅥 🍴 🎵 📶 €€€€

Burggarten, 1010 **Tel** *533 10 33* **Fax** *533 10 33 10* **Map** *4 D1, 5 B4*

In a great location – inside the Palm House and next to the Butterfly House in the Burggarten – this restaurant features a wide variety of international dishes, with something to suit all appetites, including soups, salads, fish and veal.

Sky Restaurant

♿ 🅥 🍴 🎵 €€€€

Kärntnerstrasse 19, 1010 **Tel** *513 17 12 40* **Fax** *513 17 12 20* **Map** *4 D2, 5 C5*

Right at the top of the Steffl building *(see p225)*, this impressive restaurant, café and bar offers a splendid view of the surrounding area and serves up Austrian and international cuisine. For a treat, try the lamb and steak dishes or the meals made in a wok. Reservations are recommended. Open for dinner only. Closed Sun.

Mörwald im Ambassador

♿ 🅥 🍴 €€€€€

Kärntnerstrasse 22, 1010 **Tel** *961 61 161* **Fax** *961 61 160* **Map** *5 C4*

Located in the Ambassador Hotel *(see p196)*, this restaurant serves traditional and modern Viennese fare and is popular with locals as well as tourists. Specialities include pork and veal dishes. There is a a range of unique desserts, including dumplings and pancakes with fruit. Reservations are required.

Sapori Restaurant

♿ 🅥 🍴 €€€€€

Herrengasse 12, 1010 **Tel** *22 780* **Fax** *227 80 79* **Map** *2 D5, 5 B2*

Located in the Radisson Blu Style Hotel *(see p196)*, the Sapori serves an à *la carte* breakfast as well as fine Italian cuisine in a comfortable and modern environment. A seasonal menu is also available, as are business lunches. Closed lunch and pm Sun & public hols.

SCHOTTENRING AND ALSERGRUND

Flein
V [symbols] €

Boltzmanngasse 2, 1090 **Tel** *319 76 89* **Fax** *319 76 89*   **Map** *1 C3*

Conveniently situated in the gardens of the *Lycée Français de Vienne* is this pleasant restaurant that is well-known for serving up delicious, but inexpensive, traditional Austrian and French food. Popular with locals. Try the lunch specials and some of the coffees as well. Closed Sat & Sun.

Rembetiko
[symbols] €

Porzellangasse 38, 1090 **Tel** *317 64 93* **Fax** *319 02 76*   **Map** *1 C3*

For those who hanker after Greek lamb and grilled fish, this may be the place to restore spirits. The homely interior in Grecian blue and white, along with the friendly service, attracts plenty of regular customers. Another plus is the considerable choice of Greek wines. Closed Sat & Sun.

Stomach
[symbols] €€€

Seegasse 26, 1090 **Tel** *310 20 99* **Fax** *310 20 99*   **Map** *1 C3*

The choice of food in this restaurant is eclectic and large (as are the portions). Standard fare is Viennese with some international and seasonal selections. Located in a Biedermeier house, the courtyard is one of the most attractive in Vienna for summer dining. Reservations are recommended. Closed Mon, Tue & lunch Wed–Sat.

Trattoria Martinelli
[symbols] €€€€

Freyung 3, Palais Harrach, 1010 **Tel** *533 67 21* **Fax** *533 67 21 20*   **Map** *2 D5, 5 B2*

The priority of this elegant restaurant is to offer fine and authentic Tuscan cuisine in a genuinely Italian ambience. Among the specialities are the celebrated *osso buco* and the delicious and unique wild duck ravioli. Worth visiting if you desire a taste of Italy. Extensive Italian wines are also on offer.

MUSEUM AND TOWNHALL QUARTER

Lebenbauer
V [symbols] €€

Teinfaltstrasse 3, 1010 **Tel** *533 55 56* **Fax** *533 55 56 11*   **Map** *1 C5, 5 B2*

This is an award-winning, popular, comfortable and airy vegetarian and natural foods restaurant. Here, you can select from a wide variety of attractively-served and healthy meals. Fish is also available. A pleasant outdoor patio is available for warmer weather dining. Reservations are recommended. Closed Sat, Sun and hols.

Lux-Gasthaus-Café-Bar
V [symbols] €€

Schrankgasse 4 / Spittelberggasse 3, 1070 **Tel** *526 94 91* **Fax** *526 09 84*   **Map** *3 B1*

With its choice of seating areas (glass atrium, *Gasthaus*, bistro with red leather benches), this restaurant/café/bar is excellent value. The regional and international cuisine includes seasonal dishes, soups, various salads and wonderful fish.

Spatzennest
V [symbols] €€

St. Ulrichsplatz 1, 1070 **Tel** *526 16 59* **Fax** *526 16 59*   **Map** *3 B1*

This quaint *Beisl* is in a pleasant location near St Ulrich's church and close to the lively Spittelberg pedestrian area with its eateries and stalls. It offers appetizing, traditional Viennese and regional specialities, including *Wiener Schnitzels*, smoked pork dumplings and roasted chicken. Daily specials are also served. Closed Fri & Sat.

Schnattl
V [symbols] €€€

Lange Gasse 40, 1080 **Tel** *405 34 00* **Fax** *405 34 00*   **Map** *1 B5*

A popular restaurant that features Styrian (southern Austrian) fare, the Schnattl also makes an effort to offer organic produce. Try the salad with pumpkinseed oil dressing or some game. The interior is in post-modern style. Styrian wines are available, as are daily lunch specials. Reservations are required. Closed Aug.

Selina
[symbols] €€€

Laudongasse 13, 1080 **Tel** *405 64 04* **Fax** *408 04 59*   **Map** *1 A4*

Close to City Hall, this restaurant has a pleasant and elegant interior. It specializes in Austrian cuisine as well as some international dishes, and is well-known for its Mediterranean and vegetarian meals. Also good are the fish and seafood specials. Reservations are recommended.

Zu ebener Erde und erster Stock
V [symbols] €€€

Burggasse 13, 1070 **Tel** *523 62 54*   **Map** *3 B1*

Enjoy first-rate Viennese cooking and seasonal specials in the romantic ambience of this charming Biedermeier house. The ground floor resembles a traditional *Beisl* and offers less expensive fare, while the floor above offers more elegant dining. Reservations are required. Closed Sat lunch & Sun.

Key to Price Guide *see p210* **Key to Symbols** *see back cover flap*

OPERA AND NASCHMARKT

Hungerkünstler   🚻 V 🍴   €
Gumpendorfer Strasse 48, 1060 **Tel** *581 03 70*   **Map** *3 B3*

This is a simple neighbourhood *Beisl* that offers traditional Viennese and regional cuisine along with some Italian and international specialities. The noodle dish with melted cheese is worth sampling. The interior of the restaurant is pleasant, with antique chandeliers, making for a relaxed dining experience. Closed Sun.

Kostas   📋 🚻 V 🍴   €€
Friedrichstrasse 6, 1010 **Tel** *586 37 29*   **Map** *4 D2*

Close to the Secession building and the Naschmarkt, this little Greek restaurant has been winning laurels for its authentic fare (the lamb dishes are particularly good). It provides better value than many less genuine rivals. Recorded Greek music adds to the ambience. Small portions are available on request. Closed Sun.

Restaurant Shambala   🚻 V 🍴   €€€
Opernring 13, 1010 **Tel** *588 90 70 00* **Fax** *588 90 90 90*   **Map** *4 D1, 5 B5*

This French restaurant in Le Meridien hotel *(see p198)*, near the Hofburg Palace, offers fine dining in an ultra sleek and modern environment. The nightly specials feature both healthy ingredients and classic French flair. Particularly delicious are the desserts and pastries.

Aux Gazelles   🚻 V 🍴 🎵   €€€€
Rahlgasse 5, 1060 **Tel** *585 66 45* **Fax** *585 66 45 39*   **Map** *3 C2, 5 A5*

In a unique North African-themed complex, you can relax with a candlelit dinner and indulge in some authentic Moroccan and French cuisine before going to one of the other venues nearby. Among them are Turkish steam baths, a café, bar, bazaar shop and nightclub. Reservations are recommended. Closed Sun.

Restaurant (Anna) Sacher   🚻 V 🍴 🍽   €€€€
Philharmonikerstrasse 4, 1010 **Tel** *514 56 0* **Fax** *514 56 810*   **Map** *5 C5*

In the elegant surroundings of the Sacher Hotel *(see p198)*, this gourmet restaurant offers an international menu that includes veal, chicken and beef dishes. Especially tantalizing is their world-renowned *Sacher torte*. Seven-course meals are available. Men must wear a jacket and tie. Reservations are required. Closed Mon.

BELVEDERE QUARTER

Salm Brău   V 🍴   €
Rennweg 8, 1030 **Tel** *799 59 92* **Fax** *799 59 92*   **Map** *4 F3*

There's a busy and friendly atmosphere in this good-value regional restaurant and beer cellar in the former stables of the monastic buildings flanking the Salesianerinnenkirche. The *Surstelze* (smoked pork joint) for two is a speciality, as are the beers, which are brewed on the premises.

Restaurant Sperl   🚻 V 🍴   €€
Karolinengasse 13, 1040 **Tel** *504 73 34* **Fax** *504 73 34 30*   **Map** *4 E4*

In this restaurant which dates from 1928, a cosy, traditional wooden interior provides the ideal setting for food from an extensive Viennese and Austrian menu. The spinach dumplings, pork medallions, vegetarian meals and specialities from the grill are all recommended.

Wiener Wirtschaft   V 🍴   €€
Wiedner Haupstrasse 27-29, 1040 **Tel** *501 11 364* **Fax** *501 11 350*   **Map** *3 C5*

Located in the Hotel Erzherzog Rainer *(see p198)*, this restaurant serves traditional Austrian cuisine. A speciality is the goulash, of which 14 different types are available. A "Goulash Fest" for larger groups consists of five different goulashes plus side dishes. Coffee and cake are available all day.

Cantino Restaurant   🚻 V 🍴   €€€
Seilerstätte 30, 1010 **Tel** *512 54 46* **Fax** *512 55 50 28*   **Map** *4 E1, 6 D5*

This is a popular restaurant that specializes in Mediterranean and Spanish cuisine and is well-known for the tantalising variety of tapas it offers. Also worth trying are the paella and fresh sheep cheese with paprika. Closed Sat lunch & Sun pm.

Korso   🚻 V 🍴 🍽   €€€€
Mahlerstrasse 2, 1010 **Tel** *515 16 546* **Fax** *515 16 575*   **Map** *4 D1, 5 C5*

Located in the Hotel Bristol *(see p199)*, the Korso features traditional Viennese cooking plus international dishes. The wine list is formidable. The ambience is one of elegance and wealth, and the service is excellent. Men must wear a jacket and tie. Reservations are required. Closed Sat lunch & Sun lunch in Jul.

Restaurant Imperial   €€€€€

Kärntner Ring 16, 1015 **Tel** *50110 356* **Fax** *501 10 410*   **Map** *4 D2, 6 D5*

Located in the Imperial Hotel *(see p199)*, this is a gourmet restaurant that features both Austrian and international cuisine. Particularly famous is the chocolate-covered Imperial Torte (cake). Cigars are also on offer. So, too, are set lunches and brunch; check with the hotel for when they are available.

Restaurant Kervansaray Hummerbar   €€€€

Mahlerstrasse 9, 1010 **Tel** *512 88 43* **Fax** *512 88 43-75*   **Map** *4 E1, 6 D5*

This popular seafood restaurant specializes in fresh oysters, scallops and lobster, and has a daily changing menu. Desserts include fresh fruit served with liquor, ice cream or cream. Advance orders can be given for meals that are prepared on request. Reservations are recommended. Closed Sun and hols.

FURTHER AFIELD

Das Möbel   €

Burggasse 10, 1070 **Tel** *524 94 97* **Fax** *524 94 97-13*   **Map** *3 A1, 5 A3*

The most unique feature of this popular and friendly café and restaurant is that you can buy any of the chairs you sit on, which are all made by Austrian designers. Otherwise, it's worth a visit to try one of the quiches on the international menu.

Gmoa-Keller   €

Am Heumarkt 25, 1030 **Tel** *712 53 10* **Fax** *712 53 10*   **Map** *4 E2*

Featuring both regional Austrian fare and seasonal dishes, this is a popular restaurant. Among the specialities are soups, veal and beef, plus fruit or chocolate pancakes for dessert. It is a friendly place that is much favoured by the musical fraternity from the nearby concert halls. Closed Sun.

Schweizerhaus   €

Prater 116, 1020 **Tel** *728 01 52* **Fax** *728 01 52-29*

Regional and Eastern European fare is served up in generous portions in this well-loved restaurant and beer garden inside the Prater Park. Try the beef stew or Slovakian cabbage soup. Beer-lovers may want to sample the Czech Budweiser Budvar beer. Closed Nov-mid-Mar.

Babu   €€

Stadtbahnbogen 181-184, 1090 **Tel** *479 48 49*

For those who thrive on late-night action, it's good to know that Babu offers a variety of regional and international cuisine almost round the clock in an interesting setting, underneath the elevated tracks of the subway. Babu also has a popular local bar.

Motto Club Restaurant-Bar   €€

Schönbrunner Strasse 30, 1050 **Tel** *587 06 72* **Fax** *587 06 72 11*   **Map** *3 A4*

A variety of dishes based on regional, Asian and Mediterranean cooking styles is provided in this chic and cosy restaurant and bar. Try the spinach salad or *teriyaki* tofu dish for a unique treat. Also worth trying is the mousse for dessert. DJ music is played nightly.

Restaurant Dubróvnik   €€

Am Heumarkt 5, 1030 **Tel** *713 71 02* **Fax** *713 71 02 14*   **Map** *4 E2, 6 E5*

Croatian specialities, including marinated sardines and *pljeskavica* with *ajvar* (spiced meat patties with a roasted pepper spread), are served in this lively restaurant and bar. If you're looking for authentic south-eastern European food, this is the place to be. Live Dalmatian music features occasionally.

Schloss Concordia   €€

Simmeringer Hauptstrasse 283, 1110 **Tel** *769 88 88* **Fax** *769 88 22*

Typical Austrian cuisine is served in a restaurant in an untypical location – across the street from the Central Cemetery. However bizarre the location, the food is delicious and relatively inexpensive, with an emphasis on extra large *Wiener* and chicken *Schnitzels*. A choice of beers is available.

Stadtwirt   €€

Untere Viaduktgasse 45, 1030 **Tel** *713 38 28* **Fax** *713 38 28 4*

This is a bustling restaurant, popular with locals, that has cosy corner seats and tables for groups. Also provided is superb Viennese and regional cooking at affordable prices, plus house wines, draught beer and brandies. Reservations are required. Closed Sat lunch & Sun.

Zu den drei Buchteln   €€

Wehrgasse 9, 1050 **Tel** *587 83 65*   **Map** *3C3*

The ambience here lives up to the Bohemian/Moravian culinary aspirations.Try some *svickova* (beef with seasoned cream sauce) and *brimsenbaluska* (sheep cheese dumplings), not to mention the irresistible desserts. Wash it all down with some Czech beer or Moravian wine. Closed Sun, last week Jul, first 2 weeks Aug.

Key to Price Guide *see p210* **Key to Symbols** *see back cover flap*

Zum Herkner

Dornbacher Strasse 123, 1170 **Tel** *485 43 86* **Fax** *485 43 86*

For many, the long trek out to Zum Herkner is certainly worth it. Good "bourgeois Viennese fare" as well as international cuisine is served at moderate prices in a rustic and unstuffy ambience. The seasonal menu is strong on veal dishes, chanterelle mushrooms and carp. Reservations are required. Closed Sat & Sun.

Eckel

Sieveringer Strasse 46, 1190 **Tel** *320 32 18* **Fax** *320 66 60*

This charming traditional Viennese restaurant offers a cosy interior in the winter and a garden in the summer. Viennese cooking is at its best here, with international specialities, such as lobster and crayfish, also featuring. There is a superb list of wines, mostly Austrian. Reservations are required. Closed Sun & Mon.

Green Cottage

Kettenbrückengasse 3, 1050 **Tel** *586 65 81* **Fax** *586 65 81*   **Map** *3 C3*

Jugendstil meets the Orient (the interior) and *nouvelle cuisine* goes Chinese (the menu)! The food here ranges from a *Sichuan* version of Mongolian lamb and seasoned grilled fish to deliciously light, rice-based desserts. Some dishes may be salty for the average taste. Friendly and attentive staff. Closed Sun.

Kronprinz Rudolf

Taborstrasse 12, 1020 **Tel** *211 50 423* **Fax** *211 50 160*   **Map** *2 F4, 6 E1*

Located in the Hotel Stefanie *(see p199)*, this restaurant offers traditional Viennese and Austrian cuisine in an elegant and refined setting. It is well-known for preparing meals from recipes used during the days of the Austro-Hungarian Empire. When the weather is good, try dining in the courtyard garden.

Mediterraneo Restaurant

Johannesgasse 28, 1037 **Tel** *711 22 110* **Fax** *713 44 89*   **Map** *4 E1, 6 D4*

Besides preparing a good selection of regional dishes, this restaurant serves up a wide variety of international favourites in a relaxed setting, including Italian, French, Spanish, Greek and Turkish cuisine. Breakfast is also on offer.

Silberwirt

Schlossgasse 21, 1050 **Tel** *544 49 07* **Fax** *548 84 66*   **Map** *3 C4*

Silberwirt is part of a complex of eateries built on the site of Schloss Margareten, which was devastated by the Turks during the 1683 siege of Vienna. Time-hallowed Viennese dishes are cooked with care and flair, and served in a relaxed ambience. A variety of Austrian wines are on offer too. Reservations are recommended.

SteirerStuben

Wiedner Hauptstrasse 111, 1050 **Tel** *544 43 49* **Fax** *544 08 88*   **Map** *3 C5*

Fine dining and international cuisine is what is offered at the Steirerstuben. Try their Alpine lamb, char *(Saibling)* in wild garlic sauce, or carp *gelée*. Among the excellent desserts is pineapple with mango sorbet. All meals and desserts are prepared artistically. Reservations are recommended. Closed Sun in Sep–Oct.

Tempel

Praterstrasse 56, Inner Courtyard, 1150 **Tel** *214 01 79* **Fax** *214 01 79*   **Map** *2 F4, 5 F2*

Tempel restaurant offers a wide choice of dishes, ranging from seafood to beef and veal. The good value set menu, sophisticated desserts and excellent Austrian wines makes this a popular eating place. There is outdoor seating in warmer weather. Closed Sat lunch, Sun & Mon.

Vikerl's Lokal

Wüffelgasse 4, 1150 **Tel** *894 34 30* **Fax** *892 41 83*

Viennese cooking is amiably served in this family-run restaurant. When available, try the quail, calf's liver or venison. Don't be deterred by the restaurant's location. The menu changes every two weeks. Reservations are recommended. Closed Mon.

Kim Kocht

Lustkandlgasse 6, 1090 **Tel** *319 02 42* **Fax** *319 02 42*   **Map** *1 B2*

This popular up-market Asian restaurant is often booked weeks in advance. Specialities include Asian fusion food, artistically prepared. Try some sushi and the sorbet for dessert. A gourmet food shop is also on the premises. Music is played from 6pm in the restaurant's bar. Reservations are required. Closed Sat–Tue.

Vincent

Grosse Pfarrgasse 7, 1020 **Tel** *214 15 16* **Fax** *212 14 14*   **Map** *2 E3*

The name bespeaks the owner's passion for modern art, specimens of which adorn the walls. The excellent organic fare is a *nouvelle cuisine* influenced version of Viennese, and decidedly creative. When available, try the mussels or the veal kidneys cooked in port wine. Reservations are required. Closed Sun.

Steirereck

Meierei im Stadtpark, 1030 **Tel** *713 31 68* **Fax** *713 31 68 2*   **Map** *6 F4*

With its atmospheric location, fabulous service and culinary artistry, this restaurant may be one of the best in Vienna. Menus of stunning flair show both Austrian and international influences. If you appreciate a meal that is staged as a performance, this is the place for you. Reservations are required. Closed Sat & Sun.

g a Café

...ection lists a broad cross-section of Viennese cafés, wine cellars, sandwich/self-service bars and *Konditoreien (see pp200-1)*. Both the traditional and the new and fashionable are included; bars are not listed, but some of the places featured do have lively bars. For coffee and cake expect to pay more in the famous cafés, for example Café Konditorei Demel. The main attraction of a Viennese coffee house is that once you have bought something you can relax and stay as long as you like.

STEPHANSDOM QUARTER

Café-Konditorei Gerstner

Kärntnerstrasse 13-15, 1010 **Tel** *512 49 63 77* **Fax** *512 49 63 44*   **Map** *4 D1, 6 D4*

One of the great "Imperial and Royal" *Konditoreien*, which has a marvellous selection of pastries that are not only delicious but are decorated quite artistically. Try the *Nusstorte* or *Topfenstrudel* for a special treat. Also available are confections, such as petits fours and marzipan.

Café Ministerium

Georg-Coch-Platz 4, 1010 **Tel** *512 92 25*   **Map** *2 F5, 6 F3*

Moderately-priced Austrian home cooking, including vegetarian selections, can be had at this café. Also on offer is a good selection of coffee drinks. Other attractions are chess and billiards, plus live music on Wednesdays and Thursdays. Free Wi-Fi Internet access is available for those who want to surf the net. Closed Sat & Sun.

Duran Sandwiches

Rotenturmstrasse 11, 1010 **Tel** *533 71 15* **Fax** *533 71 15*   **Map** *2 E5, 6 D3*

No-frills eat-in and takeaway restaurant, with quite a following, which offers a great selection of open sandwiches for an incredibly low price. Whether meat, fish or vegetarian, they appeal to the eye as well as the taste buds. Those on the go can fax in their order. Closed Sun.

È Tricaffè

Rotenturmstrasse 25, 1010 **Tel** *533 89 90* **Fax** *533 89 85*   **Map** *2 E5, 6 E2*

All the cafés in this trendy chain (see also Am Hof 2/Corner Bognergasse) serve excellent Italian-style specialities, such as antipasto and tiramisu. Most notable is the wine selection, from which you can choose Italian wines by the glass. The espresso is good too.

Jazzland

Franz Josefs Kai 29, 1010 **Tel** *533 25 75*   **Map** *2 D5, 6 D2*

The oldest jazz club in Austria and located in a 16th-century cellar, Jazzland features local and international musicians nightly. Food ranges from traditional Austrian fare to pasta and salads, with Serbian *cevapcici* (ground fried meat shaped like sausages) a speciality. Live music from 9pm; the cover charge varies. Closed Sun.

Vis-à-Vis

Wollzeile 5, 1010 **Tel** *512 93 50* **Fax** *512 93 50*   **Map** *2 E5, 6 D3*

One of Vienna's most loved, and oldest, wine bars, where more than 300 wines are on offer. Don't be fooled by the size of the place; a visit is essential for any wine connoisseur looking to sample something special. Sparkling wines are especially noteworthy and the glassware is top notch. Closed Sat & Sun.

HOFBURG QUARTER

Café Bräunerhof

Stallburggasse 2, 1010 **Tel** *512 38 93* **Fax** *513 05 49*   **Map** *4 D1, 5 C3*

Old-fashioned café that has an *à la carte* menu and also serves breakfast. It's reputed to be the favourite café of Austria's most celebrated author, Thomas Bernhard. Games of chess and billiards round out the offerings here. Live music on weekends.

Café Hawelka

Dorotheergasse 6, 1010 **Tel** *512 82 30*   **Map** *2 D5, 5 C3*

A Viennese institution, with a spartan but cosy interior, this is the preferred café of the city's Bohemians and their dogs. Try the café's most famous speciality, their *Buchteln*, which is a bun made from yeast dough and filled with apricot jam: simply delicious. Closed Tue.

Key to Symbols *see back cover flap*

Café-Konditorei Demel

Kohlmarkt 14, 1010 **Tel** *535 17 17 0* **Fax** *535 17 17 26*

Map *2 D5, 5 C3*

Founded in 1776, this famous "Royal and Imperial" confectioners offers a light lunch of sandwiches and a huge selection of pastries and confections. The elegant Neo-Classical interior adds to the enjoyment of a visit here, and it's a particularly popular spot for tourists.

Trzesniewski

Dorotheergasse 1, 1010 **Tel** *512 32 91* **Fax** *513 95 65*

Map *2 D5, 5 C3*

Famous stand-up fast-food eatery (eight branches are located throughout Vienna) that specializes in all sorts of open sandwiches. The fillings are made from organic produce and the food is always fresh. Lots of variety at a low cost. Great for a quick meal on the run. Closed Sun.

SCHOTTENRING AND ALSERGRUND

Tunnel

Florianigasse 39, 1080 **Tel** *947 57 20* **Fax** *405 34 65*

Map *1 A5*

This three-storey eatery and art gallery in Josefstadt serves a selection of cold sandwiches and warm food as well as a breakfast buffet. The international and varied cuisine (including pizzas) is generally inexpensive. A variety of drinks rounds out the menu.

MUSEUM AND TOWNHALL QUARTER

Café Landtmann

Dr Karl Lueger-Ring 4, 1010 **Tel** *241 00 111* **Fax** *532 06 25*

Map *1 C5, 5 B2*

A popular coffee-house, the Landtmann was once patronized by Sigmund Freud. Press conferences are frequently held here and it is always crowded in the evenings. An extensive menu includes breakfast. Coffee and tea specialities, home-made desserts, and pastries for diabetics are available.

Sluka

Rathausplatz 8, 1010 **Tel** *405 71 72* **Fax** *406 88 94 4*

Map *1 C5, 5 A3*

Tucked under the arches of the Neo-Gothic Town Hall, this café and confectioner offers a light lunch and buffet of *hors d'oeuvres*. It is also well-known for its caviar sandwiches. While here, don't forget to try at least one cake; those made of fruit are especially good. Extensive selections for diabetics. Closed Sun.

OPERA AND NASCHMARKT

Café Mozart

Albertinaplatz 2, 1010 **Tel** *241 00 211* **Fax** *241 00 219*

Map *4 D1, 5 C4*

Located next to the State Opera House, the building that houses Café Mozart was first established as a café in 1794. Today it is still a popular dining establishment among locals as well as tourists, offering traditional Austrian and gourmet cuisine and pastries in an elegant environment.

FURTHER AFIELD

Heuriger Zimmermann

Armbrustergasse 5, 1190 **Tel** *370 22 11* **Fax** *370 61 30*

Cosy and fashionable *Heuriger* of great character that offers a range of Viennese warm dishes as well as the typical *Heurigen* buffet in a friendly environment. Vegetarians will like the extensive salad buffet. The outdoor dining area is also a good place to relax on a sunny day.

Mayer am Pfarrplatz

Pfarrplatz 2, Heiligenstadt, 1190 **Tel** *370 12 87* **Fax** *370 47 14*

Popular wine tavern in the village where Beethoven wrote his "testament". Among rustic surroundings you can enjoy a delicious cold buffet or a choice of hot meals that include home-made sausages. Historians will admire the wine press dating from 1617.

SHOPS AND MARKETS

Since Vienna is a compact city, it is a pleasant place to shop. The main shopping area is pedestrianized and full of pretty cafés, and although it is not in the same league as London, Paris and New York when it comes to international stores, you can browse around at a more leisurely pace. Austrian-made glassware, food and traditional crafts all make for good buys. However, the shops tend to cater for comparatively conventional and mature tastes and purses. Vienna has a range of markets selling a variety of produce and wares from exotic fruit to old trinkets. The pedestrian shopping areas of Kärntner Strasse, the Graben, and Kohlmarkt house the more expensive shops and are pleasant to wander around. For more details of shops and markets see the Directory on page 225.

Augarten porcelain Lipizzaner

BEST BUYS

Many of the best buys in Vienna are small and readily transportable: coffee addicts shouldn't forget to buy freshly ground coffee – the city imports some of the best.

If you have a sweet tooth, you couldn't be in a more appropriate city. It is justly famous for its cakes, pastries and *Torten (see p206–7)* and any good *Café-Konditorei* (cake shop and café) will post cakes back home for you. In November and December, try the buttery Advent *Stollen* available from **Julius Meinl am Graben** *(see p223)* or any good baker. Stuffed with fruit and nuts and dusted with icing sugar, it is a tasty Christmas loaf. Alternatively, buy some prettily-packaged *Sachertorte (see p207)*, available year round. The specialist chocolate shops *(see p223)* are worth a visit, both for the unusual packaging and the chocolate itself.

Sweet *Eiswein* (so-called because the grapes are left on the vines until the first frosts) is an unusual and delicious dessert wine. **Zum Schwarzen Kameel** *(see p223)* sells the rarer red version as well.

Other Austrian-made goods include clothes manufactured in the felt-like woollen fabric known as *Loden (see p223)*. If you feel like treating yourself and have space in your car or suitcase, buy custom-made sheets or high-quality down pillows or duvets made in Austria *(see p222)*. Petit point embroidery, which adorns anything from powder compacts to handbags, is a Viennese speciality *(see p222)*.

Glassware – including superb chandeliers – and **Augarten** porcelain *(see p222)* tend to be highly original, although expensive. Many people collect crystal ornaments made by Swarovski. **Ostovics** *(see p222)* is a good cookery and glass shop for such items.

Trachten (Austrian costume) shops *(see p223)* are fun; they have a wide selection of hats, children's dresses, jackets and blouses. **Gilhofer** *(see p223)* stocks old prints and maps. Early editions of works by writers such as Freud, Kraus or Rilke can be found in Vienna's antique bookshops *(see p223)*.

Chest of drawers chocolate box from Altmann & Kühne *(see p223)*

OPENING HOURS

Shops usually open at 8:30 or 9 in the morning and close at 6 or 7 in the evening. Some of the smaller shops close for an hour at lunch time. Traditionally stores were required to close at noon on Saturday, though all now stay open until 5pm. Shops are still closed on Sundays and public holidays, although you can buy items such as groceries, flowers, camera film, books and newspapers at the major railway stations. The supermarkets at the airport and Wien Nord station are open seven days a week.

J & L Lobmeyr's glass shop on Kärntner Strasse *(see p222)*

HOW TO PAY

Vienna is now more credit (and debit) card-orientated, with many shops accepting the major cards. Some also take Eurocheques (with a card), but it is still wise to carry some cash as an alternative.

WHERE TO SHOP

The pedestrian shopping areas of Graben, Kohlmarkt and Kärntner Strasse have many of the most well-known and expensive shops in Vienna.

The more cheaply priced area is along Mariahilfer Strasse, with department stores selling household goods, and well-known chain stores such as H & M.

RIGHTS AND SERVICES

If a purchase is defective you are usually entitled to a refund, provided you have proof of purchase. This is not always the case with goods bought in the sales – inspect them carefully before you buy. Many shops in Vienna will pack goods for you – and often gift-wrap them at no extra charge – and send them anywhere in the world.

VAT EXEMPTION

VAT (value added tax) or MWSt (Mehrwertsteuer) is normally charged at 20 per cent. If you reside outside the European Union (EU), you are entitled to claim back the VAT on goods purchased in Austria. This is only the case, however, if the total purchase price (this can include the total cost of several items from one shop) exceeds €73. Take along your passport when shopping and ask the shopkeeper to complete Form U34 at the time of sale. This should also bear the shop's stamp and have the receipt attached. You may have the refund credited to your credit card account, have it posted home, or pick it up at the airport.

Purchased goods must not be used prior to exportation. If you leave Vienna by air, present the form at Customs

View down Kohlmarkt, one of Vienna's pedestrian shopping streets

before checking in, and have it stamped as proof of export. You may also have to show your purchases at Customs, so pack them somewhere accessible. Then post the stamped form to the Austrian shopkeeper or collect the refund at the airport (there is a handling fee). If leaving by car or train, present the form to Customs at the border, where you can also claim a refund. If you are not disembarking the train at the border, there is sometimes a customs official on the train to stamp your form.

When you have goods sent directly to your home outside the EU, VAT is deducted at the time of purchase.

One of the famous *Loden* coats from Loden-Plankl *(see p223)*

However, since Austria is a member of the EU, EU citizens cannot claim back VAT.

SALES

The bi-annual sales are held in January and July. The best bargains can usually be found in fashions. Electrical and household goods are also much reduced.

SHOPPING CENTRES

Shopping centres are a fairly recent innovation in Vienna. The most modern are the **Ringstrassen Galerien**, the splendid **Haas Haus** and the spruced-up **Generali Centre**. Built in the same style as the Café Central *(see pp58–61)*, **Freyung Passage** is an arcade of elegant shops in the Palais Ferstel *(see pp108 and 110)*.

ADDRESSES

Generali Centre
Mariahilfer Strasse 77–79. **Map** 3 A3.

Haas Haus
Stock-im-Eisen-Platz 4.
Map 2 D5 & 5 C3.

Freyung Passage
Palais Ferstel 1, Freyung 2.
Map 2 D5 & 5 B2.

Ringstrassen Galerien
Kärntner Ring 5–7. **Map** 6 D5.

Shops and Boutiques

Even if Vienna does not boast the wide range of shops you find in many other European capitals, it does offer certain goods that are hard to beat elsewhere. Austrian glassware is justly famous and cut-glass gifts are of a high quality. A few shops, such as **Knize** (in the Graben), designed by Adolf Loos, are in themselves worth a visit simply to admire the Jugendstil architecture. It's best to speak English in shops unless you are fluent in German – you will probably receive quicker service!

SPECIALITY SHOPS

Vienna still manufactures leather goods, although nowadays a lot are imported from Italy. **Robert Horn** designs and manufactures leather travel cases and accessories. He maintains that even he has been unable to improve on the design of a briefcase carried by Metternich at the Congress of Vienna, which he has only slightly modernized.

Petit point embroidery is another Viennese speciality. Some of the most attractive can be found at **Petit Point** (where even the shop's door handle is embroidered) and at **Maria Stransky**.

A marvellous place for party tricks, and much beloved by practical jokers, is **Zauberklingl**. **Kober** (see p232) is a "serious" toy shop which sells well-made dolls and toys. Or combine a visit to the novelty and joke shop called **Witte** with a trip to the Naschmarkt. Witte stocks masks, fancy dress outfits, and beautiful old-fashioned paper decorations that are ideal for festivals. **Metzger**, a shop specializing in beeswax, sells its own candles and candlesticks. It also stocks certain gift items, such as honey cakes and boxes of chocolates.

MUSIC

As you would expect in "the City of Music", the range of recordings available is rich and varied. The shops with the widest range of classical CDs are **EMI** and **Gramola**. However, don't expect to find many bargains: CDs are more expensive in Austria than in other countries in Europe. **Arcadia** specializes particularly in opera and operetta. The staff in all these shops are usually very knowledgeable. **Doblinger** focuses on contemporary Austrian music and is excellent for sheet music; it also has a second-hand CD department.

JEWELLERY

Viennese jewellers have long been famous for their fine workmanship. Fruit and flower brooches carved in semi-precious stones and sometimes studded with diamonds, are a more recent Austrian innovation. **Juwelier Wagner** always has a good selection. Both **Köchert** and **Heldwein** were jewellers to the Imperial Court and still produce beautiful jewellery in their own workshops today. Köchert also sells antique pieces and Heldwein are known for their multi-coloured chains of semi-precious stones. In 2010, one of the pieces designed by **Schullin** won the prestigious Diamonds International award organized by De Beers for innovative design. Their small window usually attracts a crowd of admirers to view their latest creations. Don't let that put you off – prices start at a reasonable level.

GLASSWARE

The Chandeliers at Vienna's Opera House and the Metropolitan Opera in New York are by **J & L Lobmeyr**, as are the chandeliers in numerous palaces throughout the world – including the Kremlin. This company – now run by a fifth generation of the same family – has produced beautiful glasses and crystal chandeliers since the early 19th century, often commissioning famous artists. One range of glasses still in production today was designed by Josef Hoffmann (see p56) in Jugendstil style. Its famous *Musselinglas*, a type of glass so fine that it almost bends to the touch, is exquisite. There is a small but superb glass museum on the first floor and, apart from its own glassware, Lobmeyr also sells select items of Hungarian Herend porcelain.

INTERIORS

Vienna's porcelain makers, **Augarten**, are the second oldest in Europe. The company was founded in 1718 and taken over by the House of Habsburg in 1744. Ever since, its products have been marked with the banded shield coat of arms. Each piece of porcelain at **Schloss Augarten** is still hand finished and painted: patterns and shapes are based on original models from the Baroque, Rococo, Biedermeier and Art Deco periods and on designs created by present-day artists. The Schloss Augarten factory is open to visitors. **Ostovics** stocks glass and porcelain as well as kitchen-ware, and is good for gifts.

Founded in 1849, **Backhausen** is known for its exclusive furnishing fabrics, woven in the original Jugendstil patterns, and for its silk scarves and matching velvet handbags. In addition it has a good selection of duvets and household linens. Quality bedding and linens are available at **Gans**, which conveniently has a shop at Vienna's Schwechat airport for last-minute purchases. **Gunkel** stocks household linen and bath robes, and for generations the Viennese have patronized **Zur Schwäbischen Jungfrau**, founded in 1720, where fine linens can be made to order as well as purchased ready-made.

FOOD AND WINE

One of Vienna's most renowned and almost revered food and wine shops, **Zum Schwarzen Kameel** (see p212), sells mouth-watering produce.

Julius Meinl am Graben food hall, on the pedestrianized Graben, also offers a wide selection of delicacies. Enter via its Lukullus Bar in Naglergasse if you decide you would like to stop for a snack and a drink.

There is also a good chain of wine merchants called **Wein & Co**, one of which is situated on the Jasomir-gottstrasse.

Altmann & Kühne is famous for its tiny, handmade chocolates sold in beautiful boxes shaped like miniature chests of drawers, books, horses and angels.

GIFTS

Successor of the famous Wiener Werkstätten, the outfit called **Österreichische Werkstätten** has a selection of almost exclusively Austrian goods. In stock are a range of enamelled jewellery designed by Michaela Frey, ceramics, mouth-blown glass, candles and, from late autumn onwards, Christmas tree decorations. The arts and crafts markets (see p224) are also good hunting-grounds for picking up knick-knacks. The Tirol-based firm of **Swarovksi** produces high quality crystal. Their necklaces, pins and earrings are popular world-wide, as are their animal figurines and accessories.

BOOKS

Located in the Jewish District is **Shakespeare & Co**, which stocks an extensive selection of books in English, as does the **British Bookshop** and **Frick International**. For music books in English, visit **Doblinger** (see p222). Rare old books – as well as new ones – can be purchased at **Heck**. Old prints and maps are available at the specialist **Gilhofer. Taschenbuchladen**

bookshop stocks a range of paperbacks.

NEWSPAPERS AND PERIODICALS

Most newspaper kiosks located within the Ringstrasse stock foreign newspapers – and so do the best coffee houses, where they can be read free of charge. There is no English-language Viennese newspaper. **Morawa** sells a variety of newspapers and periodicals in practically any language.

CLOTHES AND ACCESSORIES

Viennese clothes are well-made and tend to be quite formal. **Loden-Plankl** is famous for jackets, coats and capes made from *Loden*. This is a warm, felt-like fabric traditionally in dark green or grey, but now produced in a range of colours.

Tostmann is best known for traditional Austrian costumes or *Trachten*: its *Dirndl* (dresses) are made from a variety of fabrics including beautiful brocades. Its clothes for children are particularly delightful.

Fürnkranz has several branches throughout Vienna, but its main shop providing elegant day and evening wear is in Kärntner Strasse, with the shop at Neuer Markt stocking more sporty styles. Opened in 2011, the flagship store of Peek & Cloppenburg offers casual and sports wear as well as accessories. A trusted and old-established

Viennese name is **Knize**. In imperial times this was a famous tailoring establishment, but the shop now stocks ready-to-wear clothes for men and women. It also sells its own scent. **Kettner** – almost hidden down a nearby side street – stocks casual daywear for both men and women at all its branches.

Steffl department store offers fashion, toys and stationery over seven floors.

All the shoes at **Bally** are imported from Italy; the quality, as you would expect, is excellent. **D'Ambrosio**, which has several branches located in the first district, stocks trendy, up-market Italian-style shoes for both men and women at moderate prices. **Kurt Denkstein** is another shoe retailer with stock at reasonable prices.

Younger, trendier shoppers should head straight to Judengasse – this street has plenty of reasonably priced boutiques with styles to suit every taste. For menswear in particular, **D G Linnerth** stocks informal and sporty clothes designed for teenagers upwards. The branch of the trendy clothes chain **H & M**, on Graben, is worth a visit if only to view the gilded birdcage of a lift.

An optician called **Erich Hartmann** bought a shop with a large stock of horn and tortoiseshell back in 1980. Today he sells a range of handmade spectacles, combs and chains, all made from horn.

SIZE CHART

For Australian sizes follow British and American convention.

Women's clothes

Austrian	36	38	40	42	44	46	48	50
British	10	12	14	16	18	20	22	24
American	8	10	12	14	16	18	20	22

Shoes

Austrian	36	37	38	39	40	41	42	43
British	3½	4	5	5½	6½	7½	8	9
American	5	5½	6½	7	8	9	9½	10½

Men's shirts

Austrian	44	46	48	50	52	54
British	34	36	38	40	42	44
American	S	M	M	L	XL	XL

Antiques, Auctions and Markets

Many districts in Vienna have their own markets – and a few have several – where you can buy arts and crafts, food, flowers and imported and second-hand goods. The city is also known for its Christmas markets, popular with locals in the evenings. If you are interested in antiques and bric-a-brac, it is worth looking in both the specialist antique shops and the main auction house. Alternatively, enjoy browsing round the bustling ethnic stalls and mix of cultures in the Naschmarkt, Vienna's main food market.

ANTIQUES

Vienna is justly famous for its antique shops. Most are located in the Stephansdom Quarter as well as along Schönbrunner Strasse, where stock ranges from valuable antiques to simply second-hand. The **Dorotheum** *(see Auctions)*, the **Kunst und Antikmarkt** and the Floh-markt *(see Artisan Markets)* should not be missed. Jewellery and antique paintings can be particularly good finds. One of the best shops for antique jewellery is the **Galerie Rauhenstein**. It stocks rare and beautiful pieces up to and including the 1940s.

If you are interested in old jewellery and silver and other antiques, **Herbert Asenbaum** is worth a visit. For larger pieces and shops on a larger scale, try **Subal & Subal** on Spiegelgasse or **Reinhold Hofstätter** on Bräunerstrasse. They are both well established and have a good selection of fine antique furniture.

AUCTIONS

Opened in 1707 as a pawn-brokers for the "new poor", and appropriately called the *Armen Haus* (poor house), Vienna's **Dorotheum** is now the city's most important auction house. In 1788 it moved to the site of a former convent called the Dorotheerkirche, which had an altar-piece of St Dorothea in it – hence the name. This is an interesting place to browse around, and since buying is not restricted to auction times, you can often purchase items over the counter. It has other branches dotted around the city.

FOOD MARKETS

Between the Linke and Rechte Wienzeile, the **Naschmarkt** *(see p138)* is worth visiting even if you don't buy anything. Exotic fruit and vegetables, notably Greek, Turkish and Asian specialities, crowd the stalls and are piled high in the shops. It is a fascinating place to wander around and observe life. Open all year round, it acts as a meeting point for people of different nationalities who come to buy and sell fruit and vegetables, tea, herbs and spices. The section near the Karlsplatz contains the more expensive Viennese-run stalls. These gradually give way to stands run by colourful Turkish stallholders as you move further towards the flea market.

In addition to the exotic food stalls, you will see Czechs selling hand puppets, Russians selling Babushka dolls and Turks with stalls piled high with eastern clothes. The market is also a good spot for late-night revellers to feast on highly-spiced fish snacks in the early hours of the morning.

Food-lovers should not miss the farmers' market known as the **Bauernmarkt**. A whole range of organic and other country produce is on sale here on Saturday mornings.

ARTISAN MARKETS

Antique markets and arts and crafts markets are fairly new to Vienna, but the Flohmarkt (flea market) at the end of the **Naschmarkt** *(see p138)* and the **Kunst und Antikmarkt** are established hunting grounds for second-hand

goods and antiques. The price quoted is probably not the price that you are expected to pay – it's usually assumed that you will bargain.

For the better quality hand-crafted goods, head to the Spittelberg market *(see p117)* near the Volkstheater. Here artists and craftspeople sell their own products rather than mass-produced factory goods. This is a fashionable and attractive part of Vienna and, although the market is small, you are likely to find gifts of good quality. There are also small galleries and cafés where artists exhibit their works.

The **Heiligenkreuzerhof** *(see p75)* art market is in a quiet, secluded courtyard where a small, select group of exhibitors is on hand should you wish to discuss the work. The stalls sell jewellery, ceramics and other handmade goods. Further entertainment and atmosphere is provided by an Austrian folk singer dressed in traditional clothes playing his accordion.

FESTIVE MARKETS

Christmas markets in Vienna are very special, the most famous of all being the **Christkindlmarkt** *(see p64)* held in front of the Rathaus. Attractions vary from year to year, but there are always sideshows, decorated trees, performances on a temporary stage and lots of stalls, as well as a workshop for making Christmas presents and baking goodies. Items for sale include honey cakes, bees-wax candles, Christmas decorations and various crafts, although the main attraction is the joyous atmosphere. It is especially magical at night when everything is lit up.

The **Alt Wiener Christ-kindlmarkt** *(see p64)* at the Freyung is a smaller affair. Two weeks before Easter there is also an Easter market here with a large selection of blown and hand-painted eggs. Other Christmas markets take place in the Spittelberg area, Schloss Schönbrunn, Karl-skirche, Heiligenkreuzerhof and on Maria-Theresien-Platz.

DIRECTORY

SPECIALITY SHOPS

Kober
Graben 14–15. **Map** 2 D5 & 5 C3. **Tel** 53360180.

Maria Stransky
Hofburg Passage 2.
Map 5 C4. **Tel** 5336098.

Metzger
Stephansplatz 7. **Map** 2 E5 & 6 D3. **Tel** 5123433.
One of two branches.

Petit Point
Kärntner Strasse 16.
Map 4 D1 & 6 D4.
Tel 5124886.

Robert Horn
Bräunerstrasse 7.
Map 5 C4. **Tel** 5138294.

Witte
Linke Wienzeile 16.
Map 3 A4. **Tel** 58643050.

Zauberklingl
Führichgasse 4. **Map** 5 C4. **Tel** 5126868.

MUSIC

Arcadia
Kärntner Strasse 40.
Map 4 D2 & 5 C5.
Tel 5139568.

Doblinger
Dorotheergasse 10.
Map 5 C3. **Tel** 515030.

EMI
Kärntner Str 30. **Map** 4 D1 & 6 D4. **Tel** 51236750.

Gramola
Graben 16. **Map** 2 D5 & 5 C3. **Tel** 5335034.

JEWELLERY

Heldwein
Graben 13.
Map 5 C3. **Tel** 5125781.

Juwelier Wagner
Kärntnerstrasse 32.
Map 4 D1. **Tel** 5120512.

Köchert
Neuer Markt 15.
Map 5 C4. **Tel** 51258280.

Schullin
Kohlmarkt 7. **Map** 2 D5 & 5 C3. **Tel** 53390070.

GLASSWARE

J & L Lobmeyr
Kärntner Str 26. **Map** 2 D5 & 6 D4. **Tel** 5120508.

INTERIORS

Augarten
Stock-im-Eisen-Platz 3–4.
Map 2 D5 & 5 C3.
Tel 5121494.

Backhausen
Schwarzenbergstrasse 10.
Map 6 D5. **Tel** 514040.

Gans
Brandstätte 1–3. **Map** 4 D1 & 6 D3. **Tel** 5333560.
One of several branches.

Gunkel
Tuchlauben 11. **Map** 2 D5 & 5 C3. **Tel** 53363010.

Ostovics
Stephansplatz 9. **Map** 6 D3. **Tel** 5331411.

Schloss Augarten
Obere Augartenstrasse 1.
Map 2 E2. **Tel** 211240.

Zur Schwäbischen Jungfrau
Graben 26. **Map** 2 D5 & 5 C3. **Tel** 5355356.

FOOD AND WINE

Altmann & Kühne
Graben 30. **Map** 2 D5 & 5 C3. **Tel** 5330927.
One of two branches.

Julius Meinl am Graben
Graben 19. **Map** 2 D5 & 5 C3. **Tel** 5323334.

Wein & Co
Jasomirgottstrasse 3–5.
Map 6 D3. **Tel** 5330916.

Zum Schwarzen Kameel
Bognergasse 5.
Map 5 C3. **Tel** 5338125.

GIFTS

Österreichische Werkstätten
Kärntner Str 6. **Map** 4 D1 & 6 D4. **Tel** 5122418.

Swarovski
Kärntnerstrasse 24.
Map 6 D4. **Tel** 3240000.
One of several branches.

BOOKS

British Bookshop
Weihburggasse 24.
Map 6 E4. **Tel** 5121945.

Frick International
Schulerstrasse 1–3.
Map 6 D3. **Tel** 5126905.

Gilhofer
Rathausstrasse 19.
Map 1 C5. **Tel** 40961900.

Heck
Kärntner Ring 14. **Map** 4 E2 & 6 D5. **Tel** 5055152.

Shakespeare & Co
Sterngasse 2. **Map** 2 E5 & 6 D2. **Tel** 5355053.

NEWSPAPERS AND PERIODICALS

Morawa
Wollzeile 11. **Map** 2 E5 & 6 D3. **Tel** 515620.

CLOTHES AND ACCESSORIES

Bally
Am Graben 12.
Map 5 C3. **Tel** 5130505.

D'Ambrosio
Jasomirgottstrasse 6. **Map** 6 D3. **Tel** 532635223.
One of several branches.

D G Linnerth
Lugeck 1–2. **Map** 6 D3.
Tel 5125888.

Erich Hartmann
Singerstrasse 8, Corner of Lilieng. **Map** 6 D3.
Tel 5121489.

Flamm
Neuer Markt 12.
Map 5 C4. **Tel** 5122889.

Fürnkranz
Kärntner Str 39.
Map 6 D4 & 5 C5.
Tel 4884426. One of several branches.

H & M
Graben 8. **Map** 2 D5 & 5 C3. **Tel** 5125505. One of several branches.

J&R Denkstein
Stephansplatz 4. **Map** 6 D3. **Tel** 5127465.

Kettner
Plankengasse 7. **Map** 5 C4. **Tel** 5132239.

Knize
Graben 13. **Map** 2 D5 & 5 C3. **Tel** 5221190.

Loden-Plankl
Michaelerplatz 6.
Map 5 C3. **Tel** 5338032.

Steffl
Kärntnerstrasse 19.
Map 6 D3. **Tel** 514310.

Tostmann
Schottengasse 3a.
Map 5 B2. **Tel** 53353310.

ANTIQUES

Galerie Rauhenstein
Rauhensteingasse 3.
Map 6 D4. **Tel** 5133009.

Herbert Asenbaum
Kärntner Str 28. **Map** 4 D1 & 6 D4. **Tel** 5122847.

Reinhold Hofstätter
Bräunerstrasse 12.
Map 5 C4. **Tel** 5335069.

Subal & Subal
Spiegelgasse 8. **Map** 4 D1 & 5 C4. **Tel** 5131349.

AUCTIONS

Dorotheum
Dorotheergasse 17. **Map** 4 D1 & 5 C4. **Tel** 51560.

MARKETS

Alt Wiener Christkindlmarkt
Freyung. **Map** 2 D5 & 5 B2. ◯ 17 Nov–24 Dec: 9:30am–7:30pm daily.

Bauernmarkt
Freyung. **Map** 2 D5 & 5 B2. ◯ Mar–end Oct: 10am–6:30pm Tue & Thu.

Christkindlmarkt
At the Neues Rathaus.
Map 1 C5 & 5 A2. ◯ Mid-Nov–24 Dec: 10am–7pm daily.

Heiligenkreuzerhof
Map 2 E5 & 6 E3. ◯ Apr–Sep: first Sat & Sun of each month; end Nov–Mar: 10am–6pm Sat & Sun.

Kunst und Antikmarkt
Donaukanal-Promenade.
Map 6 F2. ◯ May–end Sep: 2–8pm Sat, 10am–8pm Sun.

Naschmarkt
Map 3 C2. ◯ 6am–6:30pm Mon–Fri, 6am–6pm Sat.

ENTERTAINMENT IN VIENNA

Vienna offers a wide range of entertainment, particularly of the musical variety. There is grand opera at the Opera House – Staatsoper (see pp140–41) – or the latest musical at the Theater an der Wien (see p138). Dignified orchestral concerts and elegant Viennese waltzes take place at the great balls during the Carnival season, and waltzes are played in the relaxed atmosphere of the Stadtpark. Even the famous Lipizzaner horses perform to Viennese music and no visit to the city is complete without a trip to the

Pipo at the Ronacher (see p228)

Spanish Riding School (see pp98–9). Vienna also has excellent theatres, two of which perform in English, and several cinemas which specialize in classic films. Restaurants close early, but you can still be entertained around the clock at one of Vienna's many nightspots. Within the Ringstrasse, the city buzzes with late-night revellers enjoying jazz clubs, such as the Roter Engel, discos, casinos and bars with live music. Or you can end your day sipping coffee and nibbling pastries at a latenight café (see also pp217–19).

The stage of the Theater in der Josefstadt (see p116)

PRACTICAL INFORMATION

A monthly guide to Vienna is issued free by the Wiener Tourismusverband (main Vienna Tourist Office – see p238). Posters which list the weekly programmes for the opera houses and theatres are pasted on billboard columns and displayed in most hotel lobbies. They also list casts for all the performances. Each day the four main newspapers in the city, Die Presse, Kronenzeitung, Standard and Kurier (see p245) publish programme listings. All four also give details of daily cinema performances and concerts as well as the main sporting events.

BOOKING TICKETS

You can buy tickets direct from the appropriate box office (check opening hours, since these vary), or reserve them on the telephone. The phone numbers and addresses for the booking offices are listed in the Music, Theatre and Cinema directories (see pp229–30). The four state theatres, the Burgtheater (see p132), the Akademietheater (see p230), the Opera House (see pp140–41) and the Wiener Volksoper (see p229), all have

Billboard column

one central booking office, the **Bundestheaterkassen** (see p229). However, tickets for performances at any of these four theatres can also be purchased at the box office of the Wiener Volksoper and the Burgtheater.

Tickets usually go on sale a week before the performance. Tickets for the Vienna State Opera are sold from one month in advance. However, bear in mind that tickets for September performances are sold during the month of June.

Phone reservations for credit card holders can be made from six days in advance. Written applications for tickets for the state theatre must reach the Vienna State Opera ticket office (address as Bundestheaterkassen) no later than three weeks before the date of the performance.

Standing-room tickets are sold at the evening box office one hour before the start of the performance.

Tickets for the state theatres, the Theater an der Wien (see p138), the **Raimund Theater** (see p229) and Konzerthaus (see p228) can be used on public transport for two hours before, and six hours after, all performances. Agencies are reliable – try **Reisebüro Mondial** (see p229) – and hotel staff may be able to obtain tickets. Otherwise try the box office for returns.

AT THE THEATRE

If you visit the theatre in person, you will be able to see the seating plan and make your choice accordingly. The monthly programme for the state theatres also contains individual seating plans and it is a good idea to have them in front of you when booking your tickets by telephone. Most hotel porters will also have copies of seating plans for the principal venues.

If you book by telephone remember that *Parkett* (stalls) are in front and are usually the most expensive. In some theatres the front rows of the stalls are known as *Orchestersitze*. The *Parterre* (back stalls) are cheaper and the dress circle (the grand or royal circle) is called *Erster Rang*, followed by the *Zweiter Rang* (balcony). At the Burgtheater and Opera House, there are two extra levels called the *Balkon* and *Galerie*. The higher you go, the cheaper the seats are.

Casino Wien in Esterházy Palace

Boxes are known as *Logen* and the back seats are always cheaper than the front seats.

At the **Wiener Volksoper** (see p229) they still have *Säulensitze*, seats where the view is partly obscured by a column. These cheap tickets are bought by music lovers who come to listen rather than to view. There are four tiers of boxes at the Volksoper, known in ascending order as *Parterre, Balkon, Erster Rang* and *Zweiter Rang*.

Buffets at Vienna's principal theatres provide alcoholic and non-alcoholic drinks, and tasty snacks which range from open sandwiches at the **Akademietheater** (see p230) and Volksoper to the more elaborate

Busker beneath the Pestsäule

concoctions at the Opera House and Burgtheater. Small open sandwiches with caviar, egg, smoked salmon, cheese and salami on Vienna roll-style bread are also common. Glasses of *Sekt*, a sparkling wine, are always available.

Buffets are usually open for up to one hour before the start of a performance and are often fairly empty. They are an ideal place for relaxing with a snack and a drink, and the coffee is extremely good.

It is not usual to tip ushers at theatres, unless you are being shown to a box, but you may round up the price of a theatre programme.

Coats and hats have to be left in the cloakroom before you go to your seat. There is usually no fixed charge, and tipping is at your discretion.

FACILITIES FOR THE DISABLED

A number of venues offer wheelchair access or help for those with hearing difficulties. Be sure to make your needs very clear when booking tickets.

A booklet, *Wien für Gäste mit Handicaps* (Vienna for handicapped guests), is published by the Wiener Tourismusverband (see p238) and provides information on facilities at entertainment venues, museums, hotels, restaurants, cafés, cinemas, post offices and so on.

TRANSPORT

Buses and trams run until around 11:30pm, while the underground continues until about midnight (see Getting Around Vienna, pp250–55). Night buses are popular, with eight routes operating around the city and into the suburbs. They start at 12:30am from Schwedenplatz, the Opera and Schottentor, and continue every half hour until 4am, 24hrs at weekends. Tickets usually cost around €1 and are sold on the bus (see p254).

You can phone for a taxi from your venue, or take one from outside. Taxis usually line up outside theatres after a performance, otherwise you can go to one of the many taxi ranks which are found on most street corners. Taxis which do not stop when hailed are already booked.

CASINOS

Casinos Austria has become the hallmark for superbly run casinos all over the world (you will even find them aboard luxury liners), but **Casino Wien** is a showcase. It is set in the Baroque Esterházy Palace (see p80) and you can play French or American roulette, baccarat and poker there. The complex includes a bar, a restaurant and the **Jackpot Casino**, which is a typically Viennese addition.

Casino Wien

Kärntner Strasse 41. Map 4 D1.
Casino ⬜ 3pm–4am daily.
Jackpot Casino ⬜ 10am–1am daily. **Tel** 5124836.

Dancing at the grand Opera Ball (see p141)

Music in Vienna

The Vienna Opera House (see pp140–41) is one of the greatest of its kind in the world and, like all four state theatres, is heavily subsidised. The acoustics are excellent – the world-famous conductor Arturo Toscanini advised on the rebuilding of the theatre after it was destroyed at the end of the last war. The house orchestra, the Vienna Philharmonic, performs while the Opera House is open from September until June. Most operas are sung in the original language. The city supports two principal orchestras, the Vienna Philharmonic and the Wiener Symphoniker. There are also a number of chamber music ensembles and visiting artists. Church music is often of concert quality. You can hear more informal music in the Stadtpark, where a small orchestra regularly plays waltzes in summer. Live rock music is popular in discos, and there is an annual jazz festival (see p63).

OPERA AND OPERETTA

Seat prices at the Vienna Opera House range from €10 to €192. Tickets are sold one month in advance of a performance, except standing-room tickets, which are on sale one hour before the performance starts. These are good value, but because of this there is usually a long queue. After buying your ticket you can mark your space by tying a scarf around the rail, leaving you free to wander around. The New Year's Eve performance is always Die Fledermaus by Johann Strauss, and famous guests sometimes make surprise appearances during the second act.

The **Wiener Volksoper** is renowned for its superb operetta productions of works by composers ranging from Strauss, Millöcker and Ziehrer to Lehár and Kálmán. There are also performances of musicals and light opera by Mozart, Puccini and Bizet, sung in German. Prices can range from €3 to €58, and the season is exactly the same as the Opera House.

Concealed in a small side street in the Stephansdom Quarter is one of Vienna's great little opera houses the **Wiener Kammeroper**. Many international singers such as Waldemar Kmentt, Eberhard Waechter and Walter Berry started their careers here. You can expect anything to be performed here from the early works of Rossini to classic operetta, as well as rock versions of familiar operas such as Tales of Hoffmann and Carmen, and opera parodies.

Another venue for opera is the **Theater an der Wien**. Musicals had previously been staged here. These are now put on at the historic **Ronacher**, once Vienna's most glamorous theatre, and the large **Raimund Theater**. In May and June, the Wiener Festwochen (see p62) presents theatre and music theatre productions in a variety of venues, most notably Halle G at the MuseumsQuartier.

July sees opera performances by **Oper Klosterneuburg** in the Kaiserhof courtyard of Klosterneuberg, the palatial religious foundation a short way north of Vienna. The festival **Seefestspiele Mörbisch** (see p63) takes place every weekend in July and August on a stage projecting on to Lake Neusiedl.

CLASSICAL CONCERTS

The principal venues for classical concerts are the **Musikverein** (including the Brahmsaal and the halls of Gläserner Saal and Steinerner Saal) and the concert halls of the **Konzerthaus**. Performances are also held in places such as Schubert's birthplace in Nussdorf (see p185) and in many historic palaces.

The New Year's Concert (see p65) is televised live from the Grosser Musikvereinsaal in the Musikverein every year. You can apply for tickets by writing direct to the **Wiener Philharmoniker**. However, applications must be received on 2 January (not before, not after) for the next year's concert. You can order from www.wienerphilharmoniker.at.

Waltz concerts and operetta, which include stars from the Vienna Volksoper, can be heard at the Musikverein, the Neue Burg (see p95) and the Konzerthaus on Tuesdays, Thursdays and Saturdays from April until October. Mozart and Strauss concerts are performed on Wednesdays at the Neue Burg. All tickets are the same price, so the best thing to do is to get there early if you want to make sure of getting the best seat. The Konzerthaus and Musikverein concert seasons run from October to June (for events from July to September, see p63).

CHURCH MUSIC

Details of the many church concerts performed in Vienna are published in all the daily newspapers. Look out particularly for details of Sunday mass at the following places: Augustinerkirche (see p102), Minoritenkirche (see p103), the Jesuitenkirche/Jesuit church (see pp70 and 73), Stephansdom (see p76) and Michaelerkirche (see p92). In July and August, many other churches hold organ recitals.

The Vienna Boys' Choir (see p39) can be heard during mass at the Burgkapelle (see p103) every Sunday and religious holiday at 9:15am except from July to mid-September. (Tickets are available from the Burg-kapelle; the box office is open the Friday before). You can also hear them at the **Konzerthaus** every Friday at 3:30pm in May, June, September and October. Buy tickets from hotel porters and from **Reise-büro Mondial**. Book well in advance.

INFORMAL MUSIC

The description just outside **Konzert-Café Schmid Hansl** reads, "the home of Viennese song". The original owner of this small café, which serves hot food until it closes, was Hansl Schmid, a very fine singer and musician. Guests would often visit the café just to hear him sing, and sometimes a famous artist might join him in a duet or give a solo performance. The present owner, Hansl Schmid's son, once a member of the Vienna Boys' Choir, has kept up this tradition, and you may well encounter opera stars coming in to perform unexpectedly.

Another Viennese favourite is the **Wiener Kursalon**. Dinner and waltz evenings with the Johann Strauss Salonorchester are held daily throughout the year along with classical ballet performances. Concerts take place in the Stadtpark during the summer months.

ROCK, POP AND JAZZ

What is popular one week in Vienna's lively music scene may very well be out of fashion the next. Many discos have live music on certain nights or for a limited period.

U4 disco has a different style every night (from indusrial to flower power) and Thursday is gay night. **Tanzcafé** and **Volksgarten Club Disco** are the oldest in town with house to hip-hop and salsa. Also still popular is **Take Five**. **Roter Engel** in the Bermuda Triangle has live music every night. The **Praterdome**, situated near the ferris wheel in Prater park, has popular theme nights.

Live concerts are held at the **Café Szene**, **Jazzland**, and on Sundays at **Chelsea**. The **OstClub** features live music from Eastern Europe, the Balkans and Russia.

A must for jazz fans is **Porgy & Bess Jazz & Music Club**, with live music and dancing, and the **Jazzfest** held in the first two weeks of July, with concerts in various venues such as the Opera House *(see pp140–41)*, the Volkstheater *(see p230)* and the Neues Rathaus *(see p130)* as well as many open-air events. All styles, electro and house as well as alternative music, can be found at **Café Leopold**, **Schikaneder Bar** and **Flex**.

DIRECTORY

OPERA AND OPERETTA

Bundestheaterkassen
Central Ticket Office.
Operngasse 2, A-1010.
Map 5 C4. **Tel** 5131513.
⏲ 8am–6pm Mon–Fri,
9am–noon Sat, Sun & hols.

Oper Klosterneuburg
Kaiserhof Courtyard,
Klosterneuburg.
Tel 02243444425.

Raimund Theater
Wallgasse 18, A-1060.
Tel 58885. **www.**
musicalvienna.at

Reisebüro Mondial
Faulmanngasse 4.
Map 4 D2. **Tel** 58804141.

Ronacher
Seilerstatte 9, A-1010.
Map 4 E1 & 6 D4.
Tel 58885.
www.musicalvienna.at

Seefestspiele Mörbisch
Mörbisch am,
Neusiedlersee, Burgenland.
Tel 02685 8181.
(Jul & Aug). **www.**
seefestspiele-moerbisch.at

Wiener Kammeroper
Fleischmarkt 24, A-1010.
Map 2 E5 & 6 D2.
Tel 51201-0077. **www.**
wienerkammeroper.at

Wiener Volksoper
Währinger Strasse 78,
A-1090. **Map** 1 B2.
Tel 514443670.
www.volksoper.at

CLASSICAL CONCERTS

Konzerthaus
Lothringerstrasse 20,
A-1030. **Map** 4 E2 & 6 E5.
Tel 242002.
www.konzerthaus.at

Musikverein
Bösendorferstrasse 12.
Map 6 D5. **Tel** 5058190.
www.musikverein.at

Orangery at Schönbrunn
Tel 81250040.
⏲ 7pm or 8:30pm
(concerts 8:30pm daily).
www.imagevienna.com

Wiener Hofburgorchester
Margaretenstrasse 3.
Map 4 D2. **Tel** 5872552.
www.hofburgorchester.at

Wiener Philharmoniker
Bösendorferstrasse 12,
A-1010. **Map** 4 E2 & 6 D5.
Tel 50565250. **www.**
wienerphilharmoniker.at

INFORMAL MUSIC

Konzert-Café Schmid Hansl
Schulgasse 31. **Map** 1 A2.
Tel 4063658.
⏲ 8pm–4am Tue–Sat.

Wiener Kursalon
Johannesgasse 33.
Map 6 E5. **Tel** 5125790.
www.soundofvienna.at

ROCK, POP AND JAZZ

Café Leopold
Museumsplatz 1.
Map 5 A5. **Tel** 5236732.

Café Szene
Hauffgasse 26.
Tel 7493341.

Chelsea
Stadtbahnbogen 29–31,
A-1080. **Map** 4 D2.
Tel 4079309.

Flex
Donaukanal
Augartenbrücke.
Map 1 D3. **Tel** 5337525.

Jazzfest
See text for venues.
Tel 588660 for
information.

Jazzland
Franz-Josefs-Kai 29.
Map 2 D5 & 6 D2.
Tel 5332575.

OstClub
Schwarzenbergplatz 10.
Map 4 E2. **Tel** 5056228.

Porgy & Bess Jazz & Music Club
Riemergasse 11. **Map** 5 E4.
Tel 5128811.

Praterdome
Riesenradplatz 7.
Tel 9081192990.

Roter Engel
Rabensteig 5. **Map** 6 D2.
Tel 5354105.

Schikaneder Bar
Margaretenstrasse 22–24.
Map 3 C3. **Tel** 5852867.

Take Five
Annagasse 3a. **Map** 4 D1
& 6 D4. **Tel** 5129277.

Tanzcafé Volksgarten
Burgring/Heldenplatz.
Map 3 C1 & 5 B4.
Tel 5330518.

U4
Schönbrunner Strasse 222.
Map 3 A4. **Tel** 8158307.

Theatre and Cinema

Vienna has a good choice of theatres, with an eclectic mix of styles ranging from classical drama to the avant-garde. Some places, like the early 19th-century Josef-stadt Theater *(see p116)*, are well worth visiting for their architecture alone. You can see productions in English at the English Theatre or, if you understand German, you can go and watch one of the many fringe performances. Some cinemas screen films in their original language. The classic film which is usually showing somewhere in the city is *The Third Man*, set in Vienna during the Allied occupation.

THEATRES

Viennese theatre is some of the best in Europe and the **Burgtheater** *(see p132)*, one of the City's four state theatres, is the most important venue. Classic and modern plays are performed here and even if your understanding of German is limited, you will still enjoy a new production (which can often be avant-garde) of a Shakespeare play. For classic and modern plays go to the **Akademietheater**, part of the Burgtheater.

The **Josefstadt Theater** *(see p116)* is worth a visit for the interior alone. As the house lights slowly dim, the crystal chandeliers float gently to the ceiling. It offers excellent productions of

Austrian plays as well as classics from other countries, and the occasional musical. **Kammerspiele** is the Josefstadt's "little house". The old and well-established **Volkstheater** offers more modern plays as well as the occasional classic and some operetta performances.

Vienna has a wide range of fringe theatre from one-man shows to *Kabarett* – these are satirical shows not cabarets – but fairly fluent German is needed to appreciate them. German-speakers will also enjoy the highly recommended **Kabarett Simpl**, featuring top name cabaret acts.

Theatres that give perform-ances in English include **Vienna's English Theatre** and the **International Theater**. Plays at the English Theatre are cast and rehearsed in London or New York before opening in Vienna. Some run for a short period only, but they often feature famous international stars.

The International Theater has a Vienna-based ensemble of English-speaking actors. The company presents a wide range of works, with an emphasis on the 20th century. There is also a new production of Charles Dickens' *A Christmas Carol* every year.

CINEMAS

A cinema that screens the latest films in their original language is the **Burg Kino**, while the **Haydn Cinema** and the **Artis International** show new releases in English only. Cinemas that specialize in showing old and new classics as well as the more unusual films are the **Österreichisches Filmmuseum**, **Filmhaus Stöbergasse**, **Filmcasino**, and **Votiv-Kino** (which has a special cinema breakfast on Sundays). The **Apollo Center** is a modern complex and has the largest cinema screen in Austria.

DIRECTORY

THEATRES

Akademietheater
Lisztstrasse 1, A-1030.
Map 4 E2.
Tel 514444740.

Burgtheater
Dr Karl-Lueger-Ring,
A-1014. **Map** 1 C5 &
5 A2. *Tel 514444145.*

International Theater
Porzellangasse 8, A-1090.
Map 1 C3.
Tel 3196272.

Josefstadt Theater
Josefstädt Strasse 26, A-1080. **Map** 1 B5.
Tel 427000.

Kabarett Simpl
Wollzeile 36,
A-1010.
Map 2 E5 & 6 E3.
Tel 5124742.

Kammerspiele
Rotenturmstrasse 20,
A-1010. **Map** 2 E5 & 6 E2
Tel 42700300.

Vienna's English Theatre
Josefsgasse 12, A-1080.
Map 1 B5. *Tel 4021260.*

Volkstheater
Neustiftgasse 1,
A-1070.
Map 3 B1.
Tel 52111400.

CINEMAS

Apollo Center
Gumpendorfer Strasse 63.
Map 3 A4 & 5 B5.
Tel 5879651.

Artis International
Schulgasse 5,
A-1010.
Map 1 A2.
Tel 5356570.

Burg Kino
Opernring 19.
Map 4 D1 & 5 B5.
Tel 5878406.

Filmcasino
Margaretenstrasse 78.
Map 3 C3.
Tel 5879062.

Filmhaus Stöbergasse
Stöbergasse 11–15.
Map 3 B5.
Tel 5466630.

Haydn Cinema
Mariahilfer Strasse 57.
Map 3 B2.
Tel 5872262.

Österreichisches Filmmuseum
Augustinerstrasse 1.
Map 4 D1 & 5 C4.
Tel 5337054.

Votiv-Kino
Währinger Strasse 12.
Map 1 C4.
Tel 3173571.

Sport and Dance

Outdoor activities are extremely popular. Football is followed by many locals – especially since the pre-war victories of the famous "Wonder Team". Visitors who enjoy swimming can take advantage of the pools the city has to offer. Horse racing and ice-skating also attract many locals. Flat racing takes place at the Freudenau in the Prater. The well-equipped **Stadthalle** is ideal for spectator sports like boxing and wrestling and houses its own pool, bowling alleys and ice rink. Many of Vienna's dance schools hold special waltz classes during the Carnival season *(see p65)*.

ICE-SKATING

Outdoor ice-skating is very popular in Vienna. Locals make good use of the open-air rinks at the Wiener Eislaufverein and Vienna Ice Dreams *(see p234)*.

SWIMMING

Vienna can be very warm in summer and has many outdoor pools, including the **Schönbrunner Bad** in the Schönbrunn Palace park *(see pp172–3)*. The **Krapfenwald-bad** has wonderful views over Vienna, and the **Schafbergbad** holds underwater gymnastics every Tuesday and Thursday. The **Thermalbad Oberlaa** has three open-air pools and an indoor pool. The Kinderfreibad Augarten *(see p234)* is popular with children,

and they can be left at the Kinderfreibad to be watched by the attendants. Beach huts on the Alte Donau coast can be hired daily from **Strandbad Gänsehäufel** or **Strandbad Alte Donau**, where you can also hire boats. Strandbad Gänsehäufel has a beach, a heated pool, table tennis and Punch and Judy shows. For relaxing beaches, the world's longest water slide, barbecues and a night bus at weekends, visit **Donauinsel**.

FOOTBALL

The Viennese are enthusiastic football fans, and there are two huge covered football stadiums in the city. The **Ernst Happel Stadion** (which seats 48,000) is in the Prater and the **Hanappi Stadion** (which seats 20,000) is at Hütteldorf.

HORSE RACING

The prater offers a wide range of activities *(see pp162–3)*, including trotting races at the **Krieau**.

DANCING AND DANCE SCHOOLS

During the Carnival season *(see p65)* many balls, and some fancy dress dances, are held in Vienna. Venues include the Hofburg, the Neues Rathaus *(see p130)* and the Musikverein *(see p229)*. The grandest event is the Opera Ball *(see p141)*, which takes place on the Thursday before Ash Wednesday. The opening ceremony includes a performance by the Opera House ballet. An invitation is not needed, you just buy a ticket. The Kaiserball is held at the Neue Burg on New Year's Eve *(see pp65 and 95)*. A special ball calendar is issued by the Wiener Tourismusverband – Vienna Tourist Office *(see p238)*.

The Summer Dance Festival *(see p63)* runs from July to August. You can learn a range of dances, including rock 'n' roll, at some dance schools in the city. During the Carnival season, some schools hold Viennese waltz classes. The **Elmayer-Vestenbrugg** also teaches etiquette.

DIRECTORY

GENERAL

Stadthalle
Vogelweidplatz 15.
Swimming pool
Tel 98100433.
◻ *8am–9:30pm Mon, Wed, Fri, 6:30am–9:30pm Tue & Thu, 7am–9:30pm Sat, 7am–6pm Sun & public hols.*

ICE-SKATING

Wiener Eislaufverein
Lothringerstrasse 28.
Tel 71363530. ◻ *Oct–Mar: 9am–9pm Tue, Thu & Fri, 9am–8pm Sat–Mon, 9am–10pm Wed.*

SWIMMING

Krapfenwaldbad
Krapfenwaldgasse 65–73.
Tel 3201501.
◻ *May–Sep: 9am–8pm Mon–Fri, 8am–8pm Sat & Sun.*

Schafbergbad
Josef-Redl-Gasse 2.
Tel 4791593.

Strandbad Alte Donau
Strandbad Alte Donau, Arbeiterstrandbad-strasse 91.
Tel 2636538.

Strandbad Gänsehäufel
Moissigasse 21.
Tel 2699016.

Thermalbad Oberlaa
Kurbadstrasse 14.
Tel 680090.
◻ *9am–10pm Mon–Sat (8am–10pm Sun & public hols).*

Donauinsel
U1 stop – Donauinsel.

FOOTBALL

Ernst Happel Stadion
Meiereistrasse 7.
Tel 72808540.

Hanappi Stadion
Kaisslergasse 6.
Tel 9145519.

HORSE RACING

Krieau
Prater: trotting
Nordportalstrasse 247.
Tel 7280046 (enquiries).
(see pp64 & 160).

DANCING AND DANCE SCHOOLS

Elmayer-Vestenbrugg
Bräunerstrasse 13.
Map 5 C4.
Tel 5127197 (3–8pm).
◻ *3–8pm Mon–Sat, 5–10pm Sun.*

CHILDREN'S VIENNA

Traditionally, the Viennese have a reputation for preferring dogs to children. But negative attitudes towards children are gradually disappearing as the number of families has increased since the 1960s baby boom. Most restaurants serve children's portions, and in some of the more expensive places they can eat Sunday lunch at half price. Eating out at a *Heuriger* is less formal, and you can sit outside in summer. Vienna has many playgrounds and almost all museums offer tours that cater for children. Further out there are large parks, a zoo, swimming pools and ice rinks. Various children's activities are organized throughout the year.

Children pay half price on trams

PRACTICAL ADVICE

Traffic in Vienna can be fast and drivers are not automatically obliged to stop at pelican crossings. Always cross the road at traffic lights, and watch out for speeding cyclists in the bicycle lanes.

Children up to the age of six can travel for free on public transport. Those between the ages of six and 14 must buy a half-price ticket. During the summer holidays (the end of June to the end of August) children under 18 can travel free provided they can show some form of identification when buying a ticket.

It is a good idea to carry some small change, as you will need it to use public lavatories. These are usually clean.

In shops, the assistants may offer children boiled sweets, but do not feel obliged to accept these.

The concierges at many hotels, particularly the larger establishments, can arrange for a baby-sitter. If they cannot, they may be able to suggest a reliable local agency. If you get back from an evening out after about 10 or 11pm, you may have to pay for the baby-sitter's taxi home.

CHILDREN'S SHOPS

Traditional Austrian clothing, which is still worn by some children in Vienna, can be purchased from **Lanz Trachtenmoden** on Kärntner Strasse. Traditional dress includes *Lederhosen*, leather shorts, for boys and the *Dirndl*, a traditional dress, for girls. The *Dirndl* is worn with a white lace blouse and an apron. A little bag is sometimes carried as well. Lanz Trachtenmoden also stocks a range of beautiful knitwear in a myriad of colours and designs. Children will particularly like the fine embroidered woollen slippers made in the Tyrol.

Dohnal sells Austrian-made clothes for children up to the age of 16. In addition, the large international chains such as **012 Benetton**, **Jacadi** and **H & M** stock a wide selection of good-quality children's clothes.

Haas & Haas sells delightful craft-like presents, including wooden toys and puppets. They also have a conservatory-style tea house which is an ideal place to

Children on a day out visiting Josefsplatz in the Hofburg

treat your children to lunch, or a delicious cake or *Palatschinken* (see pp206–7). A more conventional toy shop is **Kober** on the Graben. Kober stocks a superb selection of toys and games, but at high prices.

Dressing up in traditonal costume is popular during Fasching (see p65)

EATING OUT

Generally speaking, the restaurants in Vienna are not as tolerant of noisy or boisterous children as establishments in many other cities, but there are still a large number of places where children are welcome. It is worth noting that some of the more expensive hotel restaurants offer special Sunday lunch deals for families. The best is probably the **Vienna Marriott** (see p196), where children under 6 eat free and 6 to 12-year-olds eat for half price. The hotel also provides a playroom with a child minder. The **Radisson Blu Palais Hotel** offers a similar lunch deal, but does not have a playroom.

Heurige, where you can sit outside in summer, are usually

Visitors watching the penguins at Vienna's zoo

DIRECTORY

CHILDREN'S SHOPS

012 Benetton
Goldschmiedgasse 9. **Map** 5 C3.
Tel 5339005.

Dohnal
Kärntner Strasse 12.
Map 4 D1 & 6 D4. *Tel* 5127311.

H & M
Kärntner Strasse 11–15. **Map** 4 D1.

Haas & Haas
Teehandlung, Stephansplatz 4.
Map 2 E3 & 6 D3. *Tel* 5129770.

Jacadi
Trattnerhof 1. **Map** 5 C3.
Tel 5358866.

Kober
Graben 14–15. **Map** 2 D5 & 5 C3.
Tel 5336019.

Lanz Trachtenmoden
Kärntner Strasse 10.
Map 4 D1 & 6 D4. *Tel* 5122456.

EATING OUT

Da Bizi
Rotenturmstrasse 4.
Map 6 D3. *Tel* 5133705.

**Markt-Restaurant
Rosenberger**
Maysedergasse 2. **Map** 5 C4.
Tel 5123458.

McDonald's
Singerstrasse 4.
Map 4 E1 & 6 D3. *Tel* 5139279.

Radisson Blu Palais Hotel
Parkring 16. **Map** 4 E1 & 6 E4.
Tel 515170.

Wienerwald
Annagasse 3. **Map** 4 D1 & 6 D4.
Tel 5123766. Goldschmiedgasse
6. **Map** 6 D3. *Tel* 050151515.

less formal and therefore a better option for families with small children. The best time for families is from 4pm, when most of them open, as they are likely to get busier as the evening goes on. **Heuriger Zimmermann** *(see p219)* has a small zoo where children are permitted to stroke the animals.

There are also a number of well-known fast-food restaurants, including **McDonald's** and **Da Bizi**, which are an option you may decide to go for if your children are fussy about food. Most of them have special children's menus and some offer free gifts for children, especially on their birthdays. The **Wienerwald** Viennese chicken restaurants also have a children's menu. **Markt-Restaurant Rosenberger** also caters for children.

Delicious hot chocolate

SIGHTSEEING WITH CHILDREN

Vienna has an amazing variety of attractions that will appeal to children of all ages, including theme parks, funfairs, museums, sports and the zoo.

It usually costs around half the adult entrance fee for children to get into museums. However, be warned that if children touch or get too close to the exhibits, the museum attendants are likely to make a fuss.

Vienna has plenty of parks, but some are designed more for admiring from the pathways than running around in. Watch out for signs warning *Bitte nicht betreten*, which means "Please don't walk on the grass". Details of some of the more child-friendly parks and nature reserves are given on page 234, and there are several playgrounds along the first stretch of the Prater Hauptallee. A picnic in one of these parks is an ideal way to entertain children. Picnic foods and drinks can easily be obtained from a supermarket, and the delicious cakes and pastries that Vienna is famous for can be bought in a *Konditorei* (café and cake shop), of which there are many.

Children's playgrounds in Vienna are generally safe and well equipped. However, it is advisable to avoid the Karlsplatz and Stadtpark play areas because of drug dealing in the vicinity.

Family out cycling, a familiar sight at the Prater

Elephants at Tiergarten Schönbrunn in the palace gardens (see pp172–3)

THE ZOO, PARKS AND NATURE RESERVES

Situated in Schönbrunn Palace gardens (see pp172–3), this fine zoo (Tiergarten) combines historic features with a thoroughly up-to-date layout and the benefit of spacious reserves for the animals. The garden also has a superb maze, which was laid out between 1698 and 1740, and a labyrinth with various games and riddles. With its frescoed ceilings, the central pavilion serves as a charming cafe.

In the Vienna Woods, the Lainzer Tiergarten (see p171), is a nature reserve where children can see deer, wild boar and horses. There are playgrounds and a pond. An easy walk takes you to Hermes Villa hunting lodge, with its café and nature-based exhibitions.

FUNFAIR AND CHILDREN'S CITY

An ideal venue for a family outing is the atmospheric Prater (see pp162–3). Its big wheel is magical at night, and busier than by day. The Prater park also has sandpits, playgrounds, ponds and streams.

Minopolis is a child-size city, with a bank, hospital, supermarket, and fire and police stations where children aged four to 12 can play at being adults.

Minopolis

Cineplexx Reichsbrücke,
Wagramerstrasse 2. **Tel** 2633000.
◯ 1–7pm Fri–Sun & hols except
1 Jan & 25 Dec.

CHILDREN'S SPORTS

Vienna has some excellent swimming baths, free for children under six, such as the Dianabad (see p231). The **Kinderfreibad Augarten**

Ice-skating at Wiener Eislaufverein

is a shallow pool and free for children between the ages of six and 15. However, it is not open to anyone else, except accompanying adults. The

Stadionbad has three children's pools and a water slide and is free to children under 15 on Wednesdays.

In summer, you can swim in the Donauinsel coves (see p231). During winter, you can bathe in the hot geysers at Thermalbad Oberlaa (see p231).

Between October and March you can go ice-skating at **Wiener Eislaufverein** or at **Vienna Ice Dreams** in front of the Rathaus. Then enjoy hot chocolate in a Ringstrasse coffee house like Café Prückel (see pp58–61) or Café Schwarzenberg (see pp60–61) on Kärntner Ring.

Vienna Ice Dreams

Rathausplatz. **Map** 5 A2.
◯ end of Jan–Mar: 9am–11pm daily.

Wiener Eislaufverein

Lothringerstrasse 28. **Map** 4 E2.
Tel 71363530. ◯ Oct–Mar:
9am– 9pm Tue, Thu, Fri, 9am–8pm
Sat–Mon, 9am–10pm Wed.

ENTERTAINMENT

Although most theatre is performed in German, the **Märchenbühne der Apfelbaum** marionette theatre sometimes puts on shows in English of favourite fairy tales. Fairy stories with music and song can also be seen at the **Lilarum** puppet theatre. The **Wiener Konzerthaus** and Musikverein hold regular concerts for children six times

The big wheel forms a familiar landmark in the Prater park (see pp162–3)

a year on Saturday or Sunday afternoons. In November and December the Opera House *(see pp140–41)* and the Wiener Volksoper *(see p229)* have traditional children's programmes *(Kinderzyklus)*. Productions include Mozart's *The Magic Flute* and the most popular opera at the Volksoper, Engelbert Humperdink's *Hansel and Gretel*.

Several cinemas in Vienna show films in the original languages – look in the *Standard* newspaper's foreign films section. See also *Entertainment in Vienna* on pp226–31.

A Christmas market stall in front of the Rathaus *(see p130)*

SPECIAL ACTIVITIES AND WORKSHOPS

The Rathaus *(see p130)* has children's activities once a month (details from the town hall), and from mid-November there is a Christmas market *(see pp224–5)* which includes a children's train, pony rides and stalls selling toys, chestnuts and winter woollens. A Christmas workshop is held at the Volkshalle in the Rathaus from 9am to 6pm (7pm at weekends). The activities include baking, silk painting and making decorations.

Attacus atlas at the Natural History Museum (see pp128–9)

MUSEUMS

Vienna has a range of museums for children to enjoy. The Natural History Museum *(see pp128–9)* boasts an impressive collection of fossils. The **Haus des Meeres** (Vienna Aquarium) contains over 3,000 sea creatures, including piranhas, crocodiles and sharks. Feeding time is 3pm.

Popular exhibits at the Völkerkundemuseum *(see p95)* include exotic musical instruments, African masks and figurines, and Montezuma's treasures. Children aged 13 and under are allowed to enter the **Kunsthaus Wien** free. Designed by Friedensreich

Hundertwasser, this colourful private gallery has undulating floors and bright paintings. The **Wiener Strassenbahn museum** (Vienna Tram Museum) houses the largest collection of vintage trams and buses in the world. Details of tours are available from information offices at Karlsplatz and Westbahnhof *(see p238)*.

The Heeresgeschichtliches Museum *(see pp166–7)* contains a range of war memorabilia and the ZOOM Kindermuseum *(see p120)* offers interactive exhibits such as the Zoom Lab. Other options include the **Zirkus und Clownmuseum**, dressing up events at the Sisi Museum in the Hofburg and at Schönbrunn Palace, experimenting with sight and sound at the Haus der Musik *(see p80)* and learning about the mechanics of theatre on a back stage tour at the Austrian Theatre Museum in Lobkowitz Palace *(see p104)*.

Montezuma's headdress in the Völkerkundemuseum *(see p95)*

The exterior of Karl-Lueger-Kirche in winter ▷

SURVIVAL GUIDE

PRACTICAL INFORMATION

The best way to get around the centre of Vienna is on foot because many of the sights are in close proximity to each other. Museums and galleries are often crowded at weekends, so in order to avoid the tourist hordes, plan a visit during the week if possible. A useful leaflet containing up-to-date information on

Sign for tourist information

Vienna's museums is available free from tourist offices. Galleries and churches can be closed for refurbishment or special events, so it is wise to check opening hours in advance. Most shops in the city centre are open Monday to Friday from 8am–6pm, and until 5pm on Saturdays. Embassy details are listed on page 239.

VISAS AND PASSPORTS

Austria is part of the Schengen common European border treaty, which means that travellers moving from one Schengen country to another are not subject to border controls. Schengen residents need only show an identity card when entering Austria. Visitors from the UK, Ireland, US, Canada, Australia or New Zealand will need to show a full passport. Travellers from these countries do not need visas for stays of up to three months. Non-EU citizens wishing to stay in the country longer than three months will need a visa, obtained from the Austrian embassy or consulate. These must be obtained in advance. All visitors should check requirements before travelling.

CUSTOMS INFORMATION

Nationals of EU countries, including Britain and Ireland, may take home unlimited quantities of duty-paid alcoholic drinks and tobacco goods as long as these are intended for their own consumption, and it can be proven that the goods are not intended for resale. Citizens

Tourist Information office in central Vienna

of the US and Canada are limited to a duty-free maximum of 200 cigarettes or 50 cigars. Americans may bring home 1 litre (33.8 fl oz) of wine or spirits, while Canadians are allowed 1.5 litres (50.7 fl oz) of wine, or a total of 1.14 litres (38.5 fl oz) of any alcoholic beverages, or 8.5 litres (287 fl oz) of beer or ale. Residents of other countries should ask their customs authority for more details. Information is included in the free *Zollinfo* brochure available at the Austrian border and allowances are listed on the Vienna Tourist Board website. The **Austrian Foreign Ministry** website also has information on tax-free goods.

TOURIST INFORMATION

For help planning your visit you can contact the **Österreich Werbung** (Austrian National Tourist Office) and the **Wiener Tourismusverband** (Vienna Tourist Board). The main Tourist Board office is located on Albertinaplatz. Information booths at Westbahnhof (*see p248*) and Schwechat Airport (*see p246*) provide maps, brochures, public transport schedules and assistance with hotel bookings. Tickets to musical and theatrical performances are sold at the Albertinaplatz office, including discounted rates for same-day events. The Austrian National Tourist Office can also assist with planning day trips from Vienna (*see pp176–7*).

Wien Xtra-Youth Info offers plenty of multi-lingual information about cheap hostel accommodation, youth events, cinema, pop concert tickets and leisure activities.

Tourists walking near the Hofburg complex (*see pp96–101*)

ADMISSION FEES AND OPENING HOURS

Entrance prices vary considerably between museums. Any major temporary exhibition will involve an additional charge. Children pay roughly half price and there are also reductions for senior citizens and students with identity cards. Many sights are free for those under 19 years of age. Entrance fees are waived each year on 26 October – the Austrian National Day. Look out for combined tickets like the Duo (€16), which provides entry into Leopold Museum and MUMOK, or the Kombi ticket (€25), which permits entry into the Leopold Museum, MUMOK, the Kunsthalle Wien and the Architekturzentrum Wien. Many museums in the city are closed on Mondays or Tuesdays so check opening times in advance. For information on booking theatre and musical performances, *see pp226–9*.

ACCESSIBILITY TO PUBLIC CONVENIENCES

Viennese public toilets (signed as "WC") are clean, safe and well maintained. Most charge a nominal fee payable to an attendant or machine in small change. Many are open until late, especially those in underground stations. Vienna is famous for its "toilet art", and the beautiful Art Deco WC on the Graben, designed by Adolf Loos, is well worth a visit. Other lavatorial highlights include the Opera Toilet at the Karlsplatz underground station and the Toilet of Modern Art in the Hundertwasserhaus housing estate.

TRAVELLERS WITH SPECIAL NEEDS

Vienna is relatively easy to navigate as a disabled traveller. Most of the major museums have special entrances and ramps for wheelchairs, and detailed information is available from the Vienna Tourist Office. Trams and buses are equipped with seats for disabled travellers (see p254). Most major underground stations provide lifts unless otherwise indicated. Travellers who need assistance from airline staff should contact the airline at least 48 hours before they fly.

SENIOR TRAVELLERS

The Viennese are extremely respectful of older people. Senior travellers in Vienna are often given priority seating on public transport and many theatres, cinemas, attractions and museums offer generous discounts to travellers with senior ID. **Retired Backpackers**

Market stall selling fruit and vegetables

and **My Travel Companions** serve independent world travellers over 50, including those headed for Austria.

STUDENT TRAVELLERS

Vienna's main theatres offer cheap standing-room and unsold tickets at the box office before the performance. For popular shows, you may need to queue for several hours. A university identity card or international student card also entitles students to a variety of discounts, including reductions on some museum admission fees and occasional discounts on rail tickets. Tourist offices provide a list of cheaper hotels as well as a list of Vienna's youth hostels (see p195).

ELECTRICITY

Austria's voltage is 220V AC/ 50Hz with European round 2-pin plugs.

RESPONSIBLE TOURISM

Austria is one of the world's leading destinations for sustainable tourism. About 70 per cent of energy is generated from renewable sources and about 60 per cent of all waste is recycled. In the capital itself, recycling bins are located throughout the city and there are numerous organic restaurants, food shops and even clothes stores that promote sustainable fashion.

The *Österreichisches Umweltzeichen* (Austrian Environmental Seal of Approval) is awarded to hotels and restaurants that meet high environmental standards. **Hotel Stadthalle**, near to Westbahnhof station, was the first hotel in Vienna to be awarded the *European Ecolabel*. for its green efforts This hotel uses solar panels to heat up water and collects rain water to flush its toilets.

For organic, locally grown produce, head to the market at Freyung in the 1st District open from 9am to 5pm on the first and third Friday and Saturday of the month.

Personal Security and Health

Pharmacy sign

Vienna is one of Europe's safest capital cities and presents few risks to visitors who employ common sense. Crime rates are low and violence, delinquency and social disorder are rare. Austrian police are trusted and respected and are easy to contact for both minor incidents and in the case of an emergency. Most incidents involving visitors are crimes of opportunity, involving theft of personal belongings.

POLICE

Vienna's police are easily identifiable. They wear a blue uniform with a badge that reads Polizei (police) and an Austrian coat of arms and/or the Austrian flag. Most police officers are helpful and many speak good English. Only surrender your passport and wallet to a uniformed officer with official ID. To report a crime, go in person to the nearest police station or call the emergency number, "133". You will need to give a detailed account of the incident and any items stolen. The police will prepare a statement, which you will need to sign. You can request an interpreter to translate any German language documents or terms you don't understand. Should the police need to detain you for questioning, be sure to request the services of a solicitor. You are also entitled to contact the local branch of your country's embassy or consulate for assistance (see p239).

Viennese police officers in uniform

WHAT TO BE AWARE OF

When looking after your personal safety use common sense. Be alert to pickpockets, particularly in the Prater at night, as well as at crowded markets, on public transport and at stations. Keep your cash in a discreet money belt and other valuables, such as cameras and mobile phones, well out of sight. Carry bags on your front with the strap worn across your shoulder.

There are a few places to steer clear of in Vienna. Unlit parks should be avoided at night. Illegal drug users often gather at Karlsplatz (underneath the Opera), but they generally present few problems for tourists. Prostitution is legal and is centred on the Gürtel ring-road near the Westbahnhof. Schwedenplatz can also be unsavoury after dark. Always avoid street gambling and illegal money changers, as they are likely to be using counterfeit notes. Street cons and late-night petty theft are common in the "Bermuda Triangle" area (see p84). Walking on Vienna's cycle lanes is forbidden and dangerous at any time of day or night.

Austria has experienced an increase in drug trafficking operations due to its strategic location in Europe. However, unlike some other European capitals, Vienna employs a zero-tolerance approach to drug misdemeanours. Anyone found in possession of drugs faces arrest and a court appearance followed by a

heavy fine and/or a period of imprisonment.

English-speaking services and helplines available to visitors in Vienna include **Alcoholics Anonymous** and **Befrienders**, a helpline for anyone feeling lonely.

IN AN EMERGENCY

Austrians are approachable, community-minded and are often more than willing to help a person in need. Before you arrive in Austria, make a list of the emergency numbers you may require for events such as credit card theft, emergency repatriation or any specialized critical medical care you may need. Also take a photocopy of your passport, medical insurance and ID cards. Your country's consulate in Austria will be able to help in the first instance with most emergency situations. All underground stations have SOS points for emergencies from which you can call the station supervisor or halt trains. Experienced and well-trained Red Cross (Rotes Kreuz) workers are also at hand to provide aid in the event of a natural disaster or emergency situation. For ambulance, fire and police emergency numbers, see the directory opposite.

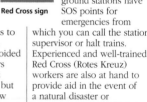

Red Cross sign

LOST AND STOLEN PROPERTY

Victims of theft should visit the police station in **Stephansplatz** as soon as possile to file a crime report. The report will take some time to complete, but you will need a copy to claim against an insurance policy for stolen property. For items misplaced on the railways or the Schnellbahn, go to the lost-and-found office in person at the **Westbahnhof**. For lost or stolen credit cards, contact the issuing company's office (see p242). For items lost elsewhere, call the **Lost Property Bureau** (Fündburo) and consult your embassy for help (see p239).

Police car

Ambulance

Fire engine

HOSPITALS AND PHARMACIES

Vienna's many pharmacies are a good source of information on medicines and the treatment of minor ailments. To locate an *Apotheke* (pharmacy), look out for a bright red "A" sign; there is generally one on every major street. Pharmacies operate a night rota system. Any closed pharmacies will display the address of the nearest one open, together with details of the **Pharmacy Information Line**.

For more serious illnesses and injuries, call the **Vienna Medical Emergency Service**. Vienna has several private hospitals, clinics and medical centres, but the main facility is **Vienna General**, which is the largest hospital in Europe. Most paramedics, doctors and clinic staff in Vienna speak English. An ambulance *(Rettungsdienst)* should be called in all medical emergencies by dialling "144" *(see Directory)*.

MINOR HAZARDS

Most visitors to Vienna will only ever need medical advice for minor ailments.

Commonly, these are sun-stroke during the city's hottest months, blisters from the excessive pavement-pounding and upset stomachs and headaches from too much rich food, wine and beer. Other annoyances over the summer include mosquitoes, noise from outdoor bars and clubs in the "Bermuda Triangle" and the pungent smells that bubble up from parts of the Danube Canal. Unlike some European cities, Vienna's water quality is excellent: freshly supplied from outlying mountains with purity assured.

Your hotel can recommend a walk-in clinic or doctor for minor medical issues.

TRAVEL AND HEALTH INSURANCE

Medical care is expensive in Vienna, so it pays to be fully insured for health purposes, however short your visit. Britain, like many other European countries, has a reciprocal arrangement with Austria whereby emergency hospital treatment is free upon presentation of a British passport. Keep all receipts for medical services, as you may need to claim costs back after you return home. EU citizens must carry a European Health Insurance Card (EHIC) to make use of medical services. The card comes with a booklet of advice and information on the procedure for claiming free medical treatment.

A travel insurance policy will also provide cover for other expenses and losses. Health and travel policies vary dramatically, so be sure to shop around for a policy that suits your particular needs, especially if you are planning on participating in adventure sports, or if you have an existing medical condition.

DIRECTORY

EMERGENCY NUMBERS

Alcoholics Anonymous
Tel 7995599.
Ask for English language AA.

Ambulance
Tel 144.

Befrienders
Tel 7133374.

Dentist
Tel 5122078.
Night and weekend line.

Doctor on Call
Tel 141.

Fire
Tel 122.

Police
Tel 133.

LOST AND STOLEN PROPERTY

Lost Property (Fundbüro)
Bastiengasse 36.
Tel 40008091.
◷ 8am–3:30pm Mon–Fri.

Police Station
Stephansplatz, 1010. **Map** 2 D5.
Tel 31347202.

Westbahnhof
Europaplatz 1.

HOSPITALS AND PHARMACIES

Internationale Apotheke
Kärntner Ring 17. **Map** 4 E2 & 6 D5.
Tel 5122825.

Pharmacy Information Line
Tel 1550.

Schweden-Apotheke, Pharmacie-Internationale
Schwedenplatz 2. **Map** 2 E2 & 6 E2.
Tel 53329110.

Vienna General Hospital
Währinger Gürtel 18–20.
Map 1 C4 & 5 A1.
Tel 40400.

Vienna Medical Emergency Service
Tel 40144.

Zum Heiligen Geist
Operngasse 16. **Map** 4 D2.
Tel 5877367.

Banking and Local Currency

Bank Austria logo

As you'd expect from a thriving European capital city, the financial services available in Vienna are excellent and funds are easily accessible. Credit and debit cards are widely accepted in major establishments, including restaurants, theatres and hotels. However, it is not unusual for smaller stores and cafés to insist on cash. ATMs are easily found in the city centre around the main tourist and shopping areas, together with money-changing machines and a number of bureaux de change.

companies may also charge a fee for using the card overseas. These charges can vary dramatically, so ask your credit card company about transaction costs before using your card abroad. Be sure to report lost or stolen cards to your own or nearest Austrian bank.

Although the popularity of traveller's cheques has declined, these fixed-amount cheques remain a safe way to carry large sums of money. A minimum commission applies, so it is uneconomical to change small sums. Cheques can be cashed at any bank or bureaux de change. Choose a well-known name such as American Express. Traveller's cheques can usually be replaced if they are lost or stolen, as long as the issuing receipt showing the serial number of the cheque is retained.

BANKING AND BUREAUX DE CHANGE

The best place to change money is at a bank. Although you can use travel agents, hotels and bureaux de change (*Wechselstuben*), banks offer a better rate. Commission applies on all currency changed and there is often a minimum charge or a handling fee of around €3.60. Exchanging a larger amount of money at one time can save on commission. You can also exchange foreign bank notes for euros at one of the automatic money-changing machines (Change-o-mats) found in the city centre and at main railway stations.

Most banks are open from 8am–12:30pm and from 1:30–3pm Monday to Friday (to 5:30pm on Thursdays). Some banks, generally those located at the main railway stations and at airports (*see Directory*), do not close for lunch and stay open longer.

The façade of Bank Austria in central Vienna

ATMS

ATMs are easy to find in Vienna's central shopping and main tourist areas. They accept a wide range of debit and credit cards; to find a cash point that accepts your card, check the logos on the machine. ATMs give instructions in German, English and French and increasingly also in Italian, Swedish and Spanish. The daily limit for withdrawals is usually £250. A fee is charged for each withdrawal. Charges for overseas usage vary, so check with your bank before you travel.

To use an ATM safely, only withdraw cash in daylight at a centrally-located machine and never carry your PIN with your card. Use your body to shield the transaction from the queue behind. Don't count your money at the ATM or walk away with cash clearly exposed.

CREDIT CARDS, DEBIT CARDS & TRAVELLERS CHEQUES

Credit cards, including **VISA, MasterCard, American Express** and **Diners Club**, are accepted in most hotels, shops and major restaurants. Many shops also accept debit cards. However, it is advisable to carry some cash, which is often preferred by smaller establishments such as side-street boutiques and cafés. Travellers planning to use a credit card should always check first to make sure it is accepted. Often a minimum expenditure applies (such as €10) when making a payment in this way. Credit card

CURRENCY

The euro (€) is the common currency of the European Union. It went into general circulation on 1 January 2002, initially for 12 participating countries. Austria was one of those 12 countries taking the euro in 2002, with the Austrian schilling phased out in the same year.

EU members using the euro as sole official currency are known as the Eurozone. Several EU members have opted out of joining this common currency.

Euro notes are identical throughout the Eurozone countries, each one portraying designs of fictional architectural structures. The coins, however, have one side identical (the value side), and one side with an image unique to each country.

Bank Notes
Euro bank notes have seven denominations. The €5 note (grey in colour) is the smallest, followed by the €10 note (pink), €20 note (blue), €50 note (orange), €100 note (green), €200 note (yellow) and €500 note (purple). All notes show the stars of the European Union.

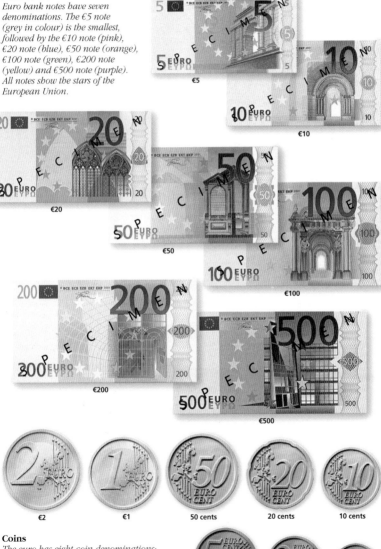

€5

€10

€20

€50

€100

€200

€500

€2

€1

50 cents

20 cents

10 cents

5 cents

2 cents

1 cent

Coins
The euro has eight coin denominations: €1 and €2; 50 cents, 20 cents, 10 cents, 5 cents, 2 cents and 1 cent. The €2 and €1 coins are both silver and gold in colour. The 50-, 20- and 10-cent coins are gold. The 5-, 2- and 1-cent coins are bronze.

Communications and Media

Telephone sign

Staying in touch in Vienna is easy. Making national and international telephone calls is uncomplicated, thanks to well-organized networks of mobile and landline services. Post offices across the city offer a range of mailing options. Vienna is also saturated with high-speed Internet and Wi-Fi networks and well served by TV (terrestrial and satellite) and radio channels, plus a range of domestic and foreign-run newspapers and magazines.

Touch-screen public telephone

INTERNATIONAL AND LOCAL TELEPHONE CALLS

Making calls within Austria and to overseas numbers is straightforward but can be pricey. For international calls it is best to avoid phoning from hotels as they tend to add a hefty surcharge. Cheap-rate calling times for international calls from Austria is between 6pm and 8am at weekends; for domestic calls it is between 8pm and 6am, and weekends. A cheap way to make calls to international numbers from a regular phone is with a phonecard, which can be purchased from any post office or from newsagents. Travellers are also increasingly

using VoIP (Voice over Internet protocol) services such as Skype. This system permits you to make phone calls anywhere in the world from a computer providing you have the right software installed and all the necessary adaptors and hardware.

MOBILE PHONES

To guarantee that your mobile phone will work in Austria, make sure you have a quad-band phone. Tri-band phones from outside the US are also usually compatible, but a US tri-band phone may have limited global coverage. Contact your service provider for clarification.

To use your mobile phone abroad, you may need to ask your provider to enable roaming on your phone. Remember that you are charged for both incoming and outgoing calls, and you pay a substantial premium for the international leg of the call.

If your handset is unlocked, you may be able to purchase a SIM card from one of the local mobile phone providers, such as **A1 Telekom, Tele-ring** or **Yesss**. Pay-as-you-go handsets can be bought from supermarkets such as Merkur or Hofer for around €15–20.

PUBLIC TELEPHONES

Telephone booths are located at most post offices; these are convenient to use as you pay at the counter rather than use coins. There are also yellow-striped public telephones located throughout the city that take phonecards known as *Telefon-Wertkarte*. Available for €3.60 and €6.90, phone-cards are sold in post offices and tobacconists. Coin-operated telephones, which are becoming less common, accept 10-, 20- and 50-cent as well as €1- and €2- coins. Most public phones have instructions in English and other languages. Directories are usually available in telephone boxes but may be too tatty to use. Post offices have directories in good condition, or contact directory enquiries *(see Reaching the Right Number below)*.

INTERNET ACCESS

Almost every major hotel, restaurant and public space in Vienna is a Wi-Fi hotspot. For an up-to-date list of locations, visit the **Freewave** website. A number of hotels charge a daily fee for Wi-Fi access but many provide it free for guests.

Tourists using Internet café in central Vienna

REACHING THE RIGHT NUMBER

- For directory enquiries in Austria, the EU and neighbouring countries, dial 118877.
- For international information, dial 0900 118877.
- All directory enquiries cost €1.35 per minute.
- For international or national telegrams, dial 0800 100190.
- For wake-up service, dial 0900 100100.
- To phone the **USA**, dial 001 followed by the number.

- To ring the **UK**, dial 0044 followed by the number (omit the 0 from the area code).
- To ring **Australia**, dial 0061 followed by the number.
- To ring **New Zealand**, dial 0064 followed by the number.
- To ring the **Irish Republic**, dial 00353 followed by the number.
- The front pages of the A–Z telephone directory list codes for each country. The cost of calls is available at post offices.

Some of the best spots in which to log on for free are the many bars, restaurants and coffee shops around the MuseumsQuartier. Vienna also boasts a rich supply of Internet cafés. Some popular options in or near Innere Stadt include **BIGnet Internet**, **Café Einstein**, **Café Stein**, **Café-Bar Blue Box** and **Surfland Internet Café**. Tourists may also use computers in public facilities such as libraries and business centres, where access is usually charged at an hourly rate.

POSTAL SERVICES

Austrian post offices are clearly identifiable by their bold yellow signs. They provide postage stamps (*Briefmarken*), telegrams and registered letters, and arrange the delivery of packages. Phonecards and collectors' stamps are also sold. Other services include *Post Restante* or *Postlagernd* (to be called for) and the cashing of travellers' cheques and giro cheques up to a maximum of €180 per cheque. Foreign currency is handled by the larger post offices.

The Austrian postal system is reliable and efficient. Letters are weighed and charged accordingly. Customers can choose between two postal tariffs: priority and economy.

For quick delivery of a package, international couriers such as **DHL** and **FedEx** offer a reliable service.

Post office opening hours are generally between 8am and noon and 2pm and 6pm Monday to Friday. Larger post offices are also open from 8am to 10am on Saturdays (not for financial dealings). The Innere Stadt's **Central Post Office** stays open 24 hours a day, and the one at Westbahnhof opens from 6am to 11pm daily. The post office at Schwechat Airport is open from 7am–8pm daily.

Postage stamps are also sold at newsagents. Letters for Europe weighing up to 20g cost 65 cents, as do postcards. You'll need a €1.40 stamp for the rest of the world. Registered letters cost €2.10.

NEWSPAPERS AND MAGAZINES

Tabloid *Kronen Zeitung* is, by far, Austria's most widely read newspaper. The second-largest, *Der Kurier*, is less sensationalist and focuses on national and international news, politics and current affairs. *Die Presse* is the oldest of Austria's national dailies, as well as the best-selling quality paper, while independent broadsheet *Der Standard* is popular with university students. *Falter* is Vienna's main listings magazine. Papers, including foreign language magazines and periodicals, can be bought from a *Tabak Trafik* (newsagent), kiosks or, on Sundays, street vendors. Online news magazines, such as the monthly English-language *viennareview.net*, are increasingly popular.

TV AND RADIO

Austria has two main radio stations. Ö1 specializes in classical music and Ö3 plays popular tunes. Radio FM4 broadcasts in English from 1am to 2pm daily on 103.8 MHz. Vienna Cable Radio transmits on FM100.8. Although terrestrial broadcast TV is German-language, many international films are shown with subtitles. Almost every hotel and sports bar has satellite television, on which large numbers of international programmes and English-language channels are broadcast.

National and foreign newspapers on sale at a street kiosk

DIRECTORY

MOBILE PHONES

A1 Telekom
www.a1.net

Tele-ring
www.telering.at

Yesss
www.yesss.at

INTERNET ACCESS

BIGnet Internet
Judengasse 4. **Map** 6 D2.
Tel 5332939.
www.bignet.at

Café Einstein
Rathausplatz 4. **Map** 1 C5 & 5 A2.
www.einstein.at

Café Stein
Währingerstrasse 6-8.
Map 1 A2 & 5 A1.
Tel 31972410.
www.cafe-stein.com

Café-Bar Blue Box
Richtergasse 8. **Map** 3 A2.
www.bluebox.at

Freeware
www.freewave.at

Surfland Internet Café
Krugerstrasse 10. **Map** 6 D5.
www.surfland.at

POSTAL SERVICES

Central Post Office
Fleischmarkt 19.
Map 2 E5 & 6 D2.
Tel 515090 or *Tel* 8921020 (for general information).
www.post.at

DHL
Tel 0820550505.
www.dhl.at

FedEx
Tel 080012380.
www.fedex.com/at

Distinctive yellow sign outside one of Vienna's post offices

GETTING TO VIENNA

Forming a strategic commercial and transit hub between Eastern and Western Europe, Vienna is well served by air, water and rail. Direct flights link to every major European city as well as to North America, Canada, Japan and Australia. An efficient hydrofoil runs between Vienna and Bratislava and river cruises arrive from Romania, Bulgaria, Germany, Budapest, Slovakia and Prague. Vienna has good motorway routes to the rest of Europe, but if you are arriving from neighbouring Germany, note that the Austrian motorway speed limit is only 130 km (80 miles) per hour. Flights into Bratislava, just 65 km (40 miles) from the centre of Vienna, arrive frequently and are often competitively priced. Taxis, trains and airport shuttle buses transfer arriving air travellers from Bratislava Central Station to Vienna.

Austrian Airlines aeroplane

The modern exterior of Schwechat International Airport

ARRIVING BY AIR

Vienna's main airport is well served by most international airlines. Several flights per day link London Heathrow with Vienna's airport at Schwechat. The main airlines with regular flights between the UK and Vienna are **British Airways, Lufthansa, KLM** and **Air France**, along with several low-cost carriers such as **easyJet** and **BMI**. The main Austrian carrier is **Austrian Airlines. Aer Lingus** serves Vienna from Gatwick and Dublin. Travellers from the United States can choose direct flights with **Delta** from New York, Orlando and Atlanta. Austrian Airlines flies direct to New York and Chicago. There are also direct flights from Sydney and Toronto. Bratislava's Milan Rastislav Štefánik Airport is less than 2 hours' drive from central Vienna with regular domestic and international flights from Europe, the Middle East and North Africa.

SCHWECHAT AIRPORT

Schwechat International, Vienna's only airport, is located 19 km (12 miles) southeast of the city centre. With two terminals, the airport is used by over 100 airlines. As one of Europe's most modern airport facilities, Schwechat International is served by the super-efficient CAT (City Airport Train), which runs to and from Wien Mitte station.

A well-maintained road also connects with central Vienna, and drivers will find a fuel station, auto repair shop, parking and several car rental outlets onsite. The airport itself is clearly signed and easy to navigate, with all the facilities that you would expect, including restaurants, duty free shops, a supermarket, banks and tourist information offices. The well-stocked supermarket is open 7 days a week from 7:30am until 7pm, including holidays. The airport is fully equipped for disabled travellers.

BRATISLAVA AIRPORT

With its low-cost flights and close proximity to Vienna, Bratislava's upgraded Milan Rastislav Štefánik Airport has become a popular transit point for visitors to the Austrian capital. Located 9 km (5.6 miles) northeast of Bratislava, Milan R Š is Slovakia's main international airport.

Scheduled flights, operated by **Czech Airlines, Danube Wings, LOT Polish Airlines, Ryanair** and **Belle Air**, connect to Europe, the Middle East and North Africa.

Most nationalities do not need a visa to enter Slovakia. You will need a valid passport or identity card. For detailed information, check with your consulate before travelling.

TICKETS AND FARES

To get the best deal on air fares, shop around and book well in advance. Cheaper tickets on scheduled flights can often be booked up to six months before the date of travel. Discount agencies also sell cut-price APEX tickets at less than the normal full fare. Charter flights are often available at very competitive prices. No-frills budget airlines represent excellent value for money, although many charge extra for checked luggage, stowed sporting equipment, priority boarding and other services. Meals are also an additional charge. Being flexible on the date and time of travel allows passengers to get the best from

Shopping mall at Schwechat International Airport

low-cost airlines. Another option is a weekend package, which will often include a two-night stay at a good Viennese hotel for less than the price of an economy-class airline ticket.

TRANSPORT FROM AIRPORT INTO TOWN

From Schwechat International, you can get to Vienna city centre either by taxi or **CAT (City Airport Train)**. Taxis take about 20 minutes to reach central Vienna and cost around €32. The CAT train departs every 30 minutes from the basement level of the airport to Wien Mitte. It costs €9 each way if you pay on the train, or €8 if booked in advance online.

The cheapest means of transport into the city is the Schnellbahn train, which also departs from the basement level of the airport. Running every half hour, the train takes roughly 30 minutes to connect with Wien Mitte and stops at Praterstern-Wien Nord. Tickets cost €3.40.

Buses run from about 6am–midnight every 30 minutes to Schwedenplatz, Meidling and Westbahnhof stations. A one-way ticket costs around €6; pay the driver on board.

From Milan Rastislav Štefánik Airport, bus shuttle transfers take 75 minutes and cost €10 each way. Shuttle buses depart from the terminal building four times a day at 10:15am, 4:30pm, 10pm and 10:50pm. Seasonal services offer the option of the **Twin City Liner** catamaran, which takes 75 minutes and costs €29 one way. However, a year-round train service remains the fastest option at around 1 hour. Trains run from 5:45am–10:45pm nearly every hour. A single journey costs €14.20. Taxis from the airport cost around €80 per person.

Slovakia is part of the Schengen agreement, which means residents from Schengen countries are not subject to border controls. Other nationalities will need to show their passport when crossing the border.

DIRECTORY

AIRPORTS

Bratislava Airport
Tel 0233 033353.
www.airportbratislava.sk

Schwechat Airport
Tel 0810 222333 or 7007 32300.
www.viennaairport.com

AIRLINES

Aer Lingus
Tel 0871 7182020.
www.aerlingus.com

Air France
Tel 50222 2400.
Airport *Tel* 700732065.
www.airfrance.com

Austrian Airlines
Tel 517661000.
Airport *Tel* 700762520.
www.austrian.com

Belle Air
www.belleair.it

British Airways
Tel 79567567.
www.ba.com

BMI
www.flybmi.com

Czech Airlines
www.czechairlines.com

Danube Wings
www.danubewings.eu

Delta
Tel 79567023.
www.delta.com

easyJet
www.easyjet.com

KLM
www.klm.com

LOT Polish Airlines
www.lot.com

Lufthansa
Tel 0810 10258080.
Flight information *Tel* 7007 or 700722233.
www.lufthansa.com

Ryanair
www.ryanair.com

TRANSPORT FROM AIRPORT INTO TOWN

CAT (City Airport Train)
www.cityairporttrain.com

Twin City Liner
www.twincityliner.com

CAT (City Airport Train) linking Schwechat to the centre of Vienna

ARRIVING BY RAIL

Vienna's rail network is in the process of being restructured and construction is under way for a main railway station, the Hauptbahnhof Wien, which will serve all international routes into Vienna. The new station is scheduled to be completed in 2015. It will be located at Südtirolerplatz, south of the city centre, with connections to the U1 underground line. The station at Südbahnhof has closed as part of these railworks.

Until the new station opens international routes are operating from one of several stations located around the city. Routes from western Austria and Germany arrive at the Westbahnhof, located to the west of the city, with connections to the U3 and U6 underground lines, the Schnellbahn and several tram and bus routes.

International routes from southern Europe arrive in Vienna at Bahnhof Meidling, which is conveniently situated on the U6 underground line in south Vienna. Routes from northern Europe terminate at Franz-Josefs-Bahnhof in the north of the city. The station is served by the Schnellbahn and the cross-city D tram that goes directly to the Ringstrasse. Trains from Neusiedl am See, Marchegg, Bratislava and Brno stop at the Ostbahnhof, a temporary station located within walking distance of the Belvedere Palace. The Ostbahnhof has connections to the Schnellbahn and D and O tramlines. As soon as

Eurolines coach connecting Vienna with the rest of Europe

services start from the Hauptbahnhof Wien, the Ostbahnhof will close and be demolished. The Westbahnhof will then serve domestic routes only. Check online at www. oebb.at or www.hauptbahn-wien.at for more information on how the works will affect your travel plans.

All the stations have taxi ranks and a range of facilities that include shops, luggage storage, food outlets and cash points. The travel agency (Reisebüro) at Westbahnhof is open from 8am to 7pm on weekdays and from 8am to 1pm on Saturdays and can provide travel information as well as assistance with booking hotel rooms. Once in Vienna, visitors can find rail information in English by calling the **Öbb Call Centre**.

Ticket offices can be found in all larger railway stations. There are many types of tickets, such as group, family and tourist travel, with or without concessions. When buying a ticket, seek advice at the ticket office as to which one is best for you. You can also book tickets through the Öbb Call Center or online at the **Austrian Federal Railways**

website. On most Eurocity journeys, buying a ticket less than 72 hours prior to departure incurs a supplement. Many of the train lines to Vienna are overnight and, for a small fee, it is possible to reserve a seat or a bed up to two months before travelling. Snacks are sometimes sold on board and most overnight routes will include a Continental breakfast if you are booked on a sleeper or couchette. Expect to pay around €40 for a trip from Vienna to Budapest, a journey of 3½ hours.

ARRIVING BY COACH

Vienna's main coach station, the Vienna International Bus Terminal (VIB), is located close to Erdberg U3 underground station. Services, run by **Eurolines**, arrive here from most major European cities including Budapest, London and Paris. Prices vary, but expect to pay around €53 from London to Vienna (senior discounts apply). **Postbus** runs routes throughout Austria and Slovakia. Coaches arrive in Vienna at the Hauptbahnhof Wein bus terminal.

ARRIVING BY CAR

Austrian roads are well constructed with good, clear signage and ample lighting for travelling after dark. Carrying your driver's licence is mandatory in Austria. You must also have car registration documents and insurance papers at hand. Visitors need an overseas extension of their annual insurance, such as a Green Card. An international driver's licence is required for anyone using a language written in a script other than Roman. Seatbelts must be worn at all times. Note that

A train near Ollersbach, en route to Vienna

children up to the age of 12 or under 1.5 m (5 ft) must be seated in suitable child-safety seats.

Tolls are compulsory on all motorways in Austria and a *vignette* sticker, should be purchased and attached to the inside of the windscreen before travel on motorways. *Vignettes* are available for 10 days (€7.90), two months (€23) or one year (€76.50) and can be purchased at fuel stations and newsagents. All hire cars should have a *vignette* provided. Drivers without a valid *vignette* can be fined up to €4,000.

There are four main routes into Vienna by road. The Südautobahn is made up of the A2 and A23 motorways, it provides access into the city from the south. The Donau-uferautobahn (A22) is the main northen motorway. The A1 (Westautobahn) and the A4 (Ostautobahn) enter Vienna from the west and east respectively. Motorways converge on the outer ring road (Gürtel). The city centre is marked *Zentrum*. The **Austrian Automobile Club (ÖAMTC)** provides daily reports on road conditions.

ARRIVING BY BOAT

From April to October you can arrive in Vienna by boat along the Danube from Bratislava, the Wachau and the Budapest. Companies such as **Viking River Cruises** also run cruises into Vienna from Budapest. Boats dock at the **DDSG–Blue Danube** landing station at the Reichsbrücke bridge. The landing station is close to the Vorgartenstrasse U-Bahn station on the U1 line. An information counter at the dock sells tickets and provides city maps and schedule information. A seasonal hydrofoil links Vienna, Visegrad, Budapest and Bratislava. Discounts apply for children (2–14) and students (ID required).

DIRECTORY

ARRIVING BY RAIL

Austrian Federal Railways
www.oebb.at

Öbb Call Centre
Tel 051717 (rail information).

ARRIVING BY COACH

Eurolines
www.eurolines.com

Postbus
www.postbus.at

ARRIVING BY CAR

Austrian Automobile Club
www.oeamtc.at

ARRIVING BY BOAT

DDSG–Blue Danube
www.ddsg-blue-danube.at

Viking River Cruises
www.vikingrivercruises.co.uk

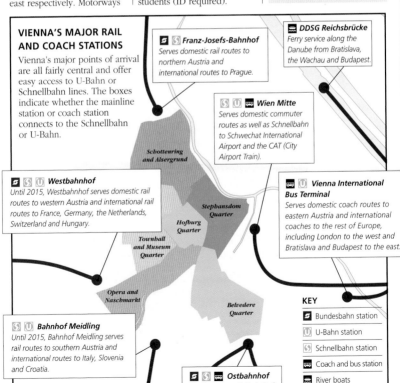

VIENNA'S MAJOR RAIL AND COACH STATIONS

Vienna's major points of arrival are all fairly central and offer easy access to U-Bahn or Schnellbahn lines. The boxes indicate whether the mainline station or coach station connects to the Schnellbahn or U-Bahn.

Franz-Josefs-Bahnhof
Serves domestic rail routes to northern Austria and international routes to Prague.

DDSG Reichsbrücke
Ferry service along the Danube from Bratislava, the Wachau and Budapest.

Wien Mitte
Serves domestic commuter routes as well as Schnellbahn to Schwechat International Airport and the CAT (City Airport Train).

Westbahnhof
Until 2015, Westbahnhof serves domestic rail routes to western Austria and international rail routes to France, Germany, the Netherlands, Switzerland and Hungary.

Vienna International Bus Terminal
Serves domestic coach routes to eastern Austria and international coaches to the rest of Europe, including London to the west and Bratislava and Budapest to the east.

Schottenring and Alsergrund

Stephansdom Quarter

Hofburg Quarter

Townhall and Museum Quarter

Opera and Naschmarkt

Belvedere Quarter

Bahnhof Meidling
Until 2015, Bahnhof Meidling serves rail routes to southern Austria and international routes to Italy, Slovenia and Croatia.

Ostbahnhof
The temporary Ostbahnhof serves rail routes to eastern Austria and Budapest.

KEY

- Bundesbahn station
- U-Bahn station
- Schnellbahn station
- Coach and bus station
- River boats

GETTING AROUND VIENNA

With so much to see, compact central Vienna is best explored on foot. Paths are well maintained with adequate signage marking major sights and attractions. Traffic-free areas offer pedestrians the opportunity to shop and sightsee away from tooting horns and congestion. Numerous cobblestone plazas, gardens, parks and cafés offer plenty of places to stop, draw breath, check the map and enjoy a cup of coffee. Viennese drivers are dissuaded from driving through the city centre by a complicated and frustrating one-way system and sky-high parking tariffs. However, if the leg-work gets too much, Vienna's network of buses comprehensively crisscross the citycentre. The underground system is also clean, efficient and easy to use. As part of the City of Vienna Transport Authority's interconnecting public transport system, it is supplemented by a coordinated tram and bus network. Services operate from 5am to 12:30am to a highly reliable timetable.

Citybike logo

Tourists walking in the gardens at Belvedere Palace

GREEN TRAVEL

As one of the greenest cities in Europe, Vienna has invested heavily in an impressive array of environmentally-friendly transport initiatives. A highly efficient public transport system and 1,500 km (900 miles) of bicycle paths offer viable eco-friendly alternatives to driving through the city. Over 1,000 rechargeable electrically-powered bicycles (an environmentally sound rental scheme) are available for hire at very affordable rates from more than 50 strategically positioned stations throughout the city *(see Cycling)*. Almost every part of the metropolis is accessible by public transport and timetables for trams, buses, underground and trains neatly dovetail each other. Inexpensive tickets and discounted fares for combined use of all modes of transport ensure the public network is very popular for locals and tourists alike.

The ultimate green transportation in Vienna are the pedicab taxis known as **Faxi Taxi** *(see p252)*, which operate in the city centre around major sights and attractions. Powered solely by a cycle mechanism, the Faxi Taxi is also cheaper than a motorized taxi. The only drawback is that Faxis accommodate just two passengers with light hand luggage.

Parking, a rare and expensive option in Vienna, also serves as a deterrent to drivers. Indeed, an entire vehicle-free housing development has been built in the capital. "Bike City" focuses on the needs of cyclists with the whole complex benefitting from easy access bicycle paths and excellent direct links to public transportation.

WALKING

There is no better way to see the city than to walk around Vienna at your own pace. Major sights and attractions are conveniently clustered together in close proximity and attractive streets are peppered with inviting cafés and cake shops. The area around Kärntner Strasse, Stock-im-Eisen-Platz and Graben is entirely traffic free. Numerous tour companies offer multi-lingual guided walks with a wide variety of fascinating cultural themes and intriguing historical topics. Contact the *Wiener Tourismusverband (see p238)* for more information.

Exploring Vienna on foot is not without its hazards; traffic rarely stops at pedestrian crossings, so it is wise to be cautious when crossing the road. British and Australian visitors should remember that motorists drive on the right. In addition, keep an eye out for cyclists; they often share the pavement with pedestrians and, if they are travelling at some speed, may not have time to stop if you stray onto their section of the pavement. At all times, pedestrians should take care not to walk along bike paths and tramlines, as this is prohibited. On the Ringstrasse, trams run against the traffic, so looking both ways is essential. Jaywalking is illegal in Vienna, and this law is enforced by police – even if the roads are quiet. To avoid a hefty fine, it is important to abide by the signals at the pedestrian crossings; do not cross a road when a red figure is showing.

Cycling in the Prater

BY FIAKER

Traditional horse-drawn open carriages or Fiakers, many driven by a bowler-hatted and whiskered coachman, are a novel and relaxing way to get around. Remember that part of the route is on the busy Ring-strasse. You can hire a Fiaker at Stephansplatz, Heldenplatz or Albertinaplatz, but to avoid an unpleasant surprise, agree the price and length of the trip with the driver before you set off. Even a short trip can be costly.

CYCLING

With its plethora of bike paths, Vienna is a great city for cyclists, as long as the main roads and tramlines are avoid-ed. A 7-km (4-mile) cycle path round the Ringstrasse takes you past many historic sights, and there are also bike paths to the Prater *(see pp162–3)* and to the Hundertwasser Haus *(see p164)*. If you are a keen cyclist, a booklet called *Rad Wege* illustrates all of Vienna's cycle routes and is available from a number of bookshops. Bicycles can be rented at some train stations and discounts are given with a train ticket, or from various **Citybike** stations. To rent a Citybike without an Austrian debit card, use a Citybike Tourist Card, which costs €2 per day. The card can be hired out on a daily basis from either the **Royal Tours** or **Pedal Power** offices. Some hotels also offer Citybike Tourist Card rental to their guests. City cycle tours take place during summer *(see below)*. Pedal Power's 3-hour city tours leave from the Prater Ferris wheel at 10am daily.

GUIDED TOURS

Vienna Sightseeing and **Cityrama** are two of the city's largest tour operators, and their buses and coaches are a common sight – especially during the summer months.

Trams are a good way of seeing the 19th-century build-ings in the Ringstrasse because you can choose where to get on and off. Organized tours are run by the **Tram Museum** in a 1920s tram from a meeting point at Otto Wagner's Karls-platz Pavilions *(see pp146–7)*. Private groups may also hire a vintage tram to go to the Prater or a *Heuriger* (tavern) or simply to tour the city.

DDSG–Blue Danube organizes tours on the Danube River and the Danube Canal to sights such as Otto Wagner's Nussdorf locks. From June to October the **Twin City Liner**, a high-speed catamaran, makes a round trip to Bratislava three times a day.

In the summer there are guided walking tours, in English, French or Italian, with a variety of themes. From May to Septem-ber, cycling enthusiasts can book tours through Pedal Power *(see Cycling)*. Tours are available in German or English, but Italian or French can be arranged. **Segway public tours** run from April to October, and the 3-hour excursion includes a brief lesson on how to ride the Segway personal transport.

DRIVING

As in many European cities, drivers in Vienna are aggressive and single-minded. Vehicles swap lanes at speed, lose patience easily and show little regard for other road users. Drivers need to be alert at all times.

Priority is always given to the right unless a "yellow diamond" indicates otherwise. Trams, buses, police cars, fire engines and ambulances all have right of way. Vienna's speed limit is 50 km (30 miles) per hour. Police carry out checks with infra-red guns and can issue fines on the spot. The limit for alcohol is 0.5 mg per ml of blood (about 1/3 litre [11 fl oz] of beer or 1–2 glasses of wine). Spot checks are common and anyone exceeding the limit is likely to face a hefty fine and the loss of their licence.

Drivers who belong to an internationally affiliated automobile association can make use of breakdown services provided by ÖAMTC (the Austrian Automobile Club). Radio station FM4 has traffic news in English.

PARKING

Apart from Sundays, when shops are closed, finding a parking spot in Vienna is a very frustrating and time-consuming exercise. *Anfang* (beginning) and *Ende* (end) signs are posted everywhere, and it is prohibited to park between them. You'll need to go to the police if your car is clamped or towed away.

The City of Vienna operates a park and pay scheme in districts 1–9 and 20 from 9am–10pm Mondays to Fridays *(see p252)*. Parking disks are sold at newsagents (*Tabak Trafiken*), some banks and petrol stations. Usually, a maximum stay of 2 hours is allowed in any space. In other districts, a blue line by the kerb indicates a pay and display scheme. Note that car parks are expensive.

Car park sign

Faxi Taxis lined up on a Vienna street

TAXIS

Taxis in Vienna are instantly recognizable by a TAXI sign on the roof. If available for hire, the sign will be illuminated. Taxis can be found at ranks across the city but they cannot be hailed in the street. Alternatively, one can be summoned by phone – there are three numbers: 31300, 40100 or 60160. For a short trip, expect to pay from €7 to €10 with additional charges for extra passengers, luggage, and late-night and weekend journeys. Tipping about 10 per cent of the fare is customary, rounding up to the nearest euro. A trip to the airport costs up to €34.

Vienna's Faxi Taxi pedicab is a quick way to get around the centre of the city (*see p250*). Find them at taxi stands or flag one down in the street. Journeys up to 2 km (1 mile) cost €5. One-way journeys more than 2 km cost €10.

PUBLIC TRANSPORT

Vienna's transport network is made up of trams (*strassenbahn*), buses (*autobus*), underground (U-Bahn) and trains (S-Bahn). The city's transport system, **Wiener Linien**, works largely on an honesty system. There are no ticket barriers at stations, allowing passengers to hop on and off. Formal checks by transport authority staff do take place – you'll be asked for your *fahrschein* (ticket) by a uniformed guard. Anyone caught without a valid ticket is fined and charged. Smoking is banned in stations and on public transport. Children under 6 travel for free year-round while those aged under 15 may travel free of charge on Sundays and holidays. The latter also qualify for half-price single tickets. Rush hour runs weekdays from about 7–9:30am, then again from about 4:30–6:30pm.

TICKETS AND TRAVEL CARDS

Vienna's public transport ticketing system is less confusing than it appears at first glance. Buying a ticket in advance is the easiest option. Tickets are sold at newsagents (*Tabak Trafiken*), from ticket machines at stations or over the counter at U-Bahn and S-Bahn offices. Vienna city is zone 100 of the regional fare system and a standard ticket covers all areas of the city and allows passengers to change trains and lines and switch from the underground to a tram or a bus, as long as they don't break their journey. A single ticket costs €1.80 if bought in advance or €2.20 on board.

Weekly season tickets (€14) are valid from Monday to Sunday. These are good value for anyone using public transport for more than four days. The *8-Tage-Karte* (€28.80) is best for groups of travellers and consists of eight strips which, when stamped, are valid for a day. Up to eight people may stamp the same ticket; start with step one or you will invalidate the other seven. Also available are 24-, 48- and 72-hour tickets costing €5.70, €10, and €13.60 respectively. The Vienna Card (€18.50) is a 72-hour ticket valid on all transport. It comes with additional discounts and benefits and only needs punching once.

DIRECTORY

GREEN TRAVEL

Faxi Taxi
Tel 0699/12005624.
www.faxi.at

CYCLING

Citybike
Tel 0810/500 500.
www.citybikewien.at

Pedal Power
Tel 7297234.
www.pedalpower.at

Royal Tours
Herrengasse.
www.royaltours.at

GUIDED TOURS

Cityrama
Börsegasse 1.
Map 2 D4 & 5 B1.
Tel 534130.

DDSG–Blue Danube
Handelskai 265.
Tel 58880.

Segway tours
www.wien.info/en/
sightseeing/tours-guides/
segway

Tram Museum
Tel 790944903.

Twin City Liner
Schwedenplatz,

Marienbrücke 103.
Map 6 E2.
Tel 72710137.

Vienna Sightseeing Tours
Stelzhamergasse 4–11.
Map 4 F1 & 6 F3.
Tel 7124683.

DRIVING

ÖAMTC
www.oamtc.at

PARKING

Am Hof.
Map 2 D5 & 5 C2.

Börsegasse.
Map 2 D4 & 5 C1.

Dr-Karl-Lueger-Ring.
Map 1 C5 & 5 A2.

Morzinplatz.
Map 2 E4 & 6 D.

Wollzeile 7.
Map 2 E5 & 6 D3.

Other car parks are shown on the Street Finder map (*see pp262–7*).

PUBLIC TRANSPORT

Wiener Linien
www.wienerlinien.at

Travelling by Underground

U-Bahn station symbol

Vienna's underground system (U-Bahn) is one of Europe's most modern networks and is a clean, fast and reliable way of crossing the city. Construction commenced in the late 1960s, with the inaugural journey taking place in the mid-1970s. It has since undergone expansion and refurbishment in phases to a total length of 75 km (50 miles). The U-Bahn now has 105 stations with ongoing development plans into 2019.

seven days a week from around 5pm–12:30am. During the day, trains depart every 5 minutes or so, less frequently after about 8pm. A 24-hour service runs at weekends and public holidays. Outside these hours, the U-Bahn service is replaced by Vienna NightLine buses *(see pp254–5)*. The U-Bahn's five colour-coded lines are U1, U2, U3, U4 & U6. Confusingly, there is no U5 line. The Vienna U-Bahn has been earmarked for extension as part of an ongoing city transport expansion project that is expected to run until 2019. This will involve constructing additional stations and new stretches of track – check the Wiener Linien website for updates *(see p252)*.

THE UNDERGROUND SYSTEM

The U-Bahn is generally safe *(see p240)*, but in case of emergencies there are help points on most platforms. Smoking is prohibited on U-Bahn platforms and on the trains themselves. Displays above the train doors show stations and connections, and a recorded voice announces stops and also connections to trams and buses. Signs indicate where prams can be stored by the doors. Bicycles are also allowed on a few carriages at set times. Be aware that doors are opened manually and can be stiff and heavy. The U-Bahn operates

MAKING A JOURNEY BY UNDERGROUND

1 To determine which line to take, travellers should look for their destination on a U-Bahn map. The five lines are distinguished by colour and number. Simply trace the line to your destination, making a note of where you need to change lines. Connections to other forms of transport are also shown.

2 Tickets can be bought from a newsagent, ticket vending machines or ticket offices. To get to the trains, insert your ticket into the ticket-stamping machine in the direction of the arrow. Wait for the ping indicating that it is validated, and pass through the barrier. Follow the signs (with the number and colour of the line) to your platform.

3 On the platform, check the direction and destination of the train on an electronic destination indicator.

4 Stops along the line are shown on a plan. A red arrow in the corner shows the direction in which the train enters the station.

5 At your destination, follow *Ausgang* signs to reach street level.

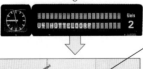

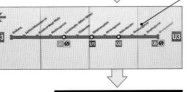

← Ausgang

Pull handle to open door

The door opens out to the side

Sign showing stops on line 3 of the U-Bahn, including connecting stops

6 At stations with more than one exit, use the map of the city to check which street or square you will come out at.

Travelling by Tram, Bus and Train

Schnellbahn logo

Travelling on the tram, bus and train is a pleasant and easy way to get around Vienna. Trams are instantly recognizable with their red and white livery, and no visit to the city is complete without a nostalgic tram ride. Little hopper buses serve the city centre, while larger buses run from the inner suburbs, Ringstrasse and Prater to the outer suburbs. Popular with commuters, the Schnellbahn (S-Bahn) runs beyond the city limits to outer suburbs and further afield.

TRAMS

Vienna's tram network is one of the largest in the world, with over 28 routes. Known locally as "Bim" for its distinctive bell sound, it is a delightful way to get around the city. For the ultimate experience, seek out one of the old, traditional models with their wooden seats and vintage interiors.

Most of the main sights in Vienna's historic centre, such as the State Opera House, Imperial Palace, Parliament and Vienna City Hall, are located on the popular Ring Tram route. Passengers will need to purchase a Round-the-Ring ticket (€7) for a complete unbroken journey or a 24-hour Ring Tram ticket (€9) for a hop-on-hop-off service.

On-board services include audio-visual information about highlights along the route, delivered via a multi-lingual multimedia system. Trams depart every 30 minutes all year round, from 10am–6pm (to 7pm in July & August).

All trams are equipped with seats for disabled travellers. However, the modern low-riding trams are a more wheelchair-friendly option. Look for vehicles with the ULF (Ultra Low Floor) sign.

BUSES

Buses are comfortable, air-conditioned and equipped with CCTV. Bus stops are marked by a green "H" for *haltestelle* or stop. All stops display bus numbers, destinations, timetables and route maps. Buses should stop automatically on main routes but if you are in any doubt, flag it down. Tickets purchased from the driver will be valid for one bus journey only. If you have already purchased a ticket from a newsagent or ticket machine, you will need to validate it in the blue ticket-stamping machine on the bus. If you have already made part of your journey by tram or U-Bahn, there is no need to stamp your ticket again. Limited services run on holidays and Christmas Day. On New Year's Eve, buses and other forms of public transport run all night. All buses are wheelchair accessible.

NIGHT BUSES

Vienna's night bus service operates every night of the week starting at 12:30am and then at 30-minute intervals until 4am in the morning. There is some variation between the service operating on weekday nights (Sunday night through to Thursday night) and those operating at the weekend and on public holidays. Night buses are marked by the letter "N". All night buses in Vienna start from Schwedenplatz, the

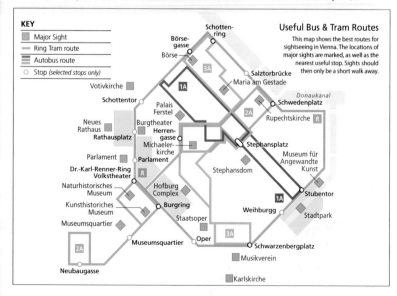

KEY

- Major Sight
- Ring Tram route
- Autobus route
- ○ Stop *(selected stops only)*

Useful Bus & Tram Routes

This map shows the best routes for sightseeing in Vienna. The locations of major sights are marked, as well as the nearest useful stop. Sights should then only be a short walk away.

Votivkirche · Schotten-ring · Börse-gasse · Börse · 3A · Salztorbrücke · Maria am Gestade · Donaukanal · Schwedenplatz · 1A · Schottentor · Palais Ferstel · 2A · Rupechtskirche · Neues Rathaus · Rathausplatz · Burgtheater · Herren-gasse · Stephansplatz · Michaeler-kirche · Museum für Angewandte Kunst · Parlament · Parlament · Dr.-Karl-Renner-Ring · Volkstheater · R · Stephansdom · Naturhistorisches Museum · Hofburg Complex · Kunsthistoriches Museum · Burgring · 1A · Stubentor · Weihburgg · Stadtpark · Museumsquartier · Staatsoper · 3A · Museumsquartier · Oper · Schwarzenbergplatz · 2A · Musikverein · Neubaugasse · Karlskirche

A typical Vienna city bus at Leopoldau bus station

Opera and Schottentor, and run out to most suburbs. Tickets can be purchased from the driver and all other pre-bought tickets and passes are valid on this service. Passengers can pre-arrange a taxi to wait at the destination stop if they are staying some distance from a night bus route. Taxis can be booked through the Transport Office in Schwedenplatz.

TRAINS

Known colloquially as the S-Bahn, the Schnellbahn (Fast Train) is recognizable by its blue and white logo and is primarily a commuter service. A metropolitan route has stops in the centre of Vienna interconnecting with mainline stations *(see p249)* but is generally used as a means of getting farther afield. The

local Bundesbahn is also a commuter service and is sometimes called the Regionalbahn on maps and timetables in order to distinguish it from national routes. Timetable information is available from station information offices and is displayed on station departures/arrivals boards. When travelling within the city limits all public transport tickets and passes are valid on the Schnellbahn. For Schnellbahn journeys outside of Vienna a ticket must be purchased in advance. See the **Austrian Federal Railways** website for more information.

DIRECTORY

Austrian Federal Railways
www.oebb.at

Wiener Linien
www.wienerlinien.at

Travelling Beyond Vienna

Vienna is a great base from which to discover other parts of Austria as well as neighbouring European destinations. The historic cities of Salzburg, Innsbruck, Graz and Linz are well-served by public transport from the city, and car hire is a viable option to reach more rural areas.

DOMESTIC FLIGHTS

Frequent domestic flights with **Austrian Airlines** link Vienna with Graz, Klagenfurt, Salzburg, Innsbruck and Linz (from about €80–90 each way). Air travel in Austria is expensive and, with extra time needed for checking in, getting to and from the airport, and for retrieving your luggage, it is not always the fastest and most convenient way of getting to another destination within Austria.

TRAINS

Trains to the west and north of Austria depart from Westbahnhof, with hourly services to Salzburg (€45, 3½ hours). Routes from Franz-Josefs-Bahnhof station connect Vienna with Tulln, Krems an der Donau, and the Wachau region.

Hertz logo

CAR HIRE AND ROAD TRAVEL

Car rental is an option for excursions outside of the city. Expect to pay about €170 for a 3-day rental. The minimum age for hiring a car is 21 years. You'll need a driver's licence, passport and third-party insurance.

BOATS

Boat trips regularly set off from Vienna along the Wachau Valley. Alternative trips in the other direction head to Bratislava (1 hour) and Budapest (4 hours). All ships have restaurants and sundecks.

A hydrofoil service runs from the DDSG–Blue Danube landing station at the Reichsbrücke bridge, connecting Vienna with Visegrad, Budapest and Bratislava. Return fares cost €39 for Vienna to Bratislava and €89 for Vienna to Visegrad and Budapest.

DIRECTORY

DOMESTIC FLIGHTS

Austrian Airlines
www.austrian.com

CAR HIRE

Avis City
Airport **Tel** 7007 32700.
www.avis.at

Budget City
Airport **Tel** 7007 32711.
www.budget.at

Europcar
Tel 7146717.
Airport **Tel** 7007 32699.
www.europcar.at

Hertz City
Tel 5128677.
Airport **Tel** 7007 32661.
www.hertz.at

STREET FINDER

The map references for all the sights, hotels, restaurants, bars, shops and entertainment venues described in this book refer to the maps in this section. A complete index of street names and all the places of interest marked on the maps can be found on the following pages. The key map (*right*) shows the area of Vienna covered by the *Street Finder*. This map includes sightseeing areas as well as districts for hotels, restaurants and entertainment venues.

All the street names in the index and on the *Street Finder* are in German – *Strasse* translating as street and *Gasse* meaning lane. *Platz* or *Hof* indicate squares or courtyards. Throughout this guide, the numbers of the houses follow the street names, in the same way that you will find them in Vienna.

View of Vienna's roof tops from Am Hof
(see p87)

KEY TO STREET FINDER

▨	Major sight
▨	Places of interest
▨	Other building
Ⓤ	U-Bahn station
🚆	Bundesbahn station
🚋	Badner Bahn stop
Ⓢ	Schnellbahn station
🚌	Bus and coach station
P	Parking
ℹ	Tourist information office
✚	Hospital with casualty unit
🚓	Police station
✚	Church
✡	Synagogue
⊠	Post office
═══	Railway line
▬▬	Pedestrian street

SCALE OF MAPS
1–4 & 5–6 RESPECTIVELY

0 metres	250	
0 yards	250	**1:14,000**

0 metres	125	
0 yards	125	**1:9,000**

Section of the Austria fountain (1846) by Schwanthaler (left) and side view of the Schottenkirche (see p110)

0 kilometres	1
0 miles	0.5

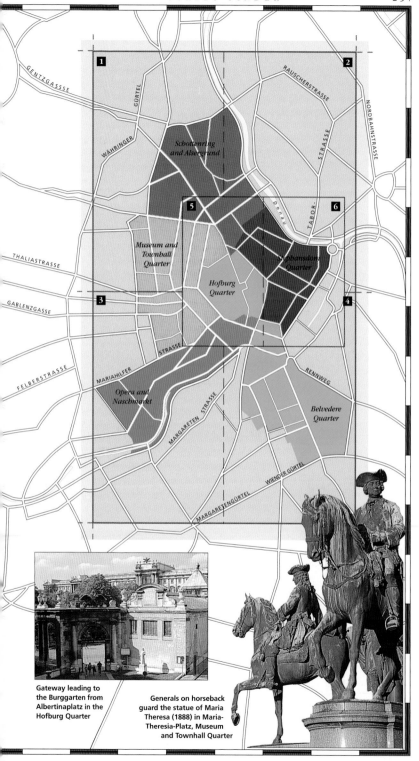

1

2

GENTZGASSE

RAUSCHERSTRASSE

GÜRTEL

STRASSE

NORDBAHNSTRASSE

WÄHRINGER

Schottenring and Alsergrund

5

6

THALIASTRASSE

Donau

TABOR

Museum and Townhall Quarter

Stephansdom Quarter

GABLENZGASSE

Hofburg Quarter

3

4

STRASSE

RENNWEG

FELBERSTRASSE

MARIAHILFER

Opera and Naschmarkt

Belvedere Quarter

MARGARETEN STRASSE

WIENER GÜRTEL

MARGARETENGÜRTEL

Gateway leading to the Burggarten from Albertinaplatz in the Hofburg Quarter

Generals on horseback guard the statue of Maria Theresa (1888) in Maria-Theresia-Platz, Museum and Townhall Quarter

Street Finder Index

Vienna's street and place names are generally spelt as one word; -platz, -strasse or -kirche are put at the end of the name, as in Essiggasse for example. Occasionally they are treated as separate words, for instance Alser Strasse. Abbreviations used in this index are Dr as in Doctor-Ignaz-Seipel-Platz, and St as in Sankt Josef Kirche. Some entries have two map references. The first refers to the smaller scale map that covers the whole of central Vienna, the second refers to the large-scale inset map that covers the Stephansdom and Hofburg Quarters.

USEFUL WORDS	
Gasse	street
Strasse	road
Platz	square
Hof	court
Kirche	church
Kapelle	chapel
Dom	cathedral
Denkmal	monument
Markt	market
(often the sight of an old market)	
Brücke	bridge

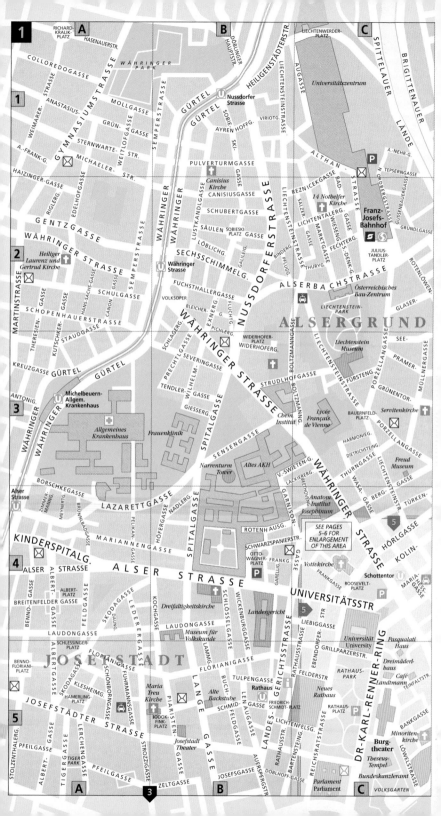

D   **E**   **F**   **2**

DRESDNER STRASSE

REBHANNGASSE

1

BRIGITTENAU

OMANOG.
DENIS-

OOSTER-

GERHARDUSGASSE

BRIG... GASSE
St Brigitta
Kirche

RAFFAELGASSE

DAMM-STRASSE

WALDMÜLLERGASSE

NORDWESTBAHNSTRASSE

TREUSTRASSE

NEUBURGER- GASSE

ROTHMAR-GASSE

KLUCKYGASSE

HANNOVERGASSE

JÄGERSTRASSE

SACHSEN-
PLATZ
STRASSE

HARTL G.

GREISENECKERGASSE

WEBER- STRASSE

HEINZELMANNGASSE

WALLENSTEINSTRASSE

WALLENSTEIN-
PLATZ

BÄUERLE-GASSE

STREFFLEURGASSE

JAN- GASSE

KARL-MEISSL-G.

HEISTERGASSE

RAUSCHERSTRASSE

NORDWESTBAHNSTRASSE

Frachtenbahnhof

LAMPIGASSE

WOLFSAUGASSE

STAUDINGERGASSE

WASNER- GASSE

KARAJ...

Friedensbrücke

CLUSIUSG.

RÖGERGASSE

GASSE

GASSE GEORG-SIGL-G.

HAHNGASSE

DONAUKANAL

ROSSAUER LÄNDE

OBERE

SCHOLZGASSE

GAUSS-
PLATZ
Muttergotteskirche

AUGARTEN
PARK

TABORSTR.

MARINELLIG.

Evang.
Kirche

AM TABOR

SCHERZERG.

TRUNNERSTR.

2

WETTSTEIN-
PARK

MOSERGASSE

GASSE

Rossauer
Lände

OBERE AUGARTENSTRASSE

LEOPOLDSTADT

LESSINGG.

VOLKERT-
STR.

DARWIN-GASSE

HEINESTRASSE

PAZMANITENGASSE

CASTELLEZGASSE

3

SERVITENGASSE

BERG- GASSE

DONAUSTRASSE

Rossauerbrücke

Augartenbrücke

REMBRANDTSTRASSE

FÖRSTERG.

HAASGASSE

FRANZ-HOCHEDLINGER-GASSE

LEOPOLDS-GASSE

SCHREYGASSE

NESTROYG.

ADAMBERGERG.

*Augarten Palais
Augarten Palace*

MALZGASSE

MIESBACHGASSE

KLEINE PFARRGASSE

POCH-
PLATZ

GROSSE PFARRGASSE

SPERL-GASSE

St Leopold
Kirche

JOSEFINENGASSE

VEREINS- GASSE

GROSSE STADTGUT-GASSE

NOVARAGASSE

PILLERSDORGASSE

BLUMAUERGASSE

GLOCKENGASSE

ODEONG.

ZIRKUSGASSE

Rossauer
Kaserne

HÖRLGASSE

STRASSE

SCHLICK-
PLATZ

GASSE

Schottenring

W. KIENZL
Park

HERMINEN-
GASSE

SCHIFFAMTSGASSE

SCHIFFGASSE

IM WERD

*Kriminal-
museum*

HAIDGASSE

GROSSE MOHREN-

KÖTHENBRÜCKG.

ROTENSTERNGASSE

WEINTRAUBENGASSE

4

FLOSS GASSE

TANDELMARKTGASSE

6

KARMELITERG.

SEE PAGES
5-6 FOR
ENLARGEMENT
OF THIS AREA

THERESIEN-

SCHOTTENRING

BÖRSEGASSE

GONZAGAGASSE

NEUTORGASSE

ZELINKA-GASSE

ESSLINGASSE

FRANZ- JOSEFS- KAI

KRUMMB.G.

KLEINE SPERLGASSE

HOLLANDSTRASSE

LILIENBRUNNGASSE

NEGERLEG.

GREDLERSTR.

TABORSTRASSE

SCHMELZG.

*Spital der
Barmherzigen
Brüder*

KOMÖDIENG.

NESTROY-
PLATZ

Nestroyplatz

CZERNING.

HOHENSTAUFENGASSE

WIPPLINGERSTRASSE

Börse

WERDERTOR-G.

HEINRICHSGASSE

Börseplatz

BÖRSESTR.

HELFERSTORFERSTR.

CONCORDIA-
PLATZ

RUDOLFS-
PLATZ

Salztor-
brücke

GONZAG.

MORZIN-
PLATZ

Marien-
brücke

HST.
SCHWEDEN-
PLATZ

FERDINAND-STRASSE

ASPERNBRÜCKENG.

PRATERSTRASSE

UNTERE

STRASSE

DONAUSTRASSE

6

INNERE
STADT

Schottenkirche

FREYUNG

Freyung
Palais

RENNGASSE

TIEFER GRABEN

STRAUCHG.

AM HOF

*Maria am
Gestade*

Altes
Rathaus

SALVATORGASSE

SALZGRIES

*Jüdisches Ghetto
Jewish District*

MARC-AUREL-STR.

FLEISCHMARKT

*Ruprechts-
kirche
Stadttempel*

Schwedenplatz

Aspern-
brücke

FRANZ- JOSEFS- KAI

Schwedenbrücke

Urania

JULIUS-
RAAB-PLATZ

RADETZKYSTRASSE

5

Herren-
gasse

NAGLERGASSE

SEITZERG.

JUDEN-
PLATZ

*Böhmische
Hofkanzlei*

Bohemian Court
Chancery

HOHER MARKT

Clock
Museum

TUCHLA UBEN

BRANDSTÄTTE

BAUERN-

KRAMERG.

HOHER MARKT

ROTGASSE

ROTENTURMSTRASSE

FLEISCHMARKT

*Akademie der
Wissenschaften
Academy of
Sciences*

Heiligenkreuzerhof

WOLLZEILE

POST-

DOMINIKANERBASTEI

Hauptpostamt

Post-
sparkasse

GEORG-
COCH-
PLATZ

BIBERSTRASSE

STUBENRING

SCHALLAUTZERSTR.

VORDERE ZOLLAMTSSTR.

Regierungs-
gebäude

Finanz-
landes-
direktion

HERREN
GASSE

WALLNER-STRASSE

Mollard-
Clary
Palace

Loos Haus

MICHAELER-
PLATZ

Michaelerkirche

D

KOHLMARKT

Demel
Konditorei

Peterskirche

GRABEN

HABSBURGERG.

DOROTHEERG.

STOCK-
IM-EISEN-
PLATZ

STEPHANS-
PLATZ

Stephansplatz

Stephansdom

Haas
Haus

Figaro-
haus

*Dom- und
Diözesanmuseum*

Cathedral Museum

SCHULERSTR.

*Dominikaner-
kirche*

E

*Jesuiten-
kirche*

WOLLZEILE

**Austrian Museum
of Applied Arts**

F

MAK

VORMARXERG.

4

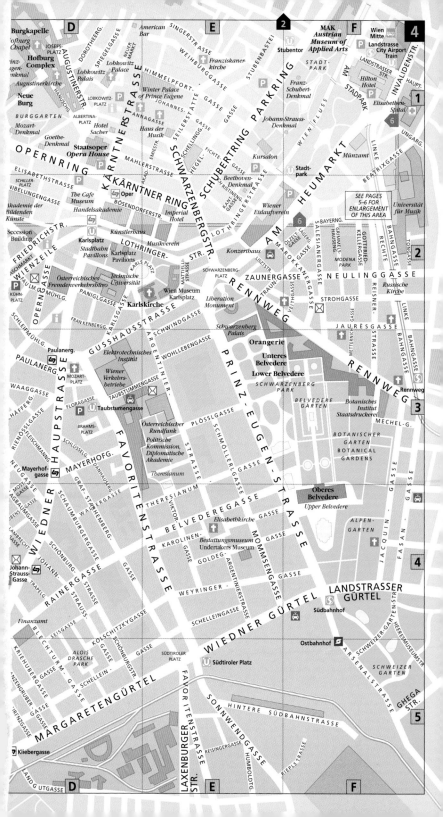

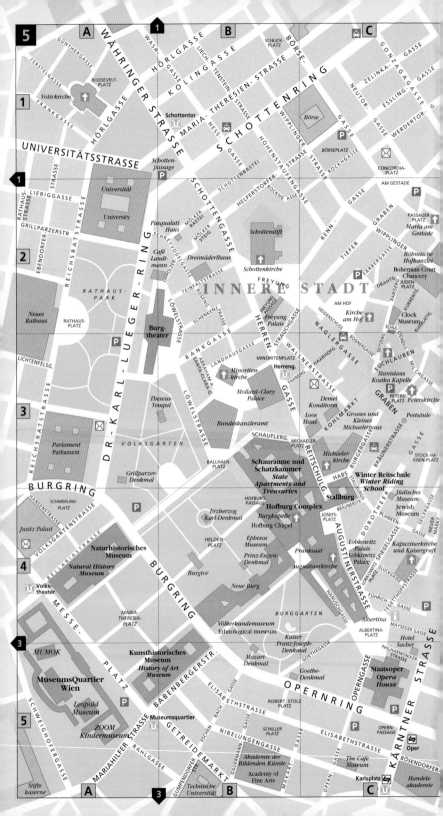

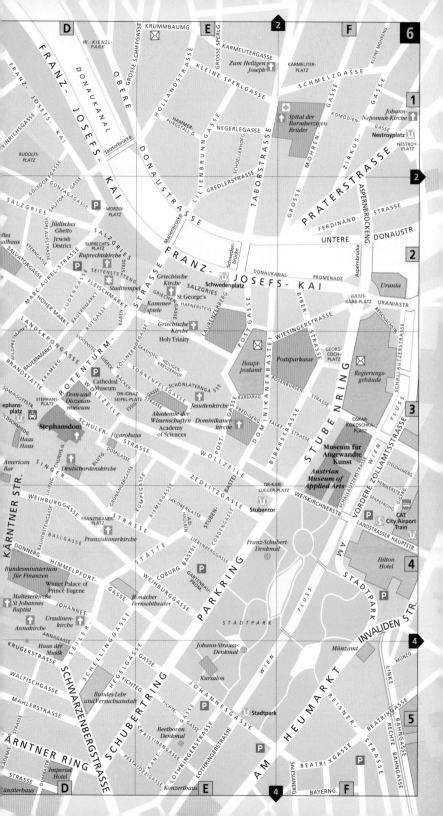

General Index

Acknowledgments

Dorling Kindersley wishes to thank the following people who contributed to the preparation of this book.

Main Contributor
Stephen Brook was born in London and educated at Cambridge. After working as an editor in Boston and London, he became a full-time writer in 1982. Among his books are *New York Days, New York Nights; The Double Eagle; Prague, L.A. Lore* and books on wine. He also writes articles on wine and travel for many newspapers and periodicals.

Additional Contributors
Gretel Beer, Rosemary Bircz, Caroline Bugler, Dierdre Coffey, Fred Mawer, Nicholas Parsons.

Proof Reader
Diana Vowles.

Design and Editorial
Managing Editor Carolyn Ryden
Managing Art Editor Steve Knowlden
Senior Editor Georgina Matthews
Senior Art Editor Vanessa Courtier
Editorial Director David Lamb
Art Director Anne-Marie Bulat
Consultant Robert Avery
Language Consultant Barbara Eichberger

DTP
Vinod Harish, Vincent Kurian, Azeem Siddiqui.

Additional Design and Editorial Assistance
Emma Anacootee, Ros Angus, Claire Baranowski, Marta Bescos, Tessa Bindloss, Jane Edmonds, Gadi Farfour, Emer FitzGerald, Fay Franklin, Rhiannon Furbear, Camilla Gersh, Sally Gordon, Emily Green, Alistair Gunn, Elaine Harries, Melanie Hartzell, Paul Hines, Laura Jones, Priya Kukadia, Joanne Lenney, Carly Madden, Hayley Maher, Ella Milroy, Sonal Modha, Kate Molan, Melanie Nicholson-Hartzell, Catherine Palmi, Helen Partington, Sangita Patel, Alice Peebles, Marianne Petrou, Robert Purnell, Nicki Rawson, Sadie Smith, Sands Publishing Solutions, Simon Ryder, Andrew Szudek, Samia Tadros, Lynda Warrington, Susannah Wolley Dod, Johanna Wurm.

Additional Illustrations
Kevin Jones, Gilly Newman, John Woodcock, Martin Woodward.

Cartography
Uma Bhattacharya, Mohammad Hassan, Jasneet Kaur, Peter Winfield, James Mills-Hicks (Dorling Kindersley Cartography)
Colourmap Scanning Limited, Contour Publishing, Cosmographics, European Map Graphics, Street Finder maps: ERA Maptec Ltd (Dublin).
Map Co-ordinators Simon Farbrother, David Pugh
Cartographic Research Jan Clark, Caroline Bowie, Claudine Zante.

Additional Photography
DK Studio/Steve Gorton, Ian O'Leary, Poppy, Rough Guides/Natascha Sturny, Steve Shott, Clive Streeter, Daniel Wurm.

Fact checker
Melanie Nicholson-Hartzell

Special Assistance
Marion Telsnig and Ingrid Pollheimer-Stadtlober at the Austrian Tourist Board, London; Frau Preller at the Heeresgeschichtliches Museum; Frau Wegscheider at the Kunsthistorisches Museum; Frau Stillfried and Mag Czap at the Hofburg; Herr Fehli-nger at the Museen der Stadt Wien; Mag Schmid at the Natural History Museum; Mag Dvorak at the Österreichischer Bundestheaterverband; Dr Michael Krapf and Mag Grabner at the Österreichische Galerie; Robert Tidmarsh and Mag Weber-Kainz at Schloss Schönbrunn; Frau Zonschits at the Tourismusverband.

Photography Permissions
Dorling Kindersley would like to thank the following for their kind permission to photograph at their establishments:

Alte Backstube, Bestattungsmuseum, Schloss Belvedere, Bundesbaudirektion, Deutschordenskirche and Treasury, Dom und Diözesanmuseum, Sigmund Freud Gesellschaft, Josephinum Institut für Geschichte der Medzin der Universität Wien, Kapuzinerkirche, Pfarramt St. Karl, Stift Klosterneuburg, Wiener Kriminalmuseum, Niederösterreichisches Landesmuseum, Österreichischer Bundestheaterverband, Österreichische Postsparkasse (P. S. K.), Dombausekretariat Sankt Stephan, Spanische Reitschule and Museum für Volkskunde. Dorling Kindersley would also like to thank all the shops, restaurants, cafés, hotels, churches and public services who aided us with photography. These are too numerous to thank individually.

Picture Credits
a = above; b = below/bottom; c = centre; f = far; l = left; r = right; t = top.

Works of art have been reproduced with the permission of the following copyright holders: *Brunnenhaus* Ernst Fuchs © DACS, London 2011; *The Tiger Lion* 1926 Oskar Kokoschka © DACS, London 2011 155t; © THE HENRY MOORE FOUNDATION: 144b.

The Publishers are grateful to the following individuals, companies and picture libraries for permission to reproduce their photographs:

4CORNERS IMAGES: Damm Stefan 11br; ALAMY IMAGES: David Coleman 238cr; Christopher Gannon 250cl; imagebroker/ Christian Handl 205tl; INSADCO: Photography/ Martin Bobrovsky 205c; Art Kowalsky 10cla; John Lens 176cr; Barry Mason 207c; mediacolor's 176 cla, 206cl; David Noble 207tl; Robert Harding Picture Library Ltd/ Richard Nebesky 204cla; Jack Sullivan 241cla; vario images/ Stefan Kiefer 245tr, 251crb; vario images/ Thomas Jantzen 245bc; Ken Welsh 10bc; GRAPHIC WoodyStock/ Helmet Ebner 180; GRAPHIC SAMMLUNG ALBERTINA, Wien: 26–7; ANCIENT ART AND ARCHITECTURE COLLECTION: 24b(d), 25t, 29ca; Akg-Images: 8–9, 16(d), 17t, 19tc(d), 19br(d), 21b, 22–3, 24t, 24–5, 25cb, 25bl, 26ca, 26br(d), 27t, 28t, 28c, 28br(d), 29t, 28–9, 29cl, 29bl, 30t(d), 30cl, 32cl, 32br, 33b, 34br, 36tl, 38br, 55b(d), 67 inset, 87b(d), 98cla, 110b(d), 149ca, 152cb, 172b, 237 inset; Erich Lessing 11tl, 38cb, 39cr, 98cla; AUSTRIAN AIRLINES: 240t; AUSTRIAN ARCHIVES: 35tl; AUSTRIAN TELEKOM: 244cla

BANK AUSTRIA. UNICREDIT BANK AUSTRIA AG: 242bl; BELVEDERE,Vienna: 156crb; Thomas Preiss 157cla; BILDARCHIV PREUSSISCHER KULTURBESITZ, Berlin: 23bl, 35cbl, 92t; CASA EDITRICE BONECHI, Firenze: 167ca; CHRISTIAN BRANDSTÄTTER VERLAG, Wien: 20ca, 31c(d), 33tl, 34bl, 83t, 99c; BRIDGEMAN ART LIBRARY, London: 133b(d); Albertina, Wien 46br; Bonhams, London

24ca; British Library, London 4t(d), 19bl(d); Kunsthistorisches Museum, Wien 19tr(d), 46cr; Museum der Stadt Wien 33tr, 38car(d), 38bcl, 39cl; Österreichische Galerie 35tr; HOTEL BRISTOL: 190cr; ©1999 BUNDESGÄRTEN, WIEN: 172tl; BUNDESMINISTERIUM FÜR FINANZEN: 27cb(d); BURGHAUPTMANNSCHAFT IN WIEN: 101ca, 101cb, 101b.

COURTESY OF CAFÉ MUSEUM: 58BR; CAFE RESTAURANT LANDTMANN: 11cl; ARCHÄOLOGISCHER PARK CARNUNTUM: 21tr; CASINOS AUSTRIA: 227c; CEPHAS PICTURE LIBRARY: Mick Rock 161b, 208tl; Wine Magazine 240br; CITYBIKE WIEN: 250tc, 251tl; CONTRAST PHOTO: Milenko Badzic 65t; Franz Hausner 166b; Michael Himml/ Transglobe 152tr; Hinterleitner 227b; Peter Kurz 63b, 141tl, 233b; Boris Mizaikoffl/Transglobe 63t; Tappeiner/Trans- globe 234c; H Valencak 178b. K.U.K HOFZUCKERBACKER CH. DEMEL'S SOHNE GMBH: 203c; DK IMAGES:(c) Judith Miller/ Sloan's 10tc; ET ARCHIVE, London: 38br; Museum für Gestaltung, Zurich 34cl; Museum der Stadt Wien 26bl, 31tl, 38cl; EUROLINES: 248tr; EUROLINES (UK) Ltd: 248cb; EUROPEAN COMMISSION: 243; MARY EVANS PICTURE LIBRARY, London: 18tl, 18bl, 18br, 19tl, 22c, 25br, 27br, 30cr, 30bl, 30br, 32t, 35b, 38t, 39t, 76tr, 175b, 189 inset.

F. A. HERBIG VERLAGSBUCHHANDLUNG GMBH, München: 98bl, 98br, 99bl, 99br. FAXI DAS FAHRRADTAXI: 252tl; ROBERT HARDING PICTURE LIBRARY: Larsen Collinge International 42cb, 232t; Adam Woolfitt 62t, 137t, 150t, 178t; HEERESGES-CHICHTLICHES MUSEUM, Wien: 47b, 166t, 166b, 167t, 167cb, 167b; HEINZ HEIDER, VOR: 252cl; HERTZ: 255cb; HISTORISCHES MUSEUM DER STADT WIEN: 17b, 20t, 21ca, 21cbr, 26t, 28cb, 32cr, 32bl, 33ca, 33cb, 43t, 47tl, 49c, 141tc, 141tr, 145ca, 169t; HOTEL SACHER: 202cr; HULTON-DEUTSCH COLLECTION: 28bl, 36tr(d), 38bcr(d), 168ca; HUTCHISON LIBRARY: John G Egan 200t. THE IMAGE BANK, London: GSO Images 11b; Fotoworld 41bl; HOTEL IMPERIAL: 190b. JOSEFSTADT THEATRE: 226c. KERN'S BEISL RESTAURANT: 203bl; WILHELM KLEIN: 23t, 26cb; KUNSTHAUS WIEN: Peter Strobel 48t; KUNSTHISTORISCHES MUSEUM, Wien: 24cb, 41cbr, 46cl, 48b, 56c, 95t, 95b, 99t, 100 all, 122–3 all, 124–5 all, 126–7 all, 175tl.

J & L LOBMEYR, Wien: 49t; LEOPOLD MUSEUM-PRIVATSTIF- TUNG: *Selbstbildnis*, 1910, by Egon Schiele 46bla, *Hockender Weiblicher Akt*, 1910, by Egon Schiele 120tr, *Self Portrait with Chinese Lantern*, 1912, by Egon Schiele 118t, *Die Schnitter*, 1922 by Egger- Lienz 120t; LONELY PLANET IMAGES: Richard Nebesky 233tl; MAGNUM PHOTOS: Erich Lessing 18tr, 20c, 20bl, 20br, 21tl, 21cbl, 22cb, 23cal, 26c, 29br, 30–1, 31b; MANSELL COLLECTION, London: 9 inset; MUSEUM JUDENPLATZ: Votava/PID 86tl; MUSEUMSQUARTIER, ERRICHTUNGS-UND BETRIEBSGESMBH: Lisi Gradnitzer 118br; Rupert Steiner MQ E+B GesmbH 41br, 119t, Martin Gendt MQ E+B GesmbH 119bl; MUMOK,

MUSEUM OF MODERN ART LUDWIG FOUNDATION VIENNA: *Homme accroupi*, 1907, by André Derain, © ADAGP, Paris & DACS, London 2011, 119br; *The Red Horseman*, 1974 by Roy Lichtenstein, © Estate of Roy Lichtenstein/DACS, London 2011, 120b. NARODNI MUSEUM, Praha: 18bc; NATURHISTORISCHES MUSEUM, Wien: 46t, 128–9 except 129br, 235cb.

ÖBB-PERSONENVERKEHR AG: 249bl, 254tl; ÖSTERREIC- HISCHE GALERIE, Wien: 47cb, 154c, 155 all, 156bl, 157cra, 157br; ÖSTERREICHISCHES MUSEUM FÜR ANGEWANDTE KUNST, Wien: 28ca, 47tl, 56t, 57c, 82–3 all except 83t; ÖSTERREICHISCHE NATIONALBANK: 243cal, 243cac; ÖSTER-REICHISCHE NATIONALBIBLIOTHEK, Wien: 20cb, 22t, 23cb, 36c; ÖSTERREICH WERBUNG: 5bl, 27ca, 31tc, 31tr, 34ca, 44b, 98cbl, 101t, 140b, 163cb, 163b, 172t, 179b, 203t, 232cr. PHOTOLIBRARY: Merten Merten 157tl; POPPERFOTO: 37tc; RAIFFEISENBANK WIEN: Gerald Zugman 34cr; RETROGRAPH ARCHIVE, London: Martin Ranicar-Breese 193br; REX FEATURES, London: Action Press 36bl, Adolfo Franzo 37tl, Sipa Press 121b, Sokol/Sipa Press 121b; GEORG RIHA: 77t; RONACHER VARIETY THEATRE/CMM: Velo Weger 226t.

HOTEL SACHER: 194t; SCHLOSS SCHÖNBRUNN KULTUR-UND BETRIEBSGES MBH, Wien: Professor Gerhard Trumler 172c, 173 all except 173b, 174 all, 175tr; SCHLOSS SCHÖNBRUNN KULTUR- UND BETRIEBSGES MBH 1999: Wolfgang Voglhuber 139b; SCIENCE PHOTO LIBRARY, London: Geospace 10t; SYGMA: Habans/ Orban 37tr, Viennareport 37ca; SURFLAND INTERNETCAFE: 244crb; T-MOBILE AUSTRIA GMBH: 244tl; TRAVEL LIBRARY: Philip Entiknapp 66–7, 221t. UNICREDIT BANK AUSTRIA AG: 242tl; VIENNA AIRPORT: 246cl, 247tl, 247bl; VIENNA POLICE: 240bl, 241tl; VIENNA TOURIST BOARD: 238bl; VIENNASLIDE: Harald A Jahn 232b; Karl Luymair 230cl; MUSEUM FÜR VÖLKERKUNDE, Wien: 49b, 235b; VOTAVA, Wien: 163t; WERNER FORMAN ARCHIVE: Museum der Stadt Wien 66t; St Stephens Cathedral Museum 23car; WIENER LINIEN GmbH & Co KG: 252 cl, 253c, 253cr, 253cb, 253br, 255tl; WIEN MUSEUM: 86br, Longcase Clock c.1762-69 David A.S. Cajetano 86c; WIENER SÄNGERKNABEN: 5cbr, 39b, 64b; WIENER STADT- UND LANDESBIBLIOTHEK, Wien: 36tc, 36bl; WIGAST AG: 193tl, 193cr. ZEFA: 153c; Anatol 98–9; Damm 248b; G Bro-Bauer 179t; Havlickek 177c; Sibelberbauer 62b; Streichan 37cb; Studio Mike 206t; V Wentzel 41cbc. ZOOM KINDERMUSEUM: Alexandra Eizinger 118cla.

MAP COVER: AWL IMAGES: Walter Bibikow.

JACKET: Front - AWL IMAGES: Walter Bibikow. Back - AWL IMAGES: Jon Arnold tl, Danita Delimont Stock bl, Travel Pix Collection clb; DORLING KINDERSLEY: Peter Wilson cla. Spine - AWL IMAGES: Walter Bibikow t.

All other images © Dorling Kindersley. For further information see: www.dkimages.com

Phrase Book

In Emergency

Help!	Hilfe!	hilf-er
Stop!	Halt!	hult
Call a doctor	Holen Sie einen Arzt	hole'n zee ine'n artst
Call an ambulance	Holen Sie einen Krankenwagen	hole'n zee ine'n krank'n-varg'n
Call the police	Holen Sie die Polizei	hole'n zee dee pol-its-eye
Call the fire brigade	Holen Sie die Feuerwehr	hole'n zee dee foy-er-vair
Where is the nearest telephone?	Wo finde ich ein Telefon in der Nähe?	voh fin-der ish ine tel-e-fone in dair nay-er?
Where is the nearest hospital?	Wo ist das nächstgelegene Krankenhaus?	voh ist duss next-g'lay-g'ner krunk'n-hows?

Communication Essentials

Yes	Ja	yah
No	Nein	nine
Please	Bitte	bitt-er
Thank you	Danke vielmals	dunk-er feel-malse
Excuse me	Gestatten	g'shtatt'n
Hello	Grüss Gott	groos got
Goodbye	Auf Wiedersehen	owf veed-er-zay-ern
Goodnight	Gute Nacht	goot-er nukht
morning	Vormittag	for-mit-targ
afternoon	Nachmittag	nakh-mit-targ
evening	Abend	ah'b'nt
yesterday	Gestern	gest'n
today	Heute	hoyt-er
tomorrow	Morgen	morg'n
here	hier	hear
there	dort	dort
What?	Was?	vuss?
When?	Wann?	vunn?
Why?	Warum?	var-room?
Where?	Wo/Wohin?	voh/vo-hin?

Useful Phrases

How are you?	Wie geht es Ihnen?	vee gayt ess een'n?
Very well, thank you	Sehr gut, danke	zair goot, dunk-er
Pleased to meet you	Es freut mich sehr, Sie kennenzulernen	ess froyt mish zair, zee ken'n-tsoo-lairn'n
See you soon	Bis bald/bis gleich	bis bult/bis gleyesh
That's fine	Sehr gut	zair goot
Where is…?	Wo befindet sich…?	voe b'find't zish…?
Where are…?	Wo befinden sich…?	voe b'find'n zish…?
How far is it to…?	Wie weit ist…?	vee vite ist…?
Which way to…?	Wie komme ich zu…?	vee komma ish tsoo…?
Do you speak English?	Sprechen Sie englisch?	shpresh'n zee eng-glish?
I don't understand	Ich verstehe nicht	ish fair-shtay-er nisht
Could you please speak slowly?	Bitte sprechen Sie etwas langsamer?	bitt-er shpresh'n zee et-vuss lung-zam-er?
I'm sorry	Es tut mir leid/ Verzeihung	es toot meer lyte/ fair-tseye-oong

Useful Words

big	gross	grohss
small	klein	kline
hot	heiss	hyce
cold	kalt	kult
good	gut	goot
bad	schlecht	shlesht
enough	genug	g'nook
well	gut	goot
open	auf/offen	owf/off'n
closed	zu/geschlossen	tsoo/g'shloss'n
left	links	links
right	rechts	reshts
straight on	geradeaus	g'rah-der-owss
near	in der Nähe	in dair nay-er
far	weit	vyte
up	auf, oben	owf, obe'n
down	ab, unten	up, oont'n
early	früh	froo
late	spät	shpate

entrance	Eingang/Einfahrt	ine-gung/ine-fart
exit	Ausgang/Ausfahrt	ows-gung/ows-fart
toilet	WC/Toilette	vay-say/toy-lett-er
free/unoccupied	frei	fry
free/no charge	frei/gratis	fry/grah-tis

Making a Telephone Call

I'd like to place a long-distance call	Ich möchte ein Ferngespräch machen	ish mer-shter ine fairn-g'shpresh mukh'n
I'd like to call collect	Ich möchte ein Rückgespräch (Collectgespräch) machen	ish mer-shter ine rook-g'shpresh (coll-ect-g'shpresh) mukh'n
local call	Ortsgespräch	orts-g'shpresh
I'll try again later	Ich versuche es noch einmal etwas später	ish fair-zookh-er ess nokh ine-mull ett-vuss shpay-ter
Can I leave a message?	Kann ich etwas ausrichten?	kunn ish ett-vuss ows-rikht'n?
Hold on	Haben Sie etwas Geduld	harb'n zee ett-vuss g'doolt
Could you speak up a little please?	Bitte sprechen Sie etwas lauter?	bitt-er shpresh'n zee ett-vuss lowt-er?

Staying in a Hotel

Do you have a vacant room?	Haben Sie ein Zimmer frei?	harb'n zee ine tsimm-er fry?
double room with double bed	ein Doppelzimmer mit Doppelbett	ine dopp'l-tsimm-er mitt dopp'l-bet
twin room	ein Doppelzimmer	ine dopp'l-tsimm-er
single room	ein Einzelzimmer	ine ine-ts'l-tsimm-er
room with a bath/shower	Zimmer mit Bad/Dusche	tsimm-er mit bart doosh-er
porter	Gepäckträger/ Concierge	g'peck-tray-ger/ kon-see-airsh
key	Schlüssel	shlooss'l
I have a reservation	Ich habe ein Zimmer reserviert	ish harb-er ine tsimm-er rezz-er-veert

Sightseeing

bus	der Bus	dair booss
tram	die Strassenbahn	dee stra-sen-barn
train	der Zug	dair tsoog
art gallery	Galerie	gall-er-ee
bus station	Busbahnhof	booss-barn-hofe
bus (tram) stop	die Haltestelle	dee hal-te-shtel-er
castle	Schloss, Burg	shloss, boorg
palace	Schloss, Palais	shloss, pall-ay
post office	das Postamt	dee pohs-taamt
cathedral	Dom	dome
church	Kirche	keersh-er
garden	Garten, Park	gart'n, parka
library	Bibliothek	bib-leo-tek
museum	Museum	moo-zay-oom
information (office)	Information (-sbüro)	in-for-mut-see-on (-zboo-roe)
closed for public holiday	Feiertags geschlossen	fire-targz g'shloss'n

Shopping

How much does this cost?	Wieviel kostet das?	vee-feel kost't duss?
I would like…	Ich hätte gern…	ish hett-er gairn…
Do you have…?	Haben Sie…?	harb'n zee…?
I'm just looking	Ich schaue nur an	ish shau-er noor un
Do you take credit cards?	Kann ich mit einer Kreditkarte bezahlen?	kunn ish mitt ine-er kred-it-kar-ter b'tsahl'n?
What time do you open?	Wann machen Sie auf?	vunn mukh'n zee owf?
What time do you close?	Wann schliessen Sie?	vunn shlees'n zee?
This one	dieses	deez'z
expensive	teuer	toy-er
cheap	billig	bill-igg
size	Grösse	grers-er
white	weiss	vyce
black	schwarz	shvarts
red	rot	roht
yellow	gelb	gelp
green	grün	groon
blue	blau	blau

Types of Shop

antique shop	Antiquitäten-geschäft	un-tick-vi-tayt'n-g'sheft
bakery	Bäckerei	beck-er-eye
bank	Bank	bunk
book shop	Buchladen/ Buchhandlung	bookh-lard'n/ bookh-hant-loong
butcher	Fleischerei	fly-sher-eye
cake shop	Konditorei	kon-ditt-or-eye
chemist		
(for prescriptions)	Apotheke	App-o-tay-ker
(for cosmetics)	Drogerie	droog-er-ree
department store	Warenhaus, Warengeschäft	vahr'n-hows, vahr'n-g'sheft
delicatessen	Feinkost (geschäft)	fine-kost (g'sheft)
fishmonger	Fischgeschäft	fish-g'sheft
gift shop	Geschenke(laden)	g'shenk-er(lahd'n)
greengrocer	Obst und Gemüse	ohbst oont g'moo-zer
grocery	Lebensmittel-geschäft	layb'nz-mitt'l-g'sheft
hairdresser	Friseur/Frisör	freezz-er/freezz-er
market	Markt	markt
newsagent/ tobacconist	Tabak Trafik	tab-ack tra-feek
travel agent	Reisebüro	rye-zer-boo-roe
café	Cafe, Kaffeehaus	kaff-ay, kaff-ay-hows

Eating Out

Have you got a table for… people?	Haben Sie einen Tisch für… Personen?	harb'n zee ine'n tish foor… pair-sohn'n?
I want to reserve a table	Ich möchte einen Tisch bestellen	ish mer-shter ine'n tish b'shtell'n
The bill please	Zahlen, bitte	tsarl'n bitt-er
I am a vegetarian	Ich bin Vegetarier	ish bin vegg-er-tah-ree-er
Waitress/waiter	Fräulein/Herr Ober	froy-line/hairoh-bare
menu	die Speisekarte	dee shpize-er-kart-er
fixed price menu	das Menü	duss men-oo
cover charge	Couvert/Gedeck	koo-vair/g'deck
wine list	Weinkarte	vine-kart-er
glass	Glas	glars
bottle	Flasche	flush-er
knife	Messer	mess-er
fork	Gabel	garb'l
spoon	Löffel	lerff'l
breakfast	Frühstück	froo-shtook
lunch	Mittagessen	mit-targ-ess'n
dinner	Abendessen/ Dinner	arb'nt-ess'n/ dee-nay
main course	Hauptspeise	howpt-shpize-er
starter, first course	Vorspeise	for-shpize-er
dish of the day	Tageskarte	targ-erz-kart-er
wine garden(s)	Heuriger (Heurige)	hoy-rigg-er (-e)
rare	englisch	eng-glish
medium	medium	may-dee-oom
well done	durch	doorsh

Menu Decoder

See also pp 202–11

Apfel	upf'l	apple
Almdudler	ahlm-dood-ler	herbal lemonade
Banane	bar-nar-ner	banana
Ei	eye	egg
Eis	ice	ice cream
Fisch	fish	fish
Fisolen	fee-soul'n	green beans (haricot)
Fleisch	flysh	meat
Garnelen	gar-nayl'n	prawns
gebacken	g'buck'n	baked/fried
gebraten	g'brart'n	roast
gekocht	g'kokht	boiled
Gemüse	g'mooz-er	vegetables
vom Grill	fom grill	grilled
Gulasch	goo-lush	stew
Hendl/Hahn/Huhn	hend'l/harn/hoon	chicken
Kaffee	kaf-fay	coffee
Kartoffel/Erdäpfel	kar-toff'l/air-dupf'l	potatoes
Käse	kayz-er	cheese
Knoblauch	k'nob-lowkh	garlic
Knödel	k'nerd'l	dumpling
Kotelett	kot-lett	chop
Lamm	lumm	lamb
Marillen	mah-ril'n	apricot
Meeresfrüchte	mair-erz-froosh-ter	seafood

Mehlspeise	mayl-shpize-er	dessert
Milch	milhk	milk
Mineralwasser	minn-er-arl-vuss-er	mineral water
Obst	ohbst	fresh fruit
Öl	erl	oil
Oliven	o-leev'n	olives
Orange	o-ronsh-er	orange
frischgepresster Orangensaft	frish-g'press-ter o-ronsh'n-zuft	fresh orange juice
Paradeissalat	pa-ra-dice-sa-lahd	tomato salad
Pfeffer	pfeff-er	pepper
pochiert	posh-eert	poached
Pommes frites	pomm-fritt	chips
Reis	rice	rice
Rind	rint	beef
Rostbraten	rohst-brart'n	steak
Rotwein	roht-vine	red wine
Salz	zults	salt
Sauce/Saft	zohss-er/zuft	sauce
Schalentiere	sharl'n-tee-rer	shellfish
Schinken/Speck	shink'n/shpeck	ham
Schlag	shlahgg	cream
Schnecken	shnek'n	snails
Schokolade	shock-o-lard-er	chocolate
Schwein	shvine	pork
Semmel	zem'l	roll
Senf	zenf	mustard
Serviettenknödel	ser-vee-ert'n-k'nerd'l	sliced dumpling
Sulz	zoolts	brawn
Suppe	zoop-er	soup
Tee	tay	tea
Topfenkuchen	topf'n-kookh'n	cheesecake
Torte	tort-er	cake
Wasser	vuss-er	water
Weinessig	vine-ess-igg	vinegar
Weisswein	vyce-vine	white wine
Wurst	voorst	sausage (fresh)
Zucker	tsook-er	sugar
Zwetschge	tsvertsh-ger	plum
Zwiebel	tsveeb'l	onions

Numbers

0	null	nool
1	eins	eye'ns
2	zwei	tsvy
3	drei	dry
4	vier	feer
5	fünf	foonf
6	sechs	zex
7	sieben	zeeb'n
8	acht	uhkht
9	neun	noyn
10	zehn	tsayn
11	elf	elf
12	zwölf	tsverlf
13	dreizehn	dry-tsayn
14	vierzehn	feer-tsayn
15	fünfzehn	foonf-tsayn
16	sechzehn	zex-tsayn
17	siebzehn	zeep-tsayn
18	achtzehn	uhkht-tsayn
19	neunzehn	noyn-tsayn
20	zwanzig	tsvunn-tsig
21	einundzwanzig	ine-oont-tsvunn-tsig
22	zweiundzwanzig	tsvy-oont-tsvunn-tsig
30	dreissig	dry-sig
40	vierzig	feer-tsig
50	fünfzig	foonf-tsig
60	sechzig	zesh-tsig
70	siebzig	zeep-tsig
80	achtzig	uhkht-tsig
90	neunzig	noyn-tsig
100	einhundert	ine hoond't
1000	eintausend	ine towz'nt

Time

one minute	eine Minute	ine-er min-oot-er
one hour	eine Stunde	ine-er shtoond-er
half an hour	eine halbe Stunde	ine-er hull-ber shtoond-er
Monday	Montag	mone-targ
Tuesday	Dienstag	deen-starg
Wednesday	Mittwoch	mitt-vokh
Thursday	Donnerstag	donn-er-starg
Friday	Freitag	fry-targ
Saturday	Samstag	zum-starg
Sunday	Sonntag	zon-targ

Vienna Transport Network

There are five U-Bahn lines running across the city, each identified by a number. The Schnellbahn is essentially a commuter service. Bundesbahn trains to the rest of Austria and Europe run from Vienna's mainline stations. The Badner Bahn operates between its terminal opposite the Opera, and Baden. For more details, see *Getting Around Vienna* on pages 250–55.

KEY

- U1
- U2
- U3
- U4
- U6
- Schnellbahn line
- Badner Bahn line
- O Interchange
- Bundesbahn station
- CAT (City Aiport Train)
- Schnellbahn terminus
- Bus Terminal
- Major sight

Oberdöbling

Krottenbachstrasse

S45

WÄHRING

Nussdorfer Strasse

Gersthof

WÄHRINGER STRASSE

Währinger Strasse Volksoper

WÄHRINGER GÜRTEL

Hernals

HERNALSER

HAUPTSTRASSE

Michelbeuern Allgem. Krankenhaus

WATTGASSE

Alser Strasse

Ottakring O

OTTAKRING

JOSEFSTA

Josefstädter Strasse

Rath

Thaliastrasse

KOPPSTRASSE

WIENER GÜRTEL BUNDESSTRASSE

Kendler Strasse

S45

Burggasse - Stadthalle

NEUBAU

Ve

Mu

g

Hüttledorfer Strasse

Johnstrasse

MARIAHIL

Neubau-gasse

Breitensee

Schweglerstrasse

Westbahnhof
S50

S50

MARIAHILFER

Ziegler-gasse

HÜTTELDORFER STRASSE

Penzing

S45, S50

Pilgram

Unter Sankt Veit

Gumpendorfer Strasse

U4
Hütteldorf

Braunschweiggasse

Hietzing

WEINER BUNDESSTRASSE

WEINER BUNDESSTRASSE

Schönbrunn

Margareten-gürtel

MARG

S15

LAINZER STRASSE

Schloss Schönbrunn

Meidling Hauptstrasse

Niederhofstrasse

Längenfeldgasse

Eichenstrasse

SCHÖNBRUNNER SCHLOSSPARK

Wolfganggasse

BRUNNER BUNDESSTRASSE

S1, S2, S3, S4

Speising

Philadelphiabrücke
S3, S4, S9

Meidling

MEIDLING

S1, S2, S8, S9

S15

Hetzendorf O

U6
Siebenhirten

Wiener Verkehrsbetriebe (Vienna Transport Authority Information) *Tel* 50130.